MAJOR
AMERICAN
AUTHORS

D. Bruce Lockerbie   General Editor
The Stony Brook School

Alden Murray   Art Editor

Lynn Landy   Art Researcher

Bruce C. Dodd, Jr.   POE

Ralph E. Gillette   CRANE

Mary K. Healy   FROST

Mark Hamilton
David Lougée   WHITMAN, DICKINSON

Letitia Lange   FAULKNER

Michael L. Lasser   THE PURITANS

D. Bruce Lockerbie   MELVILLE, HAWTHORNE,
FITZGERALD, HEMINGWAY,
JAMES, O'NEILL, TWAIN,
BALDWIN, HANSBERRY

Harvey S. Wiener   EMERSON, THOREAU

Literature Acknowledgments

The authors and publisher have made every effort to trace the owner-ship of all selections found in this book and to make full acknowledgment for their use. Several of the selections are in the public domain.

Grateful acknowledgment is hereby made to the following authors, publishers, and individuals for their special permission to reprint copyrighted material.

BEACON PRESS, for "Notes of a Native Son," copyright © 1955 by James Baldwin. And for "Stranger in the Village," copyright 1953, © 1955 by James Baldwin. Reprinted from *Notes of a Native Son* by James Baldwin by permission.

HARPER & ROW, PUBLISHERS, INC., for "Tell all the Truth but tell it slant" (#449), (in the Johnson edition #1129), from *Bolts of Melody* by Emily Dickinson, edited by Mabel Loomis Todd and Millicent Todd Bingham. Copyright 1945 by The Trustees of Amherst College. Reprinted by permission of the publisher. For an excerpt from Chapter VI (under the title "Buck Fanshaw's Funeral") from *Roughing It* by Mark Twain. For an excerpt from *The Man That Corrupted Hadleyburg* by Mark Twain. Reprinted by permission.

HARVARD UNIVERSITY PRESS and THE TRUSTEES OF AMHERST COLLEGE, for "This is my letter to the World" (#441), "As imperceptibly as Grief" (#1540), "I cannot live with You" (#640), "My life closed twice . . ." (#1732), "Because I could not stop for Death" (#712), "I heard a Fly buzz . . ." (#465), "Success is counted sweetest" (#67), "The Soul selects her own Society" (#303) by Emily Dickinson. Reprinted from *The Poems of Emily Dickinson* edited by Thomas H. Johnson (Cambridge, Mass.: The Belknap Press of Harvard University Press). Copyright 1951, 1955 by The President and Fellows of Harvard College. Reprinted by permission.

HOLT, RINEHART AND WINSTON, INC., for "Mending Wall," "A Considerable Speck," "Provide, Provide," "Design," "A Leaf

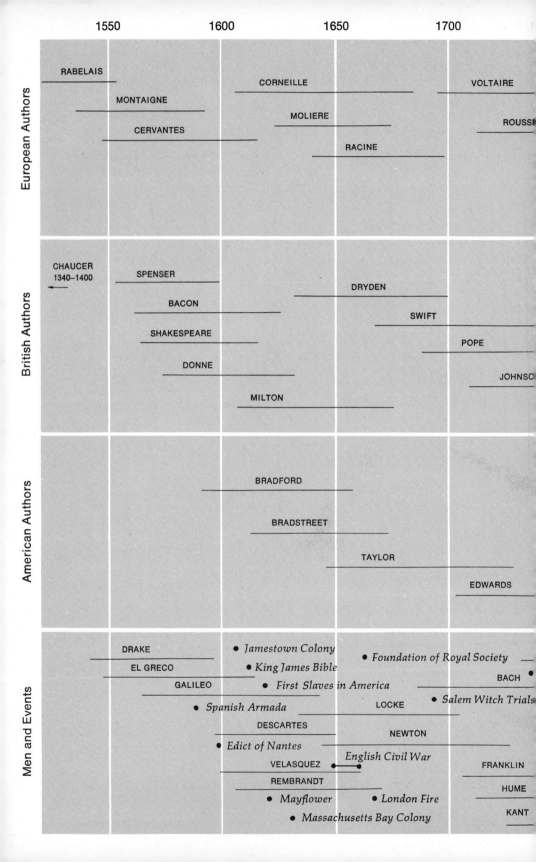

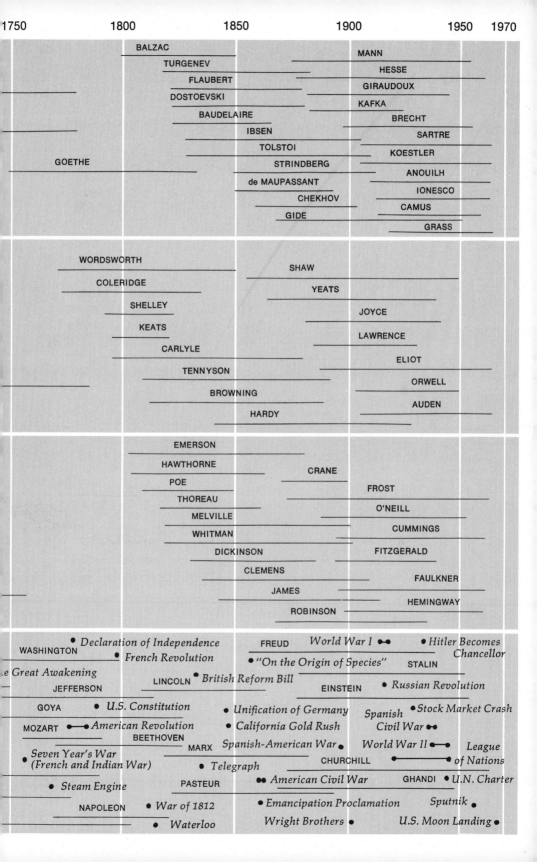

Contents

The Puritans

While American popular history traditionally celebrates the coming of the Pilgrims to Plymouth in 1620, much more important for all of us was the establishment of the Massachusetts Bay Colony ten years later. Very simply, if we are truly to understand the history, the society, and the literature of the American nation, we must begin with those colonists who came to the Massachusetts Bay to translate their religious zeal into practical action, to establish their Zion in the wilderness.

Children of the Reformation, which established Protestantism on the European continent, the English Puritans were members of the Anglican Church, whose theology and whose practices seemed to them to demand simplification and *purification*. They sought a return to the values of primitive Christianity, the removal of an elaborate religious institution which came between a man and his God, a restoration of the Bible as the sole basis of religious authority and moral judgment, and the establishment of a theocracy in which the Word of God as interpreted by His ministers was sufficient for all governing. Obviously, traditional Anglicans did not welcome these attempts to alter the Church, and with the decision of Elizabeth I to accept Anglicanism as the Church of England, disruption of the established order became not only heresy but treason. To preserve their beliefs and, in some cases, to save their skins, the Puritans sailed for America. They came, not to establish freedom for all religions or a democratic government, but to erect a theocratic oligarchy dedicated to one relatively authoritarian religious ideal.

The Puritans had English common sense; they were aware of some of the hardships they would face in the American wilderness, and they were sensitive to the political and economic pressures sure to be exerted by the crown. Thus, they pursued a middle course in planning the colony and in governing it following establishment.

Committed first and foremost to the preservation and sustenance of their religious life, they saw that its growth depended in large measure on the survival, prosperity, and independence of the colony as a whole. The clergy and their loyal followers were essential to the establishment of the new commonwealth, but so were the skilled tradesmen and craftsmen whom they encouraged to join them regardless of religious conviction. The leaders followed the advice of John Cotton, one of the colony's founders: "Neglect not walls and bulwarks and fortifications for your own defense; but ever let the name of the Lord be your refuge." In this healthy combination of the idealistic and the practical, we discover the common ancestor of the capacity for tolerance, the acceptance of political compromise, and the tone of optimism which are among the more satisfying characteristics of American life.

This should not suggest that the Puritans were therefore liberal and open-minded. They were not. But they were not fanatical either, although there were fanatics among them. They were quite capable of laughter, although depicted today as rather a stern-faced lot. A story is told of Nathaniel Ward, one of the sternest and most conservative of the early settlers, who purchased a house in which he found a mantel inscription reading, "Sobriety, Justice, Piety." To the list Ward added one more word—"Laughter." The Puritans smoked and drank and even danced on occasion. They invented rum-running and the practice of bundling. Their furniture makers attained high artistry. Furthermore, we know that they enjoyed singing psalms in church; their meetinghouse was often a social center as well as a house of worship; the classically educated clergymen possessed superb libraries and read not only the theology but also the poetry of the day.

Believing as they did, that the Bible was directly inspired by God and that reading the Bible was essential to the religious life, they also believed that the colony could prosper only if both the laity and the clergy were educated. The establishment of schools, the use of the primer, and the founding of Harvard College came early in Puritan America and were treated with due seriousness.

There is, of course, another side to the issue. Conservative, orthodox, and superstitious, Puritan theologians envisioned an ultimately utopian society in which the members of each church entered into a covenant with God. Their sacred duties were to strive to do God's will, to celebrate His choice of them as "visible saints" committed to the performance of His work, and to mourn their depraved sinfulness which kept them from fulfilling their pledge. Although Satan was the direct cause of the world's evil, the Puritans believed that he could do nothing without God's permission. Thus war, disease, storm, and famine were interpreted as signs of God's displeasure. The Puritans were believers in predestination and accepted with equanimity the conviction that all things, regardless of size or import, were controlled beforehand by the will of God. Their deity was both Creator and Sustainer; as Cotton Mather wrote, "As the world was first created, so it has ever since been preserved by the immediate hand of God."

Complacency and resignation are distinct possibilities in a society with beliefs like these—the belief that all men, suffering Original Sin, merit only damnation; the belief that God, in His infinite mercy and through the intercession of His Son, agrees to "elect" some souls to be uplifted into everlasting grace; the belief that no man can through good deeds influence his ultimate destiny or affect the Divine Mercy which rules over him. But the Puritan struggled to retain his faith, and he succeeded remarkably well, at least in the early, zealous days of highest hope. He continued to seek evidence of his conversion, the mystical experience in which God's grace is received. He tried to live a pious life both in the hope of election and to make that election secure. He could never be sure of his status and he dared not fall prey to the sinful pride of assuming his election; nevertheless, the "visible saint" was not without some quiet confidence. Finally, he sought to come closer to God and His glory to learn better how to resist the depravity and temptation which surrounded him.

The Middle Way of New England society was a continuation of the dominant moderate form of Puritanism in England. Choosing to remain in the Anglican Church and to work for reform from within despite their disapproval of its practices, the English Puritans shared their fellow Anglicans' disapproval of those extreme purifiers, the Separatists. This smaller radical group concluded that its attempts at reform were hopeless and therefore withdrew from the Church; they sought refuge in Holland and came eventually to Plymouth in 1620. But the Separatist settlers did not dominate New England, in spite of their earlier arrival. Instead, the concept of the Middle Way permeated Puritan belief and society. *Laissez-faire* capitalism and rugged individualism, for example, flourished in Massachusetts. Enterprise and economic success were accepted values among the people; if God makes the opportunity available, then it is, after all, sinful *not* to exploit it. The successful businessman combined normal acumen with a sincere though rarely otherworldly piety. His theology included seizing the present initiative, and sin was to him synonymous with wasted opportunity.

Even while the Puritans confronted a wilderness which they believed to be inhabited by Satan and his agents, they also had a sincere affection for nature. Exposed daily to its real and imagined dangers, they also perceived that here was God's Creation in its purest form. What better place than a quiet grove in which to feel the initial onrushing of God's grace. In like manner, the Puritans pursued scientific knowledge, not to increase their understanding of the physical universe as such, but to come ever closer to an insight into God's holy plan for His Creation.

To observe the New England way in any detail is to discover a whole series of paradoxes resolved through the colony's essentially moderate way of structuring its society, of conducting its religious affairs, and of maintaining its political equilibrium. As we have seen, the people were both religious and worldly; they admired individual resourcefulness and initiative in the face of their belief in pre-destination; they sought a simple life but delighted in the ornate robes of high officeholders and in the extended metaphors of their preachers; their clergymen were intellectuals who used logical argument and precise reasoning, but the faith's hold on the people was essentially irrational and superstitious; the clergy sought unity and consensus but confronted challenge after challenge to their authority; the colony experimented with nation-making but violently resisted advice, assistance, and influence from without.

In their struggles to found a nation of their own, these displaced Englishmen began the process which culminated in the American consciousness. This consciousness is most clearly marked by the twin themes of innocence and alienation, themes which mark the American experience from its first days in New England. The Puritans were the first who came to America to search for a new Eden, for the youth and innocence lost to corruption and experience. But they were not the last. Their quest for utopia or, failing that, for a sense of selfhood and integrity in the fallen world, gave impetus to the restless movement which marks the American's search for new streams from which to drink. American myths like Manifest Destiny and the "melting pot," writers like Henry David Thoreau and Walt Whitman, and characters like Hester Prynne and Holden Caulfield lend substance to this quest and name the Puritans as fathers to us all.

Puritan Poetry

Given their commitment to the task of building a civilized society according to their common ideals, it is only slightly short of amazing that the Puritans wrote as much poetry as they did. On the other hand, it should not be surprising to learn that the Puritans truly did appreciate poetic expression. The clergy read the works of Greek and Latin poets and attempted frequent translations; there were occasional imitations of current English modes; poets of some skill sought an intensity of language to record the ecstasy of their faith and the shape of their lives.

Most important and most rewarding to the Puritans was poetry's moral significance: beyond its capacity to delight, poetry must offer its readers profound spiritual insights. To the Puritans, then, the subject matter of poetry was primary, regardless of the didacticism of the presentation. While they readily accepted poetic expression, it would nonetheless be incorrect to say that the Puritans cared particularly about literary theory, about matters of style, about the development of cultivated literary judgment. Like scientific investigation, political maneuvering, and all the other secular activities of Puritan New England, poetry was a means to an end. And that end was spiritual.

At the same time that it was a high calling, however, poetry was also fraught with potential danger for the poet and his reader, for it could tempt the faithful from truth to fable. As a result of poetry's secular appeal, Cotton Mather found it necessary to warn Harvard's young divinity students that while poetic composition was a satisfying recreation, they should resist being so taken by it "as to be always poring on the *Passionate* and *Measured* pages. Let not what should be *Sauce* rather than Food for you, Engross all your Application." The Puritan might seek and find diversion and enrichment in this world and in his poetry, but he knew always where the proper emphases lay.

ANNE BRADSTREET (1612–1672)

Anne Dudley married Simon Bradstreet when she was sixteen. Two years later, in 1630, the couple sailed for America and settled on a farm in North Andover, Massachusetts. While her husband's importance grew until he became governor of the colony, Mrs. Bradstreet became America's first important woman poet and perhaps the first truly American poet in her use of both her New England experiences and the New England countryside. She was a devoted wife and mother to her large family despite the hardships of settlement and her lingering illnesses. In the difficulties she faced, however, we may find one explanation for the emotionalism, the sensitivity to life's joys, and the personalized tone in the midst of her conventional Puritan belief.

To My Dear and Loving Husband

If ever two were one, then surely we.
If ever man were loved by wife, then thee.
If ever wife was happy in a man,
Compare with me, ye women, if you can.
I prize thy love more than whole mines of gold,
Or all the riches that the East doth hold.
My love is such that rivers cannot quench,
Nor ought but love from thee give recompense.
Thy love is such I can no way repay;
The heavens reward thee manifold, I pray.
Then, while we live, in love let's so persever,
That when we live no more we may live ever.

A Letter to Her Husband, Absent Upon Publick Employment

My head, my heart, mine Eyes, my life, nay more,
My joy, my Magazine of earthly store,
If two be one, as surely thou and I,
How stayest thou there, whilst I at *Ipswich* lye?

So many steps, head from the heart to sever
If but a neck, soon should we be together:
I like the earth this season, mourn in black,
My Sun is gone so far in's Zodiack,
Whom whilst I 'joy'd, nor storms, nor frosts I felt,
His warmth such frigid colds did cause to melt.
My chilled limbs now nummed lye forlorn;
Return, return sweet *Sol* from *Capricorn*;
In this dead time, alas, what can I more
Than view those fruits which through thy heat I bore?
Which sweet contentment yield me for a space,
True living Pictures of their Fathers face.
O strange effect! now thou art *Southward* gone,
I weary grow, the tedious day so long;
But when thou *Northward* to me shalt return,
I wish my Sun may never set, but burn
Within the Cancer of my glowing breast,
The welcome house of him my dearest guest.
Where ever, ever stay, and go not thence,
Till natures sad decree shall call thee hence;
Flesh of thy flesh, bone of thy bone,
I here, thou there, yet both but one.

Before the Birth of One of Her Children

All things within this fading world hath end,
Adversity doth still our joys attend;
No ties so strong, no friends so dear and sweet,
But with death's parting blow is sure to meet.
The sentence past is most irrevocable,
A common thing, yet oh, inevitable.
How soon, my dear, death may my steps attend,
How soon't may be thy lot to lose thy friend
We both are ignorant; yet love bids me
These farewell lines to recommend to thee,
That when that knot's untied that made us one,
I may seem thine, who in effect am none.
And if I see not half my days that's due,
What nature would, God grant to yours and you.
The many faults that well you know I have,
Let be interred in my oblivion's grave;
If any worth or virtue were in me,

Let that live freshly in thy memory;
And when thou feel'st no grief, as I no harms,
Yet love thy dead, who long lay in thine arms.
And when thy loss shall be repaid with gains,
Look to my little babes, my dear remains.
And if thou love thyself, or loved'st me,
These O protect from stepdame's injury.
And if chance to thine eyes shall bring this verse,
With some sad sighs honor my absent hearse;
And kiss this paper for thy love's dear sake,
Who with salt tears this last farewell did take.

Here Followes Some Verses Upon the Burning of Our House, July 10th, 1666. Copyed out of a Loose Paper.

In silent night when rest I took,
For sorrow neer I did not look,
I waken'd was with thundring nois
And Piteous shreiks of dreadfull voice.
That fearfull sound of fire and fire,
Let no man know is my Desire.

I, starting up, the light did spye,
And to my God my heart did cry
To strengthen me in my Distresse
And not to leave me succourlesse.
Then coming out beheld a space,
The flame consumed my dwelling place.

And, when I could no longer look,
I blest his Name that gave and took,
That layd my goods now in the dust:
Yea so it was, and so 'twas just.
It was his own: it was not mine;
Far be it that I should repine.

He might of All justly bereft,
But yet sufficient for us left.
When by the Ruines oft I past,
My sorrowing eyes aside did cast,
And here and there the places spye
Where oft I sate, and long did lye.

Here stood that Trunk, and there that chest;
There lay that store I counted best:
My pleasant things in ashes lye,
And them behold no more shall I.
Under thy roof no guest shall sitt,
Nor at thy Table eat a bitt.

No pleasant tale shall 'ere be told,
Nor things recounted done of old.
No Candle 'ere shall shine in Thee,
Nor bridegroom's voice ere heard shall bee.
In silence ever shalt thou lye;
Adeiu, Adeiu; All's vanity.

Then streight I gin my heart to chide,
And did thy wealth on earth abide?
Didst fix thy hope on mouldring dust,
The arm of flesh didst make thy trust?
Raise up thy thoughts above the skye
That dunghill mists away may flie.

Thou hast an house on high erect,
Fram'd by that mighty Architect,
With glory richly furnished,
Stands permanent though: this bee fled.
It's purchaséd, and paid for too
By him who hath enough to doe.

A Prise so vast as is unknown,
Yet, by his Gift, is made thine own.
Ther's wealth enough, I need no more;
Farewell my Pelf, farewell my Store.
The world no longer let me Love,
My hope and Treasure lyes Above.

In Memory of My Dear Grand-Child Elizabeth Bradstreet

Farewell dear babe, my heart's too much content,
Farewell sweet babe, the pleasure of mine eye,
Farewell fair flower that for a space was lent,
Then ta'en away unto Eternity.
Blest babe why should I once bewail thy fate,

Or sigh the days so soon were terminate;
Sith thou are settled in an Everlasting state.

By nature trees do rot when they are grown.
And plums and apples thoroughly ripe do fall,
And corn and grass are in their season mown,
And time brings down what is both strong and tall.
But plants new set to be eradicate,
And buds new blown, to have so short a date,
Is by His hand alone that guides nature and fate.

EDWARD TAYLOR (1645?–1729)

There is an element of mystery in the case of Edward Taylor, the finest American poet before the nineteenth century. Born in Coventry, England, around 1645, Taylor came to America in 1668 and entered Harvard College where his roommate was Samuel Sewall. He then served as minister at Westfield until his death in 1729. Taylor wrote hundreds of poems in his lifetime although he never attempted publication, perhaps because he felt that his work was unworthy, perhaps because its sensuousness and richness of language were radical departures from the approved "plain style." In any case, his poems were finally discovered in 1939 and given the attention they merit.

The Preface

Infinity, when all things it beheld
In Nothing, and of Nothing all did build,
Upon what Base was fixt the Lath, wherein
He turned this Globe, and riggalld° it so trim?
Who blew the Bellows of his Furnace Vast?
Or held the Mould wherein the world was Cast?
Who laid its Corner Stone? Or whose Command?
Where stand the Pillars upon which it stands?
Who Lac'de and Fillitted° the earth so fine,
With Rivers like green Ribbons Smaragdine?°
Who made the Sea's its Selvedge, and it locks
Like a Quilt Ball within a Silver Box?
Who Spread its Canopy? Or Curtains Spun?
Who in this Bowling Alley bowld the Sun?
Who made it always when it rises set
To go at once both down, and up to get?
Who th'Curtain rods made for this Tapistry?
Who hung the twinckling Lanthorns in the Sky?

° *riggalld:* made a groove for.
° *Fillitted:* girded.
° *Smaragdine:* emerald.

Who? who did this? or who is he? Why, know
Its Onely Might Almighty this did doe.
His hand hath made this noble worke which Stands
His Glorious Handywork not made by hands.
Who spake all things from nothing; and with ease
Can speake all things to nothing, if he please.
Whose Little finger at his pleasure Can
Out mete ten thousand worlds with halfe a Span:
Whose Might Almighty can by half a looks
Root up the rocks and rock the hills by th'roots.
Can take this mighty World up in his hande,
And shake it like a Squitchen° or a Wand.
Whose single Frown will make the Heavens shake
Like as an aspen leafe the Winde makes quake.
Oh! what a might is this Whose single frown
Doth shake the world as it would shake it down?
Which All from Nothing fet,° from Nothing, All:
Hath All on Nothing set, lets Nothing fall.
Gave All to nothing Man indeed, whereby
Through nothing man all might him Glorify.
In Nothing then imbosst the brightest Gem
More pretious than all pretiousness in them.
But Nothing man did throw down all by Sin:
And darkened that lightsom Gem in him.
    That now his Brightest Diamond is grown
    Darker by far than any Coalpit Stone.

The Ebb and Flow

When first thou on me Lord wrought'st thy Sweet Print,
    My heart was made thy tinder box.
    My 'ffections were thy tinder in't.
        Where fell thy Sparkes by drops.
Those holy Sparks of Heavenly Fire that came
Did ever catch and often out would flame.

° *Squitchen:* switch.
° *fet:* fetched.
° *Gods Tender Bowells:* believed to be the source of compassion.

But now my Heart is made thy Censar trim,
    Full of thy golden Altars fire,
    To offer up Sweet Incense in
        Unto thyselfe intire:
I finde my tinder scarce thy sparks can feel
That drop out from thy Holy flint and Steel.

Hence doubts out bud for feare thy fire in mee
    'S a mocking Ignis Fatuus°
    Or lest thine Altars fire out bee,
        Its hid in ashes thus.
Yet when the bellows of thy Spirit blow
Away mine ashes, then thy fire doth glow.

Huswifery

Make me, O Lord, thy Spining Wheele compleate.
    Thy Holy Worde my Distaff° make for mee.
Make mine Affections thy Swift Flyers° neate
    And make my Soule thy holy Spoole to bee.
    My Conversation make to be thy Reele
    And reele the yarn thereon spun of thy Wheele.

Make me thy Loome then, knit therein this Twine:
    And make thy Holy Spirit, Lord, winde quills:°
Then weave the Web thyselfe. The yarn is fine.
    Thine Ordinances make my Fulling° Mills.
    Then dy the same in Heavenly Colours Choice,
    All pinkt° with Varnisht Flowers of Paradise.

Then cloath therewith mine Understanding, Will,
    Affections, Judgment, Conscience, Memory
My Words, and Actions, that their shine may fill
    My wayes with glory and thee glorify.
    Then mine apparell shall display before yee
    That I am Cloathd in Holy robes for glory.

° *Ignis Fatuus:* false light.

° The sustained imagery in "Huswifery" relates to the craft of weaving: *Distaff:* wool holder; *Flyers:* revolving arms; *quills:* spindles; *Fulling:* cloth processing; *pinkt:* ornamented with perforations.

Meditation Six

Am I thy Gold? Or Purse, Lord, for thy Wealth;
    Whether in mine, or mint refinde for thee?
Ime counted so, but count me o're thyselfe,
    Lest gold washt face, and brass in Heart I bee.
    I Feare my Touchstone touches when I try
    Mee, and my Counted Gold too overly.

Am I new minted by thy Stamp indeed?
    Mine Eyes are dim; I cannot clearly see.
Be thou my Spectacles that I may read
    Thine Image, and Inscription stampt on mee.
    If thy bright Image do upon me stand
    I am a Golden Angell° in thy hand.

Lord, make my Soule thy Plate: thine Image bright
    Within the Circle of the same enfoile.
And on its brims in golden Letters write
    Thy Superscription in an Holy style.
    Then I shall be thy Money, thou my Hord:
    Let me thy Angell bee, bee thou my Lord.

Meditation Eight
John 6:51. I am the Living Bread.

I kening° through Astronomy Divine
    The Worlds bright Battlement, wherein I spy
A Golden Path my Pensill cannot line,
    From that bright Throne unto my Threshold ly.
    And while my puzzled thoughts about it pore
    I finde the Bread of Life in't at my doore.

When that this Bird of Paradise put in
    This Wicker Cage (my Corps) to tweedle praise
Had peckt the Fruite forbad: and so did fling
    Away its Food; and lost its golden dayes;
    It fell into Celestiall Famine sore:
    And never could attain a morsell more.

° *Angell:* gold coin.
° *kening:* knowing, seeing.

Alas! alas! Poore Bird, what wilt thou doe?
  The Creatures field no food for Souls e're gave.
And if thou knock at Angells dores they show
  An Empty Barrell: they no soul bread have.
  Alas! Poore Bird, the Worlds White Loafe is done.
  And cannot yield thee here the smallest Crumb.

In this sad state, Gods Tender Bowells° run
  Out streams of Grace: And he to end all strife
The Purest Wheate in Heaven, his deare-dear Son
  Grinds, and kneads up into this Bread of Life.
  Which Bread of Life from Heaven down came and
                          stands
  Disht on thy Table up by Angells Hands.

Did God mould up this Bread in Heaven, and bake,
  Which from his Table came, and to thine goeth?
Doth he bespeake thee thus, This Soule Bread take.
  Come Eate thy fill of this thy Gods White Loafe?
  Its Food too fine for Angells, yet come, take
  And Eate thy fill. Its Heavens Sugar Cake.

What Grace is this knead in this Loafe? This thing
  Souls are but petty things it to admire.
Yee Angells, help: This fill would to the brim
  Heav'ns whelm'd-down Chrystall meele Bowle, yea and
                          higher.
  This Bread of Life dropt in thy mouth, doth Cry.
  Eate, Eate me, Soul, and thou shalt never dy.

QUESTIONS FOR DISCUSSION

Anne Bradstreet

1. To what extent does Anne Bradstreet see the world exclusively through a woman's eyes? What kind of woman is she? Make a list of descriptive terms that come to mind as she speaks in her poems.
2. What are Bradstreet's attitudes toward the world she knows: her husband, her family, her home, her community, her faith, her God?
3. How do Bradstreet's metaphors and other figures of speech contribute to the effectiveness of her poems?
4. It has been suggested that Anne Bradstreet was essentially a worldly poet who yielded to God's will and to Puritan doctrines in her poems, but not always easily. Discuss this suggestion as it seems to relate to "Upon the Burning of Our House."

Edward Taylor

1. Edward Taylor's language often constructs a figure of speech known as a conceit (an elaborate, ingenious, and extended comparison). The conceit was a particular favorite of the English metaphysical poets—John Donne, George Herbert, and others. Which particular examples of the conceit can you find represented in Taylor's poems?
2. A meditation has been described as a form of private or secret prayer, commonly developed as an application of a stated biblical text. Discuss what seem to be the paradoxes in Taylor's meditations—to express his love for the divine, he chooses to write about earthly passions.
3. What changes in the speaking voice do you find in contrasting "Meditation Six" ("Am I Thy Gold") with "Huswifery"? How do you account for these changes?
4. From what sources does Taylor draw his imagery? Speculate about the aptness of his images as they help establish the speaking voice in any one of the poems.

ASSIGNMENTS FOR WRITING

1. On the basis of your reading several of Anne Bradstreet's poems, discuss in a brief essay the character of Anne Bradstreet, the wife and mother. Use specific references from the poems to support your statements.
2. Choose one of Taylor's poems in which the conceit appeals to you, and write an analysis of the poem, explaining the intricacies of the conceit as fully as possible.

The Greatest Puritan,
Jonathan Edwards (1703-1758)

The last and perhaps the greatest of the Puritan leaders, Jonathan Edwards was also Colonial America's foremost intellectual figure. Born into the tradition of an august and austere clergy, Edwards entered Yale College at the age of thirteen, a precocious student of theology. But Edwards was far more than a theologian; he was in every sense a man of the Enlightenment. He recognized that the discoveries of science had implications for the doctrines preached from pulpits, and he determined to formulate the restatement of those doctrines that would ally the Revealed Truth of the Scriptures with the revealed truth of scientific study.

From his position as pastor of the influential Northampton, Massachusetts, church, Edwards established himself as one of the most effective evangelists of any period. In 1735, an intense spiritual movement swept new believers into the faith: this was the beginning of the Great Awakening, which spread throughout the colonies and lasted well into the 1740's. During this time Edwards preached some of his most famous sermons, including "Sinners in the Hands of an Angry God."

Ironically, this same man, the most powerful preacher of his day, was ousted by his congregation in 1750, and he went into a self-imposed exile in the frontier town of Stockbridge. There he wrote his famous philosophical tracts, including *Freedom of the Will.*

In January 1758, Edwards became president of the College of New Jersey (now Princeton University), but three months later, after receiving a small-pox inoculation, he died.

from Personal Narrative

Edwards' Personal Narrative, written in 1739, is not a complete autobiography. It covers only the years of his childhood, college study, and early career. It is a gem of clear writing, a discipline to which Edwards subjected himself with rigor because he believed that the message from God should be communicated to men in the clearest language possible.

I had a variety of concerns and exercises about my soul from my childhood, but had two more remarkable seasons of awakening, before I met with that change by which I was brought to those new dispositions, and that new sense of things, that I have since had. The first time was when I was a boy, some years before I went to college, at a time of remarkable awakening in my father's congregation, I was then very much affected for many months, and concerned about the things of religion, and my soul's salvation; and was abundant in duties. I used to pray five times a day in secret, and to spend much time in religious talk with other boys; and used to meet with them to pray together. I experienced I know not what kind of delight in religion. My mind was much engaged in it, and had much selfrighteous pleasure; and it was my delight to abound in religious duties. I with some of my schoolmates joined together, and built a booth in a swamp, in a very retired spot, for a place of prayer. And besides, I had particular secret places of my own in the woods, where I used to retire by myself; and was from time to time much affected. My affections seemed to be lively and easily moved, and I seemed to be in my element when engaged in religious duties. And I am ready to think, many are deceived with such affections, and such a kind of delight as I then had in religion, and mistake it for grace.

But in process of time, my convictions and affections wore off; and I entirely lost all those affections and delights and left off secret prayer, at least as to any constant performance of it; and returned like a dog to his vomit, and went on in the ways of sin. Indeed I was at times very uneasy, especially towards the latter part of my time at college; when it pleased God, to seize me with a pleurisy; in which he brought me nigh to the grave, and shook me over the pit of hell. And yet, it was not long after my recovery, before I fell again into my old ways of sin. But God would not suffer me to go on with any quietness; I had great and violent inward struggles, till, after many conflicts with wicked inclinations, repeated resolutions, and bonds that I laid myself under by a kind of vows to God, I was brought wholly to break off all former wicked ways, and all ways of known outward sin; and to apply myself to seek salvation, and practise many religious duties; but without that kind of affection and delight which I had formerly experienced. My concern now wrought more by inward struggles and conflicts, and selfreflections. I made seeking my salvation the main business of my life. But yet, it seems to me, I sought after a miserable manner; which has made me sometimes since to question, whether ever it issued in that which was saving; being ready to doubt, whether such miserable seeking ever succeeded. I was indeed brought to seek salvation in a manner that I never was before; I felt a spirit to part with all things in the world, for an interest in Christ. My concern continued and prevailed, with many exercising thoughts and inward struggles; but yet it never seemed to be proper to express that concern by the name of terror.

From my childhood up, my mind had been full of objections against the doctrine of God's sovereignty, in choosing whom he would to eternal life, and rejecting whom he pleased; leaving them eternally to perish, and be everlastingly tormented in hell. It used to appear like a horrible doctrine to me. But I remember the time very well, when I seemed to be convinced, and fully satisfied, as to this sovereignty of God, and his justice in thus eternally disposing of men, according to his sovereign pleasure. But never could give an account, how, or by what means, I was thus convinced, not in the least imagining at the time, nor a long time after, that there was any extraordinary influence of God's Spirit in it; but only that now I saw further, and my reason apprehended the justice and reasonableness of it. However, my mind rested in it; and it put an end to all those cavils and objections. And there has been a wonderful alteration in my mind, in respect to the doctrine of God's sovereignty, from that day to this; so that I scarce ever have found so much as the rising of an objection against it, in the most absolute sense, in God's shewing mercy to whom he will shew mercy, and hardening whom he will. God's absolute sovereignty and justice, with respect to salvation and damnation, is what my mind seems to rest assured of, as much as of any thing that I see with my eyes; at least it is so at times. But I have often, since that first conviction, had quite another kind of sense of God's sovereignty than I had then. I have often since had not only a conviction, but a delightful conviction. The doctrine has very often appeared exceeding pleasant, bright, and sweet. Absolute sovereignty is what I love to ascribe to God. But my first conviction was not so.

* * *

Once, as I rode out into the woods for my health, in 1737, having alighted from my horse in a retired place, as my manner commonly has been, to walk for divine contemplation and prayer, I had a view that for me was extraordinary, of the glory of the Son of God, as Mediator between God and man, and his wonderful, great, full, pure and sweet grace and love, and meek and gentle condescension. This grace that appeared so calm and sweet, appeared also great above the heavens. The person of Christ appeared ineffably excellent with an excellency great enough to swallow up all thought and conception . . . which continued as near as I can judge, about an hour; which kept me the greater part of the time in a flood of tears, and weeping aloud. I felt an ardency of soul to be, what I know not otherwise how to express, emptied and annihilated; to lie in the dust, and to be full of Christ alone; to love him with a holy and pure love; to trust in him; to live upon him; to serve and follow him; and to be perfectly sanctified and made pure, with a divine and heavenly purity. I have, several other times, had views very much of the same nature, and which have had the same effects.

I have many times had a sense of the glory of the third person in the Trinity, in his office of Sanctifier; in his holy operations, communicating divine light and life to the soul. God, in the communications of his Holy Spirit, has appeared as an infinite fountain of divine glory and sweetness; being full, and sufficient to fill and satisfy the soul; pouring forth itself in sweet communications; like the sun in its glory, sweetly and pleasantly diffusing light and life. And I have sometimes had an affecting sense of the excellency of the word of God, as a word of life; as the light of life; a sweet, excellent lifegiving word; accompanied with a thirsting after that word, that it might dwell richly in my heart.

Often, since I lived in this town, I have had very affecting views of my own sinfulness and vileness; very frequently to such a degree as to hold me in a kind of loud weeping, sometimes for a considerable time together; so that I have often been forced to shut myself up. I have had a vastly greater sense of my own wickedness, and the badness of my heart, than ever I had before my conversion. It has often appeared to me, that if God should mark iniquity against me, I should appear the very worst of all mankind; of all that have been, since the beginning of the world to this time; and that I should have by far the lowest place in hell. When others, that have come to talk with me about their soul concerns, have expressed the sense they have had of their own wickedness, by saying that it seemed to them, that they were as bad as the devil himself; I thought their expressions seemed exceeding faint and feeble, to represent my wickedness.

My wickedness, as I am in myself, has long appeared to me perfectly ineffable, and swallowing up all thought and imagination; like an infinite deluge, or mountain over my head. I know not how to express better what my sins appear to me to be, than by heaping infinite upon infinite, and multiplying infinite by infinite. Very often, for these many years, these expressions are in my mind, and in my mouth, "Infinite upon infinite . . . Infinite upon infinite!" When I look into my heart, and take a view of my wickedness, it looks like an abyss infinitely deeper than hell. And it appears to me, that were it not for free grace, exalted and raised up to the infinite height of all the fulness and glory of the great Jehovah, and the arm of his power and grace stretched forth in all the majesty of his power, and in all the glory of his sovereignty, I should appear sunk down in my sins below hell itself; far beyond the sight of every thing, but the eye of sovereign grace, that can pierce even down to such a depth. And yet it seems to me, that my conviction of sin is exceeding small, and faint; it is enough to amaze me, that I have no more sense of my sin. I know certainly, that I have very little sense of my sinfulness. When I have had turns of weeping and crying for my sins I thought I knew at the time, that my repentance was nothing to my sin.

I have greatly longed of late, for a broken heart, and to lie low before God; and, when I ask for humility, I cannot bear the thoughts of being no more humble than other Christians. It seems to me, that though their degrees of humility may be suitable for them, yet it would be a vile selfexaltation in me, not to be the lowest in humility of all mankind. Others speak of their longing to be "humbled to the dust;" that may be a proper expression for them, but I always think of myself, that I ought, and it is an expression that has long been natural for me to use in prayer, "to lie infinitely low before God." And it is affecting to think, how ignorant I was, when a young Christian, of the bottomless, infinite depths of wickedness, pride, hypocrisy and deceit, left in my heart.

I have a much greater sense of my universal, exceeding dependence on God's grace and strength, and mere good pleasure, of late, than I used formerly to have; and have experienced more of an abhorrence of my own righteousness. The very thought of any joy arising in me, on any consideration of my own amiableness, performances, or experiences, or any goodness of heart or life, is nauseous and detestable to me. And yet I am greatly afflicted with a proud and selfrighteous spirit, much more sensibly than I used to be formerly. I see that serpent rising and putting forth its head continually, every where, all around me.

Though it seems to me, that, in some respects, I was a far better Christian, for two or three years after my first conversion, than I am now; and lived in a more constant delight and pleasure; yet, of late years, I have had a more full and constant sense of the absolute sovereignty of God, and a delight in that sovereignty; and have had more of a sense of the glory of Christ, as a Mediator revealed in the gospel. On one Saturday night, in particular, I had such a discovery of the excellency of the gospel above all other doctrines, that I could not but say to myself, "This is my chosen light, my chosen doctrine;" and of Christ, "This is my chosen Prophet." It appeared sweet, beyond all expression, to follow Christ, and to be taught, and enlightened, and instructed by him; to learn of him, and live to him. Another Saturday night, (*January* 1739) I had such a sense, how sweet and blessed a thing it was to walk in the way of duty; to do that which was right and meet to be done, and agreeable to the holy mind of God; that it caused me to break forth into a kind of loud weeping, which held me some time, so that I was forced to shut myself up, and fasten the doors. I could not but, as it were, cry out, "How happy are they which do that which is right in the sight of God! They are blessed indeed, they are the happy ones!" I had, at the same time, a very affecting sense, how meet and suitable it was that God should govern the world, and order all things according to his own pleasure; and I rejoiced in it, that God reigned, and that his will was done.

from Sinners in the Hands of an Angry God

"*Sinners in the Hands of an Angry God*" *was preached at Enfield, Connecticut, on July 8, 1741. A witness, the Reverend Eleazar Wheelock, wrote that the sermon was delivered softly and unspectacularly; yet, "there was such a breathing of distress, and weeping, that the preacher was obliged to speak to the people and desire silence, that he might be heard."*

In this verse is threatened the vengeance of God on the wicked unbelieving Israelites, who were God's visible people, and who lived under the means of grace; but who, notwithstanding all God's wonderful works towards them, remained (as ver. 28.) void of counsel, having no understanding in them. Under all the cultivations of heaven, they brought forth bitter and poisonous fruit; as in the two verses next preceding the text.—The expression I have chosen for my text, *Their foot shall slide in due time,* seems to imply the following things, relating to the punishment and destruction to which these wicked Israelites were exposed.

1. That they were always exposed to *destruction;* as one that stands or walks in slippery places is always exposed to fall. This is implied in the manner of their destruction coming upon them, being represented by their foot sliding. The same is expressed, Psalm 73:18. "Surely thou didst set them in slippery places; thou castedst them down into destruction."

2. It implies, that they were always exposed to sudden unexpected destruction. As he that walks in slippery places is every moment liable to fall, he cannot foresee one moment whether he shall stand or fall the next; and when he does fall, he falls at once without warning: Which is also expressed in Psalm 73:18, 19. "Surely thou didst set them in slippery places; thou castedst them down into destruction: How are they brought into desolation as in a moment!"

3. Another thing implied is, that they are liable to fall *of themselves,* without being thrown down by the hand of another; as he that stands or walks on slippery ground needs nothing but his own weight to throw him down.

4. That the reason why they are not fallen already, and do not fall now, is only that God's appointed time is not come. For it is said, that when that due time, or appointed time comes, *their foot shall slide.* Then they shall be left to fall, as they are inclined by their own weight. God will not hold them up in these slippery places any longer, but will let them go; and then, at that very instant, they shall fall into destruction; as he that stands on such slippery declining ground, on the edge of a pit, he cannot stand alone, when he is let go he immediately falls and is lost.

The observation from the words that I would now insist upon is this.—"There is nothing that keeps wicked men at any one moment out of hell, but the mere pleasure of God"—By the *mere* pleasure of God, I mean his *sovereign* pleasure, his arbitrary will, restrained by no obligation, hindered by no manner of difficulty, any more than if nothing else but God's mere will had in the least degree, or in any respect whatsoever, any hand in the preservation of wicked men one moment.—

· · ·

So that, thus it is that natural men are held in the hand of God, over the pit of hell; they have deserved the fiery pit, and are already sentenced to it; and God is dreadfully provoked, his anger is as great towards them as to those that are actually suffering the executions of the fierceness of his wrath in hell, and they have done nothing in the least to appease or abate that anger, neither is God in the least bound by any promise to hold them up one moment; the devil is waiting for them, hell is gaping for them, the flames gather and flash about them, and would fain lay hold on them, and swallow them up; the fire pent up in their own hearts is struggling to break out: and they have no interest in any Mediator, there are no means within reach that can be any security to them. In short, they have no refuge, nothing to take hold of; all that preserves them every moment is the mere arbitrary will, and un-covenanted, unobliged forbearance of an incensed God.

APPLICATION

The use of this awful subject may be for awakening uncon-verted persons in this congregation. This that you have heard is the case of every one of you that are out of Christ.—That world of misery, that lake of burning brimstone, is extended abroad under you. There is the dreadful pit of the glowing flames of the wrath of God; there is hell's wide gaping mouth open; and you have nothing to stand upon, nor any thing to take hold of; there is nothing between you and hell but the air; it is only the power and mere pleasure of God that holds you up.

You probably are not sensible of this; you find you are kept out of hell, but do not see the hand of God in it; but look at other things, as the good state of your bodily constitution, your care of your own life, and the means you use for your own preser-vation. But indeed these things are nothing; if God should withdraw his hand, they would avail no more to keep you from falling, than the thin air to hold up a person that is suspended in it.

Your wickedness makes you as it were heavy as lead, and to tend downwards with great weight and pressure towards hell;

and if God should let you go, you would immediately sink and swiftly descend and plunge into the bottomless gulf, and your healthy constitution, and your own care and prudence, and best contrivance, and all your righteousness, would have no more influence to uphold you and keep you out of hell, than a spider's web would have to stop a fallen rock. Were it not for the sovereign pleasure of God, the earth would not bear you one moment; for you are a burden to it; the creation groans with you; the creature is made subject to the bondage of your corruption, not willingly; the sun does not willingly shine upon you to give you light to serve sin and Satan; the earth does not willingly yield her increase to satisfy your lusts; nor is it willingly a stage for your wickedness to be acted upon; the air does not willingly serve you for breath to maintain the flame of life in your vitals, while you spend your life in the service of God's enemies. God's creatures are good, and were made for men to serve God with, and do not willingly subserve to any other purpose, and groan when they are abused to purposes so directly contrary to their nature and end. And the world would spew you out, were it not for the sovereign hand of him who hath subjected it in hope. There are black clouds of God's wrath now hanging directly over your heads, full of the dreadful storm, and big with thunder; and were it not for the restraining hand of God, it would immediately burst forth upon you. The sovereign pleasure of God, for the present, stays his rough wind; otherwise it would come with fury, and your destruction would come like a whirlwind, and you would be like the chaff of the summer threshing floor.

The wrath of God is like great waters that are dammed for the present; they increase more and more, and rise higher and higher, till an outlet is given; and the longer the stream is stopped, the more rapid and mighty is its course, when once it is let loose. It is true, that judgment against your evil works has not been executed hitherto; the floods of God's vengeance have been withheld; but your guilt in the mean time is constantly increasing, and you are every day treasuring up more wrath; the waters are constantly rising, and waxing more and more mighty; and there is nothing but the mere pleasure of God, that holds the waters back, that are unwilling to be stopped, and press hard to go forward. If God should only withdraw his hand from the flood-gate, it would immediately fly open, and the fiery floods of the fierceness and wrath of God, would rush forth with inconceivable fury, and would come upon you with omnipotent power; and if your strength were ten thousand times greater than it is, yea, ten thousand times greater than the strength of the stoutest, sturdiest devil in hell, it would be nothing to withstand or endure it.

The bow of God's wrath is bent, and the arrow made ready on the string, and justice bends the arrow at your heart, and strains the bow, and it is nothing but the mere pleasure of God, and that of an angry God, without any promise or obligation at all, that keeps the arrow one moment from being made drunk with your blood. Thus all you that never passed under a great change of heart, by the mighty power of the Spirit of God upon your souls; all you that were never born again, and made new creatures, and raised from being dead in sin, to a state of new, and before altogether unexperienced light and life, are in the hands of an angry God. However you may have reformed your life in many things, and may have had religious affections, and may keep up a form of religion in your families and closets, and in the house of God, it is nothing but his mere pleasure that keeps you from being this moment swallowed up in everlasting destruction. However unconvinced you may now be of the truth of what you hear, by and by you will be fully convinced of it. Those that are gone from being in the like circumstances with you, see that it was so with them; for destruction came suddenly upon most of them; when they expected nothing of it, and while they were saying, Peace and safety: now they see, that those things on which they depended for peace and safety, were nothing but thin air and empty shadows.

The God that holds you over the pit of hell, much as one holds a spider, or some loathsome insect over the fire, abhors you, and is dreadfully provoked: his wrath towards you burns like fire; he looks upon you as worthy of nothing else, but to be cast into the fire; he is of purer eyes than to bear to have you in his sight; you are ten thousand times more abominable in his eyes, than the most hateful venomous serpent is in ours. You have offended him infinitely more than ever a stubborn rebel did his prince; and yet it is nothing but his hand that holds you from falling into the fire every moment. It is to be ascribed to nothing else, that you did not go to hell the last night; that you was suffered to awake again in this world, after you closed your eyes to sleep. And there is no other reason to be given, why you have not dropped into hell since you arose in the morning, but that God's hand has held you up. There is no other reason to be given why you have not gone to hell, since you have sat here in the house of God, provoking his pure eyes by your sinful wicked manner of attending his solemn worship. Yea, there is nothing else that is to be given as a reason why you do not this very moment drop down into hell.

O sinner! Consider the fearful danger you are in: it is a great furnace of wrath, a wide and bottomless pit, full of the fire of wrath, that you are held over in the hand of that God, whose wrath is provoked and incensed as much against you, as against many of the damned in hell. You hang by a slender thread, with the flames of divine wrath flashing about it, and ready every moment to singe it, and burn it asunder; and you have no interest in any Mediator, and nothing to lay hold of to save yourself, nothing to keep off the flames of wrath, nothing of your own, nothing that you ever have done, nothing that you can do, to induce God to spare you one moment.—And consider here more particularly,

1. *Whose* wrath it is: it is the wrath of the infinite God. If it were only the wrath of man, though it were of the most potent prince, it would be comparatively little to be regarded. The wrath of kings is very much dreaded, especially of absolute monarchs, who have the possessions and lives of their subjects wholly in their power, to be disposed of at their mere will. Prov. 20:2. "The fear of a king is as the roaring of a lion: Whoso provoketh him to anger, sinneth against his own soul." The subject that very much enrages an arbitrary prince, is liable to suffer the most extreme torments that human art can invent, or human power can inflict. But the greatest earthly potentates in their greatest majesty and strength, and when clothed in their greatest terrors, are but feeble, despicable worms of the dust, in comparison of the great and almighty Creator and King of heaven and earth. It is but little that they can do, when most enraged, and when they have exerted the utmost of their fury. All the kings of the earth, before God, are as grasshoppers; they are nothing, and less than nothing: both their love and their hatred is to be despised. The wrath of the great King of kings, is as much more terrible than theirs, as his majesty is greater. Luke 12:4, 5. "And I say unto you, my friends, Be not afraid of them that kill the body, and after that, have no more that they can do. But I will forewarn you whom you shall fear: fear him, which after he hath killed, hath power to cast into hell: yea, I say unto you, Fear him."

2. It is the *fierceness* of his wrath that you are exposed to. We often read of the fury of God; as in Isaiah 59:18. "According to their deeds, accordingly he will repay fury to his adversaries." So Isaiah 66:15. "For behold, the Lord will come with fire, and with his chariots like a whirlwind, to render his anger with fury, and his rebuke with flames of fire." And in many other places. So, Rev. 19: 15. we read of "the wine press of the fierceness and wrath of Almighty God." The words are exceeding terrible. If it had only been said, "the wrath of God," the words would have implied that which

is infinitely dreadful: but it is "the fierceness and wrath of God." The fury of God! the fierceness of Jehovah! Oh, how dreadful must that be! Who can utter or conceive what such expressions carry in them! But it is also "the fierceness and wrath of *Almighty* God." As though there would be a very great manifestation of his almighty power in what the fierceness of his wrath should inflict, as though omnipotence should be as it were enraged, and exerted, as men are wont to exert their strength in the fierceness of their wrath. Oh! then, what will be the consequence! What will become of the poor worms that shall suffer it! Whose hands can be strong? And whose heart can endure? To what a dreadful, inexpressible, inconceivable depth of misery must the poor creature be sunk who shall be the subject of this!

· · ·

3. The *misery* you are exposed to is that which God will inflict to that end, that he might show what that wrath of Jehovah is. God hath had it on his heart to show to angels and men, both how excellent his love is, and also how terrible his wrath is. Sometimes earthly kings have a mind to show how terrible their wrath is, by the extreme punishments they would execute on those that would provoke them. Nebuchadnezzar, that mighty and haughty monarch of the Chaldean empire, was willing to show his wrath when enraged with Shadrach, Meshech, and Abednego; and accordingly gave orders that the burning fiery furnace should be heated seven times hotter than it was before; doubtless, it was raised to the utmost degree of fierceness that human art could raise it. But the great God is also willing to show his wrath, and magnify his awful majesty and mighty power in the extreme sufferings of his enemies. Rom. 9:22. "What if God, willing to show his wrath, and to make his power known, endure with much long-suffering the vessels of wrath fitted to destruction?" And seeing this is his design, and what he has determined, even to show how terrible the unrestrained wrath, the fury and fierceness of Jehovah is, he will do it to effect. There will be something accomplished and brought to pass that will be dreadful with a witness. When the great and angry God hath risen up and executed his awful vengeance on the poor sinner, and the wretch is actually suffering the infinite weight and power of his indignation, then will God call upon the whole universe to behold that awful majesty and mighty power that is to be seen in it. Isa. 33: 12–14. "And the people shall be as the burnings of lime, as thorns cut up shall they be burnt in the fire. Hear ye that are far off, what I have done; and ye that are near, acknowledge my might.

The sinners in Zion are afraid; fearfulness hath surprised the hypocrites," &c.

．．．

4. It is *everlasting* wrath. It would be dreadful to suffer this fierceness and wrath of Almighty God one moment; but you must suffer it to all eternity. There will be no end to this exquisite horrible misery. When you look forward, you shall see a long for ever, a boundless duration before you, which will swallow up your thoughts, and amaze your soul; and you will absolutely despair of ever having any deliverance, any end, any mitigation, any rest at all. You will know certainly that you must wear out long ages, millions of millions of ages, in wrestling and conflicting with this almighty merciless vengeance; and then when you have so done, when so many ages have actually been spent by you in this manner, you will know that all is but a point to what remains. So that your punishment will indeed be infinite. Oh, who can express what the state of a soul in such circumstances is! All that we can possibly say about it, gives but a very feeble, faint representation of it; it is inexpressible and inconceivable: For "who knows the power of God's anger?"

．．．

Therefore, let every one that is out of Christ, now awake and fly from the wrath to come. The wrath of Almighty God is now undoubtedly hanging over a great part of this congregation: Let every one fly out of Sodom: "Haste and escape for your lives, look not behind you, escape to the mountain, lest you be consumed."

Sarah Pierrepont

Jonathan Edwards wrote this prose-poem about his bride-to-be before he even met her. It is indicative of their relationship that he continued to think of her in the same way throughout their forty years of marriage. He sent his last message to her from his death bed: "Tell her that the uncommon union which has so long subsisted between us has been of such a nature as I trust is spiritual, and therefore will continue forever."

They say there is a young lady in [New Haven] who is beloved of that Great Being, who made and rules the world, and that there are certain seasons in which this Great Being, in some way or other invisible, comes to her and fills her mind with exceeding sweet delight, and that she hardly cares for any thing, except to meditate on him—that she expects after a while to be received up where he is, to be raised up out of the world and caught up into heaven; being assured that he loves her too well to let her remain at a distance from him always. There she is to dwell with him, and to be ravished with his love and delight forever. Therefore, if you present all the world before her, with the richest of its treasures, she disregards it and cares not for it, and is unmindful of any pain or affliction. She has a strange sweetness in her mind, and singular purity in her affections; is most just and conscientious in all her conduct; and you could not persuade her to do any thing wrong or sinful, if you would give her all the world, lest she should offend this Great Being. She is of a wonderful sweetness, calmness and universal benevolence of mind; especially after this Great God has manifested himself to her mind. She will sometimes go about from place to place, singing sweetly; and seems to be always full of joy and pleasure; and no one knows for what. She loves to be alone, walking in the fields and groves, and seems to have some one invisible always conversing with her.

QUESTIONS FOR DISCUSSION

Personal Narrative

1. What place does nature hold in Edwards' religious experience? What is the importance, for example, of the setting for his boyhood's "place of prayer"?
2. There can be little question over the fact that Edwards expresses his faith with great joy. According to the text, what accounts for this joy?
3. Edwards cites an example of the visions he claims to have seen. After looking carefully at the description of the event, discuss how the plainness of the style in which it is written either supports or detracts from the authenticity of the experience.
4. From your reading of the excerpts of *Personal Narrative*, what do you understand to be the unqualified virtues of the man who shares Edwards' faith? What religious pitfalls must such a person avoid?

Sinners in the Hands of an Angry God

1. Look carefully at the language of the sermon, discussing the tone with which the speaker addresses his audience. How does the speaker use repetition to support this tone?
2. Examine the sermon for its figures of speech. How many extended metaphors or analogies are developed? Which seem to you to be the most effective? Which might have been the most terrifying to a mid-eighteenth-century frontier audience?
3. Sermons are written only secondarily to be read; they are intended primarily to be heard. Choose a competent reader in the class and listen as he reads the sermon's most emotional paragraph, beginning "O sinner! Consider the fearful danger . . . ," (page 26) twice: first, in a quiet voice, then stridently and with passion. Contrast the two techniques of delivery. How do you account for the sermon's effectiveness in the quiet reading?
4. Do you find similarities or differences between the God worshiped in *Personal Narrative* and the God feared in the "Sinners" sermon? What are the attributes of God represented in each work?
5. Although popular misconceptions of Jonathan Edwards generally see him as having been a "hell-fire and brimstone" extremist, contemporary evidence seems to support quite an opposite opinion. What evidence do you find in the language of *Personal Narrative* and the "Sinners" sermon to correct the misconception?

Sarah Pierrepont

1. Contrast the speaking voice you may assume to be speaking in the "Sarah Pierrepont" passage with the voices you have already examined in *Personal Narrative* and the sermon. What factors determine the difference? How does the subject of each piece of writing affect the tone in which the speaker expresses himself?
2. To what degree does young Sarah Pierrepont exemplify the qualities for which the young Edwards himself was searching, as related in *Personal Narrative*? How realistic do you think this description of the young girl is?

ASSIGNMENTS FOR WRITING

1. In *Personal Narrative*, we observe Jonathan Edwards' total submission to God and the "sweetness" he finds in it. In "Sinners" we observe a harsh God before whom man is helpless as well as a ray of hope which man can find only if he will act. Write an essay discussing these two works

in terms of the concept of the Middle Way of American Puritanism.

2. "Sinners in the Hands of an Angry God" is a carefully molded work whose structure lends itself to analysis. Write a critical essay in which you show what that structure is. Comment on the manner in which Edwards uses this structure to support one point after another.

3. Besides informing and describing, the character sketch is meant to bring the personage alive in the mind of the reader. Attempt a character sketch of someone you know well, but follow Edwards' model, "Sarah Pierrepont," to the extent that you choose one major characteristic of your subject and make it both the main idea and the primary organizing device of your paper.

Colonial Portraits

UNKNOWN: John Freake, 1674

The first artists in the colonies were known as "limners." In addition to painting likenesses, they might be called upon to turn out a coat of arms or a sign for an inn. The Freake Limner's work has a gentle, graceful quality that sets him apart from the other unknown painters of the time. Even more effective in its coloring is the companion piece, *Mrs. Freake and Baby Mary.*

JOHN SINGLETON COPLEY: Epes Sargent, c. 1760

Copley (1738-1815), virtually self-taught, the first great portrait painter the colonies produced, remained unsurpassed. He had a genius for portraying the sheer force of character that these Boston merchants, magistrates, and, eventually, revolutionaries so amply possessed. He had little to fear from the competition of Philadelphia painters like Williams (c. 1710-c. 1790). Compared to Copley's massive *Epes Sargent (above)*, his pretty lady in pink seems almost as two-dimensional as her stage scenery garden.

WILLIAM WILLIAMS: Deborah Hall, 1766

MATTHEW PRATT: The American School, 1765

Pennsylvania-born Benjamin West (1738-1820) preceded Copley to Europe by fourteen years. When this handsome prodigy from the New World appeared in Rome, he was an exotic sensation. His hosts were enchanted to hear him exclaim "How like a Mohawk warrior!" when he first saw the celebrated classical statue the *Apollo Belvedere*. In London, he set himself up as a portrait painter but won his true fame with historical subjects like *The Death of Wolfe* and *Penn's Treaty with the Indians* (both 1771). A founding member of the Royal Academy, he became its president after the death of Reynolds. The King was his friend and greatest patron. Three generations of American painters came to London and were received by West with kindness and sound advice. Matthew Pratt (1734-1805) depicted his studio *(above)* with West, standing at the left, criticizing a drawing which Pratt is showing him.

Colonel Guy Johnson (opposite) was one of the first men to hold the office of Superintendent of Indian Affairs. We see him dressed for the role and, lurking behind him, his friend and secretary, Captain Joseph Brant—the Mohawk Chief Thayendanega. In his last years, West broke new ground with his *Death on the Pale Horse*, a swirling, romantic picture that looks forward to Delacroix as his earlier works had anticipated the French neoclassicists.

BENJAMIN WEST: Colonel Guy Johnson, c. 1776

JOHN SINGLETON COPLEY: Mrs. Ezekiel Goldthwaite, 1770

Copley turns the wife of Boston's town clerk (*above*) into a miraculous display of gleaming satin, as typical of him as the peculiar airlessness of the picture. Ensconced behind their picture frames, his sitters are palpably *there* but without any atmosphere at all around them. Just before the American Revolution, Copley went to England and never returned. The painter of *Paul Revere* rounded out his career portraying *The Daughters of George the Third*.

GILBERT STUART: Mrs. Richard Yates, c. 1793

West's pupil Stuart (1755-1828) had a successful career as a portrait painter in London and Dublin. Soon after his return to New York, he painted this no-nonsense lady in a mob cap *(above)*. With her appraising glance and the exquisite tension of her hands, Stuart has achieved a masterpiece of character that rivals his *John Adams* or the famous *Athenaeum* portrait of Washington. Peale (1741-1827) named his sons after illustrious painters. *The Staircase Group* (p. 40) shows Raphaelle Peale and his younger brother Titian Ramsey. When this picture was exhibited in a door frame, with a real step in front of it, the illusion was so perfect that Washington is said to have bowed to the two young gentlemen.

CHARLES WILLSON PEALE:
The Staircase Group, 1795

Edgar Allan Poe

Edgar Allan Poe crammed his unhappy life and his brilliant literary craftsmanship into the forty years between 1809 and the California gold rush. Without his ethereal poems and chilling stories, he would doubtless have been only a tragic and unknown statistic. But what a man does is usually a product of what he is, and his circumstances play a major role in making him what he is. Perhaps Poe's circumstances both curtailed his life and triggered his genius.

The factors of Poe's life could not be considered unique, but they were unusually combined and are therefore worthy of notice. Born in Boston, the only child of an itinerant American actor and his English wife, David and Elizabeth Arnold Poe, he inherited a creative bent and perhaps the artistic temperament that drove him. The shock of being orphaned at the age of two and the change of homes to a strict and wealthy middle-class environment left emotional scars. The home of his foster parents, John and Frances Allan, in Richmond, Virginia, was characterized by erosive tension. The Allans did not legally adopt him, nor did he ever feel an accepted member of the family.

While the Allans were in England, Poe attended the Manor House School at Stoke Newington, outside London, from 1817 to 1820. Six years later, after attending several schools back in Richmond, Poe was admitted to the University of Virginia. Unfortunately, his excellence as a student did not carry over into his gambling enterprises. John Allan refused to pay his debts, and Poe was forced to withdraw in disgrace.

Shortly after his disappointing university experience, Poe's young fiancée, Sarah Elmira Royster, was marshaled into marriage with another man. Furthermore, the lack of compatibility between Poe and Allan broke into an open rift, resulting in the hasty departure of the troubled and unhappy young man into what he called "the wide world"—Boston. There he published a collection of poems, *Tamerlane and Other Poems* (1827). It was not particularly well received, and the young poet enlisted in the United States Army as Edgar A. Perry. He was sent to duty in Charleston, South Carolina. In two years he had gained the rank of regimental sergeant major. Upon his discharge in 1829, he returned to poetry and published a second volume.

Why he accepted an appointment as a cadet to the United States Military Academy at West Point is not altogether clear. He stayed only briefly, receiving an honorable discharge in 1831; soon thereafter *Poems: Second Edition* was published.

Poe turned to writing stories, and in 1833 "Ms. Found in a Bottle" won him first prize in a major literary contest. It also entered his name among those of the promising young journalists of his time. However, Poe was, for the most part, in financially desperate circumstances, and he remained so until December of 1835, when he became assistant editor of the *Southern Literary Messenger* in Richmond. Five months later, he married his very young cousin, Virginia Clemm. Poe resigned from the *Messenger* after two years to complete and publish his only attempted novel, *The Narrative of Arthur Gordon Pym*.

Editing and the writing of tales were his bread and butter. Without these he could not have supported himself and his often sickly wife. Yet quarrels, often petty, with owners and publishers of the magazines he edited prompted Poe to give up one position after another. He tried founding his own magazine but needed to produce hack work for various periodicals in order to support his ailing wife and himself.

In 1845, while he was employed by the New York *Evening Mirror*, he published "The Raven." Immediately he became popular. "The Raven" was Poe's literary home run. At last he was a major figure in literary circles, the subject of essays such as that by James Russell Lowell, in which he wrote, "Mr. Poe has attained an individual eminence in our literature."

Poe's professional star was on the rise when, on January 30, 1847, his wife, Virginia, passed away. Soon there followed what might be called "sentimental relationships" with several ladies, to whom verses were addressed. A Lowell, Massachusetts, lecture was the setting for his meeting Mrs. Nancy Locke Heywood Richmond ("Annie"). It was during this period, too, that rumors about barroom escapades, featuring Poe's literary recitations, made their rounds. Twice he journeyed to Providence, Rhode Island, for the purpose of persuading Mrs. Sarah Helen Whitman to marry him. Reports of his taking a drug called laudanum in an attempt to commit suicide followed the second trip, but not all biographers accept these rumors.

July, 1849, found Poe dickering in still another attempt to start a new magazine. Interrupting his constant lecturing, he returned to Richmond to become engaged to the now-widowed Sarah Royster Shelton, his first love. He was en route back to New York to arrange his personal affairs when he was found unconscious in Baltimore and taken to the Washington College Hospital. On October 7, 1849, Poe died of undiagnosed causes, an ironic note reminiscent of the morbid themes on which he wrote.

Biographic speculation flared as the myth of the man became confused and clouded with the eerie tales that he wove. Poe was a master of sophisticated deception and affectation for his own social purposes of holding an audience or impressing the more gullible ladies. Yet, incontestably, there appeared in the record of his life's events a good bit more than ordinary unhappiness. His were the unusual reactions of an unusual and brilliant human being, not the bizarre antics of a quasi-lunatic. In short, there were more griefs than drinks or drugs.

Poe's work emerges through a pattern of personal disasters which erupted frequently and stirred his frenzied pace. His work appealed to an unusually wide spectrum of readers in America and abroad, particularly in France and England. Both ordinary people who adored Poe's contemporary, Longfellow, and renowned continental writers and critics who held forth on Whitman have had a common interest in Poe, who was for so brief a time America's leading poet.

His writing was as varied as his audience. With Nathaniel Hawthorne, he brought the modern short story to popular life. His one novel, *Arthur Gordon Pym*, however, has been held to be either the awkward literary stepchild of a South Pole exploration or an outright hoax. Poe himself later wrote that he considered it "a silly book." Generally his critical essays remain well regarded, though they are somewhat outmoded by his psychologizing and claims for the "rules of art," which are, according to Poe, as exacting and logical as the rules of science.

Poe's style outshone the cumbersome writing which was then common. A single Poe sentence, although itself usually a labyrinth of involuted and convoluted grammatical structure, is nonetheless studded with infusions of metrical phrases which sing out his moods and etch the memory with glimpses of ominous settings. For example, note the opening sentence of "The Fall of the House of Usher":

> During the whole of a dull, dark, and soundless day in the autumn of the year, when the clouds hung oppressively low in the heavens, I had been passing alone, on horseback, through a singularly dreary tract of country, and at length found myself, as the shades of the evening drew on, within view of the melancholy House of Usher.

The unity of mood-creating words and phrases, the long-flowing rhythm of subordinating expressions, and the power of language to evoke immediately a visual impression characterize Poe's style.

The poems issue as a stream of single thoughts set off by remarkable similarities in topics, figures, and metaphors, along with vivid contrasts within a single work. Their germ is often shrouded in Poe's subconscious; hence, the poem in his mind may have been superior to its written form, as may well be true of all art. Poe's poems are embellished by internal rhyme, assonance, alliteration, and onomatopoeia. Classical references and formal diction in "To Helen," for example, recall to the reader both the denotation and the connotations of the splendid past and lend their weight to the stature of the poetic statement.

Like Chopin, his exact contemporary, Poe was an artist whose talents were ignited by life itself; they burned brilliantly and were snuffed out in the perverse atmosphere which at once wrenched from him his desperate best and decreed his early death.

Tales

Poe's tales may be divided roughly into categories that represent fantasy, terror, death, revenge and murder, and, of course, mystery. Seldom does Poe seem less than obsessed with death, often in a grotesque manner and reached through the most devious of plans and circumstances.

Around 1832 Poe began burlesquing the best-selling tales in popular magazines, writing imitations of those being published. Then he discovered that he could produce better stories himself in a quite legitimate art form. In time the stories of Edgar Allan Poe became the foremost examples of short fiction.

In addition, Poe laid a solid foundation for the critic of the short story to build upon. As its cornerstone, Poe's short story rested upon what he called "a certain *single effect*," first established in the mind of the writer, then developed to its fulfillment. In an essay written in 1845, James Russell Lowell discussed Poe's ability to accomplish "this preconceived effect."

> In his tales, Mr. Poe has chosen to exhibit his power chiefly in that dim region which stretches from the very utmost limits of the probable into the weird confines of superstition and unreality. He combines in a very remarkable manner two faculties which are seldom found united: a power of influencing the mind of the reader by the impalpable shadows of mystery, and a minuteness of details which does not leave a pin or a button unnoticed. Both are, in truth, the natural results of the predominating quality of his mind, to which we have before alluded: analysis. It is this which distinguishes the artist. His mind at once reaches forward to the effect to be produced. Having resolved to bring about certain emotions in the reader, he makes all subordinate parts tend strictly to the common center. Even his mystery is mathematical to his own mind. To him x is a known quantity all along. In any picture that he paints, he understands the chemical properties of all his colors. However vague some of his figures may seem, however formless the shadows, to him the outline is as clear and distinct as that of a geometrical diagram.

Poe's own statement on the *single effect* appeared in a review of Nathaniel Hawthorne's book of short stories, *Twice-Told Tales.*

The tale proper affords the fairest field which can be afforded by the wide domains of mere prose, for the exercise of the highest genius. Were I bidden to say how this genius could be most advantageously employed for the best display of its powers, I should answer, without hesitation, "in the composition of a rhymed poem not to exceed in length what might be perused in an hour."

Were I called upon, however, to designate that class of composition which, next to such a poem as I have suggested, should best fulfill the demands and serve the purposes of ambitious genius, should offer it the most advantageous field of exertion, and afford it the fairest opportunity of display, I should speak at once of the brief prose tale. History, philosophy, and other matters of that kind, we leave out of the question, of course. *Of course*, I say, and in spite of the graybeards. These grave topics, to the end of time, will be best illustrated by what a discriminating world, turning up its nose at the drab pamphlets, has agreed to understand as *talent*. The ordinary novel is objectionable, from its length, for reasons analogous to those which render length objectionable in the poem. As the novel cannot be read at one sitting, it cannot avail itself of the immense benefit of *totality*. Worldly interests, intervening during the pauses of perusal, modify, counteract, and annul the impressions intended. But simple cessation in reading would, of itself, be sufficient to destroy the true unity. In the brief tale, however, the author is enabled to carry out his full design without interruption. During the hour of perusal, the soul of the reader is at the writer's control.

A skillful artist has constructed a tale. He has not fashioned his thoughts to accommodate his incidents, but having deliberately conceived a certain *single effect* to be wrought, he then invents such incidents, he then combines such events, and discusses them in such tone as may best serve him in establishing this preconceived effect. If his very first sentence tend not to the outbringing of this effect, then in his very first step has he committed a blunder. In the whole composition there should be no word written of which the tendency, direct or indirect, is not to the one pre-established design. And by such means, with such care and skill, a picture is at length painted which leaves in the mind of him who contemplates it with a kindred art, a sense of the fullest satisfaction. The idea of the tale, its thesis, has been presented unblemished, because undisturbed—an end absolutely demanded, yet, in the novel, altogether unattainable.

Few, if any, of Poe's tales were intended to be didactic. He was content, as he said, to "leave that to the graybeards." Nevertheless, a severe justice is often served upon the villains. Such retribution is more often than not a double one, involving both the physical and mental torment of the wrongdoer. Other themes that recur in

Poe's tales are the personal deterioration of the guilty and the consequence of neglected soical responsibilities. However, in most of Poe's stories, the penalties of crime result naturally, although it is not uncharacteristic of Poe to rely upon the supernatural to achieve his goals.

"The Fall of the House of Usher" cannot be so easily categorized as can many other Poe tales. In each there is a fabric of emotional tones woven together toward the dominant effect. In each there is the impression that not only has the line between reality and unreality been finely drawn, but that also there is a characteristic overlapping that disguises one from the other. The story is enhanced by its setting. Perhaps the alert reader can spot the clues to the finale in "The Fall of the House of Usher"—the rankness of vegetation, the instability of the land, and the "barely perceptible fissure" in the wall. Hopefully, however, these clues will not rob the reader of the sheer pleasure of being emotionally wrung out by these twilight adventures.

"The Purloined Letter" and Poe's other mystery stories differ from his tales of the grotesque. Whereas "The Cask of Amontillado" unnerves the reader, "The Purloined Letter" offers the pieces of a puzzle to be solved. Poe's word for solving the puzzle was *ratiocination*, the process of reasoning from premises to a conclusion. Poe's other famous tales of ratiocination are "The Murders in the Rue Morgue" and "The Gold Bug."

The Cask of Amontillado

The thousand injuries of Fortunato I had borne as I best could, but when he ventured upon insult I vowed revenge. You, who so well know the nature of my soul, will not suppose, however, that I gave utterance to a threat. *At length* I would be avenged; this was a point definitely settled—but the very definitiveness with which it was resolved precluded the idea of risk. I must not only punish but punish with impunity. A wrong is unredressed when retribution overtakes its redresser. It is equally unredressed when the avenger fails to make himself felt as such to him who has done the wrong.

It must be understood that neither by word nor deed had I given Fortunato cause to doubt my good will. I continued, as was my wont, to smile in his face, and he did not perceive that my smile *now* was at the thought of his immolation.

He had a weak point—this Fortunato—although in other regards he was a man to be respected and even feared. He prided himself on his connoisseurship in wine. Few Italians have the true virtuoso spirit. For the most part their enthusiasm is adopted to suit the time and opportunity, to practice imposture upon the British and Austrian *millionaires.* In painting and gemmary, Fortunato, like his countrymen, was a quack, but in the matter of old wines he was sincere. In this respect I did not differ from him materially;—I was skillful in the Italian vintages myself, and bought largely whenever I could.

It was about dusk, one evening during the supreme madness of the carnival season, that I encountered my friend. He accosted me with excessive warmth, for he had been drinking much. The man wore motley. He had on a tight-fitting parti-striped dress, and his head was surmounted by the conical cap and bells. I was so pleased to see him that I thought I should never have done wringing his hand.

I said to him—"My dear Fortunato, you are luckily met. How remarkably well you are looking today. But I have received a pipe of what passes for Amontillado, and I have my doubts."

"How?" said he. "Amontillado? A pipe? Impossible! And in the middle of the carnival!"

"I have my doubts," I replied; "and I was silly enough to pay the full Amontillado price without consulting you in the matter. You were not to be found, and I was fearful of losing a bargain."

"Amontillado!"

"I have my doubts."

"Amontillado!"

"And I must satify them."

"Amontillado!"

"As you are engaged, I am on my way to Luchresi. If anyone has a critical turn, it is he. He will tell me—"

"Luchresi cannot tell Amontillado from Sherry."

"And yet some fools will have it that his taste is a match for your own."

"Come, let us go."

"Whither?"

"To your vaults."

"My friend, no; I will not impose upon your good nature. I perceive you have an engagement. Luchresi—"

"I have no engagement;—come."

"My friend, no. It is not the engagement, but the severe cold with which I perceive you are afflicted. The vaults are insufferably damp. They are encrusted with niter."

"Let us go, nevertheless. The cold is merely nothing. Amontillado! You have been imposed upon. And as for Luchresi, he cannot distinguish Sherry from Amontillado."

Thus speaking, Fortunato possessed himself of my arm; and putting on a mask of black silk and drawing a *roquelaire* closely about my person, I suffered him to hurry me to my palazzo.

There were no attendants at home; they had absconded to make merry in honor of the time. I had told them that I should not return until the morning, and had given them explicit orders not to stir from the house. These orders were sufficient, I well knew, to insure their immediate disappearance, one and all, as soon as my back was turned.

I took from their sconces two flambeaux, and giving one to Fortunato, bowed him through several suites of rooms to the archway that led into the vaults. I passed down a long and winding staircase, requesting him to be cautious as he followed. We came at length to the foot of the descent, and stood together upon the damp ground of the catacombs of the Montresors.

The gait of my friend was unsteady, and the bells upon his cap jingled as he strode.

"The pipe," he said.

"It is farther on," said I; "but observe the white web-work which gleams from these cavern walls."

He turned towards me, and looked into my eyes with two filmy orbs that distilled the rheum of intoxication.

"Niter?" he asked, at length.

"Niter," I replied. "How long have you had that cough?"

"Ugh! ugh! ugh!—ugh! ugh! ugh!—ugh! ugh! ugh!—ugh! ugh! ugh!—ugh! ugh! ugh!"

My poor friend found it impossible to reply for many minutes.

"It is nothing," he said, at last.

"Come," I said, with decision, "we will go back; your health is precious. You are rich, respected, admired, beloved; you are happy, as once I was. You are a man to be missed. For me it is no matter. We will go back; you will be ill, and I cannot be responsible. Besides, there is Luchresi—"

"Enough," he said; "the cough is a mere nothing; it will not kill me. I shall not die of a cough."

"True—true," I replied; "and, indeed, I had no intention of alarming you unnecessarily—but you should use all proper caution. A draught of this Medoc will defend us from the damps."

Here I knocked off the neck of a bottle which I drew from a long row of its fellows that lay upon the mold.

"Drink," I said, presenting him the wine.

He raised it to his lips with a leer. He paused and nodded to me familiarly, while his bells jingled.

"I drink," he said, "to the buried that repose around us."

"And I to your long life."

He again took my arm, and we proceeded.

"These vaults," he said, "are extensive."

"The Montresors," I replied, "were a great and numerous family."

"I forget your arms."

"A huge human foot d'or, in a field azure; the foot crushes a serpent rampant whose fangs are imbedded in the heel."

"And the motto?"

"*Nemo me impune lacessit.*"

"Good!" he said.

The wine sparkled in his eyes and the bells jingled. My own fancy grew warm with the Medoc. We had passed through long walls of piled skeletons, with casks and puncheons intermingling, into the inmost recesses of the catacombs. I paused again, and this time I made bold to seize Fortunato by an arm above the elbow.

"The niter!" I said; "see, it increases. It hangs like moss upon the vaults. We are below the river's bed. The drops of moisture trickle among the bones. Come, we will go back ere it is too late. Your cough——"

"It is nothing," he said; "let us go on. But first, another draught of the Medoc."

I broke and reached him a flagon of De Grâve. He emptied it at a breath. His eyes flashed with a fierce light. He laughed and threw the bottle upwards with a gesticulation I did not understand.

I looked at him in surprise. He repeated the movement—a grotesque one.

"You do not comprehend?" he said.

"Not I," I replied.

"Then you are not of the brotherhood."

"How?"

"You are not of the masons."

"Yes, yes," I said; "yes, yes."

"You? Impossible! A mason?"

"A mason," I replied.

"A sign," he said, "a sign."

"It is this," I answered, producing from beneath the folds of my *roquelaire* a trowel.

"You jest," he exclaimed, recoiling a few paces. "But let us proceed to the Amontillado."

"Be it so," I said, replacing the tool beneath the cloak and again offering him my arm. He leaned upon it heavily. We continued our route in search of the Amontillado. We passed through a range of low arches, descended, passed on, and descending again, arrived at a deep crypt, in which the foulness of the air caused our flambeaux rather to glow than flame.

At the most remote end of the crypt there appeared another less spacious. Its walls had been lined with human remains, piled to the vault overhead, in the fashion of the great catacombs of Paris. Three sides of this interior crypt were still ornamented in this manner. From the fourth side the bones had been thrown down, and lay promiscuously upon the earth, forming at one point a mound of some size. Within the wall thus exposed by the displacing of the bones, we perceived a still interior crypt or recess, in depth about four feet, in width three, in height six or seven. It seemed to have been constructed for no especial use within itself, but formed merely the interval between two of the colossal supports of the roof of the catacombs, and was backed by one of their circumscribing walls of solid granite.

It was in vain that Fortunato, uplifting his dull torch, endeavored to pry into the depth of the recess. Its termination the feeble light did not enable us to see.

"Proceed," I said; "herein is the Amontillado. As for Luchresi——"

"He is an ignoramus," interrupted my friend, as he stepped unsteadily foward, while I followed immediately at his heels. In an instant he had reached the extremity of the niche, and finding his progress arrested by the rock, stood stupidly bewildered. A moment more and I had fettered him to the granite. In its surface were two iron staples, distant from each other about two feet, horizontally. From one of these depended a short chain, from the other a padlock. Throwing the links about his waist, it was but the work of a few seconds to secure it. He was too much astounded to resist. Withdrawing the key I stepped back from the recess.

"Pass your hand," I said, "over the wall; you cannot help feeling the niter. Indeed, it is *very* damp. Once more let me *implore* you to return. No? Then I must positively leave you. But I must first render you all the little attentions in my power."

"The Amontillado!" ejaculated my friend, not yet recovered from his astonishment.

"True," I replied; "the Amontillado."

As I said these words I busied myself among the pile of bones of which I have before spoken. Throwing them aside, I soon uncovered a quantity of building stone and mortar. With these materials and with the aid of my trowel, I began vigorously to wall up the entrance of the niche.

I had scarcely laid the first tier of the masonry when I discovered that the intoxication of Fortunato had in a great measure worn off. The earliest indication I had of this was a low moaning cry from the depth of the recess. It was *not* the cry of a drunken man. There was then a long and obstinate silence. I laid the second tier, and the third, and the fourth; and then I heard the furious vibrations of the chain. The noise lasted for several minutes, during which, that I might hearken to it with the more satisfaction, I ceased my labors and sat down upon the bones. When at last the clanking subsided, I resumed the trowel, and finished without interruption the fifth, the sixth, and the seventh tier. The wall was now nearly upon a level with my breast. I again paused, and holding the flambeaux over the mason-work, threw a few feeble rays upon the figure within.

A succession of loud and shrill screams, bursting suddenly from the throat of the chained form, seemed to thrust me violently back. For a brief moment I hesitated, I trembled. Unsheathing my rapier, I began to grope with it about the recess; but the thought of an instant reassured me. I placed my hand upon the solid fabric of the catacombs, and felt satisfied. I reapproached the wall; I replied to the yells of him who clamored. I re-echoed, I aided, I surpassed them in volume and in strength. I did this, and the clamorer grew still.

It was now midnight, and my task was drawing to a close. I had completed the eighth, the ninth, and the tenth tier. I had finished a portion of the last and the eleventh; there remained but a single stone to be fitted and plastered in. I struggled with its weight; I placed it partially in its destined position. But now there came from out the niche a low laugh that erected the hairs upon my head. It was succeeded by a sad voice, which I had difficulty in recognizing as that of the noble Fortunato. The voice said—

"Ha! ha! ha!—he! he! he!—a very good joke, indeed—an excellent jest. We will have many a rich laugh about it at the palazzo—he! he! he!—over our wine—he! he! he!"

"The Amontillado!" I said.

"He! he! he!—he! he! he!—yes, the Amontillado. But is it not getting late? Will not they be awaiting us at the palazzo, the Lady Fortunato and the rest? Let us be gone."

"Yes," I said, "let us be gone."

"For the love of God, Montresor!"

"Yes," I said, "for the love of God!"

But to these words I harkened in vain for a reply. I grew impatient. I called aloud—

"Fortunato!"

No answer. I called again—

"Fortunato!"

No answer still. I thrust a torch through the remaining aperture and let it fall within. There came forth in return only a jingling of the bells. My heart grew sick; it was the dampness of the catacombs that made it so. I hastened to make an end of my labor. I forced the last stone into its position; I plastered it up. Against the new masonry I re-erected the old rampart of bones. For the half of a century no mortal has disturbed them. *In pace requiescat!*

QUESTIONS FOR DISCUSSION

1. Is the speaker an ordinary man, a monster, or both? Explain.
2. Which do you feel is the stronger element in this story—character or setting? Why?

3. Is there any importance attached to the specific grievance of Montresor with Fortunato? Explain.
4. Why are the circumstances of the story ironic in the setting of Mardi Gras?

ASSIGNMENT FOR WRITING

Rewrite the ending of "The Cask of Amontillado" and bring Montresor to a clever justice.

The Fall of the House of Usher

Son cœur est un luth suspendu;
Sitôt qu'on le touche il résonne.[1]—De Béranger

During the whole of a dull, dark, and soundless day in the autumn of the year, when the clouds hung oppressively low in the heavens, I had been passing alone, on horseback, through a singularly dreary tract of country, and at length found myself, as the shades of the evening drew on, within view of the melancholy House of Usher. I know not how it was—but, with the first glimpse of the building, a sense of insufferable gloom pervaded my spirit. I say insufferable; for the feeling was unrelieved by any of that half-pleasurable, because poetic, sentiment, with which the mind usually receives even the sternest natural images of the desolate or terrible. I looked upon the scene before me—upon the mere house, and the simple landscape features of the domain— upon the bleak walls—upon the vacant eyelike windows—upon a few rank sedges—and upon a few white trunks of decayed trees —with an utter depression of soul which I can compare to no earthly sensation more properly than to the after-dream of the reveler upon opium—the bitter lapse into everyday life—the hideous dropping off of the veil. There was an iciness, a sinking, a sickening of the heart—an unredeemed dreariness of thought which no goading of the imagination could torture into aught of the sublime. What was it—I paused to think—what was it that so unnerved me in the contemplation of the House of Usher? It was a mystery all insoluble; nor could I grapple with the shadowy fancies that crowded upon me as I pondered. I was forced to fall back upon the unsatisfactory conclusion, that while, beyond doubt, there *are* combinations of very simple natural objects which have the power of thus affecting us, still the analysis of this power lies among considerations beyond our depth. It was possible, I reflected, that a mere different arrangement of the particulars of the scene, of the details of the picture, would be sufficient to modify, or perhaps to annihilate, its capacity for sorrowful impression; and, acting upon this idea, I reined my horse to the pre-

[1] His heart is a suspended lute; If it is touched it resounds.

cipitous brink of a black and lurid tarn that lay in unruffled luster by the dwelling, and gazed down—but with a shudder even more thrilling than before—upon the remodeled and inverted images of the gray sedge, and the ghastly tree stems, and the vacant and eyelike windows.

Nevertheless, in this mansion of gloom I now proposed to myself a sojourn of some weeks. Its proprietor, Roderick Usher, had been one of my boon companions in boyhood; but many years had elapsed since our last meeting. A letter, however, had lately reached me in a distant part of the country—a letter from him—which, in its wildly importunate nature, had admitted of no other than a personal reply. The MS. gave evidence of nervous agitation. The writer spoke of acute bodily illness—of a mental disorder which oppressed him—and of an earnest desire to see me, as his best, and indeed his only, personal friend, with a view of attempting, by the cheerfulness of my society, some alleviation of his malady. It was the manner in which all this, and much more, was said—it was the apparent *heart* that went with his request— which allowed me no room for hesitation; and I accordingly obeyed forthwith what I still considered a very singular summons.

Although, as boys, we had been even intimate associates, yet I really knew little of my friend. His reserve had been always excessive and habitual. I was aware, however, that his very ancient family had been noted, time out of mind, for a peculiar sensibility of temperament, displaying itself, through long ages, in many works of exalted art, and manifested, of late, in repeated deeds of munificent yet unobtrusive charity, as well as in a passionate devotion to the intricacies, perhaps even more than to the orthodox and easily recognizable beauties, of musical science. I had learned, too, the very remarkable fact, that the stem of the Usher race, all time-honored as it was, had put forth, at no period, any enduring branch; in other words, that the entire family lay in the direct line of descent, and had always, with very trifling and very temporary variation, so lain. It was this deficiency, I considered, while running over in thought the perfect keeping of the character of the premises with the accredited character of the people, and while speculating upon the possible influence which the one, in the long lapse of centuries, might have exercised upon the other—it was this deficiency, perhaps, of collateral issue, and the consequent undeviating transmission, from sire to son, of the patrimony with the name, which had, at length, so identified the two as to merge the original title of the estate in the quaint and equivocal appellation of the "House of Usher"—an appellation which seemed to include, in the minds of the peasantry who used it, both the family and the family mansion.

I have said that the sole effect of my somewhat childish experiment—that of looking down within the tarn—had been to deepen the first singular impression. There can be no doubt that the consciousness of the rapid increase of my superstition—for why should I not so term it?—served mainly to accelerate the increase itself. Such, I have long known, is the paradoxical law of all sentiments having terror as a basis. And it might have been for this reason only, that, when I again uplifted my eyes to the house itself, from its image in the pool, there grew in my mind a strange fancy—a fancy so ridiculous, indeed, that I but mention it to show the vivid force of the sensations which oppressed me. I had so worked upon my imagination as really to believe that about the whole mansion and domain there hung an atmosphere peculiar to themselves and their immediate vicinity—an atmosphere which had no affinity with the air of heaven, but which had reeked up from the decayed trees, and the gray wall, and the silent tarn—a pestilent and mystic vapor, dull, sluggish, faintly discernible, and leaden-hued.

Shaking off from my spirit what *must* have been a dream, I scanned more narrowly the real aspect of the building. Its principal feature seemed to be that of an excessive antiquity. The discoloration of ages had been great. Minute fungi overspread the whole exterior, hanging in a fine tangled web-work from the eaves. Yet all this was apart from any extraordinary dilapidation. No portion of the masonry had fallen; and there appeared to be a wild inconsistency between its still perfect adaptation of parts, and the crumbling condition of the individual stones. In this there was much that reminded me of the specious totality of old woodwork which has rotted for long years in some neglected vault, with no disturbance from the breath of the external air. Beyond this indication of extensive decay, however, the fabric gave little token of instability. Perhaps the eye of a scrutinizing observer might have discovered a barely perceptible fissure, which, extending from the roof of the building in front, made its way down the wall in a zigzag direction, until it become lost in the sullen waters of the tarn.

Noticing these things, I rode over a short causeway to the house. A servant in waiting took my horse, and I entered the Gothic archway of the hall. A valet, of stealthy step, thence conducted me, in silence, through many dark and intricate passages in my progress to the *studio* of his master. Much that I encountered on the way contributed, I know not how, to heighten the vague sentiments of which I have already spoken. While the objects around me—while the carvings of the ceilings, the somber tapestries of the walls, the ebon blackness of the floors, and the phantasmagoric armorial trophies which rattled as I strode, were but matters to which, or to such as which, I had been accustomed from my infancy—while I hestitated not to acknowledge how familiar was all this—I still wondered to find how unfamiliar were the fancies which ordinary images were stirring up. On one of the staircases, I met the physician of the family. His countenance, I thought, wore a mingled expression of low cunning and perplexity. He accosted me with trepidation and passed on. The valet now threw open a door and ushered me into the presence of his master.

The room in which I found myself was very large and lofty. The windows were long, narrow, and pointed, and at so vast a distance from the black oaken floor as to be altogether inaccessible from within. Feeble gleams of encrimsoned light made their way through the trellised panes, and served to render sufficiently distinct the more prominent objects around; the eye, however, struggled in vain to reach the remoter angles of the chamber, or the recesses of the vaulted and fretted ceiling. Dark draperies hung upon the walls. The general furniture was profuse, comfortless, antique, and tattered. Many books and musical instruments lay scattered about, but failed to give any vitality to the scene. I felt that I breathed an atmosphere of sorrow. An air of stern, deep, and irredeemable gloom hung over and pervaded all.

Upon my entrance, Usher arose from a sofa on which he had been lying at full length, and greeted me with a vivacious warmth which had much in it, I at first thought, of an overdone cordiality— of the constrained effort of the *ennuyé* man of the world. A glance, however, at his countenance, convinced me of his perfect sincerity. We sat down; and for some moments, while he spoke not, I gazed upon him with a feeling half of pity, half of awe. Surely, man had never before so terribly altered, in so brief a period, as had Roderick Usher! It was with difficulty that I could bring myself to admit the identity of the wan being before me with the companion of my early boyhood. Yet the character of his face had been at all times remarkable. A cadaverousness of complexion; an eye large, liquid, and luminous beyond comparison; lips somewhat thin and very pallid, but of a surpassingly beautiful curve; a nose of delicate Hebrew model, but with a breadth of nostril unusual in similar formations; a finely molded chin, speaking, in its want of prominence, of a want of moral energy; hair of a more than weblike softness and tenuity; these features, with an inordinate expansion above the regions of the temple, made up altogether a countenance not easily to be forgotten. And now in the mere exaggeration of the prevailing character of these features, and of the expression they were wont to convey, lay so much of change that I doubted to whom I spoke. The now ghastly pallor of the skin, and the now miraculous luster of the eye, above all things startled and even awed me. The silken hair, too, had been suffered to grow all unheeded, and as, in its wild gossamer texture, it floated rather than fell about the face, I could not, even with effort, connect its arabesque expression with any idea of simple humanity.

In the manner of my friend I was at once struck with an incoherence—an inconsistency; and I soon found this to arise from a series of feeble and futile struggles to overcome an habitual trepidancy—an excessive nervous agitation. For something of this nature I had indeed been prepared, no less by his letter, than by reminiscences of certain boyish traits, and by conclusions deduced from his peculiar physical conformation and temperament. His action was alternately vivacious and sullen. His voice varied rapidly from a tremulous indecision (when the animal spirits seemed utterly in abeyance) to that species of energetic concision—that abrupt, weighty, unhurried, and hollow-sounding enunciation—that leaden, self-balanced and perfectly modulated guttural utterance, which may be observed in the lost drunkard, or the irreclaimable eater of opium, during the periods of his most intense excitement.

It was thus that he spoke of the object of my visit, of his earnest desire to see me, and of the solace he expected me to afford him. He entered, at some length, into what he conceived to be the nature of his malady. It was, he said, a constitutional and a family evil, and one for which he despaired to find a remedy—a mere nervous affection, he immediately added, which would undoubtedly soon pass off. It displayed itself in a host of unnatural sensations. Some of these, as he detailed them, interested and bewildered me; although, perhaps, the terms, and the general manner of the narration had their weight. He suffered much from a morbid acuteness of the senses; the most insipid food was alone endurable; he could wear only garments of certain texture; the odors of all flowers were oppressive; his eyes were tortured by even a faint light; and there were but peculiar sounds, and these from stringed instruments, which did not inspire him with horror.

To an anomalous species of terror I found him a bounden slave. "I shall perish," said he, "I *must* perish in this deplorable folly. Thus, thus, and not otherwise, shall I be lost. I dread the events of the future, not in themselves, but in their results. I shudder at the thought of any, even the most trivial, incident, which may operate upon this intolerable agitation of soul. I have, indeed, no abhorrence of danger, except in its absolute effect—in terror. In this unnerved—in this pitiable condition—I feel that the period will sooner or later arrive when I must abandon life and reason together, in some struggle with the grim phantasm, FEAR."

I learned, moreover, at intervals, and through broken and equivocal hints, another singular feature of his mental condition. He was enchained by certain superstitious impressions in regard to the dwelling which he tenanted, and whence, for many years, he had never ventured forth—in regard to an influence whose superstitious force was conveyed in terms too shadowy here to be restated—an influence which some peculiarities in the mere form and substance of his family mansion, had, by dint of long sufferance, he said, obtained over his spirit—an effect which the *physique* of the gray walls and turrets, and of the dim tarn into which they all looked down, had, at length, brought about upon the *morale* of his existence.

He admitted, however, although with hesitation, that much of the peculiar gloom which thus afflicted him could be traced to a more natural and far more palpable origin—to the severe and long-continued illness—indeed to the evidently approaching dissolution —of a tenderly beloved sister—his sole companion for long years— his last and only relative on earth. "Her decease," he said, with a bitterness which I can never forget, "would leave him (him the hopeless and the frail) the last of the ancient race of the Ushers." While he spoke, the lady Madeline (for so was she called) passed slowly through a remote portion of the apartment, and, without having noticed my presence, disappeared. I regarded her with an utter astonishment not unmingled with dread—and yet I found it impossible to account for such feelings. A sensation of stupor oppressed me, as my eyes followed her retreating steps. When a door, at length, closed upon her, my glance sought instinctively and eagerly the countenance of the brother—but he had buried his face in his hands, and I could only perceive that a far more than ordinary wanness had overspread the emaciated fingers through which trickled many passionate tears.

The disease of the lady Madeline had long baffled the skill of her physicians. A settled apathy, a gradual wasting away of the person, and frequent although transient affections of a partially cataleptical character, were the unusual diagnosis. Hitherto she had steadily borne up against the pressure of her malady, and had not betaken herself finally to bed; but, on the closing in of the evening of my arrival at the house, she succumbed (as her brother told me at night with inexpressible agitation) to the prostrating power of the destroyer; and I learned that the glimpse I had obtained of her person would thus probably be the last I should obtain—that the lady, at least while living, would be seen by me no more.

For several days ensuing, her name was unmentioned by either Usher or myself: and during this period I was busied in earnest endeavors to alleviate the melancholy of my friend. We painted and read together; or I listened, as if in a dream, to the wild improvisations of his speaking guitar. And thus, as a closer and still closer intimacy admitted me more unreservedly into the recesses of his spirit, the more bitterly did I perceive the futility of all attempt at cheering a mind from which darkness, as if an inherent positive quality, poured forth upon all objects of the moral and physical universe, in one unceasing radiation of gloom.

I shall ever bear about me a memory of the many solemn hours I thus spent alone with the master of the House of Usher. Yet I should fail in any attempt to convey an idea of the exact character of the studies, or of the occupations, in which he involved me, or led me the way. An excited and highly distempered ideality threw a sulfurous luster over all. His long improvised dirges will ring forever in my ears. Among other things, I hold painfully in mind a certain singular perversion and amplification of the wild air of the last waltz of Von Weber. From the paintings over which his elaborate fancy brooded, and which grew, touch by touch, into vaguenesses at which I shuddered the more thrillingly, because I shuddered knowing not why;—from these paintings (vivid as their images now are before me) I would in vain endeavor to educe more than a small portion which should lie within the compass of merely written words. By the utter simplicity, by the nakedness of his designs, he arrested and overawed attention. If ever mortal painted an idea, that mortal was Roderick Usher. For me at least— in the circumstances then surrounding me—there arose out of the pure abstractions which the hypochondriac contrived to throw upon his canvas, an intensity of intolerable awe, no shadow of which felt I ever yet in the contemplation of the certainly glowing yet too concrete reveries of Fuseli.

One of the phantasmagoric conceptions of my friend, partaking not so rigidly of the spirit of abstraction, may be shadowed forth, although feebly, in words. A small picture presented the interior of an immensely long and rectangular vault or tunnel, with low walls, smooth, white, and without interruption or device. Certain accessory points of the design served well to convey the idea that this excavation lay at an exceeding depth below the surface of the earth. No outlet was observed in any portion of its vast extent, and no torch, or other artificial source of light was discernible;

yet a flood of intense rays rolled throughout, and bathed the whole in a ghastly and inappropriate splendor.

I have just spoken of that morbid condition of the auditory nerve which rendered all music intolerable to the sufferer, with the exception of certain effects of stringed instruments. It was, perhaps, the narrow limits to which he thus confined himself upon the guitar, which gave birth, in great measure, to the fantastic character of his performances. But the fervid *facility* of his *impromptus* could not be so accounted for. They must have been, and were, in the notes, as well as in the words of his wild fantasias (for he not unfrequently accompanied himself with rhymed verbal improvisations), the result of the intense mental collectedness and concentration to which I have previously alluded as observable only in particular moments of the highest artificial excitement. The words of one of these rhapsodies I have easily remembered. I was, perhaps, the more forcibly impressed with it, as he gave it, because, in the under or mystic current of its meaning, I fancied that I perceived, and for the first time, a full consciousness on the part of Usher, of the tottering of his lofty reason upon her throne. The verses, which were entitled "The Haunted Palace," ran very nearly, if not accurately, thus:

In the greenest of our valleys,
    By good angels tenanted,
Once a fair and stately palace—
    Radiant palace—reared its head.
In the monarch Thought's dominion—
    It stood there!
Never seraph spread a pinion
    Over fabric half so fair.

Banners yellow, glorious, golden,
    On its roof did float and flow;
(This—all this—was in the olden
    Time long ago)
And every gentle air that dallied,
    In that sweet day,
Along the ramparts plumed and pallid,
    A winged odor went away.

Wanderers in that happy valley
    Through two luminous windows saw
Spirits moving musically
    To a lute's well-tunèd law,

Round about a throne, where sitting
    (Porphyrogene!)
In state his glory well befitting,
    The ruler of the realm was seen.

And all with pearl and ruby glowing
    Was the fair palace door,
Through which came flowing, flowing, flowing
    And sparkling evermore,
A troop of Echoes whose sweet duty
    Was but to sing,
In voices of surpassing beauty,
    The wit and wisdom of their king.

But evil things, in robes of sorrow,
    Assailed the monarch's high estate;
(Ah, let us mourn, for never morrow
    Shall dawn upon him, desolate!)
And, round about his home, the glory
    That blushed and bloomed
Is but a dim-remembered story
    Of the old time entombed.

And travelers now within that valley,
    Through the red-litten windows, see
Vast forms that move fantastically
    To a discordant melody;
While, like a rapid ghastly river,
    Through the pale door,
A hideous throng rush out forever,
    And laugh—but smile no more.

I well remember that suggestions arising from this ballad, led us into a train of thought wherein there became manifest an opinion of Usher's which I mention not so much on account of its novelty (for other men[2] have thought thus), as on account of the pertinacity with which he maintained it. This opinion, in its general form, was that of the sentience of all vegetable things. But, in his disordered fancy, the idea had assumed a more daring character, and trespassed, under certain conditions, upon the kingdom of inorganization. I lack words to express the full extent, or the earnest *abandon* of his persuasion. The belief, however, was connected (as I have previously hinted) with the gray stones of the home

[2] Watson, Dr. Percival, Spallanzani, and especially the Bishop of Landaff.— See *Chemical Essays*, vol. v. [E.A.P.]

of his forefathers. The conditions of the sentience had been here, he imagined, fulfilled in the method of collocation of these stones— in the order of their arrangement, as well as in that of the many *fungi* which overspread them, and of the decayed trees which stood around—above all, in the long undisturbed endurance of this arrangement, and in its reduplication in the still waters of the tarn. Its evidence—the evidence of the sentience—was to be seen, he said (and I here started as he spoke), in the gradual yet certain condensation of an atmosphere of their own about the waters and the walls. The result was discoverable, he added, in that silent, yet importunate and terrible influence which for centuries had molded the destinies of his family, and which made *him* what I now saw him—what he was. Such opinions need no comment, and I will make none.

Our books—the books which, for years, had formed no small portion of the mental existence of the invalid—were, as might be supposed, in strict keeping with this character of phantasm. We pored together over such works as the *Ververt et Chartreuse* of Gresset; the *Belphegor* of Machiavelli; the *Heaven and Hell* of Swedenborg; the *Subterranean Voyage of Nicholas Klimm* by Holberg; the *Chiromancy* of Robert Flud, of Jean D'Indaginé, and of De la Chambre; the *Journey into the Blue Distance of Tieck*; and the *City of the Sun* of Campanella. One favorite volume was a small octavo edition of the *Directorium Inquisitorum*, by the Dominican Eymeric de Gironne; and there were passages in Pomponius Mela, about the old African Satyrs and Aegipans, over which Usher would sit dreaming for hours. His chief delight, however, was found in the perusal of an exceedingly rare and curious book in quarto Gothic—the manual of a forgotten church— the *Vigiliæ Mortuorum secundum Chorum Ecclesiæ Maguntinæ.*

I could not help thinking of the wild ritual of this work, and of its probable influence upon the hypochondriac, when, one evening, having informed me abruptly that the lady Madeline was no more, he stated his intention of preserving her corpse for a fortnight (previously to its final interment) in one of the numerous vaults within the main walls of the building. The worldly reason, however, assigned for this singular proceeding, was one which I did not feel at liberty to dispute. The brother had been led to his resolution (so he told me) by consideration of the unusual character of the malady of the deceased, of certain obtrusive and eager inquiries on the part of her medical men, and of the remote and exposed situation of the burial-ground of the family. I will not deny that when I called to mind the sinister countenance of the person whom I met upon the staircase, on the day of my arrival at the house, I had no desire to oppose what I regarded as at best a harmless, and by no means an unnatural, precaution.

At the request of Usher, I personally aided him in the arrangements for the temporary entombment. The body having been encoffined, we two alone bore it to its rest. The vault in which we placed it (and which had been so long unopened that our torches, half smothered in its oppressive atmosphere, gave us little opportunity for investigation) was small, damp, and entirely without means of admission for light; lying, at great depth, immediately beneath that portion of the building in which was my own sleeping apartment. It had been used, apparently, in remote feudal times, for the worst purposes of a dungeon-keep, and, in later days, as a place of deposit for powder, or some other highly combustible substance, as a portion of its floor, and the whole interior of a long archway through which we reached it, were carefully sheathed with copper. The door, of massive iron, had been also similarly protected. Its immense weight caused an unusually sharp grating sound, as it moved upon its hinges.

Having deposited our mournful burden upon tressels within this region of horror, we partially turned aside the yet unscrewed lid of the coffin, and looked upon the face of the tenant. A striking similitude between the brother and sister now first arrested my attention; and Usher, divining, perhaps, my thoughts, murmured out some few words from which I learned that the deceased and himself had been twins, and that sympathies of a scarcely intelligible nature had always existed between them. Our glances, however, rested not long upon the dead—for we could not regard her unawed. The disease which had thus entombed the lady in the maturity of youth had left, as usual in all maladies of a strictly cataleptical character, the mockery of a faint blush upon the bosom and the face, and that suspiciously lingering smile upon the lip which is so terrible in death. We replaced and screwed down the lid, and, having secured the door of iron, made our way, with toil, into the scarcely less gloomy apartments of the upper portion of the house.

And now, some days of bitter grief having elapsed, an observable change came over the features of the mental disorder of my friend. His ordinary manner had vanished. His ordinary occupations were neglected or forgotten. He roamed from chamber to chamber with hurried, unequal, and objectless step. The pallor of his countenance had assumed, if possible, a more ghastly hue—but the luminousness of his eye had utterly gone out. The once occasional huskiness of his tone was heard no more; and a tremulous quaver, as if of extreme terror, habitually characterized his utterance. There were times, indeed, when I thought his unceasingly agitated mind was laboring with some oppressive secret, to divulge which he struggled for the necessary courage. At times, again, I was obliged to resolve all into the mere inexplicable vagaries of madness, for I beheld him gazing upon vacancy for long hours, in an attitude of the profoundest attention, as if listening to some imaginary sound. It was no wonder that his condition terrified—that it infected me. I felt creeping upon me, by slow yet certain degrees, the wild influences of his own fantastic yet impressive superstitions.

It was, especially, upon retiring to bed late in the night of the seventh or eighth day after the placing of the lady Madeline within the dungeon, that I experienced the full power of such feelings. Sleep came not near my couch—while the hours waned and waned away. I struggled to reason off the nervousness which had dominion over me. I endeavored to believe that much, if not all of what I felt, was due to the bewildering influence of the gloomy furniture of the room—of the dark and tattered draperies, which, tortured into motion by the breath of a rising tempest, swayed fitfully to and fro upon the walls, and rustled uneasily about the decorations of the bed. But my efforts were fruitless. An irrepressible tremor gradually pervaded my frame; and, at length, there sat upon my very heart an incubus of utterly causeless alarm. Shaking this off with a gasp and a struggle, I uplifted myself upon the pillows, and peering earnestly within the intense darkness of the chamber, harkened—I know not why, except that an instinctive spirit prompted me—to certain low and indefinite sounds which came, through the pauses of the storm, at long intervals, I knew not whence. Overpowered by an intense sentiment of horror, unaccountable yet unendurable, I threw on my clothes with haste (for I felt that I should sleep no more during the night), and endeavored to arouse myself from the pitiable condition into which I had fallen, by pacing rapidly to and fro through the apartment.

I had taken but few turns in this manner, when a light step on an adjoining staircase arrested my attention. I presently recognized it as that of Usher. In an instant afterward he rapped, with a gentle touch, at my door, and entered, bearing a lamp. His countenance was, as usual, cadaverously wan—but, moreover, there was a species of mad hilarity in his eyes—an evidently restrained *hysteria* in his whole demeanor. His air appalled me—but anything was preferable to the solitude which I had so long endured and I even welcomed his presence as a relief.

"And you have not seen it?" he said abruptly, after having

stared about him for some moments in silence—"you have not then seen it?—but, stay! you shall." Thus speaking, and having carefully shaded his lamp, he hurried to one of the casements, and threw it freely open to the storm.

The impetuous fury of the entering gust nearly lifted us from our feet. It was, indeed, a tempestuous yet sternly beautiful night, and one wildly singular in its terror and its beauty. A whirlwind had apparently collected its force in our vicinity; for there were frequent and violent alterations in the direction of the wind; and the exceeding density of the clouds (which hung so low as to press upon the turrets of the house) did not prevent our perceiving the lifelike velocity with which they flew careering from all points against each other, without passing away into the distance. I say that even their exceeding density did not prevent our perceiving this—yet we had no glimpse of the moon or stars—nor was there any flashing forth of the lightning. But the under surfaces of the huge masses of agitated vapor, as well as all terrestrial objects immediately around us, were glowing in the unnatural light of a faintly luminous and distinctly visible gaseous exhalation which hung about and enshrouded the mansion.

"You must not—you shall not behold this!" said I, shudderingly, to Usher, as I led him, with a gentle violence, from the window to a seat. "These appearances, which bewilder you, are merely electrical phenomena not uncommon—or it may be that they have their ghastly origin in the rank miasma of the tarn. Let us close this casement; the air is chilling and dangerous to your frame. Here is one of your favorite romances. I will read, and you shall listen; and so we will pass away this terrible night together."

The antique volume which I had taken up was the *Mad Trist* of Sir Launcelot Canning; but I had called it a favorite of Usher's more in sad jest than in earnest; for, in truth, there is little in its uncouth and unimaginative prolixity which could have had interest for the lofty and spiritual ideality of my friend. It was, however, the only book immediately at hand; and I indulged a vague hope that the excitement which now agitated the hypochondriac might find relief (for the history of mental disorder is full of similar anomalies) even in the extremeness of the folly which I should read. Could I have judged, indeed, by the wild overstrained air of vivacity with which he hearkened, or apparently hearkened, to the words of the tale, I might well have congratulated myself upon the success of my design.

I had arrived at that well-known portion of the story where Ethelred, the hero of the Trist, having sought in vain for peaceable admission into the dwelling of the hermit, proceeds to make good an entrance by force. Here, it will be remembered, the words of the narrative run thus:

"And Ethelred, who was by nature of a doughty heart, and who was now mighty withal, on account of the powerfulness of the wine which he had drunken, waited no longer to hold parley with the hermit, who, in sooth, was of an obstinate and maliceful turn, but, feeling the rain upon his shoulders, and fearing the rising of the tempest, uplifted his mace outright, and, with blows, made quickly room in the plankings of the door for his gauntleted hand; and now pulling therewith sturdily, he so cracked, and ripped, and tore all asunder, that the noise of the dry and hollow-sounding wood alarumed and reverberated throughout the forest."

At the termination of this sentence I started, and for a moment, paused; for it appeared to me (although I at once concluded that my excited fancy had deceived me)—it appeared to me that, from some very remote portion of the mansion, there came, indistinctly, to my ears, what might have been, in its exact similarity of character, the echo (but a stifled and dull one certainly) of the very cracking and ripping sound which Sir Launcelot had so particularly described. It was, beyond doubt, the coincidence alone which had arrested my attention; for, amid the rattling of the sashes of the casements, and the ordinary commingled noises of the still increasing storm, the sound, in itself, had nothing, surely, which would have interested or disturbed me. I continued the story:

"But the good champion Ethelred, now entering within the door, was sore enraged and amazed to perceive no signal of the maliceful hermit; but, in the stead thereof, a dragon of a scaly and prodigious demeanor, and of a fiery tongue, which sate in guard before a palace of gold, with a floor of silver; and upon the wall there hung a shield of shining brass with this legend enwritten—

Who entereth herein, a conqueror hath bin;
Who slayeth the dragon, the shield he shall win.

And Ethelred uplifted his mace, and struck upon the head of the dragon, which fell before him, and gave up his pesty breath, with a shriek so horrid and harsh, and withal so piercing, that Ethelred had fain to close his ears with his hands against the dreadful noise of it, the like whereof was never before heard."

Here again I paused abruptly, and now with a feeling of wild amazement—for there could be no doubt whatever that, in this instance, I did actually hear (although from what direction it proceeded I found it impossible to say) a low and apparently distant, but harsh, protracted, and most unusual screaming or grating sound—the exact counterpart of what my fancy had already conjured up for the dragon's unnatural shriek as described by the romancer.

Oppressed, as I certainly was, upon the occurrence of the second and most extraordinary coincidence, by a thousand conflicting sensations, in which wonder and extreme terror were predominant, I still retained sufficient presence of mind to avoid exciting, by any observation, the sensitive nervousness of my companion. I was by no means certain that he had noticed the sounds in question; although, assuredly, a strange alteration had, during the last few minutes, taken place in his demeanor. From a position fronting my own, he had gradually brought round his chair, so as to sit with his face to the door of the chamber; and thus I could but partially perceive his features, although I saw that his lips trembled as if he were murmuring inaudibly. His head had dropped upon his breast—yet I knew that he was not asleep, from the wide and rigid opening of the eye as I caught a glance of it in profile. The motion of his body, too, was at variance with this idea—for he rocked from side to side with a gentle yet constant and uniform sway. Having rapidly taken notice of all this, I resumed the narrative of Sir Launcelot, which thus proceeded:

"And now, the champion, having escaped from the terrible fury of the dragon, bethinking himself of the brazen shield, and of the breaking up of the enchantment which was upon it, removed the carcass from out of the way before him, and approached valorously over the silver pavement of the castle to where the shield was upon the wall; which in sooth tarried not for his full coming, but fell down at his feet upon the silver floor, with a mighty great and terrible ringing sound."

No sooner had these syllables passed my lips, than—as if a shield of brass had indeed, at the moment, fallen heavily upon a floor of silver—I became aware of a distinct, hollow, metallic, and clangorous, yet apparently muffled reverberation. Completely unnerved, I leaped to my feet; but the measured rocking movement of Usher was undisturbed. I rushed to the chair in which he sat. His eyes were bent fixedly before him, and throughout his whole countenance there reigned a stony rigidity. But, as I placed my hand upon his shoulder, there came a strong shudder over his whole person; a sickly smile quivered about his lips; and I saw that he spoke in a low, hurried, and gibbering murmur, as if unconscious of my presence. Bending closely over him, I at length drank in the hideous import of his words.

"Not hear it?—yes, I hear it, and *have* heard it. Long—long—long—many minutes, many hours, many days, have I heard it—yet I dared not—oh, pity me, miserable wretch that I am!—I dared not—I *dared* not speak! *We have put her living in the tomb!* Said I not that my senses were acute? I *now* tell you that I heard her first feeble movements in the hollow coffin. I heard them—many, many days ago—yet I dared not—*I dared not speak!* And now—tonight—Ethelred—ha! ha! the breaking of the hermit's door, and the death-cry of the dragon, and the clangor of the shield!—say, rather, the rending of her coffin, and the grating of the iron hinges of her prison, and her struggles within the coppered archway of the vault! Oh whither shall I fly? Will she not be here anon? Is she not hurrying to upbraid me for my haste? Have I not heard her footstep on the stair? Do I not distinguish that heavy and horrible beating of her heart? MADMAN!" here he sprang furiously to his feet, and shrieked out his syllables, as if in the effort he were giving up his soul—"MADMAN! I TELL YOU THAT SHE NOW STANDS WITHOUT THE DOOR!"

As if in the superhuman energy of his utterance there had been found the potency of a spell—the hung antique panels to which the speaker pointed, threw slowly back, upon the instant, their ponderous and ebony jaws. It was the work of the rushing gust—but then without those doors there DID stand the loftly and enshrouded figure of the lady Madeline of Usher. There was blood upon her white robes, and the evidence of some bitter struggle upon every portion of her emaciated frame. For a moment she remained trembling and reeling to and fro upon the threshold, then, with a low moaning cry, fell heavily inward upon the person of her brother, and in her violent and now final death-agonies, bore him to the floor a corpse, and a victim to the terrors he had anticipated.

From that chamber, and from that mansion, I fled aghast. The storm was still abroad in all its wrath as I found myself crossing the old causeway. Suddenly there shot along the path a wild light, and I turned to see whence a gleam so unusual could have issued; for the vast house and its shadows were alone behind me. The radiance was that of the full, setting, and blood-red moon which now shone vividly through that once barely discernible fissure of which I have before spoken as extending from the roof of the building, in a zigzag direction, to the base. While I gazed, this fissure rapidly widened—there came a fierce breath of the whirlwind—

the entire orb of the satellite burst at once upon my sight—my brain reeled as I saw the mighty walls rushing asunder—there was a long tumultuous shouting sound like the voice of a thousand waters— and the deep and dank tarn at my feet closed sullenly and silently over the fragments of the "HOUSE OF USHER."

QUESTIONS FOR DISCUSSION

1. At the end of paragraph five (page 57), the narrator mentions "a barely perceptible fissure" which at the end of the story causes the mansion to collapse. What larger meaning does Poe suggest with this crack or fault in the building?
2. The song that Roderick Usher sings, "The Haunted Palace," describes literally a mansion similar to his own. How far may the description of the mansion be carried symbolically? What contribution does the song make to the unity of the story?
3. The narrator calls Roderick Usher a "hypochondriac." What is the nature of his illness? What is the connection between his illness and his sister Madeline's death? What is the connection between his death and the reappearance of Madeline?
4. Did Usher create his decaying situation, or was he simply a victim of family misfortune or even of powers beyond human control? Explain your understanding of Usher's situation.
5. How far can you trust the narrator of this story in accepting his account of the facts? Is he objective in relating them? What factors might have influenced his judgment of persons or situations?
6. Do you think that Poe identifies with any of the characters in this story? If so, which character or characters?

ASSIGNMENTS FOR WRITING

1. In 150 to 200 words, unveil a setting by means of which you suggest that a grim story is about to follow.
2. Write a short story in which a decaying microcosm initiates its own end or is ended by adverse external circumstances.
3. In 150 to 200 words, introduce an unusual character whose appearance, attitudes, and actions suggest a violent past.

Poetry

Poe considered himself foremost a poet. As such, his philosophy of creative art is crucial to one's understanding of his work. He said, "With me, poetry has not been a purpose, but a passion." Many of his fifty-odd poems are correspondingly strange and sometimes puzzling expressions of this passion.

Much of Poe's poetry came quite early in his life and typifies his notion that good poetry has its own rules and reasons for being. Poetry was, in the poetic gospel according to Poe, an intricate journey from some supposed "here" to a less well-defined "there." It had to do with one of three subjects: life, death, or love. Death is the dominating theme in a resounding melodic or minor key.

In his "Letter to B——" Poe wrote:

> A poem, in my opinion, is opposed to a work of science by having, for its *immediate* object, pleasure, not truth; to romance, by having for its object an *indefinite* instead of a *definite* pleasure, being a poem only so far as this object is attained; romance presenting perceptible images with definite, poetry with *in*definite sensations, to which end music is an *essential*, since the comprehension of sweet sound is our most indefinite conception. Music, when combined with a pleasurable idea, is poetry; music without the idea is simply music; the idea without the music is prose from its very definitiveness.

Furthermore, Poe argued, poetry must not be moralistic; it must not attempt to preach. In his essay, "The Poetic Principle," he wrote:

> It has been assumed, tacitly and avowedly, directly and indirectly, that the ultimate object of all Poetry is Truth. Every poem, it is said, should inculcate a moral; and by this moral is the poetical merit of the work to be adjudged. We Americans especially have patronized this happy idea; and we Bostonians, very especially, have developed it in full. We have taken it into our heads that to write a poem simply for the poem's sake, and to acknowledge such to have been our design, would be to confess ourselves radically wanting in the true Poetic dignity and force:—but the simple fact is, that, would we but permit ourselves to look into our own souls,

we should immediately there discover that under the sun there neither exists nor *can* exist any work more thoroughly dignified—more supremely noble than this very poem—this poem *per se*—this poem which is a poem and nothing more—this poem written solely for the poem's sake.

"The Raven" is Poe's best model, combining the ideal subjects—life, death, and love—with the poetic blend of musical language; in other words, the poem for its own sake. Often, however, a poem can be a window of words and symbols through which we peer to view an idea or value. Such a poem is "Eldorado." Man apparently continues to search for a utopia, his own "Shangri-La" or "Fountain of Youth." In "Eldorado" Poe directs our search to this perfect existence. Nonetheless, the reader must keep in mind the spirit in which these poems were conceived, a spirit that elevates art above its subject and asks only that the subject be treated beautifully.

The Raven

Once upon a midnight dreary, while I pondered, weak and weary,
Over many a quaint and curious volume of forgotten lore—
While I nodded, nearly napping, suddenly there came a tapping,
As of some one gently rapping, rapping at my chamber door.
" 'T is some visitor," I muttered, "tapping at my chamber door—
       Only this and nothing more."

Ah, distinctly I remember it was in the bleak December;
And each separate dying ember wrought its ghost upon the floor.
Eagerly I wished the morrow;—vainly I had sought to borrow
From my books surcease of sorrow—sorrow for the lost Lenore—
For the rare and radiant maiden whom the angels name Lenore—
       Nameless *here* for evermore.

And the silken, sad, uncertain rustling of each purple curtain
Thrilled me—filled me with fantastic terrors never felt before;
So that now, to still the beating of my heart, I stood repeating
" 'T is some visitor entreating entrance at my chamber door—
Some late visitor entreating entrance at my chamber door;—
       This it is and nothing more."

Presently my soul grew stronger; hesitating then no longer,
"Sir," said I, "or Madam, truly your forgiveness I implore;
But the fact is I was napping, and so gently you came rapping,
And so faintly you came tapping, tapping at my chamber door,
That I scarce was sure I heard you"—here I opened wide the door;—
       Darkness there and nothing more.

Deep into that darkness peering, long I stood there wondering,
       fearing,
Doubting, dreaming dreams no mortal ever dared to dream before;
But the silence was unbroken, and the stillness gave no token,
And the only word there spoken was the whispered word, "Lenore!"
This I whispered, and an echo murmured back the word "Lenore!"
       Merely this and nothing more.

Back into the chamber turning, all my soul within me burning,
Soon again I heard a tapping somewhat louder than before.
"Surely," said I, "surely that is something at my window lattice;

Let me see, then, what thereat is, and this mystery explore—
Let my heart be still a moment and this mystery explore;—
                        'T is the wind and nothing more!"

Open here I flung the shutter, when, with many a flirt and flutter
In there stepped a stately Raven of the saintly days of yore.
Not the least obeisance made he; not a minute stopped or stayed he;
But, with mien of lord or lady, perched above my chamber door—
Perched upon a bust of Pallas just above my chamber door—
                        Perched, and sat, and nothing more.

Then this ebony bird beguiling my sad fancy into smiling,
By the grave and stern decorum of the countenance it wore,
"Though thy crest be shorn and shaven, thou," I said, "art sure
                        no craven,
Ghastly grim and ancient Raven wandering from the Nightly
                        shore—
Tell me what thy lordly name is on the Night's Plutonian shore!"
                        Quoth the Raven, "Nevermore."

Much I marveled this ungainly fowl to hear discourse so plainly,
Though its answer little meaning—little relevancy bore;
For we cannot help agreeing that no living human being
Ever yet was blessed with seeing bird above his chamber door—
Bird or beast upon the sculptured bust above his chamber door,
                        With such name as "Nevermore."

But the Raven, sitting lonely on the placid bust, spoke only
That one word, as if his soul in that one word he did outpour.
Nothing farther then he uttered—not a feather then he fluttered—
Till I scarcely more than muttered "Other friends have flown
                        before—
On the morrow *he* will leave me, as my hopes have flown before."
                        Then the bird said "Nevermore."

Startled at the stillness broken by reply so aptly spoken,
"Doubtless," said I, "what it utters is its only stock and store
Caught from some unhappy master whom unmerciful Disaster
Followed fast and followed faster till his songs one burden bore—
Till the dirges of his Hope that melancholy burden bore
                        Of 'Never—nevermore.'"

But the Raven still beguiling all my fancy into smiling,
Straight I wheeled a cushioned seat in front of bird, and bust and
                               door;
Then, upon the velvet sinking, I betook myself to linking
Fancy unto fancy, thinking what this ominous bird of yore—
What this grim, ungainly, ghastly, gaunt, and ominous bird of yore
                               Meant in croaking "Nevermore."

This I sat engaged in guessing, but no syllable expressing
To the fowl whose fiery eyes now burned into my bosom's core;
This and more I sat divining, with my head at ease reclining
On the cushion's velvet lining that the lamp-light gloated o'er.
But whose velvet violet lining with the lamp-light gloating o'er,
                               She shall press, ah, nevermore!

Then, methought, the air grew denser, perfumed from an unseen
                               censer
Swung by Seraphim whose foot-falls tinkled on the tufted floor.
"Wretch" I cried, "thy God hath lent thee—by these angels he
                               hath sent thee
Respite—respite and nepenthe from thy memories of Lenore;
Quaff, oh quaff this kind nepenthe and forget this lost Lenore!"
                               Quoth the Raven "Nevermore."

"Prophet!" said I, "thing of evil! prophet still, if bird or devil!—
Whether Tempter sent, or whether tempest tossed thee here ashore,
Desolate yet all undaunted, on this desert land enchanted—
On this home by Horror haunted—tell me truly, I implore—
Is there—*is* there balm in Gilead?—tell me—tell me, I implore!"
                               Quoth the Raven "Nevermore."

"Prophet!" said I, "thing of evil!—prophet still, if bird or devil!
By that Heaven that bends above us—by that God we both adore—
Tell this soul with sorrow laden if, within the distant Aidenn,
It shall clasp a sainted maiden whom the angels name Lenore—
Clasp a rare and radiant maiden whom the angels name Lenore."
                               Quoth the Raven "Nevermore."

"Be that word our sign of parting, bird or fiend!" I shrieked,
                               upstarting—
"Get thee back into the tempest and the Night's Plutonian shore!
Leave no black plume as a token of that lie thy soul hath spoken!

Leave my loneliness unbroken!—quit the bust above my door!
Take thy beak from out my heart, and take thy form from off my
door!"
          Quoth the Raven "Nevermore."

And the Raven, never flitting, still is sitting, *still* is sitting
On the pallid bust of Pallas just above my chamber door;
And his eyes have all the seeming of a demon's that is dreaming,
And the lamp-light o'er him streaming throws his shadow on the
floor;
And my soul from out that shadow that lies floating on the floor
          Shall be lifted—nevermore!

Eldorado

    Gaily bedight,
    A gallant knight,
In sunshine and in shadow,
    Had journeyed long,
    Singing a song,
In search of Eldorado.

    But he grew old—
    This knight so bold—
And o'er his heart a shadow
    Fell as he found
    No spot of ground
That looked like Eldorado.

    And, as his strength
    Failed him at length,
He met a pilgrim shadow—
    "Shadow," said he,
    "Where can it be—
This land of Eldorado?"

    "Over the Mountains
    Of the Moon,
Down the Valley of the Shadow,
    Ride, boldly ride,"
    The shade replied,—
"If you seek for Eldorado!"

To Helen

Helen, thy beauty is to me
  Like those Nicéan barks of yore,
That gently, o'er a perfumed sea,
  The weary, way-worn wanderer bore
  To his own native shore.

On desperate seas long wont to roam,
  Thy hyacinth hair, thy classic face,
Thy Naiad airs have brought me home
  To the glory that was Greece,
  And the grandeur that was Rome.

Lo! in yon brilliant window-niche
  How statue-like I see thee stand,
The agate lamp within thy hand!
  Ah, Psyche, from the regions which
  Are Holy-Land!

Annabel Lee

It was many and many a year ago,
  In a kingdom by the sea
That a maiden there lived whom you may know
  By the name of Annabel Lee;
And this maiden she lived with no other thought
  Than to love and be loved by me.

I was a child and *she* was a child,
  In this kingdom by the sea,
But we loved with a love that was more than love—
  I and my Annabel Lee—
With a love that the winged seraphs of heaven
  Coveted her and me.

And this was the reason that, long ago,
  In this kingdom by the sea,
A wind blew out of a cloud, chilling
  My beautiful Annabel Lee;

So that her highborn kinsmen came
    And bore her away from me,
To shut her up in a sepulchre
    In this kingdom by the sea.

The angels, not half so happy in heaven,
    Went envying her and me—
Yes!—that was the reason (as all men know,
    In this kingdom by the sea)
That the wind came out of the cloud by night,
    Chilling and killing my Annabel Lee.

But our love it was stronger by far than the love
    Of those who were older than we—
    Of many far wiser than we—
And neither the angels in heaven above,
    Nor the demons down under the sea,
Can ever dissever my soul from the soul
    Of the beautiful Annabel Lee:

For the moon never beams, without bringing me dreams
    Of the beautiful Annabel Lee;
And the stars never rise, but I feel the bright eyes
    Of the beautiful Annabel Lee;
And so, all the night-tide, I lie down by the side
Of my darling—my darling—my life and my bride,
    In the sepulchre there by the sea—
    In her tomb by the sounding sea.

The Bells

I

Hear the sledges with the bells—
    Silver bells!
What a world of merriment their melody foretells!
    How they tinkle, tinkle, tinkle,
      In the icy air of night!
    While the stars that oversprinkle
    All the heavens, seem to twinkle

With a crystalline delight;
Keeping time, time, time,
In a sort of Runic rhyme,
To the tintinnabulation that so musically wells
From the bells, bells, bells, bells,
Bells, bells, bells—
From the jingling and the tinkling of the bells.

II

Hear the mellow wedding bells—
Golden bells!
What a world of happiness their harmony foretells!
Through the balmy air of night
How they ring out their delight!—
From the molten-golden notes,
And all in tune,
What a liquid ditty floats
To the turtle-dove that listens, while she gloats
On the moon!
Oh, from out the sounding cells,
What a gush of euphony voluminously wells!
How it swells!
How it dwells
On the Future!—how it tells
Of the rapture that impels
To the swinging and the ringing
Of the bells, bells, bells—
Of the bells, bells, bells, bells,
Bells, bells, bells—
To the rhyming and the chiming of the bells!

III

Hear the loud alarum bells—
Brazen bells!
What a tale of terror, now their turbulency tells!
In the startled ear of night
How they scream out their affright!
Too much horrified to speak,
They can only shriek, shriek,
Out of tune,
In a clamorous appealing to the mercy of the fire,

In a mad expostulation with the deaf and frantic fire,
Leaping higher, higher, higher,
With a desperate desire,
And a resolute endeavor
Now—now to sit, or never,
By the side of the pale-faced moon.
Oh, the bells, bells, bells!
What a tale their terror tells
Of Despair!
How they clang, and clash, and roar!
What a horror they outpour
On the bosom of the palpitating air!
Yet the ear, it fully knows,
By the twanging,
And the clanging,
How the danger ebbs and flows;
Yet the ear distinctly tells,
In the jangling,
And the wrangling,
How the danger sinks and swells,
By the sinking or the swelling in the anger of the bells—
Of the bells—
Of the bells, bells, bells, bells,
Bells, bells, bells—
In the clamor and the clanging of the bells!

IV

Hear the tolling of the bells—
Iron bells!
What a world of solemn thought their monody compels!
In the silence of the night,
How we shiver with affright
At the melancholy menace of their tone!
For every sound that floats
From the rust within their throats
Is a groan.
And the people—ah, the people—
They that dwell up in the steeple,
All alone,
And who, tolling, tolling, tolling,
In that muffled monotone,
Feel a glory in so rolling

On the human heart a stone—
They are neither man nor woman—
They are neither brute nor human—
        They are Ghouls:—.
And their king is who tolls:—
And he rolls, rolls, rolls,
            Rolls
        A pæan from the bells!
And his merry bosom swells
        With the pæan of the bells!
And he dances, and he yells;
Keeping time, time, time,
In a sort of Runic rhyme,
    To the pæan of the bells:—
        Of the bells:
Keeping time, time, time
In a sort of Runic rhyme,
    To the throbbing of the bells—
Of the bells, bells, bells—
    To the sobbing of the bells:—
Keeping time, time, time,
    As he knells, knells, knells,
    In a happy Runic rhyme,
        To the rolling of the bells—
    Of the bells, bells, bells:—
        To the tolling of the bells—
Of the bells, bells, bells, bells,
        Bells, bells, bells—
To the moaning and the groaning of the bells.

QUESTIONS FOR DISCUSSION

The Raven

1. What is the prevailing mood in "The Raven"? Citing specific examples, trace the elements which Poe used to establish the mood of this poem.
2. In "The Philosophy of Composition," Poe wrote that "a close circumspection of space is necessary to the effect of insulated incident:— it has the force of a frame to a picture." To what degree has Poe achieved "the force of a frame to a picture" in his description of the locale in the first five stanzas?
3. List the feelings which the poet elicits at various stages of the poem. What accounts for these feelings?
4. What can you tell about the character and temperament of the speaker in the poem? Look for clues in the language of his narration of incidents and in the language of his conversations with himself and with the raven. Look at the description of furnishings in his room.
5. Where is the primary vital action of the poem taking place? Is it between the lover and the bird? in the mind of the speaker? in the mind of the poet at work? or in the response of the reader?
6. Why does "The Raven" tempt so many readers to parody it?

Eldorado

1. To what work of literature is the speaker referring with the words "the Valley of the Shadow"?
2. Why do you think Poe chose a knight as the recipient of his advice?
3. To what does the phrase "Over the Mountains Of the Moon" refer?
4. What is Poe's message in this poem?

The Conqueror Worm

1. Describe the situation in this poem: What is happening to whom and where? What are the consequences?
2. In what sense is the worm a conqueror? What is Poe's attitude toward the conqueror and the conquered?
3. Does the poet consider the play of "Man" a tragedy? Explain.

To Helen

1. Paraphrase the first stanza and show how the classical allusions relate to "the glory that was Greece,/And the grandeur that was Rome."
2. In what respects is the speaker like Ulysses (Odysseus), "the weary, way-worn wanderer"?
3. What makes the stanzas different from each other? What do these differences contribute to the unity of the poem?

4. What are the qualities of womanliness embodied in the references to Helen and Psyche?

Annabel Lee

1. What is gained by having the story within the poem presented in a mythological setting? How do you interpret the kingdom, the cloud and wind, the highborn kinsmen?
2. What is the significance of the sea in this poem? Did Annabel Lee drown?
3. What words and phrases in the poem suggest that Poe might have been speaking about his deceased wife?
4. Does the nursery-rhyme effect of the final stanza spoil a bona fide expression of anguish throughout the rest of the poem?

The Bells

1. How do the four different types of bells suggest a progression through the poem? What are the specific stages in this progression?
2. Notice the dominant vowel sounds in each of the four stanzas of the poem. How do these sounds relate to the description of each bell? What is this relationship between sound and meaning called?
3. What effect does the irregular rhyming contribute? Does it help to unify the poem? Does it distract the reader? Explain.
4. Why are some lines so much longer or shorter than others? What is the particular effect of the longest lines? What does this variety in line length do to a careful reading of the poem?

ASSIGNMENTS FOR WRITING

1. Throughout Poe's poetry one finds frequent references to angels and demons. In a brief essay, discuss Poe's use of spiritual beings as participants in his poetry. Use specific evidence from the poems.

2. In "The Raven," Poe makes particular use of the following poetic devices:

assonance	metaphor
alliteration	hyperbole
onomatopoeia	irony
simile	personification

   Choose one of the poetic devices and write an analysis of its effective use, giving several examples in the poem.

3. In a well-organized composition, state Poe's apparent view of women, basing your opinion on specific references to some of the preceding poems.

4. Citing specific examples from the poetry, trace the influence of a particular characteristic or event in Poe's biography. Be sure that you limit yourself to known facts.

5. In about three well-developed paragraphs, show the conflict or reconciliation in Poe's poetry between natural orderliness and imaginative emotionalism.

6. According to your view, what should be the purpose of poetry? Write an essay in which you argue, as Poe did, for a particular philosophy of poetry.

7. Write a short poem on one of Poe's three basic subjects: life, death, or love. Follow his principle of avoiding a moralizing tone. Let the poem exist for its own sake.

Transcendentalism

To fully understand Emerson and Thoreau, we must explore the meaning of transcendentalism, the philosophy which stimulated much of their thoughts and actions. Although American transcendentalism bears its own marks of individuality, we find the basic elements of the philosophy in a variety of literary sources. From classical civilizations the transcendentalists took the ideas of Plato and Plotinus; from England they drew upon Coleridge and Carlyle; from continental Europe they studied Goethe, Fitche, Hegel, and Kant; from the Orient they refined the lines of the *Bhagavad Gita*, the sacred text of Hindu, the essence of mysticism, solitude, and contemplation. To be sure, the transcendentalism of Emerson and Thoreau offered no orderly system of thought. Its exact nature often confused even the profoundest thinkers. Essentially, it strove to understand and explain the relationship between man, his God, and the external world of nature without relying upon those experiences rooted in the senses.

Reason and knowledge do not serve the transcendentalist; rather, *intuition* is the key, the immediate and sudden grasping of things. These moments of intuition are inconsistent and sporadic and may appear to the individual anywhere in a hurrying glow of illumination to the mind, "a certain brief experience . . . in the highway or in the market, in some place, at some time," as Emerson says. Intuition, transcending the range of a man's experience and the depth of his reason, flows into every person.

The transcendentalists made man's communication with God an aspect of *man's* will. God, to the transcendental thinker, became more of a spirit than a being, an "Over-Soul" as Emerson called it, which flowed through every living being in varying degrees. Each man, any man, could seek divine truth and communion for himself, without the aid of either logical reasoning or some figure of authority to help him. Obviously such a philosophy shifted the stress to man, proclaiming him as the central essence of the universe. As a result, the concept of individuality, like a rare and stunning flower, pushed its leaves through the old, dry earth of a Puritan theology and philosophy that too long had denied man the right to assert himself. The offshoots of this concept define even today the whole meaning of the American character; self-confidence, self-reliance, self-adjustment and development still stir up the atmosphere of romantic idealism emanating from the early transcendentalists.

Ralph Waldo Emerson

Ralph Waldo Emerson suffered early the blows and wounds of tragedy. In the eighth year of his life, 1811, he encountered death. His father, a Boston Unitarian minister whom his famous son later described as "a somewhat social gentleman, but severe to us children," passed on, leaving his family—a widow and three other sons—in poverty. Only the charity of the dead minister's congregation kept the family alive, providing them with a dwelling and the means of subsistence for some years, while the boys struggled with the housework, pursued their studies, and offered their prayers. What held the brothers together, Emerson felt, was "the iron band of poverty."

Early in life, during his years of education at the Boston Latin School and later at Harvard College, Emerson developed a need for solitude and introspection. In the journals he kept from 1819 until late in his adult life, there is abundant evidence of the growth of a mind expansive and sensitive, brilliant and critical. Meanwhile, sickness took the lives of his two younger brothers and robbed him of his first wife, Ellen Tucker, contributing to the growth in him of a skepticism toward life diametrically opposed to the essentially optimistic outlook that pervaded the essays he wrote and the lectures he gave.

In 1829, after teaching school and studying for the ministry, Emerson accepted appointment as pastor of the Second Unitarian Church of Boston; but three years later, after a dispute with his congregation over religious doctrines, he resigned. He visited Europe soon after, meeting many of its literary figures: Thomas Carlyle, William Wordsworth, Samuel Taylor Coleridge among them. With Carlyle he began a friendship that through spirited letters lasted a lifetime. All these men encouraged him in his search for new insights into moral truth and the nature of man, while fanning into flame Emerson's original love for literature. It was a love that never diminished, and his essays shimmer with quotations from Shakespeare and Swedenborg, Plutarch and Newton, Persian poetry translated into German.

In 1835, two years after his return from Europe, he married Lydia Jackson and settled in Concord, not far from Boston. There his career as a lecturer and essayist began in earnest, his first published work *Nature* appearing in 1836, the year his wife bore his first child, a son Waldo. Although *Nature* showed the first sparks of his genius as a philosopher whose faith rested in man, it was "The American Scholar" that first won for him the respect of the nation's thinkers. Oliver Wendell Holmes called "The American Scholar"—an oration Emerson delivered in 1837 to the Phi Beta Kappa Society during Harvard's commencement activities—"Our Intellectual Declaration of Independence." In 1838 his address to the Harvard Divinity School, challenging the Christian teaching of special divine Revelation and proclaiming strongly man's moral nature, exploded such a bomb of controversy and called forth such accusations of atheism that for twenty years thereafter Emerson's voice was banned from Harvard's campus.

Although his need for solitude and privacy structured much of his life, in Concord he lived amidst a distinguished group of friends. Henry David Thoreau, Elizabeth Hoar, Ellery Channing, Bronson Alcott, and Margaret Fuller: all these kindred spirits walked and talked at length together. The Transcendental Club met to argue questions at Emerson's house. There he listened to the plans of the Brook Farm community, established in 1841 by George Ripley to escape the dullness of life by combining manual labor and intellectual life in a joyous marriage. With Margaret Fuller he built up, contributed to, and for a time was editor of the *Dial*, the transcendentalists' journal.

In 1842, however, the death of his son Waldo brought him melancholy and renewed self-criticism, and increasingly he found solace only in work: poetry, lecture tours, and new essays. From this point on until his death, skepticism filled his thoughts and struggled with the faith he had come to believe in. Outwardly, however, success came with his ever-increasing fame as both speaker and writer.

Emerson was fifty-eight when the Civil War broke out, and he devoted himself wholly to the cause of freedom—writing, lecturing, traveling. Thoreau died in 1862, Hawthorne followed in 1864, and Emerson's circle of friends gradually diminished in size. But Emerson himself lived on to lecture again at Harvard and to visit England once more before his death in 1882.

The first collection of Emerson's works appeared in 1841 as *Essays: First Series. Essays: Second Series* followed in 1844. His other important works include *Representative Men* (1850), which explores the minds and spirits of great figures like Shakespeare, Goethe, Plato, and Napoleon; *English Traits* (1856), which offers impressions of a visit to England in 1847; and *Poems* (1846).

Although Emerson's poetry often lacks music, it boasts a brilliance of imagery, a sensitivity to the world of nature, and an eye for paradox. Of his prose, some critics say Emerson is over-wordy, inconsistent, sententious, repetitious, and too abstract, though the last of these complaints seems unjustified in such later works as the essay "Behavior," which deals essentially with the concrete. No one today, however, denies the magnitude and force of Emerson's ideas which burst like a stream of sunlight upon the gray windows of mid-nineteenth-century American thought.

from Nature

INTRODUCTION

Our age is retrospective. It builds the sepulchres of the fathers. It writes biographies, histories, and criticism. The foregoing generations beheld God and nature face to face; we, through their eyes. Why should not we also enjoy an original relation to the universe? Why should not we have a poetry and philosophy of insight and not of tradition, and a religion by revelation to us, and not the history of theirs? Embosomed for a season in nature, whose floods of life stream around and through us, and invite us, by the powers they supply, to action proportioned to nature, why should we grope among the dry bones of the past, or put the living generation into masquerade out of its faded wardrobe? The sun shines to-day also. There is more wool and flax in the fields. There are new lands, new men, new thoughts. Let us demand our own works and laws and worship.

Undoubtedly we have no questions to ask which are unanswerable. We must trust the perfection of the creation so far as to believe that whatever curiosity the order of things has awakened in our minds, the order of things can satisfy. Every man's condition is a solution in hieroglyphic to those inquiries he would put. He acts it as life, before he apprehends it as truth. In like manner, nature is already, in its forms and tendencies, describing its own design. Let us interrogate the great apparition that shines so peacefully around us. Let us inquire, to what end is nature?

All science has one aim, namely, to find a theory of nature. We have theories of races and of functions, but scarcely yet a remote approach to an idea of creation. We are now so far from the road to truth, that religious teachers dispute and hate each other, and speculative men are esteemed unsound and frivolous. But to a sound judgment, the most abstract truth is the most practical. Whenever a true theory appears, it will be its own evidence. Its test is, that it will explain all phenomena. Now many are thought not only unexplained but inexplicable; as language, sleep, madness, dreams, beasts, sex.

Philosophically considered, the universe is composed of Nature and the Soul. Strictly speaking, therefore, all that is separate from us, all which Philosophy distinguishes as the NOT ME, that is, both nature and art, all other men and my own body, must be ranked under this name, NATURE. In enumerating the values of nature and casting up their sum, I shall use the word in both senses;—in its common and in its philosophical import. In inquiries so general as our present one, the inaccuracy is not material; no confusion of thought will occur. *Nature,* in the common sense, refers to essences unchanged by man; space, the air, the river, the leaf. *Art* is applied to the mixture of his will with the same things, as in a house, a canal, a statue, a picture. But his operations taken together are so insignificant, a little chipping, baking, patching, and washing, that in an impression so grand as that of the world on the human mind, they do not vary the result.

NATURE

To go into solitude, a man needs to retire as much from his chamber as from society. I am not solitary whilst I read and write, though nobody is with me. But if a man would be alone, let him look at the stars. The rays that come from those heavenly worlds will separate between him and what he touches. One might think the atmosphere was made transparent with this design, to give man, in the heavenly bodies, the perpetual presence of the sublime. Seen in the streets of cities, how great they are! If the stars should appear one night in a thousand years, how would men believe and adore; and preserve for many generations the remembrance of the city of God which had been shown! But every night come out these envoys of beauty, and light the universe with their admonishing smile.

The stars awaken a certain reverence, because though always present, they are inaccessible; but all natural objects make a kindred impression, when the mind is open to their influence. Nature never wears a mean appearance. Neither does the wisest man extort her secret, and lose his curiosity by finding out all her perfection. Nature never became a toy to a wise spirit. The flowers, the animals, the mountains, reflected the wisdom of his best hour, as much as they had delighted the simplicity of his childhood.

When we speak of nature in this manner, we have a distinct but most poetical sense in the mind. We mean the integrity of impression made by manifold natural objects. It is this which distinguishes the stick of timber of the wood-cutter from the tree of the poet. The charming landscape which I saw this morning is indubitably made up of some twenty or thirty farms. Miller owns this field, Locke that, and Manning the woodland beyond. But none of them owns the landscape. There is a property in the horizon which no man has but he whose eye can integrate all the parts, that is, the poet. This is the best part of these men's farms, yet to this their warranty-deeds give no title.

To speak truly, few adult persons can see nature. Most persons do not see the sun. At least they have a very superficial seeing. The sun illuminates only the eye of the man, but shines into the eye and the heart of the child. The lover of nature is he whose inward and outward senses are still truly adjusted to each other; who has retained the spirit of infancy even into the era of manhood. His intercourse with heaven and earth becomes part of his daily food. In the presence of nature a wild delight runs through the man, in spite of real sorrows. Nature says,—he is my creature, and maugre all his impertinent griefs, he shall be glad with me. Not the sun or the summer alone, but every hour and season yields its tribute of delight; for every hour and change corresponds to and authorizes a different state of the mind, from breathless noon to grimmest midnight. Nature is a setting that fits equally well a comic or a mourning piece. In good health, the air is a cordial of incredible virtue. Crossing a bare common, in snow puddles, at twilight, under a clouded sky, without having in my thoughts any occurrence of special good fortune, I have enjoyed a perfect exhilaration. I am glad to the brink of fear. In the woods, too, a man casts off his years, as the snake his slough, and at what period soever of life, is always a child. In the woods is perpetual youth. Within these plantations of God, a decorum and sanctity reign, a perennial festival is dressed, and the guest sees not how he should tire of them in a thousand years. In the woods, we return to reason and faith. There I feel that nothing can befall me in life,—no disgrace, no calamity (leaving me my eyes), which nature cannot repair. Standing on the bare ground,—my head bathed by the blithe air, and uplifted into infinite space,—all mean egotism vanishes. I become a transparent eyeball; I am nothing, I see all; the currents of the Universal Being circulate through me; I am part or parcel of God. The name of the nearest friend sounds then foreign and accidental: to be brothers, to be acquaintances,—master or servant, is then a trifle and a disturbance. I am the lover of uncontained and immortal beauty. In the wilderness, I find something more dear and connate than in streets or villages. In the tranquil landscape, and especially in the distant line of the horizon, man beholds somewhat as beautiful as his own nature.

The greatest delight which the fields and woods minister is the suggestion of an occult relation between man and the vegetable. I am not alone and unacknowledged. They nod to me, and I to them. The waving of the boughs in the storm is new to me and old. It takes me by surprise, and yet is not unknown. Its effect is like that of a higher thought or a better emotion coming over me, when I deemed I was thinking justly or doing right.

Yet it is certain that the power to produce this delight does not reside in nature, but in man, or in a harmony of both. It is necessary to use these pleasures with great temperance. For nature is not always tricked in holiday attire, but the same scene which yesterday breathed perfume and glittered as for the frolic of the nymphs, is overspread with melancholy to-day. Nature always wears the colors of the spirit. To a man laboring under calamity, the heat of his own fire hath sadness in it. Then there is a kind of contempt of the landscape felt by him who has just lost by death a dear friend. The sky is less grand as it shuts down over less worth in the population.

• • •

QUESTIONS FOR DISCUSSION

Introduction

1. What major criticism does Emerson have for our retrospective age? How does the image "we grope among the dry bones of the past" contribute to the point he makes? What other specific word pictures help set forth his idea?
2. What inquiry does the author order us to make? What do you see as the meaning of this statement?
3. Emerson says that the universe is composed of Nature and the Soul. How does he define the word *Nature*? How do you think he would define the word *Soul*?

Nature

1. What paradox does Emerson set forth in his discussion of solitude? To achieve solitude Emerson tells us to "look at the stars." Why are the stars so important?
2. How, according to the author, is the poet distinguished from other men? Why does Emerson say "few adult persons can see nature"? Why might you agree or disagree with him?
3. Who is the true lover of nature? What does Emerson himself achieve when he confronts the wilderness?
4. Upon whom does the power to produce delight from nature's scenes rely? Do you agree that "Nature always wears the colors of the spirit"? Explain.

ASSIGNMENTS FOR WRITING

1. "All science has one aim, namely to find a theory of nature." Assuming a very general definition of the word *nature*, write a paragraph or two to show whether or not you agree with this statement. If you disagree, make sure you name what you feel is the one aim of science. If you agree, give concrete examples to establish your point.

2. Emerson senses a spiritual closeness to all living things as he stands in the presence of the fields and woods. Describe a scene you remember in which you stood close to nature, perhaps on a country vacation, an afternoon at the shore, a moment in an open field, in a forest, or on a mountain ledge—even a backyard scene. Use words that appeal vividly to the senses.

from The American Scholar

Mr. President and Gentlemen:

I greet you on the recommencement of our literary year. Our anniversary is one of hope, and, perhaps, not enough of labor. We do not meet for games of strength or skill, for the recitation of histories, tragedies, and odes, like the ancient Greeks; for parliaments of love and poesy, like the Troubadours; nor for the advancement of science, like our contemporaries in the British and European capitals. Thus far, our holiday has been simply a friendly sign of the survival of the love of letters amongst a people too busy to give to letters any more. As such it is precious as the sign of an indestructible instinct. Perhaps the time is already come when it ought to be, and will be, something else; when the sluggard intellect of this continent will look from under its iron lids and fill the postponed expectation of the world with something better than the exertions of mechanical skill. Our day of dependence, our long apprenticeship to the learning of other lands, draws to a close. The millions that around us are rushing into life, cannot always be fed on the sere remains of foreign harvests. Events, actions arise, that must be sung, that will sing themselves. Who can doubt that poetry will revive and lead in a new age, as the star in the constellation Harp, which now flames in our zenith, astronomers announce, shall one day be the pole-star for a thousand years?

In this hope I accept the topic which not only usage but the nature of our association seem to prescribe to this day—the AMERICAN SCHOLAR. Year by year we come up hither to read one more chapter of his biography. Let us inquire what light new days and events have thrown on his character and his hopes.

It is one of those fables which out of an unknown antiquity convey an unlooked-for wisdom, that the gods, in the beginning, divided Man into men, that he might be more helpful to himself; just as the hand was divided into fingers, the better to answer its end.

The old fable covers a doctrine ever new and sublime; that there is One Man—present to all particular men only partially, or through one faculty; and that you must take the whole society to find the whole man. Man is not a farmer, or a professor, or an engineer, but he is all. Man is priest, and scholar, and statesman, and producer, and soldier. In the *divided* or social state these functions are parceled out to individuals, each of whom aims to do his stint of the joint work, whilst each other performs his. The fable implies that the individual, to possess himself, must sometimes return from his own labor to embrace all the other laborers. But, unfortunately, this original unit, this fountain of power, has been so distributed to multitudes, has been so minutely subdivided and peddled out, that it is spilled into drops, and cannot be gathered. The state of society is one in which the members have suffered amputation from the trunk, and strut about so many walking monsters—a good finger, a neck, a stomach, an elbow, but never a man.

Man is thus metamorphosed into a thing, into many things. The planter, who is Man sent out into the field to gather food, is seldom cheered by any idea of the true dignity of his ministry. He sees his bushel and his cart, and nothing beyond, and sinks into the farmer, instead of Man on the farm. The tradesman scarcely ever gives an ideal worth to his work, but is ridden by the routine of his craft, and the soul is subject to dollars. The priest becomes a form; the attorney a statute-book; the mechanic a machine; the sailor a rope of the ship.

In this distribution of functions the scholar is the delegated intellect. In the right state he is *Man Thinking*. In the degenerate state, when the victim of society, he tends to become a mere thinker, or still worse, the parrot of other men's thinking.

In this view of him, as Man Thinking, the theory of his office is contained. Him Nature solicits with all her placid, all her monitory pictures; him the past instructs; him the future invites. Is not indeed every man a student, and do not all things exist for the student's behoof? And, finally, is not the true scholar the only true master? But the old oracle said, "All things have two handles: beware of the wrong one." In life, too often, the scholar errs with mankind and forfeits his privilege. Let us see him in his school, and consider him in reference to the main influences he receives.

I.   The first in time and the first in importance of the influences upon the mind is that of nature. Every day, the sun; and, after sunset, Night and her stars. Ever the winds blow; ever the grass grows. Every day, men and women, conversing—beholding and beholden. The scholar is he of all men whom this spectacle most engages. He must settle its value in his mind. What is nature to him? There is never a beginning, there is never an end, to the inexplicable continuity of this web of God, but always circular power returning into itself. Therein it resembles his own spirit, whose beginning, whose ending, he never can find—so entire, so boundless. Far too as her splendors shine, system on system shooting like rays, upward, downward, without center, without circumference—in the mass and in the particle, Nature hastens to render account of herself to the mind. Classification begins. To the young mind every thing is individual, stands by itself.

By and by, it finds how to join two things and see in them one nature; then three, then three thousand; and so, tyrannized over by its own unifying instinct, it goes on tying things together, diminishing anomalies, discovering roots running under ground whereby contrary and remote things cohere and flower out from one stem. It presently learns that since the dawn of history there has been a constant accumulation and classifying of facts. But what is classification but the perceiving that these objects are not chaotic, and are not foreign, but have a law which is also a law of the human mind? The astronomer discovers that geometry, a pure abstraction of the human mind, is the measure of planetary motion. The chemist finds proportions and intelligible method throughout matter; and science is nothing but the finding of analogy, identity, in the most remote parts. The ambitious soul sits down before each refractory fact; one after another reduces all strange constitutions, all new powers, to their class and their law, and goes on forever to animate the last fiber of organization, the outskirts of nature, by insight.

Thus to him, to this schoolboy under the bending dome of day, is suggested that he and it proceed from one root; one is leaf and one is flower; relation, sympathy, stirring in every vein. And what is that root? Is not that the soul of his soul? A thought too bold; a dream too wild. Yet when this spiritual light shall have revealed the law of more earthly natures—when he has learned to worship the soul, and to see that the natural philosophy that now is, is only the first gropings of its gigantic hand, he shall look forward to an ever expanding knowledge as to a becoming creator. He shall see that nature is the opposite of the soul, answering to it part for part. One is seal and one is print. Its beauty is the beauty of his own mind. Its laws are the laws of his own mind. Nature then becomes to him the measure of his attainments. So much of nature as he is ignorant of, so much of his own mind does he not yet possess. And, in fine, the ancient precept, "Know thyself," and the modern precept, "Study nature," become at last one maxim.

II.   The next great influence into the spirit of the scholar is the mind of the Past—in whatever form, whether of literature, of art, of institutions, that mind is inscribed. Books are the best type of the influence of the past, and perhaps we shall get at the truth—learn the amount of this influence more conveniently—by considering their value alone.

The theory of books is noble. The scholar of the first age received into him the world around; brooded thereon; gave it the new arrangement of his own mind, and uttered it again. It came into him life; it went out from him truth. It came to him short-lived actions; it went out from him immortal thoughts. It came to him business; it went from him poetry. It was dead fact; now, it is quick thought. It can stand, and it can go. It now endures, it now flies, it now inspires. Precisely in proportion to the depth of mind from which it issued, so high does it soar, so long does it sing.

Or, I might say, it depends on how far the process had gone, of transmuting life into truth. In proportion to the completeness of the distillation, so will the purity and imperishableness of the product be. But none is quite perfect. As no air-pump can by any means make a perfect vacuum, so neither can any artist entirely exclude the conventional, the local, the perishable from his book, or write a book of pure thought, that shall be as efficient, in all respects, to a remote posterity, as to contemporaries, or rather to the second age. Each age, it is found, must write its own books; or rather, each generation for the next succeeding. The books of an older period will not fit this.

Yet hence arises a grave mischief. The sacredness which attaches to the act of creation, the act of thought, is transferred to the record. The poet chanting was felt to be a divine man: henceforth the chant is divine also. The writer was a just and wise spirit: henceforward it is settled the book is perfect; as love of the hero corrupts into worship of his statue. Instantly the book becomes noxious: the guide is a tyrant. The sluggish and perverted mind of the multitude, slow to open to the incursions of Reason, having once so opened, having once received this book, stands upon it, and makes an outcry if it is disparaged. Colleges are built on it. Books are written on it by thinkers, not by Man Thinking; by men of talent, that is, who start wrong, who set out from accepted dogmas, not from their own sight of principles. Meek young men grow up in libraries, believing it their duty to accept the views which Cicero, which Locke, which Bacon, have given; forgetful that Cicero, Locke, and Bacon were only young men in libraries when they wrote these books.

Hence, instead of Man Thinking, we have the bookworm. Hence the book-learned class, who value books, as such; not as related to nature and the human constitution, but as making a sort of Third Estate with the world and the soul. Hence the restorers of readings, the emendators, the bibliomaniacs of all degrees.

Books are the best of things, well used; abused, among the worst. What is the right use? What is the one end which all means go to effect? They are for nothing but to inspire. I had better never see a book than to be warped by its attraction clean out of my own orbit, and made a satellite instead of a system. The one thing in the world, of value, is the active soul. This every man is entitled to; this every man contains within him, although in almost all men obstructed and as yet unborn. The soul active sees absolute truth and utters truth, or creates. In this action it is genius; not the privilege of here and there a favorite, but the sound estate of every man. In its essence it is progressive. The book, the college, the school of art, the institution of any kind, stop with some past utterance of genius. This is good, say they—let us hold by this. They pin me down. They look backward and not forward. But genius looks forward: the eyes of man are set in his forehead, not in his hindhead: man hopes: genius creates. Whatever talents may be, if the man create not, the pure efflux of the Deity is not his; cinders and smoke there may be, but not yet flame. There are creative manners, there are creative actions, and creative words; manners, actions, words, that is, indicative of no custom or authority, but springing spontaneous from the mind's own sense of good and fair.

On the other part, instead of being its own seer, let it receive from another mind its truth, though it were in torrents of light, without periods of solitude, inquest, and self-recovery, and a fatal disservice is done. Genius is always sufficiently the enemy of genius by over-influence. The literature of every nation bears me witness. The English dramatic poets have Shakespearized now for two hundred years.

Undoubtedly there is a right way of reading, so it be sternly subordinated. Man Thinking must not be subdued by his instruments. Books are for the scholar's idle times. When he can read God directly, the hour is too precious to be wasted in other men's transcripts of their readings. But when the intervals of darkness come, as come they must—when the sun is hid and the stars withdraw their shining —we repair to the lamps which were kindled by their ray, to guide our steps to the East again, where the dawn is. We hear, that we may speak. The Arabian proverb says, "A fig tree, looking on a fig tree, becometh fruitful."

It is remarkable, the character of the pleasure we derive from the best books. They impress us with the conviction that one nature wrote and the same reads. We read the verses of one of the great English poets, of Chaucer, of Marvell, of Dryden, with the most modern joy —with a pleasure, I mean, which is in great part caused by the abstraction of all *time* from their verses. There is some awe mixed with the joy of our surprise, when this poet, who lived in some past world, two or three hundred years ago, says that which lies close to my own soul, that which I also had well-nigh thought and said. But for the evidence thence afforded to the philosophical doctrine of the identity of all minds, we should suppose some preëstablished harmony, some foresight of souls that were to be, and some preparation of stores for their future wants, like the fact observed in insects, who lay up food before death for the young grub they shall never see.

I would not be hurried by any love of system, by any exaggeration of instincts, to underrate the Book. We all know, that as the human body can be nourished on any food, though it were boiled grass and the broth of shoes, so the human mind can be fed by any knowledge. And great and heroic men have existed who had almost no other information than by the printed page. I only would say that it needs a strong head to bear that diet. One must be an inventor to read well. As the proverb says, "He that would bring home the wealth of the Indies, must carry out the wealth of the Indies." There is then creative reading as well as creative writing. When the mind is braced by labor and invention, the page of whatever book we read becomes luminous with manifold allusion. Every sentence is doubly significant, and the sense of our author is as broad as the world. We then see, what is always true, that as the seer's hour of vision is short and rare among heavy days and months, so is its record, perchance, the least part of his volume. The discerning will read, in his Plato or Shakespeare, only that least part—only the authentic utterances of the oracles; all the rest he rejects, were it never so many times Plato's and Shakespeare's.

Of course there is a portion of reading quite indispensable to a wise man. History and exact science he must learn by laborious reading. Colleges, in like manner, have their indispensable office—to teach elements. But they can only highly serve us when they aim not to drill, but to create; when they gather from far every ray of various genius to their hospitable halls, and by the concentrated fires, set the hearts of their youth on flame. Thought and knowledge are natures in which apparatus and pretension avail nothing. Gowns and pecuniary foundations, though of towns of gold, can never countervail the least sentence or syllable of wit. Forget this, and our American colleges will recede in their public importance, whilst they grow richer every year.

III. There goes in the world a notion that the scholar should be a recluse, a valetudinarian—as unfit for any handiwork or public labor as a penknife for an axe. The so-called "practical men" sneer at speculative men, as if, because they speculate or *see*, they could do nothing. I have heard it said that the clergy—who are always, more universally than any other class, the scholars of their day—are addressed as women; that the rough, spontaneous conversation of men they do not hear, but only a mincing and diluted speech. They are often virtually disfranchised; and indeed there are advocates for their celibacy. As far as this is true of the studious classes, it is not just and wise. Action is with the scholar subordinate, but it is essential. Without it he is not yet man. Without it thought can never ripen into truth. Whilst the world hangs before the eye as a cloud of beauty, we cannot even see its beauty. Inaction is cowardice, but there can be no scholar without the heroic mind. The preamble of thought, the transition through which it passes from the unconscious to the conscious, is action. Only so much do I know, as I have lived. Instantly we know whose words are loaded with life, and whose not.

The world—this shadow of the soul, or *other me*—lies wide around. Its attractions are the keys which unlock my thoughts and make me acquainted with myself. I run eagerly into this resounding tumult. I grasp the hand of those next me, and take my place in the ring to suffer and to work, taught by an instinct that so shall the dumb abyss be vocal with speech. I pierce its order; I dissipate its fear; I dispose of it within the circuit of my expanding life. So much only of life as I know by experience, so much of the wilderness have I vanquished and planted, or so far have I extended my being, my dominion. I do not see how any man can afford, for the sake of his nerves and his nap, to spare any action in which he can partake. It is pearls and rubies to his discourse. Drudgery, calamity, exasperation, want, are instructors in eloquence and wisdom. The true scholar grudges every opportunity of action past by, as a loss of power. It is the raw material out of which the intellect molds her splendid products. A strange process too, this by which experience is converted into thought, as a mulberry leaf is converted into satin. The manufacture goes forward at all hours.

The actions and events of our childhood and youth are now matters of calmest observation. They lie like fair pictures in the air. Not so with our recent actions—with the business which we now have in hand. On this we are quite unable to speculate. Our affections as yet circulate through it. We no more feel or know it than we feel the feet, or the hand, or the brain of our body. The new deed is yet a part of life—remains for a time immersed in our unconscious life. In some contemplative hour it detaches itself from the life like a ripe fruit, to become a thought of the mind. Instantly it is raised, transfigured; the corruptible has put on incorruption. Henceforth it is an object of beauty, however base its origin and neighborhood. Observe too the impossibility of antedating this act. In its grub state, it cannot fly, it cannot shine, it is a dull grub. But suddenly, without observation, the selfsame thing unfurls beautiful wings, and is an angel of wisdom. So is there no fact, no event, in our private history, which shall not, sooner or later, lose its adhesive, inert form, and astonish us by soaring from our body into the empyrean. Cradle and infancy, school and playground, the fear of boys, and dogs, and ferrules, the love of little maids and berries, and many another fact that once filled the whole sky, are gone already; friend and relative, profession and party, town and country, nation and world, must also soar and sing.

Of course, he who has put forth his total strength in fit actions has the richest return of wisdom. I will not shut myself out of this globe of action, and transplant an oak into a flowerpot, there to hunger and pine; nor trust the revenue of some single faculty, and exhaust one vein of thought, much like those Savoyards, who, getting their livelihood by carving shepherds, shepherdesses, and smoking Dutchmen, for all Europe, went out one day to the mountain to find stock, and discovered that they had whittled up the last of their pine trees. Authors we have, in numbers, who have written out their vein, and who, moved by a commendable prudence, sail for Greece or Palestine, follow the trapper into the prairie, or ramble round Algiers, to replenish their merchantable stock.

If it were only for a vocabulary, the scholar would be covetous of action. Life is our dictionary. Years are well spent in country labors; in town; in the insight into trades and manufactures; in frank intercourse with many men and women; in science; in art; to the one end of mastering in all their facts a language by which to illustrate and embody our perceptions. I learn immediately from any speaker how much he has already lived, through the poverty or the splendor of his speech. Life lies behind us as the quarry from whence we get tiles and copestones for the masonry of to-day. This is the way to learn grammar. Colleges and books only copy the language which the field and the work-yard made.

But the final value of action, like that of books, and better than books, is that it is a resource. That great principle of Undulation in nature, that shows itself in the inspiring and expiring of the breath; in desire and satiety; in the ebb and flow of the sea; in day and night; in heat and cold; and, as yet more deeply ingrained in every atom and every fluid, is known to us under the name of Polarity—these "fits of easy transmission and reflection," as Newton called them, are the law of nature because they are the law of spirit.

The mind now thinks, now acts, and each fit reproduces the other. When the artist has exhausted his materials, when the fancy no longer paints, when thoughts are no longer apprehended and books are a weariness—he has always the resources *to live*. Character is higher than intellect. Thinking is the function. Living is the functionary. The stream retreats to its source. A great soul will be strong to live, as well as strong to think. Does he lack organ or medium to impart his truths? He can still fall back on this elemental force of living them. This is a total act. Thinking is a partial act. Let the grandeur of justice shine in his affairs. Let the beauty of affection cheer his lowly roof. Those "far from fame," who dwell and act with him, will feel the force of his constitution in the doings and passages of the day better than it can be measured by any public and designed display. Time shall teach him that the scholar loses no hour which the man lives. Herein he unfolds the sacred germ of his instinct, screened from influence. What is lost in seemliness is gained in strength. Not out of those on whom systems of education have exhausted their culture, comes the helpful giant to destroy the old or to build the new, but out of unhandseled savage nature; out of terrible Druids and Berserkers come at last Alfred and Shakespeare.

I hear therefore with joy whatever is beginning to be said of the dignity and necessity of labor to every citizen. There is virtue yet in the hoe and the spade, for learned as well as for unlearned hands. And labor is everywhere welcome; always we are invited to work; only be this limitation observed, that a man shall not for the sake of wider activity sacrifice any opinion to the popular judgments and modes of action.

· · ·

QUESTIONS FOR DISCUSSION

1. Why, according to Emerson, is this meeting taking place? What hope does he express?
2. What fable does Emerson tell? Why do you think he calls it a fable?
3. What does Emerson mean when he says of society, "the members have suffered amputation from the trunk"? How is the planter "amputated"? How are tradesmen, priests, attorneys, mechanics, sailors all made into "walking monsters"?
4. What is the difference between the scholar in "the right state" and in "the degenerate state"? What difference can you perceive between a mere thinker and a *Man Thinking*? Why does the word *Man* seem so important to Emerson?
5. What meaning do you find in the statement Emerson quotes from the oracle, "All things have two handles: beware of the wrong one"?
6. Why does Emerson find books important for the mind of the scholar? Why does he later say "Books are the best of things, well used; abused, among the worst"? What do you think he means by "creative reading"?

7. What, according to Emerson, makes a scholar a man? In what ways do you think a scholar of today could conform to this notion?

8. Why do you think Emerson inserts the simile (a comparison explicitly stated and often introduced by *like* or *as*) of the mulberry leaf when he discusses experience and thought?

9. What does Emerson mean by "Life is our dictionary"? How can a person's vocabulary, "the poverty or the splendor of his speech," reveal how much he has already lived?

10. This address was made to a college audience. What advice in this essay would a young person today find most meaningful? What ideas, if any, do you find in Emerson's talk that would not apply today?

11. What is the first important influence on the mind? What examples of transcendental thought do you find in the first paragraph of Section I?

ASSIGNMENTS FOR WRITING

1. Emerson believed that "Character is higher than intellect." Do you? In a thoughtfully planned essay, argue the merits of either character or intellect. Tell what you mean by each of these words. Where possible, use experiences drawn from your own life to illustrate your point of view.

2. A good address ought to include several of the following characteristics: it should be vivid, appealing to the listeners' senses; it should be spoken in language suitable to its audience; it should deal with a subject of interest to its listeners; it should provoke some feeling of reaction in those who hear it. In a well-written paragraph, indicate whether or not you find Emerson's talk satisfactory; base your discussion upon the qualities listed above and specific references to the address itself.

carver, he worked in turn as a cabinetmaker, ship's carpenter, and itinerant portrait painter before settling permanently in Pittsburgh. It was there that Blythe turned out the lively anecdotes for which he is remembered today. Frantic activity and jostling crowds pleased him, and he found them in his local post office (*opposite*). An element of caricature adds spice without marring the final result. This was the era when Dickens was writing his universally popular novels, and there is more than a hint here of the same attitude and atmosphere. Woodville (1825-1856) came closer than any other American to rivalling the efforts of the Dutch genre painters. He was able to see such pictures in the collection of his Baltimore patron, Robert Gilmor, who also assisted him to study abroad. His best work (*below*) is carefully composed, skillfully brushed, and glowingly colored. Woodville's pictures are all too rare. He committed suicide in Paris at the age of thirty-one.

Erastus Salisbury Field (1805-1900) painted his extraordinary nine-by-twelve-foot *Historical Monument* (p. 112) long after the other pictures in this section, but it belongs with them in spirit. For thirty years a portrait painter, he matched in technique the sturdy naiveté of his imagination. Note the steel bridges, carrying steam trains, connecting the tops of the towers.

GEORGE CATTON WOODVILLE: Waiting for the Stage, 1851

ERASTUS S. FIELD: Historical Monument of the American Republic, c. 1876

from Self-Reliance

"Ne te quaesiveris extra."

Man is his own star; and the soul that can
Render an honest and a perfect man,
Commands all light, all influence, all fate;
Nothing to him falls early or too late.
Our acts our angels are, or good or ill,
Our fatal shadows that walk by us still.

—Epilogue to Beaumont and Fletcher's *Honest Man's Fortune.*

Cast the bantling on the rocks,
Suckle him with the she-wolf's teat,
Wintered with the hawk and fox,
Power and speed be hands and feet.

I read the other day some verses written by an eminent painter which were original and not conventional. The soul always hears an admonition in such lines, let the subject be what it may. The sentiment they instill is of more value than any thought they may contain. To believe your own thought, to believe that what is true for you in your private heart is true for all men—that is genius. Speak your latent conviction, and it shall be the universal sense; for the inmost in due time becomes the outmost, and our first thought is rendered back to us by the trumpets of the Last Judgment. Familiar as the voice of the mind is to each, the highest merit we ascribe to Moses, Plato and Milton is that they set at naught books and traditions, and spoke not what men, but what *they* thought. A man should learn to detect and watch that gleam of light which flashes across his mind from within, more than the luster of the firmament of bards and sages. Yet he dismisses without notice his thought, because it is his. In every work of genius we recognize our own rejected thoughts; they come back to us with a certain alienated majesty. Great works of art have no more affecting lesson for us than this. They teach us to abide by our spontaneous impression with good-humored inflexibility then most when the whole cry of voices is on the other side. Else to-morrow a stranger will say with masterly good sense precisely what we have thought and felt all the time, and we shall be forced to take with shame our own opinion from another.

There is a time in every man's education when he arrives at the conviction that envy is ignorance; that imitation is suicide; that he must take himself for better or worse as his portion; that though the wide universe is full of good, no kernel of nourishing corn can come to him but through his toil bestowed on that plot of ground which is given to him to till. The power which resides in him is new in nature, and none but he knows what that is which he can do, nor does he know until he has tried. Not for nothing one face, one character, one fact, makes much impression on him, and another none. This sculpture in the memory is not without preëstablished harmony. The eye was placed where one ray should fall, that it might testify of that particular ray. We but half express ourselves, and are ashamed of that divine idea which each of us represents. It may be safely trusted as proportionate and of good issues, so it be faithfully imparted, but God will not have his work made manifest by cowards. A man is relieved and gay when he has put his heart into his work and done his best; but what he has said or done otherwise shall give him no peace. It is a deliverance which does not deliver. In the attempt his genius deserts him; no muse befriends; no invention, no hope.

Trust thyself: every heart vibrates to that iron string. Accept the place the divine providence has found for you, the society of your contemporaries, the connection of events. Great men have always done so, and confided themselves childlike to the genius of their age, betraying their perception that the absolutely trustworthy was seated at their heart, working through their hands, predominating in all their being. And we are now men, and must accept in the highest mind the same transcendent destiny; and not minors and invalids in a protected corner, not cowards fleeing before a revolution, but guides, redeemers and benefactors, obeying the Almighty effort and advancing on Chaos and the Dark.

What pretty oracles nature yields us on this text in the face and behavior of children, babes, and even brutes! That divided and rebel mind, that distrust of a sentiment because our arithmetic has computed the strength and means opposed to our purpose, these have not. Their mind being whole, their eye is as yet unconquered; and when we look in their faces we are disconcerted. Infancy conforms to nobody; all conform to it; so that one babe commonly makes four or five out of the adults who prattle and play to it. So God has armed youth and puberty and manhood no less with its own piquancy and charm, and made it enviable and gracious and its claims not to be put by, if it will stand by itself. Do not think the youth has no force, because he cannot speak to you and me. Hark! in the next room his voice is sufficiently clear and emphatic. It seems he knows how to speak to his contemporaries. Bashful or bold then, he will know how to make us seniors very unnecessary.

The nonchalance of boys who are sure of a dinner, and would disdain as much as a lord to do or say aught to conciliate one, is the healthy attitude of human nature. A boy is in the parlor what the pit is in the playhouse; independent, irresponsible, looking out from his corner on such people and facts as pass by, he tries and sentences them on their merits, in the swift, summary way of boys, as good, bad, interesting, silly, eloquent, troublesome. He cumbers himself never about consequences, about interests; he gives an independent, genuine verdict. You must court him; he does not court you. But the man is as it were clapped into jail by his consciousness. As soon as he has once acted or spoken with *éclat* he is a committed person, watched by the sympathy or the hatred of hundreds, whose affections must now enter into his account. There is no Lethe for this. Ah, that he could pass again into his neutrality! Who can thus avoid all pledges and, having observed, observe again from the same unaffected, unbiased, unbribable, unaffrighted innocence—must always be formidable. He would utter opinions on all passing affairs, which being seen to be not private but necessary, would sink like darts into the ear of men and put them in fear.

These are the voices which we hear in solitude, but they grow faint and inaudible as we enter into the world. Society everywhere is in conspiracy against the manhood of every one of its members. Society is a joint-stock company, in which the members agree, for the better securing of his bread to each shareholder, to surrender the liberty and culture of the eater. The virtue in most request is conformity. Self-reliance is its aversion. It loves not realities and creators, but names and customs.

Whoso would be a man, must be a nonconformist. He who would gather immortal palms must not be hindered by the name of goodness but must explore if it be goodness. Nothing is at last sacred but the integrity of your own mind. Absolve you to yourself, and you shall have the suffrage of the world. I remember an answer which when quite young I was prompted to make to a valued adviser who was wont to importune me with the dear old doctrines of the church. On my saying, "What have I to do with the sacredness of traditions, if I live wholly from within?" my friend suggested—"But these impulses may be from below, not from above." I replied, "They do not seem to me to be such; but if I am the Devil's child, I will live then from the Devil." No law can be sacred to me but that of my nature. Good and bad are but names very readily transferable to that or this; the only right is what is after my constitution; the only wrong what is against it. A man is to carry himself in the presence of all opposition as if every thing were titular and ephemeral but he. I am ashamed to think how easily we capitulate to badges and names, to large societies and dead institutions. Every decent and well-spoken individual affects and sways me more than is right. I ought to go upright and vital, and speak the rude truth in all ways. If malice and vanity wear the coat of philanthropy, shall that pass? If an angry bigot assumes this bountiful cause of Abolition, and comes to me with his last news from Barbadoes, why should I not say to him, "Go love thy infant; love thy wood-chopper; be good-natured and modest; have that grace; and never varnish your hard, uncharitable ambition with this incredible tenderness for black folk a thousand miles off. Thy love afar is spite at home." Rough and graceless would be such greeting, but truth is handsomer than the affectation of love. Your goodness must have some edge to it—else it is none. The doctrine of hatred must be preached, as the counteraction of the doctrine of love, when that pules and whines. I shun father and mother and wife and brother when my genius calls me. I would write on the lintels of the door-post, *Whim.* I hope it is somewhat better than whim at last, but we cannot spend the day in explanation. Expect me not to show cause why I seek or why I exclude company. Then again, do not tell me, as a good man did to-day, of my obligation to put all poor men in good situations. Are they *my* poor? I tell thee, thou foolish philanthropist, that I grudge the dollar, the dime, the cent I give to such men as do not belong to me and to whom I do not belong. There is a class of persons to whom by all spiritual affinity I am bought and sold; for them I will go to prison if need be; but your miscellaneous popular charities; the education at college of fools; the building of meeting-houses to the vain end to which many now stand; alms to sots, and the thousand-fold Relief Societies; though I confess with shame I sometimes succumb and give the dollar, it is a wicked dollar, which by and by I shall have the manhood to withhold.

• • •

QUESTIONS FOR DISCUSSION

1. Which sentences in this essay best assert Emerson's faith in the power of the individual? Read several of these sentences aloud. Do you find them convincing, idealistic, optimistic, or false? Why?

2. What traits of boyhood listed here by Emerson fit the youth of today?

How, according to the author, does a man differ from a boy? Why might you agree or disagree with him?

3. "Society everywhere is in conspiracy against the manhood of every one of its members." What do you think Emerson means by this remark? Why might you concur with or disapprove of his point of view?

4. Emerson says "truth is handsomer than the affectation of love." How does the incident he relates about a bigot lead him to this conclusion? Why might you agree or disagree with his statement?

5. Who, according to Emerson, are foolish philanthropists? Why does he call the dollar he gives to relief societies "a wicked dollar"? How do you think Emerson would evaluate today's welfare and charity institutions?

6. The Latin inscription at the beginning of the essay, "Ne te quaesiveris extra," means "Do not seek yourself outside yourself." What do you see as the meaning behind this statement? Why do you think Emerson chose this sentence to precede his essay "Self-Reliance"?

ASSIGNMENTS FOR WRITING

1. Emerson stresses nonconformity as the essence of existence. In a carefully planned essay, discuss your own views on the merits or disadvantages of nonconformity in a person's life. Call upon your own experiences to illustrate why you believe the way you do.

2. Many observers of contemporary America say that young people today are excessively nonconformist in their behavior. Suppose Emerson could view today's high school youth. Write a paragraph in which you indicate what you feel his reactions would be. You may wish to pretend that you are Emerson himself and write in the first person.

Gifts

Gifts of one who loved me—
'T was high time they came;
When he ceased to love me,
Time they stopped for shame.

It is said that the world is in a state of bankruptcy; that the world owes the world more than the world can pay, and ought to go into chancery and be sold. I do not think this general insolvency, which involves in some sort all the population, to be the reason of the difficulty experienced at Christmas and New Year and other times, in bestowing gifts; since it is always so pleasant to be generous, though very vexatious to pay debts. But the impediment lies in the choosing. If at any time it comes into my head that a present is due from me to somebody, I am puzzled what to give, until the opportunity is gone. Flowers and fruits are always fit presents; flowers, because they are a proud assertion that a ray of beauty outvalues all the utilities of the world. These gay natures contrast with the somewhat stern countenance of ordinary nature: they are like music heard out of a workhouse. Nature does not cocker us; we are children, not pets; she is not fond; everything is dealt to us without fear or favor, after severe universal laws. Yet these delicate flowers look like the frolic and interference of love and beauty. Men used to tell us that we love flattery even though we are not deceived by it, because it shows that we are of importance enough to be courted. Something like that pleasure, the flowers give us: what am I to whom these sweet hints are addressed? Fruits are acceptable gifts, because they are the flower of commodities, and admit of fantastic values being attached to them. If a man should send to me to come a hundred miles to visit him and should set before me a basket of fine summer-fruit, I should think there was some proportion between the labor and the reward.

For common gifts, necessity makes pertinences and beauty every day, and one is glad when an imperative leaves him no option; since if the man at the door have no shoes, you have not to consider whether you could procure him a paint-box. And as it is always pleasing to see a man eat bread, or drink water, in the house or out of doors, so it is always a great satisfaction to supply these first wants. Necessity does everything well. In our condition of universal dependence it seems heroic to let the petitioner be the judge of his necessity, and to give all that is asked, though at great inconvenience. If it be a fantastic desire, it is better to leave to others the office of punishing him. I can think of many parts I should prefer playing to that of the Furies. Next to things of necessity, the rule for a gift, which one of my friends prescribed, is that we might convey to some person that which properly belonged to his character, and was easily associated with him in thought. But our tokens of compliment and love are for the most part barbarous. Rings and other jewels are not gifts, but apologies for gifts. The only gift is a portion of thyself. Thou must bleed for me. Therefore the poet brings his poem; the shepherd, his lamb; the farmer, corn; the miner, a gem; the sailor, coral and shells; the painter, his picture; the girl, a handkerchief of her own sewing. This is right and pleasing, for it restores society in so far to the primary basis, when a man's biography is conveyed in his gift, and every man's wealth is an index of his merit. But it is a cold lifeless business when you go to the shops to buy me something which does not represent your life and talent, but a goldsmith's. This is fit for kings, and rich men who represent kings, and a false state of property, to make presents of gold and silver stuffs, as a kind of symbolical sin-offering, or payment of blackmail.

The law of benefits is a difficult channel, which requires careful sailing, or rude boats. It is not the office of a man to receive gifts. How dare you give them? We wish to be self-sustained. We do not quite forgive a giver. The hand that feeds us is in some danger of being bitten. We can receive anything from love, for that is a way of receiving it from ourselves; but not from any one who assumes to bestow. We sometimes hate the meat which we eat, because there seems something of degrading dependence in living by it:

"Brother, if Jove to thee a present make,
Take heed that from his hands thou nothing take."

We ask the whole. Nothing less will content us. We arraign society if it do not give us, besides earth and fire and water, opportunity, love, reverence and objects of veneration.

He is a good man who can receive a gift well. We are either glad or sorry at a gift, and both emotions are unbecoming. Some violence I think is done, some degradation borne, when I rejoice or grieve at a gift. I am sorry when my independence is invaded, or when a gift comes from such as do not know my spirit, and so the act is not supported; and if the gift pleases me overmuch, then I should be ashamed that the donor should read my heart, and see that I love his commodity, and not him. The gift, to be true, must be the flowing of the giver unto me, correspondent to my flowing unto him. When the waters are at level, then my goods pass to him, and his to me. All his are mine, all mine his. I say to him, How can you give me this pot of oil or this flagon of wine when all your oil and wine is mine, which belief of mine this gift seems to deny? Hence the fitness of beautiful, not useful things, for gifts. This giving is flat usurpation, and therefore when the beneficiary is ungrateful, as all beneficiaries hate all Timons, not at all considering the value of the gift but looking back to the greater store it was taken from—I rather sympathize with the beneficiary than with the anger of my lord Timon. For the expectation of gratitude is mean, and is continually punished by the total insensibility of the obliged person. It is a great happiness to get off without injury and heart-burning from one who has had the ill-luck to be served by you. It is a very onerous business, this of being served, and the debtor naturally wishes to give you a slap. A golden text for these gentlemen is that which I so admire in the Buddhist, who never thanks, and who says, "Do not flatter your benefactors."

The reason of these discords I conceive to be that there is no commensurability between a man and any gift. You cannot give anything to a magnanimous person. After you have served him he at once puts you in debt by his magnanimity. The service a man renders his friend is trivial and selfish compared with the service he knows his friend stood in readiness to yield him, alike before he had begun to serve his friend, and now also. Compared with that good-will I bear my friend, the benefit it is in my power to render him seems small. Besides, our action on each other, good as well as evil, is so incidental and at random that we can seldom hear the acknowledgments of any person who would thank us for a benefit, without some shame and humiliation. We can rarely strike a direct stroke, but must be content with an oblique one; we seldom have the satisfaction of yielding a direct benefit which is directly received. But rectitude scatters favors on every side without knowing it, and receives with wonder the thanks of all people.

I fear to breathe any treason against the majesty of love, which is the genius and god of gifts, and to whom we must not affect to prescribe. Let him give kingdoms of flower-leaves indifferently. There are persons from whom we always expect fairy-tokens; let us not cease to expect them. This is prerogative, and not to be limited by our municipal rules. For the rest, I like to see that we cannot be bought and sold. The best of hospitality and of generosity is also not in the will, but in fate. I find that I am not much to you; you do not need me; you do not feel me; then am I thrust out of doors, though you proffer me house and lands. No services are of any value, but only likeness. When I have attempted to join myself to others by services, it proved an intellectual trick—no more. They eat your service like apples, and leave you out. But love them, and they feel you and delight in you all the time.

QUESTIONS FOR DISCUSSION

1. What, in Emerson's opinion, is the reason for our difficulty at Christmas and New Year? Why is he puzzled when it comes to giving gifts?
2. Why are flowers and fruits acceptable gifts, according to the writer? Do people still give such gifts today? Why?
3. What role does necessity play in dispensing common gifts?
4. Emerson's presentation of the barefoot man at the door is an example of figurative language (various devices for speaking about one thing in terms of another). Why does he use this particular figure?
5. Why does Emerson call our tokens of love barbarous? Why does he say that "Rings and other jewels are not gifts, but apologies for gifts"? Do you agree with him? How do our modern conceptions of gift-giving compare to Emerson's?
6. "We do not quite forgive a giver." What do you think Emerson means by this remark? Is he implying that there is something wrong in giving a gift, something which punishes the giver in some way?
7. Emerson says "He is a good man who can receive a gift well." Do you agree that it is difficult to accept a gift well?
8. What, according to the author, is "the genius and god of gifts"? What does he mean?

ASSIGNMENTS FOR WRITING

1. The act of giving has interested many writers of prose and poetry. Select some story, novel, or poem which treats the presentation of a gift—perhaps O. Henry's "The Gift of the Magi," John Steinbeck's *The Red Pony*, A. E. Housman's "When I Was One and Twenty"—and compare the ideas set forth there with those offered by Emerson in "Gifts."
2. Assuming Emerson's statement "The only gift is a portion of thyself" to be true, write a paragraph in which you discuss the portion of *yourself* which you think would make a fine gift for a loved one. Tell which of your talents, abilities, skills, or successes you would offer as a gift. Indicate why you single out this one particular "portion of thyself."

Henry David Thoreau

It pleases our romantic fancy to think that as Emerson stood before his audience at Harvard and in a ringing voice liberated the American intellect in his speech to the Phi Beta Kappa Society of 1837, Henry David Thoreau, then twenty, sat hypnotized among the listeners, soaking up the Concord master's words and etching the language of "The American Scholar" upon his mind and heart. There is considerable doubt that this is true, though many assume it to be. Thoreau hated large crowds, and as a letter from a friend indicates, he was hardly seen at all immediately after the commencement ceremony. That he missed Emerson's speech, however, in no way alters the fact that in his lifetime Thoreau best fulfilled the requirements for the scholar Emerson so carefully spelled out. Indeed, to whom other than Thoreau can these words of Emerson's be better applied: "In the right state the scholar is *Man Thinking*"; "He who has put forth his total strength in fit action has the richest return of wisdom." In later years Emerson would show specifically his faith in Thoreau by introducing him as "*the* man of Concord."

One of four children, Thoreau was born in Concord on July 12, 1817. His father, after several business failures, finally enjoyed a moderate success in manufacturing pencils. Henry fell early in love with the Concord hills and the forests along the river, and in school he showed a keen ability for learning. The family singled him out from the rest to send to college. But the Harvard curriculum lacked inspiration for him, and he chose to pursue with care only those books which attracted him. Travel books ignited his imagination and carried him to exotic streets and shorelines; in Thomas Carlyle he discovered humor and a dazzling prose style; in Coleridge he learned the meditations of German transcendentalists; in John Donne, Sir Thomas Browne, and George Herbert he found the riches of sensory expression and the provocative oddities of idea and imagery. From this assiduous reading, which he pursued all his life, grew the scope and breadth of his knowledge.

Thoreau's family always thought of him as the scholar, and they never questioned the way he used his time. Much of it he spent on long walks, watching the wildlife that never tired him. For a while he tried teaching, but resigned when a school board demanded that he flog unruly pupils. At Emerson's suggestion, he kept a journal, recording faithfully in it his observations and impressions.

Emerson encouraged the younger writer and invited him to stay with his family for a while. When he offered Thoreau a piece of land just touching Walden Pond, Emerson really presented the opportunity for assured leisure and independence. Thoreau, eager to study and work at his own pace, accepted the offer. In 1845, at twenty-eight years old, he embarked upon his famous and singular experiment in independent living. For two years he lived at Walden in a cabin he built himself, welcoming animal visitors from the woods, reading in the depths that suited him, hoeing in his bean field, sitting under the sky while his flute sang to the stars, spotting the sun rise beyond the doorway, thinking, rowing on the pond and measuring its bottom, listening in solitude to the different sounds of a far-off civilization and the forest about him. What he saw and thought and felt filled the pages of his journal. At Walden, he tried to live according to Emerson's belief that self-knowledge grew from man's realization of the secrets in the world of nature.

After his attempts at self-discovery at Walden Pond, Thoreau returned to Concord and set about finding a publisher for the books and poems lying restive in the pages of his journal. *A Week on the Concord and Merrimack Rivers* appeared in 1849, but got so cold a reception that at first no one wished to risk publishing *Walden,* Thoreau's record of his life in the woods. Not until 1854, five years after *Week,* was it finally published. Even then, few reviewers noticed it. Most of those who read it marveled only at the bits of economy, the mere pennies Thoreau needed to live in the woods. They missed the lucid visions of truth and life that shone in its pages.

Reading, writing, and thinking always filled Thoreau's days. Although infected lungs plagued his life from college days on, he labored until the end, the tragic consequences of consumption warded off so long, no doubt, by the zealous outdoor living that commanded his existence. In the outdoors, behind the lush clothes of nature, a God lived, and man's life and its meaning flowed from this truth. Thoreau's God smiled from within a peaceful landscape.

Shortly before he died in his forty-fourth year on May 6, 1862, his aunt asked him, "Henry, have you made your peace with God?"

No wonder, then, that he replied, "Why, Aunt, I didn't know we had ever quarreled!"

from Walden

from ECONOMY

If I should attempt to tell how I have desired to spend my life in years past, it would probably surprise those of my readers who are somewhat acquainted with its actual history; it would certainly astonish those who know nothing about it. I will only hint at some of the enterprises which I have cherished.

In any weather, at any hour of the day or night, I have been anxious to improve the nick of time, and notch it on my stick too; to stand on the meeting of two eternities, the past and future, which is precisely the present moment; to toe that line. You will pardon some obscurities, for there are more secrets in my trade than in most men's, and yet not voluntarily kept, but inseparable from its very nature. I would gladly tell all that I know about it, and never paint "No Admittance" on my gate.

I long ago lost a hound, a bay horse, and a turtledove, and am still on their trail. Many are the travelers I have spoken concerning them, describing their tracks and what calls they answered to. I have met one or two who had heard the hound, and the tramp of the horse, and even seen the dove disappear behind a cloud, and they seemed as anxious to recover them as if they had lost them themselves.

To anticipate, not the sunrise and the dawn merely, but, if possible, Nature herself! How many mornings, summer and winter, before yet any neighbor was stirring about his business, have I been about mine! No doubt, many of my townsmen have met me returning from this enterprise, farmers starting for Boston in the twilight, or woodchoppers going to their work. It is true, I never assisted the sun materially in his rising, but, doubt not, it was of the last importance only to be present at it.

So many autumn, ay, and winter days, spent outside the town, trying to hear what was in the wind, to hear and carry it express! I well-nigh sunk all my capital in it, and lost my own breath into the bargain, running in the face of it. If it had concerned either of the political parties, depend upon it, it would have appeared in the Gazette with the earliest intelligence. At other times watching from the observatory of some cliff or tree, to telegraph any new arrival; or waiting at evening on the hill-tops for the sky to fall, that I might catch something, though I never caught much, and that, manna-wise, would dissolve again in the sun.

For a long time I was reporter to a journal, of no very wide circulation, whose editor has never yet seen fit to print the bulk of my contributions, and, as is too common with writers, I got only my labor for my pains. However, in this case my pains were their own reward.

For many years I was self-appointed inspector of snow-storms and rain-storms, and did my duty faithfully; surveyor, if not of highways, then of forest paths and all across-lot routes, keeping them open, and ravines bridged and passable at all seasons, where the public heel had testified to their utility.

I have looked after the wild stock of the town, which give a faithful herdsman a good deal of trouble by leaping fences; and I have had an eye to the unfrequented nooks and corners of the farm; though I did not always know whether Jonas or Solomon worked in a particular field to-day; that was none of my business. I have watered the red huckleberry, the sand cherry and the nettle-tree, the red pine and the black ash, the white grape and the yellow violet, which might have withered else in dry seasons.

In short, I went on thus for a long time (I may say it without boasting), faithfully minding my business, till it became more and more evident that my townsmen would not after all admit me into the list of town officers, nor make my place a sinecure with a moderate allowance. My accounts, which I can swear to have kept faithfully, I have, indeed, never got audited, still less accepted, still less paid and settled. However, I have not set my heart on that.

Not long since, a strolling Indian went to sell baskets at the house of a well-known lawyer in my neighborhood. "Do you wish to buy any baskets?" he asked. "No, we do not want any," was the reply. "What!" exclaimed the Indian as he went out the gate, "do you mean to starve us?" Having seen his industrious white neighbors so well off,—that the lawyer had only to weave arguments, and, by some magic, wealth and standing followed,—he had said to himself: I will go into business; I will weave baskets; it is a thing which I can do. Thinking that when he had made the baskets he would have done his part, and then it would be the white man's to buy them. He had not discovered that it was necessary for him to make it worth the other's while to buy them, or at least make him think that it was so, or to make something else which it would be worth his while to buy. I too had woven a kind of basket of a delicate texture, but I had not made it worth any one's while to buy them. Yet not the less, in my case, did I think it worth my while to weave them, and instead of studying how to make it worth men's while to buy my baskets, I studied rather how to avoid the necessity of selling them. The life which men praise and regard as successful is but one kind. Why should we exaggerate any one kind at the expense of the others?

Finding that my fellow-citizens were not likely to offer me any room in the court house, or any curacy or living anywhere else, but I must shift for myself, I turned my face more exclusively than ever to the woods, where I was better known. I determined to go into business at once, and not wait to acquire the usual capital, using such slender means as I had already got. My purpose in going to Walden Pond was not to live cheaply nor to live dearly there, but to transact some private business with the fewest obstacles; to be hindered from accomplishing which for want of a little common sense, a little enterprise and business talent, appeared not so sad as foolish.

•   •   •

Near the end of March, 1845, I borrowed an axe and went down to the woods by Walden Pond, nearest to where I intended to build my house, and began to cut down some tall, arrowy white pines, still in their youth, for timber. It is difficult to begin without borrowing, but perhaps it is the most generous course thus to permit your fellow-men to have an interest in your enterprise. The owner of the axe, as he released his hold on it, said that it was the apple of his eye; but I returned it sharper than I received it. It was a pleasant hillside where I worked, covered with pine woods, through which I looked out on the pond, and a small open field in the woods where pines and hickories were springing up. The ice in the pond was not yet dissolved, though there were some open spaces, and it was all dark-colored and saturated with water. There were some slight flurries of snow during the days that I worked there; but for the most part when I came out on to the railroad, on my way home, its yellow sand-heap stretched away gleaming in the hazy atmosphere, and the rails shone in the spring sun, and I heard the lark and pewee and other birds already come to commence another year with us. They were pleasant spring days, in which the winter of man's discontent was thawing as well as the earth, and the life that had lain torpid began to stretch itself. One day, when my axe had come off and I had cut a green hickory for a wedge, driving it with a stone, and had placed the whole to soak in a pond-hole in order to swell the wood, I saw a striped snake run into the water, and he lay on the bottom, apparently without inconvenience, as long as I stayed there, or more than a quarter of an hour; perhaps because he had not yet fairly come out of the torpid state. It appeared to me that for a like reason men remain in their present low and primitive condition; but if they should feel the influence of the spring of springs arousing them, they would of necessity rise to a higher and more ethereal life. I had previously seen the snakes in frosty mornings in my path with portions of their bodies still numb and inflexible, waiting for the sun to thaw them. On the 1st of April it rained and melted the ice, and in the early part of the day, which was very foggy, I heard a stray goose groping about over the pond and cackling as if lost, or like the spirit of the fog.

So I went on for some days cutting and hewing timber, and also studs and rafters, all with my narrow axe, not having many communicable or scholar-like thoughts, singing to myself,—

> Men say they know many things;
> But lo! they have taken wings,—
> The arts and sciences,
> And a thousand appliances:
> The wind that blows
> Is all that anybody knows.

I hewed the main timbers six inches square, most of the studs on two sides only, and the rafters and floor timbers on one side, leaving the rest of the bark on, so that they were just as straight and much stronger than sawed ones. Each stick was carefully mortised or tenoned by its stump, for I had borrowed other tools by this time. My days in the woods were not very long ones; yet I usually carried my dinner of bread and butter, and read the newspaper in which it was wrapped, at noon, sitting amid the green pine boughs which I had cut off, and to my bread was imparted some of their fragrance, for my hands were covered with a thick coat of pitch. Before I had done I was more the friend than the foe of the pine tree, though I had cut down some of them, having become better acquainted with it. Sometimes a rambler in the wood was attracted by the sound of my axe, and we chatted pleasantly over the chips which I had made.

By the middle of April, for I made no haste in my work, but rather made the most of it, my house was framed and ready for the raising. I had already bought the shanty of James Collins, an Irishman who worked on the Fitchburg Railroad, for boards. James Collins' shanty was considered an uncommonly fine one. When I called to see it he was not at home. I walked about the outside, at first unobserved from within, the window was so deep and high. It was of small dimensions, with a peaked cottage roof, and not much else to be seen, the dirt being raised five feet all around as if it were a compost heap. The roof was the soundest part, though a good deal warped and made brittle by the sun. Doorsill there was none, but a perennial passage for the hens under the door-board. Mrs. C. came to the door and asked me to view it from the inside. The hens were driven in by my approach. It was dark, and had a dirt floor for the most part, dank, clammy, and aguish, only here a board and there a board which would not bear removal. She lighted a lamp to show me the inside of the roof and the walls, and also that the board floor extended under the bed, warning me not to step into the cellar, a sort of dust hole two feet deep. In her own words, they were "good boards overhead, good boards all around, and a good window,"—of two whole squares originally, only the cat had passed out that way lately. There was a stove, a bed, and a place to sit, an infant in the house where it was born, a silk parasol, gilt-framed looking-glass, and a patent new coffee-mill nailed to an oak sapling, all told. The bargain was soon concluded, for James had in the meanwhile returned. I to pay four dollars and twenty-five cents to-night, he to vacate at five to-morrow morning, selling to nobody else meanwhile: I to take possession at six. It were well, he said, to be there early, and anticipate certain indistinct but wholly unjust claims on the score of ground rent and fuel. This he assured me was the only encumbrance. At six I passed him and his family on the road. One large bundle held their all,— bed, coffee-mill, looking-glass, hens,—all but the cat; she took to the woods and became a wild cat, and, as I learned afterward, trod in a trap set for woodchucks, and so became a dead cat at last.

I took down this dwelling the same morning, drawing the nails, and removed it to the pond-side by small cartloads, spreading the boards on the grass there to bleach and warp back again in the sun. One early thrush gave me a note or two as I drove along the woodland path. I was informed treacherously by a young Patrick that neighbor Seeley, an Irishman, in the intervals of the carting, transferred the still tolerable, straight, and drivable nails, staples, and spikes to his pocket, and then stood when I came back to pass the time of day, and look freshly up, unconcerned, with spring thoughts, at the devastation; there being a dearth of work, as he said. He was there to represent spectatordom, and help make this seemingly insignificant event one with the removal of the gods of Troy.

I dug my cellar in the side of a hill sloping to the south, where a woodchuck had formerly dug his burrow, down through sumach and blackberry roots, and the lowest stain of vegetation, six feet square by seven deep, to a fine sand where potatoes would not freeze in any winter. The sides were left shelving, and not stoned; but the sun having never shone on them, the sand still keeps its place. It was but two hours' work. I took particular pleasure in this breaking of ground, for in almost all latitudes men dig into the earth for an equable temperature. Under the most splendid house in the city is still to be found the cellar where they store their roots as of old, and long after the superstructure has disappeared posterity remark its dent in the earth. The house is still but a sort of porch at the entrance of a burrow.

At length, in the beginning of May, with the help of some of my acquaintances, rather to improve so good an occasion for neighborliness than from any necessity, I set up the frame of my house. No man was ever more honored in the character of his raisers than I. They are destined, I trust, to assist at the raising of loftier structures one day. I began to occupy my house on the 4th of July, as soon as it was boarded and roofed, for the boards were carefully feather-edged and lapped, so that it was perfectly impervious to rain, but before boarding I laid the foundation of a chimney at one end, bringing two cartloads of stones up the hill from the pond in my arms. I built the chimney after my hoeing in the fall, before a fire became necessary for warmth, doing my cooking in the meanwhile out of doors on the ground, early in the morning: which mode I still think is in some respects more convenient and agreeable than the usual one. When it stormed before my bread was baked, I fixed a few boards over the fire, and sat under them to watch my loaf, and passed some pleasant hours in that way. In those days, when my hands were much employed, I read but little, but the least scraps of paper which lay on the ground, my holder, or tablecloth, afforded me as much entertainment, in fact answered the same purpose as the Iliad.

It would be worth the while to build still more deliberately than I did, considering, for instance, what foundation a door, a window, a cellar, a garret, have in the nature of man, and perchance never raising any superstructure until we found a better reason for it than our temporal necessities even. There is some of the same fitness in a man's building his own house that there is in a bird's building its own nest. Who knows but if men constructed their dwellings with their own hands, and provided food for themselves and families simply and honestly enough, the poetic faculty would be universally developed, as birds universally sing when they are so engaged? But alas! we do like cowbirds and cuckoos, which lay their eggs in nests which other birds have built, and cheer no traveler with their chattering and unmusical notes. Shall we forever resign the pleasure of construction to the carpenter? What does architecture amount to in the experience of the mass of men? I never in all my walks came across a man engaged in so simple and natural an occupation as building his house. We belong to the community. It is not the tailor alone who is the ninth part of a man; it is as much the preacher, and the merchant, and the farmer. Where is this division of labor to end? and what object does it finally serve? No doubt another *may* also think for me; but it is not therefore desirable that he should do so to the exclusion of my thinking for myself.

True, there are architects so called in this country, and I have heard of one at least possessed with the idea of making architectural ornaments have a core of truth, a necessity and hence a beauty, as if it were a revelation to him. All very well perhaps from his point of view, but only a little better than the common dilettantism. A sentimental reformer in architecture, he began at the cornice, not at the foundation. It was only how to put a core of truth within the ornaments, that every sugarplum, in fact, might have an almond or caraway seed in it,—though I hold that almonds are most wholesome without the sugar,—and not how the inhabitant, the indweller, might build truly within and without, and let the ornaments take care of themselves. What reasonable man ever supposed that ornaments were something outward and in the skin merely,—that the tortoise got his spotted shell, or the shell-fish its mother-o'-pearl tints, by such a contract as the inhabitants of Broadway their Trinity Church? But a man has no more to do with the style of architecture of his house than a tortoise with that of its shell: nor need the soldier be so idle as to try to paint the precise *color* of his virtue on his standard. The enemy will find it out. He may turn pale when the trial comes. This man seemed to me to lean over the cornice, and timidly whisper his half truth to the rude occupants who really knew it better than he. What of architectural beauty I now see, I know has gradually grown from within outward, out of the necessities and character of the indweller, who is the only builder,—out of some unconscious truthfulness, and nobleness, without ever a thought for the appearance and whatever additional beauty of this kind is destined to be produced will be preceded by a like unconscious beauty of life. The most interesting dwellings in this country, as the painter knows, are the most unpretending, humble log huts and cottages of the poor commonly; it is the life of the inhabitants whose shells they are, and not any peculiarity in their surfaces merely, which makes them *picturesque:* and equally interesting will be the citizen's suburban box, when his life shall be as simple and as agreeable to the imagination, and there is as little straining after effect in the style of his dwelling. A great proportion of architectural ornaments are literally hollow, and a September gale would strip them off, like borrowed plumes, without injury to the substantials. They can do without *architecture* who have no olives nor wines in the cellar. What if an equal ado were made about the ornaments of style in literature, and the architects of our Bibles spent as much time about their cornices as the architects of our churches do? So are made the *belles-lettres* and the *beaux-arts* and their professors. Much it concerns a man, forsooth, how a few sticks are slanted over him or under him, and what colors are daubed upon his box. It would signify somewhat, if, in any earnest sense, *he* slanted them and daubed it; but the spirit having departed out of the tenant, it is of a piece with constructing his own coffin,—the architecture of the grave,—and "carpenter" is but another name for "coffin-maker." One man says, in his despair or indifference to life, take up a handful of the earth at your feet, and paint your house that color. Is he thinking of his last and narrow house? Toss up a copper for it as well. What an abundance of leisure he must have! Why do you take up a handful of dirt? Better paint your house your own complexion; let it turn pale or blush for you. An enterprise to improve the style of cottage architecture! When you have got my ornaments ready, I will wear them.

Before winter I built a chimney, and shingled the sides of my house, which were already impervious to rain, with imperfect and sappy shingles made of the first slice of the log, whose edges I was obliged to straighten with a plane.

I have thus a tight shingled and plastered house, ten feet wide by fifteen long, and eight-feet posts, with a garret and a closet, a large window on each side, two trap-doors, one door at the end, and a brick fireplace opposite. The exact cost of my house, paying the usual price for such materials as I used, but not counting the work, all of which was done by myself, was as follows; and I give the details because very few are able to tell exactly what their houses cost, and fewer still, if any, the separate cost of the various materials which compose them:—

Boards	$8 03½,	mostly shanty boards.
Refuse shingles for roof and sides	4 00	
Laths	1 25	
Two second-hand windows with glass	2 43	
One thousand old brick .	4 00	
Two casks of lime . . .	2 40	That was high.
Hair	0 31	More than I needed.
Mantle-tree iron	0 15	
Nails	3 90	
Hinges and screws . . .	0 14	
Latch	0 10	
Chalk	0 01	
Transportation	1 40	{ I carried a good part on my back.
In all	$28 12½	

These are all the materials, excepting the timber, stones, and sand, which I claimed by squatter's right. I have also a small woodshed adjoining, made chiefly of the stuff which was left after building the house.

I intend to build me a house which will surpass any on the main street in Concord in grandeur and luxury, as soon as it pleases me as much and will cost me no more than my present one.

• • •

from WHERE I LIVED, AND WHAT I LIVED FOR

When first I took up my abode in the woods, that is, began to spend my nights as well as days there, which, by accident, was on Independence Day, or the Fourth of July, 1845, my house was not finished for winter, but was merely a defense against the rain, without plastering or chimney, the walls being of rough, weather-stained boards, with wide chinks, which made it cool at night. The upright white hewn studs and freshly planed door and window casings gave it a clean and airy look, especially in the morning, when its timbers were saturated with dew, so that I fancied that by noon some sweet gum would exude from them. To my imagination it retained throughout the day more or less of this auroral character, reminding me of a certain house on a mountain which I had visited a year before. This was an airy and unplastered cabin, fit to entertain a traveling god, and where a goddess might trail her garments. The winds which passed over my dwelling were such as sweep over the ridges of mountains, bearing the broken strains, or celestial parts only, of terrestrial music. The morning wind forever blows, the poem of creation is uninterrupted; but few are the ears that hear it. Olympus is but the outside of the earth everywhere.

The only house I had been the owner of before, if I except a boat, was a tent, which I used occasionally when making excursions in the summer, and this is still rolled up in my garret; but the boat, after passing from hand to hand, has gone down the stream of time. With this more substantial shelter about me, I had made some progress toward settling in the world. This frame, so slightly clad, was a sort of crystallization around me, and reacted on the builder. It was suggestive somewhat as a picture in outlines. I did not need to go outdoors to take the air, for the atmosphere within had lost none of its freshness. It was not so much within-doors as behind a door where I sat, even in the rainiest weather. The Harivansa says, "An abode without birds is like a meal without seasoning." Such was not my abode, for I found myself suddenly neighbor to the birds; not by having imprisoned one, but having caged myself near them. I was not only nearer to some of those which commonly frequent the garden and the orchard, but to those wilder and more thrilling songsters of the forest which never, or rarely, serenade a villager,—the wood thrush, the veery, the scarlet tanager, the field sparrow, the whippoor-will, and many others.

I was seated by the shore of a small pond, about a mile and a half south of the village of Concord and somewhat higher than it, in the midst of an extensive wood between that town and Lincoln, and about two miles south of that our only field known to fame, Concord Battle Ground; but I was so low in the woods that the opposite shore, half a mile off, like the rest, covered with wood, was my most distant horizon. For the first week, whenever I looked out on the pond it impressed me like a tarn high up on the side of a mountain, its bottom far above the surface of other lakes, and, as the sun arose, I saw it throwing off its nightly clothing of mist, and here and there, by degrees, its soft ripples or its smooth reflecting surface was revealed, while the mists, like ghosts, were stealthily withdrawing in every direction into the woods, as at the breaking up of some nocturnal conventicle. The very dew seemed to hang upon the trees later into the day than usual, as on the sides of mountains.

This small lake was of most value as a neighbor in the intervals of a gentle rain-storm in August, when, both air and water being perfectly still, but the sky overcast, mid-afternoon had all the serenity of evening, and the wood thrush sang around, and was heard from shore to shore. A lake like this is never smoother than at such a time; and the clear portion of the air above it being shallow and darkened by clouds, the water, full of light and reflections, becomes a lower heaven itself so much the more important. From a hilltop near by, where the wood had been recently cut off, there was a pleasing vista southward across the pond, through a wide indentation in the hills which form the shore there, where their opposite sides sloping toward each other suggested a stream flowing out in that direction through a wooded valley, but stream there was none. That way I looked between and over the near green hills to some distant and higher ones in the horizon, tinged with blue. Indeed, by standing on tiptoe I could catch a glimpse of some of the peaks of the still bluer and more distant mountain ranges in the northwest, those true-blue coins from heaven's own mint, and also of some portion of the village. But in other directions, even from this point, I could not see over or beyond the woods which surrounded me. It is well to have some water in your neighborhood, to give buoyancy to and float the earth.

One value even of the smallest well is, that when you look into it you see that earth is not continent but insular. This is as important as that it keeps butter cool. When I looked across the pond from this peak toward the Sudbury meadows, which in time of flood I distinguished elevated perhaps by a mirage in their seething valley, like a coin in a basin, all the earth beyond the pond appeared like a thin crust insulated and floated even by this small sheet of intervening water, and I was reminded that this on which I dwelt was but *dry land.*

Though the view from my door was still more contracted, I did not feel crowded or confined in the least. There was pasture enough for my imagination. The low shrub oak plateau to which the opposite shore arose stretched away toward the prairies of the West and the steppes of Tartary, affording ample room for all the roving families of men. "There are none happy in the world but beings who enjoy freely a vast horizon,"—said Damodara, when his herds required new and larger pastures.

Both place and time were changed, and I dwelt nearer to those parts of the universe and to those eras in history which had most attracted me. Where I lived was as far off as many a region viewed nightly by astronomers. We are wont to imagine rare and delectable places in some remote and more celestial corner of the system, behind the constellation of Cassiopeia's Chair, far from noise and disturbance. I discovered that my house actually had its site in such a withdrawn, but forever new and unprofaned, part of the universe. If it were worth the while to settle in those parts near to the Pleiades or the Hyades, to Aldebaran or Altair, then I was really there, or at an equal remoteness from the life which I had left behind, dwindled and twinkling with as fine a ray to my nearest neighbor, and to be seen only in moonless nights by him. Such was that part of creation where I had squatted;—

> "There was a shepherd that did live,
>   And held his thoughts as high
> As were the mounts whereon his flocks
>   Did hourly feed him by."

What should we think of the shepherd's life if his flocks always wandered to higher pastures than his thoughts?

Every morning was a cheerful invitation to make my life of equal simplicity, and I may say innocence, with Nature herself. I have been as sincere a worshiper of Aurora as the Greeks. I got up early and bathed in the pond; that was a religious exercise, and one of the best things which I did. They say that characters were engraven on the bathing tub of King Tching-thang to this effect: "Renew thyself completely each day; do it again, and again, and forever again." I can understand that. Morning brings back the heroic ages. I was as much affected by the faint hum of a mosquito making its invisible and unimaginable tour through my apartment at earliest dawn, when I was sitting with door and windows open, as I could be by any trumpet that ever sang of fame. It was Homer's requiem; itself an Iliad and Odyssey in the air, singing its own wrath and wanderings. There was something cosmical about it; a standing advertisement, till forbidden, of the everlasting vigor and fertility of the world. The morning, which is the most memorable season of the day, is the awakening hour. Then there is least somnolence in us; and for an hour, at least, some part of us awakes which slumbers all the rest of the day and night. Little is to be expected of that day, if it can be called a day, to which we are not awakened by our Genius, but by the mechanical nudgings of some servitor, are not awakened by our own newly acquired force and aspirations from within, accompanied by the undulations of celestial music, instead of factory bells, and a fragrance filling the air—to a higher life than we fell asleep from; and thus the darkness bear its fruit, and prove itself to be good, no less than the light. That man who does not believe that each day contains an earlier, more sacred, and auroral hour than he has yet profaned, has despaired of life, and is pursuing a descending and darkening way. After a partial cessation of his sensuous life, the soul of man, or its organs rather, are reinvigorated each day, and his Genius tries again what noble life it can make. All memorable events, I should say, transpire in morning time and in a morning atmosphere. The Vedas say, "All intelligences awake with the morning." Poetry and art, and the fairest and most memorable of the actions of men, date from such an hour. All poets and heroes, like Memnon, are the children of Aurora, and emit their music at sunrise. To him whose elastic and vigorous thought keeps pace with the sun, the day is a perpetual morning. It matters not what the clocks say or the attitudes and labors of men. Morning is when I am awake and there is a dawn in me. Moral reform is the effort to throw off sleep. Why is it that men give so poor an account of their day if they have not been slumbering? They are not such poor calculators. If they had not been overcome with drowsiness, they would have performed something. The millions are awake enough for physical labor; but only one in a million is awake enough for effective intellectual exertion, only one in a hundred millions to a poetic or divine life. To be awake is to be alive. I have never yet met a man who was quite awake. How could I have looked him in the face?

We must learn to reawaken and keep ourselves awake, not by mechanical aids, but by an infinite expectation of the dawn, which does not forsake us in our soundest sleep. I know of no more encouraging fact than the unquestionable ability of man to evaluate his life by a conscious endeavor. It is something to be able to paint a particular picture, or to carve a statue, and so to make a few objects beautiful; but it is far more glorious to carve and paint the very atmosphere and medium through which we look, which morally we can do. To affect the quality of the day, that is the highest of arts. Every man is tasked to make his life, even in its details, worthy of the contemplation of his most elevated and critical hour. If we refused, or rather used up, such paltry information as we get, the oracles would distinctly inform us how this might be done.

I went to the woods because I wished to live deliberately, to front only the essential facts of life, and see if I could not learn what it had to teach, and not, when I came to die, discover that I had not lived. I did not wish to live what was not life, living is so dear; nor did I wish to practice resignation, unless it was quite necessary. I wanted to live deep and suck out all the marrow of life, to live so sturdily and Spartan-like as to put to rout all that was not life, to cut a broad swath and shave close, to drive life into a corner, and reduce it to its lowest terms, and, if it proved to be mean, why then to get the whole and genuine meanness of it, and publish its meanness to the world; or if it were sublime, to know it by experience, and be able to give a true account of it in my next excursion. For most men, it appears to me, are in a strange uncertainty about it, whether it is of the devil or of God, and have *somewhat hastily* concluded that it is the chief end of man here to "glorify God and enjoy him forever."

Still we live meanly, like ants; though the fable tells us that we were long ago changed into men; like pygmies we fight with cranes; it is error upon error, and clout upon clout, and our best virtue has for its occasion a superfluous and evitable wretchedness. Our life is frittered away by detail. An honest man has hardly need to count more than his ten fingers, or in extreme cases he may add his ten toes, and lump the rest. Simplicity, simplicity, simplicity! I say, let your affairs be as two or three, and not a hundred or a thousand; instead of a million count half a dozen, and keep your accounts on your thumb-nail. In the midst of this chopping sea of civilized life, such are the clouds and storms and quicksands and thousand-and-one items to be allowed for, that a man has to live, if he would not founder and go to the bottom and not make his port at all, by dead reckoning, and he must be a great calculator indeed who succeeds. Simplify, simplify. Instead of three meals a day, if it be necessary eat but one; instead of a hundred dishes, five; and reduce other things in proportion. Our life is like a German Confederacy, made up of petty states, with its boundary forever fluctuating, so that even a German cannot tell you how it is bounded at any moment. The nation itself, with all its so-called internal improvements, which, by the way, are all external and superficial, is just such an unwieldy and overgrown establishment, cluttered with furniture and tripped up by its own traps, ruined by luxury and heedless expense, by want of calculation and a worthy aim, as the million households in the land; and the only cure for it, as for them, is in a rigid economy, a stern and more than Spartan simplicity of life and elevation of purpose. It lives too fast. Men think that it is essential that the *Nation* have commerce, and export ice, and talk through a telegraph, and ride thirty miles an hour, without a doubt, whether *they* do or not; but whether we should live like baboons or like men, is a little uncertain. If we do not get out sleepers, and forge rails, and devote days and nights to the work, but go to tinkering upon our *lives* to improve *them*, who will build railroads? And if railroads are not built, how shall we get to Heaven in season? But if we stay at home and mind our business, who will want railroads? We do not ride on the railroad; it rides upon us. Did you ever think what those sleepers are that underlie the railroad? Each one is a man, an Irishman, or a Yankee man. The rails are laid on them, and they are covered with sand, and the cars run smoothly over them. They are sound sleepers, I assure you. And every few years a new lot is laid down and run over; so that, if some have the pleasure of riding on a rail, others have the misfortune to be ridden upon. And when they run over a man that is walking in his sleep, a supernumerary sleeper in the wrong position, and wake him up, they suddenly stop the cars, and make a hue and cry about it, as if this were an exception. I am glad to know that it takes a gang of men for every five miles to keep the sleepers down and level in their beds as it is, for this is a sign that they may sometime get up again.

Why should we live with such hurry and waste of life? We are determined to be starved before we are hungry. Men say that a stitch in time saves nine, and so they take a thousand stitches to-day to save nine to-morrow. As for *work*, we haven't any of any consequence. We have the Saint Vitus' dance, and cannot possibly keep our heads still. If I should only give a few pulls at the parish bell-rope, as for a fire, that is, without setting the bell, there is hardly a man on his farm in the outskirts of Concord, notwithstanding that press of engagements which was his excuse so many times this morning, nor a boy, nor a woman, I might almost say, but would forsake all and follow that sound, not mainly to save property from the flames, but, if we will confess the truth, much more to see it burn, since burn it must, and we, be it known, did not set it on fire,—or to see it put out, and have a hand in it, if that is done as handsomely; yes, even if it were the parish church itself. Hardly a man takes a half-hour's nap after dinner, but when he wakes he holds up his head and asks, "What's the news?" as if the rest of mankind had stood his sentinels. Some give directions to be waked every half-hour, doubtless for no other purpose; and then, to pay for it, they tell what they have dreamed. After a night's sleep the news is as indispensable as the breakfast. "Pray tell me anything new that has happened to a man anywhere on this globe,"—and he reads it over his coffee and rolls, that a man has had his eyes gouged out this morning on the Wachito River; never dreaming the while that he lives in the dark unfathomed mammoth cave of this world, and has but the rudiment of an eye himself.

For my part, I could easily do without the post-office. I think that there are very few important communications made through it. To speak critically, I never received more than one or two letters in my life—I wrote this some years ago—that were worth the postage. The penny-post is, commonly, an institution through which you seriously offer a man that penny for his thoughts which is so often safely offered in jest. And I am sure that I never read any memorable news in a newspaper. If we read of one man robbed, or murdered, or killed by accident, or one house burned, or one vessel wrecked, or one steamboat blown up, or one cow run over on the Western Rail-road, or one mad dog killed, or one lot of grasshoppers in the winter, —we never need read of another. One is enough. If you are acquainted with the principle, what do you care for a myriad instances and applications? To a philosopher all *news*, as it is called, is gossip and they who edit and read it are old women over their tea. Yet not a few are greedy after this gossip. There was such a rush, as I hear, the other day at one of the offices to learn the foreign news by the last arrival, that several large squares of plate glass belonging to the establishment were broken by the pressure,—news which I seriously think a ready wit might write a twelvemonth, or twelve years, beforehand with sufficient accuracy. As for Spain, for instance, if you know how to throw in Don Carlos and the Infanta, and Don Pedro and Seville and Granada, from time to time in the right proportions,—they may have changed the names a little since I saw the papers,—and serve up a bull-fight when other entertainments fail, it will be true to the letter, and give us as good an idea of the exact state or ruin of things in Spain as the most succinct and lucid reports under this head in the newspapers: and as for England, almost the last significant scrap of news from that quarter was the revolution of 1649; and if you have learned the history of her crops for an average year, you never need attend to that thing again, unless your speculations are of a merely pecuniary character. If one may judge who rarely looks into the newspapers, nothing new does ever happen in foreign parts, a French revolution not excepted.

What news! how much more important to know what that is which was never old! "Kieou-he-yu (great dignitary of the state of Wei) sent a man to Khoung-tseu to know his news. Khoung-tseu caused the messenger to be seated near him, and questioned him in these terms: What is your master doing? The messenger answered with respect: My master desires to diminish the number of his faults, but he cannot come to the end of them. The messenger being gone, the philosopher remarked: What a worthy messenger! What a worthy messenger!" The preacher, instead of vexing the ears of drowsy farmers on their day of rest at the end of the week,—for Sunday is the fit conclusion of an ill-spent week, and not the fresh and brave beginning of a new one,—with this one other draggle-tail of a sermon, should shout with thundering voice, "Pause! Avast! Why so seeming fast, but deadly slow?"

Shams and delusions are esteemed for soundest truths, while reality is fabulous. If men would steadily observe realities only, and not allow themselves to be deluded, life, to compare it with such things as we know, would be like a fairy tale and the Arabian Nights' Entertainments. If we respected only what is inevitable and has a right to be, music and poetry would resound along the streets. When we are unhurried and wise, we perceive that only great and worthy things have any permanent and absolute existence, that petty fears and petty pleasures are but the shadow of the reality. This is always exhilarating and sublime. By closing the eyes and slumbering, and consenting to be deceived by shows, men establish and confirm their daily life of routine and habit everywhere, which still is built on purely illusory foundations. Children, who play life, discern its true law and relations more clearly than men, who fail to live it worthily, but who think that they are wiser by experience, that is, by failure. I have read in a Hindoo book, that "there was a king's son, who, being expelled in infancy from his native city, was brought up by a forester, and, growing up to maturity in that state, imagined himself to belong to the barbarous race with which he lived. One of his father's ministers having discovered him, revealed to him what he was, and the misconception of his character was removed, and he knew himself to be a prince. So soul," continues the Hindoo philosopher, "from the circumstances in which it is placed, mistakes its own character, until the truth is revealed to it by some holy teacher, and then it knows itself to be *Brahme*." I perceive that we inhabitants of New England live this mean life that we do because our vision does not penetrate the surface of things. We think that that *is* which *appears* to be. If a man should walk through this town and see only the reality, where, think you, would the "Milldam" go to? If he should give us an account of the realities he beheld there, we should not recognize the place in his description. Look at a meeting-house, or a court-house, or a jail, or a shop, or a dwelling-house, and say what that thing really is before a true gaze, and they would all go to pieces in your account of them. Men esteem truth remote, in the outskirts of the system, behind the farthest star, before Adam and after the last man. In eternity there is indeed something true and sublime. But all these times and places and occasions are now and here. God himself culminates in the present moment, and will never be more divine in the lapse of all the ages. And we are enabled to apprehend at all what is sublime and noble only by the perpetual instilling and drenching of the reality that surrounds us. The universe constantly and obediently answers to our conceptions; whether we travel fast or slow, the track is laid for us. Let us spend our lives in conceiving then. The poet or the artist never yet had so fair and noble a design but some of his posterity at least could accomplish it.

Let us spend one day as deliberately as Nature, and not be thrown off the track by every nutshell and mosquito's wing that falls on the rails. Let us rise early and fast, or break fast, gently and without perturbation; let company come and let company go, let the bells ring and the children cry,—determined to make a day of it. Why should we knock under and go with the stream? Let us not be upset and overwhelmed in that terrible rapid and whirlpool called a dinner, situated in the meridian shallows. Weather this danger and you are safe, for the rest of the way is down hill. With unrelaxed nerves, with morning vigor, sail by it, looking another way, tied to the mast like Ulysses. If the engine whistles, let it whistle till it is hoarse for its pains. If the bell rings, why should we run? We will consider what kind of music they are like. Let us settle ourselves, and work and wedge our feet downward through the mud and slush of opinion, and prejudice, and tradition, and delusion, and appearance, that alluvion which covers the globe, through Paris and London, through New York and Boston and Concord, through Church and State, through poetry and philosophy and religion, till we come to a hard bottom and rocks in place, which we can call *reality*, and say, This is, and no mistake; and then begin, having a *point d'appui*, below freshet and frost and fire, a place where you might found a wall or a state, or set a lamp-post safely, or perhaps a gauge, not a Nilometer, but a Realometer, that future ages might know how deep a freshet of shams and appearances had gathered from time to time. If you stand right fronting and face to face to a fact, you will see the sun glimmer on both its surfaces, as if it were a cimeter, and feel its sweet edge dividing you through the heart and marrow, and so you will happily conclude your mortal career. Be it life or death, we crave only reality. If we are really dying, let us hear the rattle in our throats and feel cold in the extremities; if we are alive, let us go about our business.

Time is but the stream I go a-fishing in. I drink at it; but while I drink I see the sandy bottom and detect how shallow it is. Its thin current slides away, but eternity remains. I would drink deeper; fish in the sky, whose bottom is pebbly with stars. I cannot count one. I know not the first letter of the alphabet. I have always been regretting that I was not as wise as the day I was born. The intellect is a cleaver; it discerns and rifts its way into the secret of things. I do not wish to be any more busy with my hands than is necessary. My head is hands and feet. I feel all my best faculties concentrated in it. My instinct tells me that my head is an organ for burrowing, as some creatures use their snout and fore paws, and with it I would mine and burrow my way through these hills. I think that the richest vein is somewhere hereabouts; so by the divining-rod and thin rising vapors I judge; and here I will begin to mine.

from CONCLUSION

I left the woods for as good a reason as I went there. Perhaps it seemed to me that I had several more lives to live, and could not spare any more time for that one. It is remarkable how easily and insensibly we fall into a particular route, and make a beaten track for ourselves. I had not lived there a week before my feet wore a path from my door to the pondside; and though it is five or six years since I trod it, it is still quite distinct. It is true, I fear, that others may have fallen into it, and so helped to keep it open. The surface of the earth is soft and impressible by the feet of men; and so with the paths which the mind travels. How worn and dusty, then, must be the highways of the world, how deep the ruts of tradition and conformity! I did not wish to take a cabin passage, but rather to go before the mast and on the deck of the world, for there I could best see the moonlight amid the mountains. I do not wish to go below now.

I learned this, at least, by my experiment: that if one advances confidently in the direction of his dreams, and endeavors to live the life which he has imagined, he will meet with a success unexpected in common hours. He will put some things behind, will pass an invisible boundary; new, universal, and more liberal laws will begin to establish themselves around and within him; or the old laws be expanded, and interpreted in his favor in a more liberal sense, and he will live with the license of a higher order of beings. In proportion as he simplifies his life, the laws of the universe will appear less complex, and solitude will not be solitude, nor poverty poverty, nor weakness weakness. If you have built castles in the air, your work need not be lost; that is where they should be. Now put the foundations under them.

. . .

Rather than love, than money, than fame, give me truth. I sat at a table where were rich food and wine in abundance, and obsequious attendance, but sincerity and truth were not; and I went away hungry from the inhospitable board. The hospitality was as cold as the ices. I thought that there was no need of ice to freeze them. They talked to me of the age of the wine and the fame of the vintage; but I thought of an older, a newer, and purer wine, of a more glorious vintage, which they had not got, and could not buy. The style, the house and grounds and "entertainment" pass for nothing with me. I called on the king, but he made me wait in his hall, and conducted like a man incapacitated for hospitality. There was a man in my neighborhood who lived in a hollow tree. His manners were truly regal. I should have done better had I called on him.

How long shall we sit in our porticoes practicing idle and musty virtues, which any work would make impertinent? As if one were to begin the day with long-suffering, and hire a man to hoe his potatoes; and in the afternoon go forth to practice Christian meekness and charity with goodness aforethought! Consider the China pride and stagnant self-complacency of mankind. This generation inclines a little to congratulate itself on being the last of an illustrious line; and in Boston and London and Paris and Rome, thinking of its long descent, it speaks of its progress in art and science and literature with satisfaction. There are the Records of the Philosophical Societies, and the public Eulogies of *Great Men!* It is the good Adam contemplating his own virtue. "Yes, we have done great deeds, and sung divine songs, which shall never die,"—that is, as long as *we* can remember them. The learned societies and great men of Assyria,—where are they? What youthful philosophers and experimentalists we are! There is not one of my readers who has yet lived a whole human life. These may be but the spring months in the life of the race. If we have had the seven-years' itch, we have not seen the seventeen-year locust yet in Concord. We are acquainted with a mere pellicle of the globe on which we live. Most have not delved six feet beneath the surface, nor leaped as many above it. We know not where we are. Beside, we are sound asleep nearly half our time. Yet we esteem ourselves wise, and have an established order on the surface. Truly, we are deep thinkers, we are ambitious spirits! As I stand over the insect crawling amid the pine needles on the forest floor, and endeavoring to conceal itself from my sight, and ask myself why it will cherish those humble thoughts, and hide its head from me who might, perhaps, be its benefactor, and impart to its race some cheering information, I am reminded of the greater Benefactor and Intelligence that stands over me the human insect.

There is an incessant influx of novelty into the world and yet we tolerate incredible dullness. I need only suggest what kind of sermons are still listened to in the most enlightened countries. There are such words as joy and sorrow, but they are only the burden of a psalm, sung with a nasal twang, while we believe in the ordinary and mean. We think that we can change our clothes only. It is said that the British Empire is very large and respectable, and that the United States are a first-rate power. We do not believe that a tide rises and falls behind every man which can float the British Empire like a chip, if he should ever harbor it in his mind. Who knows what sort of seventeen-year locust will next come out of the ground? The government of the world I live in was not framed, like that of Britain, in after-dinner conversations over the wine.

The life in us is like the water in the river. It may rise this year higher than man has ever known it, and flood the parched uplands; even this may be the eventful year, which will drown out all our muskrats. It was not always dry land where we dwell. I see far inland the banks which the stream anciently washed, before science began to record its freshets. Every one has heard the story which has gone the rounds of New England, of a strong and beautiful bug which came out of the dry leaf of an old table of apple-tree wood, which had stood in a farmer's kitchen for sixty years, first in Connecticut, and afterward in Massachusetts,—from an egg deposited in the living tree many years earlier still, as appeared by counting the annual layers beyond it; which was heard gnawing out for several weeks, hatched perchance by the heat of an urn. Who does not feel his faith in a resurrection and immortality strengthened by hearing of this? Who knows what beautiful and winged life, whose egg has been buried for ages under many concentric layers of woodenness in the dead dry life of society, deposited at first in the alburnum of the green and living tree, which has been gradually converted into the semblance of its well-seasoned tomb,—heard perchance gnawing out now for years by the astonished family of man, as they sat round the festive board,—may unexpectedly come forth from amidst society's most trivial and handseled furniture, to enjoy its perfect summer life at last!

I do not say that John or Jonathan will realize all this; but such is the character of that morrow which mere lapse of time can never make to dawn. The light which puts out our eyes is darkness to us. Only that day dawns to which we are awake. There is more day to dawn. The sun is but a morning star.

QUESTIONS FOR DISCUSSION

Economy

1. What kinds of jobs does Thoreau say he has held in years past? How are these jobs different from what we think of as jobs today? What does the author mean when he says, "there are more secrets in my trade than in most men's"?

2. Suppose you asked a stranger what his occupation was and he responded, "For many years I was self-appointed inspector of snowstorms and rainstorms and did my duty faithfully." What would be your reaction? Why? Thoreau surely must have known what kind of reaction this statement would bring. Why, then, do you suppose he made it?

3. One of the best ways to analyze Thoreau's skill as a prose writer is to examine the brilliant manner in which, throughout his writing, he plays with words so that often there are double meanings. What double meanings do you observe in the following statements? What other instances can you find?
   a. "I went on thus for a long time . . . faithfully minding my business."
   b. "waiting at evening on the hilltops for the sky to fall, that I might catch something."

4. A symbol in literature is something that stands for or suggests something else by similarity or association. What do you think "a hound, a bay horse, and a turtledove" might symbolize? What does Thoreau mean when he says he lost them?

5. Why does the author insert an incident about an Indian? Why might anyone try to avoid the necessity of selling something, as Thoreau claims he would do?

6. What is Thoreau's stated purpose in going to Walden Pond? What kind of "private business" would he wish to transact?

7. How does Thoreau use the season of spring as a symbolic time of year? Why is it appropriate that he should begin building in springtime? What does he mean by "the winter of man's discontent was thawing as well as the earth"?

8. Where in this selection do you find Thoreau a skillful and conscientious observer of nature? Why does his view of the snake make him think of mankind?

9. Why does Thoreau suddenly insert a poem in the midst of this chapter? In what ways may this stylistic oddity reinforce our opinion of Thoreau as truly independent? In your opinion, is the poem appropriate here?

10. What details about the building of Thoreau's house do you find most ingenious? Which are most humorous? Why does Thoreau seem to appreciate neighbor Seeley's "spectatordom"?

11. Why does Thoreau feel it important for men to construct their dwellings with their own hands? How are most men like cuckoos and cowbirds? What, according to the author, are the most interesting dwellings in the country? Why?

12. What does "Better paint your house your own complexion" mean?

13. In what way does the last paragraph of this selection serve as a sharp comment on the houses which stand along the Concord streets? What does Thoreau seem to be proposing as essential ingredients of "grandeur and luxury"? Why might you agree or disagree?

Where I Lived, and What I Lived For

1. In verbal irony there is a difference between what is said and what is meant. Why might we feel that Thoreau is being ironical when he says he first moved to Walden Pond "which, *by accident*, was on Independence Day"?

2. What mystical undertones do you notice in Thoreau's description of the cabin?

3. Which images of the surroundings are most vivid? What pictures of the lake stand out most in your mind? How has Thoreau employed figurative language here?

4. Why does Thoreau say "Morning brings back the heroic ages"? Why does he consider the hum of a mosquito "Homer's requiem"? Would you agree that "morning . . . is the most memorable season of the day"? Why?

5. What do the words "an infinite expectation of the dawn" mean to you? How do these words affirm Thoreau's faith in the magnificent possibilities for mankind?

6. Why did Thoreau go to the woods? Would you say that his goal was admirable, foolish, unachievable, insane, idealistic? Why?

7. What would be Thoreau's advice to today's man caught up in the lightning pace of urban living? What sentences in the selection make you feel as you do? Why might you be tempted to either approve or condemn Thoreau's suggestions?

8. Why does Thoreau repeat the word *simplicity* three times, then twice more later on in the paragraph on page 137? How is our life like a German Confederacy? Would you agree with the general opinion stated in this paragraph? Why?

9. Why would Thoreau renounce the post-office and the newspaper? Why

is all the news, to a philosopher, merely gossip? What then, according to Thoreau, is important enough to be worth knowing?

10. Why are we directed to observe realities only? Would Thoreau agree with the adage "Truth is stranger than fiction"? Why might you agree or disagree?

11. In what way do children see things more clearly than men? How does the story from the Hindu book reinforce Thoreau's idea?

12. A metaphor (an implied comparison) is a device often used by writers to bring vividness and intensity to prose and poetry. Read the last paragraph of this section carefully. What metaphor does Thoreau use for Time? How does Thoreau sustain the metaphor beyond the first line?

Conclusion

1. Why did Thoreau leave the woods? Do you think his reason for leaving was as good as his reason for going there? Why?

2. What did Thoreau learn from his experiment? Do you think it possible for a person *always* to advance "confidently in the direction of his dreams"?

3. What do you think Thoreau meant by "the China pride and stagnant self-complacency of mankind"? What other sharp criticism is made of Thoreau's readers and mankind in general? With which of his comments might you agree? Why?

4. What thoughts did the crawling insect stimulate in Thoreau's mind? How is this a reflection of Thoreau's basic sympathy for transcendental philosophy?

5. Why does the author compare the life in us to water in the river?

6. What is the significance of the story of the "strong and beautiful bug"? How could you liken Thoreau himself to this insect? How does Thoreau's previous reference to insects interact with this one?

7. How do you explain the paradox in the last paragraph: "The light which puts out our eyes is darkness to us"? What do you think each of the last three sentences means? Why do you think Thoreau chose such obscure language to close his book?

ASSIGNMENTS FOR WRITING

1. Thoreau would never have encouraged every person to leave for the woods in order to live the best possible life. To go to Walden was for him, and only him, the best experiment in real living. Everyone, he felt, must choose his own experiment. What experiment in living would you choose in order to live life fully, to live the life you think best worth living? Discuss your views in a carefully constructed essay.

2. The following is Emerson's own comparison between himself and Thoreau in relation to their literary skills:

    He has muscle, and ventures on and performs feats which I am forced to decline. In reading him, I find the same thought, the same spirit that is in me, but he takes a step beyond, and illustrates by excellent images that which I should have conveyed in a sleepy generality.

    Do you agree? In your discussion, compare specific examples from the writings of both men.

3. Assume that you chose to live several days in the woods, in the manner of Thoreau, alone. Describe in a paragraph one moment during your stay there: perhaps a scene especially vivid, the construction of your dwelling, the cooking of your first meal, your first night alone under the stars. Use vivid language and rely upon words of color, sound, and touch to build a mood.

from On the Duty of Civil Disobedience

I heartily accept the motto,—"That government is best which governs least;" and I should like to see it acted up to more rapidly and systematically. Carried out, it finally amounts to this, which also I believe, —"That government is best which governs not at all;" and when men are prepared for it, that will be the kind of government which they will have. Government is at best but an expedient; but most governments are usually, and all governments are sometimes, inexpedient. The objections which have been brought against a standing army, and they are many and weighty, and deserve to prevail, may also at last be brought against a standing government. The standing army is only an arm of the standing government. The government itself, which is only the mode which the people have chosen to execute their will, is equally liable to be abused and perverted before the people can act through it. Witness the present Mexican war, the work of comparatively a few individuals using the standing government as their tool; for, in the outset, the people would not have consented to this measure.

This American government,—what is it but a tradition, though a recent one, endeavoring to transmit itself unimpaired to posterity, but each instant losing some of its integrity? It has not the vitality and force of a single living man; for a single man can bend it to his will. It is a sort of wooden gun to the people themselves. But it is not the less necessary for this; for the people must have some complicated machinery or other, and hear its din, to satisfy that idea of government which they have. Governments show thus how successfully men can be imposed on, even impose on themselves, for their own advantage. It is excellent, we must all allow. Yet this government never of itself furthered any enterprise, but by the alacrity with which it got out of its way. *It* does not keep the country free. *It* does not settle the West. *It* does not educate. The character inherent in the American people has done all that has been accomplished; and it would have done somewhat more, if the government had not sometimes got in its way. For government is an expedient by which men would fain succeed in letting one another alone; and, as has been said, when it is most expedient, the governed are most let alone by it. Trade and commerce, if they were not made of India-rubber, would never manage to bounce over the obstacles which legislators are continually putting in their way; and, if one were to judge these men wholly by the effects of their actions and not partly by their intentions, they would deserve to be classed and punished with those mischievous persons who put obstructions on the railroads.

But, to speak practically and as a citizen, unlike those who call themselves no-government men, I ask for, not at once no government, but *at once* a better government. Let every man make known what kind of government would command his respect, and that will be one step toward obtaining it.

After all, the practical reason why, when the power is once in the hands of the people, a majority are permitted, and for a long period continue, to rule is not because they are most likely to be in the right, nor because this seems fairest to the minority, but because they are physically the strongest. But a government in which the majority rule in all cases cannot be based on justice, even as far as men understand it. Can there not be a government in which majorities do not virtually decide right and wrong, but conscience?—in which majorities decide only those questions to which the rule of expediency is applicable? Must the citizen ever for a moment, or in the least degree, resign his conscience to the legislator? Why has every man a conscience, then? I think that we should be men first, and subjects afterward. It is not desirable to cultivate a respect for the law, so much as for the right. The only obligation which I have a right to assume is to do at any time what I think right. It is truly enough said, that a corporation has no conscience; but a corporation of conscientious men is a corporation *with* a conscience. Law never made men a whit more just; and, by means of their respect for it, even the well-disposed are daily made the agents of injustice. A common and natural result of an undue respect for law is, that you may see a file of soldiers, colonel, captain, corporal, privates, powder-monkeys, and all, marching in admirable order over hill and dale to the wars, against their wills, ay, against their common sense and consciences, which makes it very steep marching indeed, and produces a palpitation of the heart. They have no doubt that it is a damnable business in which they are concerned; they are all peaceably inclined. Now, what are they? Men at all? or small movable forts and magazines, at the service of some unscrupulous man in power? Visit the Navy-Yard, and behold a marine, such a man as an American government can make, or such as it can make a man with its black arts,—a mere shadow and reminiscence of humanity, a man laid out alive and standing, and already, as one may say, buried under arms with funeral accompaniments, though it may be,—

"Not a drum was heard, not a funeral note,
    As his corse to the rampart we hurried;
Not a soldier discharged his farewell shot
    O'er the grave where our hero we buried."

The mass of men serve the state thus, not as men mainly, but as machines, with their bodies. They are the standing army, and the militia, jailors, constables, posse comitatus etc. In most cases there is no free exercise whatever of the judgment or of the moral sense; but they put themselves on a level with wood and earth and stones; and wooden men can perhaps be manufactured that will serve the purpose as well. Such command no more respect than men of straw or a lump of dirt. They have the same sort of worth only as horses and dogs. Yet such as these even are commonly esteemed good citizens. Others —as most legislators, politicians, lawyers, ministers, and office-holders —serve the state chiefly with their heads; and, as they rarely make any moral distinctions, they are as likely to serve the Devil, without *intending* it, as God. A very few, as heroes, patriots, martyrs, reformers in the great sense, and *men*, serve the state with their consciences also, and so necessarily resist it for the most part; and they are commonly treated as enemies by it. A wise man will only be useful as a man, and will not submit to be "clay," and "stop a hole to keep the wind away," but leave that office to his dust at least:—

"I am too high-born to be propertied,
    To be a secondary at control,
    Or useful serving-man and instrument
    To any soverign state throughout the world."

He who gives himself entirely to his fellow-men appears to them useless and selfish; but he who gives himself partially to them is pronounced a benefactor and philanthropist.

How does it become a man to behave toward this American government to-day? I answer, that he cannot without disgrace be associated with it. I cannot for an instant recognize that political organization as *my* government which is the *slave's* government also.

．　．　．

Unjust laws exist: shall we be content to obey them, or shall we endeavor to amend them, and obey them until we have succeeded, or shall we transgress them at once? Men generally, under such a government as this, think that they ought to wait until they have persuaded the majority to alter them. They think that, if they should resist, the remedy would be worse than the evil. But it is the fault of the government itself that the remedy *is* worse than the evil. *It* makes it worse. Why is it not more apt to anticipate and provide for reform? Why does it not cherish its wise minority? Why does it cry and resist before it is hurt? Why does it not encourage its citizens to be on the alert to point out its faults, and *do* better than it would have them? Why does it always crucify Christ, and excommunicate Copernicus and Luther, and pronounce Washington and Franklin rebels?

One would think, that a deliberate and practical denial of its authority was the only offense never contemplated by government; else, why has it not assigned its definite, its suitable and proportionate penalty? If a man who has no property refuses but once to earn nine shillings for the state, he is put in prison for a period unlimited by any law that I know, and determined only by the discretion of those who placed him there; but if he should steal ninety times nine shillings from the state, he is soon permitted to go at large again.

If the injustice is part of the necessary friction of the machine of government, let it go, let it go: perchance it will wear smooth,—certainly the machine will wear out. If the injustice has a spring, or a pulley, or a rope, or a crank, exclusively for itself, then perhaps you may consider whether the remedy will not be worse than the evil; but if it is of such a nature that it requires you to be the agent of injustice to another, then, I say, break the law. Let your life be a counter friction to stop the machine. What I have to do is to see, at any rate, that I do not lend myself to the wrong which I condemn.

As for adopting the ways which the state has provided for remedying the evil, I know not of such ways. They take too much time, and a man's life will be gone. I have other affairs to attend to. I came into this world, not chiefly to make this a good place to live in, but to live in it, be it good or bad. A man has not everything to do, but something; and because he cannot do *everything*, it is not necessary that he should do *something* wrong. It is not my business to be petitioning the Governor or the Legislature any more than it is theirs to petition me; and if they should not hear my petition, what should I do then? But in this case the state has provided no way: its very Constitution is the evil. This may seem to be harsh and stubborn and unconciliatory; but it is to treat with the utmost kindness and consideration the only spirit that can appreciate or deserves it. So is all change for the better, like birth and death, which convulse the body.

I do not hesitate to say, that those who call themselves Abolitionists should at once effectually withdraw their support, both in person and property, from the government of Massachusetts and not wait till they constitute a majority of one, before they suffer the right to prevail through them. I think that it is enough if they have God on their side, without waiting for that other one. Moreover, any man more right than his neighbors constitutes a majority of one already.

I meet this American government, or its representative, the state government, directly, and face to face, once a year—no more—in the person of its tax-gatherer; this is the only mode in which a man situated as I am necessarily meets it; and it then says distinctly, Recognize me; and the simplest, most effectual, and, in the present posture of affairs, the indispensablest mode of treating with it on this head, of expressing your little satisfaction with and love for it, is to deny it then. My civil neighbor, the tax-gatherer, is the very man I have to deal with,—for it is, after all, with men and not with parchment that I quarrel,—and he has voluntarily chosen to be an agent of the government. How shall he ever know well what he is and does as an officer of the government, or as a man, until he is obliged to consider whether he shall treat me, his neighbor, for whom he has respect, as a neighbor and well-disposed man, or as a maniac and disturber of the peace, and see if he can get over this obstruction to his neighborliness without a ruder and more impetuous thought or speech corresponding with his action. I know this well, that if one thousand, if one hundred, if ten men whom I could name,—if ten *honest* men only,—ay, if *one* HONEST man, in this State of Massachusetts, *ceasing to hold slaves*, were actually to withdraw from this copartnership, and be locked up in the county jail therefor, it would be the abolition of slavery in America. For it matters not how small the beginning may seem to be: what is once well done is done forever. But we love better to talk about it: that we say is our mission. Reform keeps many scores of newspapers in its service, but not one man. If my esteemed neighbor, the State's ambassador, who will devote his days to the settlement of the question of human rights in the Council Chamber, instead of being threatened with the prisons of Carolina, were to sit down the prisoner of Massachusetts, that State which is so anxious to foist the sin of slavery upon her sister,—though at present she can discover only an act of inhospitality to be the ground of a quarrel with her,—the Legislature would not wholly waive the subject the following winter.

Under a government which imprisons any unjustly, the true place for a just man is also a prison. The proper place to-day, the only place which Massachusetts has provided for her freer and less desponding spirits, is in her prisons, to be put out and locked out of the State by her own act, as they have already put themselves out by their principles. It is there that the fugitive slave, and the Mexican prisoner on parole, and the Indian come to plead the wrongs of his race should find them; on that separate, but more free and honorable ground, where the State places those who are not *with* her, but *against* her,—the only house in a slave State in which a free man can abide with honor. If any think that their influence would be lost there, and their voices no longer afflict the ear of the State, that they would not be as an enemy within its walls, they do not know by how much truth is stronger than error, nor how much more eloquently and effectively he can combat injustice who has experienced a little in his own person. Cast your whole vote, not a strip of paper merely, but your whole influence. A minority is powerless while it conforms to the majority; it is not even a minority then; but it is irresistible when it clogs by its whole weight. If the alternative is to keep all just men in prison, or give up war and slavery, the State will not hesitate which to choose. If a thousand men were not to pay their tax-bills this year, that would not be a violent and bloody measure, as it would be to pay them, and enable the State to commit violence and shed innocent blood. This is, in fact, the definition of a peaceable revolution, if any such is possible. If the tax-gatherer, or any other public officer, asks me, as one has done, "But what shall I do?" my answer is, "If you really wish to do anything, resign your office." When the subject has refused allegiance, and the officer has resigned his office, then the revolution is accomplished. But even suppose blood should flow. Is there not a sort of blood shed when the conscience is wounded? Through this wound a man's real manhood and immortality flow out, and he bleeds to an everlasting death. I see this blood flowing now.

• • •

Some years ago, the State met me in behalf of the Church, and commanded me to pay a certain sum toward the support of a clergyman whose preaching my father attended, but never I myself. "Pay," it said, "or be locked up in the jail." I declined to pay. But, unfortunately, another man saw fit to pay it. I did not see why the schoolmaster should be taxed to support the priest, and not the priest the schoolmaster; for I was not the State's schoolmaster, but I supported myself by voluntary subscription. I did not see why the lyceum should not present its tax-bill, and have the State to back its demand, as well as the Church. However, at the request of the selectmen, I condescended to make some such statement as this in writing:—"Know all men by these presents, that I, Henry Thoreau, do not wish to be regarded as a member of any incorporated society which I have not joined." This I gave to the town clerk; and he has it. The State, having thus learned that I did not wish to be regarded as a member of that church, has never made a like demand on me since; though it said that it must adhere to its original presumption that time. If I had known how to name them, I should then have signed off in detail from all the societies which I never signed on to; but I did not know where to find a complete list.

I have paid no poll-tax for six years. I was put into a jail once on this account, for one night; and, as I stood considering the walls of solid stone, two or three feet thick, the door of wood and iron, a foot thick, and the iron grating which strained the light, I could not help being struck with the foolishness of that institution which treated me as if I were mere flesh and blood and bones, to be locked up. I wondered that it should have concluded at length that this was the best use it could put me to, and had never thought to avail itself of my services in some way. I saw that, if there was a wall of stone between me and my townsmen, there was a still more difficult one to climb or break through before they could get to be as free as I was. I did not for a moment feel confined, and the walls seemed a great waste of stone and mortar. I felt as if I alone of all my townsmen had paid my tax. They plainly did not know how to treat me, but behaved like persons who are underbred. In every threat and in every compliment there was a blunder; for they thought that my chief desire was to stand the other side of that stone wall. I could not but smile to see how industriously they locked the door on my meditations, which followed them out again without let or hindrance, and *they* were really all that was dangerous. As they could not reach me, they had resolved to punish my body; just as boys, if they cannot come at some person against whom they have a spite, will abuse his dog. I saw that the State was half-witted, that it was timid as a lone woman with her silver spoons, and that it did not know its friends from its foes, and I lost all my remaining respect for it, and pitied it.

Thus the State never intentionally confronts a man's sense, intellectual or moral, but only his body, his senses. It is not armed with superior wit or honesty, but with superior physical strength. I was not born to be forced. I will breathe after my own fashion. Let us see who is the strongest. What force has a multitude? They only can force me who obey a higher law than I. They force me to become like themselves. I do not hear of *men* being *forced* to live this way or that by masses of men. What sort of life were that to live? When I meet a government which says to me, "Your money or your life," why should I be in haste to give it my money? It may be in a great strait, and not know what to do: I cannot help that. It must help itself; do as I do. It is not worth the while to snivel about. I am not responsible for the successful working of the machinery of society. I am not the son of the engineer. I perceive that, when an acorn and a chestnut fall side by side, the one does not remain inert to make way for the other, but both obey their own laws, and spring and grow and flourish as best they can, till one, perchance, overshadows and destroys the other. If a plant cannot live according to its nature, it dies; and so a man.

• • •

The authority of government, even such as I am willing to submit to,—for I will cheerfully obey those who know and can do better than I, and in many things even those who neither know nor can do so well,—is still an impure one: to be strictly just, it must have the sanction and consent of the governed. It can have no pure right over my person and property but what I concede to it. The progress from an absolute to a limited monarchy, from a limited monarchy to a democracy, is a progress toward a true respect for the individual. Even the Chinese philosopher was wise enough to regard the individual as the basis of the empire. Is a democracy, such as we know it, the last improvement possible in government? Is it not possible to take a step further towards recognizing and organizing the rights of man? There will never be a really free and enlightened State until the State comes to recognize the individual as a higher and independent power, from which all its own power and authority are derived, and treats him accordingly. I please myself with imagining a State at last which can afford to be just to all men, and to treat the individual with respect as a neighbor; which even would not think it inconsistent with its own repose if a few were to live aloof from it, not meddling with it, nor embraced by it, who fulfilled all the duties of neighbors and fellowmen. A State which bore this kind of fruit, and suffered it to drop off as fast as it ripened, would prepare the way for a still more perfect and glorious State, which also I have imagined, but not yet anywhere seen.

QUESTIONS FOR DISCUSSION

1. How has Thoreau altered the motto which appears in the first sentence? With which would you be more likely to agree, the original or the revised motto?

2. With what would Thoreau replace majority rule in deciding right and wrong? Do you think this could effectively operate in today's societies? Why?

3. "The only obligation which I have a right to assume is to do at any time what I think is right." From this statement, upon whom does the final responsibility of right and wrong rely? Assuming all men followed

Thoreau's dictum, what positive results would you expect? What difficulties can you anticipate for a world of people who believe and behave in this way?

4. How do men serve the state as machines? Do you agree that most men do not exercise judgment or moral sense? Why are politicians "as likely to serve the Devil, without *intending* it, as God"? Do you agree?

5. What does the second poem mean? Why might it be considered a creed, in verse, of the independent man? Would you call it good poetry?

6. With the paragraph beginning "Unjust laws exist," Thoreau offers, in the form of questions, three solutions to unjust laws. Which of these do you think wisest? Why?

7. Why does Thoreau reject "the ways which the state has provided for remedying the evil"? How does this help explain the attitudes of many of today's youth toward orderly change through legislation? Do you think Thoreau's feelings here are justifiable? Why?

8. "For it matters not how small the beginning may seem to be: what is once well done is done forever." What does this statement mean? According to Thoreau, have many men lived up to this philosophy?

9. Why does Thoreau say "the true place for a just man is also a prison"? How does he define "peaceable revolution"? What aspects of this philosophy have some contemporary Civil Rights organizations adopted?

10. Why is Thoreau undisturbed by the presence of the stone wall around him? What paradox does he employ in his explanation? Why does he compare his townsmen to boys?

11. What elements of transcendental influence do you notice in the last paragraph?

12. Why do you think Thoreau chose the word *Duty* for the title: "On the Duty of Civil Disobedience"? What does the word *Duty* imply? How is its meaning different from a word like *privilege* or *right*?

ASSIGNMENTS FOR WRITING

1. Joseph Wood Krutch, in an essay on Thoreau's "On the Duty of Civil Disobedience" and its place in the modern world, says, "in practice, those whose conscience demands that they defy authority in ways that involve great consequences must be willing to accept some penalty." Write an essay in which you show first how Thoreau would have responded to this statement, and then how you feel it is relevant to contemporary society. Use concrete examples from your own readings or observations.

2. Do you feel that an individual has a right to refuse to obey a law if it opposes his moral values? Discuss this question in a paragraph. Be specific in your presentation of ideas.

Nathaniel Hawthorne

In the summer of 1850, Nathaniel Hawthorne was forty-six years old, happily married to Sophia Peabody and father of two young children. Together they enjoyed a resort in the Berkshire Mountains near Lenox, Massachusetts. Hawthorne was by profession a writer, although he had also held political appointments in what we now call the civil service. Hawthorne's published works included two volumes of short stories, *Twice-Told Tales* and *Mosses from an Old Manse,* and a recent novel, *The Scarlet Letter.* This latter publication had been well received, and although Hawthorne was not and never would be a rich man, the rewards of a favorable reception for his finest writing made him comfortable.

He had not always known such comfort. In fact, his childhood and early manhood had been years of sorrow, illness, loneliness, and self-imposed seclusion. Born in 1804 to a sailing captain and his wife in Salem, Massachusetts, the boy Nathaniel was soon aware of his heritage and its grisly history: He was a Hathorne, one of that inflexible family whose members had ruled in Puritan Salem during the formative years of the Massachusetts colony. William Hathorne had ordered a Quaker woman to be whipped through the streets of several towns; his son John had served on the tribunal of judges in 1692 that condemned Salem's alleged witches to death. Whether it was the unpleasantness of this blood-line association that caused Nathaniel Hawthorne to change the spelling of his name, adding the *w,* is mere speculation; we do know that the sins of the fathers were indeed visited upon him in the form of their haunting memory.

I know not whether these ancestors of mine bethought themselves to repent, and ask pardon of Heaven for their cruelties; or whether they are now groaning under the heavy consequences of them, in another state of being. At all events, I, the present writer, as their representative hereby take shame upon myself for their sakes, and pray that any curse incurred by them—as I have heard, and as the dreary and unprosperous condition of the race, for many a long year back, would argue to exist—may be now and henceforth removed.

So Hawthorne wrote in his introductory to *The Scarlet Letter*.

The "dreary and unprosperous condition" of his family had begun, in his experience, with the death of his father while away on a voyage. The widow moved her young family in with relatives, then from Salem to Raymond, Maine, and back again. The boy received an unsettling injury while playing ball that resulted in lameness and kept him from normal play and socializing. He learned to amuse himself with reading and contemplation, sometimes taking long walks in spite of his lameness. By the time he had been prepared for college, at age seventeen, he had made his vocational decision. He wrote to his mother, "I do not want to be a doctor and live by men's diseases, nor a minister to live by their sins, nor a lawyer and live by their quarrels. So, I don't see that there is anything left for me but to be an author."

At Bowdoin College in Brunswick, Maine, Hawthorne made friends with Horace Bridge and Franklin Pierce, both of whom were to help him in later life; he was also the classmate of Henry Wadsworth Longfellow, whose acclaim for *Twice-Told Tales* gave Hawthorne a boost in reputation. Hawthorne was an average student, adept at Latin but too nervous to fulfill the mandatory public speaking requirements. This reticence carried over into his writing, manifested in his characteristic indirectness, which some contemporary critics mistook as a morally ambiguous position.

Following graduation from Bowdoin in 1825, Hawthorne chose a life of almost total withdrawal from society—something comparable to the experience of another New England metaphysical writer in another Massachusetts village, Miss Dickinson of Amherst. Professor Mark Van Doren suggests in his critical biography that the only accurate explanation for this period, from 1825 until 1838, is this:

Hawthorne was learning how to write stories; he was struggling to reconcile the peculiar nature of his thoughts and fancies with the taste of the period; he was trying to feel his native land as the "poetic or fairy precinct" which in his conviction was necessary for romance; he was discovering and ordering his own profound, somewhat obsessive, moral ideas; he was laboring to become known, and so to justify the profession he had chosen; he was having little success, and being discouraged—each of these propositions is true, yet none of them is complete.

He wrote a puerile romance based upon his college experience, *Fanshawe*, a book which he attempted to recover from distribution almost as soon as it was printed. He managed to have published anonymously some sketches and stories, including several that were later to bring him praise: "The Gentle Boy," "The Ambitious Guest," "My Kinsman, Major Molineaux." He also ventured out of his seclusion for a brief period to edit a tawdry magazine of reprints. Most of all, he read and read the bleak histories of his ancestors' New England. All of these efforts at obtaining a sure grip on literary fame failed as individual ventures; together, however, they helped to forge a career.

In 1837, Hawthorne's friend Bridge underwrote the publication of *Twice-Told Tales,* and the long-sought literary reputation became a reality. With public exposure, Hawthorne felt able to emerge from physical seclusion as well. To prepare himself for the impending responsibilities of marriage, he took a position in the Boston Custom House, resigning two years later when the newly elected Whigs were about to turn out the Democrat appointees. Thereupon Hawthorne established his first and only immediate relationship with the Transcendentalist Movement. The Brook Farm experimenters in communal living welcomed the young writer in 1841, and Hawthorne committed himself to their goal of "plain living and high thinking." Expecting to bring his bride-to-be to Brook Farm, he paid five hundred dollars for two shares. Meanwhile he labored at his appointed task—shoveling manure. Soon disillusioned, he wrote to Sophia, "It is my opinion, dearest, that a man's soul may be buried and perish under a dung-heap or in a furrow of the field, just as well as under a pile of money."

Instead of socialism at Brook Farm, Hawthorne chose the quiet of Concord's Old Manse, the former parish home of Concord's Unitarian ministers. Here Hawthorne and his bride began their idyllic marriage; here, too, he wrote *Mosses from an Old Manse.* But the need to provide adequately for his growing family forced Hawthorne back into the political spoils system, and the years 1846–1849 found him in the Salem Custom House by day, at his desk writing by night. Such a part-time compromise of art with commerce might have continued indefinitely and to the detriment of American letters, had not the fouler side of politics intervened. Hawthorne found himself summarily dismissed from his position—a circumstance he describes in "The Custom House" introduction to *The Scarlet Letter.*

Cast upon his writing fortunes once again, Hawthorne nearly despaired of his ability to sustain his family. His health, never robust, was poorer than usual when the publisher James T. Fields of Boston visited Hawthorne in Salem. Fields urged the unhappy author to give him something to publish. "Nonsense," replied Hawthorne, "who would risk publishing a book for *me*, the most unpopular writer in America?" But Fields prevailed, and Hawthorne gave him the manuscript of a yet unfinished novel. It was *The Scarlet Letter*, which Fields published in the spring of 1850.

Throughout his career, Hawthorne had been typecast as the writer of pleasant little tales for children, sentimental sketches, and prissy, moralized allegories. Few of his critical readers had penetrated beneath the historical surface of his New England stories to find their pervasive sense of guilt and their condemnation of prideful piety. It remained for a crude, younger man, himself an aspiring serious novelist, to reveal what others had failed to see. This man was Herman Melville. His essay, "Hawthorne and His Mosses," published in August of 1850, produced the most telling criticism of Hawthorne yet written, criticism that offers us a clear insight into these tales today. To contradict the fatuous popular opinion of Hawthorne's lightheartedness, Melville wrote:

> For in spite of all the Indian-summer sunlight on the hither side of Hawthorne's soul, the other side—like the dark half of the physical sphere—is shrouded in a blackness ten times black. . . . Whether Hawthorne has simply availed himself of this mystical blackness as a means to the wondrous effects he makes it to produce in his lights and shades; or whether there really lurks in him, perhaps unknown to himself, a touch of Puritanic gloom,—this, I cannot altogether tell. Certain it is, however, that this great power of blackness in him derives its force from its appeals to that Calvinistic sense of Innate Depravity and Original Sin, from whose visitations, in some shape or other, no deeply thinking mind is always and wholly free. For, in certain moods, no man can weigh this world without throwing in something, somehow like Original Sin, to strike the uneven balance. At all events, perhaps no writer has ever wielded this terrific thought with greater terror than this same harmless Hawthorne. Still more: this black conceit pervades him through and through. You may be witched by his sunlight,— transported by the bright gildings in the skies he builds over you; but there is the blackness of darkness beyond; and even his bright gildings but fringe and play upon the edges of thunderclouds. In one word, the world is mistaken in this Nathaniel Hawthorne.

What Melville pointed out to readers of the *Literary World* magazine seems more apparent to modern readers schooled in the science of psychology and the philosophy of existentialism than may have been true for Hawthorne's contemporaries. The complexities of the human mind—the powers of the imagination and of the conscience—

are beyond the simple analysis of romantic storytelling. The ironic awareness of the individual's precarious hold on life, which informs much of modern man's thinking, corresponds more closely to Hawthorne's position than to that of his now forgotten peers. Only a mind like Hawthorne's, steeped in the curious combination of Christian theology, Puritan superstition, and Yankee independence, could create the tales of "dark necessity" and of "unpardonable sin" found in this book. Blended together with a supremely graceful style, these stories support Melville's contention that Hawthorne's piercing vision of life had given him gifts comparable to those of Dante and Shakespeare.

But after the fame of *The Scarlet Letter*, Hawthorne's literary course went strangely awry. He followed his first large success with *The House of the Seven Gables* (1851), *The Blithedale Romance*, based upon his Brook Farm experience (1852), and *The Marble Faun* (1860), a story laid in Rome, his only romance set outside his native country. His friendship with Franklin Pierce resulted in an appointment as consul in Liverpool and Manchester, England when Pierce was elected President. Yet neither popular recognition nor political preferment could eliminate a nagging sense that in these later years he had himself committed the artist's unpardonable sin, best expressed by little Pearl in her rebuke of Dimmesdale in *The Scarlet Letter:* "Thou wast not bold!—thou wast not true!" Hawthorne returned to New England from Europe in 1860, and attempted but failed to finish four novels.

The enigma of the unfulfilled artist who seems to turn away from what he most desires continues to perplex readers and literary historians. Once hailed the near equal of Shakespeare, Hawthorne refused to claim his birthright, a fact that puzzles us still. Yet in spite of this disappointment, the spell of the Hawthorne who *was* cancels out much of the envy for what might have been, leaving the reader with Melville's own conclusion: that Hawthorne's books "should be sold by the hundred thousand; and read by the million; and admired by every one who is capable of admiration."

Young Goodman Brown

Young Goodman Brown came forth at sunset into the street at Salem village; but put his head back, after crossing the threshold, to exchange a parting kiss with his young wife. And Faith, as the wife was aptly named, thrust her own pretty head into the street, letting the wind play with the pink ribbons of her cap while she called to Goodman Brown.

"Dearest heart," whispered she, softly and rather sadly, when her lips were close to his ear, "prithee put off your journey until sunrise and sleep in your own bed to-night. A lone woman is troubled with such dreams and such thoughts that she's afeared of herself sometimes. Pray tarry with me this night, dear husband, of all nights in the year."

"My love and my Faith," replied young Goodman Brown, "of all nights in the year, this one night must I tarry away from thee. My journey, as thou callest it, forth and back again, must needs be done 'twixt now and sunrise. What, my sweet, pretty wife, dost thou doubt me already, and we but three months married?"

"Then God bless you!" said Faith, with the pink ribbons; "and may you find all well when you come back."

"Amen!" cried Goodman Brown. "Say thy prayers, dear Faith, and go to bed at dusk, and no harm will come to thee."

So they parted; and the young man pursued his way until, being about to turn the corner by the meeting-house, he looked back and saw the head of Faith still peeping after him with a melancholy air, in spite of her pink ribbons.

"Poor little Faith!" thought he, for his heart smote him. "What a wretch am I to leave her on such an errand! She talks of dreams, too. Methought as she spoke there was trouble in her face, as if a dream had warned her what work is to be done to-night. But no, no; 'twould kill her to think it. Well, she's a blessed angel on earth; and after this one night I'll cling to her skirts and follow her to heaven."

With this excellent resolve for the future, Goodman Brown felt himself justified in making more haste on his present evil purpose. He had taken a dreary road, darkened by all the gloomiest trees of the forest, which barely stood aside to let the narrow path creep through, and closed immediately behind. It was all as lonely as could be; and there is this peculiarity in such a solitude, that the traveler knows not who may be concealed by the innumerable trunks and the thick boughs overhead; so that with lonely footsteps he may yet be passing through an unseen multitude.

"There may be a devilish Indian behind every tree," said Goodman Brown to himself; and he glanced fearfully behind him as he added, "What if the devil himself should be at my very elbow!"

His head being turned back, he passed a crook of the road, and, looking forward again, beheld the figure of a man, in grave and decent attire, seated at the foot of an old tree. He arose at Goodman Brown's approach and walked onward side by side with him.

"You are late, Goodman Brown," said he. "The clock of the Old South was striking as I came through Boston, and that is full fifteen minutes agone."

"Faith kept me back a while," replied the young man, with a tremor in his voice, caused by the sudden appearance of his companion, though not wholly unexpected.

It was now deep dusk in the forest, and deepest in that part of it where these two were journeying. As nearly as could be discerned, the second traveler was about fifty years old, apparently in the same rank of life as Goodman Brown, and bearing a considerable resemblance to him, though perhaps more in expression than features. Still they might have been taken for father and son. And yet, though the elder person was as simply clad as the younger, and as simple in manner too, he had an indescribable air of one who knew the world, and who would not have felt abashed at the governor's dinner table or in King William's court, were it possible that his affairs should call him thither. But the only thing about him that could be fixed upon as remarkable was his staff, which bore the likeness of a great black snake, so curiously wrought that it might almost be seen to twist and wriggle itself like a living serpent. This, of course, must have been an ocular deception, assisted by the uncertain light.

"Come, Goodman Brown," cried his fellow-traveler, "this is a dull pace for the beginning of a journey. Take my staff, if you are so soon weary."

"Friend," said the other, exchanging his slow pace for a full stop, "having kept covenant by meeting thee here, it is my purpose now to return whence I came. I have scruples touching the matter thou wot'st of."

"Sayest thou so?" replied he of the serpent, smiling apart. "Let us walk on, nevertheless, reasoning as we go; and if I convince thee not thou shalt turn back. We are but a little way in the forest yet."

"Too far! too far!" exclaimed the goodman, unconsciously resuming his walk. "My father never went into the woods on such an errand, nor his father before him. We have been a race of honest men and good Christians since the days of the martyrs; and shall I be the first of the name of Brown that ever took this path and kept"—

"Such company, thou wouldst say," observed the elder person, interpreting his pause. "Well said, Goodman Brown! I have been as well acquainted with your family as with ever a one among the Puritans; and that's no trifle to say. I helped your grandfather, the constable, when he lashed the Quaker woman so smartly through the streets of Salem; and it was I that brought your father a pitch-pine knot, kindled at my own hearth, to set fire to an Indian village, in King Philip's war. They were my good friends, both; and many a pleasant walk have we had along this path, and returned merrily after midnight. I would fain be friends with you for their sake."

"If it be as thou sayest," replied Goodman Brown, "I marvel they never spoke of these matters; or, verily, I marvel not, seeing that the least rumor of the sort would have driven them from New England. We are a people of prayer, and good works to boot, and abide no such wickedness."

"Wickedness or not," said the traveler with the twisted staff, "I have a very general acquaintance here in New England. The deacons of many a church have drunk the communion wine with me; the selectmen of divers towns make me their chairman; and a majority of the Great and General Court are firm supporters of my interest. The governor and I, too—But these are state secrets."

"Can this be so?" cried Goodman Brown, with a stare of amazement at his undisturbed companion. "Howbeit, I have nothing to do with the governor and council; they have their own ways, and are no rule for a simple husbandman like me. But, were I to go on with thee, how should I meet the eye of that good old man, our minister, at Salem village? Oh, his voice would make me tremble both Sabbath day and lecture day."

Thus far the elder traveler had listened with due gravity; but now burst into a fit of irrepressible mirth, shaking himself so violently that his snake-like staff actually seemed to wriggle in sympathy.

"Ha! ha! ha!" shouted he again and again; then composing himself, "Well, go on, Goodman Brown, go on; but, prithee, don't kill me with laughing."

"Well, then, to end the matter at once," said Goodman Brown, considerably nettled, "there is my wife, Faith. It would break her dear little heart; and I'd rather break my own."

"Nay, if that be the case," answered the other, "e'en go thy ways, Goodman Brown. I would not for twenty old women like the one hobbling before us that Faith should come to any harm."

As he spoke he pointed his staff at a female figure on the path, in whom Goodman Brown recognized a very pious and exemplary dame, who had taught him his catechism in youth, and was still his moral and spiritual adviser, jointly with the minister and Deacon Gookin.

"A marvel, truly, that Goody Cloyse should be so far in the wilderness at nightfall," said he. "But with your leave, friend, I shall take a cut through the woods until we have left this Christian woman behind. Being a stranger to you, she might ask whom I was consorting with and whither I was going."

"Be it so," said his fellow-traveler. "Betake you to the woods, and let me keep the path."

Accordingly the young man turned aside, but took care to watch his companion, who advanced softly along the road until he had come within a staff's length of the old dame. She, meanwhile, was making the best of her way, with singular speed for so aged a woman, and mumbling some indistinct words—a prayer, doubtless— as she went. The traveler put forth his staff and touched her withered neck with what seemed the serpent's tail.

"The devil!" screamed the pious old lady.

"Then Goody Cloyse knows her old friend?" observed the traveler, confronting her and leaning on his writhing stick.

"Ah, forsooth, and is it your worship indeed?" cried the good dame. "Yea, truly is it, and in the very image of my old gossip, Goodman Brown, the grandfather of the silly fellow that now is. But—would your worship believe it?—my broomstick hath strangely disappeared, stolen, as I suspect, by that unhanged witch, Goody Cory, and that, too, when I was all anointed with the juice of smallage, and cinquefoil, and wolf's bane"—

"Mingled with fine wheat and the fat of a new-born babe," said the shape of old Goodman Brown.

"Ah, your worship knows the recipe," cried the old lady, cackling aloud. "So, as I was saying, being all ready for the meeting, and no horse to ride on, I made up my mind to foot it; for they tell me there is a nice young man to be taken into communion tonight. But now your good worship will lend me your arm, and we shall be there in a twinkling."

"That can hardly be," answered her friend. "I may not spare you my arm, Goody Cloyse; but here is my staff, if you will."

So saying, he threw it down at her feet, where, perhaps, it assumed life, being one of the rods which its owner had formerly lent to the Egyptian magi. Of this fact, however, Goodman Brown could not take cognizance. He had cast up his eyes in astonishment, and, looking down again, beheld neither Goody Cloyse nor the serpentine staff, but his fellow-traveler alone, who waited for him as calmly as if nothing had happened.

"That old woman taught me my catechism," said the young man; and there was a world of meaning in this simple comment.

They continued to walk onward, while the elder traveler exhorted his companion to make good speed and persevere in the path, discoursing so aptly that his arguments seemed rather to spring up in the bosom of his auditor than to be suggested by himself. As they went, he plucked a branch of maple to serve for a walking stick, and began to strip it of the twigs and little boughs, which were wet with evening dew. The moment his fingers touched them they became strangely withered and dried up as with a week's sunshine. Thus the pair proceeded, at a good free pace, until suddenly, in a gloomy hollow of the road, Goodman Brown sat himself down on the stump of a tree and refused to go any farther.

"Friend," said he, stubbornly, "my mind is made up. Not another step will I budge on this errand. What if a wretched old woman do choose to go to the devil when I thought she was going to heaven: is that any reason why I should quit my dear Faith and go after her?"

"You will think better of this by and by," said his acquaintance, composedly. "Sit here and rest yourself a while; and when you feel like moving again, there is my staff to help you along."

Without more words, he threw his companion the maple stick, and was as speedily out of sight as if he had vanished into the deepening gloom. The young man sat a few moments by the roadside, applauding himself greatly, and thinking with how clear a conscience he should meet the minister in his morning walk, nor shrink from the eye of good old Deacon Gookin. And what calm sleep would be his that very night, which was to have been spent so wickedly, but so purely and sweetly now, in the arms of Faith! Amidst these pleasant and praiseworthy meditations, Goodman Brown heard the tramp of horses along the road, and deemed it advisable to conceal himself within the verge of the forest, conscious of the guilty purpose that had brought him thither, though now so happily turned from it.

On came the hoof tramps and the voices of the riders, two grave old voices, conversing soberly as they drew near. These mingled sounds appeared to pass along the road, within a few yards of the young man's hiding-place; but, owing doubtless to the depth of the gloom at that particular spot, neither the travelers nor their steeds were visible. Though their figures brushed the small boughs by the wayside, it could not be seen that they intercepted, even for a moment, the faint gleam from the strip of bright sky athwart which they must have passed. Goodman Brown alternately crouched and stood on tiptoe, pulling aside the branches and thrusting forth his head as far as he durst without discerning so much as a shadow. It vexed him the more, because he could have sworn, were such a thing possible, that he recognized the voices of the minister and Deacon Gookin, jogging along quietly, as they were wont to do, when bound to some ordination or ecclesiastical council. While yet within hearing, one of the riders stopped to pluck a switch.

"Of the two, reverend sir," said the voice like the deacon's, "I had rather miss an ordination dinner than to-night's meeting. They tell me that some of our community are to be here from Falmouth and beyond, and others from Connecticut and Rhode Island, besides several of Indian powwows, who, after their fashion, know almost as much deviltry as the best of us. Moreover, there is a goodly young woman to be taken into communion."

"Mighty well, Deacon Gookin!" replied the solemn old tones of the minister. "Spur up, or we shall be late. Nothing can be done you know until I get on the ground."

The hoofs clattered again; and the voices, talking so strangely in the empty air, passed on through the forest, where no church had ever been gathered or solitary Christian prayed. Whither, then, could these holy men be journeying so deep into the heathen wilderness? Young Goodman Brown caught hold of a tree for support, being ready to sink down on the ground, faint and overburdened with the heavy sickness of his heart. He looked up to the sky, doubting whether there really was a heaven above him. Yet there was the blue arch, and the stars brightening in it.

"With heaven above and Faith below, I will yet stand firm against the devil!" cried Goodman Brown.

While he still gazed upward into the deep arch of the firmament and had lifted his hands to pray, a cloud, though no wind was stir-ring, hurried across the zenith and hid the brightening stars. The blue sky was still visible, except directly overhead, where this black mass of cloud was sweeping swiftly northward. Aloft in the air, as if from the depths of the cloud, came a confused and doubtful sound of voices. Once the listener fancied that he could distinguish the accents of towns-people of his own, men, and women, both pious and ungodly, many of whom he had met at the communion table, and had seen others rioting at the tavern. The next moment, so indistinct were the sounds, he doubted whether he had heard aught but the murmur of the old forest, whispering without a wind. Then came a stronger swell of those familiar tones, heard daily in the sunshine at Salem village, but never until now from a cloud of night. There was one voice of a young woman, uttering lamentations, yet with an uncertain sorrow, and entreating for some favor, which, perhaps, it would grieve her to obtain; and all the unseen multitude, both saints and sinners, seemed to encourage her onward.

"Faith!" shouted Goodman Brown, in a voice of agony and desperation; and the echoes of the forest mocked him, crying, "Faith! Faith!" as if bewildered wretches were seeking her all through the wilderness.

The cry of grief, rage, and terror was yet piercing the night, when the unhappy husband held his breath for a response. There was a scream, drowned immediately in a louder murmur of voices, fading into far-off laughter, as the dark cloud swept away, leaving the clear and silent sky above Goodman Brown. But something fluttered lightly down through the air and caught on the branch of a tree. The young man seized it, and beheld a pink ribbon.

"My Faith is gone!" cried he, after one stupefied moment. "There is no good on earth; and sin is but a name. Come, devil; for to thee is this world given."

And, maddened with despair, so that he laughed loud and long, did Goodman Brown grasp his staff and set forth again, at such a rate that he seemed to fly along the forest path rather than to walk or run. The road grew wilder and drearier and more faintly traced, and vanished at length, leaving him in the heart of the dark wilderness, still rushing onward with the instinct that guides mortal man to evil. The whole forest was peopled with frightful sounds—the creaking of the trees, the howling of wild beasts, and the yell of Indians; while sometimes the wind tolled like a distant church bell, and sometimes gave a broad roar around the traveler, as if all Nature were laughing him to scorn. But he was himself the chief horror of the scene, and shrank not from its other horrors.

"Ha! ha! ha!" roared Goodman Brown when the wind laughed at him. "Let us hear which will laugh loudest. Think not to frighten me with your deviltry. Come witch, come wizard, come Indian powwow, come devil himself, and here comes Goodman Brown. You may as well fear him as he fears you."

In truth, all through the haunted forest there could be nothing more frightful than the figure of Goodman Brown. On he flew among the black pines, brandishing his staff with frenzied gestures, now giving vent to an inspiration of horrid blasphemy, and now shouting forth such laughter as set all the echoes of the forest laughing like demons around him. The fiend in his own shape is less hideous than when he rages in the breast of man. Thus sped the demoniac on his course, until, quivering among the trees, he saw a red light before him, as when the felled trunks and branches of a clearing have been set on fire, and throw up their lurid blaze against the sky, at the hour of midnight. He paused, in a lull of the tempest that had driven him onward, and heard the swell of what seemed a hymn, rolling solemnly from a distance with the weight of many voices. He knew the tune; it was a familiar one in the choir of the village meeting-house. The verse died heavily away, and was lengthened by a chorus, not of human voices, but of all the sounds of the benighted wilderness pealing in awful harmony together. Goodman Brown cried out, and his cry was lost to his own ear by its unison with the cry of the desert.

In the interval of silence he stole forward until the light glared full upon his eyes. At one extremity of an open space, hemmed in by the dark wall of the forest, arose a rock, bearing some rude, natural resemblance either to an altar or a pulpit, and surrounded by four blazing pines, their tops aflame, their stems untouched, like candles at an evening meeting. The mass of foliage that had overgrown the summit of the rock was all on fire, blazing high into the night and fitfully illuminating the whole field. Each pendent twig and leafy festoon was in a blaze. As the red light arose and fell, a numerous congregation alternately shone forth, then disappeared in shadow, and again grew, as it were, out of the darkness, peopling the heart of the solitary woods at once.

"A grave and dark-clad company," quoth Goodman Brown.

In truth they were such. Among them, quivering to and fro between gloom and splendor, appeared faces that would be seen next day at the council board of the province, and others which, Sabbath after Sabbath, looked devoutly heavenward, and benignantly over the crowded pews, from the holiest pulpits in the land. Some affirm that the lady of the governor was there. At least there were high dames well known to her, and wives of honored husbands, and widows, a great multitude, and ancient maidens, all of excellent repute, and fair young girls, who trembled lest their mothers should espy them. Either the sudden gleams of light flashing over the obscure field bedazzled Goodman Brown, or he recognized a score of the church members of Salem village famous for their especial sanctity. Good old Deacon Gookin had arrived, and waited at the skirts of that venerable saint, his revered pastor. But, irreverently consorting with these grave, reputable, and pious people, these elders of the church, these chaste dames and dewy virgins, there were men of dissolute lives and women of spotted fame, wretches given over to all mean and filthy vice, and suspected even of horrid crimes. It was strange to see that the good shrank not from the wicked, nor were the sinners abashed by the saints. Scattered also among their pale-faced enemies were the Indian priests, or powwows, who had often scared their native forest with more hideous incantations than any known to English witchcraft.

"But where is Faith?" thought Goodman Brown; and, as hope came into his heart, he trembled.

Another verse of the hymn arose, a slow and mournful strain, such as the pious love, but joined to words which expressed all that our nature can conceive of sin, and darkly hinted at far more. Unfathomable to mere mortals is the lore of fiends. Verse after verse was sung; and still the chorus of the desert swelled between like the deepest tone of a mighty organ; and with the final peal of that dreadful anthem there came a sound, as if the roaring wind, the rushing streams, the howling beasts, and every other voice of the unconcerted wilderness were mingling and according with the voice of guilty man in homage to the prince of all. The four blazing pines threw up a loftier flame, and obscurely discovered shapes and visages of horror on the smoke wreaths above the impious assembly. At the same moment the fire on the rock shot redly forth and formed a glowing arch above its base, where now appeared a figure. With reverence be it spoken, the figure bore no slight similitude, both in garb and manner, to some grave divine of the New England churches.

"Bring forth the converts!" cried a voice that echoed through the field and rolled into the forest.

At the word, Goodman Brown stepped forth from the shadow of the trees and approached the congregation, with whom he felt a loathful brotherhood by the sympathy of all that was wicked in his heart. He could have well-nigh sworn that the shape of his own dead father beckoned him to advance, looking downward from a smoke wreath, while a woman, with dim features of despair, threw out her hand to warn him back. Was it his mother? But he had no power to retreat one step, nor to resist, even in thought, when the minister and good old Deacon Gookin seized his arms and led him to the blazing rock. Thither came also the slender form of a veiled female, led between Goody Cloyse, that pious teacher of the catechism, and Martha Carrier, who had received the devil's promise to be queen of hell. A rampant hag was she. And there stood the proselytes beneath the canopy of fire.

"Welcome, my children," said the dark figure, "to the communion of your race. Ye have found thus young your nature and your destiny. My children, look behind you!"

They turned; and flashing forth, as it were, in a sheet of flame, the fiend worshipers were seen; the smile of welcome gleamed darkly on every visage.

"There," resumed the sable form, "are all whom ye have reverenced from youth. Ye deemed them holier than yourselves, and shrank from your own sin, contrasting it with their lives of righteousness and prayerful aspirations heavenward. Yet here are they all in my worshiping assembly. This night it shall be granted you to know their secret deeds: how hoary-bearded elders of the church have whispered wanton words to the young maids of their households; how many a woman, eager for widows' weeds, has given her husband a drink at bedtime and let him sleep his last sleep in her bosom; how beardless youths have made haste to inherit their fathers' wealth; and how fair damsels—blush not, sweet ones—have dug little graves in the garden, and bidden me, the sole guest to an infant's funeral. By the sympathy of your human hearts for sin ye shall scent out all the places—whether in church, bedchamber, street, field, or forest—where crime has been committed, and shall exult to behold the whole earth one stain of guilt, one mighty blood spot. Far more than this. It shall be yours to penetrate, in every bosom, the deep mystery of sin, the fountain of all wicked arts, and which inexhaustibly supplies more evil impulses than human power—than my power at its utmost—can make manifest in deeds. And now, my children, look upon each other."

They did so; and, by the blaze of the hell-kindled torches, the wretched man beheld his Faith, and the wife her husband, trembling before that unhallowed altar.

"Lo, there ye stand, my children," said the figure, in a deep and solemn tone, almost sad with its despairing awfulness, as if his once angelic nature could yet mourn for our miserable race. "Depending upon one another's hearts, ye had still hoped that virtue were not all a dream. Now are ye undeceived. Evil is the nature of mankind. Evil must be your only happiness. Welcome again, my children, to the communion of your race."

"Welcome," repeated the fiend worshipers, in one cry of despair and triumph.

And there they stood, the only pair, as it seemed, who were yet hesitating on the verge of wickedness in this dark world. A basin was hollowed, naturally, in the rock. Did it contain water, reddened by the lurid light? or was it blood? or, perchance, a liquid flame?

Herein did the shape of evil dip his hand and prepare to lay the mark of baptism upon their foreheads, that they might be partakers of the mystery of sin, more conscious of the secret guilt of others, both in deed and thought, than they could now be of their own. The husband cast one look at his pale wife, and Faith at him. What polluted wretches would the next glance show them to each other, shuddering alike at what they disclosed and what they saw!

"Faith! Faith!" cried the husband, "look up to heaven, and resist the wicked one."

Whether Faith obeyed he knew not. Hardly had he spoken when he found himself amid calm night and solitude, listening to a roar of the wind which died heavily away through the forest. He staggered against the rock, and felt it chill and damp; while a hanging twig, that had been all on fire, besprinkled his cheek with the coldest dew.

The next morning young Goodman Brown came slowly into the street of Salem village, staring around him like a bewildered man. The good old minister was taking a walk along the graveyard to get an appetite for breakfast and meditate his sermon, and bestowed a blessing, as he passed, on Goodman Brown. He shrank from the venerable saint as if to avoid an anathema. Old Deacon Gookin was at domestic worship, and the holy words of his prayer were heard through the open window. "What God doth the wizard pray to?" quoth Goodman Brown. Goody Cloyse, that excellent old Christian, stood in the early sunshine at her own lattice, catechizing a little girl who had brought her a pint of morning's milk. Goodman Brown snatched away the child as from the grasp of the fiend himself. Turning the corner by the meeting-house, he spied the head of Faith, with the pink ribbons, gazing anxiously forth, and bursting into such joy at sight of him that she skipped along the street and almost kissed her husband before the whole village. But Goodman Brown looked sternly and sadly into her face, and passed on without a greeting.

Had Goodman Brown fallen asleep in the forest and only dreamed a wild dream of a witch-meeting?

Be it so if you will; but, alas! it was a dream of evil omen for young Goodman Brown. A stern, a sad, a darkly meditative, a distrustful, if not a desperate man did he become from the night of that fearful dream. On the Sabbath day, when the congregation were singing a holy psalm, he could not listen because an anthem of sin rushed loudly upon his ear and drowned all the blessed strain. When the minister spoke from the pulpit with power and fervid eloquence, and, with his hand on the open Bible, of the sacred truths of our religion, and of saint-like lives and triumphant deaths, and of future bliss or misery unutterable, then did Goodman Brown turn pale, dreading lest the roof should thunder down upon the gray blasphemer and his hearers. Often, waking suddenly at midnight, he shrank from the bosom of Faith; and at morning or eventide, when the family knelt down at prayer, he scowled and muttered to himself, and gazed sternly at his wife, and turned away. And when he had lived long, and was borne to his grave a hoary corpse, followed by Faith, an aged woman, and children and grandchildren, a goodly procession, besides neighbors not a few, they carved no hopeful verse upon his tombstone, for his dying hour was gloom.

QUESTIONS FOR DISCUSSION

1. Many of the ingredients for analysis of plot, character, and setting in "Young Goodman Brown" may be found in the first three paragraphs of the story. Reread this passage and be prepared to recount the information that relates to plot, character, and setting.
2. At what point in the story does the reader know that Brown's journey is for no good purpose? From whom does this information come—from Brown himself, from Faith, or from the narrator? Why is it important to the complexity of the story that the reader should be informed as he is?
3. Who is the fellow-traveler met by Brown in the forest? What marks of identity corroborate your recognition of him? Why is it significant that the two travelers "might have been taken for father and son"?
4. This story is full of ironic statements, whose multiple meanings are made clearer upon a second reading. What, for instance, may be the double meanings of Brown's remark to the Devil, "Faith kept me back a while"? What other similarly ironic statements can you identify?
5. Knowing what you do about Hawthorne's own ancestry in Salem, do you see any relationship between Hawthorne's family history and the accusations of the Devil regarding Brown's family?
6. As the story progresses, one becomes aware of Brown's naiveté and the shocking nature of the revelations he is receiving. To what extent is such a theme prevalent in literature? What other works develop a similar theme?
7. Young Goodman Brown's surrender to the Devil is proclaimed in the words, "My Faith is gone! There is no good on earth; and sin is but a name. Come, devil; for to thee is this world given." What leads him to this conclusion? What are the immediate and long-range results of this declaration?
8. How do you answer Hawthorne's question, "Had Goodman Brown fallen asleep in the forest and only dreamed a wild dream of a witch-meeting?"

9. The final paragraph describes the unhappiness of Brown's life from that time on. Compare this description with the Devil's explanation of the false sense of righteousness with which some saintly persons are revered. What is your understanding of the reason for Brown's gloom?
10. Cynicism may be understood as the assumption that everyone else is as guilty as oneself, regardless of appearances. In *The Scarlet Letter*, Hawthorne comments on cynicism: "Such loss of faith is ever one of the saddest results of sin." In "Young Goodman Brown" there are expressions of cynicism regarding religious profession. What are these expressions? By whom are they made? Who are the subjects of the cynicism? How are these incidents related as "results of sin"?

ASSIGNMENTS FOR WRITING

1. The figure of the Devil in literature frequently appears with identifiable clues to the reader. From your own reading, write a comparison of Hawthorne's devil with any other from literature.
2. "Young Goodman Brown" describes the disillusionment of Brown with his neighbors in Salem. Write a brief narrative in which you discuss a process of disillusionment through which one may come to disbelieve in the merits of an admired person or organization. Be cautious about making sweeping charges and mass accusations, but show the development of skepticism in detail.

The Birthmark

In the latter part of the last century there lived a man of science, an eminent proficient in every branch of natural philosophy, who not long before our story opens had made experience of a spiritual affinity more attractive than any chemical one. He had left his laboratory to the care of an assistant, cleared his fine countenance from the furnace smoke, washed the stain of acids from his fingers, and persuaded a beautiful woman to become his wife. In those days when the comparatively recent discovery of electricity and other kindred mysteries of Nature seemed to open paths into the region of miracle, it was not unusual for the love of science to rival the love of woman in its depth and absorbing energy. The higher intellect, the imagination, the spirit, and even the heart might all find their congenial aliment in pursuits which, as some of their ardent votaries believed, would ascend from one step of powerful intelligence to another, until the philosopher should lay his hand on the secret of creative force and perhaps make new worlds for himself. We know not whether Aylmer possessed this degree of faith in man's ultimate control over Nature. He had devoted himself, however, too unreservedly to scientific studies ever to be weaned from them by any second passion. His love for his young wife might prove the stronger of the two; but it could only be by intertwining itself with his love of science, and uniting the strength of the latter to his own.

Such a union accordingly took place, and was attended with truly remarkable consequences and a deeply impressive moral. One day, very soon after their marriage, Aylmer sat gazing at his wife with a trouble in his countenance that grew stronger until he spoke.

"Georgiana," said he, "has it never occurred to you that the mark upon your cheek might be removed?"

"No, indeed," said she, smiling; but perceiving the seriousness of his manner, she blushed deeply. "To tell you the truth it has been so often called a charm that I was simple enough to imagine it might be so."

"Ah, upon another face perhaps it might," replied her husband; "but never on yours. No, dearest Georgiana, you came so nearly perfect from the hand of Nature that this slightest possible defect, which we hesitate whether to term a defect or a beauty, shocks me, as being the visible mark of earthly imperfection."

"Shocks you, my husband!" cried Georgiana, deeply hurt; at first reddening with momentary anger, but then bursting into tears. "Then why did you take me from my mother's side? You cannot love what shocks you!"

To explain this conversation it must be mentioned that in the center of Georgiana's left cheek there was a singular mark, deeply interwoven, as it were, with the texture and substance of her face. In the usual state of her complexion—a healthy though delicate bloom—the mark wore a tint of deeper crimson, which imperfectly defined its shape amid the surrounding rosiness. When she blushed it gradually became more indistinct, and finally vanished amid the triumphant rush of blood that bathed the whole cheek with its brilliant glow. But if any shifting motion caused her to turn pale there was the mark again, a crimson stain upon the snow, in what Aylmer sometimes deemed an almost fearful distinctness. Its shape bore not a little similarity to the human hand, though of the smallest pygmy size. Georgiana's lovers were wont to say that some fairy at her birth hour had laid her tiny hand upon the infant's cheek, and left this impress there in token of the magic endowments that were to give her such sway over all hearts. Many a desperate swain would have risked life for the privilege of pressing his lips to the mysterious hand. It must not be concealed, however, that the impression wrought by this fairy sign manual varied exceedingly, according to the difference of temperament in the beholders. Some fastidious persons—but they were exclusively of her own sex—affirmed that the bloody hand, as they chose to call it, quite destroyed the effect of Georgiana's beauty, and rendered her countenance even hideous. But it would be as reasonable to say that one of those small blue stains which sometimes occur in the purest statuary marble would convert the Eve of Powers to a monster. Masculine observers, if the birthmark did not heighten their admiration, contented themselves with wishing it away, that the world might possess one living specimen of ideal loveliness without the semblance of a flaw. After his marriage,—for he thought little or nothing of the matter before,—Aylmer discovered that this was the case with himself.

Had she been less beautiful,—if Envy's self could have found aught else to sneer at,—he might have felt his affection heightened by the prettiness of this mimic hand, now vaguely portrayed, now lost, now stealing forth again and glimmering to and fro with every pulse of emotion that throbbed within her heart; but seeing her otherwise so perfect, he found this one defect grow more and more intolerable with every moment of their united lives. It was the fatal flaw of humanity which Nature, in one shape or another, stamps ineffaceably on all her productions, either to imply that they are temporary and finite, or that their perfection must be wrought by toil and pain. The crimson hand expressed the ineludible gripe in which mortality clutches the highest and purest of earthly mold, degrading them into kindred with the lowest, and even with the very brutes, like whom their visible frames return to dust. In this manner, selecting it as the symbol of his wife's liability to sin, sorrow, decay, and death, Aylmer's somber imagination was not long in rendering the birthmark a frightful object, causing him more trouble and horror than ever Georgiana's beauty, whether of soul or sense, had given him delight.

At all the seasons which should have been their happiest, he invariably and without intending it, nay, in spite of a purpose to the contrary, reverted to this one disastrous topic. Trifling as it at first appeared, it so connected itself with innumerable trains of thought and modes of feeling that it became the central point of all. With the morning twilight Aylmer opened his eyes upon his wife's face and recognized the symbol of imperfection; and when they sat together at the evening hearth his eyes wandered stealthily to her cheek, and beheld, flickering with the blaze of the wood fire, the spectral hand that wrote mortality where he would fain have worshiped. Georgiana soon learned to shudder at his gaze. It needed but a glance with the peculiar expression that his face often wore to change the roses of her cheek into a deathlike paleness, amid which the crimson hand was brought strongly out, like a bas-relief of ruby on the whitest marble.

Late one night when the lights were growing dim, so as hardly to betray the stain on the poor wife's cheek, she herself, for the first time, voluntarily took up the subject.

"Do you remember, my dear Aylmer," said she, with a feeble attempt at a smile, "have you any recollection of a dream last night about this odious hand?"

"None! none whatever!" replied Aylmer, starting; but then he added, in a dry, cold tone, affected for the sake of concealing the real depth of his emotion, "I might well dream of it; for before I fell asleep it had taken a pretty firm hold of my fancy."

"And you did dream of it?" continued Georgiana, hastily; for she dreaded lest a gush of tears should interrupt what she had to say. "A terrible dream! I wonder that you can forget it. Is it possible to forget this one expression?—'It is in her heart now; we must have it out!' Reflect, my husband; for by all means I would have you recall that dream."

The mind is in a sad state when Sleep, the all-involving, cannot confine her specters within the dim region of her sway, but suffers them to break forth, affrighting this actual life with secrets that perchance belong to a deeper one. Aylmer now remembered his dream. He had fancied himself with his servant Aminadab, attempting an operation for the removal of the birthmark; but the deeper went the knife, the deeper sank the hand, until at length its tiny grasp appeared to have caught hold of Georgiana's heart; whence, however, her husband was inexorably resolved to cut or wrench it away.

When the dream had shaped itself perfectly in his memory, Aylmer sat in his wife's presence with a guilty feeling. Truth often finds its way to the mind close muffled in robes of sleep, and then speaks with uncompromising directness of matters in regard to which we practice an unconscious self-deception during our waking moments. Until now he had not been aware of the tyrannizing influence acquired by one idea over his mind, and of the lengths which he might find in his heart to go for the sake of giving himself peace.

"Aylmer," resumed Georgiana, solemnly, "I know not what may be the cost to both of us to rid me of this fatal birthmark. Perhaps its removal may cause cureless deformity; or it may be the stain goes as deep as life itself. Again: do we know that there is a possibility, on any terms, of unclasping the firm gripe of this little hand which was laid upon me before I came into the world?"

"Dearest Georgiana, I have spent much thought upon the subject," hastily interrupted Aylmer. "I am convinced of the perfect practicability of its removal."

"If there be the remotest possibility of it," continued Georgiana, "let the attempt be made at whatever risk. Danger is nothing to me; for life, while this hateful mark makes me the object of your horror and disgust,—life is a burden which I would fling down with joy. Either remove this dreadful hand, or take my wretched life! You have deep science. All the world bears witness of it. You have achieved great wonders. Cannot you remove this little, little mark, which I cover with the tips of two small fingers? Is this beyond your power, for the sake of your own peace, and to save your poor wife from madness?"

"Noblest, dearest, tenderest wife," cried Aylmer, rapturously, "doubt not my power. I have already given this matter the deepest thought—thought which might almost have enlightened me to create a being less perfect than yourself. Georgiana, you have led deeper than ever into the heart of science. I feel myself fully competent to render this dear cheek as faultless as its fellow; and then, most beloved, what will be my triumph when I shall have corrected what

Nature left imperfect in her fairest work! Even Pygmalion, when his sculptured woman assumed life, felt not greater ecstasy than mine will be."

"It is resolved, then," said Georgiana, faintly smiling. "And, Aylmer, spare me not, though you should find the birthmark take refuge in my heart at last."

Her husband tenderly kissed her cheek—her right cheek—not that which bore the impress of the crimson hand.

The next day Aylmer apprised his wife of a plan that he had formed whereby he might have opportunity for the intense thought and constant watchfulness which the proposed operation would require; while Georgiana, likewise, would enjoy the perfect repose essential to its success. They were to seclude themselves in the extensive apartments occupied by Aylmer as a laboratory, and where, during his toilsome youth, he had made discoveries in the elemental powers of Nature that had roused the admiration of all the learned societies in Europe. Seated calmly in this laboratory, the pale philosopher had investigated the secrets of the highest cloud region and of the profoundest mines; he had satisfied himself of the causes that kindled and kept alive the fires of the volcano; and had explained the mystery of the fountains, and how it is that they gush forth, some so bright and pure, and others with such rich medicinal virtues, from the dark bosom of the earth. Here, too, at an earlier period, he had studied the wonders of the human frame, and attempted to fathom the very process by which Nature assimilates all her precious influences from earth and air, and from the spiritual world, to create and foster man, her masterpiece. The latter pursuit, however, Aylmer had long laid aside in unwilling recognition of the truth—against which all seekers sooner or later stumble—that our great creative Mother, while she amuses us with apparently working in the broadest sunshine, is yet severely careful to keep her own secrets, and, in spite of her pretended openness, shows us nothing but results. She permits us, indeed, to mar, but seldom to mend, and, like a jealous patentee, on no account to make. Now, however, Aylmer resumed these half-forgotten investigations; not, of course, with such hopes or wishes as first suggested them; but because they involved much physiological truth and lay in the path of his proposed scheme for the treatment of Georgiana.

As he led her over the threshold of the laboratory, Georgiana was cold and tremulous. Aylmer looked cheerfully into her face, with intent to reassure her, but was so startled with the intense glow of the birthmark upon the whiteness of her cheek that he could not restrain a strong convulsive shudder. His wife fainted.

"Aminadab! Aminadab!" shouted Aylmer, stamping violently on the floor.

Forthwith there issued from an inner apartment a man of low stature, but bulky frame, with shaggy hair hanging about his visage, which was grimed with the vapors of the furnace. This personage had been Aylmer's underworker during his whole scientific career, and was admirably fitted for that office by his great mechanical readiness, and the skill with which, while incapable of comprehending a single principle, he executed all the details of his master's experiments. With his vast strength, his shaggy hair, his smoky aspect, and the indescribable earthiness that incrusted him, he seemed to represent man's physical nature; while Aylmer's slender figure, and pale, intellectual face, were no less apt a type of the spiritual element.

"Throw open the door of the boudoir, Aminadab," said Aylmer, "and burn a pastil."

"Yes, master," answered Aminadab, looking intently at the lifeless form of Georgiana; and then he muttered to himself, "If she were my wife, I'd never part with that birthmark."

When Georgiana recovered consciousness she found herself breathing an atmosphere of penetrating fragrance, the gentle potency of which had recalled her from her deathlike faintness. The scene around her looked like enchantment. Aylmer had converted those smoky, dingy, somber rooms, where he had spent his brightest years in recondite pursuits, into a series of beautiful apartments not unfit to be the secluded abode of a lovely woman. The walls were hung with gorgeous curtains, which imparted the combination of grandeur and grace that no other species of adornment can achieve; and as they fell from the ceiling to the floor, their rich and ponderous folds, concealing all angles and straight lines, appeared to shut in the scene from infinite space. For aught Georgiana knew, it might be a pavilion among the clouds. And Aylmer, excluding the sunshine, which would have interfered with his chemical processes, had supplied its place with perfumed lamps, emitting flames of various hue, but all uniting in a soft, impurpled radiance. He now knelt by his wife's side, watching her earnestly, but without alarm; for he was confident in his science, and felt that he could draw a magic circle round her within which no evil might intrude.

"Where am I? Ah, I remember," said Georgiana, faintly; and she placed her hand over her cheek to hide the terrible mark from her husband's eyes.

"Fear not, dearest!" exclaimed he. "Do not shrink from me!

Believe me, Georgiana, I even rejoice in this single imperfection, since it will be such a rapture to remove it."

"Oh, spare me!" sadly replied his wife. "Pray do not look at it again. I never can forget that convulsive shudder."

In order to soothe Georgiana, and, as it were, to release her mind from the burden of actual things, Aylmer now put in practice some of the light and playful secrets which science had taught him among its profounder lore. Airy figures, absolutely bodiless ideas, and forms of unsubstantial beauty came and danced before her, imprinting their momentary footsteps on beams of light. Though she had some indistinct idea of the method of these optical phenomena, still the illusion was almost perfect enough to warrant the belief that her husband possessed sway over the spiritual world. Then again, when she felt a wish to look forth from her seclusion, immediately, as if her thoughts were answered, the procession of external existence flitted across a screen. The scenery and the figures of actual life were perfectly represented, but with that bewitching, yet indescribable difference which always makes a picture, an image, or a shadow so much more attractive than the original. When wearied of this Aylmer bade her cast her eyes upon a vessel containing a quantity of earth. She did so, with little interest at first; but was soon startled to perceive the germ of a plant shooting upward from the soil. Then came the slender stalk; the leaves gradually unfolded themselves; and amid them was a perfect and lovely flower.

"It is magical!" cried Georgiana. "I dare not touch it."

"Nay, pluck it," answered Aylmer,—"pluck it, and inhale its brief perfume while you may. The flower will wither in a few moments and leave nothing save its brown seed vessels; but thence may be perpetuated a race as ephemeral as itself."

But Georgiana had no sooner touched the flower than the whole plant suffered a blight, its leaves turning coal-black as if by the agency of fire.

"There was too powerful a stimulus," said Aylmer, thoughtfully.

To make up for this abortive experiment, he proposed to take her portrait by a scientific process of his own invention. It was to be effected by rays of light striking upon a polished plate of metal. Georgiana assented; but, on looking at the result, was affrighted to find the features of the portrait blurred and indefinable; while the minute figure of a hand appeared where the cheek should have been. Aylmer snatched the metallic plate and threw it into a jar of corrosive acid.

Soon, however, he forgot these mortifying failures. In the intervals of study and chemical experiment he came to her flushed and exhausted, but seemed invigorated by her presence, and spoke in glowing language of the resources of his art. He gave a history of the long dynasty of the alchemists, who spent so many ages in quest of the universal solvent by which the golden principle might be elicited from all things vile and base. Aylmer appeared to believe that, by the plainest scientific logic, it was altogether within the limits of possibility to discover this long-sought medium; "but," he added, "a philosopher who should go deep enough to acquire the power would attain too lofty a wisdom to stoop to the exercise of it." Not less singular were his opinions in regard to the elixir vitae. He more than intimated that it was at his option to concoct a liquid that should prolong life for years, perhaps interminably; but that it would produce a discord in Nature which all the world, and chiefly the quaffer of the immortal nostrum, would find cause to curse.

"Aylmer, are you in earnest?" asked Georgiana, looking at him with amazement and fear. "It is terrible to possess such power, or even to dream of possessing it."

"Oh, do not tremble, my love," said her husband. "I would not wrong either you or myself by working such inharmonious effects upon our lives; but I would have you consider how trifling, in comparison, is the skill requisite to remove this little hand."

At the mention of the birthmark, Georgiana, as usual, shrank as if a redhot iron had touched her cheek.

Again Aylmer applied himself to his labors. She could hear his voice in the distant furnace room giving directions to Aminadab, whose harsh, uncouth, misshapen tones were audible in response, more like the grunt or growl of a brute than human speech. After hours of absence, Aylmer reappeared and proposed that she should now examine his cabinet of chemical products and natural treasures of the earth. Among the former he showed her a small vial, in which, he remarked, was contained a gentle yet most powerful fragrance, capable of impregnating all the breezes that blow across a kingdom. They were of inestimable value, the contents of that little vial; and, as he said so, he threw some of the perfume into the air and filled the room with piercing and invigorating delight.

"And what is this?" asked Georgiana, pointing to a small crystal globe containing a gold-colored liquid. "It is so beautiful to the eye that I could imagine it the elixir of life."

"In one sense it is," replied Aylmer; "or, rather, the elixir of immortality. It is the most precious poison that ever was concocted in this world. By its aid I could apportion the lifetime of any mortal at whom you might point your finger. The strength of the dose would determine whether he were to linger out years, or drop dead in the midst of a breath. No king on his guarded throne could keep his life if I, in my private station, should deem that the welfare of millions justified me in depriving him of it."

"Why do you keep such a terrific drug?" inquired Georgiana in horror.

"Do not mistrust me, dearest," said her husband, smiling; "its virtuous potency is yet greater than its harmful one. But see! here is a powerful cosmetic. With a few drops of this in a vase of water, freckles may be washed away as easily as the hands are cleansed. A stronger infusion would take the blood out of the cheek, and leave the rosiest beauty a pale ghost."

"Is it with this lotion that you intend to bathe my cheek?" asked Georgiana, anxiously.

"Oh, no," hastily replied her husband; "this is merely superficial. Your case demands a remedy that shall go deeper."

In his interviews with Georgiana, Aylmer generally made minute inquiries as to her sensations and whether the confinement of the rooms and the temperature of the atmosphere agreed with her. These questions had such a particular drift that Georgiana began to conjecture that she was already subjected to certain physical influences, either breathed in with the fragrant air or taken with her food. She fancied likewise, but it might be altogether fancy, that there was a stirring up of her system—a strange, indefinite sensation creeping through her veins, and tingling, half painfully, half pleasurably, at her heart. Still, whenever she dared to look into the mirror, there she beheld herself pale as a white rose and with the crimson birthmark stamped upon her cheek. Not even Aylmer now hated it so much as she.

To dispel the tedium of the hours which her husband found it necessary to devote to the processes of combination and analysis, Georgiana turned over the volumes of his scientific library. In many dark old tomes she met with chapters full of romance and poetry. They were the works of philosophers of the middle ages, such as Albertus Magnus, Cornelius Agrippa, Paracelsus, and the famous friar who created the prophetic Brazen Head. All these antique naturalists stood in advance of their centuries, yet were imbued with some of their credulity, and therefore were believed, and perhaps imagined themselves to have acquired from the investigation of Nature a power above Nature, and from physics a sway over the spiritual world. Hardly less curious and imaginative were the early volumes of the Transactions of the Royal Society, in which the members, knowing little of the limits of natural possibility, were continually recording wonders or proposing methods whereby wonders might be wrought.

But to Georgiana the most engrossing volume was a large folio from her husband's own hand, in which he had recorded every experiment of his scientific career, its original aim, the methods adopted for its development, and its final success or failure, with the circumstances to which either event was attributable. The book, in truth, was both the history and emblem of his ardent, ambitious, imaginative, yet practical and laborious life. He handled physical details as if there were nothing beyond them; yet spiritualized them all, and redeemed himself from materialism by his strong and eager aspiration towards the infinite. In his grasp the veriest clod of earth assumed a soul. Georgiana, as she read, reverenced Aylmer and loved him more profoundly than ever, but with a less entire dependence on his judgment than heretofore. Much as he had accomplished, she could not but observe that his most splendid successes were almost invariably failures, if compared with the ideal at which he aimed. His brightest diamonds were the merest pebbles, and felt to be so by himself, in comparison with the inestimable gems which lay hidden beyond his reach. The volume, rich with achievements that had won renown for its author, was yet as melancholy a record as ever mortal hand had penned. It was the sad confession and continual exemplification of the shortcomings of the composite man, the spirit burdened with clay and working in matter, and of the despair that assails the higher nature at finding itself so miserably thwarted by the earthly part. Perhaps every man of genius in whatever sphere might recognize the image of his own experience in Aylmer's journal.

So deeply did these reflections affect Georgiana that she laid her face upon the open volume and burst into tears. In this situation she was found by her husband.

"It is dangerous to read in a sorcerer's books," said he with a smile, though his countenance was uneasy and displeased. "Georgiana, there are pages in that volume which I can scarcely glance over and keep my senses. Take heed lest it prove as detrimental to you."

"It has made me worship you more than ever," said she.

"Ah, wait for this one success," rejoined he, "then worship me if you will. I shall deem myself hardly unworthy of it. But come, I have sought you for the luxury of your voice. Sing to me, dearest."

So she poured out the liquid music of her voice to quench the thirst of his spirit. He then took his leave with a boyish exuberance of gaiety, assuring her that her seclusion would endure but a little longer, and that the result was already certain. Scarcely had he departed when Georgiana felt irresistibly impelled to follow him. She had forgotten to inform Aylmer of a symptom which for two or three hours past had begun to excite her attention. It was a sensation in the fatal birthmark, not painful, but which induced a restlessness throughout her system. Hastening after her husband, she intruded for the first time into the laboratory.

The first thing that struck her eye was the furnace, that hot and feverish worker, with the intense glow of its fire, which by the quantities of soot clustered above it seemed to have been burning for ages. There was a distilling apparatus in full operation. Around the room were retorts, tubes, cylinders, crucibles, and other apparatus of chemical research. An electrical machine stood ready for immediate use. The atmosphere felt oppressively close, and was tainted with gaseous odors which had been tormented forth by the processes of science. The severe and homely simplicity of the apartment, with its naked walls and brick pavement, looked strange, accustomed as Georgiana had become to the fantastic elegance of her boudoir. But what chiefly, indeed almost solely, drew her attention, was the aspect of Aylmer himself.

He was pale as death, anxious and absorbed, and hung over the furnace as if it depended upon his utmost watchfulness whether the liquid which it was distilling should be the draught of immortal happiness or misery. How different from the sanguine and joyous mien that he had assumed for Georgiana's encouragement!

"Carefully now, Aminadab; carefully, thou human machine; carefully, thou man of clay!" muttered Aylmer, more to himself than his assistant. "Now if there be a thought too much or too little, it is all over."

"Ho! ho!" mumbled Aminadab. "Look, master! look!"

Aylmer raised his eyes hastily, and at first reddened, then grew paler than ever, on beholding Georgiana. He rushed towards her and seized her arm with a gripe that left the print of his fingers upon it.

"Why do you come hither? Have you no trust in your husband?" cried he, impetuously. "Would you throw the blight of that fatal birthmark over my labors? It is not well done. Go, prying woman, go!"

"Nay, Aylmer," said Georgiana with the firmness of which she possessed no stinted endowment, "it is not you that have a right to complain. You mistrust your wife; you have concealed the anxiety with which you watch the development of this experiment. Think not so unworthily of me, my husband. Tell me all the risk we run, and fear not that I shall shrink; for my share in it is far less than your own."

"No, no, Georgiana!" said Aylmer, impatiently; "it must not be."

"I submit," replied she calmly. "And, Aylmer, I shall quaff whatever draught you bring me; but it will be on the same principle that would induce me to take a dose of poison if offered by your hand."

"My noble wife," said Aylmer, deeply moved, "I knew not the height and depth of your nature until now. Nothing shall be concealed. Know, then, that this crimson hand, superficial as it seems, has clutched its grasp into your being with a strength of which I had no previous conception. I have already administered agents powerful enough to do aught except to change your entire physical system. Only one thing remains to be tried. If that fail us we are ruined."

"Why did you hesitate to tell me this?" asked she.

"Because, Georgiana," said Aylmer, in a low voice, "there is danger."

"Danger? There is but one danger—that this horrible stigma shall be left upon my cheek!" cried Georgiana. "Remove it, remove it, whatever be the cost, or we shall both go mad!"

"Heaven knows your words are too true," said Aylmer, sadly. "And now, dearest, return to your boudoir. In a little while all will be tested."

He conducted her back and took leave of her with a solemn tenderness which spoke far more than his words how much was now at stake. After his departure, Georgiana became rapt in musings. She considered the character of Aylmer, and did it completer justice than at any previous moment. Her heart exulted, while it trembled, at his honorable love—so pure and lofty that it would accept nothing less than perfection nor miserably make itself contented with an earthlier nature than he had dreamed of. She felt how much more precious was such a sentiment than that meaner kind which would have borne with the imperfection for her sake, and have been guilty of treason to holy love by degrading its perfect idea to the level of the actual; and with her whole spirit she prayed that, for a single moment, she might satisfy his highest and deepest conception. Longer than one moment she well knew it could not be; for his spirit was ever on the march, ever ascending, and each instant required something that was beyond the scope of the instant before.

The sound of her husband's footsteps aroused her. He bore a

crystal goblet containing a liquor colorless as water, but bright enough to be the draught of immortality. Aylmer was pale; but it seemed rather the consequence of a highly-wrought state of mind and tension of spirit than of fear or doubt.

"The concoction of the draught has been perfect," said he, in answer to Georgiana's look. "Unless all my science have deceived me, it cannot fail."

"Save on your account, my dearest Aylmer," observed his wife, "I might wish to put off this birthmark of mortality by relinquishing mortality itself in preference to any other mode. Life is but a sad possession to those who have attained precisely the degree of moral advancement at which I stand. Were I weaker and blinder it might be happiness. Were I stronger, it might be endured hopefully. But being what I find myself, methinks I am of all mortals the most fit to die."

"You are fit for heaven without tasting death!" replied her husband. "But why do we speak of dying? The draught cannot fail. Behold its effect upon this plant."

On the window seat there stood a geranium diseased with yellow blotches, which had overspread all its leaves. Aylmer poured a small quantity of the liquid upon the soil in which it grew. In a little time, when the roots of the plant had taken up the moisture, the unsightly blotches began to be extinguished in a living verdure.

"There needed no proof," said Georgiana, quietly. "Give me the goblet. I joyfully stake all upon your word."

"Drink, then, thou lofty creature!" exclaimed Aylmer, with fervid admiration. "There is no taint of imperfection on thy spirit. Thy sensible frame, too, shall soon be all perfect."

She quaffed the liquid and returned the goblet to his hand.

"It is grateful," said she with a placid smile. "Methinks it is like water from a heavenly fountain; for it contains I know not what of unobtrusive fragrance and deliciousness. It allays a feverish thirst that had parched me for many days. Now, dearest, let me sleep. My earthly senses are closing over my spirit like the leaves around the heart of a rose at sunset."

She spoke the last words with a gentle reluctance, as if it required almost more energy than she could command to pronounce the faint and lingering syllables. Scarcely had they loitered through her lips ere she was lost in slumber. Aylmer sat by her side, watching her aspect with the emotions proper to a man the whole value of whose existence was involved in the process now to be tested. Mingled with this mood, however, was the philosophic investigation characteristic of the man of science. Not the minutest symptom escaped him. A heightened flush of the cheek, a slight irregularity of breath, a quiver of the eyelid, a hardly perceptible tremor through the frame,—such were the details which, as the moments passed, he wrote down in his folio volume. Intense thought had set its stamp upon every previous page of that volume, but the thoughts of years were all concentrated upon the last.

While thus employed, he failed not to gaze often at the fatal hand, and not without a shudder. Yet once, by a strange and unaccountable impulse, he pressed it with his lips. His spirit recoiled, however, in the very act; and Georgiana, out of the midst of her deep sleep, moved uneasily and murmured as if in remonstrance. Again Aylmer resumed his watch. Nor was it without avail. The crimson hand, which at first had been strongly visible upon the marble paleness of Georgiana's cheek, now grew more faintly outlined. She remained not less pale than ever; but the birthmark, with every breath that came and went, lost somewhat of its former distinctness. Its presence had been awful; its departure was more awful still. Watch the stain of the rainbow fading out the sky, and you will know how that mysterious symbol passed away.

"By Heaven! it is well-nigh gone!" said Aylmer to himself, in almost irrepressible ecstasy. "I can scarcely trace it now. Success! success! And now it is like the faintest rose color. The lightest flush of blood across her cheek would overcome it. But she is so pale!"

He drew aside the window curtain and suffered the light of natural day to fall into the room and rest upon her cheek. At the same time he heard a gross, hoarse chuckle, which he had long known as his servant Aminadab's expression of delight.

"Ah, clod! ah, earthly mass!" cried Aylmer, laughing in a sort of frenzy, "you have served me well! Matter and spirit—earth and heaven—have both done their part in this! Laugh, thing of the senses! You have earned the right to laugh."

These exclamations broke Georgiana's sleep. She slowly unclosed her eyes and gazed into the mirror which her husband had arranged for that purpose. A faint smile flitted over her lips when she recognized how barely perceptible was now that crimson hand which once blazed forth with such disastrous brilliancy as to scare away all their happiness. But then her eyes sought Aylmer's face with a trouble and anxiety that he could by no means account for.

"My poor Aylmer!" murmured she.

"Poor? Nay, richest, happiest, most favored!" exclaimed he. "My peerless bride, it is successful! You are perfect!"

"My poor Aylmer," she repeated, with a more than human tenderness, "you have aimed loftily; you have done nobly. Do not repent that with so high and pure a feeling, you have rejected the best the earth could offer. Aylmer, dearest Aylmer, I am dying!"

Alas! it was too true! the fatal hand had grappled with the mystery of life, and was the bond by which an angelic spirit kept itself in union with a mortal frame. As the last crimson tint of the birthmark—that sole token of human imperfection—faded from her cheek, the parting breath of the now perfect woman passed into the atmosphere, and her soul, lingering a moment near her husband, took its heavenward flight. Then a hoarse, chuckling laugh was heard again! Thus ever does the gross fatality of earth exult in its invariable triumph over the immortal essence which, in this dim sphere of half development, demands the completeness of a higher state. Yet, had Aylmer reached a profounder wisdom, he need not thus have flung away the happiness which would have woven his mortal life of the selfsame texture with the celestial. The momentary circumstance was too strong for him; he failed to look beyond the shadowy scope of time, and, living once for all in eternity, to find the perfect future in the present.

QUESTIONS FOR DISCUSSION

1. Aylmer is called "a man of science" who "had devoted himself, however, too unreservedly to scientific studies." What qualities in Aylmer's personality and temperament reveal the accuracy of this description? Do you think that Hawthorne is making a judgment about the scientist?

2. What is the significance of the shape of the birthmark? What does the narrator suggest may be held in the grip of the birthmark?

3. One of Hawthorne's devices throughout his fiction is the unresolved multiple choice. In this story, the attitudes of Georgiana's acquaintances toward her birthmark are represented by the narrator. What are these attitudes? How and why do they differ? What do these differences contribute to the reader's understanding of Georgiana or of Aylmer himself? Is Hawthorne's technique effective?

4. Aylmer calls the blemish on his wife's cheek "the visible mark of earthly imperfection." The narrator refers to it as "the fatal flaw of humanity." What is the meaning of the birthmark? What is the relationship between the birthmark and Aristotle's idea of the "tragic flaw," expressed in his *Poetics*?

5. What is Aylmer's attitude toward himself and his scientific technology? What limits does he recognize? By what standards does he evaluate his actions?

6. What role does Aminadab fulfill in the story? In what sense is he Aylmer's "double" or opposite?

7. What are the specific evidences of Aylmer's powers? Is he a scientist, an alchemist, or a sorcerer?
8. Why are Georgiana's encounters with the plant and with Aylmer's photographic process so seemingly destructive? What is the effect of these encounters upon her relationship with Aylmer?
9. Why is the revelation of Aylmer's failures important to the growth of Georgiana's love for and trust in him? What is ironic about her sense of Aylmer's "honorable love—so pure and lofty that it would accept nothing less than perfection"?

ASSIGNMENTS FOR WRITING

1. Read Edgar Allan Poe's story, "The Oval Portrait," and write a brief essay in which you compare and contrast the characters of Hawthorne's Aylmer and Poe's artist.
2. In the experience of Georgiana and Aylmer, what at first bothers only him becomes an obsession for her also. Such an obsession, of course, contributes eventually to her death. From either your imagination or actual experience, choose a similar type of situation—a person obsessed by a desire—and discuss the obsession and its effects.

Landscape

WASHINGTON ALLSTON: Elijah Fed by the Ravens, 1818

Allston (1779-1843) was the heir to a plantation in South Carolina. After graduating from Harvard, he sold it to finance his seven years of study and travel abroad. He developed his technique in London and his taste in Paris, where the Louvre then housed, thanks to Napoleon, most of the portable art treasures of the Continent. Greatly impressed by the poetry of color he found in Venetian painting, Allston went on to Rome and firsthand acquaintance with the Italian landscape. The *Elija (above)* shows his romantic temperament responding to the picturesque style of Salvator Rosa—which complemented the classical views of Claude and Poussin in the seventeenth century. The gaunt, blasted tree is a more important character in this drama than Elija himself, more expressive than the ragged clouds or rugged cliffs. It took Allston only three weeks to paint, and we prefer it today to his more highly finished work.

ASHER B. DURAND: Kindred Spirits, 1849

Never has landscape so dominated American painting as it did in the heyday of the Hudson River School. We might place its beginnings around 1820, when Thomas Doughty (1793-1856) gave up the leather business to devote himself full-time to landscape painting, or 1826, when Thomas Cole (1801/1848), a wandering painter born in England, settled on the west bank of the Hudson in the village of Catskill. His best pictures were not painted until the late 1830's, but they had a vision that went far beyond the typical woodland and water scenes of Doughty. Cole could be

J. ALDEN WEIR: The Red Bridge, c. 1897

Weir's customary palette contained all the shades of spring and summer greenery. Sometimes he made use of a device which gave additional form to his landscapes: putting in some building or other man-made object to offer contrast with the realm of nature. Once it was the white building of the *Willimantic Thread Factory;* here it is an iron bridge over the Shetucket River near Windham, Connecticut. Whoever painted the bridge did so to keep it from rusting, but Weir made telling use of the red lead color as the perfect complement to the dominant green of the surrounding landscape. The same aesthetic decision, after much argument, determined the final color of the Golden Gate Bridge. Ben Shahn used delicate patterns of red ironwork, in the form of city fire escapes, in several paintings, and they cropped up once more, hovering overhead, in the scenery for *West Side Story.*

From the time of Homer and Sargent in the late nineteenth century, some of the best American painting has been done in watercolor. Prendergast's scenes of Venice and New York (p. 737) show how he had absorbed and domesticated the vital trends in contemporary French painting. John Marin (1870-1953) was past forty before his talent was fully recognized. His steady development into the greatest watercolor master of his time owed much to the perception and encouragement of Alfred Stieglitz. As a photographer, Stieglitz had already made his mark with such classics as *Winter, Fifth Avenue* and the famous *Steerage* when, in 1905, he opened The Little Galleries of the Photo-Secession at 291 Fifth Avenue. Before long he was showing not only photographs but Rodin watercolors, Cézanne, Toulouse-Lautrec, Matisse, and Picasso, plus a group of young Americans which included Marsden Hartley, Max Weber, Arthur Dove, Stanton Macdonald-Wright, and Georgia O'Keeffe. Marin had his first one-man show at "291" in 1910. Turning from New York subjects like the Woolworth Building and the Brooklyn Bridge, Marin became fascinated with the landscape of Maine. For the approximate cost of three watercolors he was able to buy his own rocky little island off its coast.

JOHN MARIN: Maine Islands, 1922

Herman Melville

"I love all men who *dive*. Any fish can swim near the surface, but it takes a great whale to go down stairs five miles or more." So wrote Herman Melville in a letter to his friend, Evert Duyckinck in 1849. The writing of *Moby-Dick* was still a year and more away; the reference to "a great whale" is not, then, literal. But in the metaphor of "men who *dive*"—men who plunge into the depths of life's perplexities—one can see the direction of Melville's thought and begin to comprehend what transformed the writer of popular adventure novels into the rejected writer whose enigmatic and profound books would not sell enough to support him.

Born on August 1, 1819, to parents bound down by financial misfortune, Herman Melville was raised in New York City and later in Albany. But the family found no greater relief from poverty in the provinces; the father died in debt when Herman was thirteen. Conditions did not improve, and Melville, after his own scant schooling had prepared him for teaching elementary school, went to sea, first in 1838, and again in 1841, this time aboard the whaler *Acushnet*.

The *Acushnet* was bound from New Bedford for the whaling grounds of the South Sea islands. But by the time the ship reached the Marquesas, Melville was ready for life ashore. He deserted with a shipmate, Richard Tobias Greene, and for two years lived the idyllic life of a beachcomber with a beautiful Polynesian mistress, the prototype for Fayaway of *Typee*. This book, published in 1846 upon his return to civilization, earned Melville his early renown as "the man who had lived among the cannibals." He was quick to capitalize on his fame with a sequel, *Omoo* (1847); thereafter, the reading public expected more of the same.

Melville could not oblige. Lacking the formal education of most of his peers—"A whaleship was my Yale College and my Harvard"—

he had nonetheless begun to read widely. Evert Duyckinck, writing to his brother in the spring of 1848, observed of Melville:

> By the way Melville reads old Books. He has borrowed Sir Thomas Browne of me and says finely of the speculations of the *Religio Medici* that Browne is a kind of "crack'd Archangel." Was ever any thing of this sort said before by a sailor?

This unusual sailor had also begun to study the complex and philosophical problems of life. His copies of Shakespeare and the Bible were becoming thoroughly underscored and annotated. His next book, *Mardi* (1849), reflects the change. Allegorical in form, *Mardi* recounts the voyage of five men in search of Absolute Truth; but Melville's departure angered and confused readers who had expected more cannibal tales. He now struggled with the dilemma—not uncommon to the artist—of whether to write for money or for truth. A letter to Nathaniel Hawthorne expresses his despair:

> Dollars damn me; and the malicious Devil is forever grinning in upon me, holding the door ajar. . . . What I feel most moved to write, that is banned,—it will not pay. Yet, altogether, write the *other* way I cannot. So the product is a final hash, and all my books are botches.

Through the financially disastrous *Mardi* experience Melville was to learn an essential lesson about the integrity of the artist. From that time on, in spite of public disfavor, Melville knew his course. True, he did write *Redburn* (1849) and *White-Jacket* (1850), both based on his life at sea, as economic necessities; but when he came to the crucial decision of his career, he chose art over commercial success.

That turning point was the apparent altering of the concept behind *Moby-Dick* (1851)—the hyphen in the title was Melville's own means of differentiating the name of the book from the name of the whale. It was a revision both of purpose and of scope that resulted in Melville's writing the epic American novel rather than another pedestrian, romantic travelogue, as he seemed to have intended. The factors effecting such a change of direction were wholly circumstantial; yet, as often happens, a man's most dramatic reshaping can result from his being in the right place at the right time. In Melville's case, the right place was a summer home in Pittsfield, Massachusetts, a Berkshire Mountains resort for several literary families. The right time was August 1850, when Melville was introduced to Nathaniel Hawthorne, his close neighbor in Lenox, by their mutual friend Duyckinck. From this arranged meeting and from the intimate friendship that followed surged an outpouring of the metaphysical perplexities in Melville's soul, an upwelling of "bold and nervous lofty language," the language of spiritual metaphor.

Melville's style, as may be seen from his early letters and books, had always possessed an odd combination of ornate and crude language that often made for cumbersome reading. The formality, the stiffness of his style, with its awkward and pretentious diction, suggested the bookishness of the younger Melville. But hidden even within such disagreeable passages were the seeds of narrative genius, the power of metaphor used to evoke a concrete image in the reader's mind.

Melville cultivated this power, especially after his encounter with Hawthorne, and although he never quite refined his prose enough to be free of the occasional rough-edged word, he did become a master of evocative writing. Witness this portion of the concluding paragraph to "The Whiteness of the Whale," Chapter XLII of *Moby-Dick.*

> Is it that by its indefiniteness it shadows forth the heartless voids and immensities of the universe, and thus stabs us from behind with the thought of annihilation, when beholding the white depths of the milky way? Or is it, that as in essence whiteness is not so much a color as the visible absence of color, and at the same time the concrete of all colors, is it for these reasons that there is such a dumb blankness, full of meaning, in a wide landscape of snows—a colorless, all-color of atheism from which we shrink?

Once having set himself on a course which he knew would take him ever further from a popular audience, Melville seemed to accept the challenge with an almost demonic zeal. *Moby-Dick* was followed by an even more resounding critical failure, *Pierre, or the Ambiguities* (1852). After this rejection, Melville lost much of his intensity; his writing pace slackened, and his style was shortened to the story form. He maintained, however, the same determination to deal with "the ambiguities," the dark, deep issues of life, rather than the sun-bright and superficial fiction being written by his rivals.

The principal stories composed by Melville during the period 1853–1856 were collected in *The Piazza Tales* (1856). "Bartleby the Scrivener," subtitled "A Story of Wall Street," focuses on a legal copyist—something of a human mimeograph machine—who rejects the world around him and withdraws behind his own wall. To all attempts at ending his alienation, his response is a laconic, "I prefer not to." Critics often read this story as Melville's personal declaration of independence from a world that expected him, like Bartleby, to be no more than a copier.

"Benito Cereno" is masterful in its controlled irony. The story is told through the eyes of a good-hearted and trusting Yankee captain who went aboard a becalmed Spanish slave trader to offer his assistance. Slowly he became aware that the distress of the vessel, its crew, and its human cargo was not the result of scurvy alone but of a violent revolt and massacre by the slaves. The Spanish captain, Benito Cereno, was in fact a prisoner, both served and terrified by the feigning slave Babo.

"The Encantadas" or "The Enchanted Isles" is a set of ten sketches, mostly devoid of dramatic action. Of these, "Norfolk Isle and the Chola Widow" is impressive in its simple grandeur and its sense of human dignity. But in another sketch, Melville again made a point that synthesizes much of his world view and accounts once more for his unpopularity. Discontent with sugary misrepresentations of life, he wrote,

> Moreover, every one knows that tortoises as well as turtles are of such a make that if you but put them on their backs you thereby expose their bright sides without the possibility of their recovering themselves, and turning into view the other. But after you have done this, and because you have done this, you should not swear that the tortoise has no dark side. Enjoy the bright, keep it turned up perpetually if you can, but be honest, and don't deny the black.

But the mid-nineteenth-century American reading public would not accept this dark view of the world, and Melville sank into almost complete obscurity.

In his later years he turned to poetry. Reduced to clerking in the New York Customs House, Melville began to write for a wholly private reason. *Battle-Pieces* (1866) gave his impression of the Civil War: "All wars are boyish and are fought by boys." An immensely long poem, *Clarel* (1876), retraces Melville's journey to Jerusalem; other, briefer, volumes of verse followed.

But nothing written after *Moby-Dick* approached the same sublimity and power—until the posthumous discovery and publication of *Billy Budd, Foretopman* (1924). In a remarkable return to fictional prose, Melville recapitulated most of the paradoxes of life that had puzzled him forty years before. Begun in 1888, *Billy Budd, Foretopman* was completed just five months before Melville's death in September 1891. It is not a perfect story. Like much of Melville's work, it lacks the leanness of language that marks the work of such newcomers as Stephen Crane and Joseph Conrad. Melville's tendency to obtrude, to tell too much, was still a fault. But it is nonetheless a great story.

Drawing upon his reminiscences of life at sea and using the

historical framework of the Napoleonic Wars for his setting, Melville again created the synecdoche of life aboard ship as symbolic of man's experience. But whereas in previous books he had concentrated upon the common metaphysical and philosophical problems facing mankind, in *Billy Budd* Melville drove straight to the source of these problems—the primeval spiritual struggle between Good and Evil. Once more a mytho-poetic Adam faces a beguiling Serpent; once more he falls; once more the Loving Father utters judgment, but with that judgment comes the added promise of forgiveness: "At the last Assizes it shall acquit." In the writing of *Billy Budd*, it seems clear, Melville made his own final peace with art and with his view of life.

Having drifted into anonymity, Melville died on September 28, 1891, his books out of print, his name forgotten by his contemporaries. Ironically, today Melville stands among America's greatest writers. Perhaps in the twentieth century, racked by wars and threatened with total destruction, we have sufficiently sobered to recognize the importance of men who tell us the unpleasantness we do not wish to hear; who remind us, when considering even the most minute aspects of our lives, that "all these things are not without their meanings." Such men as Melville are "men who *dive*," whose minds explore the fathomless and inexpressible depths of human thought.

Billy Budd, Foretopman

Dedicated to Jack Chase, Englishman, wherever that great heart may now be here on earth or harbored in paradise. Captain of the maintop in the year 1843 in the U.S. Frigate United States.

PREFACE

The year 1797, the year of this narrative, belongs to a period which as every thinker now feels, involved a crisis for Christendom not exceeded in its undetermined momentousness at the time by any other era whereof there is record. The opening proposition made by the Spirit of that Age involved the rectification of the Old World's hereditary wrongs. In France to some extent this was bloodily effected. But what then? Straightway the Revolution itself became a wrong-doer, one more oppressive than the kings. Under Napoleon it enthroned upstart kings, and initiated that prolonged agony of continual war whose final throe was Waterloo. During those years not the wisest could have foreseen that the outcome of all would be what to some thinkers apparently it has since turned out to be, a political advance along nearly the whole line for Europeans.

Now, as elsewhere hinted, it was something caught from the Revolutionary Spirit that at Spithead emboldened the man-of-war's men to rise against real abuses, long-standing ones, and afterwards at the Nore to make inordinate and aggressive demands, successful resistance to which was confirmed only when the ringleaders were hung for an admonitory spectacle to the anchored fleet. Yet in a way analogous to the operation of the Revolution at large, the Great Mutiny, though by Englishmen naturally deemed monstrous at the time, doubtless gave the first latent prompting to most important reforms in the British Navy.

I

In the time before steamships, or then more frequently than now, a stroller along the docks of any considerable seaport would occasionally have his attention arrested by a group of bronzed mariners, man-of-war's men or merchant-sailors in holiday attire ashore on liberty. In certain instances they would flank or, like a body-guard, quite surround some superior figure of their own class, moving along with them like Aldebaran among the lesser lights of his constellation. That signal object was the "Handsome Sailor" of the less prosaic time alike of the military and merchant navies. With no perceptible trace of the vainglorious about him, rather with the off-hand unaffectedness of natural regality, he seemed to accept the spontaneous homage of his shipmates. A somewhat remarkable instance recurs to me. In Liverpool, now half a century ago, I saw under the shadow of the great dingy street-wall of Prince's Dock (an obstruction long since removed) a common sailor, so intensely black that he must needs have been a native African of the unadulterate blood of Ham. A symmetric figure much above the average height. The two ends of a gay silk handkerchief thrown loose about the neck danced upon the displayed ebony of his chest; in his ears were big hoops of gold, and a Scotch Highland bonnet with a tartan band set off his shapely head.

It was a hot noon in July; and his face, lustrous with perspiration, beamed with barbaric good humor. In jovial sallies right and left his white teeth flashing into view, he rollicked along, the center of a company of his shipmates. These were made up of such an assortment of tribes and complexions as would have well fitted them to be marched up by Anacharsis Cloots before the bar of the first French Assembly as Representatives of the Human Race. At each spontaneous tribute rendered by the wayfarers to this black pagoda of a fellow—the tribute of a pause and stare, and less frequent an exclamation,—the motley retinue showed that they took that sort of pride in the evoker of it which the Assyrian priests doubtless showed for their grand sculptured Bull when the faithful prostrated themselves.

To return.

If in some cases a bit of nautical Murat in setting forth his person ashore, the handsome sailor or the period in question evinced nothing of the dandified Billy-be-Damn, an amusing character all but extinct now, but occasionally to be encountered, and in a form yet more amusing than the original, at the tiller of the boats on the tempestuous Erie Canal or, more likely, vaporing in the groggeries along the tow-path. Invariably a proficient in his perilous calling, he was also more or less of a mighty boxer or wrestler. It was strength and beauty. Tales of his prowess were recited. Ashore he was the champion; afloat the spokesman; on every suitable occasion always foremost. Close-reefing topsails in a gale, there he was, astride the weather yard-arm-end, foot in the Flemish horse as "stirrup," both hands tugging at the "earring" as at a bridle, in very much the attitude of young Alexander curbing the fiery Bucephalus. A superb figure, tossed up as by the horns of Taurus against the thunderous sky, cheerily hallooing to the strenuous file along the spar.

The moral nature was seldom out of keeping with the physical make. Indeed, except as toned by the former, the comeliness and power, always attractive in masculine conjunction, hardly could have drawn the sort of honest homage the Handsome Sailor in some examples received from his less gifted associates.

Such a cynosure, at least in aspect, and something such too in nature, though with important variations made apparent as the story proceeds, was welkin-eyed Billy Budd, or Baby Budd as more familiarly under circumstances hereafter to be given he at last came to be called, aged twenty-one, a foretopman of the British fleet toward the close of the last decade of the eighteenth century. It was not very long prior to the time of the narration that follows that he had entered the King's Service, having been impressed on the Narrow Seas from a homewardbound English merchantman into a seventy-four outwardbound, H.M.S. *Indomitable;* which ship, as was not unusual in those hurried days had been obliged to put to sea short of her proper complement of men. Plump upon Billy at first sight in the gangway the boarding officer Lieutenant Ratcliffe pounced, even before the merchantman's crew formally was mustered on the quarter-deck for his deliberate inspection. And him only he elected. For whether it was because the other men when ranged before him showed to ill advantage after Billy, or whether he had some scruples in view of the merchantman being rather short-handed, however it might be, the officer contented himself with his first spontaneous choice. To the surprise of the ship's company, though much to the Lieutenant's satisfaction Billy made no demur. But, indeed, any demur would have been as idle as the protest of a goldfinch popped into a cage.

Noting his uncomplaining acquiescence, all but cheerful one might say, the shipmates turned a surprised glance of silent reproach at the sailor. The shipmaster was one of those worthy mortals found in every vocation even the humbler ones—the sort of person whom everybody agrees in calling "a respectable man." And—nor so strange to report as it may appear to be—though a plowman of the troubled waters, life-long contending with the intractable elements, there was nothing this honest soul at heart loved better than simple peace and quiet. For the rest, he was fifty or thereabouts, a little inclined to corpulence, a prepossessing face, unwhiskered, and of an agreeable color—a rather full face, humanely intelligent in expression. On a fair day with a fair wind and all going well, a certain musical chime in his voice seemed to be the veritable unobstructed outcome of the innermost man. He had much prudence, much conscientiousness, and there were occasions when these virtues were the cause of overmuch disquietude in him. On a passage, so long as his craft was in any proximity to land, no sleep for Captain Graveling. He took to heart those serious responsibilities not so heavily borne by some shipmasters.

Now while Billy Budd was down in the forecastle getting his kit together, the *Indomitable*'s lieutenant, burly and bluff, nowise disconcerted by Captain Graveling's omitting to proffer the customary hospitalities on an occasion so unwelcome to him, an omission simply caused by preoccupation of thought, unceremoniously invited himself into the cabin, and also to a flask from the spirit-locker, a receptacle which his experienced eye instantly discovered. In fact he was one of those sea-dogs in whom all the hardship and peril of naval life in the great prolonged wars of his time never impaired the natural instinct for sensuous enjoyment. His duty he always faithfully did; but duty is sometimes a dry obligation, and he was for irrigating its aridity whensoever possible with a fertilizing decoction of strong waters. For the cabin's proprietor there was nothing left but to play the part of the enforced host with whatever grace and alacrity were practicable. As necessary adjuncts to the flask, he silently placed tumbler and water-jug before the irrepressible guest. But excusing himself from partaking just then, he dismally watched the unembarrassed officer deliberately diluting his grog a little, then tossing it off in three swallows, pushing the empty tumbler away, yet not so far as to be beyond easy reach, at the same time settling himself in his seat and smacking his lips with high satisfaction, looking straight at the host.

These proceedings over, the Master broke the silence; and there lurked a rueful reproach in the tone of his voice; "Lieutenant, you are going to take my best man from me, the jewel of 'em."

"Yes, I know" rejoined the other, immediately drawing back the tumbler preliminary to a replenishing; "Yes I know. Sorry."

"Beg pardon, but you don't understand, Lieutenant. See here now. Before I shipped that young fellow, my forecastle was a rat-pit of quarrels. It was black times, I tell you, aboard the 'Rights' here. I was worried to that degree my pipe had no comfort for me. But Billy came; and it was like a Catholic priest striking peace in an Irish shindy. Not that he preached to them or said or did anything in particular; but a virtue went out of him, sugaring the sour ones. They took to him like hornets to treacle; all but the bluffer of the gang, the big shaggy chap with the fire-red whiskers. He indeed out of envy, perhaps, of the newcomer, and thinking such a 'sweet and pleasant fellow,' as he mockingly designated him to the others, could hardly have the spirit of a game-cock, must needs bestir himself in trying to get up an ugly row with him. Billy forebore with him and reasoned with him in a pleasant way—he is something like myself, Lieutenant, to whom aught like a quarrel is hateful—but nothing served. So, in the second dog-watch one day the Red Whiskers in presence of the others, under pretence of showing Billy just whence a sirloin steak was cut—for the fellow had once been a butcher—insultingly gave him a dig under the ribs. Quick as lightning Billy let fly his arm. I dare say he never meant to do quite as much as he did, but anyhow he gave the burly fool a terrible drubbing. It took about half a minute, I should think. And, Lord bless you, the lubber was astonished at the celerity. And will you believe it, Lieutenant, the Red Whiskers now really loves Billy—loves him, or is the biggest hypocrite that ever I heard of. But they all love him. Some of 'em do his washing, darn his old trousers for him; the carpenter is at odd times making a pretty little chest of drawers for him. Anybody will do anything for Billy Budd; and it's the happy family here. But now Lieutenant, if that young fellow goes—I know how it will be aboard the 'Rights.' Not again very soon shall I, coming up from dinner, lean over the capstan smoking a quiet pipe—no, not very soon again, I think. Ay, Lieutenant, you are going to take away the jewel of 'em; you are going to take away my peacemaker!" And with that the good soul had really some ado in checking a rising sob.

"Well," said the officer who had listened with amused interest to all this, and now waxing merry with his tipple; "Well, blessed are the peacemakers especially the fighting peacemakers! And such are the seventy-four beauties some of which you see poking their noses out of the port-holes of yonder warship lying-to for me," pointing through the cabin window of the *Indomitable*. "But courage! don't look so downhearted, man. Why, I pledge you in advance the royal approbation. Rest assured that His Majesty will be delighted to know that in a time when his hardtack is not sought for by sailors with such avidity as should be; a time also when some shipmasters privily resent the borrowing from them a tar or two for the service; His Majesty, I say, will be delighted to learn that *one* shipmaster at least cheerfully surrenders to the King, the flower of his flock, a sailor who with equal loyalty makes no dissent.—But where's my beauty? Ah," looking through the cabin's open door, "here he comes; and, by Jove—lugging along his chest—Apollo with his portmanteau!—My man," stepping out to him, "you can't take that big box on board a warship. The boxes there are mostly shot-boxes. Put your duds in a bag, lad. Boot and saddle for the cavalryman, bag and hammock for the man-of-war's man."

The transfer from chest to bag was made. And, after seeing his man into the cutter and then following him down, the lieutenant pushed off from the *Rights-of-Man*. That was the merchant ship's name; though by her master and crew abbreviated in sailor fashion into the *Rights*. The hard-headed Dundee owner was a staunch admirer of Thomas Paine whose book in rejoinder to Burke's arraignment of the French Revolution had then been published for some time and had gone everywhere. In christening his vessel after the title of Paine's volume, the man of Dundee was something like his contemporary shipowner, Stephen Girard of Philadelphia, whose sympathies, alike with his native land and its liberal philosophers, he evinced by naming his ships after Voltaire, Diderot, and so forth.

But now, when the boat swept under the merchantman's stern, and officer and oarsmen were noting—some bitterly and others with a grin,—the name emblazoned there; just then it was that the new recruit jumped up from the bow where the coxswain had directed him to sit, and waving his hat to his silent shipmates sorrowfully looking over at him from the taffrail, bade the lads a genial good-by. Then making a salutation as to the ship herself, "And good-by to you, too, old *Rights-of-Man!*"

"Down, Sir!" roared the lieutenant, instantly assuming all the rigor of his rank, though with difficulty repressing a smile.

To be sure, Billy's action was a terrible breach of naval decorum. But in that decorum he had never been instructed; in consideration of which the lieutenant would hardly have been so energetic in reproof but for the concluding farewell to the ship. This he rather took as meant to convey a covert sally on the new recruit's part, a sly slur at impressment in general, and that of himself in especial. And yet, more likely, if satire it was in effect, it was hardly so by intention, for Billy, though happily endowed with the gaiety of high health, youth and a free heart, was yet by no means of a satirical turn. The will to it and the sinister dexterity were alike wanting. To deal in double meaning and insinuations of any sort was quite foreign to his nature.

As to his enforced enlistment, that he seemed to take pretty much as he was wont to take any vicissitude of weather. Like the animals, though no philosopher, he was, without knowing it, practically a fatalist. And, it may be, that he rather liked this adventurous turn in his affairs, which promised an opening into novel scenes and martial excitements.

Aboard the *Indomitable* our merchant-sailor was forthwith rated as an able-seaman and assigned to the starboard watch of the foretop. He was soon at home in the service, not at all disliked for his unpretentious good looks and a sort of genial happy-go-lucky air. No merrier man in his mess: in marked contrast to certain other individuals included like himself among the impressed portions of the ship's company; for these when not actively employed were sometimes, and more particularly in the last dog-watch when the drawing near of twilight induced revery, apt to fall into a saddish mood which in some partook of sullenness. But they were not so young as our foretopman, and no few of them must have known a hearth of some sort, others may have had wives and children left, too probably, in uncertain circumstances, and hardly any but must have acknowledged kith and kin, while for Billy, as will shortly be seen, his entire family was practically invested in himself.

II

Though our new-made foretopman was well received in the top and on the gun-decks, hardly here was he that cynosure he had previously been among those minor ship's companies of the merchant marine, with which companies only had he hiterto consorted.

He was young; and despite his all but fully developed frame in aspect looked even younger than he really was, owing to a lingering adolescent expression in the as yet smooth face all but feminine in purity in natural complexion but where, thanks to his seagoing, the lily was quite suppressed and the rose had some ado visibly to flush through the tan.

To one essentially such a novice in the complexities of factitious life, the abrupt transition from his former and simpler sphere to the ampler and more knowing world of a great warship; this might well have abashed him had there been any conceit or vanity in his composition. Among her miscellaneous multitude, the *Indomitable* mustered several individuals who however inferior in grade were of no common natural stamp, sailors more signally susceptive of that air which continuous martial discipline and repeated presence in battle can in some degree impart even to the average man. As the *handsome sailor* Billy Budd's position aboard the seventy-four was something analogous to that of a rustic beauty transplanted from the provinces and brought into competition with the high-born dames of the court. But this change of circumstances he scarce noted. As little did he observe that something about him provoked an ambiguous smile in one or two harder faces among the blue-jackets. Nor less unaware was he of the peculiar favorable effect his person and demeanor had upon the more intelligent gentlemen of the quarter-deck. Nor could this well have been otherwise. Cast in a mold peculiar to the finest physical examples of those Englishmen in whom the Saxon strain would seem not at all to partake of any Norman or other admixture, he showed in face that humane look of reposeful good nature which the Greek sculptor in some instances gave to his heroic strong man, Hercules. But this again was subtly modified by another and pervasive quality. The ear, small and shapely, the arch of the foot, the curve in mouth and nostril, even the indurated hand dyed to the orange-tawny of the toucan's bill, a hand telling alike of the halyards and tar-bucket; but, above all, something in the mobile expression, and every chance attitude and movement, something suggestive of a mother eminently favored by Love and the Graces; all this strangely indicated a lineage in direct contradiction to his lot. The mysteriousness here, became less mysterious through a matter-of-fact elicited when Billy at the capstan was being formally mustered into the service. Asked by the officer, a small brisk little gentleman as it chanced among other questions, his place of birth, he replied, "Please, Sir, I don't know."

"Don't know where you were born?—Who was your father?"

"God knows, Sir."

Struck by the straightforward simplicity of these replies, the officer next asked "Do you know anything about your beginning?"

"No, Sir. But I have heard that I was found in a pretty silk-lined basket hanging one morning from the knocker of a good man's door in Bristol."

"*Found* say you? Well," throwing back his head and looking up and down the new recruit; "Well it turns out to have been a pretty good find. Hope they'll find some more like you, my man; the fleet sadly needs them."

Yes, Billy Budd was a foundling, a presumable bye-blow, and, evidently, no ignoble one. Noble descent was as evident in him as in a blood horse.

For the rest, with little or no sharpness of faculty or any trace of the wisdom of the serpent, nor yet quite a dove, he possessed that kind a degree of intelligence going along with the unconventional rectitude of a sound human creature, one to whom not yet has been proffered the questionable apple of knowledge. He was illiterate; he could not read, but he could sing, and like the illiterate nightingale was sometimes the composer of his own song.

Of self-consciousness he seemed to have little or none, or about as much as we may reasonably impute to a dog of St. Bernard's breed.

Habitually living with the elements and knowing little more of the land than as a beach, or, rather, that portion of the terraqueous globe providentially set apart for dance-houses doxies and tapsters, in short what sailors call a "fiddlers' green," his simple nature remained unsophisticated by those moral obliquities which are not in every case incompatible with that manufacturable thing known as respectability. But are sailors, frequenters of "fiddlers' greens," without vices? No; but less often than with landsmen do their vices, so called, partake of crookedness of heart, seeming less to proceed from viciousness than exuberance of vitality after long constraint; frank manifestations in accordance with natural law. By his original constitution aided by the cooperating influences of his lot, Billy in many respects was little more than a sort of upright barbarian, much such perhaps as Adam presumably might have been ere the urbane Serpent wriggled himself into his company.

And here be it submitted that apparently going to corroborate the doctrine of man's fall, a doctrine now popularly ignored, it is observable that where certain virtues pristine and unadulterate peculiarly characterize anybody in the external uniform of civilization, they will upon scrutiny seem not to be derived from custom or convention but rather to be out of keeping with these, as if indeed exceptionally transmitted from a period prior to Cain's city and citified man. The character marked by such qualities has to an unvitiated taste an untampered-with flavor like that of berries while the man thoroughly civilized even in a fair specimen of the breed has to the same moral palate a questionable smack as of a compounded wine. To any stray inheritor of these primitive qualities found, like Caspar Hauser, wandering dazed in any Christian capital of our time the good-natured poet's famous invocation, near two thousand years ago, of the good rustic out of his latitude in the Rome of the Caesars, still appropriately holds:—

> "Honest and poor, faithful in word and thought,
> What has Thee, Fabian, to the city brought."

Though our Handsome Sailor had as much of masculine beauty as one can expect anywhere to see; nevertheless, like the beautiful woman in one of Hawthorne's minor tales, there was just one thing amiss in him. No visible blemish, indeed, as with the lady; no, but an occasional liability to a vocal defect. Though in the hour of elemental uproar or peril, he was everything that a sailor should be, yet under sudden provocation of strong heart-feeling his voice otherwise singularly musical, as if expressive of the harmony within, was apt to develop an organic hesitancy, in fact more or less of a stutter or even worse. In this particular Billy was a striking instance that the arch interferer, the envious marplot of Eden still has more or less to do with every human consignment to this planet of earth. In every case, one way or another, he is sure to slip in his little card as much as to remind us—I too have a hand here.

The avowal of such an imperfection in the Handsome Sailor should be evidence not alone that he is not presented as a conventional hero, but also that the story in which he is the main figure is no romance.

III

At the time of Billy Budd's arbitrary enlistment into the *Indomitable* that ship was on her way to join the Mediterranean fleet. No long time elapsed before the junction was effected. As one of that fleet the seventy-four participated in its movements, though at times on account of her superior sailing qualities, in the absence of frigates, despatched on separate duty as a scout and at times on less temporary service. But with all this the story has little concernment, restricted as it is to the inner life of one particular ship and the career of an individual sailor.

It was the summer of 1797. In the April of that year had occurred the commotion at Spithead followed in May by a second and yet more serious outbreak in the fleet at the Nore. The latter is known, and without exaggeration in the epithet, as the Great Mutiny. It was indeed a demonstration more menacing to England than the contempoary manifestoes and conquering and proselyting armies of the French Directory.

To the British Empire the Nore Mutiny was what a strike in the fire-brigade would be to London threatened by general arson. In a crisis when the Kingdom might well have anticipated the famous signal that some years later published along the naval line of battle what it was that upon occasion England expected of Englishmen; *that* was the time when at the mastheads of the three-deckers and seventy-fours moored in her own roadstead—a fleet, the right arm of a Power then all but the sole free conservative one of the Old World, the blue-jackets, to be numbered by thousands, ran up with hurras the British colors with the union and cross wiped out; by that cancellation transmuting the flag of founded law and freedom defined, into the enemy's red meteor of unbridled and unbounded revolt. Reasonable discontent growing out of practical grievances in the fleet had been ignited into irrational combustion as by live cinders blown across the Channel from France in flames.

The event converted into irony for a time those spirited strains of

Dibdin—as a song-writer no mean auxiliary to the English Government at the European conjuncture—strains celebrating, among other things, the patriotic devotion of the British tar:

"And as for my life, 'tis the King's!"

Such an episode in the Island's grand naval story her naval historians naturally abridge; one of them (G. P. R. James) candidly acknowledging that fain would he pass it over did not "impartiality forbid fastidiousness." And yet his mention is less a narration than a reference, having to do hardly at all with details. Nor are these readily to be found in the libraries. Like some other events in every age befalling states everywhere including America, the Great Mutiny was of such character that national pride along with views of policy would fain shade it off into the historical background. Such events cannot be ignored, but there is a considerate way of historically treating them. If a well-constituted individual refrains from blazoning aught amiss or calamitous in his family; a nation in the like circumstance may without reproach be equally discreet.

Though after parleyings between Government and the ringleaders, and concessions by the former as to some glaring abuses, the first uprising—that at Spithead—with difficulty was put down, or matters for a time pacified; yet at the Nore the unforeseen renewal of insurrection on a yet larger scale, and emphasized in the conferences that ensued by demands deemed by the authorities not only inadmissible but aggressively insolent, indicated—if the red flag did not sufficiently do so, what was the spirit animating the men. Final suppression, however, there was; but only made possible perhaps by the unswerving loyalty of the marine corps and a voluntary resumption of loyalty among influential sections of the crews.

To some extent the Nore Mutiny may be regarded as analogous to the distempering irruption of contagious fever in a frame constitutionally sound, and which anon throws it off.

At all events, of these thousands of mutineers were some of the tars who not so very long afterwards—whether wholly prompted thereto by patriotism, or pugnacious instinct, or by both,—helped to win a coronet for Nelson at the Nile, and the naval crown of crowns for him at Trafalgar. To the mutineers those battles and especially Trafalgar were a plenary absolution and a grand one: For all that goes to make up scenic naval display, heroic magnificence in arms, those battles especially Trafalgar stand unmatched in human annals.

IV

Concerning "The greatest sailor since the
world began"—Tennyson?

In this matter of writing, resolve as one may to keep to the main
road, some bypaths have an enticement not readily to be withstood.
I am going to err into such a bypath. If the reader will keep me
company I shall be glad. At the least we can promise ourselves that
pleasure which is wickedly said to be in sinning, for a literary sin
the divergence will be.

Very likely it is no new remark that the inventions of our time
have at last brought about a change in sea-warfare in degree corresponding to the revolution in all warfare effected by the original
introduction from China into Europe of gunpowder. The first European
fire-arm, a clumsy contrivance, was, as is well known, scouted by no
few of the knights as a base implement good enough peradventure for
weavers too craven to stand up crossing steel with steel in frank fight.
But as ashore knightly valor though shorn of its blazonry did not
cease with the knights, neither on the seas though nowadays in
encounters there a certain kind of displayed gallantry be fallen out
of date as hardly applicable under changed circumstances, did the
nobler qualities of such naval magnates as Don John of Austria,
Doria, Van Tromp, Jean Bart, the long line of British admirals and
the American Decaturs of 1812 become obsolete with their wooden
walls.

Nevertheless, to anybody who can hold the Present at its worth
without being inappreciative of the Past, it may be forgiven, if to
such a one the solitary old hulk at Portsmouth, Nelson's *Victory*,
seems to float there, not alone as the decaying monument of a
fame incorruptible, but also as a poetic reproach, softened by its
picturesqueness, to the *Monitors* and yet mightier hulls of the
European iron-clads. And this not altogether because such craft are
unsightly, unavoidably lacking the symmetry and grand lines of the
old battleships, but equally for other reasons.

There are some, perhaps, who while not altogether inaccessible to
that poetic reproach just alluded to, may yet on behalf of the new
order, be disposed to parry it; and this to the extent of iconoclasm,
if need be. For example, prompted by the sight of the star inserted
in the *Victory*'s quarter-deck designating the spot where the Great
Sailor fell, these martial utilitarians may suggest considerations implying that Nelson's ornate publication of his person in battle was not
only unnecessary, but not military, nay, savored of foolhardiness and

vanity. They may add, too, that at Trafalgar it was in effect nothing less than a challenge to death; and death came; and that but for his bravado the victorious admiral might possibly have survived the battle, and so, instead of having his sagacious dying injunction over-ruled by his immediate successor in command he himself when the contest was decided might have brought his shattered fleet to anchor, a proceeding which might have averted the deplorable loss of life by shipwreck in the elemental tempest that followed the martial one.

Well, should we set aside the more disputable point whether for various reasons it was possible to anchor the fleet, then plausibly enough the Benthamites of war may urge the above.

But the *might have been* is but boggy ground to build on. And certainly in foresight as to the larger issue of an encounter, and anxious preparation for it—buoying the deadly way and mapping it out, as at Copenhagen—few commanders have been so painstakingly circumspect as this same reckless declarer of his person in fight.

Personal prudence even when dictated by quite other than selfish considerations is surely no special virtue in a military man; while an excessive love of glory, impassioning a less burning impulse the honest sense of duty, is the first. If the name *Wellington* is not so much a trumpet to the blood as the simpler name *Nelson*, the reason for this may perhaps be inferred from the above. Alfred in his funeral ode on the victor of Waterloo ventures not to call him the greatest soldier of all time, though in the same ode he invokes Nelson as "the greatest sailor since the world began."

At Trafalgar Nelson, on the brink of opening the fight, sat down and wrote his last brief will and testament. If under the presentiment of the most magnificent of all victories to be crowned by his own glorious death, a sort of priestly motive led him to dress his person in the jewelled vouchers of his own shining deeds; if thus to have adorned himself for the altar and the sacrifice were indeed vainglory, then affectation and fustian is each more heroic line in the great epics and dramas, since in such lines the poet but embodies in verse those exaltations of sentiment that a nature like Nelson, the opportunity being given, vitalizes into acts.

V

Yes, the outbreak at the Nore was put down. But not every grievance was redressed. If the contractors, for example, were no longer permitted to ply some practices peculiar to their tribe everywhere, such as providing shoddy cloth, rations not sound, or false in the measure; not the less impressment, for one thing, went on. By custom sanctioned for centuries, and judicially maintained by a Lord Chancellor as late as Mansfield, that mode of manning the fleet, a mode now fallen into a sort of abeyance but never formally renounced, it was not practicable to give up in those years. Its abrogation would have crippled the indispensable fleet, one wholly under canvas, no steam-power, its innumerable sails and thousands of cannon, everything in short, worked by muscle alone; a fleet the more insatiate in demand for men, because then multiplying its ships of all grades against contingencies present and to come of the convulsed Continent.

Discontent foreran the Two Mutinies, and more or less it lurkingly survived them. Hence it was not unreasonable to apprehend some return of trouble sporadic or general. One instance of such apprehensions: In the same year with this story, Nelson, then Vice-Admiral Sir Horatio, being with the fleet off the Spanish coast, was directed by the Admiral in command to shift his pennant from the *Captain* to the *Theseus;* and for this reason: that the latter ship having newly arrived in the station from home where it had taken part in the Great Mutiny, danger was apprehended from the temper of the men; and it was thought that an officer like Nelson was the one, not indeed to terrorize the crew into base subjection, but to win them, by force of his mere presence back to an allegiance if not as enthusiastic as his own, yet as true. So it was that for a time on more than one quarter-deck anxiety did exist. At sea precautionary vigilance was strained against relapse. At short notice an engagement might come on. When it did, the lieutenants assigned to batteries felt it incumbent on them, in some instances to stand with drawn swords behind the men working the guns.

VI

But on board the seventy-four in which Billy now swung his hammock, very little in the manner of the men and nothing obvious in the demeanor of the officers would have suggested to an ordinary observer that the Great Mutiny was a recent event. In their general bearing and conduct the commissioned officers of a warship naturally take their tone from the commander, that is if he has that ascendancy of character that ought to be his.

Captain the Honorable Edward Fairfax Vere, to give his full title, was a bachelor of forty or thereabouts, a sailor of distinction even in a time prolific of renowned seamen. Though allied to the higher nobility, his advancement had not been altogether owing to influences connected with that circumstance. He had seen much service, been in various engagements, always acquitting himself as an officer mindful of the welfare of his men, but never tolerating an infraction of discipline; thoroughly versed in the science of his profession, and intrepid to the verge of temerity, though never injudiciously so. For his gallantry in the West Indian waters as flag-lieutenant under Rodney in that Admiral's crowning victory over De Grasse, he was made a post-captain.

Ashore in the garb of a civilian scarce any one would have taken him for a sailor, more especially that he never garnished unprofessional talk with nautical terms, and grave in his bearing, evinced little appreciation of mere humor. It was not out of keeping with these traits that on a passage when nothing demanded his paramount action, he was the most undemonstrative of men. Any landsman observing this gentleman not conspicuous by his stature and wearing no pronounced insignia, emerging from his cabin retreat to the open deck and noting the silent deference of the officers retiring to leeward, might have taken him for the King's guest, a civilian aboard the King's ship, some highly honorable discreet envoy on his way to an important post. But in fact this unobtrusiveness of demeanor may have proceeded from a certain unaffected modesty of manhood sometimes accompanying a resolute nature, a modesty evinced at all times not calling for pronounced action, and which shown in any rank of life suggests a virtue aristocratic in kind.

As with some others engaged in various departments of the world's more heroic activities, Captain Vere though practical enough upon occasion would at times betray a certain dreaminess of mood. Standing alone on the weather-side of the quarter-deck, one hand holding by the rigging he would absently gaze off at the blank sea. At the presentation to him then of some minor matter interrupting the current of his thoughts he would show more or less irascibility; but instantly he would control it.

In the navy he was popularly known by the appellation Starry Vere. How such a designation happened to fall upon one who whatever his sterling qualities was without brilliant ones was in this wise: a favorite kinsman, Lord Denton, a freehearted fellow, had been the first to meet and congratulate him upon his return to England from the West Indian cruise; and but the day previous turning over a copy of Andrew Marvell's poems had lighted, not for the first time however, upon the lines entitled *Appleton House*, the name of one of the seats of their common ancestor, a hero in the German wars of the seventeenth century, in which poem occur the lines,

> "This 'tis to have been from the first
> In a domestic heaven nursed,
> Under the discipline severe
> Of Fairfax and the starry Vere."

And so, upon embracing his cousin fresh from Rodney's victory wherein he had played so gallant a part, brimming over with just family pride in the sailor of their house, he exuberantly exclaimed, "Give ye joy, Ed; give ye joy, my starry Vere!" This got currency, and the novel prefix serving in familiar parlance readily to distinguish the *Indomitable's* Captain from another Vere his senior, a distant relative an officer of like rank in the navy, it remained permanently attached to the surname.

VII

In view of the part that the commander of the *Indomitable* plays in scenes shortly to follow, it may be well to fill out that sketch of him outlined in the previous chapter. Aside from his qualities as a sea-officer Captain Vere was an exceptional character. Unlike no few of England's renowned sailors, long and arduous service with signal devotion to it, had not resulted in absorbing and *salting* the entire man. He had a marked leaning towards everything intellectual. He loved books, never going to sea without a newly replenished library, compact but of the best. The isolated leisure, in some cases so wearisome, falling at intervals to commanders even during a war-cruise, never was tedious to Captain Vere. With nothing of that literary taste which less heeds the thing conveyed than the vehicle, his bias was towards those books to which every serious mind of superior order occupying any active post of authority in the world, naturally inclines: books treating of actual men and events no matter of what era— history, biography and unconventional writers, who, free from cant and convention, like Montaigne, honestly, and in the spirit of common sense philosophize upon realities.

In this love of reading he found confirmation of his own more reserved thoughts—confirmation which he had vainly sought in social converse, so that as touching most fundamental topics, there had got to be established in him some positive convictions which he forefelt would abide in him essentially unmodified so long as his intelligent part remained unimpaired. In view of the troubled period in which his lot was cast this was well for him. His settled convictions were as a dyke against those invading waters of novel opinion social political and otherwise, which carried away as in a torrent no few minds in those days, minds by nature not inferior to his own. While other members of that aristocracy to which by birth he belonged were incensed at the innovators mainly because their theories were inimical to the privileged classes, not alone Captain Vere disinterestedly opposed them because they seemed to him incapable of embodiment in lasting institutions, but at war with the peace of the world and the true welfare of mankind.

With minds less stored than his and less earnest, some officers of his rank, with whom at times he would necessarily consort, found him lacking in the companionable quality, a dry and bookish gentleman as they deemed. Upon any chance withdrawal from their company one would be apt to say to another something like this: "Vere is a noble fellow, Starry Vere. 'Spite the gazettes, Sir Horatio" meaning him with the Lord title "is at bottom scarce a better seaman or fighter. But between you and me now don't you think there is a queer streak of the pedantic running through him? Yes, like the King's yarn in a coil of navy-rope?"

Some apparent ground there was for this sort of confidential criticism; since not only did the Captain's discourse never fall into the jocosely familiar, but in illustrating any point touching the stirring personages and events of the time he would be as apt to cite some historic character or incident of antiquity as he would to cite from the moderns. He seemed unmindful of the circumstance that to his bluff company such remote allusions however pertinent they might really be were altogether alien to men whose reading was mainly confined to the journals. But considerateness in such matters is not easy to natures constituted like Captain Vere's. Their honesty prescribes to them directness, sometimes far-reaching like that of a migratory fowl that in its flight never heeds when it crosses a frontier.

VIII

The lieutenants and other commissioned gentlemen forming Captain Vere's staff it is not necessary here to particularize nor needs it to make any mention of any of the warrant-officers. But among the petty officers was one who having much to do with the story, may as well be forthwith introduced. This portrait I essay, but shall never hit it. This was John Claggart, the master-at-arms. But that sea-title may to landsmen seem somewhat equivocal. Originally doubtless that petty-officer's function was the instruction of the men in the use of arms, sword or cutlass. But very long ago, owing to the advance in gunnery making hand-to-hand encounters less frequent and giving to niter and sulfur the preeminence over steel, that function ceased; the master-at-arms of a great warship becoming a sort of chief of police charged among other matters with the duty of preserving order on the populous lower gun-decks.

Claggart was a man of about five-and-thirty, somewhat spare and tall, yet of no ill figure upon the whole. His hand was too small and shapely to have been accustomed to hard toil. The face was a notable one; the features all except the chin cleanly cut as those on a Greek medallion; yet the chin, beardless as Tecumseh's, had something of the strange protuberant heaviness in its make that recalled the prints of the Rev. Dr. Titus Oates, the historic deponent with the clerical drawl in the time of Charles II and the fraud of the alleged Popish Plot. It served Claggart in his office that his eye could cast a tutoring glance. His brow was of the sort phrenologically associated with more than average intellect; silken jet curls partly clustering over it, making a foil to the pallor below, a pallor tinged with a faint shade of amber akin to the hue of time-tinted marbles of old. This complexion, singularly contrasting with the red or deeply bronzed visages of the sailors, and in part the result of his official seclusion from the sunlight, though it was not exactly displeasing, nevertheless seemed to hint of something defective or abnormal in the constitution and blood. But his general aspect and manner were so suggestive of an education and career incongruous with his naval function that when not actively engaged in it he looked like a man of high quality, social and moral, who for reasons of his own was keeping *incog.* Nothing was known of his former life. It might be that he was an Englishman; and yet there lurked a bit of accent in his speech suggesting that possibly he was not such by birth, but through naturalization in early childhood. Among certain grizzled sea-gossips of the gun-decks and forecastle went a rumor perdue that the master-at-arms was a *chevalier* who had volunteered into the King's navy by way of compounding for some mysterious swindle whereof he had been arraigned at the King's Bench. The fact that nobody could substantiate this report was, of course, nothing against its secret currency. Such a rumor once started on the gun-decks in reference to almost anyone below the rank of a commissioned officer would, during the period assigned to this narrative, have seemed not altogether wanting in credibility to the tarry old wiseacres of a man-of-war crew. And indeed a man of Claggart's accomplishments, without prior nautical experience entering the navy at mature life, as he did, and necessarily allotted at the start to the lowest grade in it; a man too who never made allusion to his previous life ashore; these were circumstances which in the dearth of exact knowledge as to his true antecedents opened to the invidious a vague field for unfavorable surmise.

But the sailors' dog-watch gossip concerning him derived a vague plausibility from the fact that now for some period the British Navy could so little afford to be squeamish in the matter of keeping up the muster-rolls, that not only were pressgangs notoriously abroad both afloat and ashore, but there was little or no secret about another matter, namely that the London police were at liberty to capture any able-bodied suspect, any questionable fellow at large and summarily ship him to the dock-yard or fleet. Furthermore, even among voluntary enlistments there were instances where the motive thereto partook neither of patriotic impulse nor yet of a random desire to experience a bit of sea-life and martial adventure. Insolvent debtors of minor grade, together with the promiscuous lame ducks of morality, found in the navy a convenient and secure refuge. Secure, because once enlisted aboard a King's-Ship, they were as much in sanctuary as the transgressor of the middle ages harboring himself under the shadow of the altar. Such sanctioned irregularities which for obvious reasons the Government would hardly think to parade at the time and which consequently, and as affecting the least influential class of mankind, have all but dropped into oblivion lend color to something for the truth whereof I do not vouch, and hence have some scruple in stating; something I remember having seen in print, though the book I cannot recall; but the same thing was personally communicated to me now more than forty years ago by an old pensioner in a cocked hat with whom I had a most interesting talk on the terrace at Greenwich, a Baltimore Negro, a Trafalgar man. It was to this effect: In the case of a warship short of hands whose speedy sailing was imperative, the deficient quota in lack of any other way of making it good, would be eked out by drafts called direct from the jails. For reasons previously suggested it would not perhaps be very easy at the present day directly to prove or disprove the allegation. But allowed as a verity, how significant would it be of England's straits at the time confronted by those wars which like a flight of harpies rose shrieking from the din and dust of the fallen Bastille. That era appears measurably clear to us who look back at it, and but read of it. But to the grandfathers of us gray-beards, the more thoughtful of them, the genius of it presented an aspect like that of Camoëns' Spirit of the Cape, an eclipsing menace mysterious and prodigious. Not America was exempt from apprehension. At the height of Napoleon's unexampled conquests, there were Americans who had fought at Bunker Hill who looked forward to the possibility that the Atlantic might prove no barrier against the ultimate schemes of this French portentous upstart from the revolutionary chaos who seemed in act of fulfilling judgment prefigured in the Apocalypse.

But the less credence was to be given to the gun-deck talk touching Claggart, seeing that no man holding his office in a man-of-war can ever hope to be popular with the crew. Besides, in derogatory comments upon anyone against whom they have a grudge, or for any reason or no reason mislike, sailors are much like landsmen, they are apt to exaggerate or romance it.

About as much was really known to the *Indomitable*'s tars of the master-at-arms' career before entering the service as an astronomer knows about a comet's travels prior to its first observable appearance in the sky. The verdict of the sea quidnunc's has been cited only by way of showing what sort of moral impression the man made upon rude uncultivated natures whose conceptions of human wickedness were necessarily of the narrowest, limited to ideas of vulgar rascality,— a thief among the swinging hammocks during a night-watch, or the man-brokers and land-sharks of the sea-ports.

It was no gossip, however, but fact, that though, as before hinted, Claggart upon his entrance into the navy was, as a novice, assigned to the least honorable section of a man-of-war's crew, embracing the drudgery, he did not long remain there.

The superior capacity he immediately evinced, his constitutional sobriety, ingratiating deference to superiors, together with a peculiar ferreting genius manifested on a singular occasion, all this capped by a certain austere patriotism abruptly advanced him to the position of master-at-arms.

Of this maritime chief of police the ship's corporals, so called, were the immediate subordinates, and compliant ones; and this, as is to be noted in some business departments ashore, almost to a degree inconsistent with entire moral volition. His place put various converging wires of underground influence under the chief's control, capable when astutely worked through his under-strappers of operating to the mysterious discomfort if nothing worse, of any of the sea-commonalty.

IX

Life in the foretop well agreed with Billy Budd. There, when not actually engaged on the yards yet higher aloft, the topmen, who as such had been picked out for youth and activity, constituted an aerial club lounging at ease against the smaller stunsails rolled up into cushions, spinning yarns like the lazy gods, and frequently amused with what was going on in the busy world of the decks below. No wonder then that a young fellow of Billy's disposition was well content in such society. Giving no cause of offense to anybody, he was always alert at a call. So in the merchant service it had been with him. But now such punctiliousness in duty was shown that his topmates would sometimes good-naturedly laugh at him for it. This heightened alacrity had its cause, namely, the impression made upon him by the first formal gangway-punishment he had ever witnessed, which befell the day following his impressment. It had been incurred by a little fellow, young, a novice, an afterguardsman absent from his assigned post when the ship was being put about; a dereliction resulting in a rather serious hitch to that maneuver, one demanding instantaneous promptitude in letting go and making fast. When Billy saw the culprit's naked back under the scourge gridironed with red welts, and worse; when he marked the dire expression in the liberated man's face as with his woolen shirt flung over him by the executioner he rushed forward from the spot to bury himself in the crowd, Billy was horrified. He resolved that never through remissness would he make himself liable to such a visitation or do or omit aught that might merit even verbal reproof. What then was his surprise and concern when ultimately he found himself getting into petty trouble occasionally about such matters as the stowage of his bag or something amiss in his hammock, matters under the police oversight of the ship's corporals of the lower decks, and which brought down on him a vague threat from one of them.

So heedful in all things as he was, how could this be? He could not understand it, and it more than vexed him. When he spoke to his young topmates about it, they were either lightly incredulous, or found something comical in his unconcealed anxiety. "Is it your bag, Billy?" said one. "Well, sew yourself up in it, bully boy, and then you'll be sure to know if anybody meddles with it."

Now there was a veteran aboard who because his years began to disqualify him for more active work had been recently assigned duty as mainmast-man in his watch, looking to the gear belayed at the rail round about that great spar near the deck. At off-times the foretopman had picked up some acquaintance with him, and now in his trouble it occurred to him that he might be the sort of person to go to for wise counsel. He was an old Dansker long anglicized in the service, of few words, many wrinkles and some honorable scars. His wizened face, time-tinted and weather-stained to the complexion of an antique parchment, was here and there peppered blue by the chance explosion of a gun-cartridge in action. He was an *Agamemnon*-man; some two years prior to the time of this story having served under Nelson, when but Sir Horatio, in that ship immortal in naval memory, and which dismantled and in part broken up to her bare ribs is seen a grand skeleton in Haydon's etching. As one of a boarding-party from the *Agamemnon* he had received a cut slantwise along one temple and cheek, leaving a long pale scar like a streak of dawn's light falling athwart the dark visage. It was on account of that scar and the affair in which it was known that he had received it, as well as from his blue-peppered complexion that the Dansker went among the *Indomitable*'s crew by the name of "Board-her-in-the-smoke."

Now the first time that his small weazel-eyes happened to light on Billy Budd, a certain grim internal merriment set all his ancient wrinkles into antic play. Was it that his eccentric unsentimental old sapience primitive in its kind saw or thought it saw something which in contrast with the warship's environment looked oddly incongruous in the handsome sailor? But after shyly studying him at intervals, the old Merlin's equivocal merriment was modified; for now when the twain would meet, it would start in his face a quizzing sort of look, but it would be but momentary and sometimes replaced by an expression of speculative query as to what might eventually befall a nature like that, dropped into a world not without some man-traps and against whose subtleties simple courage lacking experience and address and without any touch of defensive ugliness, is of little avail; and where such innocence as man is capable of does yet in a moral emergency not always sharpen the faculties or enlighten the will.

However it was the Dansker in his ascetic way rather took to Billy. Nor was this only because of a certain philosophic interest in such a character. There was another cause. While the old man's eccentricities, sometimes bordering on the ursine, repelled the juniors, Billy, undeterred thereby, revering him as a salt hero would make advances, never passing the old *Agamemnon*-man without a salutation marked by that respect which is seldom lost on the aged however crabbed at times or whatever their station in life. There was a vein of dry humor, or what not, in the mastman; and, whether in freak of patriarchal irony touching Billy's youth and athletic frame, or for some other and more recondite reason, from the first in addressing him he always substituted Baby for Billy. The Dansker in fact being the originator of the name by which the foretopman eventually became known aboard ship.

Well then, in his mysterious little difficulty going in quest of the wrinkled one, Billy found him off duty in a dog-watch ruminating by himself seated on a shot-box of the upper gun-deck now and then surveying with a somewhat cynical regard certain of the more swaggering promenaders there. Billy recounted his trouble, again wondering how it all happened. The salt seer attentively listened, accompanying the foretopman's recital with queer twitching of his wrinkles and problematical little sparkles of his small ferret eyes. Making an end of his story, the foretopman asked, "And now, Dansker, do tell me what you think of it."

The old man, shoving up the front of his tarpaulin and deliberately rubbing the long slant scar at the point where it entered the thin hair, laconically said, "Baby Budd, *Jemmy Legs*" (meaning the master-at-arms) "is down on you."

"*Jemmy Legs!*" ejaculated Billy, his welkin eyes expanding; "what for? Why he calls me *the sweet and pleasant young fellow*, they tell me."

"Does he so?" grinned the grizzled one, then said, "ay Baby Lad, a sweet voice has *Jemmy Legs*."

"No, not always. But to me he has. I seldom pass him but there comes a pleasant word."

"And that's because he's down upon you, Baby Budd."

Such reiteration along with the manner of it, incomprehensible to a novice, disturbed Billy almost as much as the mystery for which he had sought explanation. Something less unpleasingly oracular he tried to extract; but the old sea-Chiron, thinking perhaps that for the nonce he had sufficiently instructed his young Achilles, pursed his lips, gathered his wrinkles together, and would commit himself to nothing further.

Years, and those experiences which befall certain shrewder men subordinated life-long to the will of superiors, all this had developed in the Dansker the pithy guarded cynicism that was his leading characteristic.

X

The next day an incident served to confirm Billy Budd in his incredulity as to the Dansker's strange summing up of the case submitted.

The ship at noon going large before the wind was rolling on her course, and he below at dinner and engaged in some sportful talk with the members of his mess, chanced in a sudden lurch to spill the entire contents of his soup-pan upon the new scrubbed deck. Claggart, the master-at-arms, official rattan in hand, happened to be passing along the battery in a bay of which the mess was lodged, and the greasy liquid streamed just across his path. Stepping over it, he was proceeding on his way without comment, since the matter was nothing to take notice of under the circumstances, when he happened to observe who it was that had done the spilling. His countenance changed. Pausing, he was about to ejaculate something hasty at the sailor, but checked himself, and pointing down to the streaming soup, playfully tapped him from behind with his rattan, saying in a low musical voice peculiar to him at times, "Handsomely done, my lad! And handsome is as handsome did it too!" and with that passed on. Not noted by Billy as not coming within his view was the involuntary smile, or rather grimace, that accompanied Claggart's equivocal words. Aridly it drew down the thin corners of his shapely mouth. But everybody taking his remark as meant for humorous, and at which therefore as coming from a superior they were bound to laugh, "with counterfeited glee" acted accordingly; and Billy tickled, it may be, by the allusion to his being the handsome sailor, merrily joined in; then addressing his messmates exclaimed "There now, who says that *Jemmy Legs* is down on me!"

"And who said he was, Beauty?" demanded one Donald with some surprise. Whereat the foretopman looked a little foolish recalling that it was only one person, Board-her-in-the-smoke, who had suggested what to him was the smoky idea that this master-at-arms was in any peculiar way hostile to him. Meantime that functionary resuming his path must have momentarily worn some expression less guarded than that of the bitter smile and, usurping the face from the heart, some distorting expression perhaps for a drummer-boy, heedlessly frolicking along from the opposite direction, and chancing to come into light collision with his person was strangely disconcerted by his aspect. Nor was the impression lessened when the official, impulsively giving him a sharp cut with the rattan, vehemently exclaimed, "Look where you go!"

XI

What was the matter with the master-at-arms? And, be the matter what it might, how could it have direct relation to Billy Budd with whom prior to the affair of the spilled soup he had never come into any special contact official or otherwise? What indeed could the trouble have to do with one so little inclined to give offense as the merchantship's *peacemaker*, even him who in Claggart's own phrase was "the sweet and pleasant young fellow"? Yes, why should *Jemmy Legs*, to borrow the Dansker's expression, be *down* on the Handsome Sailor?

But at heart and not for nothing, as the late chance encounter may indicate to the discerning, down on him, secretly down on him, he assuredly was.

Now to invent something touching the more private career of Claggart, something involving Billy Budd, of which something the latter should be wholly ignorant, some romantic incident implying that Claggart's knowledge of the young blue-jacket began at some period anterior to catching sight of him on board the seventy-four—all this, not so difficult to do, might avail in a way more or less interesting to account for whatever enigma may appear to lurk in the case. But in fact there was nothing of the sort. And yet the cause, necessarily to be assumed as the sole one assignable, is in its very realism as much charged with that prime element of Radcliffian romance, *the mysterious,* as any that the ingenuity of the author of *The Mysteries of Udolpho* could devise. For what can more partake of the mysterious than an antipathy spontaneous and profound such as is evoked in certain exceptional mortals by the mere aspect of some other mortal, however harmless he may be? if not called forth by this very harmlessness itself.

Now there can exist no irritating juxtaposition of dissimilar personalities comparable to that which is possible aboard a great warship fully manned and at sea. There, every day among all ranks almost every man comes into more or less of contact with almost every other man. Wholly there to avoid even the sight of an aggravating object one must needs give it Jonah's toss or jump overboard himself. Imagine how all this might eventually operate on some peculiar human creature the direct reverse of a saint?

But for the adequate comprehending of Claggart by a normal nature, these hints are insufficient. To pass from a normal nature to him one must cross "the deadly space between." And this is best done by indirection.

Long ago an honest scholar, my senior, said to me in reference to one who like himself is now no more, a man so unimpeachably respectable that against him nothing was ever openly said though among the few something was whispered, "Yes, X—— is a nut not to be cracked by the tap of a lady's fan. You are aware that I am the adherent of no organized religion much less of any philosophy built into a system. Well, for all that, I think that to try and get into X——, enter his labyrinth and get out again, without a clue derived from some source other than what is known as *knowledge of the world* —that were hardly possible, at least for me."

"Why," said I, "X—— however singular a study to some, is yet human, and knowledge of the world assuredly implies the knowledge of human nature, and in most of its varieties."

"Yes, but a superficial knowledge of it, serving ordinary purposes. But for anything deeper, I am not certain whether to know the world and to know human nature be not two distinct branches of knowledge, which while they may coexist in the same heart, yet either may exist with little or nothing of the other. Nay, in an average man of the world, his constant rubbing with it blunts that fine spiritual insight indispensable to the understanding of the essential in certain exceptional characters, whether evil ones or good. In a matter of some importance I have seen a girl wind an old lawyer about her little finger. Nor was it the dotage of senile love. Nothing of the sort. But he knew law better than he knew the girl's heart. Coke and Blackstone hardly shed so much light into obscure spiritual places as the Hebrew prophets. And who were they? Mostly recluses."

At the time my inexperience was such that I did not quite see the drift of all this. It may be that I see it now. And, indeed, if that lexicon which is based on Holy Writ were any longer popular, one might with less difficulty define and denominate certain phenomenal men. As it is, one must turn to some authority not liable to the charge of being tinctured with biblical element.

In a list of definitions included in the authentic translation of Plato, a list attributed to him, occurs this: "Natural Depravity: a depravity according to nature." A definition which though savoring of Calvinism, by no means involves Calvin's dogma as to total mankind. Evidently its intent makes it applicable but to individuals. Not many are the examples of this depravity which the gallows and jail supply. At any rate for notable instances, since these have no vulgar alloy of the brute in them, but invariably are dominated by intellectuality, one must go elsewhere. Civilization, especially if of the austerer sort, is auspicious to it. It folds itself in the mantle of respectability. It has its certain negative virtues serving as silent auxiliaries. It never allows wine to get within its guard. It is not going too far to say that it is without vices or small sins. There is a phenomenal pride in it that excludes them from anything mercenary or avaricious. In short the depravity here meant partakes nothing of the sordid or sensual. It is serious, but free from acerbity. Though no flatterer of mankind it never speaks ill of it.

But the thing which in eminent instances signalizes so exceptional a nature is this: though the man's even temper and discreet bearing would seem to intimate a mind peculiarly subject to the law of reason, not the less in his heart he would seem to riot in complete exemption from that law having apparently little to do with reason further than to employ it as an ambidexter implement for effecting the irrational. That is to say: toward the accomplishment of an aim which in wantonness of malignity would seem to partake of the insane, he will direct a cool judgment sagacious and sound.

These men are true madmen, and of the most dangerous sort, for their lunacy is not continuous but occasional evoked by some special object; it is probably secretive which is as much to say it is self-contained, so that when moreover, most active it is to the average mind not distinguishable from sanity, and for the reason above suggested that whatever its aims may be, and the aim is never declared, the method and the outward proceeding are always perfectly rational.

Now something such was Claggart, in whom was the mania of an evil nature, not engendered by vicious training or corrupting books or licentious living, but born with him and innate, in short "a depravity according to nature."

XII

Lawyers, Experts, Clergy
An Episode

By the way, can it be the phenomenon, disowned or at least concealed, that in some criminal cases puzzles the courts? For this cause have our juries at times not only to endure the prolonged contentions of lawyers with their fees, but also the yet more perplexing strife of the medical experts with theirs? But why leave it to them? Why not subpoena as well the clerical proficients? Their vocation bringing them into peculiar contact with so many human beings, and sometimes in their least guarded hour, in interviews very much more confidential than those of physician and patient; this would seem to qualify them to know something about those intricacies involved in the question of moral responsibility; whether in a given case, say, the crime proceeded from mania in the brain or rabies of the heart. As to any differences among themselves these clerical proficients might develop on the stand, these could hardly be greater than the direct contradictions exchanged between the remunerated medical experts.

Dark sayings are these, some will say. But why? Is it because they somewhat savor of Holy Writ in its phrase "mysteries of iniquity"? If they do, such savor was foreign from my intention, for little will it commend these pages to many a reader of today.

The point of the present story turning on the hidden nature of the master-at-arms has necessitated this chapter. With an added hint or two in connection with the incident at the mess, the resumed narrative must be left to vindicate as it may, its own credibility.

XIII

Pale ire, envy and despair

That Claggart's figure was not amiss, and his face, save the chin, well molded, has already been said. Of these favorable points he seemed not insensible, for he was not only neat but careful in his dress. But the form of Billy Budd was heroic; and if his face was without the intellectual look of the pallid Claggart's, not the less was it lit, like his, from within, though from a different source. The bonfire in his heart made luminous the rose-tan in his cheek.

In view of the marked contrast between the persons of the twain, it is more than probable that when the master-at-arms in the scene last given applied to the sailor the proverb *Handsome is as handsome does;* he there let escape an ironic inkling, not caught by the young sailors who heard it, as to what it was that had first moved him against Billy, namely, his significant personal beauty.

Now envy and antipathy passions irreconcilable in reason, nevertheless in fact may spring conjoined like Chang and Eng in one birth. Is Envy then such a monster? Well, though many an arraigned mortal has in hopes of mitigated penalty pleaded guilty to horrible actions, did ever anybody seriously confess to envy? Something there is in it universally felt to be more shameful than even felonious crime. And not only does everybody disown it but the better sort are inclined to incredulity when it is in earnest imputed to an intelligent man. But since its lodgment is in the heart not the brain, no degree of intellect supplies a guarantee against it. But Claggart's was no vulgar form of the passion. Nor, as directed toward Billy Budd, did it partake of that streak of apprehensive jealousy which marred Saul's visage perturbedly brooding on the comely young David. Claggart's envy struck deeper. If askance he eyed the good looks, cherry health and frank enjoyment of young life in Billy Budd, it was because these went along with a nature that as Claggart magnetically felt, had in its simplicity never willed malice or experienced the reactionary bite of that serpent. To him, the spirit lodged within Billy, and looking out from his welkin eyes as from windows, that ineffability it was which made the dimple in his dyed cheek, suppled his joints, and dancing in his yellow curls made him preeminently the Handsome Sailor. One person who excepted the master-at-arms was perhaps the only man in the ship intellectually capable of adequately appreciating the moral phenomenon presented in Billy Budd. And the insight but intensified his passion, which assuming various secret forms within him, at times assumed that of cynic disdain—disdain of innocence—to be nothing more than innocent! Yet in an aesthetic way he saw the charm of it, the courageous free-and-easy temper of it, and fain would have shared it, but he despaired of it.

With no power to annul the elemental evil in him, though readily enough he could hide it; apprehending the good, but powerless to be it; a nature like Claggart's surcharged with energy as such natures almost invariably are, what recourse is left to it but to recoil upon itself and, like the scorpion for which the Creator alone is responsible, act out to the end the part alloted it.

XIV

Passion, and passion in its profoundest, is not a thing demanding a palatial stage whereon to play its part. Down among the groundlings, among the beggars and rakers of the garbage, profound passion is enacted. And the circumstances that provoke it, however trivial or mean, are no measure of its power. In the present instance the stage is a scrubbed gun-deck, and one of the external provocations a man-of-war's man's spilled soup.

Now when the master-at-arms noticed whence came that greasy fluid streaming before his feet, he must have taken it—to some extent willfully, perhaps not for the mere accident it assuredly was, but for the sly escape of a spontaneous feeling on Billy's part more or less answering to the antipathy on his own. In effect a foolish demonstration he must have thought, and very harmless, like the futile kick of a heifer, which yet were the heifer a shod stallion would not be so harmless. Even so was it that into the gall of Claggart's envy he infused the vitriol of his contempt. But the incident confirmed to him certain tell-tale reports purveyed to his ear by *Squeak*, one of his more cunning corporals, a grizzled little man, so nicknamed by the sailors on account of his squeaky voice, and sharp visage ferreting about the dark corners of the lower decks after interlopers, satirically suggesting to them the idea of a rat in a cellar.

From his chief's employing him as an implicit tool in laying little traps for the worriment of the foretopman—for it was from the master-at-arms that the petty persecutions heretofore adverted to had proceeded—the corporal having naturally enough concluded that his master could have no love for the sailor, made it his business, faithful understrapper that he was, to foment the ill blood by perverting to his chief certain innocent frolics of the good-natured foretopman, besides inventing for his mouth sundry contumelious epithets he claimed to have overheard him let fall. The master-at-arms never suspected the veracity of these reports, more especially as to the epithets, for he well knew how secretly unpopular may become a master-at-arms at least a master-at-arms of those days zealous in his function, and how the blue-jackets shoot at him in private their raillery and wit; the nickname by which he goes among them (*Jemmy Legs*) implying under the form of merriment their cherished disrespect and dislike.

But in view of the greediness of hate for patrolmen, it hardly needed a purveyor to feed Claggart's passion. An uncommon prudence is habitual with the subtler depravity, for it has everything to hide. And in case of an injury but suspected its secretiveness voluntarily cuts it off from enlightenment or disillusion; and, not unreluctantly, action is taken upon surmise as upon certainty. And the retaliation is apt to be in monstrous disproportion to the supposed offense; for when in anybody was revenge in its exactions aught else but an inordinate usurer? But how with Claggart's conscience? For though consciences are unalike as foreheads, every intelligence, not excluding the scriptural devils who "believe and tremble," has one. But Claggart's conscience being but the lawyer to his will, made ogres of trifles, probably arguing that the motive imputed to Billy in spilling the soup just when he did, together with the epithets alleged, these, if nothing more, made a strong case against him; nay, justified animosity into a sort of retributive righteousness. The Pharisee is the Guy Fawkes prowling in the hid chambers underlying the Claggarts. And they can really form no conception of an unreciprocated malice. Probably, the master-at-arms' clandestine persecution of Billy was started to try the temper of the man; but it had not developed any quality in him that enmity could make official use of or even pervert into even plausible self-justification; so that the occurrence at the mess, petty if it were, was a welcome one to that peculiar conscience assigned to be the private mentor of Claggart; and for the rest, not improbably it put him upon new experiments.

XV

Not many days after the last incident narrated something befell Billy Budd that more graveled him than aught that had previously occurred.

It was a warm night for the latitude; and the foretopman, whose watch at the time was properly below, was dozing on the uppermost deck whither he had ascended from his hot hammock one of hundreds suspended so closely wedged together over a lower gun-deck that there was little or no swing to them. He lay as in the shadow of a hill-side stretched under the lee of the *booms,* a piled ridge of spare spars amidships between foremast and mainmast and among which the ship's largest boat, the launch, was stowed. Alongside of three other slumberers from below, he lay near that end of the booms which approached the foremast; his station aloft on duty as a foretopman being just over the deck station of the forecastlemen entitling him according to usage to make himself more or less at home in that neighborhood.

Presently he was stirred into semi-consciousness by somebody, who must have previously sounded the sleep of the others, touching his shoulder, and then as the foretopman raised his head, breathing into his ear in a quick whisper, "Slip into the lee forechains, Billy; there is something in the wind. Don't speak. Quick. I will meet you there;" and disappeared.

Now Billy like sundry other essentially good-natured ones had some of the weaknesses inseparable from essential good nature; and among these was a reluctance, almost an incapacity of plumply saying *no* to an abrupt proposition not obviously absurd, on the face of it, nor obviously unfriendly, nor iniquitous. And being of warm blood he had not the phlegm tacitly to negative any proposition by an unresponsive inaction. Like his sense of fear, his apprehension as to aught outside of the honest and natural was seldom very quick. Besides, upon the present occasion, the drowse from his sleep still hung upon him.

However it was, he mechanically rose and, sleepily wondering what could be in the wind, betook himself to the designated place, a narrow platform, one of six, outside of the high bulwarks and screened by the great dead-eyes and multiple columned lanyards of the shrouds and back-stays; and, in a great warship of that time, of dimensions commensurate to the hull's magnitude; a tarry balcony in short overhanging the sea, and so secluded that one mariner of the *Indomitable,* a nonconformist old tar of serious turn, made it even in daytime his private oratory.

In this retired nook the stranger soon joined Billy Budd. There was no moon yet; a haze obscured the starlight. He could not distinctly see the stranger's face. Yet from something in the outline and carriage, Billy took him to be, and correctly, one of the afterguard.

"Hist! Billy," said the man; in the same quick cautionary whisper as before, "you were impressed, weren't you? Well, so was I"; and he paused as to mark the effect. But Billy not knowing exactly what to make of this said nothing. Then the other: "we are not the only impressed ones, Billy. There's a gang of us.—Couldn't you—help—at a pinch?"

"What do you mean?" demanded Billy here shaking off his drowse.

"Hist, hist!" the hurried whisper now growing husky, "see here"; and the man held up two small objects faintly twinkling in the night light; "see, they are yours, Billy if you'll only—"

But Billy here broke in, and in his resentful eagerness to deliver himself his vocal infirmity somewhat intruded; "D-D-Damme, I don't know what you are d-driving at, or what you mean, but you had better g-g-go where you belong!" For the moment the fellow, as confounded, did not stir; and Billy, springing to his feet, said, "If you d-don't start, I'll t-t-toss you back over the r-rail!" There was no mistaking this and the mysterious emissary decamped, disappearing in the direction of the mainmast in the shadow of the booms.

"Hello, what's the matter here?" came growling from a forecastleman awakened from his deck-doze by Billy's raised voice. And as the foretopman reappeared and was recognized by him; "Ah, *Beauty,* is it you? Well, something must have been the matter for you st-st-stuttered."

"Oh," rejoined Billy, now mastering the impediment; "I found an afterguardsman in our part of the ship here and I bid him be off where he belongs."

"And is that all you did about it, foretopman?" gruffly demanded another, an irascible old fellow of brick-colored visage and hair, and who was known to his associate forecastlemen as *Red Pepper;* "such sneaks I should like to marry to the gunner's daughter!" by that expression meaning that he would like to subject them to disciplinary castigation over a gun.

However, Billy's rendering of the matter satisfactorily accounted to these inquirers for the brief commotion, since of all the sections of a ship's company the forecastlemen, veterans for the most part and bigoted in their sea-prejudices, are the most jealous in resenting territorial encroachments, especially on the part of any of the afterguard, of whom they have but a sorry opinion, chiefly landsmen, never going aloft except to reef or furl the mainsail, and in no wise competent to handle a marline-spike or turn in a *dead-eye,* say.

XVI

This incident sorely puzzled Billy Budd. It was an entirely new experience; the first time in his life that he had ever been personally approached in underhand intriguing fashion. Prior to this encounter he had known nothing of the afterguardsman, the two men being stationed wide apart, one forward and aloft during his watch, the other on deck and aft.

What could it mean? And could they really be guineas, those two glittering objects the interloper had held up to his (Billy's) eyes? Where could the fellow get guineas? Why even buttons, spare buttons, are not so plentiful at sea. The more he turned the matter over, the more he was nonplussed, and made uneasy and discomfited. In his disgustful recoil from an overture which though he but ill comprehended he instinctively knew must involve evil of some sort, Billy Budd was like a young horse fresh from the pasture suddenly inhaling a vile whiff of some chemical factory and by repeated snortings trying to get it out of his nostrils and lungs. This frame of mind barred all desire of holding further parley with the fellow, even were it but for the purpose of gaining some enlightenment as to his design in approaching him. And yet he was not without natural curiosity to see how such a visitor in the dark would look in broad day.

He espied him the following afternoon in his first dog-watch below one of the smokers on the forward part of the upper gundeck allotted to the pipe. He recognized him by his general cut and build, more than by his round freckled face and glassy eyes of pale blue, veiled with lashes all but white. And yet Billy was a bit uncertain whether indeed it were he—yonder chap about his own age, chatting and laughing in free-hearted way, leaning against a gun; a genial young fellow enough to look at, and something of a rattlebrain, to all appearance. Rather chubby too for a sailor even an afterguardsman. In short the last man in the world, one would think, to be overburdened with thoughts, especially those perilous thoughts that must needs belong to a conspirator in any serious project, or even to the underling of such a conspirator.

Although Billy was not aware of it, the fellow, with one sidelong watchful glance had perceived Billy first, and then noting that Billy was looking at him, thereupon nodded a familiar sort of friendly recognition as to an old acquaintance, without interrupting the talk he was engaged in with the group of smokers. A day or two afterwards chancing in the evening promenade on a gun-deck, to pass Billy, he offered a flying word of good-fellowship as it were, which by its unexpectedness, and equivocalness under the circumstances so embarrassed Billy that he knew not how to respond to it, and let it go unnoticed.

Billy was now left more at a loss than before. The ineffectual speculations into which he was led were so disturbingly alien to him that he did his best to smother them. It never entered his mind that here was a matter which from its extreme questionableness, it was his duty as a loyal blue-jacket to report in the proper quarter. And, probably, had such a step been suggested to him, he would have been deterred from taking it by the thought, one of novice-magnanimity, that it would savor overmuch of the dirty work of a tell-tale. He kept the thing to himself. Yet upon one occasion, he could not forbear a little disburdening himself to the old Dansker, tempted thereto perhaps by the influence of a balmy night when the ship lay becalmed; the twain, silent for the most part, sitting together on deck, their heads propped against the bulwarks. But it was only a partial and anonymous account that Billy gave, the unfounded scruples above referred to preventing full disclosure to anybody. Upon hearing Billy's version, the sage Dansker seemed to divine more than he was told; and after a little meditation during which his wrinkles were pursed as into a point, quite effacing for the time that quizzing expression his face sometimes wore,—"Didn't I say so, Baby Budd?"

"Say what?" demanded Billy.

"Why, *Jemmy Legs* is *down* on you."

"And what," rejoined Billy in amazement, "has *Jemmy Legs* to do with that cracked afterguardsman?"

"Ho, it was an afterguardsman, then. A cat's-paw, a cat's-paw!" And with that exclamation, which, whether it had reference to a light puff of air just then coming over the calm sea, or subtler relation to the afterguardsman, there is no telling, the old Merlin gave a twisting wrench with his black teeth at his plug of tobacco, vouchsafing no reply to Billy's impetuous question, though now repeated, for it was his wont to relapse into grim silence when interrogated in skeptical sort as to any of his sententious oracles, not always very clear ones, but rather partaking of that obscurity which invests most Delphic deliverances from any quarter.

XVII

Long experience had very likely brought this old man to that bitter prudence which never interferes in aught and never gives advice.

Yes, despite the Dansker's pithy insistence as to the master-at-arms being at the bottom of these strange experiences of Billy on board the *Indomitable*, the young sailor was ready to ascribe them to almost anybody but the man who, to use Billy's own expression, "always had a pleasant word for him." This is to be wondered at.

Yet not so much to be wondered at. In certain matters, some sailors even in mature life remain unsophisticated enough. But a young seafarer of the disposition of our athletic foretopman is much of a child-man. And yet a child's utter innocence is but its blank ignorance, and the innocence more or less wanes as intelligence waxes. But in Billy Budd intelligence such as it was, had advanced, while yet his simple-mindedness remained for the most part unaffected. Experience is a teacher indeed; yet did Billy's years make his experience small. Besides, he had none of that intuitive knowledge of the bad which in natures not good or incompletely so foreruns experience, and therefore may pertain, as in some instances it too clearly does pertain, even to youth.

And what could Billy know of man except of man as a mere sailor? And the old-fashioned sailor, the veritable man-before-the-mast, the sailor from boyhood up, he, though indeed of the same species as a landsman is in some respects singularly distinct from him. The sailor is frankness, the landsman is finesse. Life is not a game with the sailor, demanding the long head; no intricate game of chess where few moves are made in straightforwardness, and ends are attained by indirection; an oblique, tedious, barren game hardly worth that poor candle burnt out in playing it.

Yes, as a class, sailors are in character a juvenile race. Even their deviations are marked by juvenility. And this more especially holding true with the sailors of Billy's time. Then, too, certain things which apply to all sailors do more pointedly operate here and there, upon the junior one. Every sailor, too, is accustomed to obey orders without debating them; his life afloat is externally ruled for him; he is not brought into that promiscuous commerce with mankind where unobstructed free agency on equal terms—equal superficially, at least —soon teaches one that unless upon occasion he exercises a distrust keen in proportion to the fairness of the appearance, some foul turn may be served him. A ruled undemonstrative distrustfulness is so habitual, not with business-men so much, as with men who know their kind in less shallow relations than business, namely certain men-of-the-world, that they come at last to employ it all but unconsciously; and some of them would very likely feel real surprised at being charged with it as one of their general characteristics.

XVIII

But after the little matter at the mess Billy Budd no more found himself in strange trouble at times about his hammock or his clothes-bag or what not. While, as to that smile that occasionally sunned him, and the pleasant passing word, these were if not more frequent, yet if anything more pronounced than before.

But for all that, there were certain other demonstrations now. When Claggart's unobserved glance happened to light on belted Billy rolling along the upper gun-deck in the leisure of the second dog-watch exchanging passing broadsides of fun with other young promenaders in the crowd; that glance would follow the cheerful sea-Hyperion with a settled meditative and melancholy expression, his eyes strangely suffused with incipient feverish tears. Then would Claggart look like the man of sorrows. Yes, and sometimes the melancholy expression would have in it a touch of soft yearning, as if Claggart could even have loved Billy but for fate and ban. But this was an evanescence, and quickly repented of, as it were, by an immitigable look, pinching and shrivelling the visage into the momentary semblance of a wrinkled walnut. But sometimes catching sight in advance of the foretopman coming in his direction, he would, upon their nearing, step aside a little to let him pass, dwelling upon Billy for the moment with the glittering dental satire of a Guise. But upon any abrupt unforeseen encounter a red light would flash forth from his eye like a spark from an anvil in a dusk smithy. That quick fierce light was a strange one, darted from orbs which in repose were of a color nearest approaching a deeper violet, the softest of shades.

Though some of these caprices of the pit could not but be observed by their object, yet were they beyond the construing of such a nature. And the *thews* of Billy were hardly compatible with that sort of sensitive spiritual organization which in some cases instinctively conveys to ignorant innocence an admonition of the proximity of the malign. He thought the master-at-arms acted in a manner rather queer at times. That was all. But the occasional frank air and pleasant word went for what they purported to be, the young sailor never having heard as yet of the "too fair-spoken man."

Had the foretopman been conscious of having done or said anything to provoke the ill will of the official, it would have been different with him, and his sight might have been purged if not sharpened. As it was, innocence was his blinder.

So was it with him in yet another matter. Two minor officers—the armorer, and captain of the hold, with whom he had never exchanged a word, his position on the ship not bringing him into contact with them; these men now for the first began to cast upon Billy when they chanced to encounter him, that peculiar glance which evidences that the man from whom it comes has been some way tampered with and to the prejudice of him upon whom the glance lights. Never did it occur to Billy as a thing to be noted or a thing suspicious, though he well knew the fact that the armorer and captain of the hold, with the ship's yeoman, apothecary and others of that grade, were by naval usage, messmates of the master-at-arms, men with ears convenient to his confidential tongue.

But the general popularity that our Handsome Sailor's manly forwardness upon occasion, and irresistible good nature indicating no mental superiority tending to excite an invidious feeling; this good will on the part of most of his shipmates made him the less to concern himself about such mute aspects toward him as those whereto allusion has just been made as far as he could not so fathom as to infer their whole import.

As to the afterguardsman, though Billy for reasons already given necessarily saw little of him, yet when the two did happen to meet, invariably came the fellow's offhand cheerful recognition, sometimes accompanied by a passing pleasant word or two. Whatever that equivocal young person's original design may really have been, or the design of which he might have been the deputy, certain it was from his manner upon these occasions, that he had wholly dropped it.

It was as if his precocity of crookedness (and every vulgar villain is precocious) had for once deceived him, and the man he had sought to entrap as a simpleton had, through his very simplicity, ignominiously baffled him.

But shrewd ones may opine that it was hardly possible for Billy to refrain from going up to the afterguardsman and bluntly demanding to know his purpose in the initial interview, so abruptly closed in the fore-chains. Shrewd ones may also think it but natural in Billy to set about sounding some of the other impressed men of the ship in order to discover what basis, if any, there was for the emissary's obscure suggestions as to plotting disaffection aboard. Yes, the shrewd may so think. But something more, or rather, something else than mere shrewdness is perhaps needful for the due understanding of such a character as Billy Budd's.

As to Claggart, the monomania in the man—if that indeed it were—as involuntarily disclosed by starts in the manifestations detailed, yet in general covered over by his self-contained and rational demeanor; this, like a subterranean fire was eating its way deeper and deeper in him. Something decisive must come of it.

XIX

After the mysterious interview in the fore-chains, the one so abruptly ended there by Billy, nothing especially germane to the story occurred until the events now about to be narrated.

Elsewhere it has been said that owing to the lack of frigates (of course better sailers than line-of-battle ships) in the English squadron up the Straits at that period, the *Indomitable* was occasionally employed not only as an available substitute for a scout, but at times on detached service of more important kind. This was not alone because of her sailing qualities, not common in a ship of her rate, but quite as much, probably, that the character of her commander, it was thought, specially adapted him for any duty where under unforseen difficulties a prompt initiative might have to be taken in some matter demanding knowledge and ability in addition to those qualities implied in good seamanship. It was on an expedition of the latter sort, a somewhat distant one, and when the *Indomitable* was almost at her furthest remove from the fleet that in the latter part of an afternoon-watch she unexpectedly came in sight of a ship of the enemy. It proved to be a frigate. The latter, perceiving through the glass that the weight of men and metal would be heavily against her, invoking her light heels crowded sail to get away. After a chase urged almost against hope and lasting until about the middle of the first dog-watch, she signally succeeded in effecting her escape.

Not long after the pursuit had been given up, and ere the excitement incident thereto had altogether waned away, the master-at-arms ascending from his cavernous sphere made his appearance cap in hand by the mainmast respectfully awaiting the notice of Captain Vere then solitary walking the weather-side of the quarter-deck, doubtless somewhat chafed at the failure of the pursuit. The spot where Claggart stood was the place allotted to the men of lesser grades when seeking some more particular interview either with the officer-of-the-deck or the Captain himself. But from the latter it was not often that a sailor or petty-officer of those days would seek a hearing; only some exceptional cause, would, according to established custom, have warranted that.

Presently, just as the Commander absorbed in his reflections was on the point of turning aft in his promenade, he became sensible of Claggart's presence, and saw the doffed cap held in deferential expectancy. Here be it said that Captain Vere's personal knowledge of this petty-officer had only begun at the time of the ship's last sailing from home, Claggart then for the first, in transfer from a ship detained for repairs, supplying on board the *Indomitable* the place of a previous master-at-arms disabled and ashore.

No sooner did the Commander observe who it was that now so deferentially stood awaiting his notice, than a peculiar expression came over him. It was not unlike that which uncontrollably will flit across the countenance of one at unawares encountering a person who though known to him indeed has hardly been long enough known for thorough knowledge, but something in whose aspect nevertheless now for the first provokes a vaguely repellent distaste. But coming to a stand and resuming much of his wonted official manner, save that a sort of impatience lurked in the intonation of the opening word, he said, "Well? what is it, master-at-arms?"

With the air of a subordinate grieved at the necessity of being a messenger of ill tidings, and while conscientiously determined to be frank, yet equally resolved upon shunning overstatement, Claggart at this invitation or rather summons to disburden, spoke up. What he said, conveyed in the language of no uneducated man, was to the effect following if not altogether in these words, namely, that during the chase and preparations for the possible encounter he had seen enough to convince him that at least one sailor aboard was a dangerous character in a ship mustering some who not only had taken a guilty part in the late serious troubles, but others also who, like the man in question, had entered His Majesty's service under another form than enlistment.

At this point Captain Vere with some impatience, interrupted him:

"Be direct, man; say impressed men."

Claggart made a gesture of subservience and proceeded.

Quite lately whereof he (Claggart) had begun to suspect that on the gun-decks some sort of movement prompted by the sailor in question was covertly going on, but he had not thought himself warranted in reporting the suspicion so long as it remained indistinct. But from what he had that afternoon observed in the man referred to, the suspicion of something clandestine going on had advanced to a point less removed from certainty. He deeply felt, he added, the serious responsibility assumed in making a report involving such possible consequences to the individual mainly concerned, besides tending to augment those natural anxieties which every naval commander must feel in view of extraordinary outbreaks so recent as those which, he sorrowfully said it, it needed not to name.

Now at the first broaching of the matter Captain Vere taken by surprise, could not wholly dissemble his disquietude. But as Claggart went on, the former's aspect changed into restiveness under something in the witness's manner in giving his testimony. However, he refrained from interrupting him. And Claggart, continuing, concluded with this:

"God forbid, your honor, that the Indomitable's should be the experience of the—"

"Never mind that!" here preremptorily broke in the superior, his face altering with anger, instinctively divining the ship that the other was about to name, one in which the Nore Mutiny had assumed a singularly tragical character that for a time jeopardized the life of its commander. Under the circumstances he was indignant at the purposed allusion. When the commissioned officers themselves were on all occasions very heedful how they referred to the recent events, for a petty-officer unnecessarily to allude to them in the presence of his captain, this struck him as a most immodest presumption. Besides, to his quick sense of self-respect, it even looked under the circumstances something like an attempt to alarm him. Nor at first was he without some surprise that one who so far as he had hitherto come under his notice had shown considerable tact in his function should in this particular evince such lack of it.

But these thoughts and kindred dubious ones flitting across his mind were suddenly replaced by an intuitional surmise which though as yet obscure in form served practically to affect his reception of the ill tidings. Certain it is, that long versed in everything pertaining to the complicated gun-deck life, which like every other form of life has its secret mines and dubious side the side popularly disclaimed, Captain Vere did not permit himself to be unduly disturbed by the general tenor of his subordinate's report. Furthermore, if in view of recent events prompt action should be taken at the first palpable sign of recurring insubordination, for all that, not judicious would it be, he thought, to keep the idea of lingering disaffection alive by undue forwardness in crediting an informer even if his own subordinate and charged among other things with police surveillance of the crew. This feeling would not perhaps have so prevailed with him were it not that upon a prior occasion the patriotic zeal officially evinced by Claggart had somewhat irritated him as appearing rather supersensible and strained. Furthermore something even in the official's self-possessed and somewhat ostentatious manner in making his specifications strangely reminded him of a bandsman, a perjurous witness in a capital case before a court-martial ashore of which when a lieutenant he, Captain Vere, had been a member.

Now the preemptory check given to Claggart in the matter of the arrested allusion was quickly followed up by this: "You say that there is at least one dangerous man aboard. Name him."

"William Budd. A foretopman, your honor—"

"William Budd," repeated Captain Vere with unfeigned astonishment; "and mean you the man that Lieutenant Ratcliffe took from the merchantman not very long ago—the young fellow who seems to be so popular with the men—Billy, the Handsome Sailor, as they call him?"

"The same, your honor; but for all his youth and good looks, a deep one. Not for nothing does he insinuate himself into the good will of his shipmates, since at the least all hands will at a pinch say a good word for him at all hazards. Did Lieutenant Ratcliffe happen to tell your honor of that adroit fling of Budd's jumping up in the cutter's bow under the merchant-man's stern when he was being taken off? It is even masked by that sort of good-humored air that at heart he resents his impressment. You have but noted his fair cheek. A man-trap may be under his ruddy-tipped daisies."

Now the Handsome Sailor, as a signal figure among the crew, had naturally enough attracted the Captain's attention from the first. Though in general not very demonstrative to his officers, he had congratulated Lieutenant Ratcliffe upon his good fortune in lighting on such a fine specimen of the genus *Homo* who in the nude might have posed for a statue of young Adam before the fall.

As to Billy's adieu to the ship *Rights-of-Man*, which the boarding lieutenant had indeed reported to him, but in a deferential way more as a good story than aught else, Captain Vere, though mistakenly understanding it as a satiric sally, had but thought so much the better of the impressed man for it; as a military sailor, admiring the spirit that could take an arbitrary enlistment so merrily and sensibly. The foretopman's conduct, too, so far as it had fallen under the Captain's notice had confirmed the first happy augury, while the new recruit's qualities as a *sailor-man* seemed to be such that he had thought of recommending him to the executive officer for promotion to a place that would more frequently bring him under his own observation, namely, the captaincy of the mizzentop, replacing there in the starboard-watch a man not so young whom partly for that reason he deemed less fitted for the post. Be it parenthesized here that since the mizzentopmen have not to handle such breadths of heavy canvas as the lower sails on the mainmast and foremast, a young man if of the right stuff not only seems best adapted to duty there, but in fact is generally selected for the captaincy of that top, and the company under him are light hands and often but striplings. In sum, Captain Vere had from the beginning deemed Billy Budd to be what in the naval parlance of the time was called a *"King's bargain,"* that is to say, for His Britannic Majesty's navy a capital investment at small outlay or none at all.

After a brief pause during which the reminiscences above mentioned passed vividly through his mind, he weighed the import of Claggart's last suggestion, conveyed in the phrase "pitfall under the clover," and the more he weighed it the less reliance he felt in the informer's good faith. Suddenly he turned upon him and in a low voice: "Do you come to me, master-at-arms, with so foggy a tale?

As to Budd, cite me an act or spoken word of his confirmatory of what you in general charge against him. Stay," drawing nearer to him, "heed what you speak. Just now and in a case like this, there is a yard-arm-end for the false witness."

"Ah, your honor!" sighed Claggart mildly shaking his shapely head as in sad deprecation of such unmerited severity of tone. Then, bridling—erecting himself as in virtuous self-assertion, he circumstantially alleged certain words and acts, which collectively if credited, led to presumptions mortally inculpating Budd. And for some of these averments, he added, substantiating proof was not far.

With gray eyes impatient and distrustful essaying to fathom to the bottom Claggart's calm violet ones, Captain Vere again heard him out; then for the moment stood ruminating. The mood he evinced, Claggart—himself for the time liberated from the other's scrutiny—steadily regarded with a look difficult to render,—a look curious of the operation of his tactics, a look such as might have been that of the spokesman of the envious children of Jacob deceptively imposing upon the troubled patriarch the blood-dyed coat of young Joseph.

Though something exceptional in the moral quality of Captain Vere made him, in earnest encounter with a fellow-man, a veritable touch-stone of that man's essential nature, yet now as to Claggart and what was really going on in him his feeling partook less of intuitional conviction than of strong suspicion clogged by strange dubieties. The perplexity he evinced proceeded less from aught touching the man informed against—as Claggart doubtless opined— than from considerations how best to act in regard to the informer. At first indeed he was naturally for summoning that substantiation of his allegations which Claggart said was at hand. But such a proceeding would result in the matter at once getting abroad which in the present stage of it, he thought, might undesirably affect the ship's company. If Claggart was a false witness,—that closed the affair. And therefore before trying the accusation, he would first practically test the accuser; and he thought this could be done in a quiet undemonstrative way.

The measure he determined upon involved a shifting of the scene, a transfer to a place less exposed to observation than the broad quarter-deck. For although the few gun-room officers there at the time had, in due observance of naval etiquette, withdrawn to leeward the moment Captain Vere had begun his promenade on the deck's weather-side; and though during the colloquy with Claggart they of course ventured not to diminish the distance; and though throughout the interview Captain Vere's voice was far from high, and Claggart's silvery and low; and the wind in the cordage and the wash of the sea helped the more to put them beyond earshot; nevertheless, the interview's continuance already had attracted observation from some topmen aloft and other sailors in the waist or further forward.

Having determined upon his measures, Captain Vere forthwith took action. Abruptly turning to Claggart he asked "Master-at-arms, is it now Budd's watch aloft?"

"No, your honor." Whereupon, "Mr. Wilkes!" summoning the nearest midshipman, "tell Albert to come to me." Albert was the Captain's hammock-boy, a sort of sea-valet in whose discretion and fidelity his master had much confidence. The lad appeared. "You know Budd the foretopman?"

"I do, Sir."

"Go find him. It is his watch off. Manage to tell him out of earshot that he is wanted aft. Contrive it that he speaks to nobody. Keep him in talk yourself. And not till you get well aft here, not till then let him know that the place where he is wanted is my cabin. You understand. Go.—Master-at-arms, show yourself on the decks below, and when you think it time for Albert to be coming with his man, stand by quietly to follow the sailor in."

XX

Now when the foretopman found himself closeted there, as it were, in the cabin with the Captain and Claggart, he was surprised enough. But it was a surprise unaccompanied by apprehension or distrust. To an immature nature essentially honest and humane, forewarning intimations of subtler danger from one's kind come tardily if at all. The only thing that took shape in the young sailor's mind was this: Yes, the Captain, I have always thought, looks kindly upon me. Wonder if he's going to make me his coxswain. I should like that. And maybe now he is going to ask the master-at-arms about me.

"Shut the door there, sentry," said the commander; "stand without and let nobody come in.—Now, master-at-arms, tell this man to his face what you told of him to me"; and stood prepared to scrutinize the mutually confronting visages.

With the measured step and calm collected air of an asylum physician approaching in the public hall some patient beginning to show indications of a coming paroxysm, Claggart deliberately advanced within short range of Billy, and mesmerically looking him in the eye, briefly recapitulated the accusation.

Not at first did Billy take it in. When he did the rose-tan of his cheek looked struck as by white leprosy. He stood like one impaled and gagged. Meanwhile the accuser's eyes removing not as yet from the blue dilated ones, underwent a phenomenal change, their wonted rich violet color blurring into a muddy purple. Those lights of human intelligence losing human expression, gelidly protruding like the alien eyes of certain uncatalogued creatures of the deep. The first mesmeric glance was one of serpent fascination; the last was as the hungry lurch of the torpedo-fish.

"Speak, man!" said Captain Vere to the transfixed one struck by his aspect even more than by Claggart's, "Speak! Defend yourself." Which appeal caused but a strange dumb gesturing and gurgling in Billy; amazement at such an accusation so suddenly sprung on inexperienced nonage; this, and it may be horror at the accuser, serving to bring out his lurking defect and in this instance for the time intensifying it into a convulsed tongue-tie; while the intent head and entire form straining forward in an agony of ineffectual eagerness to obey the injunction to speak and defend himself, gave an expression to the face like that of a condemned vestal priestess in the moment of being buried alive, and in the first struggle against suffocation.

Though at the time Captain Vere was quite ignorant of Billy's liability to vocal impediment, he now immediately divined it, since vividly Billy's aspect recalled to him that of a bright young school-mate of his whom he had seen struck by much the same startling impotence in the act of eagerly rising in the class to be foremost in response to a testing question put to it by the master. Going close up to the young sailor, and laying a soothing hand on his shoulder, he said: "There is no hurry, my boy. Take your time, take your time." Contrary to the effect intended, these words so fatherly in tone, doubtless touching Billy's heart to the quick, prompted yet more violent efforts at utterance—efforts soon ending for the time in confirming the paralysis, and bringing to the face an expression which was a crucifixion to behold. The next instant, quick as the flame from a discharged cannon at night, his right arm shot out, and Claggart dropped to the deck. Whether intentionally or but owing to the young athlete's superior height, the blow had taken effect full upon the forehead, so shapely and intellectual-looking a feature in the master-at-arms; so that the body fell over lengthwise, like a heavy plank tilted from erectness. A gasp or two and he lay motionless.

"Fated boy," breathed Captain Vere in tone so low as to be almost a whisper, "what have you done! But here, help me."

The twain raised the felled one from the loins up into a sitting position. The spare form flexibly acquiesced, but inertly. It was like handling a dead snake. They lowered it back. Regaining erectness Captain Vere with one hand covering his face stood to all appearance as impassive as the object at his feet. Was he absorbed in taking in all the bearings of the event and what was best not only now at once to be done, but also in the sequel? Slowly he uncovered his face; and the effect was as if the moon emerging from eclipse should reappear with quite another aspect than that which had gone into hiding. The father in him, manifested towards Billy thus far in the scene, was replaced by the military disciplinarian. In his official tone he bade the foretopman retire to a state-room aft (pointing it out) and there remain till thence summoned. This order Billy in silence mechanically obeyed. Then, going to the cabin door where it opened on the quarter-deck, Captain Vere said to the sentry without, "Tell somebody to send Albert here." When the lad appeared his master so contrived it that he should not catch sight of the prone one. "Albert," he said to him, "tell the Surgeon I wish to see him. You need not come back till called."

When the Surgeon entered—a self-poised character of that grave sense and experience that hardly anything could take him aback,—Captain Vere advanced to meet him, thus unconsciously intercepting his view of Claggart and interrupting the other's wonted ceremonious salutation, said, "Nay, tell me how it is with yonder man," directing his attention to the prostrate one.

The Surgeon looked, and for all his self-command, somewhat started at the abrupt revelation. On Claggart's always pallid complexion, thick black blood was now oozing from mouth and ear. To the gazer's professional eye it was unmistakably no living man that he saw.

"Is it so then?" said Captain Vere intently watching him. "I thought it. But verify it." Whereupon the customary tests confirmed the Surgeon's first glance, who now looking up in unfeigned concern, cast a look of intense inquisitiveness upon his superior. But Captain Vere, with one hand to his brow was standing motionless. Suddenly, catching the Surgeon's arm convulsively, he exclaimed pointing down to the body—"It is the divine judgment of Ananias! Look!"

Disturbed by the excited manner he had never before observed in the *Indomitable's* Captain, and as yet wholly ignorant of the affair, the prudent Surgeon nevertheless held his peace, only again looking an earnest interrogation as to what it was that had resulted in such a tragedy.

But Captain Vere was now again motionless standing absorbed in thought. But again starting, he vehemently exclaimed—"Struck dead by an angel of God. Yet the angel must hang!"

At these passionate interjections, mere incoherences to the listener as yet unapprised of the antecedent events, the Surgeon was profoundly discomposed. But now as recollecting himself, Captain Vere in less passionate tone briefly related the circumstances leading up to the event.

"But come; we must dispatch" he added. "Help me to remove him" (meaning the body) "to yonder compartment," designating one opposite that where the foretopman remained immured. Anew disturbed by a request that as implying a desire for secrecy, seemed unaccountably strange to him, there was nothing for the subordinate to do but comply.

"Go now," said Captain Vere with something of his wonted manner, "go now. I shall presently call a drum-head court. Tell the lieutenants what has happened, and tell Mr. Mordant," meaning the captain of marines, "and charge them to keep the matter to themselves."

XXI

Full of disquietude and misgivings the Surgeon left the cabin. Was Captain Vere suddenly affected in his mind, or was it but a transient excitement brought about by so strange and extraordinary happening? As to the drum-head court, it struck the Surgeon as impolitic, if nothing more. The thing to do, he thought, was to place Billy Budd in confinement, and in a way dictated by usage, and postpone further action in so extraordinary a case to such time as they should again join the squadron, and then refer it to the Admiral. He recalled the unwonted agitation of Captain Vere and his excited exclamations so at variance with his normal manner. Was he unhinged? But assuming that he is, it is not so susceptible to proof. What then could he do? No more trying situation is conceivable than that of an officer subordinated under a captain whom he suspects to be, not mad indeed, but yet not quite unaffected in his intellect. To argue his order to him would be insolence. To resist him would be mutiny. In obedience to Captain Vere he communicated what had happened to the lieutenants and captain of marines saying nothing as to the Captain's state. They fully shared his own surprise and concern. Like him they seemed to think that such a matter should be reported to the Admiral.

XXII

Who in the rainbow can draw the line where the violet tint ends and the orange tint begins? Distinctly we see the difference of the color, but where exactly does the one first visibly enter into the other? So with sanity and insanity. In pronounced cases there is no question about them. But in some supposed cases, in various degrees supposedly less pronounced, to draw the exact line of demarkation few will undertake though for a fee some professional experts will. There is nothing namable but that some men will undertake to do it for pay.

Whether Captain Vere, as the Surgeon professionally and privately surmised, was really the sudden victim of any degree of aberration, one must determine for himself by such light as this narrative may afford.

That the unhappy event which has been narrated could not have happened at a worse juncture was but too true. For it was close on the heel of the suppressed insurrections, an aftertime very critical to naval authority, demanding from every English sea-commander two qualities not readily interfusable—prudence and rigor. Moreover there was something crucial in the case.

In the jugglery of circumstances preceding and attending the event on board the *Indomitable* and in the light of martial code whereby it was formally to be judged, innocence and guilt personified in Claggart and Budd—in effect changed places.

In the legal view the apparent victim of the tragedy was he who had sought to victimize a man blameless; and the indisputable deed of the latter, navally regarded, constituted the most heinous of military crimes. Yet more. The essential right and wrong involved in the matter, the clearer that might be, so much the worse for the responsibility of a loyal sea-commander inasmuch as he was not authorized to determine the matter on that primitive basis.

Small wonder then that the *Indomitable*'s Captain, though in general a man of rapid decision, felt that circumspectness not less than promptitude was necessary. Until he could decide upon his course, and in each detail; and not only so, but until the concluding measure was upon the point of being enacted, he deemed it advisable, in view of all the circumstances to guard as much as possible against publicity. Here he may or may not have erred. Certain it is however that subsequently in the confidential talk of more than one or two gun-rooms and cabins, he was not a little criticized by some officers, a fact imputed by his friends, and vehemently by his cousin Jack Denton, to professional jealousy of *Starry Vere*. Some imaginative ground for invidious comment there was. The maintenance of secrecy in the matter, the confining all knowledge of it for a time to the place where the homicide occurred, the quarter-deck cabin; in these particulars lurked some resemblance to the policy adopted in those tragedies of the palace which have occurred more than once in the capital founded by Peter the Barbarian.

The case indeed was such that fain would the *Indomitable*'s Captain have deferred taking any action whatever respecting it further than to keep the foretopman a closed prisoner till the ship rejoined the squadron and then submitting the matter to the judgment of his Admiral.

But a true military officer is in one particular like a true monk. Not with more of self-abnegation will the latter keep his vows of monastic obedience than the former his vows of allegiance to martial duty.

Feeling that unless quick action were taken on it, the deed of the foretopman, so soon as it should be known on the gun-decks, would tend to awaken any slumbering embers of the Nore among the crew, a sense of the urgency of the case overruled in Captain Vere every other consideration. But though a conscientious disciplinarian he was no lover of authority for mere authority's sake. Very far was he from embracing opportunities for monopolizing to himself the perils of moral responsibility none at least that could properly be referred to an official superior or shared with him by his official equals or even subordinates. So thinking he was glad it would not be at variance with usage to turn the matter over to a summary court of his own officers, reserving to himself as the one on whom the ultimate accountability would rest, the right of maintaining a supervision of it, or formally or informally interposing at need. Accordingly a drum-head court was summarily convened, he electing the individuals composing it, the first lieutenant, the captain of marines, and the sailing master.

In associating an officer of marines with the sea-lieutenants in a case having to do with a sailor, the Commander perhaps deviated from general custom. He was prompted thereto by the circumstance that he took that soldier to be a judicious person, thoughtful, and not altogether incapable of grappling with a difficult case unprecedented in his prior experience. Yet even as to him he was not without some latent misgiving, for withal he was an extremely good-natured man, an enjoyer of his dinner, a sound sleeper, and inclined to obesity. A man who though he would always maintain his manhood in battle might not prove altogether reliable in a moral dilemma involving aught of the tragic. As to the first lieutenant and the sailing master, Captain Vere could not but be aware that though honest natures of approved gallantry upon occasion, their intelligence was mostly confined to the matter of active seamanship and the fighting demands of their profession. The court was held in the same cabin where the unfortunate affair had taken place. This cabin, the Commander's, embraced the entire area under the poop-deck. Aft, and on either side was a small state-room the one room temporarily a jail and the other a dead-house and a yet smaller compartment leaving a space between expanding forward into a goodly oblong of length coinciding with the ship's beam. A skylight of moderate dimension was overhead and at each end of the oblong space were two sashed port-hole windows easily convertible back into embrasures for short carronades.

All being quickly in readiness, Billy Budd was arraigned, Captain Vere necessarily appearing as the sole witness in the case, and as such temporarily sinking his rank, though singularly maintaining it in a matter apparently trivial, namely, that he testified from the ship's weather-side with that object having caused the court to sit on the lee-side. Concisely he narrated all that had led up to the catastrophe, omitting nothing in Claggart's accusation and deposing as to the manner in which the prisoner had received it. At this testimony the three officers glanced with no little surprise at Billy Budd, the last man they would have suspected either of mutinous design alleged by Claggart, or of the undeniable deed he himself had done. The first lieutenant, taking judicial primacy and turning toward the prisoner, said, "Captain Vere has spoken. Is it or is it not as Captain Vere says?" In response came syllables not so much impeded in the utterance as might have been anticipated. They were these: "Captain Vere tells the truth. It is just as Captain Vere says, but it is not as the master-in-arms said. I have eaten the King's bread and I am true to the King."

"I believe you, my man," said the witness, his voice indicating a suppressed emotion not otherwise betrayed.

"God will bless you for that, your honor!" not without stammering said Billy, and all but broke down. But immediately was recalled to self-control by another question, to which with the same emotional difficulty of utterance, he said, "No, there was no malice between us. I never bore malice against the master-at-arms. I am sorry that he is dead. I did not mean to kill him. Could I have used my tongue, I would not have struck him. But he foully lied to my face and in the presence of my Captain, and I had to say something, and I could only say it with a blow, God help me!"

In the impulsive above-board manner of the frank one, the court saw confirmed all that was implied in words that just previously had perplexed them coming as they did from the testifier to the tragedy and promptly following Billy's impassioned disclaimer of mutinous intent—Captain Vere's words, "I believe you, my man."

Next it was asked of him whether he knew of or suspected aught savoring of incipient trouble (meaning mutiny, though the explicit term was avoided) going on in any section of the ship's company.

The reply lingered. This was naturally imputed by the court to the same vocal embarrassment which had retarded or obstructed previous answers. But in main it was otherwise here; the question immediately recalling to Billy's mind the interview with the after-guardsman in the fore-chains. But an innate repugnance to playing a part at all approaching that of an informer against one's own ship-mates—the same erring sense of uninstructed honor which had stood in the way of his reporting the matter at the time though as a loyal man-of-war-man it was incumbent on him, and failure so to do if charged against him and proven, would have subjected him to the heaviest of penalties; this, with the blind feeling now his, that nothing really was being hatched, prevailing with him. When the answer came it was a negative.

"One question more," said the officer of marines now first speaking and with a troubled earnestness, "You tell us that what the master-at-arms said against you was a lie. Now why should he have so lied, so maliciously lied, since you declare there was no malice between you?"

At that question unintentionally touching on a spiritual sphere wholly obscure to Billy's thoughts, he was nonplussed, evincing a confusion indeed that some observers, such as can readily be imagined, would have construed into involuntary evidence of hidden guilt. Nevertheless he strove some way to answer, but all at once relinquished the vain endeavor, at the same time turning an appealing glance towards Captain Vere as deeming him his best helper and friend. Captain Vere who had been seated for a time, rose to his feet, addressing the interrogator. "The question you put to him comes naturally enough. But can he rightly answer it? Or anybody else? Unless indeed it be he who lies within there," designating the compartment where lay the corpse. "But the prone one there will not rise to our summons. In effect though, as it seems to me, the point you make is hardly material. Quite aside from any conceivable motive actuating the master-at-arms, and irrespective of the provocation of the blow, a martial court must needs in the present case confine its attention to the blow's consequence, which consequence justly is to be deemed not otherwise than as the striker's deed."

This utterance, the full significance of which it was not at all likely that Billy took in, nevertheless caused him to turn a wistful interrogative look towards the speaker, a look in its dumb expressiveness not unlike that which a dog of generous breed might turn upon his master seeking in his face some elucidation of a previous gesture ambiguous to the canine intelligence. Nor was the same utterance without marked effect upon the three officers, more especially the soldier. Couched in it seemed to them a meaning unanticipated, involving a prejudgment on the speaker's part. It served to augment a mental disturbance previously evident enough.

The soldier once more spoke; in a tone of suggestive dubiety addressing at once his associates and Captain Vere: "Nobody is present—none of the ship's company, I mean, who might shed lateral light, if any is to be had, upon what remains mysterious in this matter."

"That is thoughtfully put," said Captain Vere; "I see your drift. Ay, there is a mystery; but to use a scriptural phrase, it is 'a mystery of iniquity,' a matter for psychologic theologians to discuss. But what has a military court to do with it? Not to add that for us any possible investigation of it is cut off by the lasting tongue-tie of—him—in yonder," again designating the mortuary state-room. "The prisoner's deed,—with that alone we have to do."

To this, and particularly the closing reiteration, the marine soldier knowing not how aptly to reply, sadly abstained from saying aught. The first lieutenant who at the outset had not unnaturally assumed primacy in the court, now overrulingly instructed by a glance from Captain Vere, a glance more effective than words, resumed that primacy. Turning to the prisoner, "Budd," he said, and scarce in equable tones, "Budd, if you have aught further to say for yourself, say it now."

Upon this the young sailor turned another quick glance towards Captain Vere; then, as taking a hint from that aspect, a hint confirming his own instinct that silence was now best, replied to the lieutenant, "I have said all, Sir."

The marine—the same who had been the sentinel without the cabin door at the time that the foretopman followed by the master-at-arms, entered it—he, standing by the sailor throughout their judicial proceedings, was now directed to take him back to the after compartment originally assigned to the prisoner and his custodian. As the twain disappeared from view, the three officers as partially liberated from some inward constraint associated with Billy's mere presence, simultaneously stirred in their seats. They exchanged looks of troubled indecision, yet feeling that decide they must and without long delay. For Captain Vere was for the time standing unconsciously with his back towards them, apparently in one of his absent fits, gazing out from a sashed port-hole to windward upon the monotonous blank of the twilight sea. But the court's silence, continuing, broken only at moments by brief consultations in low earnest tones, this seemed to assure him and encourage him. Turning, he to-and-fro paced the cabin athwart; in the returning ascent to windward, climbing the slant deck in the ship's lee roll; without knowing it symbolizing thus in his action a mind resolute to surmount difficulties even if against primitive instincts strong as the wind and the sea. Presently he came to a stand before the three. After scanning their faces he stood less as mustering his thoughts for expression, than as one inly deliberating how best to put them to well-meaning men not intellectually mature, men with whom it was necessary to demonstrate certain principles that were axioms to himself. Similar impatience as to talking is perhaps one reason that deters some minds from adressing any popular assemblies.

When speak he did, something both in the substance of what he said and his manner of saying it, showed the influence of unshared studies modifying and tempering the practical training of an active career. This, along with his phraseology now and then was suggestive of the grounds whereon rested that imputation of a certain pedantry socially alleged against him by certain naval men of wholly practical cast, captains who nevertheless would frankly concede that His Majesty's navy mustered no more efficient officer of their grade than *Starry Vere*.

What he said was to this effect: "Hitherto I have been but the witness, little more; and I should hardly think now to take another tone, that of your coadjutor, for the time, did I not perceive in you—at the crisis too—a troubled hesitancy, proceeding, I doubt not from the clashing of military duty with moral scruple—scruple vitalized by compassion. For the compassion how can I otherwise than share it. But, mindful of paramount obligation I strive against scruples that may tend to enervate decision. Not, gentlemen, that I hide from myself that the case is an exceptional one. Speculatively regarded, it well might be referred to a jury of casuists. But for us here acting not as casuists or moralists, it is a case practical and under martial law practically to be dealt with.

"But your scruples: do they move as in a dusk? Challenge them. Make them advance and declare themselves. Come now: do they import something like this: If, mindless of palliating circumstances, we are bound to regard the death of the master-at-arms as the prisoner's deed, then does that deed constitute a capital crime whereof the penalty is a mortal one. But in natural justice is nothing but the prisoner's overt act to be considered? How can we adjudge to summary and shameful death a fellow-creature innocent before God, and whom we feel to be so?—Does that state it aright? You sign sad assent. Well, I too feel that, the full force of that. It is Nature. But do these buttons that we wear attest that our allegiance is to Nature? No, to the King. Though the ocean, which is inviolate Nature primeval, though this be the element where we move and have our being as sailors, yet as the King's officers lies our duty in a sphere correspondingly natural? So little is that true, that in receiving our commissions we in the most important regards ceased to be natural free-agents. When war is declared, are we the commissioned fighters previously consulted? We fight at command. If our judgments approve the war, that is but coincidence. So in other particulars. So now. For suppose condemnation were to follow these present proceedings. Would it be so much we ourselves that would condemn as it would be martial law operating through us? For that law and the rigor of it, we are not responsible. Our vowed responsibility is in this: That however pitilessly that law may operate, we nevertheless adhere to it and administer it.

"But the exceptional in the matter moves the heart within you. Even so too is mine moved. But let not warm hearts betray heads that should be cool. Ashore in a criminal case will an upright judge allow himself off the bench to be waylaid by some tender kinswoman of the accused seeking to touch him with her tearful plea? Well the heart, sometimes the feminine in man, here is as that piteous woman. And hard though it be, she must here be ruled out."

He paused, earnestly studying them for a moment; then resumed.

"But something in your aspect seems to urge that it is not solely that heart that moves in you, but also the conscience, the private conscience. But tell me whether or not, occupying the position we do, private conscience should not yield to that imperial one formulated in the code under which alone we officially proceed?"

Here the three men moved in their seats, less convinced than agitated by the course of an argument troubling but the more the spontaneous conflict within. Perceiving which, the speaker paused for a moment; then abruptly changing his tone, went on.

"To steady us a bit, let us recur to the facts.—In war-time at sea a man-of-war's-man strikes his superior in grade, and the blow kills. Apart from its effect the blow itself is, according to the Articles of War, a capital crime. Furthermore—"

"Ay, Sir," emotionally broke in the officer of marines, "in one

sense it was. But surely Budd purposed neither mutiny nor homicide."

"Surely not, my good man. And before a court less arbitrary and
more merciful than a martial one that plea would largely extenuate.
At the last Assizes it shall acquit. But how here? We proceed under
the law of the Mutiny Act. In feature no child can resemble his
father more than that Act resembles in spirit the thing from which
it derives—War. In His Majesty's service—in this ship indeed—there
are Englishmen forced to fight for the King against their will. Against
their conscience, for aught we know. Though as their fellow-creatures
some of us may appreciate their position, yet as navy officers, what
reck we of it? Still less recks the enemy. Our impressed men he
would fain cut down in the same swath with our volunteers. As
regards the enemy's naval conscripts, some of whom may even share
our own abhorrence of the regicidal French Directory, it is the same
on our side. War looks but to the frontage, the appearance. And the
Mutiny Act, War's child, takes after the father. Budd's intent or
non-intent is nothing to the purpose.

"But while, put to it by those anxieties in you which I cannot
but respect, I only repeat myself—while thus strangely we prolong
proceedings that should be summary—the enemy may be sighted and
an engagement result. We must do; and one of two things must we
do—condemn or let go."

"Can we not convict and yet mitigate the penalty?" asked the
junior lieutenant here speaking, and falteringly, for the first.

"Lieutenant, were that clearly lawful for us under the circumstances, consider the consequence of such clemency. The people"
(meaning the ship's company) "have native sense; most of them are
familiar with our naval usage and tradition; and how would they
take it? Even could you explain to them—which our official position
forbids—they, long molded by arbitrary discipline, have not that kind
of intelligent responsiveness that might qualify them to comprehend
and discriminate. No, to the people the foretopman's deed, however
it be worded in the announcement will be plain homicide committed
in a flagrant act of mutiny. What penalty for that should follow,
they know. But it does not follow. Why? they will ruminate. You
know what sailors are. Will they not revert to the recent outbreak
at the Nore? Ay, they know the well-founded alarm—the panic it
struck throughout England. Your clement sentence they would account
pusillanimous. They would think that we flinch, that we are afraid
of them—afraid of practicing a lawful rigor singularly demanded at
this juncture lest it should provoke new troubles. What shame to us
such a conjecture on their part, and how deadly to discipline. You

see then, whither prompted by duty and the law I steadfastly drive. But I beseech you, my friends, do not take me amiss. I feel as you do for this unfortunate boy. But did he know our hearts, I take him to be of that generous nature that he would feel even for us on whom in this military necessity so heavy a compulsion is laid."

With that, crossing the deck he resumed his place by the sashed port-hole, tacitly leaving the three to come to a decision. On the cabin's opposite side the troubled court sat silent. Loyal lieges, plain and practical, though at bottom they dissented from some points Captain Vere had put to them, they were without the faculty, hardly had the inclination to gainsay one whom they felt to be an earnest man, one too not less their superior in mind than in naval rank. But it is not improbable that even such of his words as were not without influence over them, less came home to them than his closing appeal to their instinct as sea-officers in the forethought he threw out as to the practical consequences to discipline, considering the uncon-firmed tone of the fleet at the time should a man-of-war's-man's violent killing at sea of a superior in grade be allowed to pass for aught else than a capital crime demanding prompt infliction of the penalty.

Not unlikely they were brought to something more or less akin to that harassed frame of mind which in the year 1842 actuated the command of the U.S. brig-of-war *Somers* to resolve, under the so-called Articles of War, Articles modeled upon the English Mutiny Act, to resolve upon the execution at sea of a midshipman and two petty-officers as mutineers designing the seizure of the brig. Which resolution was carried out though in a time of peace and within not many days' sail of home. An act vindicated by a naval court of inquiry subsequently convened ashore. History, and here cited without comment. True, the circumstances on board the *Somers* were different from those on board the *Indomitable*. But the urgency felt, well-warranted or otherwise, was much the same.

Says a writer whom few know, "Forty years after a battle it is easy for a non-combatant to reason about how it ought to have been fought. It is another thing personally and under fire to direct the fighting while involved in the obscuring smoke of it. Much so with respect to other emergencies involving considerations both practical and moral, and when it is imperative promptly to act. The greater the fog the more it imperils the steamer, and speed is put on though at the hazard of running somebody down. Little ween the snug card-players in the cabin of the responsibilities of the sleepless man on the bridge."

In brief, Billy Budd was formally convicted and sentenced to be hung at the yard-arm in the early morning-watch, it being now night. Otherwise, as is customary in such cases, the sentence would forthwith have been carried out. In war-time on the field or in the fleet, a mortal punishment decreed by a drum-head court—on the field sometimes decreed by but a nod from the general—follows without a delay on the heel of conviction without appeal.

XXIII

It was Captain Vere himself who of his own motion communicated the finding of the court to the prisoner; for that purpose going to the compartment where he was in custody and bidding the marine there to withdraw for the time.

Beyond the communication of the sentence, what took place at this interview was never known. But in view of the character of the twain briefly closeted in that state-room, each radically sharing in the rarer qualities of our nature—so rare indeed as to be all but incredible to average minds however much cultivated—some conjectures may be ventured.

It would have been in consonance with the spirit of Captain Vere should he on this occasion have concealed nothing from the condemned one—should he indeed have frankly disclosed to him the part he himself had played in bringing about the decision, at the same time revealing his actuating motives. On Billy's side it is not improbable that such a confession would have been received in much the same spirit that prompted it. Not without a sort of joy indeed he might have appreciated the brave opinion of him implied in his Captain making such a confidant of him. Nor, as to the sentence itself could he have been insensible that it was imparted to him as to one not afraid to die. Even more may have been. Captain Vere in the end may have developed the passion sometimes latent under an exterior stoical or indifferent. He was old enough to have been Billy's father. The austere devotee of military duty letting himself melt back into what remains primeval in our formalized humanity may in the end have caught Billy to his heart even as Abraham may have caught young Isaac on the brink of resolutely offering him up in obedience to the exacting behest. But there is no telling the sacrament, seldom if in any case revealed to the gadding world wherever under circumstances at all akin to those here attempted to be set forth two of great Nature's nobler order embrace. There is privacy at the time, inviolable to the survivor, and holy oblivion the sequel to each diviner magnanimity, providentially covers all at last.

The first to encounter Captain Vere in act of leaving the compartment was the senior lieutenant. The face he beheld, for the moment one expressive of the agony of the strong, was to that officer, though a man of fifty, a startling revelation. That the condemned one suffered less than he who mainly had effected the condemnation was apparently indicated by the former's exclamation in the scene soon perforce to be touched upon.

XXIV

Of a series of incidents within a brief term rapidly following each other, the adequate narration may take up a term less brief, especially if explanation or comment here and there seems requisite to the better understanding of such incidents. Between the entrance into the cabin of him who never left it alive and him who when he did leave it left it as one condemned to die; between this and the closeted interview just given, less than an hour and a half had elapsed. It was an interval long enough however to awaken speculations among no few of the ship's company as to what it was that could be detaining in the cabin the master-at-arms and the sailor; for a rumor that both of them had been seen to enter it and neither of them had been seen to emerge, this rumor had got abroad upon the gun-decks and in the tops; the people of a great warship being in one respect like villagers, taking microscopic note of every outward movement or non-movement going on. When therefore in weather not at all tempestuous all hands were called in the second dog-watch, a summons under such circumstances not usual in those hours, the crew were not wholly unprepared for some announcement extraordinary, one having connection too with the continual absence of the two men from their wonted haunts.

There was a moderate sea at the time; and the moon, newly risen and near to being at its full, silvered the white spar-deck wherever not blotted by the clear-cut shadows horizontally thrown of fixtures and moving men. On either side the quarter-deck the marine guard under arms was drawn up; and Captain Vere, standing in his place surrounded by all the ward-room officers, addressed his men. In so doing his manner showed neither more nor less than that properly pertaining to his supreme position aboard his own ship. In clear terms and concise he told them what had taken place in the cabin; that the master-at-arms was dead; that he who had killed him had been already tried by a summary court and condemned to death; and that the execution would take place in the early morning watch. The word *mutiny* was not named in what he said. He refrained too from making the occasion an opportunity for any preachment as to the maintenance of discipline, thinking perhaps that under existing circumstances in the navy the consequence of violating discipline should be made to speak for itself.

Their Captain's announcement was listened to by the throng of standing sailors in a dumbness like that of a seated congregation of believers in hell listening to the clergyman's announcement of his Calvinistic text.

At the close, however, a confused murmur went up. It began to wax. All but instantly, then, at a sign, it was pierced and suppressed by shrill whistles of the boatswain and his mates piping down one watch.

To be prepared for burial Claggart's body was delivered to certain petty-officers of his mess. And here, not to clog the sequel with lateral matters, it may be added that at a suitable hour, the master-at-arms was committed to the sea with every funeral honor properly belonging to his naval grade.

In this proceeding as in every public one growing out of the tragedy, strict adherence to usage was observed. Nor in any point could it have been at all deviated from either with respect to Claggart or Billy Budd without begetting undesirable speculations in the ship's company, sailors, and more particularly men-of-war's men, being of all men the greatest sticklers for usage.

For similar cause all communication between Captain Vere and the condemned one ended with the closeted interview already given, the latter being now surrendered to the ordinary routine preliminary to the end. This transfer under guard from the Captain's quarters was effected without unusual precautions—at least no visible ones.

If possible not to let the men so much as surmise that their officers anticipate aught amiss from them is the tacit rule in a military ship. And the more that some sort of trouble should really be apprehended, the more do the officers keep that apprehension to themselves; though not the less unostentatious vigilance may be augmented.

In the present instance the sentry placed over the prisoner had strict orders to let no one have communication with him but the chaplain. And certain unobtrusive measures were taken absolutely to insure this point.

XXV

In a seventy-four of the old order the deck known as the upper gun-deck was the one covered over by the spar-deck which last though not without its armament was for the most part exposed to the weather. In general it was at all hours free from hammocks; those of the crew swinging on the lower gun-deck, and berth-deck, the latter being not only a dormitory but also the place for the stowing of the sailors' bags, and on both sides lined with the large chests of movable pantries of the many messes of the men.

On the starboard side of the *Indomitable's* upper gun-deck, behold Billy Budd under sentry lying prone in irons in one of the bays formed by the regular spacing of the guns comprising the batteries on either side. All these pieces were of the heavier caliber of that period. Mounted on lumbering wooden carriages they were hampered with cumbersome harness of breeching and strong side-tackles for running them out. Guns and carriages, together with the long rammers and shorter lintstocks lodged in loops overhead—all these, as customary, were painted black; and the heavy hempen breechings tarred to the same tint wore the like livery of the undertakers. In contrast with the funereal tone of these surroundings, the prone sailor's exterior apparel, white *jumper* and white duck trousers, each more or less soiled, dimly glimmered in the obscure light of the bay like a patch of discolored snow in early April lingering at some upland cave's black mouth. In effect he is already in his shroud of the garments that shall serve him in lieu of one. Over him but scarce illuminating him, two battle-lanterns swing from two massive beams of the deck above. Fed with the oil supplied by the war-contractors (whose gains, honest or otherwise, are in every land an anticipated portion of the harvest of death) with flickering splashes of dirty yellow light they pollute the pale moonshine all but ineffectually struggling in obstructed flecks through the open ports from which the tompioned cannon protrude. Other lanterns at intervals serve but to bring out somewhat the obscurer bays which like small confessionals or side-chapels in a cathedral branch from the long dim-vistaed broad aisle between the two batteries of that covered tier.

Such was the deck where now lay the Handsome Sailor. Through the rose-tan of his complexion, no pallor could have shown. It would have taken days of sequestration from the winds and the sun to have brought about the effacement of that. But the skeleton in the cheek-bone at the point of its angle was just beginning delicately to be defined under the warm-tinted skin. In fervid hearts self-contained, some brief experiences devour our human tissues as secret fire in a ship's hold consumes cotton in the bale.

But now lying between the two guns, as nipped in the vice of fate, Billy's agony, mainly proceeding from a generous young heart's virgin experience of the diabolical incarnate and effective in some men—the tension of that agony was over now. It survived not the something healing in the closeted interview with Captain Vere.

Without movement, he lay as in a trance. That adolescent expression previously noted as his, taking on something akin to the look of a child's slumbering in the cradle when the warm hearth-glow of the still chamber at night plays on the dimples that at whiles mysteriously form in the cheek, silently coming and going there. For now and then in the gyved one's trance a serene happy light born of some wandering reminiscence or dream would diffuse itself over his face, and then wane away only anew to return.

The chaplain coming to see him and finding him thus, and perceiving no sign that he was conscious of his presence, attentively regarded him for a space, then slipping aside, withdrew for the time, peradventure feeling that even he the minister of Christ though receiving his stipend from Mars had no consolation to proffer which could result in a peace transcending that which he beheld. But in the small hours he came again. And the prisoner now awake to his surroundings noticed his approach and civilly, all but cheerfully, welcomed him. But it was to little purpose that in the interview following the good man sought to bring Billy Budd to some Godly understanding that he must die, and at dawn. True, Billy himself freely referred to his death as a thing close at hand; but it was something in the way that children will refer to death in general, who yet among their other sports will play a funeral with hearse and mourners.

Not that like children Billy was incapable of conceiving what death really is. No, but he was wholly without irrational fear of it, a fear more prevalent in highly civilized communities than those so-called barbarous ones which in all respects stand nearer to unadulterate Nature. And, as elsewhere said, a barbarian Billy radically was; as much so, for all the costume, as his countrymen the British captives, living trophies, made to march in the Roman triumph of Germanicus. Quite as much so as those later barbarians, young men probably, and picked specimens among the earlier British converts of Christianity, at least nominally such and taken to Rome (as today converts from lesser isles of the sea may be taken to London) of whom the Pope of that time, admiring the strangeness of their personal beauty so unlike the Italian stamp, their clear ruddy complexions and curled flaxen locks, exclaimed, "Angles" (meaning *English* the modern derivative) "Angles do you call them? And is it because they look so like angels?" Had it been later in time, one would think that the Pope had in mind Fra Angelico's seraphs some of whom, plucking apples in gardens of the Hesperides, have the faint rosebud complexion of the more beautiful English girls.

If in vain the good chaplain sought to impress the young barbarian with ideas of death akin to those conveyed in the skull, dial and cross-bones on old tombstones; equally futile to all appearance were his efforts to bring home to him the thought of salvation and a Savior. Billy listened, but less out of awe or reverence perhaps than from a certain natural politeness; doubtless at bottom regarding all that in much the same way that most mariners of his class take any discourse abstract or out of the common tone of the work-a-day world. And this sailor way of taking clerical discourse is not wholly unlike the way in which the pioneer of Christianity full of transcendent miracles was received long ago on tropic isles by any superior *savage* so called—a Tahitian say of Captain Cook's time or shortly after that time. Out of natural courtesy he received but did not appropriate. It was like a gift placed on the palm of an outstretched hand upon which the fingers do not close.

But the *Indomitable*'s chaplain was a discreet man possessing the good sense of a good heart. So he insisted not in his vocation here. At the instance of Captain Vere, a lieutenant had apprised him of pretty much everything as to Billy; and since he felt that innocence was even a better thing than religion wherewith to go to Judgment, he reluctantly withdrew; but in his emotion not without first performing an act strange enough in an Englishman, and under the circumstances yet more so in any regular priest. Stooping over, he kissed on the fair cheek his fellow man, a felon in martial law, one who though in the confines of death he felt he could never convert to a dogma; nor for all that did he fear for his future.

Marvel not that having been made acquainted with the young sailor's essential innocence (an irruption of heretic thought hard to suppress) the worthy man lifted not a finger to avert the doom of such a martyr to martial discipline. So to do would not only have been as idle as invoking the desert, but would also have been an audacious transgression of the bounds of his function, one as exactly prescribed to him by military law as that of the boatswain or any other naval officer. Bluntly put, a chaplain is the minister of the Prince of Peace serving in the host of the God of War—Mars. As such, he is as incongruous as that musket of Blücher etc. at Christmas. Why then is he there? Because he indirectly subserves the purpose attested by the cannon; because too he lends the sanction of the religion of the meek to that which practically is the abrogation of everything but brute force.

XXVI

The night so luminous on the spar-deck but otherwise on the cavernous ones below, levels so like the tiered galleries in a coal-mine—the luminous night passed away. But, like the prophet in the chariot disappearing in heaven and dropping his mantle to Elisha, the withdrawing night transferred its pale robe to the breaking day. A meek shy light appeared in the east, where stretched a diaphanous fleece of white furrowed vapor. That light slowly waxed. Suddenly *eight bells* was struck aft, responded to by one louder metallic stroke from forward. It was four o'clock in the morning. Instantly the silver whistles were heard summoning all hands to witness punishment. Up through the great hatchways rimmed with racks of heavy shot the watch below came pouring overspreading with the watch already on deck the space between the mainmast and foremast including that occupied by the capacious *launch* and the black booms tiered on either side of it, boat and booms making a summit of observation for the powder-boys and younger tars. A different group comprising one watch of topmen leaned over the side of the rail of that sea-balcony, no small one in a seventy-four, looking down on the crowd below. Man or boy none spake but in whisper, and few spake at all. Captain Vere—as before, the central figure among the assembled commissioned officers—stood nigh the break of the poop-deck facing forward. Just below him on the quarter-deck the marines in full equipment were drawn up much as at the scene of the promulgated sentence.

At sea in the old time, the execution by halter of a military sailor was generally from the fore-yard. In the present instance for special reasons the main-yard was assigned. Under an arm of that weather or lee yard, the prisoner was presently brought up, the chaplain attending him. It was noted at the time and remarked upon afterwards, that in this final scene the good man evinced little or nothing of the perfunctory. Brief speech indeed he had with the condemned one, but the genuine Gospel was less on his tongue than in his aspect and manner towards him. The final preparations personal to the latter being speedily brought to an end by two boatswain's-mates, the consummation impended. Billy stood facing aft. At the penultimate moment, his words, his only ones, words wholly unobstructed in the utterance were these—"God bless Captain Vere!" Syllables so unanticipated coming from one with the ignominious hemp about his neck—a conventional felon's benediction directed aft towards the quarters of honor; syllables too delivered in the clear melody of a singing-bird on the point of launching from the twig, had a phenomenal effect, not unenhanced by the rare personal beauty of the young sailor spiritualized now through late experiences so poignantly profound.

Without volition as it were, as if indeed the ship's populace were the vehicles of some vocal current electric, with one voice from alow and aloft, came a resonant sympathetic echo—"God bless Captain

Vere!" And yet at that instant Billy alone must have been in their hearts, even as he was in their eyes.

At the pronounced words and the spontaneous echo that voluminously rebounded them, Captain Vere, either through stoic self-control or a sort of momentary paralysis induced by emotional shock, stood erectly rigid as a musket in the ship-armorer's rack.

The hull deliberately recovering from the periodic roll to leeward was just regaining an even keel, when the last signal the preconcerted dumb one was given. At the same moment it chanced that the vapory fleece hanging low in the east, was shot through with a soft glory as of the fleece of the Lamb of God seen in mystical vision and simultaneously therewith, watched by the wedged mass of upturned faces, Billy ascended; and ascending, took the full rose of the dawn.

In the pinioned figure arrived at the yard-end, to the wonder of all no motion was apparent save that created by the ship's motion, in moderate weather so majestic in a great ship ponderously cannoned.

XXVII

A Digression

When some days afterwards in reference to the singularity just mentioned, the purser a rather ruddy rotund person more accurate as an accountant than profound as a philosopher said at mess to the surgeon, "What testimony to the force lodged in will-power," the latter—saturnine, spare and tall, one in whom a discreet causticity went along with a manner less genial than polite, replied, "Your pardon, Mr. Purser. In a hanging scientifically conducted—and under special orders I myself directed how Budd's was to be effected—any movement following the completed suspension and originating in the body suspended, such movement indicates mechanical spasm in the muscular system. Hence the absence of that is no more attributable to will-power as you call it than to horse-power—begging your pardon."

"But this muscular spasm you speak of, is not that in a degree more or less invariable in these cases?"

"Assuredly so, Mr. Purser."

"How then, my good Sir, do you account for its absence in this instance?"

"Mr. Purser, it is clear that your sense of the singularity in this matter equals not mine. You account for it by what you call will-power, a term not yet included in the lexicon of science. For me I do not with my present knowledge pretend to account for it at all. Even should one assume the hypothesis that at the first touch of the halyards the action of Budd's heart, intensified by extraordinary emotion at its climax, abruptly stopped—much like a watch when in carelessly winding it up you strain at the finish, thus snapping the chain—even under that hypothesis how account for the phenomenon that followed?"

"You admit then that the absence of spasmodic movement was phenomenal."

"It was phenomenal, Mr. Purser, in the sense that it was an appearance the cause of which is not immediately to be assigned."

"But tell me, my dear Sir," pertinaciously continued the other, "was the man's death effected by the halter, or was it a species of euthanasia?"

"*Euthanasia*, Mr. Purser, is something like your *will-power*; I doubt its authenticity as a scientific term—begging your pardon again. It is at once imaginative and metaphysical,—in short, Greek. But," abruptly changing his tone, "there is a case in the sick-bay which I do not care to leave to my assistants. Beg your pardon, but excuse me." And rising from the mess, he formally withdrew.

XXVIII

The silence at the moment of execution and for a moment or two continuing thereafter, a silence but emphasized by the regular wash of the sea against the hull or the flutter of a sail caused by the helmsman's eyes being tempted astray, this emphasized silence was gradually disturbed by a sound not easily to be here verbally rendered. Whoever has heard the freshet-wave of a torrent suddenly swelled by pouring showers in the tropical mountains, showers not shared by the plain; whoever has heard the first muffled murmur of its sloping advance through precipitous woods may form some conception of the sound now heard. The seeming remoteness of its source was because of its murmurous indistinctness since it came from close by even from the men massed on the ship's open deck. Being inarticulate, it was dubious in significance further than it seemed to indicate some capricious revulsion of thought or feeling such as mobs ashore are liable to in the present instance possibly implying a sullen revocation on the men's part of their involuntary echoing of Billy's benediction. But ere the murmur had time to wax into clamor, it was met by a strategic command, the more telling that it came with abrupt unexpectedness.

"Pipe down the starboard watch Boatswain, and see that they go."

Shrill as the shriek of the sea-hawk the whistles of the boatswain and his mates pierced that ominous low sound, dissipating it; and yielding to the mechanism of discipline the throng was thinned by one half. For the remainder most of them were set to temporary employments connected with trimming the yards and so forth, business readily to be got up to serve occasion by any officer-of-the-deck.

Now each proceeding that follows a mortal sentence pronounced at sea by a drum-head court is characterized by a promptitude not perceptibly merging into hurry, though bordering that. The hammock, the one which had been Billy's bed when alive, having already been ballasted with shot and otherwise prepared to serve for his canvas coffin, the last offices of the sea-undertakers, the sail-maker's mates, were now speedily completed. When everything was in readiness a second call for all hands made necessary by the strategic movement before mentioned was sounded and now to witness burial.

The details of this closing formality it needs not to give. But when the tilted plank let slide its freight into the sea, a second strange human murmur was heard, blended now with another inarticulate sound proceeding from certain larger sea-fowl whose attention having been attracted by the peculiar commotion in the water resulting from the heavy sloped dive of the shotted hammock into the sea flew screaming to the spot. So near the hull did they come, that the stridor or bony creak of their gaunt double-jointed pinions was audible. As the ship under light airs passed on, leaving the burial spot astern, they still kept circling it low down with the moving shadow of their outstretched wings and the croaked requiem of their cries.

Upon sailors as superstitious as those of the age preceding ours, men-of-war's men too who had just beheld the prodigy of repose in the form suspended in air and now foundering in the deeps; to such mariners the action of the sea-fowl, though dictated by a mere animal greed for prey, was big with no prosaic significance. An uncertain movement began among them, in which some encroachment was made. It was tolerated but for a moment. For suddenly the drum beat to quarters, which familiar sound happening at least twice a day, had upon the present occasion some signal peremptoriness in it. True martial discipline long continued superinduces in an average man a sort of impulse of docility whose operation at the official sound of command much resembles in its promptitude the effect of an instinct.

The drum-beat dissolved the multitude, distributing most of them along the batteries of the two covered gun-decks. There, as wont, the gun's crews stood by their respective cannon erect and silent. In due course the first officer, sword under arm and standing in his place on the quarter-deck formally received the successive reports of the sworded lieutenants commanding the sections of batteries below; the last of which reports being made the summed report he delivered with the customary salute to the Commander. All this occupied time, which, in the present case, was the object of beating to quarters at an hour prior to the customary one. That such variance from usage was authorized by an officer like Captain Vere, a martinet as some deemed him, was evidence of the necessity for unusual action implied in what he deemed to be temporarily the mood of his men. "With mankind," he would say, "forms, measured forms, are everything; and that is the import couched in the story of Orpheus with his lyre spell-binding the wild denizens of the woods." And this he once applied to the disruption of forms going on across the Channel and the consequences thereof.

At this unwonted muster at quarters, all proceeded as at the regular hour. The band on the quarter-deck played a sacred air. After which the chaplain went through with the customary morning service. That done, the drum beat the retreat, and toned by music and religious rites subserving the discipline and purpose of war, the men in their wonted orderly manner dispersed to the places allotted them when not at the guns.

And now it was full day. The fleece of low-hanging vapor had vanished, licked up by the sun that late had so glorified it. And the circumambient air in the clearness of its serenity was like smooth white marble in the polished block not yet removed from the marble-dealer's yard.

XXIX

The symmetry of form attainable in pure fiction cannot so readily be achieved in a narration essentially having less to do with fable than with fact. Truth uncompromisingly told will always have its ragged edges; hence the conclusion of such a narration is apt to be less finished than an architectural finial.

How it fared with the Handsome Sailor during the year of the great mutiny has been faithfully given. But though properly the story ends with his life, something in way of sequel will not be amiss. Three brief chapters will suffice.

In the general re-christening under the Directory of the craft originally forming the navy of the French Monarchy, the *St. Louis* line-of-battle ship was named the *Athéiste*. Such a name, like some other substituted ones in the Revolutionary fleet while proclaiming the infidel audacity of the ruling power was yet, though not so intended to be, the aptest name, if one consider it, ever given to a warship; far more so indeed than the *Devastation*, the *Erebus* (the *Hell*) and similar names bestowed upon fighting ships.

On the return passage to the English fleet from the detached cruise during which occurred the events already recorded, the *Indomitable* fell in with the *Athéiste*. An engagement ensued; during which Captain Vere, in the act of putting his ship alongside the enemy with a view of throwing his boarders across the bulwarks, was hit by a musket-ball from a port-hole of the enemy's main cabin. More than disabled he dropped to the deck and was carried below to the same cock-pit where some of his men already lay. The senior lieutenant took command. Under him the enemy was finally captured and though much crippled was by rare good fortune successfully taken into Gibraltar, an English port not very distant from the scene of the fight. There, Captain Vere with the rest of the wounded was put ashore. He lingered for some days, but the end came. Unhappily he was cut off too early for the Nile and Trafalgar. The spirit that spite its philosophic austerity may yet have indulged in the most secret of all passions, ambition, never attained to the fullness of fame.

Not long before death while lying under the influence of that magical drug which soothing the physical frame mysteriously operates on the subtler element in man, he was heard to murmur words inexplicable to his attendant—"Billy Budd, Billy Budd." That these were not the accents of remorse would seem clear from what the attendant said to the *Indomitable*'s senior officer of marines who as the most reluctant to condemn of the members of the drum-head court, too well knew though here he kept the knowledge to himself, who Billy Budd was.

<h1 style="text-align:center">XXX</h1>

Some few weeks after the execution, among other matters under the main head of *News from the Mediterranean*, there appeared in a naval chronicle of the time, an authorized weekly publication, an account of the affair. It was doubtless for the most part written in good faith, though the medium, partly rumor, through which the facts must have reached the writer, served to deflect and in part falsify them. The account was as follows:—

"On the tenth of the last month a deplorable occurrence took place on board H.M.S. *Indomitable*. John Claggart, the ship's master-at-arms, discovering that some sort of plot was incipient among an inferior section of the ship's company, and that the ring-leader was one William Budd; he, Claggart in the act of arraigning the man before the Captain was vindictively stabbed to the heart by the suddenly drawn sheath-knife of Budd.

"The deed and the implement employed, sufficiently suggest that though mustered into the service under an English name, the assassin was no Englishman, but one of those aliens adopting English cognomens whom the present extraordinary necessities of the service have caused to be admitted into it in considerable numbers.

"The enormity of the crime and the extreme depravity of the criminal, appear the greater in view of the character of the victim, a middle-aged man respectable and discreet, belonging to that minor official grade, the petty-officers, upon whom, as none know better than the commissioned gentlemen, the efficiency of His Majesty's navy so largely depends. His function was a responsible one; at once onerous and thankless and his fidelity in it the greater because of his strong patriotic impulse. In this instance as in so many other instances in these days, the character of this unfortunate man signally refutes, if refutation were needed, that peevish saying attributed to the late Dr. Johnson, that patriotism is the last refuge of a scoundrel.

"The criminal paid the penalty of his crime. The promptitude of the punishment has proved salutary. Nothing amiss is now apprehended aboard the H.M.S. *Indomitable*."

The above item appearing in a publication now long ago superannuated and forgotten is all that hitherto has stood in human record to attest what manner of men respectively were John Claggart and Billy Budd.

XXXI

Everything is for a term remarkable in navies. Any tangible object associated with some striking incident of the service is converted into a monument. The spar from which the foretopman was suspended, was for some few years kept trace of by the blue-jackets. Their knowledge followed it from ship to dock-yard and again from dock-yard to ship, still pursuing it even when at last reduced to a mere dock-yard boom. To them a chip of it was as a piece of the Cross. Ignorant though they were of the secret facts of the tragedy, and not thinking but that the penalty was somehow unavoidably inflicted from the naval point of view, for all that they instinctively felt that Billy was a sort of man as incapable of mutiny as of willful murder. They recalled the fresh young image of the Handsome Sailor, that face never deformed by a sneer or subtler vile freak of the heart within! This impression of him was doubtless deepened by the fact that he was gone, and in a measure mysteriously gone. On the gun-decks of the *Indomitable* the general estimate of his nature and its unconscious simplicity eventually found rude utterance from another foretopman, one of his own watch, gifted as some sailors are with an artless poetic temperament. The tarry hands made some lines which after circulating among the shipboard crew for a while finally got rudely printed at Portsmouth as a ballad. The title given to it was the sailor's.

BILLY IN THE DARBIES

Good of the chaplain to enter Lone Bay
And down on his marrow-bones here and pray
For the likes just o' me, Billy Budd.—But look:
Through the port comes the moon-shine astray!
It tips the guard's cutlass and silvers this nook;
But 'twill die in the dawning of Billy's last day.
A jewel-block they'll make of me to-morrow,
Pendant pearl from the yard-arm-end
Like the ear-drop I gave to Bristol Molly—
O, 'tis me, not the sentence they'll suspend
Ay, Ay, all is up; and I must up too
Early in the morning, aloft from alow.
On an empty stomach, now, never it would do.
They'll give me a nibble—bit o' biscuit ere I go.
Sure, a messmate will reach me the last parting cup;
But, turning heads away from the hoist and the belay,
Heaven knows who will have the running of me up!
No pipe to those halyards—but aren't it all sham?
A blur's in my eyes; it is dreaming that I am.
A hatchet to my hawser? all adrift to go?
The drum roll to grog, and Billy never know?
But Donald he has promised to stand by the plank;
So I'll shake a friendly hand ere I sink.
But—no! It is dead then I'll be, come to think.—
I remember Taff the Welshman when he sank.
And his cheek it was like the budding pink.
But me they'll lash me in hammock, drop me deep.
Fathoms down, fathoms down, how I'll dream fast asleep.
I feel it stealing now. Sentry, are you there?
Just ease these darbies at the wrist,
And roll me over fair.
I am sleepy, and the oozy weeds about me twist.

QUESTIONS FOR DISCUSSION

Preface to Chapter VIII

1. What is the purpose of the Preface? Why was the period at the end of the eighteenth century one which "involved a crisis . . . not exceeded in its undetermined momentousness . . . by any other era"? What were the ironic results of the French Revolution? What is the connection between the French Revolution and the mutinies in the British navy?

2. The narrator says that the crew of the *Rights-of-Man* resembled the delegation of Anacharsis Cloots before the French Assembly. Cloots was a Prussian baron who called himself "Orator of the Human Race." With a band of derelicts and social outcasts, he appeared before the revolutionary assembly to plead for social justice. Why is it especially fitting to find such a comparison for the crew of a ship named *Rights-of-Man?*

3. What is the system under which Billy Budd was taken from the *Rights-of-Man* to serve on the H.M.S. *Indomitable?* How does that system differ from forms of compulsory military service today? Was Billy's farewell to his former ship a comment on his impressment? Was it thought to be so?

4. What was Billy's background? What was his character? What was his effect on his fellows? What can be connoted in the phrase "the Handsome Sailor"?

5. In Hawthorne's story, "The Birthmark," an apothecary married a beautiful woman, whose only physical flaw was an insignificant birthmark. He tried to remove it, hoping thereby to make his wife perfect. What was Billy's physical fault? Why is it necessary for both the woman and Billy to have some physical imperfection?

6. Why did Melville digress to tell of the exploits and character of Lord Horatio Nelson? What is Nelson's relevance to this story?

7. What was the character of Captain the Honorable Edward Fairfax Vere? Why was he called Starry Vere? Why is it important to establish about him the characteristics given in Chapter VII?

8. What was the character of John Claggart, the master-at-arms? Why was so much of his characterization dependent upon conjecture? What sort of subordinates and associates did he attract?

9. Through Chapter VIII, what has Melville achieved toward the telling of his story? Why is it necessary to make such a slow beginning in a story like *Billy Budd, Foretopman?*

Chapters IX to XVIII

1. What motivated Billy to take such care in avoiding rebuke? Why was the navy so strict in its punishments? why particularly so in 1797?

2. What role did the old Danish sailor serve for Billy? for Melville as storyteller? Why was the Dansker's message so incredible to Billy? What incident helped to delude Billy?
3. Why was the seriousness of Claggart's remark to Billy—"Handsomely done, my lad! And handsome is as handsome did it too!"—so readily misconstrued by the crew? Why did they laugh? What is being shown through this incident?
4. Melville made a serious point of explaining the complexity of Claggart's enmity against Billy. What are the reasons he gave?
5. In a letter to Hawthorne, Melville had written: "I stand for the heart. To the dogs with the head!" Hawthorne's opinion was that the division of the intellect from the emotions, at its most extreme, is indeed "the Unpardonable Sin." How close did Claggart come, in these terms, to committing "the Unpardonable Sin"?
6. What is meant when Melville says in Chapter XIV, "The Pharisee is the Guy Fawkes prowling in the hid chambers underlying the Claggarts"? In what respects was Claggart guilty of Pharisaism? Who was Guy Fawkes?
7. What is the importance of the incident with the afterguardsman? What did he hold in his fingers? What did the Dansker mean when he called the afterguardsman "a cats-paw"?

Chapters XIX to XXIII

1. What was Captain Vere's attitude toward Claggart's suggestion of disloyalty among the crew? What of the accusation against Billy? Why did he deal so summarily with the charges?
2. In what sense had "innocence and guilt personified in Claggart and Budd—in effect changed places"?
3. Why did Billy lie when Captain Vere asked whether he knew of any "incipient trouble . . . going on in any section of the ship's company"? What did Melville mean in this connection by "the same erring sense of uninstructed honor"?
4. What was Captain Vere's argument against the scruples of his officers in their reluctance to condemn Billy? Do you accept his argument? If not, how would you refute it?
5. Melville offered "some conjectures" as to what may have happened in the interview between Captain Vere and Billy when the sentence was announced. Do you accept these conjectures?

Chapters XXIV to XXXI

1. Why was Captain Vere so cautious in making his announcement of Billy's fate to the crew? What is particularly apt about Melville's description of the sailors "in a dumbness like that of a seated congrega-

tion of believers in hell listening to the clergyman's announcement of his Calvinistic text"?

2. During the discussion of the chaplain's duties in Chapter XXV, Melville returned to an old antagonism: foreign missionary work. In his voyages he had come upon English and American missionaries in the Pacific islands. What was his complaint about them?
3. What was unusual about Billy's last words? What was their effect upon the crew?
4. What is the comparison being made when Melville wrote:

At the same moment it chanced that the vapory fleece hanging low in the east was shot through with a soft glory as of the fleece of the Lamb of God seen in mystical vision and simultaneously therewith, watched by the wedged mass of upturned faces, Billy ascended; and ascending, took the full rose of dawn.

5. What is remarkable about the fact that Billy's body was motionless while being hanged? What is the purpose of the digression of Chapter XXVII? Where do Melville's sympathies lie in this discussion? Why?
6. What significance is there to the fact that Captain Vere died in a battle with a French ship named *Athéiste?* Why were his last words "Billy Budd"?
7. Why did Melville include the erroneous dispatch from the naval chronicle in Chapter XXX?
8. Why is it fitting to the nature of this story that sailors regarded a chip of the spar from which Billy was hanged "as a piece of the Cross"? How does this statement affect your understanding of the story?
9. What does the poem by one of Billy's shipmates add to the story?

Comprehensive Questioning

1. Throughout the story, the shadow of mutiny darkens every act. What effect had recent events upon the outcome of the story?
2. Claggart, like Captain Ahab, is described as suffering from a mono-mania, "like a subterranean fire . . . eating its way deeper and deeper in him." What was Claggart's monomania? What was its cause? Why was Claggart one of the "true madmen"?
3. Melville's favorite source for metaphors and allusions in *Billy Budd, Foretopman* was the Bible. What references can you identify? How do the allusions from both the Old and New Testaments unify the story?
4. If indeed *Billy Budd, Foretopman* is more than a story of an unfortunate sailor, how do you interpret it? What characters and incidents support the meaning you suggest?

ASSIGNMENTS FOR WRITING

1. A fine motion picture version of *Billy Budd* has been made, starring Peter Ustinov as Captain Vere. If you are able to see the film, write a review of it. Criticize the film as an artistic entity all its own, rather than for its closeness in plot or in characterization to Melville's story.
2. In *Billy Budd*, a rigid respect for the naval code overcomes natural human emotions. How does society today react in similar circumstances? What is the obligation of those to whom the responsibility for maintaining justice has been given? Answer in an essay supported by evidence from literature and from current events.
3. In *Billy Budd*, Melville appears to have been constructing a symbolic story based upon biblical allusions. Write an analysis of a symbol or symbols, carefully explaining the development of the story from a literal reading to its figurative meanings. Use specific textual references to support your argument.
4. Create your own version of the Garden of Eden story in a narrative. Establish the sequence of innocence, temptation, and guilt so that your reader can readily identify the allusion.
5. Read W. H. Auden's poem, "Herman Melville," and write an essay in which you discuss Auden's view of Melville's work and the place he gives *Billy Budd* in the poem. Add your own commentary and criticism.

Walt Whitman

Until recently very little has been known about Walt Whitman. In fact, of all noted American poets, none has had less critical attention in his own country. In the past thirty years, however, the number of books and articles about Whitman and his poetry has increased significantly, as readers and critics have at last come to recognize his uniquely comprehensive genius. Because so little has really been known about this engaging and mysterious American, the tendency has been to interpret his comprehensive spirit and subject matter in whatever way is convenient in order to make a point or support a theory. Consequently, there has arisen a multiplicity of legends, and very little truth, about Walt Whitman.

It is not strange that legends grew up about Whitman's life and artistic development even before his death in 1892, for he was at once a boisterously American figure and a grand, universal one. He was born on May 31, 1819 at the family farmhouse in West Hills, Long Island. His ancestry in America can be traced back to 1640, when the brothers John and Jechariah Whitman sailed to the New World from their homes in England. His maternal ancestors were the Van Velsors, Dutchmen who had also settled in America some generations before his birth. He later noted them for their robust health and their love of farming, horses, and the Quaker religion.

Some of the poet's dearest reminiscences in later life were of his early boyhood at West Hills and of the fondness he developed then for the eastern and northern shores of Long Island, where he frequently made trips to catch eels or gather sea gulls' eggs. Soon there was a change, however, for when Walt was four his father moved the family to the growing town of Brooklyn, where they were to rent, build, and lose a succession of houses as a result of the elder Whitman's precarious trade of carpentry. Two of the poet's most vivid memories of his childhood in Brooklyn were of the visit in 1824 of old General Lafayette, when the General embraced the five-year-old boy, and of the night in 1829 when his parents took him to see the Quaker preacher Elias Hicks, whose spirit and eloquence impressed the child deeply.

Brooklyn at this time was a thriving trade center and seaport, where young Walt had ample opportunity to observe the myriad activities of building and commerce which went on about the docks and warehouses, and which were later to invest the images of his poems. He attended public school more or less regularly, though the classes were rigorous and oppressive, and his performance undistinguished. (We can assess his fondness for the place from the title of a piece he wrote later, called "Death in the School-Room (A Fact).") He read eagerly on his own, however, especially after a friend gave him a subscription to a large circulating library nearby. Among the books he remembered reading as a child were the *Arabian Nights* and the novels and poetry of Walter Scott, as well as other romantic works popular at the time. Whitman himself, in summing up those years, declared that there were three major influences operating on his character throughout his childhood:

> . . . the maternal nativity-stock brought hither from far-away Netherlands, for one, (doubtless the best)—the subterranean tenacity and central bony structure (obstinacy, wilfulness) which I get from my paternal English elements, for another—and the combination of my Long Island birth-spot, seashores, childhood's scenes, absorptions, with teeming Brooklyn and New York . . . for the third.

Walt Whitman's working life began at the age of eleven, when he was employed as a clerk in a law office. One year later, in 1831, he went to work in his first of a long succession of newspaper jobs, as a printer's assistant on the Long Island *Patriot*. By 1835 his family had moved back to Long Island, where Walt took summer vacations from his work. When he was seventeen he worked on a newspaper in New York as a compositor, while developing a keen interest in debate and maintaining several memberships in debate societies. At eighteen he became an itinerate schoolteacher for a brief period, in Long Island and counties bordering New York City. Finally, in 1838, at the age of twenty, Whitman started his first newspaper, in Huntington, Long Island.

Between the years of 1839 and 1855 Whitman held a number of newspaper jobs in and around New York City, with varying, though never great, success. At the same time he developed an interest in politics, probably out of his experiences in debate, and by 1848 he had become a leading speaker for the younger wing of the Democratic Party around New York. But in neither of these fields did he really distinguish himself, and he published no significant poetry or prose until 1855, when he produced and distributed on his own the first edition of *Leaves of Grass,* which then contained only twelve poems. Whitman has left us no record of how he suddenly turned into a poet in 1855, after a mediocre career as a journalist and orator. It is a mystery which still eludes the critics, though there are several causes which are commonly assumed to have influenced his artistic awakening.

Perhaps the first impetus to Whitman's poetic sensibilities was the result of his trip south in 1848. He had been engaged for a short stint on a newspaper in New Orleans, and his trip from New York to Louisiana was his first extended journey through the states and his first chance to observe the American scenery and way of life on a national scale. The journey made a deep impression on him, and was to be the first of many trips around the country north and south, and as far west as the Rocky Mountains. Because he was to devote so much of his poetry, from the beginning, to the subject of America— fervently describing, eulogizing, and even cataloguing its people and places—it is logical to assume the importance to the poet of his first journey in 1848. With his own awakening to the vistas of his country came the awakening of one of his most persistent and intense poetic concerns: the beauty and power of America.

A second influence helped to suggest America to Whitman as a poetic concern: the theories of the great American thinker and essayist, Ralph Waldo Emerson. In several of his essays, Emerson had suggested the need for a purely American poet who would mold from the subject matter of his native country all of the universal themes which foreign literatures had been dealing with for centuries. Whitman's reading of these essays, combined with the recent excitement of his trip south, must have awakened in him the desire to "sing" the themes of America with all the beauty and force which the growing country itself displayed. As Whitman himself admitted, "I was simmering . . . and Emerson brought me to a boil." By the time they evolved into poetry, Whitman's ideas about America and its democracy had become fused with his general theories about the essential vitality of raw nature in the individual or the country. As he said later in *Specimen Days:*

> I conceive of no flourishing and heroic elements of Democracy in the United States, or of Democracy maintaining itself at all, without the Nature-element forming a main part—to be its health-element and beauty-element—to really underlie the whole politics, sanity, religion and art of the New World.

These thoughts, too, are reminiscent of Emerson, and Whitman's indebtedness to the essayist is widely acknowledged.

A third important influence on Whitman's poetic development was his religious background. His youthful exposure to the Quaker religion remained with him throughout his life, as did his memories of his Quaker grandmother and her "deeply intuitive and spiritual" nature. His early recognition of the life of the spirit contributed in large part to one of his most important themes: that of the soul. Later, Whitman's general though deeply spiritual religious bent permitted him to fuse Eastern religious concepts with the developing science of his day into a concept of the soul as a receiver and as an individual expression of the meanings of the universe. A list of references for these thoughts would include Quaker, Hindu, and Transcendental theories, but they would never have been expressed at all without the early intuitive spirituality and freedom of thought which Whitman eventually found it so invigorating to translate into poetry.

As an influence on the shape and subject matter of Whitman's work, the importance of his contemporary America, then, can hardly be overestimated. Its scenes, its vitality, its religious climate, and even its great thinkers all contributed to the scope and dynamism with which Whitman represented the human condition as he experienced it. From his diverse experiences on the Brooklyn docks to his reading of Emerson, Whitman remained open to the sensual, intellectual, and spiritual suggestions of this country whose growth and future in those realms never ceased to occupy and delight him.

It is also important to note the influence on Whitman, by 1855, of European music and European theories of poetry and of art in general. These played a significant role in helping Whitman to develop his ways of expressing himself in poetry, and especially his techniques of imagery. By 1848 Whitman was attending a great many operas in New York, and his "musical passion," as he called it in an essay on plays and operas, had important consequences for his poetic sensibilities. It was in music, above all, that the young man found the kind of spiritual transfiguration which was to become such an important aim and subject in his poetry. Once at a Beethoven concert, he said, "I allow'd myself, as I sometimes do, to wander out of myself." He described having been "carried away, seeing, absorbing many wonders."

The most significant of the European influences on Whitman, however, were the specific poetic and artistic theories with which he had come in contact. His poetic technique came to exemplify—and indeed to forecast—the symbolistic and imagistic techniques of

European art so well that he has been consciously imitated rather thoroughly in Europe, more so than in his own America! He expressed the foundations of his imagistic technique in an essay entitled "Poetry To-day in America" as follows: ". . . the poetry of the future aims at the free expression of emotion, (which means far, far more than appears at first,) and to arouse and initiate, more than to define or finish. Like all modern tendencies, it has direct or indirect reference continually to the reader, to you or me, to the central identity of everything, the mighty Ego." This kind of suggestive imagery, to the great degree to which Whitman was successful with it, was then and remains now a rare thing in America, though it was to gain great expression in French and German literature and in French painting, largely *after* Whitman had finished his work. Later in the same essay, Whitman quotes a French critic whom he had read before 1855, as saying: "For us the greatest poet is he who in his works most stimulates the reader's imagination and reflection, who excites him the most himself to poetize. The greatest poet is not he who has done the best; it is he who suggests the most."

Considering all the influences which contributed to the awakening of Whitman's poetic genius, we see that Whitman made perhaps the fullest use in American literature of the American nation and idiom which had first excited him to explore the themes of the self, the country, and the cosmos. On the other hand, perhaps it was the European influences on Whitman which were to prove the most artistically significant. European critics claim that this is the case. Since they have studied him longer and harder than we Americans, they may well be right. But for us Whitman holds a special appeal because as a self-consciously American man and poet, he sang of America, in our own language. Even those great suggestive images of his self and his universe are American in a way only we can enjoy; and they are meant for us—

> I bequeath myself to the dirt to grow from the grass I love,
> If you want me again look for me under your boot-soles.
>
> You will hardly know who I am or what I mean,
> But I shall be good health to you nevertheless,
> And filter and fibre your blood.
>
> Failing to fetch me at first keep encouraged,
> Missing me at one place search another,
> I stop somewhere waiting for you.

Inscriptions

One's-Self I Sing

One's-Self I sing, a simple separate person,
Yet utter the word Democratic, the word En-Masse.

Of physiology from top to toe I sing,
Not physiognomy alone nor brain alone is worthy for the
        Muse, I say the Form complete is worthier far,
The Female equally with the Male I sing.

Of Life immense in passion, pulse, and power,
Cheerful, for freest action form'd under the laws divine,
The Modern Man I sing.

Calamus

I Saw in Louisiana a Live-Oak Growing

I saw in Louisiana a live-oak growing,
All alone stood it and the moss hung down from the branches,
Without any companion it grew there uttering joyous leaves
        of dark green,
And its look, rude, unbending, lusty, made me think of
        myself,
But I wonder'd how it could utter joyous leaves standing
        alone there without its friend near, for I knew I could
        not,
And I broke off a twig with a certain number of leaves upon
        it, and twined around it a little moss,
And brought it away, and I have placed it in sight in my
        room,
It is not needed to remind me as of my own dear friends,
(For I believe lately I think of little else than of them,)
Yet it remains to me a curious token, it makes me think
        of manly love;   10
For all that, and though the live-oak glistens there in Loui-
        siana solitary in a wide flat space,

Uttering joyous leaves all its life without a friend a lover
near,
I know very well I could not.

Crossing Brooklyn Ferry

1

Flood-tide below me! I see you face to face!
Clouds of the west—sun there half an hour high—I see you
also face to face.
Crowds of men and women attired in the usual costumes,
how curious you are to me!
On the ferry boats the hundreds and hundreds that cross,
returning home, are more curious to me than you
suppose,
And you that shall cross from shore to shore years hence are
more to me, and more in my meditations, than you
might suppose.

2

The impalpable sustenance of me from all things at all
hours of the day,
The simple, compact, well-join'd scheme, myself disintegrated, every one disintegrated yet part of the scheme,
The similitudes of the past and those of the future,
The glories strung like beads on my smallest sights and
hearings, on the walk in the street and the passage
over the river,
The current rushing so swiftly and swimming with me far
away,   10
The others that are to follow me, the ties between me and
them,
The certainty of others, the life, love, sight, hearing of
others.

Others will enter the gates of the ferry and cross from
shore to shore,
Others will watch the run of the flood-tide,
Others will see the shipping of Manhattan north and west,
and the heights of Brooklyn to the south and east,
Others will see the islands large and small;

Fifty years hence, others will see them as they cross, the
    sun half an hour high,
A hundred years hence, or ever so many hundred years
    hence, others will see them,
Will enjoy the sunset, the pouring-in of the flood-tide, the
    falling-back to the sea of the ebb-tide.

3

It avails not, time nor place—distance avails not,   20
I am with you, you men and women of a generation, or
    ever so many generations hence,
Just as you feel when you look on the river and sky, so I
    felt,
Just as any of you is one of a living crowd, I was one of
    a crowd,
Just as you are refresh'd by the gladness of the river and
    the bright flow, I was refresh'd,
Just as you stand and lean on the rail, yet hurry with the
    swift current, I stood yet was hurried,
Just as you look on the numberless masts of ships and the
    thick-stemm'd pipes of steamboats, I look'd.
I too many and many a time cross'd the river of old,
Watched the Twelfth-month sea-gulls, saw them high in
    the air floating with motionless wings, oscillating their
    bodies,
Saw how the glistening yellow lit up parts of their bodies
    and left the rest in strong shadow,
Saw the slow-wheeling circles and the gradual edging to-
    ward the south,   30
Saw the reflection of the summer sky in the water,
Had my eyes dazzled by the shimmering track of beams,
Look'd at the fine centrifugal spokes of light round the
    shape of my head in the sunlit water,
Look'd on the haze on the hills southward and south-
    westward,
Look'd on the vapor as it flew in fleeces tinged with violet,
Look'd toward the lower bay to notice the vessels arriving,
Saw their approach, saw aboard those that were near me,
Saw the white sails of schooners and sloops, saw the ships
    at anchor,
The sailors at work in the rigging or out astride the spars,

The round masts, the swinging motion of the hulls, the
    slender serpentine pennants,   40
The large and small steamers in motion, the pilots in their
    pilot-houses,
The white wake left by the passage, the quick tremulous
    whirl of the wheels,
The flags of all nations, the falling of them at sunset,
The scallop-edged waves in the twilight, the ladled cups,
    the frolicsome crests and glistening,
The stretch afar growing dimmer and dimmer, the gray walls
    of the granite storehouses by the docks,
On the river the shadowy group, the big steam-tug closely
    flank'd on each side by the barges, the hay-boat, the
    belated lighter,
On the neighboring shore the fires from the foundry chim-
    neys burning high and glaringly into the night,
Casting their flicker of black contrasted with wild red and
    yellow light over the tops of houses, and down into
    the clefts of streets.

4

These and all else were to me the same as they are to you,
I loved well those cities, loved well the stately and rapid
    river,   50
The men and women I saw were all near to me,
Others the same—others who look back on me because I
    look'd forward to them,
(The time will come, though I stop here to-day and to-
    night.)

5

What is it then between us?
What is the count of the scores or hundreds of years be-
    tween us?

Whatever it is, it avails not—distance avails not, and place
    avails not,
I too lived, Brooklyn of ample hills was mine,
I too walk'd the streets of Manhattan island, and bathed in
    the waters around it,
I too felt the curious abrupt questionings stir within me,
In the day among crowds of people sometimes they came
    upon me,   60

In my walks home late at night or as I lay in my bed they
     came upon me,
I too had been struck from the float forever held in solution,
I too had receiv'd identity by my body,
That I was I knew was of my body, and what I should be
     I knew I should be of my body.

6

It is not upon you alone the dark patches fall,
The dark threw its patches down upon me also,
The best I had done seem'd to me blank and suspicious,
My great thoughts as I supposed them,   re they not in
     reality meager?
Nor is it you alone who know what it is to be evil,
I am he who knew what it was to be evil,   70
I too knitted the old knot of contrariety,
Blabb'd, blush'd, resented, lied, stole, grudg'd,
Had guile, anger, lust, hot wishes I dared not speak,
Was wayward, vain, greedy, shallow, sly, cowardly, malignant,
The wolf, the snake, the hog, not wanting in me,
The cheating look, the frivolous word, the adulterous wish,
     not wanting,
Refusals, hates, postponements, meanness, laziness, none of
     these wanting,
Was one with the rest, the days and haps of the rest,
Was call'd by my nighest name by clear loud voices of
     young men as they saw me approaching or passing,
Felt their arms on my neck as I stood, or the negligent lean-
     ing of their flesh against me as I sat,   80
Saw many I loved in the street or ferry-boat or public assem-
     bly, yet never told them a word,
Lived the same life with the rest, the same old laughing,
     gnawing, sleeping,
Play'd the part that still looks back on the actor or actress,
The same old role, the role that is what we make it, as great
     as we like,
Or as small as we like, or both great and small.

7

Closer yet I approach you,
What thought you have of me now, I had as much of you—
     I laid in my stores in advance,

I consider'd long and seriously of you before you were born.
Who was to know what should come home to me?
Who knows but I am enjoying this?   90
Who knows, for all the distance, but I am as good as look-
    ing at you now, for all you cannot see me?

8

Ah, what can ever be more stately and admirable to me
    than mast-hemm'd Manhattan?
River and sunset and scallop-edg'd waves of flood-tide?
The sea-gulls oscillating their bodies, the hay-boat in the
    twilight, and the belated lighter?

What gods can exceed these that clasp me by the hand,
    and with voices I love call me promptly and loudly
    by my nighest name as I approach?
What is more subtle than this which ties me to the woman
    or man that looks in my face?
Which fuses me into you now, and pours my meaning into
    you?

We understand then do we not?
What I promis'd without mentioning it, have you not
    accepted?
What the study could not teach—what the preaching could
    not accomplish is accomplish'd, is it not?   100

9

Flow on, river! flow with the flood-tide, and ebb with the
    ebb-tide!
Frolic on, crested and scallop-edg'd waves!
Gorgeous clouds of the sunset! drench with your splendor
    me, or the men and women generations after me!
Cross from shore to shore, countless crowds of passengers!
Stand up, tall masts of Mannahattan! stand up, beautiful hills
    of Brooklyn!
Throb, baffled and curious brain! throw out questions and
    answers!
Suspend here and everywhere, eternal float of solution!
Gaze, loving and thirsting eyes, in the house or street or
    public assembly!
Sound out, voices of young men! loudly and musically call
    me by my nighest name!

CROSSING BROOKLYN FERRY 289

Live, old life! play the part that looks back on the actor or
 actress!   110
Play the old role, the role that is great or small according
 as one makes it!
Consider, you who peruse me, whether I may not in unknown ways be looking upon you;
Be firm, rail over the river, to support those who lean idly,
 yet haste with the hasting current;
Fly on, sea-birds! fly sideways or wheel in large circles high
 in the air;
Receive the summer sky, you water, and faithfully hold it
 till all downcast eyes have time to take it from you!
Diverge, fine spokes of light, from the shape of my head, or
 any one's head, in the sunlit water!
Come on, ships from the lower bay! pass up or down,
 white-sail'd schooners, sloops, lighters!
Flaunt away, flags of all nations! be duly lower'd at sunset!
Burn high your fires, foundry chimneys! cast black shadows
 at nightfall! cast red and yellow light over the tops
 of the houses!
Appearances, now or henceforth, indicate what you are, 120
You necessary film, continue to envelop the soul,
About my body for me, and your body for you, be hung
 our divinest aromas,
Thrive, cities—bring your freight, bring your shows, ample
 and sufficient rivers,
Expand, being than which none else is perhaps more
 spiritual,
Keep your places, objects than which none else is more
 lasting.

You have waited, you always wait, you dumb, beautiful
 ministers,
We receive you with free sense at last, and are insatiate
 hence-forward,
Not you any more shall be able to foil us, or withhold
 yourselves from us,
We use you, and do not cast you aside—we plant you
 permanently within us,
We fathom you not—we love you—there is perfection in
 you also,   130
You furnish your parts toward eternity,
Great or small, you furnish your parts toward the soul.

By the Roteside

When I Heard the Learn'd Astronomer

When I heard the learn'd astronomer,
When the proofs, the figures, were ranged in columns be-
    fore me,
When I was shown the charts and diagrams, to add, divide,
    and measure them,
When I sitting heard the astronomer where he lectured
    with much applause in the lecture-room,
How soon unaccountable I became tired and sick,
Till rising and gliding out I wander'd off by myself,
In the mystical moist night-air, and from time to time,
Look'd up in perfect silence at the stars.

Memories of President Lincoln

When Lilacs Last in the Dooryard Bloom'd

1

When lilacs last in the dooryard bloom'd,
And the great star early droop'd in the western sky in the
    night,
I mourn'd, and yet shall mourn with ever-returning spring.

Ever-returning spring, trinity sure to me you bring,
Lilac blooming perennial and drooping star in the west,
And thought of him I love.

2

O powerful western fallen star!
O shades of night—O moody, tearful night!
O great star disappear'd—O the black murk that hides the
    star!
O cruel hands that hold me powerless—O helpless soul of
    me!   10
O harsh surrounding cloud that will not free my soul.

3

In the dooryard fronting an old farm-house near the white-
   wash'd palings,
Stands the lilac-bush tall-growing with heart-shaped leaves
   of rich green,
With many a pointed blossom rising delicate, with the perfume strong I love,
With every leaf a miracle—and from this bush in the door-
   yard,
With delicate-color'd blossoms and heart-shaped leaves of
   rich green,
A sprig with its flower I break.

4

In the swamp in secluded recesses,
A shy and hidden bird is warbling a song.
Solitary the thrush,   20
The hermit withdrawn to himself, avoiding the settlements,
Sings by himself a song.

Song of the bleeding throat,
Death's outlet song of life, (for well dear brother I know,
If thou wast not granted to sing thou would'st surely die.)

5

Over the breast of the spring, the land, amid cities,
Amid lanes and through old woods, where lately the violets
   peep'd from the ground, spotting the gray debris,
Amid the grass in the fields each side of the lanes, passing
   the endless grass,
Passing the yellow-spear'd wheat, every grain from its
   shroud in the dark-brown fields uprisen,
Passing the apple-tree blows of white and pink in the
   orchards,   30
Carrying a corpse to where it shall rest in the grave,
Night and day journeys a coffin.

6

Coffin that passes through lanes and streets,
Through day and night with the great cloud darkening the
   land,
With the pomp of the inloop'd flags with the cities draped
   in black,

With the show of the States themselves as of crape-veil'd
    women standing,
With processions long and winding and the flambeaus of
    the night,
With the countless torches lit, with the silent sea of faces
    and the unbared heads,
With the waiting depot, the arriving coffin, and the sombre
    faces,
With dirges through the night, with the thousand voices
    rising strong and solemn,   40
With all the mournful voices of the dirges pour'd around
    the coffin,
The dim-lit churches and the shuddering organs—where
    amid these you journey,
With the tolling tolling bells' perpetual clang,
Here, coffin that slowly passes,
I give you my sprig of lilac.

                        7
(Nor for you, for one alone,
Blossoms and branches green to coffins all I bring,
For fresh as the morning, thus would I chant a song for
    you O sane and sacred death.

All over bouquets of roses,
O death, I cover you over with roses and early lilies,   50
But mostly and now the lilac that blooms the first,
Copious I break, I break the sprigs from the bushes,
With loaded arms I come, pouring for you,
For you and the coffins all of you O death.)

                        8
O western orb sailing the heaven,
Now I know what you must have meant as a month since I
    walk'd,
As I walk'd in silence the transparent shadowy night,
As I saw you had something to tell as you bent to me
    night after night,
As you droop'd from the sky low down as if to my side,
    (while the other stars all look'd on,)
As we wander'd together the solemn night, (for something I
    know not what kept me from sleep,)   60
As the night advanced, and I saw on the rim of the west
    how full you were of woe,

As I stood on the rising ground in the breeze in the cool
    transparent night,
As I watch'd where you pass'd and was lost in the nether-
    ward black of the night,
As my soul in its trouble dissatisfied sank, as where you
    sad orb,
Concluded, dropt in the night, and was gone.

9

Sing on there in the swamp,
O singer bashful and tender, I hear your notes, I hear your
    call,
I hear, I come presently, I understand you,
But a moment I linger, for the lustrous star has detain'd
    me,
The star my departing comrade holds and detains me.   70

10

O how shall I warble myself for the dead one there I loved?
And how shall I deck my song for the large sweet soul that
    has gone?
And what shall my perfume be for the grave of him I love?

Sea-winds blown from east and west,
Blown from the Eastern sea and blown from the Western
    sea, till there on the prairies meeting,
These and with these and the breath of my chant,
I'll perfume the grave of him I love.

11

O what shall I hang on the chamber walls?
And what shall the pictures be that I hang on the walls,
To adorn the burial-house of him I love?   80

Pictures of growing spring and farms and homes,
With the Fourth-month eve at sundown, and the gray smoke
    lucid and bright,
With floods of the yellow gold of the gorgeous, indolent,
    sinking sun, burning, expanding the air,
With the fresh sweet herbage under foot, and the pale green
    leaves of the trees prolific,
In the distance the flowing glaze, the breast of the river, with
    a wind-dapple here and there,

With ranging hills on the banks, with many a line against
    the sky, and shadows,
And the city at hand with dwellings so dense, and stacks
    of chimneys,
And all the scenes of life and the workshops, and the work-
    men homeward returning.

12

Lo, body and soul—this land,
My own Manhattan with spires, and the sparkling and
    hurrying tides, and the ships,   90
The varied and ample land, the South and the North in the
    light, Ohio's shores and flashing Missouri,
And ever the far-spreading prairies cover'd with grass and
    corn.

Lo, the most excellent sun so calm and haughty,
The violet and purple morn with just-felt breezes,
The gentle soft-born measureless light,
The miracle spreading bathing all, the fulfill'd noon,
The coming eve delicious, the welcome night and the stars,
Over my cities shining all, enveloping man and land.

13

Sing on, sing on you gray-brown bird,
Sing from the swamps, the recesses, pour your chant from
    the bushes,   100
Limitless out of the dusk, out of the cedars and pines.

Sing on dearest brother, warble your reedy song,
Loud human song, with voice of uttermost woe.

O liquid and free and tender!
O wild and loose to my soul—O wondrous singer!
You only I hear—yet the star holds me, (but will soon de-
    part,)
Yet the lilac with mastering odor holds me.

14

Now while I sat in the day and look'd forth,
In the close of the day with its light and the fields of
    spring, and the farmers preparing their crops,
In the large unconscious scenery of my land with its lakes
    and forests,   110

In the heavenly aerial beauty, (after the perturb'd winds
and the storms,)
Under the arching heavens of the afternoon swift passing,
and the voices of children and women,
The many-moving sea-tides, and I saw the ships how they
sail'd,
And the summer approaching with richness, and the fields
all busy with labor,
And the infinite separate houses, how they all went on,
each with its meals and minutia of daily usages,
And the streets how their throbbings throbb'd, and the
cities pent—lo, then and there,
Falling upon them all and among them all, enveloping me
with the rest,
Appear'd the cloud, appear'd the long black trail,
And I knew death, its thought, and the sacred knowledge
of death.

Then with the knowledge of death as walking one side of
me,   120
And the thought of death close-walking the other side of me,
And I in the middle as with companions, and as holding
the hands of companions,
I fled forth to the hiding receiving night that talks not,
Down to the shores of the water, the path by the swamp in
the dimness,
To the solemn shadowy cedars and ghostly pines so still.

And the singer so shy to the rest receiv'd me,
The gray-brown bird I know receiv'd us comrades three,
And he sang the carol of death, and a verse for him I love.

From deep secluded recesses,
From the fragrant cedars and the ghostly pines so still,   130
Came the carol of the bird.

And the charm of the carol rapt me,
As I held as if by their hands my comrades in the night,
And the voice of my spirit tallied the song of the bird.

Come lovely and soothing death,
Undulate round the world, serenely arriving, arriving,
In the day, in the night, to all, to each,
Sooner or later delicate death.

Prais'd be the fathomless universe,

For life and joy, and for objects and knowledge curious,   140
And for love, sweet love—but praise! praise! praise!
For the sure-enwinding arms of cool-enfolding death.

Dark mother always gliding near with soft feet,
Have none chanted for thee a chant of fullest welcome?
Then I chant it for thee, I glorify thee above all,
I bring thee a song that when thou must indeed come, come unfal-
      teringly.

Approach strong deliveress,
When it is so, when thou hast taken them I joyously sing the dead,
Lost in the loving floating ocean of thee,
Laved in the flood of thy bliss O death.   150
From me to thee glad serenades,
Dances for thee I propose saluting thee, adornments and feastings
      for thee,
And the sights of the open landscape and the high-spread sky are
      fitting,
And life and the fields, and the huge and thoughtful night.

The night in silence under many a star,
The ocean shore and the husky whispering wave whose voice I know,
And the soul turning to thee O vast and well-veil'd death,
And the body gratefully nestling close to thee.

Over the tree-tops I float thee a song,
Over the rising and sinking waves, over the myriad fields and the
      prairies wide,   160
Over the dense-pack'd cities all and the teeming wharves and ways,
I float this carol with joy, with joy to thee O death.

            15
To the tally of my soul,
Loud and strong kept up the gray-brown bird,
With pure deliberate notes spreading filling the night.

Loud in the pines and cedars dim,
Clear in the freshness moist and the swamp-perfume,
And I with my comrades there in the night.

While my sight that was bound in my eyes unclosed,
As to long panoramas of visions.   170

And I saw askant the armies,
I saw as in noiseless dreams hundreds of battle-flags,

Borne through the smoke of the battles and pierc'd with
    missiles I saw them,
And carried hither and yon through the smoke, and torn
    and bloody,
And at last but a few shreds left on the staffs, (and all in
    silence,)
And the staffs all splinter'd and broken.

I saw battle-corpses, myriads of them,
And the white skeletons of young men, I saw them,
I saw the debris and debris of all the slain soldiers of the war,
But I saw they were not as was thought,   180
They themselves were fully at rest, they suffer'd not,
The living remain'd and suffer'd, the mother suffer'd,
And the wife and the child and the musing comrade suffer'd,
And the armies that remain'd suffer'd.

16

Passing the visions, passing the night,
Passing, unloosing the hold of my comrades' hands,
Passing the song of the hermit bird and the tallying song
    of my soul,
Victorious song, death's outlet song, yet varying ever-altering
    song,
As low and wailing, yet clear the notes, rising and falling,
    flooding the night,
Sadly sinking and fainting, as warning and warning, and yet
    again bursting with joy,   190
Covering the earth and filling the spread of the heaven,
As that powerful psalm in the night I heard from recesses,
Passing, I leave thee lilac with heart-shaped leaves,
I leave thee there in the door-yard, blooming, returning
    with spring.

I cease from my song for thee,
From my gaze on thee in the west, fronting the west, com-
    muning with thee,
O comrade lustrous with silver face in the night.

Yet each to keep and all, retrievements out of the night,
The song, the wondrous chant of the gray-brown bird,
And the tallying chant, the echo arous'd in my soul,   200
With the lustrous and drooping star with the countenance
    full of woe,

With the holders holding my hand nearing the call of the
      bird,
Comrades mine and I in the midst, and their memory ever
      to keep, for the dead I loved so well,
For the sweetest, wisest soul of all my days and lands—
      and this for his dear sake,
Lilac and star and bird twined with the chant of my soul,
There in the fragrant pines and the cedars dusk and dim.

Whispers of Heavenly Death

A Noiseless Patient Spider

A noiseless patient spider,
I mark'd where on a little promontory it stood isolated,
Mark'd how to explore the vacant vast surrounding,
It launch'd forth filament, filament, filament, out of itself,
Ever unreeling down, ever tirelessly speeding them.

And you O my soul where you stand,
Surrounded, detached, in measureless oceans of space,
Ceaselessly musing, venturing, throwing, seeking the spheres
      to connect them,
Till the bridge you will need be form'd, till the ductile anchor
      hold,
Till the gossamer thread you fling catch somewhere, O my
      soul.

From Noon to Starry Night

Spirit That Form'd This Scene

Written in Platte Cañon, Colorado

Spirit that form'd this scene,
These tumbled rock-piles grim and red,

These reckless heaven-ambitious peaks,
These gorges, turbulent-clear streams, this naked freshness,
These formless wild arrays, for reasons of their own,
I know thee, savage spirit—we have communed together,
Mine too such wild arrays, for reasons of their own;
Was't charged against my chants they had forgotten art?
To fuse within themselves its rules precise and delicatesse?
The lyrist's measur'd beat, the wrought-out temple's grace—
     column and polish'd arch forgot?   10
But thou that revelest here—spirit that form'd this scene,
They have remember'd thee.

QUESTIONS FOR DISCUSSION

One's-Self I Sing

1. In one of Walt Whitman's early poems, the poet refers to himself as a "kosmos." Look up the word in the dictionary (under the spelling "cosmos"), and decide which of its meanings applies best to the Self which the poet sings in the present poem. In the first two lines of the poem, what is the slight contradiction implied by the word *Yet?* How is the contradiction resolved?
2. Whitman's next declaration of his poetic purpose comes in the second stanza. What subject does he proclaim in these lines?
3. Why is line 6 ("Of Life . . .") a natural outgrowth of the preceding lines in imagery and theme? Note the alliteration of the final three nouns in the line, and explain their relation to the life of the body.
4. How, in line 7, does the poet associate human freedom of action with the divine order of creation? Discuss the possible thematic reasons for Whitman's placing of this line near the end of the poem.
5. How, in this poem, does Whitman identify himself with the "Modern Man"? Refer back to the first two lines, which can now be re-evaluated. Note that he does not say "My-Self," but "One's-Self."

I Saw in Louisiana a Live-Oak Growing

1. Before you reach the fourth line and the phrase, "made me think of myself," what image in line 3 makes a connection between the poet and his metaphorical subject? Did you notice this connection when you read "uttering joyous leaves," and if so, why?
2. In what way, in line 5, does the poet first draw a contrast between himself and the tree?

3. How does Whitman use the metaphor of the tree to express the relationship between love and poetry throughout the poem?
4. What sort of poetic inspiration does the "curious token" represent for the poet?

Crossing Brooklyn Ferry

1. This long poem has been called the greatest of Whitman's early works—the most balanced and unified in its exposition of the cosmic unity of nature and the spirit. Using the setting of the ferry crossing between New York and Brooklyn at flood-tide, Whitman confronts first himself and then the ages of men to follow him. How, in section 1, does Whitman work the progression from nature and the self to a concern with all men?
2. What relationship between men and nature is suggested by the images in the first seven lines of section 2?
3. What are the "ties between me and them" based on as the poet describes them in the final seven lines of section 2? Through what medium is the human unity fused? What allegorical role do the ferry and its journey take on in the fusion these lines describe?
4. How does section 3 relate to the final three lines of section 1? Explain how the poet sets forth and fulfills his thematic purpose, from the first line on in section 3. Trace the development of the imagery: what seasons are described here? what kinds of natural sights?
5. Concentrate on several lines or a group of lines which please you in section 3, and make a study of their rhythm and meter. Do you find the section's metric qualities fitting to its subject and imagery?
6. Whitman's original title for this poem was "The Sun Down Poem." In what ways is that title applicable to the poem? What effect is created through the accumulation of images of sun and light through stanza 3, for example?
7. What do the final lines in section 5 suggest about man's sense of physical identity as an unnatural cause of spiritual disharmony? How are the "questionings" in line 59 related to this bewilderment of the physical being? Are they the questionings of unnatural guilt? How do the final three lines support this interpretation? What do you understand Whitman to mean by "the float forever held in solution"?
8. Would you agree that section 6 develops the theme of the "questionings" introduced in section 5? What sort of continuity do you perceive between the fifth and sixth sections? Illustrate your answer with references to the images in both sections, and be sure to discuss the kind of imagery which invests section 6.
9. Section 7 begins with the poet's claim that he has already demonstrated a human unity ("Closer yet I approach you.") How is this claim a natural outgrowth of his revealing and universalizing of his own "questionings" in section 5? Could you say, then, that the poet

has transformed man's traditional bewilderment about his physical self into a bond between men, in sections 5, 6, and 7? Discuss this idea, with specific references to the three sections.

10. How does section 8 continue this progression? Discuss, with reference to the first two stanzas. What meaning does the progression give to the final three lines? Why have study and preaching failed to accomplish what Whitman has? Is the poet in some sense repudiating the past? Discuss.

11. Describe the several kinds of unity which Whitman expresses in section 9. What sort of unity in the poem does line 115 invoke, and how does this line relate to the images in the poem's opening lines?

12. Notice how, in lines 126–132 the poet returns to the objects of nature. Of what transcendental event are they the "dumb, beautiful ministers"? How do the final three lines of section 9 again express the unity of men and nature? How does the "soul" in the final line relate to the images in the previous two lines?

13. Discuss the role of the poet in this transcendental poem, tracing his presence and function throughout. Also trace the unifying force exerted by the allegory of the ferry and by the natural setting through which it passes. Illustrate your discussion with examples from imagery throughout the poem.

When I Heard the Learn'd Astronomer

1. How are the activities and atmosphere of the lecture-room in the opening four lines contrasted with the last four lines of the poem? In your discussion, mention especially the difference between the verbs and nouns in line 3 and those in lines 6 and 7. Is the contrast effective?

2. How does the "perfect silence" contrast with the sounds of the lecture-room?

3. How does the difference between the stars and the lecture about the stars contrast *knowledge* with *experience*? Discuss the effect of Whitman's techniques of contrast throughout the poem.

When Lilacs Last in the Dooryard Bloom'd

1. This poem is one of the most famous and revered elegies of all time, in any language. Whitman wrote it to commemorate the death, in the spring of 1865, of Abraham Lincoln. It would be well to understand, while reading it, what the critic Malcolm Cowley has called the "symphonic" organization of the poem: how Whitman has interwoven, or *orchestrated*, several groups of images and themes in the poem. The three dominant images are of the lilacs, the evening star, and the thrush and its song. Notice the introduction of these images in the first four sections of the poem. Trace specifically the significance of each, and the intertwining, or orchestration, of them throughout the

poem to its conclusion. What happens to them in the final lines of the poem, and what unifying effect does this have on the poem's imagistic development?

2. Likewise, there are three major themes to be dealt with in this poem: those of death, of the spring as a symbol for rebirth, and of the song, both of the bird and of the poet. The themes, too, are orchestrated throughout the poem, and give meaning and relevance to each other as the poet blends them. Trace the theme of death through the poem. Concentrate especially on sections 5, 6, 7, 14, and 15. How, in these sections, does the poet move from the particular to the universal, from the tragic to the joyous? Could you call section 14 the climax in the development of this theme? Discuss.

3. Trace the symbol of spring and the theme of rebirth through the poem, as you did with the theme of death. Concentrate on sections 1, 3, 5, 11, 12, and 14. Notice how this theme, too, is brought to a climax in section 14. What is its significance as both theme and image here? In what ways are the symbol of spring and the theme of rebirth more constant throughout than the theme of death? What significance does this have for the meaning of the poem as a whole? What unifying effect?

4. Trace the symbol of the bird's song and the theme of the poet's song through the poem. Look especially at sections 4, 9, 10, 13, 14, and 15. How are the two songs related? What does the poet's song mean and represent to him? Analyze its climactic exposition in section 14. How, and where, does the motif of the songs help to unify the poem?

5. Discuss specifically the poet's song in section 14. What is its thematic relation to section 15? What view of death does the "companions" imagery suggest?

6. Analyze the final section of the poem. In what ways does this section tie together the three dominant themes you have studied? In what line does the poet specifically express the twining of his images and themes?

7. Would you agree with Malcolm Cowley, who asserts that in this poem Whitman is not so much mourning Lincoln as expounding his philosophy of death in general? Cowley says: "Lincoln?—is he really mourning Lincoln? The grief is personal, but it seems to have no personal object." Discuss this idea that the poem is one of universal concerns, and not of any particular and specific grief. Include your observations about the themes and images you have analyzed.

A Noiseless Patient Spider

1. This is an example of a short poem in which Whitman takes one image, expands it, and then draws his meaning from it in a single unified progression. Analyze the balance between the two stanzas, and between the corresponding lines in each stanza.

2. Analyze the images the poet uses to describe the spider. Do you find them fitting to their subject?
3. What correlations does the poet draw between his soul and the spider in the final stanza? Do you find the images apt in relation to both the spider and the poet's soul?

Spirit That Form'd This Scene

1. This poem provides a rare example of Whitman writing about the kind of artistry he has employed in his work. What spirit do you think the poet is addressing in the first line?
2. How does the natural description in lines 2–5 resemble Whitman's own style in his poetry? What phrase in line 5 gives a special clue to the connection?
3. Do you consider Whitman's poetry open to the charges he cites in lines 8–10? Why, or why not?
4. How, by sound and meter, does line 10 prove Whitman to be master of those rules of art which he is accused of having forgotten?
5. In the two final lines, what spirit has the poet "remember'd," and why has it been of such significance to him? Is that spirit in a sense incompatible with the rules of art? How does Whitman reveal himself on that question, and in which lines?

ASSIGNMENTS FOR WRITING

1. In "I Saw in Louisiana a Live-Oak Growing" Whitman is really dealing with the subject of his poetry itself and of his role as a poet. In a few paragraphs, analyze this idea with reference to the poem.
2. Consider the imagery of nature in "Crossing Brooklyn Ferry." In a short essay, point out the most important natural elements of the poem's setting, and discuss the relationship of the setting to the themes of the poem as you understand them.
3. If you view "One's-Self I Sing" as a program or prospectus of Whitman's poetic intentions, how fully does he fulfill those intentions in *Leaves of Grass*? Analyze the themes he proposes in "One's-Self I Sing" as they appear in the poems you have read.

Emily Dickinson

Emily Dickinson led one of the most outwardly uneventful lives of any great poet in literary history. It was a life that in later years became one of deliberate seclusion, a seclusion moreover which faithfully followed its own set of rituals and observances—as though, for this witty and once vivacious lady from a small valley town in Massachusetts, life had quietly taken on all the trappings of a very personal religious order. It was from this world—a world partly the result of temperament, of mental and spiritual outlook, and partly the result of early experiences we shall never have full knowledge of—that Emily Dickinson wrote some of the greatest lyric poetry in the English language.

It was in the town of Amherst, Massachusetts, in 1830, that the poet was born to Edward and Emily Norcross Dickinson. Amherst, at that time, was one of the last remaining outposts of Calvinistic Puritanism, and prided itself on being able, in the words of Noah Webster, one of the founders of Amherst College, "to check the progress of errors which are propagated from Cambridge"—by which was meant such liberal religious doctrines as Unitarianism and deism, which were threatening to undo completely the once binding orthodoxy of New England life and culture. And yet rigid and provincial as life in Amherst must undoubtedly have been, a life hardly suited to the growth of an imaginative mind, Emily Dickinson did from the start enjoy certain advantages that helped to sustain her as a person and even contribute to her art. One of these was the intense unity of the family group, the affection and loyalty exhibited among its members, and the social status that her family commanded through the figure of Edward Dickinson.

Edward Dickinson was the town's most prominent citizen. A successful and prosperous lawyer, he was prominent in church affairs, treasurer of Amherst College, the man responsible for having brought the railroad to town, an appointee to the Governor's Council, and a member of both the Massachusetts Legislature and the national Congress. It was this prominence in community and state affairs that not only made the Dickinson household a focal point for village gatherings but brought to it a variety of distinguished visitors from the world outside. For Emily Dickinson, this tended to counter the surrounding atmosphere of isolation and to offset for some time her own latent inclination toward anonymity and withdrawal. And it should be remembered that Amherst was within easy traveling distance of Boston, Philadelphia, and Washington, and that both before and during her twenties Emily Dickinson spent some time in each. She was by no means the unaware, introverted young girl many have imagined her, and her seven years as a student, first at Amherst Academy and then at Mount Holyoke Seminary, provide more than sufficient evidence that the part of her nature first to reveal itself was lively, confident, and completely outgoing.

It is necessary to understand the extraordinary power that the doctrines of orthodox Calvinism exerted over nearly all the inhabitants of the Connecticut River Valley until the second quarter of the nineteenth century. This power had continued unabated into the Amherst of Emily Dickinson's time. For an evangelical creed which stressed the innate sinfulness of man, his consequent separation from the Creator, the reality of hell, and the salvation by faith of only those whom God had chosen, the rhetorical persuasions at its command were immense. There was, however, one important distinction between the Calvinism preached by such figures as Cotton Mather and Jonathan Edwards and the slightly later dogmas to which Emily Dickinson was exposed. The earlier, orthodox position had been that admission to church membership rested on one's ability to show evidence of some inner change and new-found worthiness, whereas by the turn of the nineteenth century the more liberal approach based religious acceptance on one's proven desire for worthiness and God's grace. This served to increase greatly the number of those willing, even anxious, to declare their faith, and when Amherst experienced one of its periodic revivals in 1846, Emily Dickinson found herself at 16 under sudden pressure to convert.

There was nothing unusual in young people of that day being made conscious, almost from childhood, of the need for early conversion. As Thomas H. Johnson, in his biography of Emily Dickinson, has written:

Today it is routine that all students undergo a physical examination at the beginning of the year. It was then routine that all students entering the Seminary be examined on the state of their spiritual health. The concern was not so much that unconverted persons would be hazards to others; for their own welfare the impenitent must be brought at the earliest possible moment to an awareness of their peril and wakened to a desire for conversion.

And so, first at the Academy, where the closest of her classmates, such as Abiah Wood, were leaning toward conversion and then at Mount Holyoke, where during that period the entire college seemed to center on the question of acceptance or rejection of the evangelical calling, Emily Dickinson knew that the problem of faith would be an important one for her to solve. But she chose to decide the question from a firm standpoint outside the organized Christian community.

The ways in which Emily Dickinson expressed her feelings on her refusal to make a commitment, tantamount in the community to professing herself a non-Christian, are interesting and curious. To her classmates she said it was her inability to give up the world, even for Christ. But she could also look on the matter with humor and a certain indulgent satisfaction, and the degree to which she was able, on a later occasion, to become openly intransigent, as willing and proud to defend her own convictions as she was to acknowledge those of others, is exhibited in the letter she wrote in 1854 to Sue Gilbert. Sue was the intimate friend Emily Dickinson had loved and felt closest to since the start of her twenties, and who two years later was to marry her brother, Austin Dickinson. An attractive, scintillating person, known for her social adroitness and quick repartee, Sue had apparently been hectoring both her fiance and future sister-in-law to convert and become church members as she had already done. It had reached a point where Emily Dickinson finally wrote to her,

> Sue—I have lived by this. It is the lingering emblem of the heaven I once dreamed, and though if this is taken, I shall remain alone, and though in that last day, the Jesus Christ you love, remark he does not know me—there is a darker spirit will not disown its child.
>
> Few have been given me—and if I love them so, that for *idolatry*, they are removed from me—I simply murmur *gone*, and the billow dies away into the boundless blue, and no one knows but me, that one went down today. We have walked very pleasantly—Perhaps this is the point at which our paths diverge—then pass on singing Sue, and up the distant hill I journey on.

One or two references are private and perhaps lost to us, but the fortitude of conviction and spirit of independence that first enabled the poet to stand alone eight years earlier are here clearly expressed, matured into a quiet nobleness of utterance.

The explanation that Emily Dickinson gave for choosing to remain outside the church has been troublesome and unsatisfying. But the truth is that Emily Dickinson was simply incapable of accepting the doctrines of orthodox Calvinism. Yet if many of its basic tenets were foreign and repellent to her, there was one compensating feature so familiar to her that she could hardly have been aware of it, and whose implications she could not foresee: the emphasis which this religion placed on death, immortality, and the uniqueness of each individual's experience of God provided the perfect atmosphere in which her poetic genius would grow and flourish. These were the subjects to which she was returning constantly, which the eschatological nature of the Puritan tradition served to heighten and focus, and that became the foundations on which her art was built. It is conceivable that her early exposure to Calvinism left Emily Dickinson with the single greatest problem she faced in ordering her world-view, and the one she was wrestling with in the majority of her greatest poetry. As a child, she heard constantly of a God who was the one great center and arbiter of the universe. When her faith in this God failed, she was left with a gap which she tried to fill with various kinds of deism, or alternately with principles of friendship or love. She needed to conceive some universal design which might, in justifying the workings of the whole, justify to her those brutal and mysterious aspects of life and death which had confounded her from the beginning.

Emily Dickinson's attempt to replace the Calvinistic God-figure with a universal principle of her own gave her little lasting comfort, but her poetry, as the medium of the struggle, provides us with a remarkable view of a great poet attempting to order her world in her work. She continued, until the time of her death in 1886, to try to construct a metaphysical view of the universe which could reconcile her to all that hurt or confused her.

Hers was one of the most withdrawn lives in literary history and more like that of a religious aesthetic than a literary figure. But, at times, we feel in reading Dickinson that we are reading pure meditations and, at that, some of the profoundest meditations ever written on the life and spirit of the universe.

Strangely enough, Dickinson's early religious environment also had its effect on the prosodic shape of her verse, and led to some of her most characteristic stylistic devices. Her most frequent stanza form is that of four lines of three or four iambic feet alternating, with either an a/b/a/b or a/b/c/b rhyme scheme. In its strictest form, this stanzaic organization derives from the classic Isaac Watts hymn stanza, and it is a form which, with some variation in line length, Emily Dickinson was to use throughout her life. As is fitting to the suggestive, compact nature of her poetic insight and imagination, a large number of her poems comprise from two to five such stanzas, though many do exceed that length. Yet some of her most powerful statements are made in only four, or even two lines.

Emily Dickinson's poetry is singular in two further special respects: her use of dashes and capitalization. Her frequent capitalization is a device for thematic emphasis, and is consistent only within a particular poem. It is a natural device, if frequently employed, in poetry whose epigrammatic economy often depends on making the meanings stand out as much as possible. Dickinson's use of dashes, on the other hand, is a bit more enigmatic. Her singular way of punctuating her thoughts with dashes has excited a certain controversy about their specific purpose; all that is necessary here, however, is to note that in general the dash is employed either to break up two separate concepts or images, to emphasize an idea or example by surrounding it with dashes, or simply to provide a break in the reading of the poem—a sort of restful emotional transition. Dickinson's dashes and capitalization create very little difficulty at any rate, and her use of them, once the reader is acclimatized, is as adroit and natural as one would expect from this consummate poet.

Any student of Dickinson should acknowledge his debt to the work of Thomas E. Johnson, whose three-volume edition of Dickinson's poetry is the outstanding authoritative collection as well as a monumental work of scholarship. In the Johnson edition, for the first time, the original capitalization and dashes of the poet have been reproduced, and all relevant manuscript drafts made available. Very few of Dickinson's poems were published during her lifetime, and the Johnson numbering in order of almost 2000 poems is the closest estimate we have of the original order and date of the poems. Johnson's transcription and numbering of the poems, besides being canon in Dickinson studies, are of inestimable value both to beginning readers and to seasoned scholars.

441

This is my letter to the World
That never wrote to Me—
The simple News that Nature told—
With tender Majesty

Her Message is committed
To Hands I cannot see—
For love of Her—Sweet—countrymen—
Judge tenderly—of Me

1540

As imperceptibly as Grief
The Summer lapsed away—
Too imperceptible at last
To seem like Perfidy—
A Quietness distilled
As Twilight long begun,
Or Nature spending with herself
Sequestered Afternoon—
The Dusk drew earlier in—
The Morning foreign shone—   10
A courteous, yet harrowing Grace,
As Guest, that would be gone—
And thus, without a Wing
Or service of a Keel
Our Summer made her light escape
Into the Beautiful.

640

I cannot live with You—
It would be Life—
And Life is over there—
Behind the Shelf

The Sexton keeps the Key to—
Putting up

Our Life—His Porcelain—
Like a Cup—

Discarded of the Housewife—
Quaint—or Broke—
A newer Sevres pleases—
Old Ones crack—

I could not die—with You—
For One must wait
To shut the Other's Gaze down—
You—could not—

And I—Could I stand by
And see You—freeze—
Without my Right of Frost—
Death's privilege?

Nor could I rise—with You—
Because Your Face
Would put out Jesus'—
That New Grace

Glow plain—and foreign
On my homesick Eye—
Except that You than He
Shone closer by—

They'd judge Us—How—
For You—served Heaven—You know,
Or sought to—
I could not—

Because You saturated Sight—
And I had no more Eyes
For sordid excellence
As Paradise

And were You lost, I would be—
Though My Name
Rang loudest
On the Heavenly fame—

And were You—saved—
And I—condemned to be
Where You were not—
That self—were Hell to Me—

So We must meet apart—
You there—I—here—
With just the Door ajar
That Oceans are—and Prayer—
And that White Sustenance—
Despair—

49

I never lost as much but twice,
And that was in the sod.
Twice have I stood a beggar
Before the door of God!

Angels—twice descending
Reimbursed my store—
Burglar! Banker—Father!
I am poor once more!

1732

My life closed twice before its close;
It yet remains to see
If Immortality unveil
A third event to me,

So huge, so hopeless to conceive
As these that twice befel.
Parting is all we know of heaven,
And all we need of hell.

712

Because I could not stop for Death—
He kindly stopped for me—
The Carriage held but just Ourselves—
And Immortality.

We slowly drove—He knew no haste
And I had put away
My labor and my leisure too,
For His Civility—

We passed the School, where Children strove
At Recess—in the Ring—   10
We passed the Fields of Gazing Grain—
We passed the Setting Sun—

Or rather—He passed Us—
The Dews drew quivering and chill—
For only Gossamer, my Gown—
My Tippet—only Tulle—

We paused before a House that seemed
A Swelling of the Ground—
The Roof was scarcely visible—
The Cornice—in the Ground—   20

Since then—'tis Centuries—and yet
Feels shorter than the Day
I first surmised the Horses Heads
Were toward Eternity—

341

After great pain, a formal feeling comes—
The Nerves sit ceremonious, like Tombs—
The stiff Heart questions was it He, that bore,
And Yesterday, or Centuries before?

The Feet, mechanical, go round—
Of Ground, or Air, or Ought—
A Wooden way
Regardless grown,
A Quartz contentment, like a stone—

This is the Hour of Lead—   10
Remembered, if outlived,
As Freezing persons, recollect the Snow—
First—Chill—then Stupor—then the letting go—

465

I heard a Fly buzz—when I died—
The Stillness in the Room
Was like the Stillness in the Air—
Between the Heaves of Storm—

The Eyes around—had wrung them dry—
And Breaths were gathering firm
For that last Onset—when the King
Be witnessed—in the Room—

I willed my Keepsakes—Signed away
What portion of me be   10
Assignable—and then it was
There interposed a Fly—

With Blue—uncertain stumbling Buzz—
Between the light—and me—
And then the Windows failed—and then
I could not see to see—

1551

Those—dying then,
Knew where they went—
They went to God's Right Hand—
That Hand is amputated now
And God cannot be found—

The abdication of Belief
Makes the Behavior small—
Better an ignis fatuus
Than no illume at all—

322

There came a Day at Summer's full,
Entirely for me—
I thought that such were for the Saints,
Where Resurrections—be—

The Sun, as common, went abroad,
The flowers, accustomed, blew,
As if no soul the solstice passed
That maketh all things new—

The time was scarce profaned, by speech—
The symbol of a word   10
Was needless, as at Sacrament,
The Wardrobe—of our Lord—

Each was to each The Sealed Church,
Permitted to commune this—time—
Lest we too awkward show
At Supper of the Lamb.

The Hours slid fast—as Hours will,
Clutched tight, by greedy hands—
So faces on two Decks, look back,
Bound to opposing lands—   20

And so when all the time had leaked,
Without external sound
Each bound the Other's Crucifix—
We gave no other Bond—

Sufficient troth, that we shall rise—
Deposed—at length, the Grave—
To that new Marriage,
Justified—through Calvaries of Love—

185

"Faith" is a fine invention
When Gentlemen can *see*—
But *Microscopes* are prudent
In an Emergency.

338

I know that He exists.
Somewhere—in Silence—

He has hid his rare life
From our gross eyes.

'Tis an instant's play.
'Tis a fond Ambush—
Just to make Bliss
Earn her own surprise!

But—should the play
Prove piercing earnest—   10
Should the glee—glaze—
In Death's—stiff—stare—

Would not the fun
Look too expensive!
Would not the jest—
Have crawled too far!

67

Success is counted sweetest
By those who ne'er succeed.
To comprehend a nectar
Requires sorest need.

Not one of all the purple Host
Who took the Flag today
Can tell the definition
So clear of Victory

As he defeated—dying—
On whose forbidden ear   10
The distant strains of triumph
Burst agonized and clear!

1129

Tell all the Truth but tell it slant—
Success in Circuit lies
Too bright for our infirm Delight
The Truth's superb surprise
As Lightning to the Children eased

With explanation kind
The Truth must dazzle gradually
Or every man be blind—

435

Much Madness is divinest Sense—
To a discerning Eye—
Much Sense—the starkest Madness—
'Tis the Majority
In this, as All, prevail—
Assent—and you are sane—
Demur—you're straightway dangerous—
And handled with a Chain—

303

The Soul selects her own Society—
Then—shuts the Door—
To her divine Majority—
Present no more—

Unmoved—she notes the Chariots—pausing—
At her low Gate—
Unmoved—an Emperor be kneeling
Upon her Mat—

I've known her—from an ample nation—
Choose One—   10
Then—close the Valves of her attention—
Like Stone—

QUESTIONS FOR DISCUSSION

This is my letter to the World (441)

1. From what you have learned of Emily Dickinson's life in the introduction to this collection, how could the opening two lines of the present

poem be interpreted? What other interpretations are possible?

2. Describe what you feel to be the type of "News" referred to in the third line of the poem.

3. From the evidence of this poem, you can begin to understand how Emily Dickinson regarded nature as it related to her personally and to her poetry. Discuss this double significance of nature to the poet, and keep this question in mind as you read the other poems in this section.

As imperceptibly as Grief (1540)

1. How do the opening four lines reveal the poet's attitude toward the passing of summer? What is the significance of the words *Grief* and *Perfidy* in lines 1 and 4?

2. How do lines 9–12 give the impression of an increasing distance between the poet and the season? With what sort of attitude is the summer endowed in line 11?

3. Discuss the event described in the last two lines, first in terms of the attitude of the human observer, and second in terms of the personified figure of summer.

I cannot live with You (640)

1. This poem seems to be addressed to a young Boston minister who had frequently corresponded with Emily Dickinson. Explain how stanzas 1–3 indicate the poet's feeling that her life was not adaptable to the love she contemplated.

2. Bearing in mind that this poem was probably addressed to a minister, comment on the appropriateness and the specific Christian significance of the three phases of existence which the poet develops in the first seven stanzas: the phases of life, death, and rising, or resurrection. Cite examples from the imagery of each phase in the poet's exposition of her theme.

3. How are religious elements used to elucidate and amplify the theme of love throughout the poem? What is the function of the biblical reference to be found in stanza 6? What is your general impression of the kind and quality of love expressed in this poem?

4. What key word in line 1 of the last stanza contradicts all of the images, or dreams, which have preceded it?

5. Explain the two final lines, and especially the phrase "White Sustenance." Why is despair to be a sustenance to Emily Dickinson after her declaration in the opening stanza?

I never lost as much but twice (49)

1. In the first stanza, Emily Dickinson reveals the intense personal meaning

of the deaths of people for whom she cared. Discuss this idea, with special reference to the image in lines 3 and 4.

2. Does the situation described in the second stanza seem a cyclical and futile one? Discuss this interpretation with emphasis on the poet's three names for the God she sees as the controlling influence on this situation.

My life closed twice before its close (1732)

1. A glance at the hymn "O God Our Help in Ages Past" (St. Anne's) should reveal an interesting correspondence, both in meter and message, between the hymn form and this poem. Look up the hymn, and discuss the implications for parody which the metric correspondence initiates.
2. From your reading of lines 1-6, do you think that the "third event" described in line four is likely to be a happier one than the first two? What exactly is this third event likely to be?
3. How does the word *hopeless* in line 5 relate to the lines preceding it, especially to lines 3 and 4?

Because I could not stop for Death (712)

1. This poem is one of the best examples of an extended image in the whole of Dickinson's work. Trace through the poem the sustained effectiveness with which she uses the metaphor of the carriage and its riders.
2. Do you agree that in this poem Emily Dickinson expresses a gentler, more accepting attitude toward death than is to be found in many of her other poems on the subject?
3. Which passages in the poem best communicate her gentleness, or "civility," toward Death?

After great pain, a formal feeling comes (341)

1. In this poem it is as if Emily Dickinson were delving into the very feelings of death. What word in line 2 alerts us to this possibility from the outset?
2. How do the images in the second stanza achieve their vividness in describing pain? To whom do the "Feet" in line 1 of this stanza belong? Explain the desperation of their "Wooden way."
3. How do the frequent images of heaviness and immobility in the poem contribute to the connotations begun by the metaphor of the "Tombs" in line 2?
4. How effective do you find the final two lines of the poem in conveying the experience of death? How do they relate to the imagery of heaviness in the poem?

I heard a Fly buzz—when I died (465)

1. This is one of Emily Dickinson's most remarkable poems, never falter-
   ing in its dramatic focus and execution of significant detail. It is important to note how the image of the fly with which the poem opens
   controls both the action and the meaning of the poem. Why might the
   poet have chosen so common and familiar an object as the fly to hold
   a dominant position in the speaker's failing consciousness?
2. In what way does the simile contained in the first stanza emphasize
   the particular "Stillness" of the room? Explain the metaphor introduced
   in line 3 of the second stanza. What attribute is shared by these two
   figures of speech when compared with the image of the fly?
3. Analyze the imagery which describes the fly in the final stanza. How
   has Emily Dickinson made the fly so real and vivid? What is the poetic
   effect of the fly as a participant in this death-scene?
4. What is meant by the last two lines of the poem?
5. Throughout the poem, what means of juxtaposition does the poet use
   to heighten the speaker's final moments of consciousness? Discuss her
   success in this, citing lines from the poem to amplify your estimate.

Those—dying then (1551)

1. In this poem Emily Dickinson contrasts the early Christian faith which
   she decided to give up with the independence she had adopted since
   that decision. Do lines 4 and 5 sound familiar in the light of any current
   religious controversies?
2. Do lines 4 and 5 sound as if the condition they describe is the result
   only of the poet's lack of belief, or also of the lack of a divine presence?
3. From the evidence of this poem, do you think that the poet envies
   "Those—dying then," or that she means to comment on them and their
   belief by irony and by contrast to her own decision?
4. *Ignis fatuus,* in Latin, means roughly "false light." How does this phrase
   support or relate to your answer to question 3? What meaning does it
   give to the final line of the poem?

There came a Day at Summer's full (322)

1. In this poem Emily Dickinson gives a full exposition of the deepest
   meanings she conceives for faith and love. In the first stanza, what
   clue do the two final lines give about the transcendental importance
   of the experience about to be described?
2. The second stanza contains two images which are central to the development of the poem. What is the sense of the first two lines of this
   stanza? How do the last two lines imply that the coming experience will
   symbolize the re-making or re-birth of souls?
3. The third stanza, by its renunciation of "speech" and "The symbol of a
   word," demonstrates the extraordinary significance of this transcendental

experience to the poet, for it suggests a falling-away, or super-fluousness of poetry itself. What sort of experience do you think will replace poetry?

4. How does the fourth stanza attribute a religious nature to love between two people, and, in particular, imply the love of Christ as a precedent?
5. What dire, realistic turn does this transcendental experience take in the fifth stanza? What happens to the two souls involved here?
6. Why is the "Crucifix" (line 3 of stanza 6) a good symbol for this parting? In your answer, discuss the earlier references to Christ as an archtypal love figure in stanzas 1, 3, and 4.
7. In this illustration of the weight her faith must carry, Emily Dickinson has built an admirably tight poetic structure in which the various sets of symbols interrelate in such detail as to create an intricate and yet unified impression of the relation between love and faith. Discuss this relation with special reference to the final stanza and its grim implications about the fate of love in this world: "through Calvaries of Love." ("Calvary" is a name for the place where Christ was crucified.) Does it make sense to know that Emily Dickinson frequently referred to herself as the "Queen of Calvary"? (See, for example, "I dreaded that first Robin, so," line 24.)

"Faith" is a fine invention (185)

1. How does this poem communicate the poet's reasons for her loss of faith? Discuss the metaphor centering around vision in these lines.
2. In what way does line 2 represent the poet's need to understand the problems posed in the four poems which precede it in this group?
3. What sort of "Emergency" could the poet be speaking of in the final line? Your answer should refer specifically to other poems in this selection.

I know that He exists (338)

1. Discuss the detached and yet serious quality of the poet's statement of her question of faith in the first stanza. Do you consider the tone of the stanza effective in view of the seriousness of its subject?
2. How do you interpret the second stanza? How does the word *Bliss* express hope in her search?
3. Explain the game of Hide and Seek described in this poem, tracing its development from line 3. What key word in that line initiates the imagery of the game? Who is hiding, and who seeking? How does the title relate to these questions?
4. Discuss the ideas and images in the third stanza. How do they communicate to us the poet's sense of dread and urgency? Notice especially how the "play" image is picked up here and used as a device for dramatic effect.

5. In the famous fourth stanza, to what does "the fun" refer? Why, then, does it "Look too expensive"? Because the price of horror and death is too high? What view of God does this imply? Discuss also what this "jest" implies in terms of human sacrifice. Is it really a "jest," or does the poet imply a more serious situation here, by using "jest" ironically? What are *your* answers to the questions asked in this stanza?

Success is counted sweetest (67)

1. This is one of Emily Dickinson's earliest mature poems, and one of those most frequently anthologized. In later work, she was to approach the same theme in a deeper, more complex manner. Do the two opening lines present an explicit statement of the poem's theme? Some readers have thought these lines overly didactic. Do you agree, and if so, are they the only such lines in the poem?
2. In the second and third stanzas, what dramatic situation has the poet created to give concrete substance to her theme?
3. To whom is the poet referring in the opening line of the final stanza? In what way is the ear "forbidden" in the second line of this stanza?

Tell all the Truth but tell it slant (1129)

1. Explicate, or transcribe in your own words, the meaning of the two opening lines of the poem.
2. Explain, with reference to Emily Dickinson's acute consciousness of the transitoriness of things, the phrase "infirm Delight" in line 3.
3. Do you like the image in lines 5 and 6? How does the image serve the total meaning of the poem?
4. What does the statement in the two final lines imply about the nature of truth? Do the lines refer back to the lightning imagery? Discuss all the connotations, then, which the poem has built around the word *Truth* before we even reach the next to last line.

Much Madness is divinest Sense (435)

1. Two words in the first two lines should be clues about what value the poet places on the quality of madness. What meanings do "divinest" and "discerning" impart?
2. Discuss the polarity which the poet sets up in lines 6 and 7 between "Assent" and "Demur" in terms of her own religious struggle and what it must have meant not to conform to her strongly religious environment.
3. Do you detect that the poet is speaking loyally of herself when she speaks of madness in this poem? How does the tone of the poem and of her reference to the "Majority" bear out your conclusion?
4. Do you find the poet's complaint about how society decides who is

"sane" and who is "dangerous" relevant to conditions of social unrest today? Is Dickinson's interpretation true in the way society usually treats its dissenters?

The Soul selects her own Society (303)

1. In what way do the two opening lines of the poem strike you? Are they emphatic or tentative and open to revision?
2. The poem's dominant or controlling imagery is introduced in line 3. It is a kind frequently met with in Emily Dickinson's work. How would you describe it?
3. Explain the last two lines of the first stanza. What number of people comprise the "divine Majority" of line 3? Could there be more than one answer to this question?
4. Comment on what you feel is the meaning of the second stanza. What effect is achieved by juxtaposing "Emperor" and "Mat"?
5. Discuss the third line of the final stanza. Consult a dictionary for the various meanings of "valve" and choose those you feel are best suited to the line.
6. Comment on the brief, stark line that closes the poem. What connotations does the poet's use of the word *Stone* have for you? Do you find the ending effective?
7. This poem has received various interpretations. It has been read as a personal statement of independence, the poet's decision to preserve her privacy from outside encroachments; a commitment to art at the expense of other interests; a love poem in which one individual is irrevocably singled out above all others; a renunciation of the world in order to serve only God. Which of these readings is closest to your own interpretation? Is it necessary for the reader to limit himself to one interpretation, or may more than one exist at the same time? Explain, citing lines from the poem to support your answer.

ASSIGNMENTS FOR WRITING

1. Write a long essay examining the idea that the anguish which Emily Dickinson experienced resulted not so much from the events in her life as from the lack of a unified and comfortable point of view with which she could order her perceptions and come to terms with her disappointments. Refer specifically to several poems.
2. Discuss the kinds of events and ideas which the poet chose to write about. Can you trace a consistent thread of personal significance to Emily Dickinson in the subjects she chose? Secondly, how do these poems strike you? Do her themes arouse much internal difference in you as a reader? Are they deep meanings with which you, too, are concerned?

Mark Twain

Shortly before he died, Mark Twain said, "I came in with Halley's comet in 1835. It is coming again next year, and I expect to go out with it. It will be the greatest disappointment of my life if I don't go out with Halley's comet. The Almighty has said, no doubt: 'Now here are these two unaccountable freaks, they came in together, they must go out together.' Oh! I am looking forward to that."

Samuel Langhorne Clemens' birth, on November 30, 1835, had indeed coincided with the appearance of Halley's comet, a fact which may have seemed more ominous than auspicious throughout much of his life. His father, John Marshall Clemens, was a frustrated inventor whose sense of failure brought little joy to his Florida, Missouri home. At the age of four, Sam Clemens was taken with his impoverished family to the river-edge town of Hannibal, Missouri, which was to serve as the imaginative setting for many of his stories.

When his father died in 1847, young Clemens was apprenticed as a printer's helper; thus he entered journalism, the trade in which he was to remain, off and on, throughout the next twenty years. His first published work was mostly filler items, humorous and sometimes silly pieces, appearing in weekly newspapers. Gradually Sam Clemens gained the confidence to submit his work for a broader audience; by the time he left Hannibal in 1853, looking for work in New York and Philadelphia, he had already been published in eastern magazines.

Two of the more significant interruptions in Clemens' career as a newspaperman, however, were the four years he spent on the Mississippi steamboats as a pilot (1857-1861) and his abortive military service as a Confederate volunteer during the early weeks of the Civil War. This latter escapade he retells in a sketch, "The

Private History of a Campaign that Failed." The effect of both these experiences may not be immediately discernible to the casual reader of an account of Clemens' life; the fact is, however, that the coincidences of history collaborated in turning a rootless hack-writer and river rat toward the West and to his first writing of real quality.

Orion Clemens, the older brother, had received a federal appointment in the Nevada Territory. He encouraged Sam Clemens to accompany him to the frontier. After a brief and futile attempt to strike it rich as a prospector, Samuel Clemens threw away the gold pans and settled in to work as a newspaper correspondent for the Virginia City *Territorial Enterprise*. In February, 1863, "Mark Twain" was born. This famous pseudonym—meaning that the water measures two fathoms—was borrowed from the jargon of the Mississippi River pilots. There is also reliable evidence to suggest that Clemens had acquired the nickname before he used it as a pen name, for in the frontier saloons where he maintained credit, calling out for the bartender to "mark twain," meant "charge two more drinks to my account."

From Nevada, Clemens took his pen name to San Francisco and wrote for various periodicals. Of these early bits and pieces, little of note remains, except "The Celebrated Jumping Frog of Calaveras County," which when published in a New York magazine in 1865 gave national recognition to Mark Twain. From that point, his career as a humorist was settled.

The particular pattern of Mark Twain's subsequent works reflects the popularity of the frontiersman's tall tale. Beginning ostensibly as a factual account, the narrative quickly branches away from the strictest truth into ever-blossoming extravagances and hyperboles. The language is raw and uncultured, the idiomatic speech of an American rube, usually taking the measure of his favorite antagonist, the city slicker. Artemus Ward and Josh Billings had parlayed their characterizations into national fame. Even so proper a poet as James Russell Lowell had imitated this form of satire in his creation of Hosea Biglow and *The Biglow Papers*. Mark Twain now aspired to this success.

His first major opportunity came in 1867, when he sailed as a correspondent with pilgrims bound for a tour of Christian shrines in Palestine. Twain had been commissioned by a San Francisco paper to write a series of travel notes, which he then expanded into *The Innocents Abroad* (1869). His observations showed just enough of the reverence expected by most contemporary readers who were already mistaking for mere foolery the searing irony that would mark his greatest work.

Clemens' marriage in 1870 to Olivia Langdon has been considered by some critics to be of greater importance than most authors' marriages. Van Wyck Brooks bases a good deal of the substance of his argument in *The Ordeal of Mark Twain* upon the refining influence of Livy Clemens' Calvinist conscience. Her disapproval, such critics claim, kept Sam Clemens from allowing Mark Twain full scope to the social criticism—acidic and blasphemous— that he might have written. She was his censor, they claim. Other critics, however, blame Clemens' own duplicity and point to his adoption of a pseudonym as proof of this quality. To them, the field was open for Samuel Langhorne Clemens to be as profane as he wished. The fact that Samuel Clemens allowed Mark Twain to speak for him suggests a reticence that disguised truth under the bald-faced and laugh-provoking lie.

Mark Twain perfected, as few men have been able, the art of transferring his writing to speaking. Shortly after the journey to the Holy Land, Twain offered himself as a lecturer, using sketches from his published work. His talks consisted of "a running narrative-plank, with square holes in it, six inches apart, all the length of it." Into these "holes" the speaker jammed anecdotes that alternated between serious and comic, "according to the temper of the audience," he told his wife. Here once more, the tall tale became Mark Twain's favorite vehicle, and his books, which came now in a steady procession, received the double exposure to both readers and listeners. *Roughing It* (1872) and *Life on the Mississippi* (1883) recalled his experiences in Nevada and as a river pilot. *The Adventures of Tom Sawyer* (1876) crystallized the development of Hannibal as his Athens, his Camelot, his Globe Theater.

By 1885, Clemens was enormously successful. He had founded his own publishing company; he had also completed *Adventures of Huckleberry Finn*. In these two events, much of the rest of Clemens' career may be summarized. The business enterprises— the publishing firm and the subsequent investment in an impractical typesetting machine—robbed Clemens of his prosperity and, undoubtedly, contributed to his ultimate despair. Yet the creation of the boy-narrator, the vagabond Huck Finn, who speaks the truth to the face of falsehood, preserved Mark Twain. The grandeur of the river, the intertwining of philosophy and picaresque adventure, the nobility and humanity of the relationship between the slave Jim and the child Huckleberry had produced a paradigm in world literature—so much so that Ernest Hemingway could say, "all modern American literature comes from one book by Mark Twain called *Huckleberry Finn* . . . it's the best book we've had."

Thereafter, the story of Samuel L. Clemens becomes the description of demise. The bankruptcy of his business interests drove him into forced lecturing. The deaths of three of his children and, in 1904, of Livy herself almost maddened him. Increasingly his prose and his public speaking reflected the bitterness of his heart against "the damned human race." Still, however, his audiences chuckled at what seemed to them the amusing antics of a clown with rheumatism.

One needs only to examine "The Man That Corrupted Hadleyburg" (1899) to see the direction in which Mark Twain's readers were being led, even if unknowingly and against their will. It was the direction toward personal annihilation, articulated in his unfinished allegory, *The Mysterious Stranger*. Satan declares to mankind,

> There is no God, no universe, no human race, no earthly life, no heaven, no hell. It is all a dream—a grotesque and foolish dream. Nothing exists but you. And you are but a *thought*—a vagrant thought, a useless thought, a homeless thought, wandering forlorn among the empty eternities.

The evaporation of idealism, especially in the sentimental and romantic mind, is always accompanied by bitterness and cynicism. Religious disaffection (although one of Clemens' closest friends was the Hartford clergyman, the Reverend Joe Twichell) and social disgust pervaded most of Mark Twain's last years which were lightened only by his personal satisfaction at having been honored with a doctorate by Oxford University in 1907.

Mark Twain had his wish fulfilled in death: he did "go out with Halley's comet," dying within days of the 1910 return of the spectacle. It was, of course, Samuel Langhorne Clemens, eulogized by his friend William Dean Howells as "the Lincoln of our literature," who died. Mark Twain lives on; like Huckleberry Finn, he has chosen to "light out for the Territory ahead of the rest."

(*Continued on page 337*)

Still Life and Birds

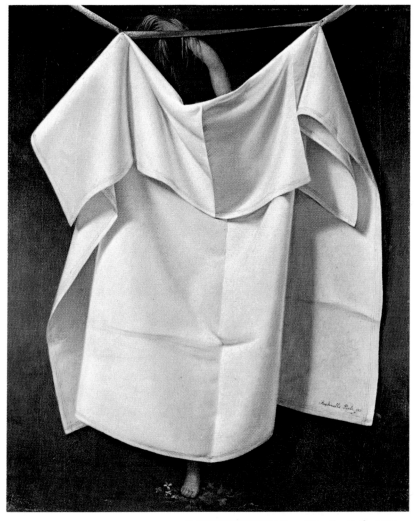

RAPHAELLE PEALE: After the Bath, 1823

Since the days of the ancient Greeks, artists have made *trompe l'oeil* (fool-the-eye) pictures of fruit, flowers, bric-a-brac, and dead game. Birds flew down to peck at the grapes painted by Zeuxis, but he was topped by his rival Parrhasios, who produced a picture covered by a veil. When Zeuxis tried to pull it away, he discovered the veil was part of the painting itself. A similar story is told about Mrs. Peale attempting to remove the sheet from her husband's *After the Bath (above)* when it was still on the easel at home.

JOHN JAMES AUDUBON: Ivory-Billed Woodpeckers

Later specialists in ornithology may have equaled Audubon (1785-1851)
in the scientific rendering of our native birds and their brilliant plumage,
but none have produced such memorable works of art. They are American
classics. Heade (1819-1904) went to South America in 1863 to paint
close-up views of hummingbirds against vast, steamy, tropical landscapes. The book they were to illustrate was never published. Graves (born
1910) has painted many birds, using a quasi-oriental technique, imbued
with his own unique mysticism.

MORRIS GRAVES: Blind Bird, 1940

MARTIN J. HEADE: Hummingbirds and Passion Flowers, c. 1865/70

WILLIAM HARNETT: Old Models, 1892

Other Philadelphia painters took up still life painting where the Peales left off. Harnett (1848-1892) was such a master of illusion that one of his five-dollar bills caused him to be arrested for counterfeiting. When he began to be appreciated again in the 1930's, the supply of his pictures could barely keep up with the demand. The critic Alfred Frankenstein was puzzled by the fact that the rediscovered Harnetts came in two quite different styles—one glossy and hard-edged, the other more diffused and soft—and by such mysteries as the posthumous date "1900" in a typical letter rack picture (below). His detective work revealed that all the "soft" pictures were painted by Harnett's forgotten friend Peto (1854-1907) and the Harnett signatures (envelope, upper right) were later additions by forgers. As a result, Peto rose from oblivion to take his place beside Harnett in museums and private collections.

JOHN FREDERICK PETO: Old Reminiscences, 1900

ARTHUR G. DOVE: Grandmother, 1925

Dove (1880-1946), another artist in the Stieglitz circle, painted the first American abstract pictures. *Grandmother (above)* is a collage (which means something pasted) of actual things: old cross-stitched needlework, a page from a hymnal, pressed ferns, and weathered shingles. If we merely look at it, it seems to be an unusual still life; if we believe the title, it is a portrait. As such, it belongs with two similiar portraits by Hartley (p. 812) and Demuth (p. 816). Dove made twenty-five collages between 1924 and 1932. His portrait of a critic he didn't care for has an empty head, roller skates, and a flat newspaper body.

Nobody could accuse Loren MacIver (born 1909) of being a "literary" painter, but her work comes closer to poetry than that of any other artist in this book. *Morning Cart (opposite)* is typical of her feminine sensibility and her lyrical celebration of the commonplace. Her subjects have included a hopscotch game chalked on a decaying asphalt pavement, a taxi in the rain—seen from the inside, the pinpoint pattern made by holes in a worn window shade, red votive lights, and the whole skyline of Venice leaking into its blue lagoon.

Some of the most disturbing pictures of all time have been painted by Ivan Albright (born 1897) of Chicago. The French artist Jean Dubuffet found his portrayal of a door (p. 334) worth going to the ends of the earth to see, and said that he had never encountered a painting that gave him "immediately such a strong sense of commotion." He visited Albright's studio and saw his old hats and gloves, his collection of dust and spiderwebs, and the setup for his picture *Poor Room—there is no time, no end, no today, no yesterday, no tomorrow, only forever, and forever and forever without end,* which he worked on for twenty years. Albright paints people in the same style of opalescent decay that he uses for still life. For Hollywood's *Picture of Dorian Grey* he provided the portrait which became a putrescent horror while Wilde's hero enjoyed sin and eternal youth. He has written poetry and book reviews.

LOREN MACIVER: Morning Cart, 1960

IVAN ALBRIGHT:
That Which I Should Have
Done I Did Not Do, 1931/41

from Roughing It

BUCK FANSHAW'S FUNERAL

Somebody has said that in order to know a community, one must observe the style of its funerals and know what manner of men they bury with most ceremony. I cannot say which class we buried with most éclat in our "flush times," the distinguished public benefactor or the distinguished rough—possibly the two chief grades or grand divisions of society honored their illustrious dead about equally; and hence, no doubt, the philosopher I have quoted from would have needed to see two representative funerals in Virginia before forming his estimate of the people.

There was a grand time over Buck Fanshaw when he died. He was a representative citizen. He had "killed his man"—not in his own quarrel, it is true, but in defense of a stranger unfairly beset by numbers. He had kept a sumptuous saloon. He had been the proprietor of a dashing helpmeet whom he could have discarded without the formality of a divorce. He had held a high position in the fire department and been a very Warwick in politics. When he died there was great lamentation throughout the town, but especially in the vast bottom-stratum of society.

On the inquest it was shown that Buck Fanshaw, in the delirium of a wasting typhoid fever, had taken arsenic, shot himself through the body, cut his throat, and jumped out of a four-story window and broken his neck—and after due deliberation, the jury, sad and tearful, but with intelligence unblinded by its sorrow, brought in a verdict of death "by the visitation of God." What could the world do without juries?

Prodigious preparations were made for the funeral. All the vehicles in town were hired, all the saloons put in mourning, all the municipal and fire-company flags hung at half-mast, and all the firemen ordered to muster in uniform and bring their machines duly draped in black. Now—let us remark in parentheses—as all the peoples of the earth had representative adventurers in the Silverland, and as each adventurer had brought the slang of his nation or his locality with him, the combination made the slang of Nevada the richest and the most infinitely varied and copious that had ever existed anywhere in the world, perhaps, except in the mines of California in the "early days." Slang was the language of Nevada.

It was hard to preach a sermon without it, and be understood. Such phrases as "You bet!" "Oh, no, I reckon not!" "No Irish need apply," and a hundred others, became so common as to fall from the lips of a speaker unconsciously—and very often when they did not touch the subject under discussion and consequently failed to mean anything.

After Buck Fanshaw's inquest, a meeting of the short-haired brotherhood was held, for nothing can be done on the Pacific coast without a public meeting and an expression of sentiment. Regretful resolutions were passed and various committees appointed; among others, a committee of one was deputed to call on the minister, a fragile, gentle, spiritual new fledgling from an Eastern theological seminary, and as yet unacquainted with the ways of the mines. The committeeman, "Scotty" Briggs, made his visit; and in after days it was worth something to hear the minister tell about it. Scotty was a stalwart rough, whose customary suit, when on weighty official business, like committee work, was a fire-helmet, flaming red flannel shirt, patent-leather belt with spanner and revolver attached, coat hung over arm, and pants stuffed into boot-tops. He formed something of a contrast to the pale theological student. It is fair to say of Scotty, however, in passing, that he had a warm heart, and a strong love for his friends, and never entered into a quarrel when he could reasonably keep out of it. Indeed, it was commonly said that whenever one of Scotty's fights was investigated, it always turned out that it had originally been no affair of his, but that out of native good-heartedness he had dropped in of his own accord to help the man who was getting the worst of it. He and Buck Fanshaw were bosom friends, for years, and had often taken adventurous "pot-luck" together. On one occasion, they had thrown off their coats and taken the weaker side in a fight among strangers, and after gaining a hard-earned victory, turned and found that the men they were helping had deserted early, and not only that, but had stolen their coats and made off with them. But to return to Scotty's visit to the minister. He was on a sorrowful mission, now, and his face was the picture of woe. Being admitted to the presence he sat down before the clergyman, placed his fire-hat on an unfinished manuscript sermon under the minister's nose, took from it a red silk handkerchief, wiped his brow and heaved a sigh of dismal impressiveness, explanatory of his business. He choked, and even shed tears; but with an effort he mastered his voice and said in lugubrious tones:

"Are you the duck that runs the gospel-mill next door?"

"Am I the—pardon me, I believe I do not understand?"

With another sigh and a half-sob, Scotty rejoined:

"Why you see we are in a bit of trouble, and the boys thought maybe you would give us a lift, if we'd tackle you—that is, if I've got the rights of it and you are the head clerk of the doxology-works next door."

"I am the shepherd in charge of the flock whose fold is next door."

"The which?"

"The spiritual adviser of the little company of believers whose sanctuary adjoins these premises."

Scotty scratched his head, reflected a moment, and then said:

"You ruther hold over me, pard. I reckon I can't call that hand. Ante and pass the buck."

"How? I beg pardon. What did I understand you to say?"

"Well, you've ruther got the bulge on me. Or maybe we've both got the bulge, somehow. You don't smoke me and I don't smoke you. You see, one of the boys has passed in his checks, and we want to give him a good send-off, and so the thing I'm on now is to roust out somebody to jerk a little chin-music for us and waltz him through handsome."

"My friend, I seem to grow more and more bewildered. Your observations are wholly incomprehensible to me. Cannot you simplify them in some way? At first I thought perhaps I understood you, but I grope now. Would it not expedite matters if you restricted yourself to categorical statements of fact unencumbered with obstructing accumulations of metaphor and allegory?"

Another pause, and more reflection. Then, said Scotty:

"I'll have to pass, I judge."

"How?"

"You've raised me out, pard." '

"I still fail to catch your meaning."

"Why, that last lead of yourn is too many for me—that's the idea. I can't neither trump nor follow suit."

The clergyman sank back in his chair perplexed. Scotty leaned his head on his hand and gave himself up to thought. Presently his face came up, sorrowful but confident.

"I've got it now, so's you can savvy," he said. "What we want is a gospel-sharp. See?"

"A what?"

"Gospel-sharp. Parson."

"Oh! Why did you not say so before? I am a clergyman—a parson."

"Now you talk! You see my blind and straddle it like a man.

Put it there!"—extending a brawny paw, which closed over the minister's small hand and gave it a shake indicative of fraternal sympathy and fervent gratification.

"Now we're all right, pard. Let's start fresh. Don't you mind my snuffling a little—becuz we're in a power of trouble. You see, one of the boys has gone up the flume—"

"Gone where?"

"Up the flume—throwed up the sponge, you understand."

"Thrown up the sponge?"

"Yes—kicked the bucket—"

"Ah—has departed to that mysterious country from whose bourne no traveler returns."

"Return! I reckon not. Why, pard, he's *dead!*"

"Yes, I understand."

"Oh, you do? Well I thought maybe you might be getting tangled some more. Yes, you see he's dead again—"

"*Again!* Why, has he ever been dead before?"

"Dead before? No! Do you reckon a man has got as many lives as a cat? But you bet you he's awful dead now, poor old boy, and I wish I'd never seen this day. I don't want no better friend than Buck Fanshaw. I knowed him by the back; and when I know a man and like him, I freeze to him—you hear *me*. Take him all round, pard, there never was a bullier man in the mines. No man ever knowed Buck Fanshaw to go back on a friend. But it's all up, you know, it's all up. It ain't no use. They've scooped him."

"Scooped him?"

"Yes—death has. Well, well, well, we've got to give him up. Yes, indeed. It's a kind of a hard world, after all, *ain't* it? But pard, he was a rustler! You ought to seen him get started once. He was a bully boy with a glass eye! Just spit in his face and give him room according to his strength, and it was just beautiful to see him peel and go in. He was the worst son of a thief that ever drawed breath. Pard, he was *on* it! He was on it bigger than an Injun!"

"On it? On what?"

"On the shoot. On the shoulder. On the fight, you understand. *He* didn't give a continental for *any*body. *Beg* your pardon, friend, for coming so near saying a cuss-word—but you see I'm on an awful strain, in this palaver, on account of having to cramp down and draw everything so mild. But we've got to give him up. There ain't any getting around that, I don't reckon. Now if we can get you to help plant him—"

"Preach the funeral discourse? Assist at the obsequies?"

"Obs'quies is good. Yes. That's it—that's our little game. We are going to get the thing up regardless, you know. He was always nifty himself, and so you bet you his funeral ain't going to be no slouch—solid-silver door-plate on his coffin, six plumes on the hearse, and a nigger on the box in a biled shirt and a plug hat—how's that for high? And we'll take care of *you*, pard. We'll fix you all right. There'll be a kerridge for you; and whatever you want, you just 'scape out and we'll 'tend to it. We've got a shebang fixed up for you to stand behind, in No. 1's house, and don't you be afraid. Just go in and toot your horn, if you don't sell a clam. Put Buck through as bully as you can, pard, for anybody that knowed him will tell you that he was one of the whitest men that was ever in the mines. You can't draw it too strong. He never could stand it to see things going wrong. He's done more to make this town quiet and peaceable than any man in it. I've seen him lick four Greasers in eleven minutes, myself. If a thing wanted regulating, *he* warn't a man to go browsing around after somebody to do it, but he would prance in and regulate it himself. He warn't a Catholic. Scasely. He was down on 'em. His word was, 'No Irish need apply!' But it didn't make no difference about that when it came down to what a man's rights was—and so, when some roughs jumped the Catholic boneyard and started in to stake out town lots in it he *went* for 'em! And he *cleaned* 'em, too! I was there, pard, and I seen it myself."

"That was very well indeed—at least the impulse was—whether the act was strictly defensible or not. Had deceased any religious convictions? That is to say, did he feel a dependence upon, or acknowledge alliance to a higher power?"

More reflection.

"I reckon you've stumped me again, pard. Could you say it over once more, and say it slow?"

"Well, to simplify it somewhat, was he, or rather had he ever been connected with any organization sequestered from secular concerns and devoted to self-sacrifice in the interests of morality?"

"All down but nine—set 'em up on the other alley, pard."

"What did I understand you to say?"

"Why, you're most too many for me, you know. When you get in with your left I hunt grass every time. Every time you draw, you fill; but I don't seem to have any luck. Let's have a new deal."

"How? Begin again?"

"That's it."

"Very well. Was he a good man, and—"

"There—I see that; don't put up another chip till I look at my hand. A good man, says you? Pard, it ain't no name for it. He was the best man that ever—pard, you would have doted on that man. He could lam any galoot of his inches in America. It was him that put down the riot last election before it got a start; and everybody said he was the only man that could have done it. He waltzed in with a spanner in one hand and a trumpet in the other, and sent fourteen men home on a shutter in less than three minutes. He had that riot all broke up and prevented nice before anybody ever got a chance to strike a blow. He was always for peace, and he would *have* peace—he could not stand disturbances. Pard, he was a great loss to this town. It would please the boys if you could chip in something like that and do him justice. Here once when the Micks got to throwing stones through the Methodis' Sunday-school windows, Buck Fanshaw, all of his own notion, shut up his saloon and took a couple of six-shooters and mounted guard over the Sunday-school. Says he, 'No Irish need apply!' And they didn't. He was the bulliest man in the mountains, pard! He could run faster, jump higher, hit harder, and hold more tanglefoot whisky without spilling it than any man in seventeen counties. Put that in, pard—it'll please the boys more than anything you could say. And you can say, pard, that he never shook his mother."

"Never shook his mother?"

"That's it—any of the boys will tell you so."

"Well, but why *should* he shake her?"

"That's what *I* say—but some people does."

"Not people of any repute?"

"Well, some that averages pretty so-so."

"In my opinion the man that would offer personal violence to his own mother, ought to—"

"Cheese it, pard; you've banked your ball clean outside the string. What I was a drivin' at, was, that he never *throwed* off on his mother—don't you see? No indeedy. He give her a house to live in, and town lots, and plenty of money; and he looked after her and took care of her all the time; and when she was down with the smallpox I'm d—d if he didn't set up nights and nuss her himself! *Beg* your pardon for saying it, but it hopped out too quick for yours truly. You've treated me like a gentleman, pard, and I ain't the man to hurt your feelings intentional. I think you're white. I think you're a square man, pard. I like you, and I'll lick any man that don't. I'll lick him till he can't tell himself from a last year's corpse! Put it *there!*" [Another fraternal handshake—and exit.]

The obsequies were all that "the boys" could desire. Such a

marvel of funeral pomp had never been seen in Virginia. The plumed hearse, the dirge-breathing brass-bands, the closed marts of business, the flags drooping at half-mast, the long, plodding procession of uniformed secret societies, military battalions and fire companies, draped engines, carriages of officials, and citizens in vehicles and on foot, attracted multitudes of spectators to the sidewalks, roofs, and windows; and for years afterward, the degree of grandeur attained by any civic display in Virginia was determined by comparison with Buck Fanshaw's funeral.

Scotty Briggs, as a pall-bearer and a mourner, occupied a prominent place at the funeral, and when the sermon was finished and the last sentence of the prayer for the dead man's soul ascended, he responded, in a low voice, but with feeling:

"AMEN. No Irish need apply."

As the bulk of the response was without apparent relevancy, it was probably nothing more than a humble tribute to the memory of the friend that was gone; for, as Scotty had once said, it was "his word."

Scotty Briggs, in after days, achieved the distinction of becoming the only convert to religion that was ever gathered from the Virginia roughs; and it transpired that the man who had it in him to espouse the quarrel of the weak out of inborn nobility of spirit was no mean timber whereof to construct a Christian. The making him one did not warp his generosity or diminish his courage; on the contrary it gave intelligent direction to the one and a broader field to the other. If his Sunday-school class progressed faster than the other classes, was it matter for wonder? I think not. He talked to his pioneer small-fry in a language they understood! It was my large privilege, a month before he died, to hear him tell the beautiful story of Joseph and his brethren to his class "without looking at the book." I leave it to the reader to fancy what it was like, as it fell, riddled with slang, from the lips of that grave, earnest teacher, and was listened to by his little learners with a consuming interest that showed that they were as unconscious as he was that any violence was being done to the sacred properties!

QUESTIONS FOR DISCUSSION

1. What does the unnamed philosopher mean by his statement that "to know a community, one must observe the style of its funerals"? What do funerals tell about a society?

2. From the second paragraph, what details can you cite to qualify Buck Fanshaw as "a representative citizen" of Virginia City?
3. The third paragraph is typical of the style of the tall tale. What specific qualities of this narrative form can you see in this passage?
4. Although the title suggests that Buck Fanshaw's funeral is of primary concern, paragraph four shows the real subject of this story. What is it? Why does Twain make so much of this subject? Is there a more important aspect to the subject than its humor?
5. What seems to be Mark Twain's estimate of the frontier minister? How do Twain's preachers compare or contrast with clergymen in the works of other American writers?
6. What is the first phrase in Scotty Briggs' slang that the preacher understands? From what literal settings do Briggs' expressions come? What happens to these expressions when they are transferred to another context?
7. Both Briggs and Fanshaw seem to have shared the typical prejudices of the time. What proof, however, does Briggs offer to show that Buck Fanshaw was concerned for "a man's rights"?
8. What does Briggs intend by his "AMEN. No Irish need apply"? Why is its effect upon the reader so ludicrous?
9. To the narrator, why was Briggs such an effective Sunday School teacher after his conversion? What is Mark Twain saying about communication in general, religious expression in particular?

ASSIGNMENTS FOR WRITING

1. "Buck Fanshaw's Funeral" illustrates the inability of two men to communicate with each other, as long as each persists in using language unsuited to the occasion and to his audience. Write an essay, using this story for your support; argue for a sensible attitude toward language, neither overly prescriptive nor undisciplined.
2. Write a paragraph using the slang expressions currently in vogue. In a second paragraph restate your original ideas in conventional language. Try reading your first paragraph to persons of different ages. What do you learn about problems in communication?
3. The language of prejudice often reduces itself in time to sloganeering, such as Buck Fanshaw's favorite expression, "No Irish need apply." In Briggs' usage, the phrase had been reduced virtually to an offhand remark. What expressions of racial, national, or religious prejudice have similar effect in our time? In a brief essay, show how some specific prejudicial slur has lost much of its incendiary quality and become a commonplace of speech. Account for this fact, if you can. Support your essay with evidence from your reading, observation, or personal experience.

The Man That Corrupted Hadleyburg

1

It was many years ago. Hadleyburg was the most honest and upright town in all the region around about. It had kept that reputation unsmirched during three generations, and was prouder of it than of any other of its possessions. It was so proud of it, and so anxious to insure its perpetuation, that it began to teach the principles of honest dealing to its babies in the cradle, and made the like teachings the staple of their culture thenceforward through all the years devoted to their education. Also, throughout the formative years temptations were kept out of the way of the young people, so that their honesty could have every chance to harden and solidify, and become a part of their very bone. The neighboring towns were jealous of this honorable supremacy, and affected to sneer at Hadleyburg's pride in it and call it vanity; but all the same they were obliged to acknowledge that Hadleyburg was in reality an incorruptible town; and if pressed they would also acknowledge that the mere fact that a young man hailed from Hadleyburg was all the recommendation he needed when he went forth from his natal town to seek for responsible employment.

But at last, in the drift of time, Hadleyburg had the ill luck to offend a passing stranger—possibly without knowing it, certainly without caring, for Hadleyburg was sufficient unto itself, and cared not a rap for strangers or their opinions. Still, it would have been well to make an exception in this one's case, for he was a bitter man and revengeful. All through his wanderings during a whole year he kept his injury in mind, and gave all his leisure moments to trying to invent a compensating satisfaction for it. He contrived many plans, and all of them were good, but none of them was quite sweeping enough; the poorest of them would hurt a great many individuals, but what he wanted was a plan which would comprehend the entire town, and not let so much as one person escape unhurt. At last he had a fortunate idea, and when it fell into his brain it lit up his whole head with an evil joy. He began to form a plan at once, saying to himself, "That is the thing to do— I will corrupt the town."

Six months later he went to Hadleyburg, and arrived in a buggy at the house of the old cashier of the bank about ten at night. He got a sack out of the buggy, shouldered it, and staggered with it through the cottage yard, and knocked at the door. A woman's voice said "Come in," and he entered, and set his sack behind the stove in the parlor, saying politely to the old lady who sat reading the *Missionary Herald* by the lamp:

"Pray keep your seat, madam, I will not disturb you. There—now it is pretty well concealed; one would hardly know it was there. Can I see your husband a moment, madam?"

No, he was gone to Brixton, and might not return before morning.

"Very well, madam, it is no matter. I merely wanted to leave that sack in his care, to be delivered to the rightful owner when he shall be found. I am a stranger; he does not know me; I am merely passing through the town to-night to discharge a matter which has been long in my mind. My errand is now completed, and I go pleased and a little proud, and you will never see me again. There is a paper attached to the sack which will explain everything. Good night, madam."

The old lady was afraid of the mysterious big stranger, and was glad to see him go. But her curiosity was roused, and she went straight to the sack and brought away the paper. It began as follows:

TO BE PUBLISHED; *or, the right man sought out by private inquiry —either will answer. This sack contains gold coin weighing a hundred and sixty pounds four ounces—*

"Mercy on us, and the door not locked!"

Mrs. Richards flew to it all in a tremble and locked it, then pulled down the window-shades and stood frightened, worried, and wondering if there was anything else she could do toward making herself and the money more safe. She listened awhile for burglars, then surrendered to curiosity and went back to the lamp and finished reading the paper:

I am a foreigner, and am presently going back to my own country, to remain there permanently. I am grateful to America for what I have received at her hands during my long stay under her flag; and to one of her citizens—a citizen of Hadleyburg—I am especially grateful for a great kindness done me a year or two ago. Two great kindnesses, in fact. I will explain. I was a gambler. I say I WAS. I was a ruined gambler. I arrived in this village at night, hungry and without a penny. I asked for help—in the dark; I was ashamed to beg in the light. I begged of the right man. He gave me twenty dollars—that is to say, he gave me life, as I considered it. He also gave me fortune; for out of that money I have made myself rich at the gaming-table. And finally, a remark which he made to me has remained with me to this day, and has at last conquered me; and in conquering has saved the remnant of my morals; I shall gamble no more. Now I have no idea who that man was, but I want him found, and I want him to have this money, to give away, throw away, or keep, as he pleases. It is merely my way of testifying my gratitude to him. If I could stay, I would find him myself; but no matter, he will be found. This is an honest town, an incorruptible town, and I know I can trust it without fear. This man can be identified by the remark which he made to me; I feel persuaded that he will remember it.

And now my plan is this: If you prefer to conduct the inquiry privately, do so. Tell the contents of this present writing to any one who is likely to be the right man. If he shall answer, 'I am the man; the remark I made was so-and-so,' apply the test—to wit: open the sack, and in it you will find a sealed envelope containing that remark. If the remark mentioned by the candidate tallies with it, give him the money, and ask no further questions, for he is certainly the right man.

But if you shall prefer a public inquiry, then publish this present writing in the local paper—with these instructions added, to wit: Thirty days from now, let the candidate appear at the townhall at eight in the evening (Friday), and hand his remark, in a sealed envelope, to the Rev. Mr. Burgess (if he will be kind enough to act); and let Mr. Burgess there and then destroy the seals of the sack, open it, and see if the remark is correct; if correct, let the money be delivered with my sincere gratitude, to my benefactor thus identified.

Mrs. Richards sat down, gently quivering with excitement, and was soon lost in thinkings—after this pattern: "What a strange thing it is! . . . And what a fortune for that kind man who set his bread afloat upon the waters! . . . If it had only been my husband that did it!—for we are so poor, so old and poor! . . ." Then, with a sigh—"But it was not my Edward; no, it was not he that gave a stranger twenty dollars. It is pity, too; I see it now. . . ." Then, with a shudder—"But it is *gambler's* money! the wages of sin: we couldn't take it; we couldn't touch it. I don't like to be near it; it seems a defilement." She moved to a farther chair.... "I wish Edward would come and take it to the bank; a burglar might come at any moment; it is dreadful to be here all alone with it."

At eleven Mr. Richards arrived, and while his wife was saying, "I am *so* glad you've come!" he was saying, "I'm so tired—tired clear out; it is dreadful to be poor, and have to make these dismal journeys at my time of life. Always at the grind, grind, grind, on a salary—another man's slave, and he sitting at home in his slippers, rich and comfortable."

"I am so sorry for you, Edward, you know that; but be comforted: we have our livelihood; we have our good name—"

"Yes, Mary, and that is everything. Don't mind my talk—it's just a moment's irritation and doesn't mean anything. Kiss me—there, it's all gone now, and I am not complaining any more. What have you been getting? What's in the sack?"

Then his wife told him the great secret. It dazed him for a moment; then he said:

"It weighs a hundred and sixty pounds? Why, Mary, it's for-ty thousand dollars—think of it—a whole fortune! Not ten men in this village are worth that much. Give me the paper."

He skimmed through it and said:

"Isn't it an adventure! Why, it's a romance; it's like the impossible things one reads about in books, and never sees in life." He was well stirred up now; cheerful, even gleeful. He tapped his old wife on the cheek, and said, humorously, "Why, we're rich, Mary, rich; all we've got to do is to bury the money and burn the papers. If the gambler ever comes to inquire, we'll merely look coldly upon him and say: 'What is this nonsense you are talking! We have never heard of you and your sack of gold before'; and then he would look foolish, and—"

"And in the mean time, while you are running on with your jokes, the money is still here, and it is fast getting along toward burglar-time."

"True. Very well, what shall we do—make the inquiry private? No, not that; it would spoil the romance. The public method is better. Think what a noise it will make! And it will make all the other towns jealous; for no stranger would trust such a thing to any town but Hadleyburg, and they know it. It's a great card for us. I must get to the printing-office now, or I shall be too late."

"But stop—stop—don't leave me here alone with it, Edward!"

But he was gone. For only a little while, however. Not far from his own house he met the editor-proprietor of the paper, and gave him the document, and said, "Here is a good thing for you, Cox—put it in."

"It may be too late, Mr. Richards, but I'll see."

At home again he and his wife sat down to talk the charming mystery over; they were in no condition for sleep. The first question was, Who could the citizen have been who gave the stranger the twenty dollars? It seemed a simple one; both answered it in the same breath:

"Barclay Goodson."

"Yes," said Richards, "he could have done it, and it would have been like him, but there's not another in the town."

"Everybody will grant that, Edward—grant it privately, anyway. For six months, now, the village has been its own proper self once more—honest, narrow, self-righteous, and stingy."

"It is what he always called it, to the day of his death—said it right out publicly, too."

"Yes, and he was hated for it."

"Oh, of course; but he didn't care. I reckon he was the best-hated man among us, except the Reverend Burgess."

"Well, Burgess deserves it—he will never get another congregation here. Mean as the town is, it knows how to estimate *him*. Edward, doesn't it seem odd that the stranger should appoint Burgess to deliver the money?"

"Well, yes—it does. That is—that is—"

"Why so much that-*is*-ing? Would *you* select him?"

"Mary, maybe the stranger knows him better than this village does."

"Much *that* would help Burgess!"

The husband seemed perplexed for an answer; the wife kept a steady eye upon him, and waited. Finally Richards said, with the hesitancy of one who is making a statement which is likely to encounter doubt:

"Mary, Burgess is not a bad man."

His wife was certainly surprised.

"Nonsense!" she exclaimed.

"He is not a bad man. I know. The whole of his unpopularity had its foundation in that one thing—the thing that made so much noise."

"That 'one thing,' indeed! As if that 'one thing' wasn't enough, all by itself."

"Plenty. Plenty. Only he wasn't guilty of it."

"How you talk! Not guilty of it! Everybody knows he *was* guilty."

"Mary, I give you my word—he was innocent."

"I can't believe it, and I don't. How do you know?"

"It is a confession. I am ashamed, but I will make it. I was the only man who knew he was innocent. I could have saved him, and—and—well, you know how the town was wrought up—I hadn't the pluck to do it. It would have turned everybody against me. I felt mean, ever so mean; but I didn't dare; I hadn't the manliness to face that."

Mary looked troubled, and for a while was silent. Then she said, stammeringly:

"I—I don't think it would have done for you to—to—One mustn't—er—public opinion—one has to be so careful—so—" It was a difficult road, and she got mired; but after a little she got started again. "It was a great pity, but—Why, we couldn't afford it, Edward—we couldn't indeed. Oh, I wouldn't have had you do it for anything!"

"It would have lost us the good will of so many people, Mary; and then—and then—"

"What troubles me now is, what *he* thinks of us, Edward."

"He? *He* doesn't suspect that I could have saved him."

"Oh," exclaimed the wife, in a tone of relief, "I am glad of that! As long as he doesn't know that you could have saved him, he—he—well, that makes it a great deal better. Why, I might have known he didn't know, because he is always trying to be friendly with us, as little encouragement as we give him. More than once people have twitted me with it. There's the Wilsons, and the Wilcoxes, and the Harknesses, they take a mean pleasure in saying, '*Your friend* Burgess,' because they know it pesters me. I wish he wouldn't persist in liking us so; I can't think why he keeps it up."

"I can explain it. It's another confession. When the thing was new and hot, and the town made a plan to ride him on a rail, my conscience hurt me so that I couldn't stand it, and I went privately and gave him notice, and he got out of the town and stayed out till it was safe to come back."

"Edward! If the town had found it out—"

"*Don't!* It scares me yet, to think of it. I repented of it the minute it was done; and I was even afraid to tell you, lest your face might betray it to somebody. I didn't sleep any that night, for worrying. But after a few days I saw that no one was going to suspect me, and after that I got to feeling glad I did it. And I feel glad yet, Mary—glad through and through."

"So do I, now, for it would have been a dreadful way to treat him. Yes, I'm glad; for really you did owe him that, you know. But, Edward, suppose it should come out yet, some day!"

"It won't."

"Why?"

"Because everybody thinks it was Goodson."

"Of course they would!"

"Certainly. And of course *he* didn't care. They persuaded poor old Sawlsberry to go and charge it on him, and he went blustering over there and did it. Goodson looked him over, like as if he was hunting for a place on him that he could despise the most, then he says, 'So you are the Committee of Inquiry, are you?' Sawlsberry said that was about what he was. 'Hm. Do they require particulars, or do you reckon a kind of a *general* answer will do?' 'If they require particulars, I will come back. Mr. Goodson; I will take the general answer first.' 'Very well, then, tell them to go to hell—I reckon that's general enough. And I'll give you some advice, Sawlsberry; when you come back for the particulars, fetch a basket to carry the relics of yourself home in.'"

"Just like Goodson; it's got all the marks. He had only one vanity: he thought he could give advice better than any other person."

"It settled the business, and saved us, Mary. The subject was dropped."

"Bless you, I'm not doubting *that*."

Then they took up the gold-sack mystery again, with strong interest. Soon the conversation began to suffer breaks—interruptions caused by absorbed thinkings. The breaks grew more and more frequent. At last Richards lost himself wholly in thought. He sat long, gazing vacantly at the floor, and by and by he began to punctuate his thoughts with little nervous movements of his hands that seemed to indicate vexation. Meantime his wife too had relapsed into a thoughtful silence, and her movements were beginning to show a troubled discomfort. Finally Richards got up and strode aimlessly about the room, plowing his hands through his hair, much as a somnambulist might do who was having a bad dream. Then he seemed to arrive at a definite purpose; and without a word he put on his hat and passed quickly out of the house. His wife sat brooding, with a drawn face, and did not seem to be aware that she was alone. Now and then she murmured, "Lead us not into t— . . . but—but—we are so poor, so poor! . . . Lead us not into . . . Ah, who would be hurt by it?—and no one would ever know. . . . Lead us . . ." The voice died out in mumblings. After a little she glanced up and muttered in a half-frightened, half-glad way:

"He is gone! But, oh dear, he may be too late—too late. . . . Maybe not—maybe there is still time." She rose and stood thinking, nervously clasping and unclasping her hands. A slight shudder shook her frame, and she said, out of a dry throat, "God forgive me

—it's awful to think such things—but . . . Lord, how we are made—how strangely we are made!"

She turned the light low, and slipped stealthily over and kneeled down by the sack and felt of its ridgy sides with her hands, and fondled them lovingly; and there was a gloating light in her poor old eyes. She fell into fits of absence; and came half out of them at times to mutter, "If we had only waited!—oh, if we had only waited a little, and not been in such a hurry!"

Meantime Cox had gone home from his office and told his wife all about the strange thing that had happened, and they had talked it over eagerly, and guessed that the late Goodson was the only man in the town who could have helped a suffering stranger with so noble a sum as twenty dollars. Then there was a pause, and the two became thoughtful and silent. And by and by nervous and fidgety. At last the wife said, as if to herself:

"Nobody knows this secret but the Richardses . . . and us . . . nobody."

The husband came out of his thinkings with a slight start, and gazed wistfully at his wife, whose face was become very pale; then he hesitatingly rose, and glanced furtively at his hat, then at his wife—a sort of mute inquiry. Mrs. Cox swallowed once or twice, with her hand at her throat, then in place of speech she nodded her head. In a moment she was alone, and mumbling to herself.

And now Richards and Cox were hurrying through the deserted streets, from opposite directions. They met, panting, at the foot of the printing-office stairs; by the night light there they read each other's face. Cox whispered:

"Nobody knows about this but us?"

The whispered answer was,

"Not a soul—on honor, not a soul!"

"If it isn't too late to—"

The men were starting up-stairs; at this moment they were overtaken by a boy, and Cox asked:

"Is that you, Johnny?"

"Yes, sir."

"You needn't ship the early mail—nor *any* mail; wait till I tell you."

"It's already gone, sir."

"*Gone?*" It had the sound of an unspeakable disappointment in it.

"Yes, sir. Time-table for Brixton and all the towns beyond

changed to-day, sir—had to get the papers in twenty minutes earlier than common. I had to rush; if I had been two minutes later—"

The men turned and walked slowly away, not waiting to hear the rest. Neither of them spoke during ten minutes; then Cox said, in a vexed tone:

"What possessed you to be in such a hurry, *I* can't make out."

The answer was humble enough:

"I see it now, but somehow I never thought, you know, until it was too late. But the next time—"

"Next time be hanged! It won't come in a thousand years."

Then the friends separated without a good night, and dragged themselves home with the gait of mortally stricken men. At their homes their wives sprang up with an eager "Well?"—then saw the answer with their eyes and sank down sorrowing, without waiting for it to come in words. In both houses a discussion followed of a heated sort—a new thing; there had been discussions before, but not heated ones, not ungentle ones. The discussions to-night were a sort of seeming plagiarisms of each other. Mrs. Richards said,

"If you had only waited, Edward—if you had only stopped to think; but no, you must run straight to the printing-office and spread it all over the world."

"It *said* publish it."

"That is nothing; it also said do it privately, if you liked. There, now—is that true, or not?"

"Why, yes—yes, it is true; but when I thought what stir it would make, and what a compliment it was to Hadleyburg that a stranger should trust it so—"

"Oh, certainly, I know all that; but if you had only stopped to think, you would have seen that you *couldn't* find the right man, because he is in his grave, and hasn't left chick nor child nor relation behind him; and as long as the money went to somebody that awfully needed it, and nobody would be hurt by it, and—and—"

She broke down, crying. Her husband tried to think of some comforting thing to say, and presently came out with this:

"But after all, Mary, it must be for the best—it *must* be; we know that. And we must remember that it was so ordered—"

"Ordered! Oh, everything's *ordered*, when a person has to find some way out when he has been stupid. Just the same, it was *ordered* that the money should come to us in this special way, and it was you that must take it on yourself to go meddling with the designs of Providence—and who gave you the right? It was wicked, that is what it was—just blasphemous presumption, and no more becoming to a meek and humbled professor of—"

"But, Mary, you know how we have been trained all our lives long, like the whole village, till it is absolutely second nature to us to stop not a single moment to think when there's an honest thing to be done—"

"Oh, I know it, I know it—it's been one everlasting training and training and training in honesty—honesty shielded, from the very cradle, against every possible temptation, and so it's *artificial* honesty, and weak as water when temptation comes, as we have seen this night. God knows I never had shade nor shadow of a doubt of my petrified and indestructible honesty until now—and now, under the very first big and real temptation, I—Edward, it is my belief that this town's honesty is as rotten as mine is; as rotten as yours is. It is a mean town, a hard, stingy town, and hasn't a virtue in the world but this honesty it is so celebrated for and so conceited about; and so help me, I do believe that if ever the day comes that its honesty falls under great temptation, its grand reputation will go to ruin like a house of cards. There, now, I've made confession, and I feel better; I am a humbug, and I've been one all my life, without knowing it. Let no man call me honest again—I will not have it."

"I—well, Mary, I feel a good deal as you do; I certainly do. It seems strange, too, so strange. I never could have believed it—never."

A long silence followed; both were sunk in thought. At last the wife looked up and said:

"I know what you are thinking, Edward."

Richards had the embarrassed look of a person who is caught.

"I am ashamed to confess it, Mary, but—"

"It's no matter, Edward, I was thinking the same question myself."

"I hope so. State it."

"You were thinking, if a body could only guess out *what the remark was* that Goodson made to the stranger."

"It's perfectly true. I feel guilty and ashamed. And you?"

"I'm past it. Let us make a pallet here; we've got to stand watch till the bank vault opens in the morning and admits the sack. . . . Oh dear, oh dear—if we hadn't made the mistake!"

The pallet was made, and Mary said:

"The open sesame—what could it have been? I do wonder what that remark could have been? But come; we will get to bed now."

"And sleep?"

"No: think."

"Yes, think."

By this time the Coxes too had completed their spat and their reconciliation, and were turning in—to think, to think, and toss, and fret, and worry over what the remark could possibly have been which Goodson made to the stranded derelict; that golden remark; that remark worth forty thousand dollars, cash.

The reason that the village telegraph-office was open later than usual that night was this: The foreman of Cox's paper was the local representative of the Associated Press. One might say its honorary representative, for it wasn't four times a year that he could furnish thirty words that would be accepted. But this time it was different. His despatch stating what he had caught got an instant answer:

Send the whole thing—all the details—twelve hundred words.

A colossal order! The foreman filled the bill; and he was the proudest man in the State. By breakfast-time the next morning the name of Hadleyburg the Incorruptible was on every lip in America, from Montreal to the Gulf, from the glaciers of Alaska to the orange-groves of Florida; and millions and millions of people were discussing the stranger and his money-sack, and wondering if the right man would be found, and hoping some more news about the matter would come soon—right away.

2

Hadleyburg village woke up world-celebrated—astonished—happy—vain. Vain beyond imagination. Its nineteen principal citizens and their wives went about shaking hands with each other, and beaming, and smiling, and congratulating, and saying *this* thing adds a new word to the dictionary—*Hadleyburg*, synonym for *incorruptible*—destined to live in dictionaries forever! And the minor and unimportant citizens and their wives went around acting in much the same way. Everybody ran to the bank to see the gold-sack; and before noon grieved and envious crowds began to flock in from Brixton and all neighboring towns; and that afternoon and next day reporters began to arrive from everywhere to verify the sack and its history and write the whole thing up anew, and make dashing free-hand pictures of the sack, and of Richards' house, and the bank, and the Presbyterian church, and the Baptist church, and the public square, and the town-hall where the test would be applied and the money delivered; and damnable portraits of the Richardses, and Pinkerton the banker, and Cox, and the foreman, and Reverend Burgess, and the postmaster—and even of Jack Halliday, who was the loafing, good-natured, no-account, irreverent fisherman, hunter, boys' friend, stray-dogs' friend, typical "Sam Lawson" of the town. The little mean, smirking, oily Pinkerton showed the sack to all comers, and rubbed his sleek palms together pleasantly, and enlarged upon the town's fine old reputation for honesty and upon this wonderful endorsement of it, and hoped and believed that the example would now spread far and wide over the American world, and be epoch-making in the matter of moral regeneration. And so on, and so on.

By the end of a week things had quieted down again; the wild intoxication of pride and joy had sobered to a soft, sweet, silent delight—a sort of deep, nameless, unutterable content. All faces bore a look of peaceful, holy happiness.

Then a change came. It was a gradual change: so gradual that its beginnings were hardly noticed; maybe were not noticed at all, except by Jack Halliday, who always noticed everything; and always made fun of it, too, no matter what it was. He began to throw out chaffing remarks about people not looking quite so happy as they did a day or two ago; and next he claimed that the new aspect was deepening to positive sadness; next, that it was taking on a sick look; and finally he said that everybody was become so moody, thoughtful, and absentminded that he could rob the meanest man in town of a cent out of the bottom of his breeches pocket and not disturb his revery.

At this stage—or at about this stage—a saying like this was dropped at bedtime—with a sigh, usually—by the head of each of the nineteen principal households: "Ah, what *could* have been the remark that Goodson made?"

And straightway—with a shudder—came this, from the man's wife:

"Oh, *don't!* What horrible thing are you mulling in your mind? Put it away from you, for God's sake!"

But that question was wrung from those men again the next night—and got the same retort. But weaker.

And the third night the men uttered the question yet again—with anguish, and absently. This time—and the following night—the wives fidgeted feebly, and tried to say something. But didn't.

And the night after that they found their tongues and responded—longingly:

"Oh, if we *could* only guess!"

Halliday's comments grew daily more and more sparklingly disagreeable and disparaging. He went diligently about, laughing at the town, individually and in mass. But his laugh was the only one left in the village: it fell upon a hollow and mournful vacancy and emptiness. Not even a smile was findable anywhere. Halliday carried a cigar-box around on a tripod, playing that it was a camera, and halted all passers and aimed the thing and said, "Ready!—now look pleasant, please," but not even this capital joke could surprise the dreary faces into any softening.

So three weeks passed—one week was left. It was Saturday evening—after supper. Instead of the aforetime Saturday-evening flutter and bustle and shopping and larking, the streets were empty and desolate. Richards and his old wife sat apart in their little parlor—miserable and thinking. This was become their evening habit now: the lifelong habit which had preceded it, of reading, knitting, and contented chat, or receiving or paying neighborly calls, was dead and gone and forgotten, ages ago—two or three weeks ago; nobody talked now, nobody read, nobody visited—the whole village sat at home, sighing, worrying, silent. Trying to guess out that remark.

The postman left a letter, Richards glanced listlessly at the superscription and the postmark—unfamiliar, both—and tossed the letter on the table and resumed his might-have-beens and his hopeless dull miseries where he had left them off. Two or three hours later his wife got wearily up and was going away to bed without a good night—custom now—but she stopped near the letter and eyed it awhile with a dead interest, then broke it open, and began to skim it over. Richards, sitting there with his chair tilted back against the wall and his chin between his knees, heard something fall. It was his wife. He sprang to her side, but she cried out:

"Leave me alone, I am too happy. Read the letter—read it!"

He did. He devoured it, his brain reeling. The letter was from a distant state, and it said:

I am a stranger to you, but no matter: I have something to tell. I have just arrived home from Mexico, and learned about that episode. Of course you do not know who made that remark, but I know, and I am the only person living who does know. It was GOODSON. I knew him well, many years ago. I passed through your village that very night, and was his guest till the midnight train came along. I overheard him make that remark to the stranger in the dark—it was in Hale Alley. He and I talked of it the rest of the way home, and while smoking in his house. He mentioned many of your villagers in the course of his talk—most of them in a very uncomplimentary way, but two or three favorably; among these latter yourself. I say "favorably"—nothing stronger. I remember his saying he did not actually LIKE any person in the town —not one; but that you—I THINK he said you—am almost sure— had done him a very great service once, possibly without knowing the full value of it, and he wished he had a fortune, he would leave it to you when he died, and a curse apiece for the rest of the citizens. Now, then, if it was you that did him that service, you are his legitimate heir, and entitled to the sack of gold. I know that I can trust to your honor and honesty, for in a citizen of Hadleyburg these virtues are an unfailing inheritance, and so I am going to reveal to you the remark, well satisfied that if you are not the right man you will seek and find the right one and see that poor Goodson's debt of gratitude for the service referred to is paid. This is the remark: "YOU ARE FAR FROM BEING A BAD MAN: GO, AND REFORM."

HOWARD L. STEPHENSON

"Oh, Edward, the money is ours, and I am so grateful, *oh,* so grateful—kiss me, dear, it's forever since we kissed—and we needed it so—the money—and now you are free of Pinkerton and his bank, and nobody's slave any more; it seems to me I could fly for joy."

It was a happy half-hour that the couple spent there on the settee caressing each other; it was the old days come again—days that had begun with their courtship and lasted without a break till the stranger brought the deadly money. By and by the wife said:

"Oh, Edward, how lucky it was you did him that grand service, poor Goodson! I never liked him, but I love him now. And it was fine and beautiful of you never to mention it or brag about it." Then, with a touch of reproach, "But you ought to have told *me,* Edward, you ought to have told your wife, you know."

"Well, I—er—well, Mary, you see—"

"Now stop hemming and hawing, and tell me about it, Edward. I always loved you, and now I'm proud of you. Everybody believes there was only one good generous soul in this village, and now it turns out that you—Edward, why don't you tell me?"

"Well—er—er—Why, Mary, I can't!"

"You *can't?* Why can't you?"

"You see, he—well, he—he made me promise I wouldn't."

The wife looked him over, and said, very slowly:

"Made—you—promise? Edward, what do you tell me that for?"

"Mary, do you think I would lie?"

She was troubled and silent for a moment, then she laid her hand within his and said:

"No . . . no. We have wandered far enough from our bearings —God spare us that! In all your life you have never uttered a lie. But now—now that the foundations of things seem to be crumbling from under us, we—we—" She lost her voice for a moment, then said, brokenly, "Lead us not into temptation. . . . I think you made the promise, Edward. Let it rest so. Let us keep away from that ground. Now—that is all gone by; let us be happy again; it is no time for clouds."

Edward found it something of an effort to comply, for his mind kept wandering—trying to remember what the service was that he had done Goodson.

The couple lay awake the most of the night, Mary happy and busy, Edward busy but not so happy. Mary was planning what she would do with the money. Edward was trying to recall that service. At first his conscience was sore on account of the lie he had told Mary—if it was a lie. After much reflection—suppose it *was* a lie? What then? Was it such a great matter? Aren't we always *acting* lies? Then why not *tell* them? Look at Mary—look what she had done. While he was hurrying off on his honest errand, what was she doing? Lamenting because the papers hadn't been destroyed and the money kept! Is theft better than lying?

That point lost its sting—the lie dropped into the background and left comfort behind it. The next point came to the front: *Had* he rendered that service? Well, here was Goodson's own evidence as reported in Stephenson's letter; there could be no better evidence than that—it was even *proof* that he had rendered it. Of course. So that point was settled. . . . No, not quite. He recalled with a wince that this unknown Mr. Stephenson was just a trifle unsure as to whether the performer of it was Richards or some other—and, oh dear, he had put Richards on his honor! He must himself decide whither that money must go—and Mr. Stephenson was not doubting that if he was the wrong man he would go honorably and find the right one. Oh, it was odious to put a man in such a situation—ah, why couldn't Stephenson have left out that doubt! What did he want to intrude that for?

Further reflection. How did it happen that *Richards'* name remained in Stephenson's mind as indicating the right man, and not some other man's name? That looked good. Yes, that looked very good. In fact, it went on looking better and better, straight along—until by and by it grew into positive *proof*. And then Richards put the matter at once out of his mind, for he had a private instinct that a proof once established is better left so.

He was feeling reasonably comfortable now, but there was still one other detail that kept pushing itself on his notice: of course he had done that service—that was settled; but what *was* that service? He must recall it—he would not go to sleep till he had recalled it; it would make his peace of mind perfect. And so he thought and thought. He thought of a dozen things—possible services, even probable services—but none of them ꞓ ꞵmed adequate, none of them seemed large enough, none of them seemed worth the money—worth the fortune Goodson had wished he could leave in his will. And besides, he couldn't remember having done them, anyway. Now, then—now, then—what *kind* of a service would it be that would make a man so inordinately grateful? Ah—the saving of his soul! That must be it. Yes, he could remember, now, how he once set himself the task of converting Goodson, and labored at it as much as—he was going to say three months; but upon closer examination it shrunk to a month, then to a week, then to a day, then to nothing. Yes, he remembered now, and with unwelcome vividness, that Goodson had told him to go to thunder and mind his own business—*he* wasn't hankering to follow Hadleyburg to heaven!

So that solution was a failure—he hadn't saved Goodson's soul. Richards was discouraged. Then after a little came another idea: had he saved Goodson's property? No, that wouldn't do—he hadn't any. His life? That is it! Of course. Why, he might have thought of it before. This time he was on the right track, sure. His imagination-mill was hard at work in a minute, now.

Thereafter during a stretch of two exhausting hours he was busy saving Goodson's life. He saved it in all kinds of difficult and perilous ways. In every case he got it saved satisfactorily up to a certain point; then, just as he was beginning to get well persuaded that it had really happened, a troublesome detail would turn up which made the whole thing impossible. As in the matter of drowning, for instance. In that case he had swum out and tugged Goodson ashore in an unconscious state with a great crowd looking on and applauding, but when he had got it all thought out and was just beginning to remember all about it, a whole swarm of disqualifying details arrived on the ground: the town would have known of the circumstance, Mary would have known of it, it would glare like a limelight in his own memory instead of being an inconspicuous service which he had possibly rendered "without knowing its full value." And at this point he remembered that he couldn't swim, anyway.

Ah—*there* was a point which he had been overlooking from the start: it had to be a service which he had rendered "possibly without knowing the full value of it." Why, really, that ought to be an easy hunt—much easier than those others. And sure enough, by and by he found it. Goodson, years and years ago, came near marrying a very sweet and pretty girl, named Nancy Hewitt, but in some way or other the match had been broken off; the girl died, Goodson remained a bachelor, and by and by became a soured one and a frank despiser of the human species. Soon after the girl's death the village found out, or thought it had found out, that she carried a spoonful of Negro blood in her veins. Richards worked at these details a good while, and in the end he thought he remembered things concerning them which must have gotten mislaid in his memory through long neglect. He seemed to dimly remember that it was *he* that found out about the Negro blood; that it was he that told the village; that the village told Goodson where they got it; that he thus saved Goodson from marrying the tainted girl; that he had done him this great service "without knowing the full value of it," in fact without knowing that he *was* doing it; but that Goodson knew the value of it, and what a narrow escape he had had, and so went to his grave grateful to his benefactor and wishing he had a fortune to leave him. It was all clear and simple now, and the more he went over it the more luminous and certain it grew; and at last, when he nestled to sleep satisfied and happy, he remembered the whole thing just as if it had been yesterday. In fact, he dimly remembered Goodson *telling* him his gratitude once. Meantime Mary had spent six thousand dollars on a new house for herself and a pair of slippers for her pastor, and then had fallen peacefully to rest.

That same Saturday evening the postman had delivered a letter to each of the other principal citizens—nineteen letters in all. No two of the envelopes were alike, and no two of the superscriptions were in the same hand, but the letters inside were just like each other in every detail but one. They were exact copies of the letter received by Richards—handwriting and all—and were all signed by Stephenson, but in place of Richards' name each receiver's own name appeared.

All night long eighteen principal citizens did what their caste-brother Richards was doing at the same time—they put in their energies trying to remember what notable service it was that they had unconsciously done Barclay Goodson. In no case was it a holiday job; still they succeeded.

And while they were at this work, which was difficult, their wives put in the night spending the money, which was easy. During that one night the nineteen wives spent an average of seven thousand dollars each out of the forty thousand in the sack—a hundred and thirty-three thousand altogether.

Next day there was a surprise for Jack Halliday. He noticed that the faces of the nineteen chief citizens and their wives bore that expression of peaceful and holy happiness again. He could not understand it, neither was he able to invent any remarks about it that could damage it or disturb it. And so it was his turn to be dissatisfied with life. His private guesses at the reasons for the happiness failed in all instances, upon examination. When he met Mrs. Wilcox and noticed the placid ecstasy in her face, he said to himself, "Her cat has had kittens"—and went and asked the cook: it was not so; the cook had detected the happiness, but did not know the cause. When Halliday found the duplicate ecstasy in the face of "Shadbelly" Billson (village nickname), he was sure some neighbor of Billson's had broken his leg, but inquiry showed that this had not happened. The subdued ecstasy in Gregory Yates' face could mean but one thing—he was a mother-in-law short; it was another mistake. "And Pinkerton—Pinkerton—he has collected ten cents that he thought he was going to lose." And so on, and so on. In some cases the guesses had to remain in doubt, in the others they proved distinct errors. In the end Halliday said to himself, "Anyway it foots up that there's nineteen Hadleyburg families temporarily in heaven: I don't know how it happened; I only know Providence is off duty to-day."

An architect and builder from the next state had lately ventured to set up a small business in this unpromising village, and his sign had now been hanging out a week. Not a customer yet; he was a discouraged man, and sorry he had come. But his weather changed suddenly now. First one and then another chief citizen's wife said to him privately:

"Come to my house Monday week—but say nothing about it for the present. We think of building."

He got eleven invitations that day. That night he wrote his daughter and broke off her match with her student. He said she could marry a mile higher than that.

Pinkerton the banker and two or three other well-to-do men planned country-seats—but waited. That kind don't count their chickens until they are hatched.

The Wilsons devised a grand new thing—a fancy-dress ball. They made no actual promises, but told all their acquaintanceship in confidence that they were thinking the matter over and thought they should give it—"and if we do, you will be invited, of course." People were surprised, and said, one to another, "Why, they are crazy, those poor Wilsons, they can't afford it." Several among the nineteen said privately to their husbands, "It is a good idea: we will keep still till their cheap thing is over, then *we* will give one that will make it sick."

The days drifted along, and the bill of future squanderings rose higher and higher, wilder and wilder, more and more foolish and reckless. It began to look as if every member of the nineteen would not only spend his whole forty thousand dollars before receiving-day, but be actually in debt by the time he got the money. In some cases light-headed people did not stop with planning to spend, they really spent—on credit. They bought land, mortgages, farms, speculative stocks, fine clothes, horses, and various other things, paid down the bonus, and made themselves liable for the rest—at ten days. Presently the sober second thought came, and Halliday noticed that a ghastly anxiety was beginning to show up in a good many faces. Again he was puzzled, and didn't know what to make of it. "The Wilcox kittens aren't dead, for they weren't born; nobody's broken a leg; there's no shrinkage in mother-in-laws; *nothing* has happened—it is an unsolvable mystery."

There was another puzzled man, too—the Rev. Mr. Burgess. For days, wherever he went, people seemed to follow him or to be watching out for him; and if he ever found himself in a retired spot, a member of the nineteen would be sure to appear, thrust an envelope privately into his hand, whisper "To be opened at the town-hall Friday evening," then vanish away like a guilty thing. He was expecting that there might be one claimant for the sack —doubtful, however, Goodson being dead—but it never occurred to him that all this crowd might be claimants. When the great Friday came at last, he found that he had nineteen envelopes.

3

The town-hall had never looked finer. The platform at the end of it was backed by a showy draping of flags; at intervals along the walls were festoons of flags; the gallery fronts were clothed in flags; the supporting columns were swathed in flags; all this was to impress the stranger, for he would be there in considerable force, and in a large degree he would be connected with the press. The house was full. The 412 fixed seats were occupied; also the 68 extra chairs which had been packed into the aisles; the steps of the platform were occupied; some distinguished strangers were given seats on the platform; at the horseshoe of tables which fenced the front and sides of the platform sat a strong force of special correspondents who had come from everywhere. It was the best-dressed house the town had ever produced. There were some tolerably expensive toilets there, and in several cases the ladies who wore them had the look of being unfamiliar with that kind of clothes. At least the town thought they had that look, but the notion could have arisen from the town's knowledge of the fact that these ladies had never inhabited such clothes before.

The gold-sack stood on a little table at the front of the platform where all the house could see it. The bulk of the house gazed at it with a burning interest, a mouth-watering interest, a wistful and pathetic interest; a minority of nineteen couples gazed at it tenderly, lovingly, proprietarily, and the male half of this minority kept saying over to themselves the moving little impromptu speeches of thankfulness for the audience's applause and congratulations which they were presently going to get up and deliver. Every now and then one of these got a piece of paper out of his vest pocket and privately glanced at it to refresh his memory.

Of course there was a buzz of conversation going on—there always is; but at last when the Rev. Mr. Burgess rose and laid his hand on the sack he could hear his microbes gnaw, the place was so still. He related the curious history of the sack, then went on to speak in warm terms of Hadleyburg's old and well-earned reputation for spotless honesty, and of the town's just pride in this reputation. He said that this reputation was a treasure of priceless value; that under Providence its value had now become inestimably enhanced, for the recent episode had spread this fame far and wide, and thus had focused the eyes of the American world upon this village, and made its name for all time, as he hoped and believed, a synonym for commercial incorruptibility. [*Applause.*] "And who is to be the guardian of this noble treasure—the community as a whole? No! The responsibility is individual, not communal. From this day forth each and every one of you is in his own person its special guardian, and individually responsible that no harm shall come to it. Do you—does each of you—accept this great trust? [*Tumultuous assent.*] Then all is well. Transmit it to your children and to your children's children. To-day your purity is beyond reproach—see to it that it shall remain so. To-day there is not a person in your community who could be beguiled to touch a penny not his own—see to it that you abide in this grace. ["*We will! we will!*"] This is not the place to make comparisons between ourselves and other communities—some of them ungracious toward us; they have their ways, we have ours; let us be content. [*Applause.*] I am done. Under my hand, my friends, rests a stranger's eloquent recognition of what we are; through him the world will always henceforth know what we are. We do not know who he is, but in your name I utter your gratitude, and ask you to raise your voices in endorsement."

The house rose in a body and made the walls quake with the thunders of its thankfulness for the space of a long minute. Then it sat down, and Mr. Burgess took an envelope out of his pocket. The house held its breath while he slit the envelope open and took from it a slip of paper. He read its contents—slowly and impressively—the audience listening with tranced attention to this magic document, each of whose words stood for an ingot of gold:

" 'The remark which I made to the distressed stranger was this. "*You are very far from being a bad man: go, and reform.*" ' " Then he continued:

"We shall know in a moment now whether the remark here quoted corresponds with the one concealed in the sack; and if that shall prove to be so—and it undoubtedly will—this sack of gold belongs to a fellow-citizen who will henceforth stand before the nation as the symbol of the special virtue which has made our town famous throughout the land—Mr. Billson!"

The house had gotten itself all ready to burst into the proper tornado of applause; but instead of doing it, it seemed stricken with a paralysis; there was a deep hush for a moment or two, then a wave of whispered murmurs swept the place—of about this tenor: "*Billson!* oh, come, this is *too* thin! Twenty dollars to a stranger—or *anybody—Billson!* tell it to the marines!" And now at this point the house caught its breath all of a sudden in a new access of astonishment, for it discovered that whereas in one part of the hall Deacon Billson was standing up with his head meekly bowed, in another part of it Lawyer Wilson was doing the same. There was a wondering silence now for a while.

Everybody was puzzled, and nineteen couples were surprised and indignant.

Billson and Wilson turned and stared at each other. Billson asked, bitingly:

"Why do *you* rise, Mr. Wilson?"

"Because I have a right to. Perhaps you will be good enough to explain to the house why *you* rise?"

"With great pleasure. Because I wrote that paper."

"It is an impudent falsity! I wrote it myself."

It was Burgess' turn to be paralyzed. He stood looking vacantly at first one of the men and then the other, and did not seem to know what to do. The house was stupefied. Lawyer Wilson spoke up, now, and said,

"I ask the Chair to read the name signed to that paper."

That brought the Chair to itself, and it read out the name:

" 'John Wharton *Billson.*' "

"There!" shouted Billson, "what have you got to say for yourself, now? And what kind of apology are you going to make to me and to this insulted house for the imposture which you have attempted to play here?"

"No apologies are due, sir; and as for the rest of it, I publicly charge you with pilfering my note from Mr. Burgess and substituting a copy of it signed with your own name. There is no other way by which you could have gotten hold of the test-remark; I alone, of living men, possessed the secret of its wording."

There was likely to be a scandalous state of things if this went on; everybody noticed with distress that the shorthand scribes were scribbling like mad; many people were crying "Chair, Chair! Order! order!" Burgess rapped with his gavel, and said:

"Let us not forget the proprieties due. There has evidently been a mistake somewhere, but surely that is all. If Mr. Wilson gave me an envelope—and I remember now that he did—I still have it."

He took one out of his pocket, opened it, glanced at it, looked surprised and worried, and stood silent a few moments. Then he waved his hand in a wandering and mechanical way, and made an effort or two to say something, then gave it up, despondently. Several voices cried out:

"Read it! read it! What is it?"

So he began in a dazed and sleep-walker fashion:

" '*The remark which I made to the unhappy stranger was this:* "*You are far from being a bad man.* [The house gazed at him, marveling.] *Go, and reform.*" ' [*Murmurs:* "Amazing! what can this mean?"] This one," said the Chair, "is signed Thurlow G. Wilson."

"There!" cried Wilson. "I reckon that settles it! I knew perfectly well my note was purloined."

"Purloined!" retorted Billson. "I'll let you know that neither you nor any man of your kidney must venture to—"

THE CHAIR "Order, gentlemen, order! Take your seats, both of you, please."

They obeyed, shaking their heads and grumbling angrily. The house was profoundly puzzled; it did not know what to do with this curious emergency. Presently Thompson got up. Thompson was the hatter. He would have liked to be a Nineteener; but such was not for him: his stock of hats was not considerable enough for the position. He said:

"Mr. Chairman, if I may be permitted to make a suggestion, can both of these gentlemen be right? I put it to you, sir, can both have happened to say the very same words to the stranger? It seems to me—"

The tanner got up and interrupted him. The tanner was a disgruntled man; he believed himself entitled to be a Nineteener, but he couldn't get recognition. It made him a little unpleasant in his ways and speech. Said he:

"Sho, *that's* not the point! *That* could happen—twice in a hundred years—but not the other thing. *Neither* of them gave the twenty dollars!"

[*A ripple of applause.*]

BILLSON "I did!"

WILSON "I did!"

Then each accused the other of pilfering.

THE CHAIR "Order! Sit down, if you please—both of you. Neither of the notes has been out of my possession at any moment."

A VOICE "Good—that settles *that!*"

THE TANNER "Mr. Chairman, one thing is now plain: one of these men have been eavesdropping under the other one's bed, and filching family secrets. If it is not unparliamentary to suggest it, I will remark that both are equal to it. [*The Chair*. "Order! order!"] I withdraw the remark, sir, and will confine myself to suggesting that *if* one of them has overheard the other reveal the test-remark to his wife, we shall catch him now."

A VOICE "How?"

THE TANNER "Easily. The two have not quoted the remark in exactly the same words. You would have noticed that, if there hadn't been a considerable stretch of time and an exciting quarrel inserted between the two readings."

A VOICE "Name the difference."

THE TANNER "The word *very* is in Billson's note, and not in the other."

MANY VOICES "That's so—he's right!"

THE TANNER "And so, if the Chair will examine the test-remark in the sack, we shall know which of these two frauds—[*The Chair*.

"Order!"]—which of these two adventurers—[*The Chair.* "Order! order!"]—which of these two gentlemen—[*laughter and applause*] —is entitled to wear the belt as being the first dishonest blather-skite ever bred in this town—which he has dishonored, and which will be a sultry place for him from now out!" [*Vigorous applause.*]

MANY VOICES "Open it!—open the sack!"

Mr. Burgess made a slit in the sack, slid his hand in and brought out an envelope. In it were a couple of folded notes. He said:

"One of these is marked, 'Not to be examined until all written communications which have been addressed to the Chair—if any— shall have been read.' The other is marked '*The Test.*' Allow me. It is worded—to wit:

" 'I do not require that the first half of the remark which was made to me by my benefactor shall be quoted with exactness, for it was not striking, and could be forgotten; but its closing fifteen words are quite striking, and I think easily rememberable; unless *these* shall be accurately reproduced, let the applicant be regarded as an imposter. My benefactor began by saying he seldom gave advice to anyone, but that it always bore the hall-mark of high value when he did give it. Then he said this—and it has never faded from my memory: "*You are far from being a bad man*—" ' "

FIFTY VOICES "That settles it—the money's Wilson's! Wilson! Wilson! Speech! Speech!"

People jumped up and crowded around Wilson, wringing his hand and congratulating fervently—meantime the Chair was hammering with the gavel and shouting:

"Order, gentlemen! Order! Order! Let me finish reading, please." When quiet was restored, the reading was resumed—as follows:

" ' "*Go, and reform—or, mark my words—some day, for your sins, you will die and go to hell or Hadleyburg*—TRY AND MAKE IT THE FORMER.*" ' "

A ghastly silence followed. First an angry cloud began to settle darkly upon the faces of the citizenship; after a pause the cloud began to rise, and a tickled expression tried to take its place; tried so hard that it was only kept under with great and painful difficulty; the reporters, the Brixtonites, and other strangers, bent their heads down and shielded their faces with their hands, and managed to hold in by main strength and heroic courtesy. As this most inopportune time burst upon the stillness the roar of a solitary voice—Jack Halliday's:

"*That's* got the hall-mark on it!"

Then the house let go, strangers and all. Even Mr. Burgess'

gravity broke down presently, then the audience considered itself officially absolved from all restraint, and it made the most of its privilege. It was a good long laugh, and a tempestuously whole-hearted one, but it ceased at last—long enough for Mr. Burgess to try to resume, and for the people to get their eyes partially wiped; then it broke out again; and afterward yet again; then at last Burgess was able to get out these serious words:

"It is useless to try to disguise the fact—we find ourselves in the presence of a matter of grave import. It involves the honor of your town, it strikes at the town's good name. The difference of a single word between the test-remarks offered by Mr. Wilson and Mr. Billson was itself a serious thing, since it indicated that one or the other of these gentlemen had committed a theft—"

The two men were sitting limp, nerveless, crushed; but at these words both were electrified into movement, and started to get up—

"Sit down!" said the Chair, sharply, and they obeyed. "That, as I have said, was a serious thing. And it was—but for only one of them. But the matter has become graver; for the honor of *both* is now in formidable peril. Shall I go even further, and say in inextricable peril? *Both* left out the crucial fifteen words." He paused. During several moments he allowed the pervading still-ness to gather and deepen its impressive effects, then added: "There would seem to be but one way whereby this could happen. I ask these gentlemen—Was there *collusion?—agreement?*"

A low murmur sifted through the house; its import was, "He's got them both."

Billson was not used to emergencies; he sat in a helpless col-lapse. But Wilson was a lawyer. He struggled to his feet, pale and worried, and said:

"I ask the indulgence of the house while I explain this most painful matter. I am sorry to say what I am about to say, since it must inflict irreparable injury upon Mr. Billson, whom I have always esteemed and respected until now, and in whose invulner-ability to temptation I entirely believed—as did you all. But for the preservation of my own honor I must speak—and with frank-ness. I confess with shame—and I now beseech your pardon for it—that I said to the ruined stranger all of the words contained in the test-remark, including the disparaging fifteen. [*Sensation.*] When the late publication was made I recalled them, and I re-solved to claim the sack of coin, for by every right I was entitled to it. Now I will ask you to consider this point, and weigh it well: that stranger's gratitude to me that night knew no bounds; he said himself that he could find no words for it that were adequate, and that if he should ever be able he would repay me a thousandfold. Now, then, I ask you this: Could I expect—could I believe—could I even remotely imagine—that, feeling as he did, he would do so ungrateful a thing as to add those quite unnecessary fifteen words to his test?—set a trap for me?—expose me as a slanderer of my own town before my own people assembled in a public hall? It was preposterous; it was impossible. His test would contain only the kindly opening clause of my remark. Of that I had no shadow of doubt. You would have thought as I did. You would not have expected a base betrayal from one whom you had befriended and against whom you had committed no offense. And so, with perfect confidence, perfect trust, I wrote on a piece of paper the opening words—ending with 'Go, and reform,'—and signed it. When I was about to put it in an envelope I was called into my back office, and without thinking I left the paper lying open on my desk." He stopped, turned his head slowly toward Billson, waited a moment, then added: "I ask you to note this: when I returned, a little later, Mr. Billson was retiring by my street door." [*Sensation.*]

In a moment Billson was on his feet and shouting:

"It's a lie! It's an infamous lie!"

THE CHAIR "Be seated, sir! Mr. Wilson has the floor."

Billson's friends pulled him into his seat and quieted him, and Wilson went on:

"Those are the simple facts. My note was now lying in a different place on the table from where I had left it. I noticed that, but attached no importance to it, thinking a draught had blown it there. That Mr. Billson would read a private paper was a thing which could not occur to me; he was a honorable man, and he would be above that. If you will allow me to say it, I think his extra word '*very*' stands explained; it is attributable to a defect of memory. I was the only man in the world who could furnish here any detail of the test-remark—by *honorable* means. I have finished."

There is nothing in the world like a persuasive speech to fuddle the mental apparatus and upset the convictions and debauch the emotions of an audience not practiced in the tricks and delusions of oratory. Wilson sat down victorious. The house submerged him in tides of approving applause; friends swarmed to him and shook him by the hand and congratulated him, and Billson was shouted down and not allowed to say a word. The Chair hammered and hammered with its gavel, and kept shouting:

"But let us proceed, gentlemen, let us proceed!"

At last there was a measurable degree of quiet, and the hatter said:

"But what is there to proceed with, sir, but to deliver the money?"

VOICES "That's it! That's it! Come forward, Wilson!"

THE HATTER "I move three cheers for Mr. Wilson, Symbol of the special virtue which—"

The cheers burst forth before he could finish; and in the midst of them—and in the midst of the clamor of the gavel also—some enthusiasts mounted Wilson on a big friend's shoulder and were going to fetch him in triumph to the platform. The Chair's voice now rose above the noise—

"Order! To your places! You forget there is still a document to be read." When quiet had been restored he took up the document, and was going to read it, but laid it down again, saying, "I forgot; this is not to be read until all written communications received by me have first been read." He took an envelope out of his pocket, removed its inclosure, glanced at it—seemed astonished—held it out and gazed at it—stared at it.

Twenty or thirty voices cried out:

"What is it? Read it! read it!"

And he did—slowly, and wondering:

" 'The remark which I made to the stranger—[Voices. "Hello! how's this?"]—was this: "You are far from being a bad man." [Voices. "Great Scott!"] "Go, and reform." ' [Voices. "Oh, saw my leg off!"] Signed by Mr. Pinkerton, the banker.' "

The pandemonium of delight which turned itself loose now was of a sort to make the judicious weep. Those whose withers were unwrung laughed till the tears ran down; the reporters, in throes of laughter, set down disordered pot-hooks which would never in the world be decipherable; and a sleeping dog jumped up, scared out of its wits, and barked itself crazy at the turmoil. All manner of cries were scattered through the din: "We're getting rich—*two* Symbols of Incorruptibility!—without counting Billson!" "*Three!*—count Shadbelly in—we can't have too many!" "All right —Billson's elected!" "Alas, poor Wilson—victim of *two* thieves!"

A POWERFUL VOICE "Silence! The Chair's fishing up something more out of its pocket."

VOICES "Hurrah! Is it something fresh? Read it! read! read!"

THE CHAIR [*reading*] " 'The remark which I made,' etc.: ' "You are far from being a bad man. Go," ' etc. Signed, 'Gregory Yates.' "

TORNADO OF VOICES "Four Symbols!" " 'Rah for Yates!" "Fish again!"

The house was in a roaring humor now, and ready to get all the fun out of the occasion that might be in it. Several Nineteeners,

THE MAN THAT CORRUPTED HADLEYBURG 371

looking pale and distressed, got up and began to work their way toward the aisles, but a score of shouts went up:

"The doors, the doors—close the doors; no Incorruptible shall leave this place! Sit down, everybody!"

The mandate was obeyed.

"Fish again! Read! read!"

The Chair fished again, and once more the familiar words began to fall from its lips—" *'You are far from being a bad man.'* "

"Name! name! What's his name?"

" *'L. Ingoldsby Sargent.'* "

"Five elected! Pile up the Symbols! Go on, go on!"

" *'You are far from being a bad—'* "

"Name! name!"

" *'Nicholas Whitworth.'* "

"Hooray! hooray! it's a symbolic day!"

Somebody wailed in, and began to sing this rhyme (leaving out "it's") to the lovely "Mikado" tune of "When a man's afraid, a beautiful maid—"; the audience joined in, with joy; then, just in time, somebody contributed another line—

And don't you this forget—

The house roared it out. A third line was at once furnished—

Corruptibles far from Hadleyburg are—

The house roared that one too. As the last note died, Jack Halliday's voice rose high and clear, freighted with a final line—

But the Symbols are here, you bet!

That was sung, with booming enthusiasm. Then the happy house started in at the beginning and sang the four lines through twice, with immense swing and dash, and finished up with a crashing three-times-three and a tiger for "Hadleyburg the Incorruptible and all Symbols of it which we shall find worthy to receive the hall-mark to-night."

Then the shoutings at the Chair began again, all over the place:

"Go on! go on! Read! read some more! Read all you've got!"

"That's it—go on! We are winning eternal celebrity!"

A dozen men got up now and began to protest. They said that this farce was the work of some abandoned joker, and was an insult to the whole community. Without a doubt these signatures were all forgeries—

"Sit down! sit down! Shut up! You are confessing. We'll find *your* names in the lot."

"Mr. Chairman, how many of those envelopes have you got?"

The Chair counted.

"Together with those that have been already examined, there are nineteen."

A storm of derisive applause broke out.

"Perhaps they all contain the secret. I move that you open them all and read every signature that is attached to a note of that sort—and read also the first eight words of the note."

"Second the motion!"

It was put and carried—uproariously. Then poor old Richards got up, and his wife rose and stood at his side. Her head was bent down, so that none might see that she was crying. Her husband gave her his arm, and so supporting her, he began to speak in a quavering voice:

"My friends, you have known us two—Mary and me—all our lives, and I think you have liked us and respected us—"

The Chair interrupted him:

"Allow me. It is quite true—that which you are saying, Mr. Richards: this town *does* know you two; it *does* like you; it *does* respect you; more—it honors you and *loves* you—"

Halliday's voice rang out:

"That's the hall-marked truth, too! If the Chair is right, let the house speak up and say it. Rise! Now, then—hip! hip! hip!—all together!"

The house rose in mass, faced toward the old couple eagerly, filled the air with a snow-storm of waving handkerchiefs, and delivered the cheers with all its affectionate heart.

The Chair then continued:

"What I was going to say is this: We know your good heart, Mr. Richards, but this is not a time for the exercise of charity toward offenders. [*Shouts of "Right! right!"*] I see your generous purpose in your face, but I cannot allow you to plead for these men—"

"But I was going to—"

"Please take your seat, Mr. Richards. We must examine the rest of these notes—simple fairness to the men who have already been exposed requires this. As soon as that has been done—I give you my word for this—you shall be heard."

MANY VOICES "Right!—the Chair is right—no interruption can be permitted at this stage! Go on!—the names! the names!—according to the terms of the motion!"

The old couple sat reluctantly down, and the husband whispered to the wife, "It is pitifully hard to have to wait; the shame will be greater than ever when they find we were only going to plead for *ourselves*."

Straightway the jollity broke loose again with the reading of the names.

" '*You are far from being a bad man*—' Signature, 'Robert J. Titmarsh.'

" '*You are far from being a bad man*—' Signature, 'Eliphalet Weeks.'

" '*You are far from being a bad man*—' Signature, 'Oscar B. Wilder.' "

At this point the house lit upon the idea of taking the eight words out of the Chairman's hands. He was not unthankful for that. Thenceforth he held up each note in its turn, and waited. The house droned out the eight words in a massed and measured and musical deep volume of sound (with a daringly close resemblance to a well-known church chant)—" '*You are f-a-r from being a b-a-a-d man.*' " Then the Chair said, "Signature, 'Archibald Wilcox.' " And so on, and so on, name after name, and everybody had an increasingly and gloriously good time except the wretched Nineteen. Now and then, when a particularly shining name was called, the house made the Chair wait while it chanted the whole of the test-remark from the beginning to the closing words, "And go to hell or Hadleyburg—try and make it the for-or-m-e-r!" and in these special cases they added a grand and agonized and imposing "A-a-a-a-*men!*"

The list dwindled, dwindled, dwindled, poor old Richards keeping tally of the count, wincing when a name resembling his own was pronounced, and waiting in miserable suspense for the time to come when it would be his humiliating privilege to rise with Mary and finish his plea, which he was intending to word thus: ". . . for until now we have never done any wrong thing, but have gone our humble way unreproached. We are very poor, we are old, and have no chick nor child to help us; we were sorely tempted, and we fell. It was my purpose when I got up before to make confession and beg that my name might not be read out in this public place, for it seemed to us that we could not bear it; but I was prevented. It was just; it was our place to suffer with the rest. It has been hard for us. It is the first time we have ever heard our name fall from any one's lips—sullied. Be merciful—for the sake of the better days; make our shame as light to bear as in your charity you can." At this point in his revery Mary nudged him, perceiving that his mind was absent. The house was chanting, "You are f-a-r," etc.

"Be ready," Mary whispered. "Your name comes now; he has read eighteen."

The chant ended.

"Next! next! next!" came volleying from all over the house.

Burgess put his hand into his pocket. The old couple, trembling, began to rise. Burgess fumbled a moment, then said,

"I find I have read them all."

Faint with joy and surprise, the couple sank into their seats, and Mary whispered:

"Oh, bless God, we are saved!—he has lost ours—I wouldn't give this for a hundred of those sacks!"

The house burst out with its "Mikado" travesty, and sang it three times with ever-increasing enthusiasm, rising to its feet when it reached for the third time the closing line—

But there's one Symbol left, you bet!

and finishing up with cheers and a tiger for "Hadleyburg purity and our eighteen immortal representatives of it."

Then Wingate, the saddler, got up and proposed cheers "for the cleanest man in town, the one solitary important citizen in it who didn't try to steal that money—Edward Richards."

They were given with great and moving heartiness; then somebody proposed that Richards be elected sole guardian and Symbol of the now Sacred Hadleyburg Tradition, with power and right to stand up and look the whole sarcastic world in the face.

Passed, by acclamation; then they sang the "Mikado" again, and ended it with:

And there's one Symbol left, you bet!

There was a pause; then—

A VOICE "Now, then, who's to get the sack?"

THE TANNER (*with bitter sarcasm*) "That's easy. The money has to be divided among the eighteen Incorruptibles. They gave the suffering stranger twenty dollars apiece—and that remark—each in his turn—it took twenty-two minutes for the procession to move past. Staked the stranger—total contribution, $360. All they want is just the loan back—and interest—forty thousand dollars altogether."

MANY VOICES [*derisively*] "That's it! Divvy! divvy! Be kind to the poor—don't keep them waiting!"

THE CHAIR "Order! I now offer the stranger's remaining document. It says: 'If no claimant shall appear [*grand chorus of groans*]

I desire that you open the sack and count out the money to the principal citizens of your town, they to take it in trust [*cries of "Oh! Oh! Oh!"*], and use it in such ways as to them shall seem best for the propagation and preservation of your community's noble reputation for incorruptible honesty [*more cries*]—a reputation to which their names and their efforts will add a new and far-reaching luster.' [*Enthusiastic outburst of sarcastic applause.*] That seems to be all. No—here is a postscript:

'P.S.—CITIZENS OF HADLEYBURG: *There is no test-remark—nobody made one.* [Great sensation.] *There wasn't any pauper stranger, nor any twenty-dollar contribution, nor any accompanying benediction and compliment—these are all inventions.* [General buzz and hum of astonishment and delight.]*Allow me to tell my story—it will take but a word or two. I passed through your town at a certain time, and received a deep offense which I had not earned. Any other man would have been content to kill one or two of you and call it square, but to me that would have been a trivial revenge, and inadequate; for the dead do not suffer. Besides, I could not kill you all—and, anyway, made as I am, even that would not have satisfied me. I wanted to damage every man in the place, and every woman—and not in their bodies or in their estate, but in their vanity—the place where feeble and foolish people are most vulnerable. So I disguised myself and came back and studied you. You were easy game. You had an old and lofty reputation for honesty, and naturally you were proud of it—it was your treasure of treasures, the very apple of your eye. As soon as I found out that you carefully and vigilantly kept yourselves and your children out of temptation, I knew how to proceed. Why, you simple creatures, the weakest of all weak things is a virtue which has not been tested in the fire. I laid a plan, and gathered a list of names. My project was to corrupt Hadleyburg the Incorruptible. My idea was to make liars and thieves of nearly half a hundred smirchless men and women who had never in their lives uttered a lie or stolen a penny. I was afraid of Goodson. He was neither born nor reared in Hadleyburg. I was afraid that if I started to operate my scheme by getting my letter laid before you, you would say to yourselves, "Goodson is the only man among us who would give away twenty dollars to a poor devil"—and then you might not bite at my bait. But Heaven took Goodson; then I knew I was safe, and I set my trap and baited it. It may be that I shall not catch all the men to whom I mailed the pretended test secret, but I shall catch the most of them, if I know Hadleyburg nature.* [Voices. "Right—he got every last one of* *them."*] *I believe they will even steal ostensible* gamble-money, *rather than miss, poor, tempted, and mistrained fellows. I am hoping to eternally and everlastingly squelch your vanity and give Hadleyburg a new renown—one that will stick—and spread far. If I have succeeded, open the sack and summon the Committee on Propagation and Preservation of the Hadleyburg Reputation.'*

A CYCLONE OF VOICES "Open it! Open it! The Eighteen to the front! Committee on Propagation of the Tradition! Forward—the Incorruptibles!"

The Chair ripped the sack wide, and gathered up a handful of bright, broad, yellow coins, shook them together, then examined them—

"Friends, they are only gilded disks of lead!"

There was a crashing outbreak of delight over this news, and when the noise had subsided, the tanner called out:

"By right of apparent seniority in this business, Mr. Wilson is Chairman of the Committee on Propagation of the Tradition. I suggest that he step forward on behalf of his pals, and receive in trust the money."

A HUNDRED VOICES "Wilson! Wilson! Wilson! Speech! Speech!"

WILSON [*in a voice trembling with anger*] "You will allow me to say, and without apologies for my language, *damn* the money!"

A VOICE "Oh, and him a Baptist!"

A VOICE "Seventeen Symbols left! Step up, gentlemen, and assume your trust!"

There was a pause—no response.

THE SADDLER "Mr. Chairman, we've got *one* clean man left, anyway, out of the late aristocracy; and he needs money, and deserves it. I move that you appoint Jack Halliday to get up there and auction off that sack of gilt twenty-dollar pieces, and give the result to the right man—the man whom Hadleyburg delights to honor—Edward Richards."

This was received with great enthusiasm, the dog taking a hand again; the saddler started the bids at a dollar, the Brixton folk and Barnum's representative fought hard for it, the people cheered every jump that the bids made, the excitement climbed moment by moment higher and higher, the bidders got on their mettle and grew steadily more and more daring, more and more determined, the jumps went from a dollar up to five, then to ten, then to twenty, then fifty, then to a hundred, then—

At the beginning of the auction Richards whispered in distress to his wife: "O Mary, can we allow it? It—it—you see, it is an honor-reward, a testimonial to purity of character, and—and—can we allow it? Hadn't I better get up and—O Mary, what ought we to do?—what do you think we—[*Halliday's voice.* "*Fifteen I'm bid!—fifteen for the sack!—twenty!—ah, thanks!—thirty—thanks again! Thirty, thirty, thirty!—do I heard forty?—forty it is! Keep the ball rolling, gentlemen, keep it rolling!—fifty! thanks, noble Roman! going at fifty, fifty!—seventy!—ninety!—splendid!—a hundred!—pile it up, pile it up!—hundred and twenty—forty!—just in time!—hundred and fifty!—*TWO *hundred!—superb! Do I hear two h—thanks!—two hundred and fifty!—*"]

"It is another temptation, Edward—I'm all in a tremble—but, oh, we've escaped *one* temptation, and that ought to warn us to— ["*Six did I hear?—thanks!—six-fifty, six-f—*SEVEN *hundred!*"] And yet, Edward, when you think—nobody susp— ["*Eight hundred dollars!—hurrah!—make it nine!—Mr. Parsons, did I hear you say—thanks—nine!—this noble sack of virgin lead going at only nine hundred dollars, gilding and all—come! do I hear—a thousand!—gratefully yours!—did some one say eleven?—a sack which is going to be the most celebrated in the whole Uni—*] O Edward" (beginning to sob), "we are *so* poor!—but—but—do as you think best—do as you think best."

Edward fell—that is, he sat still; sat with a conscience which was not satisfied, but which was overpowered by circumstances.

Meantime a stranger, who looked like an amateur detective gotten up as an impossible English earl, had been watching the evening's proceedings with manifest interest, and with a contented expression in his face; and he had been privately commenting to himself. He was now soliloquizing somewhat like this: "None of the Eighteen are bidding; that is not satisfactory; I must change that— the dramatic unities require it; they must buy the sack they tried to steal; they must pay a heavy price, too—some of them are rich. And another thing, when I make a mistake in Hadleyburg nature the man that puts that error upon me is entitled to a high honorarium, and some one must pay it. This poor old Richards has brought my judgment to shame; he is an honest man:—I don't understand it, but I acknowledge it. Yes, he saw my deuces *and* with a straight flush, and by rights the pot is his. And it shall be a jack-pot, too, if I can manage it. He disappointed me, but let that pass."

He was watching the bidding. At a thousand, the market broke; the prices tumbled swiftly. He waited—and still watched. One competitor dropped out; then another, and another. He put in a bid or two, now. When the bids had sunk to ten dollars, he added a five; some one raised him a three; he waited a moment, then flung in a fifty-dollar jump, and the sack was his—at $1,282. The house broke out in cheers—then stopped; for he was on his feet, and had lifted his hand. He began to speak.

"I desire to say a word, and ask a favor. I am a speculator in rarities, and I have dealings with persons interested in numismatics all over the world. I can make a profit on this purchase, just as it stands; but there is a way, if I can get your approval, whereby I can make every one of these leaden twenty-dollar pieces worth its face in gold, and perhaps more. Grant me that approval, and I will give part of my gains to your Mr. Richards, whose invulnerable probity you have so justly and so cordially recognized to-night; his share shall be ten thousand dollars, and I will hand him the money to-morrow. [*Great applause from the house.* But the "invulnerable probity" made the Richardses blush prettily; however, it went for modesty, and did no harm.] If you will pass my proposition by a good majority—I would like a two-thirds vote—I will regard that as the town's consent, and that is all I ask. Rarities are always helped by any device which will rouse curiosity and compel remark. Now if I may have your permission to stamp upon the faces of each of these ostensible coins the names of the eighteen gentlemen who—"

Nine-tenths of the audience were on their feet in a moment—dog and all—and the proposition was carried with a whirlwind of approving applause and laughter.

They sat down, and all the Symbols except "Dr." Clay Harkness got up, violently protesting against the proposed outrage, and threatening to—

"I beg you not to threaten me," said the stranger, calmly. "I know my legal rights, and am not accustomed to being frightened at bluster." [*Applause.*] He sat down. "Dr." Harkness saw an opportunity here. He was one of the two very rich men of the place, and Pinkerton was the other. Harkness was proprietor of a mint; that is to say, a popular patent medicine. He was running for the legislature on one ticket, and Pinkerton on the other. It was a close race and a hot one, and getting hotter every day. Both had strong appetites for money; each had bought a great tract of land, with a purpose; there was going to be a new railway, and each wanted to be in the legislature and help locate the route to his own advantage; a single vote might make the decision, and with it two or three fortunes. The stake was large, and Harkness was a daring speculator. He was sitting close to the stranger. He leaned over while one or another of the other Symbols was entertaining the house with protests and appeals, and asked, in a whisper.

"What is your price for the sack?"

"Forty thousand dollars."

"I'll give you twenty."

"No."

"Twenty-five."

"No."

"Say thirty."

"The price is forty thousand dollars; not a penny less."

"All right, I'll give it. I will come to the hotel at ten in the morning. I don't want it known: will see you privately."

"Very good." Then the stranger got up and said to the house:

"I find it late. The speeches of these gentlemen are not without merit, not without interest, not without grace; yet if I may be excused I will take my leave. I thank you for the great favor which you have shown me in granting my petition. I ask the Chair to keep the sack for me until to-morrow, and to hand these three five-hundred-dollar notes to Mr. Richards." They were passed up to the Chair. "At nine I will call for the sack, and at eleven will deliver the rest of the ten thousand to Mr. Richards in person, at his home. Good night."

Then he slipped out, and left the audience making a vast noise which was composed of a mixture of cheers, the "Mikado" song, dog-disapproval, and the chant, "You are f-a-r from being a b-a-a-d man—a-a-a-a-men!"

4

At home the Richardses had to endure congratulations and compliments until midnight. Then they were left to themselves. They looked a little sad, and they sat silent and thinking. Finally Mary sighed and said,

"Do you think we are to blame, Edward—*much* to blame?" and her eyes wandered to the accusing triplet of big banknotes lying on the table, where the congratulators had been gloating over them and reverently fingering them. Edward did not answer at once; then he brought out a sigh and said, hesitatingly:

"We—we couldn't help it, Mary. It—well, it was ordered. *All* things are."

Mary glanced up and looked at him steadily, but he didn't return the look. Presently she said:

"I thought congratulations and praises always tasted good. But —it seems to me, now—Edward?"

"Well?"

"Are you going to stay in the bank?"

"N-no."

"Resign?"

"In the morning—by note."

"It does seem best."

Richards bowed his head in his hands and muttered:

"Before, I was not afraid to let oceans of people's money pour through my hands, but—Mary, I am so tired, so tired—"

"We will go to bed."

At nine in the morning the stranger called for the sack and took it to the hotel in a cab. At ten Harkness had a talk with him privately. The stranger asked for and got five checks on a metropolitan bank—drawn to "Bearer"—four for $1,500 each, and one for $34,000. He put one of the former in his pocketbook, and the remainder, representing $38,500, he put in an envelope, and with these he added a note, which he wrote after Harkness was gone. At eleven he called at the Richards house and knocked. Mrs. Richards peeped through the shutters, then went and received the envelope, and the stranger disappeared without a word. She came back flushed and a little unsteady on her legs, and gasped out:

"I am sure I recognized him! Last night it semed to me that maybe I had seen him somewhere before."

"He is the man that brought the sack here?"

"I am almost sure of it."

"Then he is the ostensible Stephenson, too, and sold every important citizen in this town with his bogus secret. Now if he has sent checks instead of money, we are sold, too, after we thought we had escaped. I was beginning to feel fairly comfortable once more, after my night's rest, but the look of that envelope makes me sick. It isn't fat enough; $8,500 in even the largest bank-notes makes more bulk than that."

"Edward, why do you object to checks?"

"Checks signed by Stephenson! I am resigned to take the $8,500 if it could come in bank-notes—for it does seem that it was so ordered, Mary—but I have never had much courage, and I have not the pluck to try to market a check signed with that disastrous name. It would be a trap. That man tried to catch me; we escaped somehow or other; and now he is trying a new way. If it is checks—"

"Oh, Edward, it is *too* bad!" and she held up the checks and began to cry.

"Put them in the fire! quick! we mustn't be tempted. It is a trick to make the world laugh at *us*, along with the rest, and—Give them to *me*, since you can't do it!" He snatched them and tried to hold his grip till he could get to the stove; but he was human, he was a cashier, and he stopped a moment to make sure of the signature. Then he came near to fainting.

"Fan me, Mary, fan me! They are the same as gold!"

"Oh, how lovely, Edward! Why?"

"Signed by Harkness. What can the mystery of that be, Mary?"

"Edward, do you think—"

"Look here—look at this! Fifteen—fifteen—fifteen—thirty-four. Thirty-eight thousand five hundred! Mary, the sack isn't worth twelve dollars, and Harkness—apparently—has paid about par for it."

"And does it all come to us, do you think—instead of the ten thousand?"

"Why, it looks like it. And the checks are made to 'Bearer,' too."

"Is that good, Edward? What is it for?"

"A hint to collect them at some distant bank, I reckon. Perhaps Harkness doesn't want the matter known. What is that—a note?"

"Yes. It was with the checks."

It was in the "Stephenson" handwriting, but there was no signature. It said:

"*I am a disappointed man. Your honesty is beyond the reach of temptation. I had a different idea about it, but I wronged you in that, and I beg pardon, and do it sincerely. I honor you—and that is sincere too. This town is not worthy to kiss the hem of your garment. Dear sir, I made a square bet with myself that there were nineteen debauchable men in your self-righteous community. I have lost. Take the whole pot, you are entitled to it.*"

Richards drew a deep sigh, and said:

"It seems written with fire—it burns so. Mary—I am miserable again."

"I, too. Ah, dear, I wish—"

"To think, Mary—he *believes* in me."

"Oh, don't, Edward—I can't bear it."

"If those beautiful words were deserved, Mary—and God knows I believed I deserved them once—I think I could give the forty thousand dollars for them. And I would put that paper away, as representing more than gold and jewels, and keep it always. But now— We could not live in the shadow of its accusing presence, Mary."

He put it in the fire.

A messenger arrived and delivered an envelope.

Richards took from it a note and read it; it was from Burgess.

"You saved me, in a difficult time. I saved you last night. It was at cost of a lie, but I made the sacrifice freely, and out of a grateful heart. None in this village knows so well as I know how brave and good and noble you are. At bottom you cannot respect me, knowing as you do of that matter of which I am accused, and by the general voice condemned; but I beg that you will at least believe that I am grateful man; it will help me to bear my burden."

[Signed]   BURGESS

"Saved, once more. And on such terms!" He put the note in the fire. "I—I wish I were dead, Mary, I wish I were out of it all."

"Oh, these are bitter, bitter days, Edward. The stabs, through their very generosity, are so deep—and they come so fast!"

Three days before the election each of two thousand voters suddenly found himself in possession of a prized memento—one of the renowned bogus double-eagles. Around one of its faces was stamped these words: "THE REMARK I MADE TO THE POOR STRANGER WAS—" Around the other face was stamped these: "GO, AND REFORM. [SIGNED] PINKERTON." Thus the entire remaining refuse of the renowned joke was emptied upon a single head, and with calamitous effect. It revived the recent vast laugh and concentrated it upon Pinkerton; and Harkness's election was a walkover.

Within twenty-four hours after the Richardses had received their checks their consciences were quieting down, discouraged; the old couple were learning to reconcile themselves to the sin which they had committed. But they were to learn, now, that a sin takes on new and real terrors when there seems a chance that it is going to be found out. This gives it a fresh and most substantial and important aspect. At church the morning sermon was of the usual pattern; it was the same old things said in the same old way; they had heard them a thousand times and found them innocuous, next to meaningless, and easy to sleep under; but now it was different: the sermon seemed to bristle with accusations; it seemed aimed straight and specially at people who were concealing deadly sins. After church they got away from the mob of congratulators as soon as they could, and hurried homeward, chilled to the bone at they did not know what—vague, shadowy, indefinite fears. And by chance they caught a glimpse of Mr. Burgess as he turned a corner. He paid no attention to their nod of recognition! He hadn't seen it; but they did not know that. What could his conduct mean? It might mean—it might mean—oh, a dozen dreadful things. Was it possible that he knew that Richards could have cleared him of guilt in that bygone time, and had been silently waiting for a chance to even up accounts? At home, in their distress they got to imagining that their servant might have been in the next room listening when Richards revealed the secret to his wife that he knew of Burgess' innocence; next Richards began to imagine that he had heard the swish of a gown in there at that time; next, he was sure he *had* heard it. They would call Sarah in, on a pretext, and watch her face: if she had been betraying them to Mr. Burgess, it would show in her manner. They asked her some questions—questions which were so random and incoherent and seemingly purposeless that the girl felt sure that the old people's minds had been affected by their sudden good fortune; the sharp and watchful gaze which they bent upon her frightened her, and that completed the business. She blushed, she became nervous and confused, and to the old people these were plain signs of guilt—guilt of some fearful sort or other—without doubt she was a spy and a traitor. When they were alone again they began to piece many unrelated things together and get horrible results out of the combination. When things had got about to the worst, Richards was delivered of a sudden gasp, and his wife asked:

"Oh, what is it?—what is it?"

"The note—Burgess's note! Its language was sarcastic, I see it now." He quoted: " 'At bottom you cannot respect me, *knowing*, as you do, of *that matter* of which I am accused'—oh, it is perfectly plain, now, God help me! He knows that I know! You see the ingenuity of the phrasing. It was a trap—and like a fool, I walked into it. And Mary—?"

"Oh, it is dreadful—I know what you are going to say—he didn't return your transcript of the pretended test-remark."

"No—kept it to destroy us with. Mary, he has exposed us to some already. I know it—I know it well. I saw it in a dozen faces after church. Ah, he wouldn't answer our nod of recognition—*he* knew what he had been doing!"

In the night the doctor was called. The news went around in the morning that the old couple were rather seriously ill—prostrated by the exhausting excitement growing out of their great windfall, the congratulations, and the late hours, the doctor said. The town was sincerely distressed; for these old people were about all it had left to be proud of, now.

Two days later the news was worse. The old couple were delirious, and were doing strange things. By witness of the nurses,

Richards had exhibited checks—for $8,500? No—for an amazing sum—$38,500! What could be the explanation of this gigantic piece of luck?

The following day the nurses had more news—and wonderful. They had concluded to hide the checks, lest harm come to them; but when they searched they were gone from under the patient's pillow—vanished away. The patient said:

"Let the pillow alone; what do you want?"

"We thought it best that the checks—"

"You will never see them again—they are destroyed. They came from Satan. I saw the hell-brand on them, and I knew they were sent to betray me to sin." Then he fell to gabbling strange and dreadful things which were not clearly understandable, and which the doctor admonished them to keep to themselves.

Richards was right; the checks were never seen again.

A nurse must have talked in her sleep, for within two days the forbidden gabblings were the property of the town; and they were of a surprising sort. They seemed to indicate that Richards had been a claimant for the sack himself, and that Burgess had concealed that fact and then maliciously betrayed it.

Burgess was taxed with this and stoutly denied it. And he said it was not fair to attach weight to the chatter of a sick old man who was out of his mind. Still, suspicion was in the air, and there was much talk.

After a day or two it was reported that Mrs. Richards' delirious deliveries were getting to be duplicates of her husband's. Suspicion flamed up into conviction, now, and the town's pride in the purity of its one undiscredited important citizen began to dim down and flicker toward extinction.

Six days passed, then came more news. The old couple were dying. Richards' mind cleared in his latest hour, and he sent for Burgess. Burgess said:

"Let the room be cleared. I think he wishes to say something in privacy."

"No!" said Richards: "I want witnesses. I want you all to hear my confession, so that I may die a man, and not a dog. I was clean —artifically—like the rest; and like the rest I fell when temptation came. I signed a lie, and claimed the miserable sack. Mr. Burgess remembered that I had done him a service, and in gratitude (and ignorance) he suppressed my claim and saved me. You know the thing that was charged against Burgess years ago. My testimony, and mine alone, could have cleared him, and I was a coward, and left him to suffer disgrace—"

"No—no—Mr. Richards, you—"

"My servant betrayed my secret to him—"

"No one has betrayed anything to me—"

—"and then he did a natural and justifiable thing, he repented of the saving kindness which he had done me, and he *exposed* me —as I deserved—"

"Never!—I make oath—"

"Out of my heart I forgive him."

Burgess's impassioned protestations fell upon deaf ears; the dying man passed away without knowing that once more he had done poor Burgess a wrong. The old wife died that night.

The last of the sacred Nineteen had fallen a prey to the fiendish sack; the town was stripped of the last rag of its ancient glory. Its mourning was not showy, but it was deep.

By act of the Legislature—upon prayer and petition—Hadleyburg was allowed to change its name to (never mind what—I will not give it away), and leave one word out of the motto that for many generations had graced the town's official seal.

It is an honest town once more, and the man will have to rise early that catches it napping again.

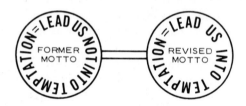

QUESTIONS FOR DISCUSSION

1. In the first paragraph Mark Twain says that, in Hadleyburg, "temptations were kept out of the way of the young people." Mrs. Richards recognizes the fault in this method of preserving incorruptibility. What does she call Hadleyburg's method of instruction?
2. What can you tell about the true nature of Hadleyburg's reputation from Mrs. Richards' early reactions to the sack of gold?
3. Throughout the story veiled references are made to the Reverend Mr. Burgess and his scandal. What might that scandal have been? What does Mark Twain achieve by leaving it vague?
4. Mrs. Richards finds increasing difficulty in saying the phrase, "Lead us not into temptation." What are the source and context of this phrase? What is its importance to Hadleyburg?

5. While Part 1 is narrated mostly from the point of view of the Richards couple, much of Part 2 is shown as Jack Halliday sees it. What does Mark Twain tell us about Halliday? Why is his presence in Hadleyburg so important? For whom does Halliday speak?

6. After Edward Richards lies to his wife, through what stages of rationalization does he pass?

7. This story contains several overt twists and contrivances that result in ironic shifts; for example, the paragraph explaining that nineteen identical letters were delivered. What is your critical opinion of Mark Twain's reliance upon this technique? What does he gain by sacrificing subtlety?

8. In Part 3, Mark Twain shifts from narrative to dramatic form, imitating, at points, a playscript. How does this change affect the scene being shown?

9. How do you explain the relationship between Edward Richards and the Reverend Mr. Burgess? How does Mark Twain use this relationship to manipulate the story? What does Twain mean when he says, near the story's end, that "once more he [Richards] had done Burgess a wrong"?

10. Why does Mark Twain introduce the vengeful stranger to the reader and not to the town meeting? How does he preserve the stranger's humanity without permitting him to be mistaken for a supernatural personage, either divine or devilish?

11. Part 4 reveals the psychological breakdown of what Twain calls "a conscience which was not satisfied, but which was overpowered by circumstances." What is the process of this breakdown?

12. Explain Edward Richards' last words. Is he sincere and straightforward or insincere and ironic? What effect does the narrator wish to create with this death-bed confession?

13. Can you tell from the final paragraphs and from the two seals what is the narrator's attitude toward self-righteousness and the notion of incorruptibility? Beyond mere entertainment, what is Mark Twain's purpose in writing this story?

ASSIGNMENTS FOR WRITING

1. The title of this story, "The Man That Corrupted Hadleyburg," focuses upon the vengeful stranger. But the reader knows how small a part the stranger has in the story. Could not the title have a broader application? Who is the man responsible for the corrupting of Hadleyburg? Who is responsible for the corrupting of any society? Write an essay in which you develop your theory of social responsibility, based upon the example of this story.

2. Clearly the Mark Twain who wrote "The Man That Corrupted

Hadleyburg" (1899) is not the same personality responsible for "Buck Fanshaw's Funeral" (1872) or any of the lighter amusements credited to him. After examining these stories carefully, write a critical essay in which you show the differences between stories written by the younger and by the older Samuel L. Clemens.

3. In *Mark Twain: The Development of a Writer,* the critic Henry Nash Smith says that "The Man That Corrupted Hadleyburg" "is not tragic, even potentially, but merely smug and hypocritical. The story nevertheless attains a considerable distinction by its tightness of construction, its evenness of tone, and its hard, sparse prose." In a critical essay, support or oppose Nash's statement, using ample evidence from the text to give your argument validity.

Henry James

The life of Henry James lies primarily in his work. Other American writers—Melville, Whitman, Twain, Fitzgerald, or Hemingway—may have created publicity for themselves by their extra-literary activities. Melville bemoaned the fact that he would go down in history as "the man who had lived among the cannibals." Whitman was a journalist, a petty politican, and a volunteer nurse in Civil War hospitals. Twain had an assortment of vocations, from riverboat pilot and prospector to inventor and platform humorist. Fitzgerald and Hemingway belonged to the Roaring Twenties that fostered their notoriety. But Henry James is scarcely a subject for biographical study, apart from his prodigious accomplishments as a novelist and story-teller. As in the case of Emily Dickinson, he was content to live behind his art, to let it stand for him as his "letter to the world."

Henry James was born in New York City on April 15, 1843 in a house just off Washington Square that later became the setting for one of his novels, *Washington Square* (1880). His father, Henry James, Sr., was by all reports an eccentric man, given to endless projects he thought would improve the minds and souls of his family. As a convert to the beliefs of Emanuel Swedenborg, the elder James sought a morality that would bring into harmony the creature and the Creator. Never orthodox in matters of theology, however, James Sr., offered his family no fixed creed and made no demands for commitment on their part. He even rejected the possibility of a stable education, fearing the effects of overexposing young minds to a single system. For this reason, Henry James, Sr., moved his family from home to home—New York City, England, France, Switzerland, Germany, and Newport, Rhode Island. In any one location Henry James and his older brother William attended several schools and had a roster of private tutors. In his memoirs, *A Small Boy and Others*, Henry James wrote:

We were day-boys, William and I, at dispensaries of learning the number and succession of which to-day excite my wonder; we couldn't have changed oftener, it strikes me as I look back, if our presence had been inveterately objected to, and yet I enjoy an inward certainty that, my brother being vividly bright and I quite blankly innocuous, this reproach was never brought home to our house.

William James was indeed "vividly bright." Known as one of America's earliest psychologists, he was the progenitor of the philosophy of pragmatism and author of a celebrated study called *The Varieties of Religious Experience.* Henry James was a very different person, shy and retiring, though not without a sense of humor. Although he attempted to imitate his brother's interests, he seemed at age 14 already inclined toward bookishness. His father wrote of him:

> Harry is not so fond of study, properly so-called, as of reading. He is a devourer of libraries, and an immense writer of novels and dramas. He has considerable talent as a writer, but I am at a loss to know whether he will ever accomplish much.

Henry James' only gesture at formal study beyond his succession of tutors was a year spent at the Harvard Law School. In 1865 his first story was published in the *Atlantic Monthly,* which later serialized many of his novels. Students of James' work have divided into periods the years that follow. From 1865 through 1881, James wrote several novels and stories of consequence, including *The American* (1877), *Daisy Miller: a Study* (1878), and *The Portrait of a Lady* (1881). *The American* presents Christopher Newman—James had an almost Dickensian preoccupation with the appropriate name for his character—a crude, unsophisticated manufacturer of washtubs who, on his first tour of Europe, meets and falls in love with a beautiful French widow. In spite of his wealth and her family's impoverished condition, the snobbery of onetime aristocrats cannot allow the marriage.

This insurmountable barrier between the Old World and the New became a constant motif throughout much of James' major work. In *The Portrait of a Lady,* James combined the intercontinental class struggle with an examination of unhappy marriage and the nobility of unrequited love. With this novel he also established his claim as the foremost exponent of the novel as a form subject to analytical scrutiny.

James insisted upon conveying the limited viewpoint of his narrator, never allowing his own knowledge as author to intrude upon the prescribed experience of his characters. To give his novels flexibility and mobility, James introduced many narrative devices, some of which he had discovered in the works of Gustave Flaubert and Ivan

Turgenev, some of which he named, if not invented, for the English critical vocabulary. Among these are *foreshortening*, the technique of compressing time while maintaining the realistic effect, and *ficelle*, the use of characters who obtain their importance from the way they are treated, rather than from their relation to the subject. These devices and others James used to serve one purpose, "to make art truth."

From 1882 until 1897, he experimented further with the novel form and with plays. He had lived in England since 1876. The only woman with whom his name was ever joined, a cousin named Minny Temple, had died in 1870. He was now given to periods of unsociability, and the depth of his insight into the human personality was sometimes mistaken for mere sophistry. In fact once when called to the stage of a London theater and identified as the playwright of the current production, James was met with loud hisses of rejection.

Perhaps as a result of his failure in the theater, Henry James returned to the novel and experimented with the *nouvelle*, a long short story or short novel. From 1898 on, Henry James wrote his most complex stories and books in his most elaborate and intense style. Included in this period were *The Turn of the Screw*, a ghost tale of psychological haunting, *The Wings of the Dove* (1902), *The Ambassadors* (1903), and *The Golden Bowl* (1904). These are the works of his maturity, his confidence, his supreme sense of the minute particle that makes a human personality unique. As Percy Lubbock says, in *The Craft of Fiction:*

> Henry James was the first writer of fiction, I judge, to use all the possibilities of the method with intention and thoroughness, and the full extent of the opportunity which is thus revealed is very great. The range of method is permanently enlarged; it is proved, once for all, that the craft of fiction has larger resources than might have been suspected before.

James concluded his life as a British subject, returning to his native country in 1904–1905 only for the purpose of collecting his work for revision and republication as The New York Edition. For these new volumes he wrote a series of prefaces, long and complicated essays in which he related the circumstances and problems involved in the writing of each work. These self-critical prefaces reveal the soul of the artist, the man thoroughly committed to the sanctity of his art. At his death in London in 1916, Henry James represented the highest pinnacle to which the Anglo-American man of letters might aspire.

Daisy Miller

Les Trois Couronnes

At the little town of Vevey, in Switzerland, there is a particularly comfortable hotel. There are, indeed, many hotels; for the entertainment of tourists is the business of the place, which, as many travelers will remember, is seated upon the edge of a remarkably blue lake—a lake that it behooves every tourist to visit. The shore of the lake presents an unbroken array of establishments of this order, of every category, from the "grand hotel" of the newest fashion, with a chalk-white front, a hundred balconies, and a dozen flags flying from its roof, to the little Swiss *pension* of an elder day, with its name inscribed in German-looking lettering upon a pink or yellow wall, and an awkward summer-house in the angle of the garden. One of the hotels at Vevay, however, is famous, even classical, being distinguished from any of its upstart neighbors by an air both of luxury and of maturity. In this region, the month of June, American travelers are extremely numerous; it may be said, indeed, that Vevay assumes at this period some of the characteristics of an American watering-place. There are sights and sounds which evoke a vision, an echo, of Newport and Saratoga. There is a flitting hither and thither of "stylish" young girls, a rustling of muslin flounces, a rattle of dance-music in the morning hours, a sound of high-pitched voices at all times. You receive an impression of these things at the excellent inn of the Trois Couronnes, and are transported in fancy to the Ocean House or to Congress Hall. But at the Trois Couronnes, it must be added, there are other features that are much at variance with these suggestions: neat German waiters, who look like secretaries of legation, Russian princesses sitting in the garden; little Polish boys walking about, held by the hand, with their governors; a view of the sunny crest of the Dent du Midi and the picturesque towers of the Castle of Chillon.

I hardly know whether it was the analogies or the differences that were uppermost in the mind of a young American, who, two or three years ago, sat in the garden of the Trois Couronnes, looking about him, rather idly, at some of the graceful objects I have mentioned. It was a beautiful summer morning, and in whatever fashion the young American looked at things they must have seemed to him charming. He had come from Geneva the day before by the little steamer to see his aunt, who was staying at the hotel—Geneva having been for a long time his place of residence. But his aunt had a headache—his aunt had almost always a headache—and now she was shut up in her room, smelling camphor, so that he was at liberty to wander about. He was some seven-and-twenty years of age. When his friends spoke of him, they usually said that he "was at Geneva studying"; when his enemies spoke of him, they said—but, after all, he had no enemies; he was an extremely amiable fellow, and universally liked. What I should say is, simply, that when certain persons spoke of him they affirmed that the reason of his spending so much time at Geneva was that he was extremely devoted to a lady who lived there—a foreign lady—a person older than himself. Very few Americans—indeed, I think none—had ever seen this lady, about whom there were some singular stories. But Winterbourne had an old attachment for the little metropolis of Calvinism; he had been put to school there as a boy, and he had afterwards gone to college there—circumstances which had let to his forming a great many youthful friendships. Many of these he had kept, and they were a source of great satisfaction to him.

After knocking at his aunt's door, and learning that she was indisposed, he had taken a walk about the town, and then he had come in to his breakfast. He had now finished his breakfast; but he was drinking a small cup of coffee, which had been served to him on a little table in the garden by one of the waiters who looked like an attaché. At last he finished his coffee and lit a cigarette. Presently a small boy came walking along the path—an urchin of nine or ten. The child, who was diminutive for his years, had an aged expression of countenance: a pale complexion, and sharp little features. He was dressed in knickerbockers, with red stockings, which displayed his poor little spindle-shanks; he also wore a brilliant red cravat. He carried in his hand a long alpenstock, the sharp point of which he thrust into everything that he approached—the flower-beds, the garden-benches, the trains of the ladies' dresses. In front of Winterbourne he paused, looking at him with a pair of bright, penetrating little eyes.

"Will you give me a lump of sugar?" he asked, in a sharp, hard little voice—a voice immature, and yet, somehow, not young.

Winterbourne glanced at the small table near him, on which his coffee-service rested, and saw that several morsels of sugar remained. "Yes, you may take one," he answered; "but I don't think sugar is good for little boys."

This little boy stepped forward and carefully selected three of the coveted fragments, two of which he buried in the pocket of his knickerbockers, depositing the other as promptly in another place.

He poked his alpenstock, lance-fashion, into Winterbourne's bench, and tried to crack the lump of sugar with his teeth.

"Oh, blazes; it's har-r-d!" he exclaimed, pronouncing the adjective in a peculiar manner.

Winterbourne had immediately perceived that he might have the honor of claiming him as a fellow countryman. "Take care you don't hurt your teeth," he said, paternally.

"I haven't got any teeth to hurt. They have all come out. I have only got seven teeth. My mother counted them last night, and one came out right afterwards. She said she'd slap me if any more came out. I can't help it. It's this old Europe. It's the climate that makes them come out. In America they didn't come out. It's these hotels."

Winterbourne was much amused. "If you eat three lumps of sugar, your mother will certainly slap you," he said.

"She's got to give me some candy, then," rejoined his young interlocutor. "I can't get any candy here—any American candy. American candy's the best candy."

"And are American little boys the best little boys?" asked Winterbourne.

"I don't know. I'm an American boy," said the child.

"I see you are one of the best!" laughed Winterbourne.

"Are you an American man?" pursued this vivacious infant. And then, on Winterbourne's affirmative reply—"American men are the best!" he declared.

His companion thanked him for the compliment; and the child, who had now got astride his alpenstock, stood looking about him, while he attacked a second lump of sugar. Winterbourne wondered if he himself had been like this in his infancy, for he had been brought to Europe at about this age.

"Here comes my sister!" cried the child, in a moment. "She's an American girl."

Winterbourne looked along the path and saw a beautiful young lady advancing. "American girls are the best girls!" he said, cheerfully, to his young companion.

"My sister ain't the best!" the child declared. "She's always blowing at me."

"I imagine that is your fault, not hers," said Winterbourne. The young lady meanwhile had drawn near. She was dressed in white muslin, with a hundred frills and flounces, and knots of pale-colored ribbon. She was bareheaded; but she balanced in her hand a large parasol, with a deep border of embroidery; and she was strikingly, admirably pretty. "How pretty they are!" thought Winterbourne, straightening himself in his seat, as if he were prepared to rise.

The young lady paused in front of his bench, near the parapet of the garden, which overlooked the lake. The little boy had now converted his alpenstock into a vaulting-pole, by the aid of which he was springing about in the gravel, and kicking it up a little.

"Randolph," said the young lady, "what *are* you doing?"

"I'm going up the Alps," replied Randolph. "This is the way!" And he gave another little jump, scattering the pebbles about Winterbourne's ears.

"That's the way they come down," said Winterbourne.

"He's an American man!" cried Randolph, in his hard little voice.

The young lady gave no heed to this announcement, but looked straight at her brother. "Well, I guess you had better be quiet," she simply observed.

It seemed to Winterbourne that he had been in a manner presented. He got up and stepped slowly towards the young girl, throwing away his cigarette. "This little boy and I have made acquaintance," he said, with great civility. In Geneva, as he had been perfectly aware, a young man was not at liberty to speak to a young unmarried lady except under certain rarely occurring conditions; but here at Vevey, what conditions could be better than these?—a pretty American girl coming and standing in front of you in a garden. This pretty American girl, however, on hearing Winterbourne's observation, simply glanced at him; she then turned her head and looked over the parapet, at the lake and the opposite mountains. He wondered whether he had gone too far; but he decided that he must advance farther, rather than retreat. While he was thinking of something else to say, the young lady turned to the little boy again.

"I should like to know where you got that pole?" she said.

"I bought it," responded Randolph.

"You don't mean to say you're going to take it to Italy?"

"Yes, I am going to take it to Italy," the child declared.

The young girl glanced over the front of her dress, and smoothed out a knot or two of ribbon. Then she rested her eyes upon the prospect again. "Well, guess you had better leave it somewhere," she said, after a moment.

"Are you going to Italy?" Winterbourne inquired, in a tone of great respect.

The young lady glanced at him again. "Yes, sir," she replied. And she said nothing more.

"Are you—a—going over the Simplon?" Winterbourne pursued, a little embarrassed.

"I don't know," she said. "I suppose it's some mountain. Randolph, what mountain are we going over?"

"Going where?" the child demanded.

"To Italy," Winterbourne explained.

"I don't know," said Randolph. "I don't want to go to Italy. I want to go to America."

"Oh, Italy is a beautiful place!" rejoined the young man.

"Can you get candy there?" Randolph loudly inquired.

"I hope not," said his sister. "I guess you have had enough candy, and mother thinks so, too."

"I haven't had any for ever so long—for a hundred weeks!" cried the boy, still jumping about.

The young lady inspected her flounces and smoothed her ribbons again, and Winterbourne presently risked an observation upon the beauty of the view. He was ceasing to be embarrassed, for he had begun to perceive that she was not in the least embarrassed herself. There had not been the slightest alteration in her charming complexion; she was evidently neither offended nor fluttered. If she looked another way when he spoke to her, and seemed not particularly to hear him, this was simply her habit, her manner. Yet, as he talked a little more, and pointed out some of the objects of interest in the view, with which she appeared quite unacquainted, she gradually gave him more of the benefit of her glance; and then he saw that this glance was perfectly direct and unshrinking. It was not, however, what would have been called an immodest glance, for the young girl's eyes were singularly honest and fresh. They were wonderfully pretty eyes; and, indeed, Winterbourne had not seen for a long time anything prettier than his fair countrywoman's various features—her complexion, her nose, her ears, her teeth. He had a great relish for feminine beauty; he was addicted to observing and analyzing it; and as regards this young lady's face he made several observations. It was not at all insipid, but it was not exactly expressive; and though it was eminently delicate, Winterbourne mentally accused it—very forgivingly—of a want of finish. He thought it very possible that Master Randolph's sister was a coquette; he was sure she had a spirit of her own; but in her bright, sweet, superficial little visage there was no mockery, no irony. Before long it became obvious that she was much disposed towards conversation. She told him that they were going to Rome for the winter—she and her mother and Randolph. She asked him if he was a "real American"; she shouldn't have taken him for one; he seemed more like a German—this was said after a little hesitation—especially when he spoke. Winterbourne, laughing, answered that he had met Germans who spoke like Americans; but that he had not, so far as he remembered, met an American who spoke like a German. Then he asked her if she should not be more comfortable in sitting upon the bench which he had just quitted. She answered that she liked standing up and walking about; but she presently sat down. She told him she was from New York State—"if you know where that is." Winterbourne learned more about her by catching hold of her small, slippery brother, and making him stand a few minutes by his side.

"Tell me your name, my boy," he said.

"Randolph C. Miller," said the boy, sharply. "And I'll tell you her name;" and he leveled his alpenstock at his sister.

"You had better wait till you are asked!" said this young lady, calmly.

"I should like very much to know your name," said Winterbourne.

"Her name is Daisy Miller!" cried the child. "But that isn't her real name; that isn't her name on her cards."

"It's a pity you haven't got one of my cards!" said Miss Miller.

"Her real name is Annie P. Miller," the boy went on.

"Ask him *his* name," said his sister, indicating Winterbourne.

But on this point Randolph seemed perfectly indifferent; he continued to supply information with regard to his own family. "My father's name is Ezra B. Miller," he announced. "My father ain't in Europe; my father's in a better place than Europe."

Winterbourne imagined for a moment that this was the manner in which the child had been taught to intimate that Mr. Miller had been removed to the sphere of celestial rewards. But Randolph immediately added, "My father's in Schenectady. He's got a big business. My father's rich, you bet!"

"Well!" ejaculated Miss Miller, lowering her parasol and looking at the embroidered border. Winterbourne presently released the child, who departed, dragging his alpenstock along the path. "He doesn't like Europe," said the young girl. "He wants to go back,"

"To Schenectady, you mean?"

"Yes; he wants to go right home. He hasn't got any boys here. There is one boy here, but he always goes round with a teacher; they won't let him play."

"And your brother hasn't any teacher?" Winterbourne inquired.

"Mother thought of getting him one to travel round with us. There was a lady told her of a very good teacher; an American lady—perhaps you know her—Mrs. Sanders. I think she came from Boston. She told her of this teacher, and we thought of getting him to travel round with us. But Randolph said he didn't want a teacher traveling round with us. He said he wouldn't have lessons when he was in the cars. And we *are* in the cars about half the time. There was an English lady we met in the cars—I think her name was Miss Featherstone;

perhaps you know her. She wanted to know why I didn't give Randolph lessons—give him 'instructions,' she called it. I guess he could give me more instruction than I could give him. He's very smart."

"Yes," said Winterbourne; "he seems very smart."

"Mother's going to get a teacher for him as soon as we get to Italy. Can you get good teachers in Italy?"

"Very good, I should think," said Winterbourne.

"Or else she's going to find some school. He ought to learn some more. He's only nine. He's going to college." And in this way Miss Miller continued to converse upon the affairs of her family, and upon other topics. She sat there with her extremely pretty hands, ornamented with very brilliant rings, folded in her lap, and with her pretty eyes now resting upon those of Winterbourne, now wandering over the garden, the people who passed by, and the beautiful view. She talked to Winterbourne as if she had known him a long time. He found it very pleasant. It was many years since he had heard a young girl talk so much. It might have been said of this unknown young lady, who had come and sat down beside him upon a bench, that she chattered. She was very quiet; she sat in a charming, tranquil attitude, but her lips and her eyes were constantly moving. She had a soft, slender, agreeable voice, and her tone was decidedly sociable. She gave Winterbourne a history of her movements and intentions, and those of her mother and brother, in Europe, and enumerated, in particular, the various hotels at which they had stopped. "That English lady in the cars," she said—"Miss Featherstone—asked me if we didn't all live in hotels in America. I told her I had never been in so many hotels in my life as since I came to Europe. I have never seen so many—it's nothing but hotels." But Miss Miller did not make this remark with a querulous accent; she appeared to be in the best humor with everything. She declared that the hotels were very good, when once you got used to their ways, and that Europe was perfectly sweet. She was not disappointed—not a bit. Perhaps it was because she had heard so much about it before. She had ever so many intimate friends that had been there ever so many times. And then she had ever so many dresses and things from Paris. Whenever she put on a Paris dress she felt as if she were in Europe.

"It was a kind of a wishing-cap," said Winterbourne.

"Yes," said Miss Miller, without examining this analogy; "it always made me wish I was here. But I needn't have done that for dresses. I am sure they send all the pretty ones to America; you see the most frightful things here. The only thing I don't like," she proceeded, "is the society. There isn't any society; or, if there is, I don't know where it keeps itself. Do you? I suppose there is some society somewhere, but I haven't seen anything of it. I'm very fond of society, and I have always had a great deal of it. I don't mean only in Schenectady, but in New York. I used to go to New York every winter. In New York I had lots of society. Last winter I had seventeen dinners given me; and three of them were by gentlemen," added Daisy Miller. "I have more friends in New York than in Schenectady—more gentlemen friends; and more young lady friends, too," she resumed in a moment. She paused again for an instant; she was looking at Winterbourne with all her prettiness in her lively eyes, and in her light, slightly monotonous smile. "I have always had," she said, "a great deal of gentlemen's society."

Poor Winterbourne was amused, perplexed, and decidedly charmed. He had never yet heard a young girl express herself in just this fashion—never, at least, save in cases where to say such things seemed a kind of demonstrative evidence of a certain laxity of deportment. And yet was he to accuse Miss Daisy Miller of actual or potential *inconduite,*[1] as they said at Geneva? He felt that he had lived at Geneva so long that he had lost a good deal; he had become dishabituated to the American tone. Never, indeed, since he had grown old enough to appreciate things had he encountered a young American girl of so pronounced a type as this. Certainly she was very charming, but how deucedly sociable! Was she simply a pretty girl from New York State? Were they all like that, the pretty girls who had a good deal of gentlemen's society? Or was she also a designing, an audacious, an unscrupulous young person? Winterbourne had lost his instinct in this matter, and his reason could not help him. Miss Daisy Miller looked extremely innocent. Some people had told him that, after all, American girls were exceedingly innocent; and others had told him that, after all, they were not. He was inclined to think Miss Daisy Miller was a flirt—a pretty American flirt. He had never, as yet, had any relations with young ladies of this category. He had known, here in Europe, two or three women—persons older than Miss Daisy Miller, and provided, for respectability's sake, with husbands—who were great coquettes—dangerous, terrible women, with whom one's relations were liable to take a serious turn. But this young girl was not a coquette in that sense; she was very unsophisticated; she was only a pretty American flirt. Winterbourne was almost grateful for having found the formula that applied to Miss Daisy Miller. He leaned back in his seat; he remarked to himself that she had the most charming nose he had ever seen; he wondered what were the regular conditions and limitations of one's intercourse with a pretty American flirt. It presently became apparent that he was on the way to learn.

[1] misconduct.

"Have you been to that old castle?" asked the young girl, pointing with her parasol to the far-gleaming walls of the Château de Chillon.

"Yes, formerly, more than once," said Winterbourne. "You, too, I suppose, have seen it?"

"No; we haven't been there. I want to go there dreadfully. Of course I mean to go there. I wouldn't go away from here without having seen that old castle."

"It's a very pretty excursion," said Winterbourne, "and very easy to make. You can drive or go by the little steamer."

"You can go in the cars," said Miss Miller.

"Yes; you can go in the cars," Winterbourne assented.

"Our courier says they take you right up to the castle," the young girl continued. "We were going last week; but my mother gave out. She suffers dreadfully from dyspepsia. She said she couldn't go. Randolph wouldn't go either; he says he doesn't think much of old castles. But I guess we'll go this week, if we can get Randolph."

"Your brother is not interested in ancient monuments?" Winterbourne inquired, smiling.

"He says he don't care much about old castles. He's only nine. He wants to stay at the hotel. Mother's afraid to leave him alone, and the courier won't stay with him; so we haven't been to many places. But it will be too bad if we don't go up there." And Miss Miller pointed again at the Château de Chillon.

"I should think it might be arranged," said Winterbourne. "Couldn't you get some one to stay for the afternoon with Randolph?"

Miss Miller looked at him a moment, and then very placidly, "I wish *you* would stay with him!" she said.

Winterbourne hesitated a moment. "I should much rather go to Chillon with you."

"With me?" asked the young girl, with the same placidity.

She didn't rise, blushing, as a young girl at Geneva would have done; and yet Winterbourne, conscious that he had been very bold, thought it possible that she was offended. "With your mother," he answered, very respectfully.

But it seemed that both his audacity and his respect were lost upon Miss Daisy Miller. "I guess my mother won't go, after all," she said. "She don't like to ride round in the afternoon. But did you really mean what you said just now, that you would like to go up there?"

"Most earnestly," Winterbourne declared.

(*Continued on page 409*)

Realists and
Romantics

WINSLOW HOMER: The Bridal Path, White Mountains, 1868

For many years, Homer, Eakins, and Ryder have been, by common consent, held up as America's Old Masters. The miraculous vision of pale horse and fair rider seen against the sun in the thin mountain air *(above)* will serve to introduce the formidable talent of Winslow Homer (1836-1910), equally at home with oil or watercolor, figure or landscape, light or serious subjects. His mother was an amateur painter, and Homer began to draw as a child. He did not perfect his art in an academy but rather during his apprenticeship to a firm of Boston lithographers. What did this strong-minded Yankee do on his first visit to Paris in the Exhibition year of 1867? It is said that he avoided the art schools and even the Louvre, but that he instinctively responded to Japanese prints (then the rage of Parisian art circles) and absorbed their lessons of color and composition. From that time on, the quality of his own work showed a marked improvement.

THOMAS EAKINS: The Pathetic Song, 1881

THOMAS EAKINS: Mrs. Edith Mahon, 1904

Eakins (1844-1916), our foremost master of realism, was born in Philadelphia and, except for his studies in Paris and Spain, spent his life there.
The essential seriousness of his attitude may be judged by *The Pathetic
Song (opposite)*, which takes a tone unprecedented in the painting of
genre, and astonishes the viewer with its satin and shadows. The pianist,
Susan Macdowell, was the future Mrs. Eakins. As if attracted by their
unique gift, Eakins frequently portrayed musicians, surrounding them
with awe and silence. *Edith Mahon (above)* was a pianist but, confronted
with the overwhelming sense of sadness and pain conveyed by her expression, that seems of small importance. She is an American Niobe, an image
of tragedy only Rembrandt could equal.

THOMAS EAKINS: Max Schmitt in a Single Scull, 1871

When Eakins went to France in 1866, it was only with difficulty that he gained admission to the government-operated Ecole des Beaux Arts and the class of Jean-Léon Gérôme. This painter, then the most respected in Paris, suffered such a downgrading after the eventual triumph of Impressionism (of which he was an outspoken opponent) that many critics have wondered how Eakins escaped ruin at his hands, and what could he possibly have taught him? The answer lies in *Max Schmitt in a Single Scull* (*above*), always ranked high among Eakins' masterpieces. Painted in the year after he returned to Philadelphia, its perfect organization in perspective and precise touch are the direct legacy of Gérôme's own practice and teaching. The singer's gown in *The Pathetic Song* is another passage which Gérôme would have admired. Eakins continued to hold his teacher in high esteem for the rest of his life, a fact which can only suggest a fresh examination of Gérôme's achievements.

Max Schmitt turns and looks out of the picture as if someone were taking a snapshot. It cannot be Eakins, for he is skimming over the mirrored surface in the direction of the bridges, like an indigenous insect. His signature, on the stern of his scull, is unnecessary, for Eakins' personal stamp is all over the picture. He has taken an autumn afternoon on the Schuykill, a moment extracted from time, and made it immortal.

Eakins painted *The Swimming Hole*, athletes boxing and wrestling, as well as other pictures of sculling, all a part of his intense interest in scientific anatomy and his conviction that the human body was the supreme vehicle of expression. Had he been born in another time and place, the nude would have been his chief subject. In Philadelphia, it merely contributed to his being dismissed from the Pennsylvania Academy for using the model for teaching purposes as would be done in Paris.

His place was taken by Anshutz (1851-1912), a painter of far less intellectual vigor than Eakins. So it came about that the teaching of Eakins reached Henri, Glackens, and Sloan (p. 740) only at second hand. *Steel-workers, Noontime*, impressively early in date, is the masterpiece of Anshutz. Its basic origin, as yet another anatomical study, has been successfully disguised by the natural grouping and the strong diagonal recession.

THOMAS ANSHUTZ: Steel Workers, Noontime, 1871

Ryder (1847-1917) was the most original romantic visionary artist America ever produced. His style is the emotional equivalent of his storm-tossed ships and lurid moonlit skies. His unforgettable manner tempts forgers to increase the limited supply of Ryders, and restorers are struggling to save the ones we have because the artist's habit of incessantly reworking his pictures, laying on the paint too thickly without allowing enough time for the varnish to dry, is causing them to disintegrate.

Rimmer (1816-1879) was a physician so obsessed with anatomy that he switched to sculpture and painting. *Flight and Pursuit* (p. 408) is a nightmare in costume which might be the illustration to one of Poe's tales of horror. For another bad dream, see p. 743.

ALBERT PINKHAM RYDER: Moonlight Marine

WINSLOW HOMER: High Cliff, Coast of Maine, 1894

Critics divide Homer's career into two periods. In the first, he was concerned with humanity—as Civil War "artist correspondent," magazine
illustrator, and painter of small genre scenes. After 1881, he lived as a
recluse at Prout's Neck on the rugged coast of Maine. Unless people were
engaged in battling with the elements, they didn't appear in his pictures
at all. As a prelude to his marine period, he spent 1881/82 at Tynemouth,
on the North Sea coast of England, notorious for its shipwrecks and the
location of England's first lifesaving station. Homer's heroic canvases
Undertow and *The Life Line* were inspired by Tynemouth but painted in
the United States. The large seascapes of the 1890's contain only three
elements: sea, sky, and rock. *High Cliff (above)* is noteworthy for its canny
diagonal composition and the miniscule size of its human figures. Whenever Prout's Neck got too grim, Homer was in the habit of taking off for
the Adirondacks or Canada in the summer and spending his winters in the
Caribbean. These busman's holidays produced hunting scenes, watercolors of warmer seas, and finally his masterpiece, *The Gulf Stream*, with
its shipwrecked Negro adrift on the shark-infested blue-green waters.

WILLIAM RIMMER: Flight and Pursuit, 1872

"Then we may arrange it. If mother will stay with Randolph, I guess Eugenio will."

"Eugenio?" the young man inquired.

"Eugenio's our courier. He doesn't like to stay with Randolph; he's the most fastidious man I ever saw. But he's a splendid courier. I guess he'll stay at home with Randolph if mother does, and then we can go to the castle."

Winterbourne reflected for an instant as lucidly as possible— "we" could only mean Miss Daisy Miller and himself. This program seemed almost too agreeable for credence; he felt as if he ought to kiss the young lady's hand. Possibly he would have done so, and quite spoiled the project; but at this moment another person, presumably Eugenio, appeared. A tall, handsome man, with superb whiskers, wearing a velvet morning-coat and a brilliant watch-chain, approached Miss Miller, looking sharply at her companion. "Oh, Eugenio!" said Miss Miller, with the friendliest accent.

Eugenio had looked at Winterbourne from head to foot; he now bowed gravely to the young lady. "I have the honor to inform mademoiselle that luncheon is upon the table."

Miss Miller slowly rose. "See here, Eugenio!" she said; "I'm going to that old castle, anyway."

"To the Château de Chillon, mademoiselle?" the courier inquired. "Mademoiselle has made arrangements?" he added, in a tone which struck Winterbourne as very impertinent.

Eugenio's tone apparently threw, even to Miss Miller's own apprehension, a slightly ironical light upon the young girl's situation. She turned to Winterbourne, blushing a little—a very little. "You won't back out?" she said.

"I shall not be happy till we go!" he protested.

"And you are staying in this hotel?" she went on. "And you are really an American?"

The courier stood looking at Winterbourne offensively. The young man, at least, thought his manner of looking an offense to Miss Miller; it conveyed an imputation that she "picked up" acquaintances. "I shall have the honor of presenting to you a person who will tell you all about me," he said, smiling, and referring to his aunt.

"Oh, well, we'll go some day," said Miss Miller. And she gave him a smile and turned away. She put up her parasol and walked back to the inn beside Eugenio. Winterbourne stood looking after her; and as she moved away, drawing her muslin furbelows over the gravel, said to himself that she had the *tournure*[2] of a princess.

---

[2] bearing.

He had, however, engaged to do more than proved feasible, in promising to present his aunt, Mrs. Costello, to Miss Daisy Miller. As soon as the former lady had got better of her headache he waited upon her in her apartment; and, after the proper inquiries in regard to her health, he asked her if she had observed in the hotel an American family—a mamma, a daughter, and a little boy.

"And a courier?" said Mrs. Costello. "Oh yes, I have observed them. Seen them—heard them—and kept out of their way." Mrs. Costello was a widow with a fortune; a person of much distinction, who frequently intimated that, if she were not so dreadfully liable to sick-headaches, she would probably have left a deeper impress upon her time. She had a long, pale face, a high nose, and a great deal of very striking white hair, which she wore in large puffs and *rouleaux* over the top of her head. She had two sons married in New York, and another who was now in Europe. This young man was amusing himself at Hombourg; and, though he was on his travels, was rarely perceived to visit any particular city at the moment selected by his mother for her own appearance there. Her nephew, who had come up to Vevey expressly to see her, was therefore more attentive than those who, as she said, were nearer to her. He had imbibed at Geneva the idea that one must always be attentive to one's aunt. Mrs. Costello had not seen him for many years, and she was greatly pleased with him, manifesting her approbation by initiating him into many of the secrets of that social sway which, as she gave him to understand, she exerted in the American capital. She admitted that she was very exclusive; but, if he were acquainted with New York, he would see that one had to be. And her picture of the minutely hierarchical constitution of the society of that city, which she presented to him in many different lights, was, to Winterbourne's imagination, almost oppressively striking.

He immediately perceived, from her tone, that Miss Daisy Miller's place in the social scale was low. "I am afraid you don't approve of them," he said.

"They are very common," Mrs. Costello declared. "They are the sort of Americans that one does one's duty by not—not accepting."

"Ah, you don't accept them?" said the young man.

"I can't, my dear Frederick. I would if I could, but I can't."

"The young girl is very pretty," said Winterbourne, in a moment.

"Of course she's pretty. But she is very common."

"I see what you mean, of course," said Winterbourne, after another pause.

"She has that charming look that they all have," his aunt resumed. "I can't think where they pick it up; and she dresses in perfection—no, you don't know how well she dresses. I can't think where they get their taste."

"But, my dear aunt, she is not, after all, a Comanche savage."

"She is a young lady," said Mrs. Costello, "who has an intimacy with her mamma's courier."

"An intimacy with the courier?" the young man demanded.

"Oh, the mother is just as bad! They treat the courier like a familiar friend—like a gentleman. I shouldn't wonder if he dines with them. Very likely they have never seen a man with such good manners, such fine clothes, so like a gentleman. He probably corresponds to the young lady's idea of a count. He sits with them in the garden in the evening. I think he smokes."

Winterbourne listened with interest to these disclosures; they helped him to make up his mind about Miss Daisy. Evidently she was rather wild.

"Well," he said, "I am not a courier, and yet she was very charming to me."

"You had better have said at first," said Mrs. Costello, with dignity, "that you had made her acquaintance."

"We simply met in the garden, and we talked a bit."

"*Tout bonnement!*[3] And pray what did you say?"

"I said I should take the liberty of introducing her to my admirable aunt."

"I am much obliged to you."

"It was to guarantee my respectability," said Winterbourne.

"And pray who is to guarantee hers?"

"Ah, you are cruel," said the young man. "She's a very nice young girl."

"You don't say that as if you believed it," Mrs. Costello observed.

"She is completely uncultivated," Winterbourne went on. "But she is wonderfully pretty, and, in short, she is very nice. To prove that I believe it, I am going to take her to the Château de Chillon."

"You two are going off there together? I should say it proved just the contrary. How long had you known her, may I ask, when this interesting project was formed? You haven't been twenty-four hours in the house."

"I had known her half an hour!" said Winterbourne, smiling.

"Dear me!" cried Mrs. Costello. "What a dreadful girl!"

Her nephew was silent for some moments. "You really think, then," he began, earnestly, and with a desire for trustworthy information—"you really think that—" But he paused again.

[3] Really!

"Think what, sir?" said his aunt.

"That she is the sort of young lady who expects a man, sooner or later, to carry her off?"

"I haven't the least idea what such young ladies expect a man to do. But I really think that you had better not meddle with little American girls that are uncultivated, as you call them. You have lived too long out of the country. You will be sure to make some great mistake. You are too innocent."

"My dear aunt, I am not so innocent," said Winterbourne, smiling and curling his mustache.

"You are too guilty, then!"

Winterbourne continued to curl his mustache, meditatively. "You won't let the poor girl know you, then?" he asked at last.

"Is it literally true that she is going to the Château de Chillon with you?"

"I think that she fully intends it."

"Then, my dear Frederick," said Mrs. Costello, "I must decline the honor of her acquaintance. I am an old woman, but I am not too old, thank Heaven, to be shocked!"

"But don't they all do these things—the young girls in America?" Winterbourne inquired.

Mrs. Costello stared a moment. "I should like to see my grand-daughters do them!" she declared, grimly.

This seemed to throw some light upon the matter, for Winterbourne remembered to have heard that his pretty cousins in New York were "tremendous flirts." If, therefore, Miss Daisy Miller exceeded the liberal margin allowed to these young ladies, it was probable that anything might be expected of her. Winterbourne was impatient to see her again, and he was vexed with himself that, by instinct, he should not appreciate her justly.

Though he was impatient to see her, he hardly knew what he should say to her about his aunt's refusal to become acquainted with her; but he discovered, promptly enough, that with Miss Daisy Miller there was no great need of walking on tiptoe. He found her that evening in the garden, wandering about in the warm starlight like an indolent sylph, and swinging to and fro the largest fan he had ever beheld. It was ten o'clock. He had just dined with his aunt, had been sitting with her since dinner, and had just taken leave of her till the morrow. Miss Daisy Miller seemed very glad to see him; she declared it was the longest evening she had ever passed.

"Have you been all alone?" he asked.

"I have been walking round with mother. But mother gets tired walking round," she answered.

"Has she gone to bed?"

"No; she doesn't like to go to bed," said the young girl. "She doesn't sleep—not three hours. She says she doesn't know how she lives. She's dreadfully nervous. I guess she sleeps more than she thinks. She's gone somewhere after Randolph; she wants to try to get him to go to bed. He doesn't like to go to bed."

"Let us hope she will persuade him," observed Winterbourne.

"She will talk to him all she can; but he doesn't like her to talk to him," said Miss Daisy, opening her fan. "She's going to try to get Eugenio to talk to him. But he isn't afraid of Eugenio. Eugenio's a splendid courier, but he can't make much impression on Randolph! I don't believe he'll go to bed before eleven." It appeared that Randolph's vigil was in fact triumphantly prolonged, for Winterbourne strolled about with the young girl for some time without meeting her mother. "I have been looking round for that lady you want to introduce me to," his companion resumed. "She's your aunt." Then, on Winterbourne's admitting the fact, and expressing some curiosity as to how she had learned it, she said she had heard all about Mrs. Costello from the chambermaid. She was very quiet, and very *comme il faut*;[4] she wore white puffs; she spoke to no one, and she never dined at the *table d'hôte*. Every two days she had a headache. "I think that's a lovely description, headache and all!" said Miss Daisy, chattering along in her thin, gay voice. "I want to know her ever so much. I know just what *your* aunt would be; I know I should like her. She would be very exclusive. I like a lady to be exclusive; I'm dying to be exclusive myself. Well, we *are* exclusive, mother and I. We don't speak to every one—or they don't speak to us. I suppose it's about the same thing. Anyway, I shall be ever so glad to know your aunt."

Winterbourne was embarrassed. "She would be most happy," he said; "but I am afraid those headaches will interfere."

The young girl looked at him through the dusk. "But I suppose she doesn't have a headache every day," she said, sympathetically.

Winterbourne was silent a moment. "She tells me she does," he answered at last, not knowing what to say.

Miss Daisy Miller stopped, and stood looking at him. Her prettiness was still visible in the darkness; she was opening and closing her enormous fan. "She doesn't want to know me!" she said, suddenly. "Why don't you say so? You needn't be afraid. I'm not afraid!" And she gave a little laugh.

Winterbourne fancied there was a tremor in her voice; he was

---

4 proper.

touched, shocked, mortified by it. "My dear young lady," he protested, "she knows no one. It's her wretched health."

The young girl walked on a few steps, laughing still. "You needn't be afraid," she repeated. "Why should she want to know me?" Then she paused again; she was close to the parapet of the garden, and in front of her was the starlit lake. There was a vague sheen upon its surface, and in the distance were dimly-seen mountain forms. Daisy Miller looked out upon the mysterious prospect, and then she gave another little laugh. "Gracious! she *is* exclusive!" she said. Winterbourne wondered whether she was seriously wounded, and for a moment almost wished that her sense of injury might be such as to make it becoming in him to attempt to reassure and comfort her. He had a pleasant sense that she would be very approachable for consolatory purposes. He felt then, for the instant, quite ready to sacrifice his aunt, conversationally; to admit that she was a proud, rude woman, and to declare that they needn't mind her. But before he had time to commit himself to this perilous mixture of gallantry and impiety, the young lady, resuming her walk, gave an exclamation in quite another tone. "Well, here's mother! I guess she hasn't got Randolph to go to bed." The figure of a lady appeared, at a distance, very indistinct in the darkness, and advancing with a slow and wavering movement. Suddenly it seemed to pause.

"Are you sure it is your mother? Can you distinguish her in this thick dusk?" Winterbourne asked.

"Well!" cried Miss Daisy Miller, with a laugh; "I guess I know my own mother. And when she has got on my shawl, too! She is always wearing my things."

The lady in question, ceasing to advance, hovered vaguely about the spot at which she had checked her steps.

"I am afraid your mother doesn't see you," said Winterbourne. "Or perhaps," he added, thinking, with Miss Miller, the joke permissible—"perhaps she feels guilty about your shawl."

"Oh, it's a fearful old thing!" the young girl replied, serenely. "I told her she could wear it. She won't come here, because she sees you."

"Ah, then," said Winterbourne, "I had better leave you."

"Oh, no; come on!" urged Miss Daisy Miller.

"I'm afraid your mother doesn't approve of my walking with you."

Miss Miller gave him a serious glance. "It isn't for me; it's for you—that is, it's for *her*. Well, I don't know who it's for! But mother doesn't like any of my gentlemen friends. She's right down timid. She always makes a fuss if I introduce a gentleman. But I *do* introduce them—almost always. If I didn't introduce my gentlemen friends to mother," the young girl added, in her little soft, flat monotone, "I shouldn't think it was natural."

"To introduce me," said Winterbourne, "you must know my name." And he proceeded to pronounce it to her.

"Oh, dear, I can't say all that!" said his companion with a laugh. But by this time they had come up to Mrs. Miller, who, as they drew near, walked to the parapet of the garden and leaned upon it, looking intently at the lake, and turning her back to them. "Mother!" said the young girl, in a tone of decision. Upon this the elder lady turned round. "Mr. Winterbourne," said Miss Daisy Miller, introducing the young man very frankly and prettily. "Common," she was, as Mrs. Costello had pronounced her; yet it was a wonder to Winterbourne that, with her commonness, she had a singularly delicate grace.

Her mother was a small, spare, light person, with a wandering eye, a very exiguous nose, and a large forehead, decorated with a certain amount of thin, much-frizzled hair. Like her daughter, Mrs. Miller was dressed with extreme elegance; she had enormous diamonds in her ears. So far as Winterbourne could observe, she gave him no greeting—she certainly was not looking at him. Daisy was near her, pulling her shawl straight. "What are you doing, poking round here?" this young lady inquired, but by no means with that harshness of accent which her choice of words may imply.

"I don't know," said her mother, turning toward the lake again.

"I shouldn't think you'd want that shawl!" Daisy exclaimed.

"Well, I do!" her mother answered, with a little laugh.

"Did you get Randolph to go to bed?" asked the young girl.

"No; I couldn't induce him," said Mrs. Miller, very gently. "He wants to talk to the waiter. He likes to talk to that waiter."

"I was telling Mr. Winterbourne," the young girl went on; and to the young man's ear her tone might have indicated that she had been uttering his name all her life.

"Oh yes!" said Winterbourne; "I have the pleasure of knowing your son."

Randolph's mamma was silent; she turned her attention to the lake. But at last she spoke. "Well, I don't see how he lives!"

"Anyhow, it isn't so bad as it was at Dover," said Daisy Miller.

"And what occurred at Dover?" Winterbourne asked.

"He wouldn't go to bed at all. I guess he sat up all night in the public parlor. He wasn't in bed at twelve o'clock; I know that."

"It was half-past twelve," declared Mrs. Miller, with mild emphasis.

"Does he sleep much during the day?" Winterbourne demanded.

"I guess he doesn't sleep much," Daisy rejoined.

"I wish he would!" said her mother. "It seems as if he couldn't."

"I think he's real tiresome," Daisy pursued.

Then for some moments there was silence. "Well, Daisy Miller," said the elder lady, presently, "I shouldn't think you'd want to talk against your own brother!"

"Well, he *is* tiresome, mother," said Daisy, quite without the asperity of a retort.

"He's only nine," urged Mrs. Miller.

"Well, he wouldn't go to that castle," said the young girl. "I'm going there with Mr. Winterbourne."

To this announcement, very placidly made, Daisy's mamma offered no response. Winterbourne took for granted that she deeply disapproved of the projected excursion; but he said to himself that she was a simple, easily-managed person, and that a few deferential protestations would take the edge from her displeasure. "Yes," he began; "your daughter has kindly allowed me the honor of being her guide."

Mrs. Miller's wandering eyes attached themselves, with a sort of appealing air, to Daisy, who, however, strolled a few steps farther, gently humming to herself. "I presume you will go in the cars," said her mother.

"Yes, or in the boat," said Winterbourne.

"Well, of course, I don't know," Mrs. Miller rejoined. "I have never been to that castle."

"It's a pity you shouldn't go," said Winterbourne, beginning to feel reassured as to her opposition. And yet he was quite prepared to find that, as a matter of course, she meant to accompany her daughter.

"We've been thinking ever so much about going," she pursued; "but it seems as if we couldn't. Of course Daisy, she wants to go round. But there's a lady here—I don't know her name—she says she shouldn't think we'd want to go to see castles *here;* she should think we'd want to wait till we got to Italy. It seems as if there would be so many there," continued Mrs. Miller, with an air of increasing confidence. "Of course we only want to see the principal ones. We visited several in England," she presently added.

"Ah, yes! in England there are beautiful castles," said Winterbourne. "But Chillon, here, is very well worth seeing."

"Well, if Daisy feels up to it—" said Mrs. Miller, in a tone impregnated with a sense of the magnitude of the enterprise. "It seems as if there was nothing she wouldn't undertake."

"Oh, I think she'll enjoy it!" Winterbourne declared. And he desired more and more to make it a certainty that he was to have the privilege of a tête-à-tête with the young lady, who was still strolling along in front of them, softly vocalizing. "You are not disposed, madam," he inquired, "to undertake it yourself?"

Daisy's mother looked at him an instant askance, and then walked forward in silence. Then—"I guess she had better go alone," she said, simply. Winterbourne observed to himself that this was a very different type of maternity from that of the vigilant matrons who massed themselves in the forefront of social intercourse in the dark old city at the other end of the lake. But his meditations were interrupted by hearing his name very distinctly pronounced by Mrs. Miller's unprotected daughter.

"Mr. Winterbourne!" murmured Daisy.

"Mademoiselle!" said the young man.

"Don't you want to take me out in a boat?"

"At present?" he asked.

"Of course!" said Daisy.

"Well, Annie Miller!" exclaimed her mother.

"I beg you, madam, to let her go," said Winterbourne, ardently; for he had never yet enjoyed the sensation of guiding through the summer starlight a skiff freighted with a fresh and beautiful young girl.

"I shouldn't think she'd want to," said her mother. "I should think she'd rather go indoors."

"I'm sure Mr. Winterbourne wants to take me," Daisy declared. "He's so awfully devoted!"

"I will row you over to Chillon in the starlight."

"I don't believe it!" said Daisy.

"Well!" ejaculated the elder lady again.

"You haven't spoken to me for half an hour," her daughter went on.

"I have been having some very pleasant conversation with your mother," said Winterbourne.

"Well, I want you to take me out in a boat!" Daisy repeated. They had all stopped, and she had turned round and was looking at Winterbourne. Her face wore a charming smile, her pretty eyes were gleaming, she was swinging her great fan about. No; it's impossible to be prettier than that, thought Winterbourne.

"There are half a dozen boats moored at that landing-place," he said, pointing to certain steps which descended from the garden to the lake. "If you will do me the honor to accept my arm, we will go and select one of them."

Daisy stood there smiling; she threw back her head and gave a little light laugh. "I like a gentleman to be formal!" she declared.

"I assure you it's a formal offer."

"I was bound I would make you say something," Daisy went on.

"You see, it's not very difficult," said Winterbourne. "But I am afraid you are chaffing me."

"I think not, sir," remarked Mrs. Miller, very gently.

"Do, then, let me give you a row," he said to the young girl.

"It's quite lovely, the way you say that!" cried Daisy.

"It will be still more lovely to do it."

"Yes, it would be lovely!" said Daisy. But she made no movement to accompany him; she only stood there laughing.

"I should think you had better find out what time it is," interposed her mother.

"It is eleven o'clock, madam," said a voice, with a foreign accent, out of the neighboring darkness, and Winterbourne, turning, perceived the florid personage who was in attendance upon the two ladies. He had apparently just approached.

"Oh, Eugenio," said Daisy, "I am going out in a boat!"

Eugenio bowed. "At eleven o'clock, mademoiselle?"

"I am going with Mr. Winterbourne—this very minute."

"Do tell her she can't," said Mrs. Miller to the courier.

"I think you had better not go out in a boat, mademoiselle," Eugenio declared.

Winterbourne wished to Heaven this pretty girl were not so familiar with her courier; but he said nothing.

"I suppose you don't think it's proper!" Daisy exclaimed. "Eugenio doesn't think anything's proper."

"I am at your service," said Winterbourne.

"Does mademoiselle propose to go alone?" asked Eugenio of Mrs. Miller.

"Oh, no; with this gentleman!" answered Daisy's mamma.

The courier looked for a moment at Winterbourne—the latter thought he was smiling—and then, solemnly, with a bow, "As mademoiselle pleases!" he said.

"Oh, I hoped you would make a fuss!" said Daisy. "I don't care to go now."

"I myself shall make a fuss if you don't go," said Winterbourne.

"That's all I want—a little fuss!" And the young girl began to laugh again.

"Mr. Randolph has gone to bed!" the courier announced, frigidly.

"Oh, Daisy; now we can go!" said Mrs. Miller.

Daisy turned away from Winterbourne, looking at him, smiling, and fanning herself. "Good-night," she said; "I hope you are disappointed, or disgusted, or something!"

He looked at her, taking the hand she offered him. "I am puzzled," he answered.

"Well, I hope it won't keep you awake!" she said, very smartly; and, under the escort of the privileged Eugenio, the two ladies passed towards the house.

Winterbourne stood looking after them; he was indeed puzzled. He lingered beside the lake for a quarter of an hour, turning over the mystery of the young girl's sudden familiarities and caprices. But the only very definite conclusion he came to was that he should enjoy deucedly "going off" with her somewhere.

Two days afterwards he went off with her to the Castle of Chillon. He waited for her in the large hall of the hotel, where the couriers, the servants, the foreign tourists, were lounging about and staring. It was not the place he should have chosen, but she had appointed it. She came tripping downstairs, buttoning her long gloves, squeezing her folded parasol against her pretty figure, dressed in the perfection of a soberly elegant traveling costume. Winterbourne was a man of imagination and, as our ancestors used to say, sensibility; as he looked at her dress and—on the great staircase—her little rapid, confiding step, he felt as if there were something romantic going forward. He could have believed he was going to elope with her. He passed out with her among all the idle people that assembled there; they were all looking at her very hard; she had begun to chatter as soon as she joined him. Winterbourne's preference had been that they should be conveyed to Chillon in a carriage; but she expressed a lively wish to go in the little steamer; she declared that she had a passion for steamboats. There was always such a lovely breeze upon the water, and you saw such lots of people. The sail was not long, but Winterbourne's companion found time to say a great many things. To the young man himself their little excursion was so much of an escapade—an adventure—that, even allowing for her habitual sense of freedom, he had some expectation of seeing her regard it in the same way. But it must be confessed that, in this particular, he was disappointed. Daisy Miller was extremely animated, she was in charming spirits; but she was apparently not at all excited; she was not fluttered; she avoided neither his eyes nor those of any one else; she blushed neither when she looked at him nor when she felt that people were looking at her. People continued to look at her a great deal, and Winterbourne took much satisfaction in his pretty companion's distinguished air. He had been a little afraid that she would talk loud, laugh overmuch, and even, perhaps, desire to move about the boat a good deal. But he quite forgot his fears; he sat smiling, with his eyes upon her face, while, without moving from her place, she delivered herself of a great number of original reflections. It was the most charming garrulity he had ever heard. He had assented to the idea that she was "common"; but was she so, after all, or was he simply getting used to her commonness? Her conversation was chiefly of what metaphysicians term the objective cast; but every now and then it took a subjective turn.

"What on *earth* are you so grave about?" she suddenly demanded, fixing her agreeable eyes upon Winterbourne's.

"Am I grave?" he asked. "I had an idea I was grinning from ear to ear."

"You look as if you were taking me to a funeral. If that's a grin, your ears are very near together."

"Should you like me to dance a hornpipe on the deck?"

"Pray do, and I'll carry round your hat. It will pay the expenses of our journey."

"I never was better pleased in my life," murmured Winterbourne.

She looked at him a moment, and then burst into a little laugh. "I like to make you say those things! You're a queer mixture!"

In the castle, after they had landed, the subjective element decidedly prevailed. Daisy tripped about the vaulted chambers, rustled her skirts in the corkscrew staircases, flirted back with a pretty little cry and a shudder from the edge of the *oubliettes*,[5] and turned a singularly well-shaped ear to everything that Winterbourne told her about the place. But he saw that she cared very little for feudal antiquities, and that the dusky traditions of Chillon made but a slight impression upon her. They had the good-fortune to have been able to walk about without other companionship than that of the custodian; and Winterbourne arranged with this functionary—that they should not be hurried—that they should linger and pause wherever they chose. The custodian interpreted the bargain generously—Winterbourne, on his side, had been generous—and ended by leaving them quite to themselves. Miss Miller's observations were not remarkable for logical consistency; for anything she wanted to say she was sure to find a pretext. She found a great many pretexts in the rugged embrasures of Chillon for asking Winterbourne sudden questions about himself—his family, his previous history, his tastes, his habits, his intentions—and for supplying information upon corresponding points in her own personality. Of her own tastes, habits, and intentions Miss Miller was prepared to give the most definite, and, indeed, the most favorable account.

"Well, I hope you know enough!" she said to her companion, after he had told her the history of the unhappy Bonnivard. "I never

[5] secret dungeons.

saw a man that knew so much!" The history of Bonnivard had evidently, as they say, gone into one ear and out of the other. But Daisy went on to say that she wished Winterbourne would travel with them, and "go round" with them; they might know something, in that case. "Don't you want to come and teach Randolph?" she asked. Winterbourne said that nothing could possibly please him so much, but that he had unfortunately other occupations. "Other occupations? I don't believe it!" said Miss Daisy. "What do you mean? You are not in business." The young man admitted that he was not in business; but he had engagements which, even within a day or two, would force him to go back to Geneva. "Oh, bother!" she said; "I don't believe it!" and she began to talk about something else. But a few moments later, when he was pointing out to her the pretty design of an antique fireplace, she broke out irrelevantly, "You don't mean to say you are going back to Geneva?"

"It is a melancholy fact that I shall have to return tomorrow."

"Well, Mr. Winterbourne," said Daisy, "I think you're horrid!"

"Oh, don't say such dreadful things!" said Winterbourne—"just at the last!"

"The last!" cried the young girl; "I call it the first. I have half a mind to leave you here and go straight back to the hotel alone." And for the next ten minutes she did nothing but call him horrid. Poor Winterbourne was fairly bewildered; no young lady had as yet done him the honor to be so agitated by the announcement of his movements. His companion, after this, ceased to pay any attention to the curiosities of Chillon or the beauties of the lake; she opened fire upon the mysterious charmer of Geneva, whom she appeared to have instantly taken it for granted that he was hurrying back to see. How did Miss Daisy Miller know that there was a charmer in Geneva? Winterbourne, who denied the existence of such a person, was quite unable to discover; and he was divided between amazement at the rapidity of her induction and amusement at the frankness of her *persiflage.*[6] She seemed to him, in all this, an extraordinary mixture of innocence and crudity. "Does she never allow you more than three days at a time?" asked Daisy, ironically. "Doesn't she give you a vacation in summer? There is no one so hard worked but they can get leave to go off somewhere at this season. I suppose, if you stay another day, she'll come after you in a boat. Do wait over till Friday, and I will go down to the landing to see her arrive!" Winterbourne began to think he had been wrong to feel disappointed in the temper in which the young lady had embarked. If he had missed the personal

[6] frivolous talk or manner.

accent, the personal accent was now making its appearance. It sounded very distinctly, at last, in her telling him she would stop "teasing" him if he would promise her solemnly to come down to Rome in the winter.

"That's not a difficult promise to make," said Winterbourne. "My aunt has taken an apartment in Rome for the winter, and has already asked me to come and see her."

"I don't want you to come for your aunt," said Daisy; "I want you to come for me." And this was the only allusion that the young man was ever to hear her make to his invidious kinswoman. He declared that, at any rate, he would certainly come. After this Daisy stopped teasing. Winterbourne took a carriage, and they drove back to Vevey in the dusk. The young girl was very quiet.

In the evening Winterbourne mentioned to Mrs. Costello that he had spent the afternoon at Chillon with Miss Daisy Miller.

"The Americans—of the courier?" asked this lady.

"Ah, happily," said Winterbourne, "the courier stayed at home."

"She went with you all alone?"

"All alone."

Mrs. Costello sniffed a little at her smelling-bottle. "And that," she exclaimed, "is the young person whom you wanted me to know!"

2

Rome

Winterbourne, who had returned to Geneva the day after his excursion to Chillon, went to Rome towards the end of January. His aunt had been established there for several weeks, and he had received a couple of letters from her. "Those people you were so devoted to last summer at Vevey have turned up here, courier and all," she wrote. "They seem to have made several acquaintances, but the courier continues to be the most *intime*. The young lady, however, is also very intimate with some third-rate Italians, with whom she rackets about in a way that makes much talk. Bring me that pretty novel of Cherbuliez's—*Paule Méré*—and don't come later than the 23rd."

In the natural course of events, Winterbourne, on arriving in Rome, would presently have ascertained Mrs. Miller's address at the American banker's, and have gone to pay his compliments to Miss Daisy. "After what happened at Vevey, I think I may certainly call upon them," he said to Mrs. Costello.

"If, after what happens—at Vevey and everywhere—you desire to keep up the acquaintance, you are very welcome. Of course a man may know every one. Men are welcome to the privilege!"

"Pray, what is it that happens—here, for instance?" Winterbourne demanded.

"The girl goes about alone with her foreigners. As to what happens further, you must apply elsewhere for information. She has picked up half a dozen of the regular Roman fortune-hunters, and she takes them about to people's houses. When she comes to a party she brings with her a gentleman with a good deal of manner and a wonderful mustache."

"And where is the mother?"

"I haven't the least idea. They are very dreadful people."

Winterbourne meditated a moment. "They are very ignorant—very innocent only. Depend upon it they are not bad."

"They are hopelessly vulgar," said Mrs. Costello. "Whether or no being hopelessly vulgar is being 'bad' is a question for the metaphysicians. They are bad enough to dislike, at any rate; and for this short life that is quite enough."

The news that Daisy Miller was surrounded by half a dozen wonderful mustaches checked Winterbourne's impulse to go straightway to see her. He had, perhaps, not definitely flattered himself that he had made an ineffaceable impression upon her heart, but he was annoyed at hearing of a state of affairs so little in harmony with an image that had lately flitted in and out of his own meditations; the image of a very pretty girl looking out of an old Roman window and asking herself urgently when Mr. Winterbourne would arrive. If, however, he determined to wait a little before reminding Miss Miller of his claims to her consideration, he went very soon to call upon two or three other friends. One of these friends was an American lady who had spent several winters at Geneva, where she had placed her children at school. She was a very accomplished woman, and she lived in the Via Gregoriana. Winterbourne found her in a little crimson drawing-room on a third floor; the room filled with southern sunshine. He had not been there ten minutes when the servant came in, announcing "Madama Mila!" This announcement was presently followed by the entrance of little Randolph Miller, who stopped in the middle of the room and stood staring at Winterbourne. An instant later his pretty sister crossed the threshold; and then, after a considerable interval, Mrs. Miller slowly advanced.

"I know you!" said Randolph.

"I'm sure you know a great many things," exclaimed Winterbourne, taking him by the hand. "How is your education coming on?"

Daisy was exchanging greetings very prettily with her hostess;

but when she heard Winterbourne's voice she quickly turned her head. "Well, I declare!" she said.

"I told you I should come, you know," Winterbourne rejoined, smiling.

"Well, I didn't believe it," said Miss Daisy.

"I am much obliged to you," laughed the young man.

"You might have come to see me!" said Daisy.

"I arrived only yesterday."

"I don't believe that!" the young girl declared.

Winterbourne turned with a protesting smile to her mother; but this lady evaded his glance, and, seating herself, fixed her eyes upon her son. "We've got a bigger place than this," said Randolph. "It's all gold on the walls."

Mrs. Miller turned uneasily in her chair. "I told you if I were to bring you, you would say something!" she murmured.

"I told *you!*" Randolph exclaimed. "I tell *you,* sir!" he added, jocosely, giving Winterbourne a thump on the knee. "It *is* bigger, too!"

Daisy had entered upon a lively conversation with her hostess, and Winterbourne judged it becoming to address a few words to her mother. "I hope you have been well since we parted at Vevey," he said.

Mrs. Miller now certainly looked at him—at his chin. "Not very well, sir," she answered.

"She's got the dyspepsia," said Randolph. "I've got it, too. Father's got it. I've got it most!"

This announcement, instead of embarrassing Mrs. Miller, seemed to relieve her. "I suffer from the liver," she said. "I think it's this climate; it's less bracing than Schenectady, especially in the winter season. I don't know whether you know we reside at Schenectady. I was saying to Daisy that I certainly hadn't found any one like Dr. Davis, and I didn't believe I should. Oh, at Schenectady he stands first; they think everything of him. He has so much to do, and yet there was nothing he wouldn't do for me. He said he never saw anything like my dyspepsia, but he was bound to cure it. I'm sure there was nothing he wouldn't try. He was just going to try something new when we came off. Mr. Miller wanted Daisy to see Europe for herself. But I wrote to Mr. Miller that it seems as if I couldn't get on without Dr. Davis. At Schenectady he stands at the very top; and there's a great deal of sickness there, too. It affects my sleep."

Winterbourne had a good deal of pathological gossip with Dr. Davis's patient, during which Daisy chatted unremittingly to her own companion. The young man asked Mrs. Miller how she was pleased with Rome. "Well, I must say I am disappointed," she answered.

"We had heard so much about it; I suppose we had heard too much. But we couldn't help that. We had been led to expect something different."

"Ah, wait a little, and you will become very fond of it," said Winterbourne.

"I hate it worse and worse every day!" cried Randolph.

"You are like the infant Hannibal," said Winterbourne.

"No, I ain't!" Randolph declared, at a venture.

"You are not much like an infant," said his mother. "But we have seen places," she resumed, "that I should put a long way before Rome." And in reply to Winterbourne's interrogation, "There's Zürich," she concluded, "I think Zürich is lovely; and we hadn't heard half so much about it."

"The best place we've seen is the City of Richmond!" said Randolph.

"He means the ship," his mother explained. "We crossed in that ship. Randolph had a good time on the *City of Richmond*."

"It's the best place I've seen," the child repeated. "Only it was turned the wrong way."

"Well, we've got to turn the right way some time," said Mrs. Miller, with a little laugh. Winterbourne expressed the hope that her daughter at least found some gratification in Rome, and she declared that Daisy was quite carried away. "It's on account of the society—the society's splendid. She goes round everywhere; she has made a great number of acquaintances. Of course she goes round more than I do. I must say they have been very sociable; they have taken her right in. And then she knows a great many gentlemen. Oh, she thinks there's nothing like Rome. Of course, it's a great deal pleasanter for a young lady if she knows plenty of gentlemen."

By this time Daisy had turned her attention again to Winterbourne. "I've been telling Mrs. Walker how mean you were!" the young girl announced.

"And what is the evidence you have offered?" asked Winterbourne, rather annoyed at Miss Miller's want of appreciation of the zeal of an admirer who on his way down to Rome had stopped neither at Bologna nor at Florence, simply because of a certain sentimental impatience. He remembered that a cynical compatriot had once told him that American women—the pretty ones, and this gave a largeness to the axiom—were at once the most exacting in the world and the least endowed with a sense of indebtedness.

"Why, you were awfully mean at Vevey," said Daisy. "You wouldn't do anything. You wouldn't stay there when I asked you."

"My dearest young lady," cried Winterbourne, with eloquence, "have I come all the way to Rome to encounter your reproaches?"

"Just hear him say that!" said Daisy to her hostess, giving a twist to a bow on this lady's dress. "Did you ever hear anything so quaint?"

"So quaint, my dear?" murmured Mrs. Walker, in the tone of a partisan of Winterbourne.

"Well, I don't know," said Daisy, fingering Mrs. Walker's ribbons. "Mrs. Walker, I want to tell you something."

"Mother-r," interposed Randolph, with his rough ends to his words, "I tell you you've got to go. Eugenio'll raise—something!"

"I'm not afraid of Eugenio," said Daisy, with a toss of her head. "Look here, Mrs. Walker," she went on, "you know I'm coming to your party."

"I am delighted to hear it."

"I've got a lovely dress!"

"I am very sure of that."

"But I want to ask a favor—permission to bring a friend."

"I shall be happy to see any of your friends," said Mrs. Walker, turning with a smile to Mrs. Miller.

"Oh, they are not my friends," answered Daisy's mamma, smiling shyly, in her own fashion. "I never spoke to them."

"It's an intimate friend of mine—Mr. Giovanelli," said Daisy, without a tremor in her clear little voice, or a shadow on her brilliant little face.

Mrs. Walker was silent a moment; she gave a rapid glance at Winterbourne. "I shall be glad to see Mr. Giovanelli," she then said.

"He's an Italian," Daisy pursued with the prettiest serenity. "He's a great friend of mine; he's the handsomest man in the world—except Mr. Winterbourne! He knows plenty of Italians, but he wants to know some Americans. He thinks ever so much of Americans. He's tremendously clever. He's perfectly lovely!"

It was settled that this brilliant personage should be brought to Mrs. Walker's party, and then Mrs. Miller prepared to take her leave. "I guess we'll go back to the hotel," she said.

"You may go back to the hotel, mother, but I'm going to take a walk," said Daisy.

"She's going to walk with Mr. Giovanelli," Randolph proclaimed.

"I am going to the Pincio," said Daisy, smiling.

"Alone, my dear—at this hour?" Mrs. Walker asked. The afternoon was drawing to a close—it was the hour for the throng of carriages and of contemplative pedestrians. "I don't think it's safe, my dear," said Mrs. Walker.

"Neither do I," subjoined Mrs. Miller. "You'll get the fever, as sure as you live. Remember what Dr. Davis told you!"

"Give her some medicine before she goes," said Randolph.

The company had risen to its feet; Daisy, still showing her pretty teeth, bent over and kissed her hostess. "Mrs. Walker, you are too perfect," she said. "I'm not going alone; I am going to meet a friend."

"Your friend won't keep you from getting the fever," Mrs. Miller observed.

"Is it Mr. Giovanelli?" asked the hostess.

Winterbourne was watching the young girl; at this question his attention quickened. She stood there smiling and smoothing her bonnet ribbons; she glanced at Winterbourne. Then, while she glanced and smiled, she answered, without a shade of hesitation, "Mr. Giovanelli—the beautiful Giovanelli."

"My dear young friend," said Mrs. Walker, taking her hand, pleadingly, "don't walk off to the Pincio at this unhealthy hour to meet a beautiful Italian."

"Well, he speaks English," said Mrs. Miller.

"Gracious me!" Daisy exclaimed, "I don't want to do anything improper. There's an easy way to settle it." She continued to glance at Winterbourne. "The Pincio is only a hundred yards distant; and if Mr. Winterbourne were as polite as he pretends, he would offer to walk with me!"

Winterbourne's politeness hastened to affirm itself, and the young girl gave him gracious leave to accompany her. They passed downstairs before her mother, and at the door Winterbourne perceived Mrs. Miller's carriage drawn up, with the ornamental courier whose acquaintance he had made at Vevey, seated within. "Good-by, Eugenio!" cried Daisy; "I'm going to take a walk." The distance from the Via Gregoriana to the other end of the Pincian Hill is, in fact rapidly traversed. As the day was splendid, however, and the concourse of vehicles, walkers, and loungers numerous, the young Americans found their progress much delayed. This fact was highly agreeable to Winterbourne, in spite of his consciousness of his singular situation. The slow-moving, idly-gazing Roman crowd bestowed much attention upon the extremely pretty young foreign lady who was passing through it upon his arm; and he wondered what on earth had been in Daisy's mind when she proposed to expose herself, unattended, to its appreciation. His own mission, to her sense, apparently, was to consign her to the hands of Mr. Giovanelli; but Winterbourne, at once annoyed and gratified, resolved that he would do no such thing.

"Why haven't you been to see me?" asked Daisy. "You can't get out of that."

"I have had the honor of telling you that I have only just stepped out of the train."

"You must have stayed in the train a good while after it stopped!" cried the young girl, with her little laugh. "I suppose you were asleep. You have had time to go to see Mrs. Walker."

"I knew Mrs. Walker—" Winterbourne began to explain.

"I know where you knew her. You knew her at Geneva. She told me so. Well, you knew me at Vevey. That's just as good. So you ought to have come." She asked him no other questions than this; she began to prattle about her own affairs. "We've got splendid rooms at the hotel; Eugenio says they're the best rooms in Rome. We are going to stay all winter, if we don't die of the fever; and I guess we'll stay then. It's a great deal nicer than I thought; I thought it would be fearfully quiet; I was sure it would be awfully poky. I was sure we should be going round all the time with one of those dreadful old men that explain about the pictures and things. But we only had about a week of that, and now I'm enjoying myself. I know ever so many people, and they are all so charming. The society's extremely select. There are all kinds—English and Germans and Italians. I think I like the English best. I like their style of conversation. But there are some lovely Americans. I never saw anything so hospitable. There's something or other every day. There's not much dancing; but I must say I never thought dancing was everything. I was always fond of conversation. I guess I shall have plenty at Mrs. Walker's, her rooms are so small." When they had passed the gate of the Pincian Gardens, Miss Miller began to wonder where Mr. Giovanelli might be. "We had better go straight to that place in front," she said, "where you look at the view."

"I certainly shall not help you to find him," Winterbourne declared.

"Then I shall find him without you," said Miss Daisy.

She burst into her little laugh. "Are you afraid you'll get lost—or run over? But there's Giovanelli, leaning against that tree. He's staring at the women in the carriages; did you ever see anything so cool?"

Winterbourne perceived at some distance a little man standing with folded arms nursing his cane. He had a handsome face, an artfully poised hat, a glass in one eye, and a nosegay in his buttonhole. Winterbourne looked at him a moment, and then said, "Do you mean to speak to that man?"

"Do I mean to speak to him? Why, you don't suppose I mean to communicate by signs?"

"Pray understand, then," said Winterbourne, "that I intend to remain with you."

Daisy stopped and looked at him, without a sign of troubled consciousness in her face; with nothing but the presence of her charming eyes and her happy dimples. "Well, she's a cool one!" thought the young man.

"I don't like the way you say that," said Daisy. "It's too imperious."

"I beg your pardon if I say it wrong. The main point is to give you an idea of my meaning."

The young girl looked at him more gravely, but with eyes that were prettier than ever. "I have never allowed a gentleman to dictate to me, or to interfere with anything I do."

"I think you have made a mistake," said Winterbourne. "You should sometimes listen to a gentleman—the right one."

Daisy began to laugh again. "I do nothing but listen to gentlemen!" she exclaimed. "Tell me if Mr. Giovanelli is the right one."

The gentleman with the nosegay in his bosom had now perceived our two friends, and was approaching the young girl with obsequious rapidity. He bowed to Winterbourne as well as to the latter's companion; he had a brilliant smile, an intelligent eye; Winterbourne thought him not a bad-looking fellow. But he nevertheless said to Daisy, "No, he's not the right one."

Daisy evidently had a natural talent for performing introductions; she mentioned the name of each of her companions to the other. She strolled along with one of them on each side of her; Mr. Giovanelli, who spoke English very cleverly—Winterbourne afterwards learned that he had practiced the idiom upon a great many American heiresses—addressed to her a great deal of very polite nonsense; he was extremely urbane, and the young American, who said nothing, reflected upon that profundity of Italian cleverness which enables people to appear more gracious in proportion as they are more acutely disappointed. Giovanelli, of course, had counted upon something more intimate; he had not bargained for a party of three. But he kept his temper in a manner which suggested far-stretching intentions. Winterbourne flattered himself that he had taken his measure. "He is not a gentleman," said the young American; "he is only a clever imitation of one. He is a music-master, or a penny-a-liner, or a third-rate artist. D—n his good looks!" Mr. Giovanelli had certainly a very pretty face; but Winterbourne felt a superior indignation at his own lovely fellow-countrywoman's not knowing the difference between a spurious gentleman and a real one. Giovanelli chattered and jested, and made himself wonderfully agreeable. It was true that, if he was an imitation, the imitation was brilliant. "Nevertheless," Winterbourne said to himself, "a nice girl ought to know!" And then he came back to the question whether this was, in fact, a nice girl. Would a nice girl, even allowing for her being a little American flirt, make a rendezvous with a presumably low-lived foreigner? The rendezvous in this case, indeed, had been in broad daylight, and in the most crowded corner of Rome; but was it not impossible to regard the choice of these circumstances as a proof of extreme cynicism? Singular though it may seem, Winterbourne was vexed that the young girl, in joining her *amoroso,* should not appear more impatient of his own company, and he was vexed because of his inclination. It was impossible to regard her as a perfectly well-conducted young lady; she was wanting in a certain indispensable delicacy. It would therefore simplify matters greatly to be able to treat her as the object of one of those sentiments which are called by romancers "lawless passions." That she should seem to wish to get rid of him would help him to think more lightly of her, and to be able to think more lightly of her would make her much less perplexing. But Daisy, on this occasion, continued to present herself as an inscrutable combination of audacity and innocence.

She had been walking some quarter of an hour, attended by her two cavaliers, and responding in a tone of very childish gayety, as it seemed to Winterbourne, to the pretty speeches of Mr. Giovanelli, when a carriage that had detached itself from the revolving train drew up beside the path. At the same moment Winterbourne perceived that his friend Mrs. Walker—the lady whose house he had lately left—was seated in the vehicle, and was beckoning to him. Leaving Miss Miller's side, he hastened to obey her summons. Mrs. Walker was flushed; she wore an excited air. "It is really too dreadful," she said. "That girl must not do this sort of thing. She must not walk here with you two men. Fifty people have noticed her."

Winterbourne raised his eyebrows. "I think it's a pity to make too much fuss about it."

"It's a pity to let the girl ruin herself."

"She is very innocent," said Winterbourne.

"She's very crazy!" cried Mrs. Walker. "Did you ever see anything so imbecile as her mother? After you had all left me just now I could not sit still for thinking of it. It seemed too pitiful not even to attempt to save her. I ordered the carriage and put on my bonnet, and came here as quickly as possible. Thank Heaven I have found you!"

"What do you propose to do with us?" asked Winterbourne, smiling.

"To ask her to get in, to drive her about here for half an hour, so that the world may see that she is not running absolutely wild, and then to take her safely home."

"I don't think it's a very happy thought," said Winterbourne; "but you can try."

Mrs. Walker tried. The young man went in pursuit of Miss Miller, who had simply nodded and smiled at his interlocutor in the carriage, and had gone her way with her companion. Daisy, on learning that Mrs. Walker wished to speak to her, retraced her steps with a perfect good grace and with Mr. Giovanelli at her side. She declared that she was delighted to have a chance to present this gentleman to Mrs. Walker. She immediately achieved the introduction, and declared that she had never in her life seen anything so lovely as Mrs. Walker's carriage-rug.

"I am glad you admire it," said this lady, smiling sweetly. "Will you get in and let me put it over you?"

"Oh no, thank you," said Daisy. "I shall admire it much more as I see you driving round with it."

"Do get in and drive with me!" said Mrs. Walker.

"That would be charming, but it's so enchanting just as I am!" and Daisy gave a brilliant glance at the gentlemen on either side of her.

"It may be enchanting, dear child, but it is not the custom here," urged Mrs. Walker, leaning forward in her victoria, with her hands devoutly clasped.

"Well, it ought to be, then!" said Daisy. "If I didn't walk I should expire."

"You should walk with your mother, dear," cried the lady from Geneva, losing patience.

"With my mother, dear!" exclaimed the young girl. Winterbourne saw that she scented interference. "My mother never walked ten steps in her life. And then, you know," she added, with a laugh, "I am more than five years old."

"You are old enough to be more reasonable. You are old enough, dear Miss Miller, to be talked about."

Daisy looked at Mrs. Walker, smiling intensely. "Talked about? What do you mean?"

"Come into my carriage, and I will tell you."

Daisy turned her quickened glance again from one of the gentlemen beside her to the other. Mr. Giovanelli was bowing to and fro, rubbing down his gloves and laughing very agreeably; Winterbourne thought it a most unpleasant scene. "I don't think I want to know what you mean," said Daisy, presently. "I don't think I should like it."

Winterbourne wished that Mrs. Walker would tuck in her carriage-rug and drive away; but this lady did not enjoy being defied, as she afterwards told him. "Should you prefer being thought a very reckless girl?" she demanded.

"Gracious!" exclaimed Daisy. She looked again at Mr. Giovanelli, then she turned to Winterbourne. There was a little pink flush in her cheek; she was tremendously pretty. "Does Mr. Winterbourne think," she asked slowly, smiling, throwing back her head and glancing at him from head to foot, "that, to save my reputation, I ought to get into the carriage?"

Winterbourne colored; for an instant he hesitated greatly. It seemed so strange to hear her speak that way of her "reputation." But he himself, in fact, must speak in accordance with gallantry. The finest gallantry here was simply to tell her the truth, and the truth for Winterbourne—as the few indications I have been able to give have made him known to the reader—was that Daisy Miller should have taken Mrs. Walker's advice. He looked at her exquisite prettiness, and then said, very gently, "I think you should get into the carriage." Daisy gave a violent laugh. "I never heard anything so stiff! If this is improper, Mrs. Walker," she pursued, "then I am all improper, and you must give me up. Good-bye; I hope you'll have a lovely ride!" and, with Mr. Giovanelli, who made a triumphantly obsequious salute, she turned away.

Mrs. Walker sat looking after her, and there were tears in Mrs. Walker's eyes. "Get in here, sir," she said to Winterbourne, indicating the place beside her. The young man answered that he felt bound to accompany Miss Miller; whereupon Mrs. Walker declared that if he refused her this favor she would never speak to him again. She was evidently in earnest. Winterbourne overtook Daisy and her companion, and, offering the young girl his hand, told her that Mrs. Walker had made an imperious claim upon his society. He expected that in answer she would say something rather free, something to commit herself still further to that "recklessness" from which Mrs. Walker had so charitably endeavored to dissuade her. But she only shook his hand, hardly looking at him; while Mr. Giovanelli bade him a farewell with a too emphatic flourish of the hat.

Winterbourne was not in the best possible humor as he took his seat in Mrs. Walker's victoria. "That was not clever of you," he said, candidly, while the vehicle mingled again with the throng of carriages.

"In such a case," his companion answered, "I don't wish to be clever; I wish to be *earnest!*"

"Well, your earnestness has only offended her and put her off."

"It has happened very well," said Mrs. Walker. "If she is so perfectly determined to compromise herself, the sooner one knows it the better; one can act accordingly."

"I suspect she meant no harm," Winterbourne rejoined.

"So I thought a month ago. But she has been going too far."

"What has she been doing?"

"Everything that is not done here. Flirting with any man she could pick up; sitting in corners with mysterious Italians; dancing all the evening with the same partners; receiving visits at eleven o'clock at night. Her mother goes away when visitors come."

"But her brother," said Winterbourne, laughing, "sits up till midnight."

"He must be edified by what he sees. I'm told that at their hotel every one is talking about her, and that a smile goes round among all the servants when a gentleman comes and asks for Miss Miller."

"The servants be hanged!" said Winterbourne, angrily. "The poor girl's only fault," he presently added, "is that she is very uncultivated."

"She is naturally indelicate," Mrs. Walker declared. "Take that example this morning. How long had you known her at Vevey?"

"A couple of days."

"Fancy, then, her making it a personal matter that you should have left the place?"

Winterbourne was silent for some moments; then he said, "I suspect, Mrs. Walker, that you and I have lived too long at Geneva!" And he added a request that she should inform him with what particular design she had made him enter the carriage.

"I wished to beg you to cease your relations with Miss Miller—not to flirt with her—to give her no further opportunity to expose herself—to let her alone, in short."

"I'm afraid I can't do that," said Winterbourne. "I like her extremely."

"All the more reason that you shouldn't help her to make a scandal."

"There shall be nothing scandalous in my attentions to her."

"There certainly will be in the way she takes them. But I have said what I had on my conscience," Mrs. Walker pursued. "If you wish to rejoin the young lady I will put you down. Here, by-the-way, you have a chance."

The carriage was traversing that part of the Pincian Garden that overhangs the wall of Rome and overlooks the beautiful Villa Borghese. It is bordered by a large parapet, near which there are several seats. One of the seats at a distance was occupied by a gentleman and a lady, towards which Mrs. Walker gave a toss of her head. At the same moment these persons rose and walked towards the parapet. Winterbourne had asked the coachman to stop; he now descended from the carriage. His companion looked at him a moment in silence; then, while he raised his hat, she drove majestically away. Winterbourne stood there; he had turned his eyes towards Daisy and her cavalier. They evidently saw no one; they were too deeply occupied with each other. When they reached the low garden-wall they stood a moment looking off at the great flat-topped pine-clusters of the Villa Borghese; then Giovanelli seated himself familiarly upon the broad ledge of the wall. The western sun in the opposite sky sent out a brilliant shaft through a couple of cloud-bars, whereupon Daisy's companion took her parasol out of her hands and opened it. She came a little nearer, and he held the parasol over her; then, still holding it, he let it rest upon her shoulder, so that both of their heads were hidden from Winterbourne. This young man lingered a moment, then he began to walk. But he walked—not toward the couple with the parasol—towards the residence of his aunt, Mrs. Costello.

He flattered himself on the following day that there was no smiling among the servants when he, at least, asked for Mrs. Miller at her hotel. This lady and her daughter, however, were not at home; and on the next day after, repeating his visit, Winterbourne again had the misfortune not to find them. Mrs. Walker's party took place on the evening of the third day, and, in spite of the frigidity of his last interview with the hostess, Winterbourne was among the guests. Mrs. Walker was one of those American ladies who, while residing abroad, make a point, in their own phrase, of studying European society; and she had on this occasion collected several specimens of her diversely-born fellow-mortals s to serve, as it were, as text-books. When Winterbourne arrived, Daisy Miller was not there, but in a few moments he saw her mother come in alone, very shyly and ruefully. Mrs. Miller's hair above her exposed-looking temples was more frizzled than ever. As she approached Mrs. Walker, Winterbourne also drew near.

"You see I've come all alone," said poor Mrs. Miller. "I'm so frightened I don't know what to do. It's the first time I've ever been to a party alone, especially in this country. I wanted to bring Randolph, or Eugenio, or some one, but Daisy just pushed me off by myself. I ain't used to going round alone."

"And does not your daughter intend to favor us with her society?" demanded Mrs. Walker, impressively.

"Well, Daisy's all dressed," said Mrs. Miller, with that accent of the dispassionate, if not of the philosophic, historian with which she always recorded incidents of her daughter's career. "She got dressed on purpose before dinner. But she's got a friend of hers there; that gentleman—the Italian—that she wanted to bring. They've got going at the piano; it seems as if they couldn't leave off. Mr. Giovanelli sings splendidly. But I guess they'll come before very long," concluded Mrs. Miller, hopefully.

"I'm sorry she should come in that way," said Mrs. Walker.

"Well, I told her that there was no use in her getting dressed before dinner if she was going to wait three hours," responded Daisy's mamma. "I didn't see the use of her putting on such a dress as that to sit around with Mr. Giovanelli."

"This is most horrible!" said Mrs. Walker, turning away and addressing herself to Winterbourne. *"Elle s'affiche.*[7] It's her revenge for my having ventured to remonstrate with her. When she comes I shall not speak to her."

Daisy came after eleven o'clock; but she was not, on such an occasion, a young lady to wait to be spoken to. She rustled forward in radiant loveliness, smiling and chattering, carrying a large bouquet, and attended by Mr. Giovanelli. Every one stopped talking, and turned and looked at her. She came straight to Mrs. Walker. "I'm afraid you thought I never was coming so I sent mother off to tell you. I wanted to make Mr. Giovanelli practice some things before he came; you know he sings beautifully, and I want you to ask him to sing. This is Mr. Giovanelli; you know I introduced him to you; he's got the most lovely voice, and he knows the most charming set of songs. I made him go over them this evening on purpose; we had the greatest time at the hotel." Of all this Daisy delivered herself with the sweetest, brightest audibleness, looking now at her hostess and now round the room, while she gave a series of little pats round her shoulders to the edges of her dress. "Is there any one I know?" she asked.

"I think every one knows you!" said Mrs. Walker, pregnantly, and she gave a very cursory greeting to Mr. Giovanelli. This gentleman bore himself gallantly. He smiled and bowed, and showed his white teeth; he curled his mustaches and rolled his eyes, and performed all the proper functions of a handsome Italian at an evening party. He sang very prettily half a dozen songs, though Mrs. Walker afterwards declared that she had been quite unable to find out who asked him. It was apparently not Daisy who had given him his orders. Daisy sat at a distance from the piano; and though she had publicly, as it were, professed a high admiration for his singing, talked, not inaudibly, while it was going on.

"It's a pity these rooms are so small; we can't dance," she said to Winterbourne, as if she had seen him five minutes before.

"I am not sorry we can't dance," Winterbourne answered; "I don't dance."

"Of course you don't dance; you're too stiff," said Miss Daisy. "I hope you enjoyed your drive with Mrs. Walker."

[7] She is seeking notoriety.

"No, I didn't enjoy it; I preferred walking with you."

"We paired off; that was much better," said Daisy. "But did you ever hear anything so cool as Mrs. Walker's wanting me to get into her carriage and drop poor Mr. Giovanelli, and under the pretext that it was proper? People have different ideas! It would have been most unkind; he had been talking about that walk for ten days."

"He should not have talked about it at all," said Winterbourne; "he would never have proposed to a young lady of this country to walk about the streets with him."

"About the streets?" cried Daisy, with her pretty stare. "Where, then, would he have proposed to her to walk? The Pincio is not the streets, either; and I, thank goodness, am not a young lady of this country. The young ladies of this country have a dreadfully poky time of it, so far as I can learn; I don't see why I should change my habits for *them*."

"I am afraid your habits are those of a flirt," said Winterbourne, gravely.

"Of course they are," she cried, giving him her little smiling stare again. "I'm a fearful, frightful flirt! Did you ever hear of a nice girl that was not? But I suppose you will tell me now that I am not a nice girl."

"You're a very nice girl; but I wish you would flirst with me, and me only," said Winterbourne.

"Ah! thank you—thank you very much; you are the last man I should think of flirting with. As I have had the pleasure of informing you, you are too stiff."

"You say that too often," said Winterbourne.

Daisy gave a delighted laugh. "If I could have the sweet hope of making you angry, I should say it again."

"Don't do that; when I am angry I'm stiffer than ever. But if you won't flirt with me, do cease, at least, to flirt with your friend at the piano; they don't understand that sort of thing here."

"I thought they understood nothing else!" exclaimed Daisy.

"Not in young unmarried women."

"It seems to me much more proper in young unmarried women than in old married ones," Daisy declared.

"Well," said Winterbourne, "when you deal with natives you must go by the custom of the place. Flirting is a purely American custom; it doesn't exist here. So when you show yourself in public with Mr. Giovanelli, and without your mother—"

"Gracious! poor mother!" interposed Daisy.

"Though you may be flirting, Mr. Giovanelli is not; he means something else."

"He isn't preaching, at any rate," said Daisy, with vivacity. "And if you want very much to know, we are too good friends for that: we are very intimate friends."

"Ah!" rejoined Winterbourne, "if you are in love with each other, it is another affair."

She had allowed him up to this point to talk so frankly that he had no expectation of shocking her by this ejaculation; but she immediately got up, blushing visibly, and leaving him to exclaim mentally that little American flirts were the queerest creatures in the world. "Mr. Giovanelli, at least," she said, giving her interlocutor a single glance, "never says such very disagreeable things to me."

Winterbourne was bewildered; he stood staring. Mr. Giovanelli had finished singing. He left the piano and came over to Daisy. "Won't you come into the other room and have some tea?" he asked, bending before her with his ornamental smile.

Daisy turned to Winterbourne, beginning to smile again. He was still more perplexed, for this inconsequent smile made nothing clear, though it seemed to prove, indeed, that she had a sweetness and softness that reverted instinctively to the pardon of offenses. "It has never occurred to Mr. Winterbourne to offer me any tea," she said, with her little tormenting manner.

"I have offered you advice," Winterbourne rejoined.

"I prefer weak tea!" cried Daisy, and she went off with the brilliant Giovanelli. She sat with him in the adjoining room, in the embrasure of the window, for the rest of the evening. There was an interesting performance at the piano, but neither of these young people gave heed to it. When Daisy came to take leave of Mrs. Walker, this lady conscientiously repaired the weakness of which she had been guilty at the moment of the young girl's arrival. She turned her back straight upon Miss Miller, and left her to depart with what grace she might. Winterbourne was standing near the door; he saw it all. Daisy turned very pale, and looked at her mother; but Mrs. Miller was humbly unconscious of any violation of the usual social forms. She appeared, indeed, to have felt an incongruous impulse to draw attention to her own striking observance of them. "Good-night, Mrs. Walker," she said; "we've had a beautiful evening. You see, if I let Daisy come to parties without me, I don't want her to go away without me." Daisy turned away, looking with a pale, grave face at the circle near the door; Winterbourne saw that, for the first moment, she was too much shocked and puzzled even for indignation. He on his side was greatly touched.

"That was very cruel," he said to Mrs. Walker.

"She never enters my drawing-room again!" replied his hostess.

Since Winterbourne was not to meet her in Mrs. Walker's drawing-room, he went as often as possible to Mrs. Miller's hotel. The ladies were rarely at home; but when he found them the devoted Giovanelli was always present. Very often the brilliant little Roman was in the drawing-room with Daisy alone, Mrs. Miller being apparently constantly of the opinion that discretion is the better part of surveillance. Winterbourne noted, at first with surprise, that Daisy on these occasions was never embarrassed or annoyed by his own entrance; but he very presently began to feel that she had no more surprises for him; the unexpected in her behavior was the only thing to expect. She showed no displeasure at her tête-à-tête with Giovanelli being interrupted; she could chatter as freshly and freely with two gentlemen as with one; there was always, in her conversation, the same odd mixture of audacity and puerility. Winterbourne remarked to himself that if she was seriously interested in Giovanelli, it was very singular that she should not take more trouble to preserve the sanctity of their interviews; and he liked her the more for her innocent-looking indifference and her apparently inexhaustible good-humor. He could hardly have said why, but she seemed to him a girl who would never be jealous. At the risk of exciting a somewhat derisive smile on the reader's part, I may affirm that with regard to the women who had hitherto interested him, it very often seemed to Winterbourne among the possibilities that, given certain contingencies, he should be afraid—literally afraid—of these ladies; he had a pleasant sense that he should never be afraid of Daisy Miller. It must be added that this sentiment was not altogether flattering to Daisy; it was part of his conviction, or rather of his apprehension, that she would prove a very light young person.

But she was evidently very much interested in Giovanelli. She looked at him whenever he spoke; she was perpetually telling him to do this and to do that; she was constantly "chaffing" and abusing him. She appeared completely to have forgotten that Winterbourne had said anything to displease her at Mrs. Walker's little party. One Sunday afternoon, having gone to St. Peter's with his aunt, Winterbourne perceived Daisy strolling about the great church in company with the inevitable Giovanelli. Presently he pointed out the young girl and her cavalier to Mrs. Costello. This lady looked at them a moment through her eye-glass, and then she said,

"That's what makes you so pensive in these days, eh?"

"I had not the least idea I was pensive," said the young man.

"You are very much preoccupied; you are thinking of something."

"And what is it," he asked, "that you accuse me of thinking of?"

"Oh that young lady's—Miss Baker's, Miss Chandler's—what's her name?—Miss Miller's intrigue with that little barber's block."

"Do you call it an intrigue," Winterbourne asked—an affair that goes on with such peculiar publicity?"

"That's their folly," said Mrs. Costello; "it's not their merit."

"No," rejoined Winterbourne, with something of that pensiveness to which his aunt had alluded. "I don't believe that there is anything to be called an intrigue."

"I have heard a dozen people speak of it; they say she is quite carried away by him."

"They're certainly very intimate," said Winterbourne.

Mrs. Costello inspected the young couple again with her optical instrument. "He is very handsome. One easily sees how it is. She thinks him the most elegant man in the world—the finest gentleman. She has never seen anything like him; he is better, even, than the courier. It was the courier, probably, who introduced him; and if he succeeds in marrying the young lady, the courier will come in for a magnificent commission."

"I don't believe she thinks of marrying him," said Winterbourne, " and I don't believe he hopes to marry her."

"You may be very sure she thinks of nothing. She goes on from day to day, from hour to hour, as they did in the Golden Age. I can imagine nothing more vulgar. And at the same time," added Mrs. Costello, "depend upon it that she may tell you any moment that she is 'engaged.' "

"I think that is more than Giovanelli expects," said Winterbourne.

"Who is Giovanelli?"

"The little Italian. I have asked questions about him, and learned something. He is apparently a perfectly respectable little man. I believe he is, in a small way, a *cavaliere avvocato*.[8] But he doesn't move in what are called the first circles. I think it is really not absolutely impossible that the courier introduced him. He is evidently immensely charmed with Miss Miller. If she thinks him the finest gentleman in the world, he, on his side, has never found himself in personal contact with such splendor, such opulence, such expensiveness, as this young lady's. And then she must seem to him wonderfully pretty and interesting. I rather doubt that he dreams of marrying her. That must appear to him too impossible a piece of luck. He has nothing but his handsome face to offer, and there is a substantial Mr. Miller in that mysterious land of dollars. Giovanelli knows that he hasn't a title to offer. If he were only a count or a *marchese!* He must wonder at his luck, at the way they have taken him up."

[8] respectable lawyer.

"He accounts for it by his handsome face, and thinks Miss Miller a young lady *qui se passe ses fantaisies!*"[9] said Mrs. Costello.

"It is very true," Winterbourne pursued, "that Daisy and her mamma have not yet risen to that stage of—what shall I call it?—of culture, at which the idea of catching a count or a *marchese* begins. I believe that they are intellectually incapable of that conception."

"Ah! but the *avvocato* can't believe it," said Mrs. Costello.

Of the observation excited by Daisy's "intrigue," Winterbourne gathered that day at St. Peter's sufficent evidence. A dozen of the American colonists in Rome came to talk with Mrs. Costello, who sat on a little portable stool at the base of one of the great pilasters. The vesper service was going forward in splendid chants and organ-tones in the adjacent choir, and meanwhile, between Mrs. Costello and her friends, there was a great deal said about poor little Miss Miller's going really "too far." Winterbourne was not pleased with what he heard; but when, coming out upon the great steps of the church, he saw Daisy, who had emerged before him, get into an open cab with her accomplice and roll away through the cynical streets of Rome, he could not deny to himself that she was going very far indeed. He felt very sorry for her—not exactly that he believed that she had completely lost her head, but because it was painful to hear so much that was pretty and undefended and natural assigned to a vulgar place among the categories of disorder. He made an attempt after this to give a hint to Mrs. Miller. He met one day in the Corso a friend, a tourist like himself, who had just come out of the Doria Palace, where he had been walking through the beautiful gallery. His friend talked for a moment about the superb portrait of Innocent X., by Velasquez, which hangs in one of the cabinets of the palace, and then said, "And in the same cabinet, by-the-way, I had the pleasure of contemplating a picture of a different kind—that pretty American girl whom you pointed out to me last week." In answer to Winterbourne's inquiries, his friend narrated that the pretty American girl—prettier than ever—was seated with a companion in the secluded nook in which the great papal portrait was enshrined.

"Who was her companion?" asked Winterbourne.

"A little Italian with a bouquet in his button-hole. The girl is delightfully pretty, but I thought I understood from you the other day that she was a young lady *du meilleur monde.*"[10]

"So she is!" answered Winterbourne; and having assured himself that his informant had seen Daisy and her companion but five minutes before, he jumped into a cab and went to call on Mrs. Miller. She

[9] who indulges in her whims.   [10] from the best world.

was at home, but she apologized to him for receiving him in Daisy's absence.

"She's gone out somewhere with Mr. Giovanelli," said Mrs. Miller. "She's always going round with Mr. Giovanelli."

"I have noticed that they are very intimate," Winterbourne observed.

"Oh, it seems as if they couldn't live without each other!" said Mrs. Miller. "Well, he's a real gentleman, anyhow. I keep telling Daisy she's engaged!"

"And what does Daisy say?"

"Oh, she says she isn't engaged. But she might as well be!" this impartial parent resumed; "she goes on as if she was. But I've made Mr. Giovanelli promise to tell me, if *she* doesn't. I should want to write to Mr. Miller about it—shouldn't you?"

Winterbourne replied that he certainly should; and the state of mind of Daisy's mamma struck him as so unprecedented in the annals of parental vigilance that he gave up as utterly irrelevant the attempt to place her upon her guard.

After this Daisy was never at home, and Winterbourne ceased to meet her at the house of their common acquaintances, because, as he perceived, these shrewd people had quite made up their minds that she was going too far. They ceased to invite her; and they intimated that they desired to express to observant Europeans the great truth that, though Miss Daisy Miller was a young American lady, her behavior was not representative—was regarded by her compatriots as abnormal. Winterbourne wondered how she felt about all the cold shoulders that were turned towards her, and sometimes it annoyed him to suspect that she did not feel at all. He said to himself that she was too light and childish, too uncultivated and unreasoning, too provincial, to have reflected upon her ostracism, or even to have perceived it. Then at other moments he believed that she carried about in her elegant and irresponsible little organism a defiant, passionate, perfectly observant consciousness of the impression she produced. He asked himself whether Daisy's defiance came from the consciousness of innocence, or from her being, essentially, a young person of the reckless class. It must be admitted that holding one's self to a belief in Daisy's "innocence" came to seem to Winterbourne more and more a matter of fine-spun gallantry. As I have already had occasion to relate, he was angry at finding himself reduced to chopping logic about this young lady; he was vexed at his want of instinctive certitude as to how far her eccentricities were generic, national, and how far they were personal. From either view of them he had somehow missed her, and now it was too late. She was "carried away" by Mr. Giovanelli.

A few days after his brief interview with her mother, he encountered her in that beautiful abode of flowering desolation known as the Palace of the Cæsars. The early Roman spring had filled the air with bloom and perfume, and the rugged surface of the Palatine was muffled with tender verdure. Daisy was strolling along the top of one of those great mounds of ruin that are embanked with mossy marble and paved with monumental inscriptions. It seemed to him that Rome had never been so lovely as just then. He stood looking off at the enchanting harmony of line and color that remotely encircles the city, inhaling the softly humid odors, and feeling the freshness of the year and the antiquity of the place reaffirm themselves in mysterious interfusion. It seemed to him, also, that Daisy had never looked so pretty; but this had been an observation of his whenever he met her. Giovanelli was at her side, and Giovanelli, too, wore an aspect of even unwonted brilliancy.

"Well," said Daisy, "I should think you would be lonesome!"

"Lonesome?" asked Winterbourne.

"You are always going round by yourself. Can't you get any one to walk with you?"

"I am not so fortunate," said Winterbourne, "as your companion."

Giovanelli, from the first, had treated Winterbourne with distinguished politeness. He listened with a deferential air to his remarks; he laughed punctiliously at his pleasantries; he seemed disposed to testify to his belief that Winterbourne was a superior young man. He carried himself in no degree like a jealous wooer; he had obviously a great deal of tact; he had no objection to your expecting a little humility of him. It even seemed to Winterbourne at times that Giovanelli would find a certain mental relief in being able to have a private understanding with him—to say to him, as an intelligent man, that, bless you, *he* knew how extraordinary was this young lady, and didn't flatter himself with delusive—or, at least, *too* delusive—hopes of matrimony and dollars. On this occasion he strolled away from his companion to pluck a sprig of almond-blossom, which he carefully arranged in his button-hole.

"I know why you say that," said Daisy, watching Giovanelli. "Because you think I go round too much with *him.*" And she nodded at her attendant.

"Everyone thinks so—if you care to know," said Winterbourne.

"Of course I care to know!" Daisy exclaimed, seriously. "But I don't believe it. They are only pretending to be shocked. They don't really care a straw what I do. Besides, I don't go round so much."

"I think you will find they do care. They will show it disagreeably."

Daisy looked at him a moment. "How disagreeably?"

"Haven't you noticed anything?" Winterbourne asked.

"I have noticed you. But I noticed you were as stiff as an umbrella the first time I saw you."

"You will find I am not so stiff as several others," said Winterbourne, smiling.

"How shall I find it?"

"By going to see the others."

"What will they do to me?"

"They will give you the cold shoulder. Do you know what that means?"

Daisy was looking at him intently; she began to color.

"Do you mean as Mrs. Walker did the other night?"

"Exactly!" said Winterbourne.

She looked away at Giovanelli, who was decorating himself with his almond-blossom. Then, looking back at Winterbourne, "I shouldn't think you would let people be so unkind!" she said.

"How can I help it?" he asked.

"I should think you would say something."

"I did say something;" and he paused a moment. "I say that your mother tells me that she believes you are engaged."

"Well, she does," said Daisy, very simply.

Winterbourne began to laugh. "And does Randolph believe it?" he asked.

"I guess Randolph doesn't believe anything," said Daisy. Randolph's skepticism excited Winterbourne to further hilarity, and he observed that Giovanelli was coming back to them. Daisy, observing it too, addressed herself again to her countryman. "Since you have mentioned it," she said, "I *am* engaged." ... Winterbourne looked at her; he had stopped laughing. "You don't believe it!" she added.

He was silent a moment; and then, "Yes, I believe it," he said.

"Oh, no, you don't!" she answered. "Well, then—I am not!"

The young girl and her cicerone were on their way to the gate of the enclosure, so that Winterbourne, who had but lately entered, presently took leave of them. A week afterwards he went to dine at a beautiful villa on the Cælian Hill, and, on arriving, dismissed his hired vehicle. The evening was charming, and he promised himself the satisfaction of walking home beneath the Arch of Constantine and past the vaguely-lighted monuments of the Forum. There was a waning moon in the sky, and her radiance was not brilliant, but she was veiled in a thin cloud-curtain which seemed to diffuse and equalize it. When, on his return from the villa (it was eleven o'clock), Winterbourne approached the dusky circle of the Colosseum, it occurred to him, as a lover of the picturesque, that the interior, in the pale moonshine, would be well worth a glance. He turned aside and walked to one of the empty arches, near which, as he observed, an open carriage—one of the little Roman street-cabs—was stationed. Then he passed in, among the cavernous shadows of the great structure, and emerged upon the clear and silent arena. The place had never seemed to him more impressive. One-half of the gigantic circus was in deep shade, the other was sleeping in the luminous dusk. As he stood there he began to murmur Byron's famous lines, out of "Manfred"; but before he had finished his quotation he remembered that if nocturnal meditations in the Colosseum are recommended by the poets, they are deprecated by the doctors. The historic atmosphere was there, certainly; but the historic atmosphere, scientifically considered, was no better than a villainous miasma. Winterbourne walked to the middle of the arena, to take a more general glance, intending thereafter to make a hasty retreat. The great cross in the center was covered with shadow; it was only as he drew near it that he made it out distinctly. Then he saw that two persons were stationed upon the low steps which formed its base. One of these was a woman, seated; her companion was standing in front of her.

Presently the sound of the woman's voice came to him distinctly in the warm night air: "Well, he looks at us as one of the old lions or tigers may have looked at the Christian martyrs!" These were the words he heard in the familiar accent of Miss Daisy Miller.

"Let us hope he is not very hungry," responded the ingenious Giovanelli. "He will have to take me first; you will serve for dessert!"

Winterbourne stopped, with a sort of horror, and, it must be added, with a sort of relief. It was as if a sudden illumination had been flashed upon the ambiguity of Daisy's behavior, and the riddle had become easy to read. She was a young lady whom a gentleman need no longer be at pains to respect. He stood there looking at her—looking at her companion, and not reflecting that though he saw them vaguely, he himself must have been more brightly visible. He felt angry with himself that he had bothered so much about the right way of regarding Miss Daisy Miller. Then, as he was going to advance again, he checked himself; not from the fear that he was doing her injustice, but from the sense of the danger of appearing unbecomingly exhilarated by this sudden revulsion from cautious criticism. He turned away towards the entrance of the place, but, as he did so, he heard Daisy speak again.

"Why, it was Mr. Winterbourne! He saw me, and he cuts me!"

What a clever little reprobate she was, and how smartly she played at injured innocence! But he wouldn't cut her. Winterbourne came forward again, and went towards the great cross. Daisy had got up; Giovanelli lifted his hat. Winterbourne had now begun to think simply of the craziness, from a sanitary point of view, of a delicate young girl lounging away the evening in this nest of malaria. What if she *were* a clever little reprobate? That was no reason for her dying of the *perniciosa.* "How long have you been here?" he asked, almost brutally.

Daisy, lovely in the flattering moonlight, looked at him a moment. Then—"All the evening," she answered, gently. . . . "I never saw anything so pretty."

"I am afraid," said Winterbourne, "that you will not think Roman fever very pretty. This is the way people catch it. I wonder," he added, turning to Giovanelli, "that you, a native Roman, should countenance such a terrible indiscretion."

"Ah," said the handsome native, "for myself I am not afraid."

"Neither am I—for you! I am speaking for this young lady."

Giovanelli lifted his well-shaped eyebrows and showed his brilliant teeth. But he took Winterbourne's rebuke with docility. "I told the signorina it was a grave indiscretion; but when was the signorina ever prudent?"

"I never was sick, and I don't mean to be!" the signorina declared. "I don't look like much, but I'm healthy! I was bound to see the Colosseum by moonlight; I shouldn't have wanted to go home without that; and we have had the most beautiful time, haven't we, Mr. Giovanelli? If there has been any danger, Eugenio can give me some pills. He has got some splendid pills."

"I should advise you," said Winterbourne, "to drive home as fast as possible and take one!"

"What you say is very wise," Giovanelli rejoined. "I will go and make sure the carriage is at hand." And he went forward rapidly.

Daisy followed with Winterbourne. He kept looking at her; she seemed not in the least embarrassed. Winterbourne said nothing; Daisy chattered about the beauty of the place. "Well, I *have* seen the Colosseum by moonlight!" she exclaimed. "That's one good thing." Then, noticing Winterbourne's silence, she asked him why he didn't speak. He made no answer; he only began to laugh. They passed under one of the dark archways; Giovanelli was in front with the carriage. Here Daisy stopped a moment, looking at the young American. "*Did* you believe I was engaged the other day?" she asked.

"It doesn't matter what I believed the other day," said Winterbourne, still laughing.

"Well, what do you believe now?"

"I believe that it makes very little difference whether you are engaged or not!"

He felt the young girl's pretty eyes fixed upon him through the thick gloom of the archway; she was apparently going to answer. But Giovanelli hurried her forward. "Quick! quick!" he said; "if we get in by midnight we are quite safe."

Daisy took her seat in the carriage, and the fortunate Italian placed himself beside her. "Don't forget Eugenio's pills!" said Winterbourne, as he lifted his hat.

"I don't care," said Daisy, in a little strange tone, "whether I have Roman fever or not!" Upon this the cabdriver cracked his whip, and they rolled away over the desultory patches of the antique pavement.

Winterbourne, to do him justice, as it were, mentioned to no one that he had encountered Miss Miller, at midnight, in the Colosseum with a gentleman; but, nevertheless, a couple of days later, the fact of her having been there under these circumstances was known to every member of the little American circle, and commented accordingly. Winterbourne reflected that they had of course known it at the hotel, and, that, after Daisy's return there had been an exchange of remarks between the porter and the cab-driver. But the young man was conscious, at the same moment, that it had ceased to be a matter of serious regret to him that the little American flirt should be "talked about" by low-minded menials. These people, a day or two later, had serious information to give: the little American flirt was alarmingly ill. Winterbourne, when the rumor came to him, immediately went to the hotel for more news. He found that two or three charitable friends had preceded him, and that they were being entertained in Mrs. Miller's salon by Randolph.

"It's going round at night," said Randolph—"that's what made her sick. She's always going round at night. I shouldn't think she'd want to, it's so plaguy dark. You can't see anything here at night, except when there's a moon! In America there's always a moon!" Mrs. Miller was invisible; she was now, at least, giving her daughter the advantage of her society. It was evident that Daisy was dangerously ill.

Winterbourne went often to ask for news of her, and once he saw Mrs. Miller, who, though deeply alarmed, was, rather to his surprise, perfectly composed, and, as it appeared, a most efficient and judicious nurse. She talked a good deal about Dr. Davis, but Winterbourne paid her the compliment of saying to himself that she was not, after all, such a monstrous goose. "Daisy spoke of you the other day," she said to him. "Half the time she doesn't know what she's saying, but that time I think she did. She gave me a message.

She told me to tell you—she told me to tell you that she never was engaged to that handsome Italian. I am sure I am very glad. Mr. Giovanelli hasn't been near us since she was taken ill. I thought he was so much of a gentleman; but I don't call that very polite! A lady told me that he was afraid I was angry with him for taking Daisy round at night. Well, so I am; but I suppose he knows I'm a lady. I would scorn to scold him. Anyway, she says she's not engaged. I don't know why she wanted you to know; but she said to me three times, 'Mind you tell Mr. Winterbourne.' And then she told me to ask if you remembered the time you went to that castle in Switzerland. But I said I wouldn't give any such messages as that. Only, if she is not engaged, I'm sure I'm glad to know it."

But, as Winterbourne had said, it mattered very little. A week after this the poor girl died; it had been a terrible case of the fever. Daisy's grave was in the little Protestant cemetery, in an angle of the wall of imperial Rome, beneath the cypresses and the thick spring-flowers. Winterbourne stood there beside it, with a number of other mourners—a number larger than the scandal excited by the young lady's career would have led you to expect. Near him stood Giovanelli, who came nearer still before Winterbourne turned away. Giovanelli was very pale: on this occasion he had no flower in his button-hole; he seemed to wish to say something. At last he said, "She was the most beautiful young lady I ever saw, and the most amiable"; and then he added in a moment, "and she was the most innocent."

Winterbourne looked at him, and presently repeated his words, "And the most innocent?"

"The most innocent!"

Winterbourne felt sore and angry. "Why, the devil," he asked, "did you take her to that fatal place?"

Mr. Giovanelli's urbanity was apparently imperturbable. He looked on the ground a moment, and then he said, "For myself I had no fear; and she wanted to go."

"That was no reason!" Winterbourne declared.

The subtle Roman again dropped his eyes. "If she had lived, I should have got nothing. She would never have married me, I am sure."

"She would never have married you?"

"For a moment I hoped so. But no. I am sure."

Winterbourne listened to him: he stood staring at the raw protuberance among the April daisies. When he turned away again, Mr. Giovanelli with his light, slow step, had retired.

Winterbourne almost immediately left Rome; but the following summer he again met his aunt, Mrs. Costello, at Vevey. Mrs. Costello was fond of Vevey. In the interval Winterbourne had often thought of Daisy Miller and her mystifying manners. One day he spoke of her to his aunt—said it was on his conscience that he had done her injustice.

"I am sure I don't know," said Mrs. Costello. "How did your injustice affect her?"

"She sent me a message before her death which I didn't understand at the time; but I have understood it since. She would have appreciated one's esteem."

"Is that a modest way," asked Mrs. Costello, "of saying that she would have reciprocated one's affection?"

Winterbourne offered no answer to this question; but he presently said, "You were right in that remark that you made last summer. I was booked to make a mistake. I have lived too long in foreign parts."

Nevertheless, he went back to live at Geneva, whence there continue to come the most contradictory accounts of his motives of sojourn: a report that he is "studying" hard—an intimation that he is much interested in a very clever foreign lady.

QUESTIONS FOR DISCUSSION

Part I

1. James introduces his audience to "some of the characteristics of an American watering-place." What are these characteristics? What impression would they give a European of the visiting Americans?

2. Frederick Winterbourne is introduced as a 27-year old American "studying" in Geneva. What is the narrator's attitude toward Winterbourne? What specific phrases from the narrator's description seem to characterize him best for you? Do you share the narrator's attitude toward Winterbourne?

3. Randolph Miller is a brat, but Winterbourne is attracted to him because he is reminded of his own childhood. Why is this seemingly minor and passing thought integral to the development of Winterbourne's attitude toward Daisy Miller?

4. *Daisy Miller* depends for much of its psychological tension upon the reader's sympathetic appreciation for the code of manners acceptable

to all well-bred Europeans and Americans in the 1870's. The first reference to social decorum is the narrator's statement, "It seemed to Winterbourne that he had been in a manner presented." What does this mean? Is there a contemporary obligation to fulfill this matter of decorum? How many other social regulations can you infer from the events of this story?

5. Winterbourne is readily attracted to Daisy Miller. What are the qualities in her appearance and character that attract him? What is his first impression of her?

6. Like others of Henry James' Americans abroad, the Miller family represents the *nouveau riche*, industrialists who have become wealthy quickly but have not had time to acquire the manners and breeding that Europeans thought should accompany wealth. Christopher Newman, the manufacturer of washtubs in *The American*, is another example. What are the evidences of the Millers' lack of culture? What marks Mrs. Miller, for example, as a drearily provincial person?

7. Daisy Miller complains to Winterbourne that Europe has no society: "There isn't any society; or, if there is, I don't know where it keeps itself." What has she failed to realize about herself and her behavior in Europe? What is ironic about her later statement, "We don't speak to everyone—or they don't speak to us"?

8. Perhaps the most important paragraph in Part I is that which begins, "Poor Winterbourne was amused, perplexed, and decidedly charmed." Reread this paragraph with great care and discuss the narrator's success at working from inside Winterbourne's conscious rationalization to show the variety of alternatives in his thinking. In what ways does the decision he reaches in this paragraph determine the rest of Winterbourne's behavior toward Daisy Miller?

9. The castle of Chillon on Lake Geneva had been the prison of François de Bonnivard in the sixteenth century. Lord Byron wrote two poems, "Sonnet on Chillon" and "The Prisoner of Chillon," romanticizing the location. As such it seems like the perfect place for Winterbourne to escort Daisy Miller. But she has her own reasons for wishing to be taken there. What are these reasons? How far does she fulfill them?

10. Winterbourne thinks to himself that Daisy has the bearing (*tournure*) of a princess. In what respects is Henry James presenting Daisy Miller as an American counterpart to European royalty?

11. Mrs. Costello is herself an American; yet she says of Daisy's family that "they are the sort of Americans that one does one's duty by not—not accepting." What does she mean? Where does Mrs. Costello fit into the social hierarchy being established in this story? Where do the others fit?

12. Even from the indirect language employed by James, the reader can confirm the fact that Winterbourne himself is not sexually naive. As he tells his aunt, "I am not so innocent." What statements made by the narrator express Winterbourne's passion for Daisy Miller? Which of these statements show him to be an opportunist in romance?

13. By the end of Part I, what is your estimate of the relationship between Winterbourne and Daisy Miller? What evidences can you find to support Professor F. W. Dupee's contention that "she is entirely in love with him"?

Part II

14. "Roman fever" was a malarial disease. Superstition attributed the sickness to the unwholesome miasma emanating from the swamps after dark. Hence it was thought dangerous to be out late at night in the streets of Rome. The Colosseum was considered particularly dangerous. How does James prepare the reader for Daisy Miller's eventual sickness and death? Why is "Roman fever" so dramatically well chosen as the disease she should contract?

15. After hearing about Daisy's associations with various men and then meeting Giovanelli, what revision in opinion does Winterbourne reach? What does he fail to understand?

16. F. W. Dupee says that this story is "both a love story and a story of comparative manners." When Winterbourne asks Mrs. Walker to tell what Daisy has been doing, she says, "Everything that is not done here," and proceeds with a condemning list. Look carefully at that list and discuss what was objectionable in the 1870's and why. Which of these definitions of improper conduct remain today?

17. Giovanelli is presented as a "Roman fortune-hunter." What descriptive mannerisms does James employ to make Giovanelli appear like the stereotyped and cynical romantic adventurer? What action confirms this impression? How does Giovanelli's conversation with Winterbourne affect your impression?

18. Winterbourne tells Daisy, "Flirting is a purely American custom; it doesn't exist here." What is the importance of this remark to an understanding of Daisy and the rest of her story?

19. Do you find any significance to the elements of the scene in the Colosseum: Winterbourne in the arena, Daisy and Giovanelli at the cross, the mention of wild animals and Christian martyrs?

20. What do you make of Winterbourne's remark to Mrs. Costello, "I have lived too long in foreign parts"? Discuss the implications of this self-criticism in light of the story's final paragraph.

21. *Daisy Miller* is regarded by many readers as one of Henry James' most comic stories. Leon Edel, for example, says of the story, "The comedy concealed the essential pathos of Daisy, a girl bright and shimmering, yet ill-prepared for life." What are the elements of comedy that you find in this story?

22. Examine two or three paragraphs at random and note the particular aspects of James' style—his diction, syntax, length of sentences, punctuation. In what respects is this style especially suitable in narrating a story of manners and society?

ASSIGNMENTS FOR WRITING

1. F. W. Dupee writes:

    Daisy is a tribute to the American girl, whose radical innocence is
    shown to triumph over the evil-mindedness of the old world as well
    as over her own rash conduct and indifferent manners.

    In a critical essay, argue in support of or in opposition to Professor
    Dupee's statement. Use the text of the story to support your argument.

2. Leon Edel has said of Henry James' work:

    James's tales belong to an old society and are governed by old laws
    and old conventions. These may seem quaint and outmoded now, but
    . . . Americans are still critical of Europe; and we know how the
    Europeans feel about Americans. Customs may have changed; auto-
    mobiles have replaced James's carriages; yet the life, the situations,
    the problems, in some of these early stories, remain as vivid and as
    dramatic as they were a century ago.

    On the basis of your experience—in travel, in conversation with travel-
    ers, in reading—discuss the validity of this description of James' work.
    Give current examples, if you can, to support your observations.

3. Most of us have known European visitors or immigrants to America.
    Write an informal essay or a short story in which you describe the
    problems of a European adjusting to American customs.

4. What are the essential characteristics of the American girl today? Write
    a thoughtful analysis of the American girl's behavior one hundred
    years after Daisy Miller. How is she different? What factors in history,
    in politics and economics, in legislation and mores, in education and
    belief have contributed to change? In what respects is she the same?
    Why?

Stephen Crane

Stephen Crane, the son of a Methodist minister, was born on November 1, 1871, in Newark, New Jersey. Twenty-nine years later, on June 5, 1900, he died of tuberculosis, far from home and family, far from the traditions that worked to keep so many Americans of the late nineteenth century rigidly Victorian. Early in his life Crane broke with the religious teachings of his father to journey on his own. His journey was not well charted, but it did have a destination: Stephen Crane was in search of truth.

His rebellion was not so much against God or Christianity as it was against the stifling legalism he found in institutionalized religion. Stephen Crane could not accept any man or institution whose religious principles failed to account for the day-to-day problems of life. He felt that its preoccupation with temperance and the sins of worldly amusement had left the church without energy to combat the real evils of poverty and social inequality. In place of a religious creed, Crane adopted a personal code: "To keep close to this personal honesty is my supreme ambition."

The quest to satisfy his own integrity took Crane away from home at sixteen; thereafter, he never found more than a temporary stopping place. He attended college briefly, both Lafayette and Syracuse, but soon dropped out. Sports and newspaper writing appealed to Crane more than the classroom. From spotty, free-lance assignments in small New York and New Jersey towns, he moved to New York City in 1892, bringing with him the manuscript of *Maggie: A Girl of the Streets*. This short novel about a wretched slum child passed through several revisions, made after Crane's firsthand observation of life on the Bowery authenticated his desperately unhappy tale, without satisfying a publisher. One prospective publisher called the book "cruel," its characters showing "no tenderness and no restraint of action to excuse their callousness." Crane felt that what the critic really meant was that the novel was too straightforward in its treatment of human conditions. He was determined to see *Maggie* in print. Borrowing enough to pay a printer, Crane had his wish fulfilled in March, 1893. He used the pseudonym "Johnston Smith" to protect his family from any possible embarrassment resulting from the book's presentation of prostitution and suicide.

Crane scarcely needed to have been so discreet; *Maggie* passed almost unnoticed from the literary scene. Major booksellers refused to sell it. But *Maggie* did obtain a select audience of distinguished writers, including the influential man of letters William Dean Howells and his younger friend Hamlin Garland. Howells and Garland had shared their private enthusiasm over the book and its uniqueness of language. They saw *Maggie* as a development toward the realism in literature that they both advocated. Howells, for example, had written *A Modern Instance* (1882), the first American novel to treat divorce as a fact of life. Garland's stories about the privations of rural life in the "Middle Border" had proved him to be one of Howells' disciples. In urging realism, both men were demanding no more than a respect for life as it is, rather than as it may be idealized by the frail and the prudish.

Howells and Garland encouraged Crane to continue his career as a writer, in spite of financial precariousness. To Garland Crane confided another literary interest—poetry. In 1894, Crane took Garland some of his poems to evaluate. Impressed with their stabbing power, Garland asked if Crane had any others. Crane pointed to his head and answered, "I've got five or six all in a little row up here. That's the way they come—in little rows, all made up, ready to be put down on paper." Indeed, this characteristic immediacy—an apparent spontaneity of expression in meter and in metaphor—remains one of the most positive qualities of Crane's poetry. Frequently marred by problems of diction and rhythm, Crane's poems nonetheless retain the power to stamp a lasting impression on the reader's mind.

Garland was particularly helpful during the writing of the one novel that was to establish Crane's reputation—*The Red Badge of Courage*, published in 1895. Much was made of the fact that, when he wrote *The Red Badge of Courage*, Crane had never seen a battle, yet his battle scenes were powerful and genuine. The tribute is, of course, in praise of Crane's imagination and evocative language which produce a realistic description of war at its worst.

But Crane was shortly to experience war firsthand. His fame

increased after the popular success of *The Red Badge of Courage*, and he received assignments as a war correspondent in both the Greco-Turkish and the Spanish-American wars. Some of his best stories and sketches—among them "The Upturned Face," "An Episode of War," and "Regulars Get No Glory"—developed from these experiences. Crane threw himself wholeheartedly into his role as a combat journalist; he was, in the minds of some colleagues, foolhardy about risking injury in the pursuit of the closest possible contact with the action. Such personal involvement shows itself clearly in his journalistic accounts. He was not the cool, aloof reporter, the objective observer of the scene before him. Instead, he identified with the troops he favored, describing, for instance, a group of marines after a night of fighting as "utterly worn to rags, with their nerves standing on end like so many bristles."

Nor could Stephen Crane content himself with the essentials of factual reporting; he often gave in to the urge to editorialize on what he saw. In "Regulars Get No Glory," he offered a subjective interpretation of an ambush into which Teddy Roosevelt's Rough Riders had been stupidly ordered: "It was simply a gallant blunder."

From his experiences as a correspondent came two of his most enduring imaginative works. On New Year's Eve, 1896, Crane shipped aboard the *Commodore*, a vessel used to run guns from Florida to Cuba. On the ocean off Daytona Beach, the ship foundered, and although Crane and the crew worked to save the ship, they were at last forced to abandon ship in a small dinghy. Crane and his companions spent most of two perilous days and nights staving off the ocean, as "Stephen Crane's Own Story" reports. After their rescue Crane wrote "The Open Boat," the story of the captain, the cook, the oiler, and the correspondent, who struggle against nature's "abominable injustice." The story is memorable for its introspection, for its sustained mood of crisis. Perhaps most memorable, however, is the quiet understatement of the story, as in the opening sentence: "None of them knew the color of the sky."

The *Commodore* experience is also clearly reflected in the poem, "A man adrift on a slim spar," which Crane wrote shortly after the catastrophe at sea. Out of this experience, then, came three distinct aspects of Crane the artist at work: as journalist, as fiction writer, and as poet. In each of these forms, Crane held the same opinion of man's courage in the face of inexorable doom. Only in the poetry, however, is man's lifelong struggle with an indifferent God clearly revealed. The poet Amy Lowell observed that "Crane's soul was heaped with bitterness and this bitterness he flung back at the theory of life which had betrayed him."

Since to Crane's mind God was indifferent, man's only alternative was to declare his individuality and to fight those restrictions placed upon his individuality by society and religion. If, furthermore, the force of man's individuality collided with a malign or indifferent deity, the fault was not man's for asserting himself. Like the speaker in a poem who addresses the universe, "Sir, I exist!" Crane insisted upon man's uniqueness; he was not cowed by the universe's heartless reply:

> "However," replied the universe,
> "The fact has not created in me
> A sense of obligation."

Stephen Crane saw the plight of the individual in such a universe, and what he saw, he saw increasingly through the perspective of naturalism. Naturalism developed out of the realism of writers such as Howells and Garland; but naturalism is more than a literary fashion, for the naturalist holds particular philosophical connections with Darwin's hypothesis and with the theories of heredity and environmental influence. Idealism and emotional commitment are irrelevant; brutish desires and animal instincts are emphasized.

Where the realist writer would see a war, Crane the naturalist saw a dying soldier passing through "this spectacle of gradual strangulation." Where some might see a civil rights issue, Crane saw society's predictable rejection of a Negro who had been horribly disfigured saving a white man's child. Where many might see the passion of a shipload of drowning victims, Crane saw a noble futility in the struggle of the oiler Billy Higgins against the sea.

Crane's concern for the individual was, however, more than merely aesthetic or psychological; it was also distinctly social. The American novelist Ralph Ellison praised Crane's story, "The Monster," and spoke of "the timeliness of its implications." Although Henry Johnson was grotesquely burned in a fire, it was not his hideous scars alone which accounted for his ostracism by society. He was a Negro, whose rejection by those for whom he sacrificed his body and risked his life is only the outward manifestation of a latent barrier to his acceptance as a human being. How remarkable that, in the period when the Supreme Court's decision in *Plessy* v. *Ferguson* (1896) was upholding the doctrine of "separate but equal" segregation, Crane should speak out boldly against the monstrosity of supposed racial supremacy.

Crane's naturalism represents men and their environment with a stark, brutal, naked honesty which reveals all their defects as well as their assets. In fact, Crane was the first American author to exhibit, as a major characteristic of his writing, a terse directness of style and a rapidly moving skeletal prose which have earned him recognition as a forerunner of Ernest Hemingway. For example, his description of wounded soldiers in *The Red Badge of Courage* leaves no doubt of his straightforwardness: "red, live bones sticking out through slits in the faded uniforms."

Such vividness causes the reader to see and to feel; the force of emotional impact is achieved not through lengthy, heartrending accounts but by simple, direct description which hides no hideous facts. To be concise and to be of crashing effect are typically Crane.

But Crane was also a writer with vast creative and figurative power, the genius of originality. With most authors we sense a somewhat familiar sound in their comparisons. The incongruities of Crane's comparisons, however, are often their very strength. In *Maggie*, for example, Crane describes a man who has just purchased round after round of drinks for those crowded next to the bar: "He was in a proper mood of missionaries," says Crane, the Methodist preacher's son, knowing well the incongruity of his metaphor for sharing. In "The Monster," Crane describes the rapid dispersion of a street-corner gang by saying that they vanished "like a snowball disrupted by dynamite." Once more, the incongruity of juxtaposing two incompatible terms appeals to the imagination, creating a vivid and telling image.

Crane relied heavily on irony to convey his impressions. Frequently this ironic method touches a scene with the humor inherent when a character fails to recognize himself as he appears to others. In *The Red Badge of Courage*, for instance, young Henry Fleming sought desperately to prove himself worthy of his comrades' respect. In the moments of his most courageous acts, he saw himself "shrieking mad calls," feeling "the daring spirit of a savage religion mad." Later though, Henry's maturer reflections recall that "he had been an animal blistered and sweating in the heat and pain of war." There is massive irony implicit in a man's returning to animalistic behavior to prove his manhood and to gain acceptance by other men. The irony encompasses not only Henry Fleming, but also war itself, which Crane described as "the red animal—war, the blood-swollen god."

In many respects, the intensity of Crane's treatment of his themes reveals his youth—his harsher critics would say, his immaturity. Yet in a day when man is struggling to assert and to retain his individuality, when religious and social traditions are coming under serious scrutiny, Stephen Crane's work takes on an added relevance. His honesty in language and in subject has fulfilled his "supreme ambition," earning for him Hemingway's praise as one of the three or four authentically American writers.

An Episode of War

The lieutenant's rubber blanket lay on the ground, and upon it he had poured the company's supply of coffee. Corporals and other representatives of the grimy and hot-throated men who lined the breastwork had come for each squad's portion.

The lieutenant was frowning and serious at this task of division. His lips pursed as he drew with his sword various crevices in the heap, until brown squares of coffee, astoundingly equal in size, appeared on the blanket. He was on the verge of a great triumph in mathematics, and the corporals were thronging forward, each to reap a little square, when suddenly the lieutenant cried out and looked quickly at a man near him as if he suspected it was a case of personal assault. The others cried out also when they saw blood upon the lieutenant's sleeve.

He had winced like a man stung, swayed dangerously, and then straightened. The sound of his hoarse breathing was plainly audible. He looked sadly, mystically, over the breastwork at the green face of a wood, where now were many little puffs of white smoke. During this moment the men about him gazed statuelike and silent, astonished and awed by this catastrophe which happened when catastrophes are not expected—when they had leisure to observe it.

As the lieutenant stared at the wood, they too swung their heads, so that for another instant all hands, still silent, contemplated the distant forest as if their minds were fixed upon the mystery of a bullet's journey.

The officer had, of course, been compelled to take his sword into his left hand. He did not hold it by the hilt. He gripped it at the middle of the blade, awkwardly. Turning his eyes from the hostile wood, he looked at the sword as he held it there, and seemed puzzled as to what to do with it, where to put it. In short, this weapon had of a sudden become a strange thing to him. He looked at it in a kind of stupefaction, as if he had been endowed with a trident, a scepter, or a spade.

Finally he tried to sheathe it. To sheathe a sword held by the left hand, at the middle of the blade, in a scabbard hung at the left hip, is a feat worthy of a sawdust ring. This wounded officer engaged in a desperate struggle with the sword and the wobbling scabbard, and during the time of it he breathed like a wrestler.

But at this instant the men, the spectators, awoke from their stonelike poses and crowded forward sympathetically. The orderly-sergeant took the sword and tenderly placed it in the scabbard. At the time, he leaned nervously backward and did not allow even his finger to brush the body of the lieutenant. A wound gives strange dignity to him who bears it. Well men shy from this new and terrible majesty. It is as if the wounded man's hand is upon the curtain which hangs before the revelations of all existence—the meaning of ants, potentates, wars, cities, sunshine, snow, a feather dropped from a bird's wing; and the power of it sheds radiance upon a bloody form, and makes the other men understand sometimes that they are little. His comrades look at him with large eyes thoughtfully. Moreover, they fear vaguely that the weight of a finger upon him might send him headlong, precipitate the tragedy, hurl him at once into the dim, gray unknown. And so the orderly-sergeant, while sheathing the sword, leaned nervously backward.

There were others who proffered assistance. One timidly presented his shoulder and asked the lieutenant if he cared to lean upon it, but the latter waved him away mournfully. He wore the look of one who knows he is the victim of a terrible disease and understands his helplessness. He again stared over the breastwork at the forest, and then, turning, went slowly rearward. He held his right wrist tenderly in his left hand as if the wounded arm was made of very brittle glass.

And the men in silence stared at the wood, then at the departing lieutenant—then at the wood, then at the lieutenant.

As the wounded officer passed from the line of battle, he was enabled to see many things which as a participant in the fight were unknown to him. He saw a general on a black horse gazing over the lines of blue infantry at the green woods which veiled his problems. An aide galloped furiously, dragged his horse suddenly to a halt, saluted, and presented a paper. It was, for a wonder, precisely like a historical painting.

To the rear of the general and his staff a group, composed of a bugler, two or three orderlies, and the bearer of the corps standard, all upon maniacal horses, were working like slaves to hold their ground, preserve their respectful interval, while the shells boomed in the air about them and caused their chargers to make furious quivering leaps.

A battery, a tumultuous and shining mass, was swirling toward the right. The wild thud of hoofs, the cries of the riders shouting blame and praise, menace and encouragement, and, last, the roar of the wheels, the slant of the glistening guns, brought the lieutenant to an intent pause. The battery swept in curves that stirred the heart; it made halts as dramatic as the crash of a wave on the rocks, and when it fled onward this aggregation of wheels, levers, motors had a beautiful unity, as if it were a missile. The sound of it was a war-chorus that reached into the depths of man's emotion.

The lieutenant, still holding his arm as if it were of glass, stood watching this battery until all detail of it was lost, save the figures of the riders, which rose and fell and waved lashes over the black mass.

Later, he turned his eyes toward the battle, where the shooting sometimes crackled like bush fires, sometimes sputtered with exasperating irregularity, and sometimes reverberated like the thunder. He saw the smoke rolling upward and saw crowds of men who ran and cheered, or stood and blazed away at the inscrutable distance.

He came upon some stragglers, and they told him how to find the field hospital. They described its exact location. In fact, these men, no longer having part in the battle, knew more of it than others. They told the performance of every corps, every division, the opinion of every general. The lieutenant, carrying his wounded arm rearward, looked upon them with wonder.

At the roadside a brigade was making coffee and buzzing with talk like a girls' boarding school. Several officers came out to him and inquired concerning things of which he knew nothing. One, seeing his arm, began to scold. "Why, man, that's no way to do. You want to fix that thing." He appropriated the lieutenant and the lieutenant's wound. He cut the sleeve and laid bare the arm, every nerve of which softly fluttered under his touch. He bound his handkerchief over the wound, scolding away in the meantime. His tone allowed one to think that he was in the habit of being wounded every day. The lieutenant hung his head, feeling, in this presence, that he did not know how to be correctly wounded.

The low white tents of the hospital were grouped around an old schoolhouse. There was here a singular commotion. In the foreground two ambulances interlocked wheels in the deep mud. The drivers were tossing the blame of it back and forth, gesticulating and berating, while from the ambulances, both crammed with wounded, there came an occasional groan. An interminable crowd of bandaged men were coming and going. Great numbers sat under the trees nursing heads or arms or legs. There was a dispute of some kind raging on the steps of the schoolhouse. Sitting with his back against a tree a man with a face as gray as a new army blanket was serenely smoking a corncob pipe. The lieutenant wished to rush forward and inform him that he was dying.

A busy surgeon was passing near the lieutenant. "Good morning," he said, with a friendly smile. Then he caught sight of the lieutenant's arm, and his face at once changed. "Well, let's have a look at it." He seemed possessed suddenly of a great contempt for the lieutenant. This wound evidently placed the latter on a very low social plane. The doctor cried out impatiently: "What muttonhead had tied it up that way anyhow?" The lieutenant answered, "Oh, a man."

When the wound was disclosed, the doctor fingered it disdainfully. "Humph," he said. "You come along with me and I'll tend to you." His voice contained the same scorn as if he were saying: "You will have to go to jail."

The lieutenant had been very meek, but now his face flushed, and he looked into the doctor's eyes. "I guess I won't have it amputated," he said.

"Nonsense, man! Nonsense! Nonsense!" cried the doctor. "Come along, now. I won't amputate it. Come along. Don't be a baby."

"Let go of me," said the lieutenant, holding back wrathfully, his glance fixed upon the door of the old schoolhouse, as sinister to him as the portals of death.

And this is the story of how the lieutenant lost his arm. When he reached home, his sisters, his mother, his wife, sobbed for a long time at the sight of the flat sleeve. "Oh, well," he said, standing shamefaced amid these tears, "I don't suppose it matters so much as all that."

QUESTIONS FOR DISCUSSION

1. Crane made effective use of repetition. Sometimes the repeated words follow immediately and sometimes paragraphs separate them. Observe the repetition regarding the lieutenant's breathing; his

treatment of his arm; the other soldiers as they view him in a statuelike manner, as the orderly-sergeant sheathes his sword, and as he departs rearward. What effect is created by this repetition?

2. Trace the lieutenant's reactions to others following his wound: to his own men, the stragglers, the brigade, the surgeon, and his family. What is most characteristic of his reaction? Can this attitude be understood in view of how the wound was received? Explain.

3. Crane's irony relates to several incidents: the lieutenant's division of the coffee, the immense knowledge of the stragglers, the arm-bandaging officer, and the time-consuming argument of the ambulance drivers. Explain in what sense each of these incidents is ironic.

ASSIGNMENT FOR WRITING

Crane excelled in the use of colorful verbs. The lieutenant "winced like a man stung, swayed dangerously, and then straightened." The shooting "sometimes crackled like bush fires, sometimes sputtered with exasperating irregularity, and sometimes reverberated like the thunder." Often Crane's vivid verbs are joined to similes and metaphors. Write a paragraph portraying intense action, such as that at a sports event or political rally. Attempt to use precise and colorful verbs, similes, and metaphors. The reader of your paragraph should experience a rapidly moving panorama as he visualizes the action you depict.

The Upturned Face

"What will we do now?" said the adjutant, troubled and excited.

"Bury him," said Timothy Lean.

The two officers looked down close to their toes, where lay the body of their comrade. The face was chalk-blue; gleaming eyes stared at the sky. Over the two upright figures was a windy sound of bullets, and on the top of the hill Lean's prostrate company of Spitzbergen infantry was firing measured volleys.

"Don't you think it would be better—" began the adjutant. "We might leave him until tomorrow."

"No," said Lean. "I can't hold that post an hour longer. I've got to fall back, and we've got to bury old Bill."

"Of course," said the adjutant, at once. "Your men got entrenching tools?"

Lean shouted back to his little line, and two men came slowly, one with a pick, one with a shovel. They started in the direction of the Rostina sharpshooters. Bullets cracked near their ears. "Dig here," said Lean gruffly. The men, thus caused to lower their glances to the turf, became hurried and frightened, merely because they could not look to see whence the bullets came. The dull beat of the pick striking the earth sounded amid the swift snap of close bullets. Presently the other private began to shovel.

"I suppose," said the adjutant, slowly, "we'd better search his clothes for—things."

Lean nodded. Together in curious abstraction they looked at the body. Then Lean stirred his shoulders suddenly, arousing himself.

"Yes," he said, "we'd better see what he's got." He dropped to his knees, and his hands approached the body of the dead officer. But his hands wavered over the buttons of the tunic. The first button was brick-red with drying blood, and he did not seem to dare touch it.

"Go on," said the adjutant, hoarsely.

Lean stretched his wooden hand, and his fingers fumbled the bloodstained buttons. At last he rose with ghastly face. He had gathered a watch, a whistle, a pipe, a tobacco pouch, a handkerchief, a little case of cards and papers. He looked at the adjutant.

There was a silence. The adjutant was feeling that he had been a coward to make Lean do all the grisly business.

"Well," said Lean, "that's all, I think. You have his sword and revolver?"

"Yes," said the adjutant, his face working, and then he burst out in a sudden strange fury at the two privates. "Why don't you hurry up with that grave? What are you doing, anyhow? Hurry, do you hear? I never saw such stupid—"

Even as he cried out in his passion the two men were laboring for their lives. Ever overhead the bullets were spitting.

The grave was finished. It was not a masterpiece—a poor little shallow thing. Lean and the adjutant again looked at each other in a curious silent communication.

Suddenly the adjutant croaked out a weird laugh. It was a terrible laugh, which had its origin in that part of the mind which is first moved by the singing of the nerves. "Well," he said humorously to Lean, "I suppose we had best tumble him in."

"Yes," said Lean. The two privates stood waiting, bent over their implements. "I suppose," said Lean, "it would be better if we laid him in ourselves."

"Yes," said the adjutant. Then, apparently remembering that he had made Lean search the body, he stooped with great fortitude and took hold of the dead officer's clothing. Lean joined him. Both were particular that their fingers should not feel the corpse. They tugged away; the corpse lifted, heaved, toppled, flopped into the grave, and the two officers, straightening, looked again at each other—they were always looking at each other. They sighed with relief.

The adjutant said, "I suppose we should—we should say something. Do you know the service, Tim?"

"They don't read the service until the grave is filled in," said Lean, pressing his lips to an academic expression.

"Don't they?" said the adjutant, shocked that he had made the mistake. "Oh, well," he cried, suddenly, "let us—let us say something—while he can hear us."

"All right," said Lean. "Do you know the service?"

"I can't remember a line of it," said the adjutant.

Lean was extremely dubious. "I can repeat two lines, but—"

"Well, do it," said the adjutant. "Go as far as you can. That's better than nothing. And the beasts have got our range exactly."

Lean looked at his two men. "Attention," he barked. The privates came to attention with a click, looking much aggrieved. The adjutant lowered his helmet to his knee. Lean, bareheaded, stood over the grave. The Rostina sharpshooters fired briskly.

"O Father, our friend has sunk in the deep waters of death, but his spirit has leaped toward Thee as the bubble arises from the lips of the drowning. Perceive, we beseech, O Father, the little flying bubble, and—"

Lean, although husky and ashamed, had suffered no hesitation up to this point, but he stopped with a hopeless feeling and looked at the corpse.

The adjutant moved uneasily. "And from Thy superb heights—" he began, and then he too came to an end.

"And from Thy superb heights," said Lean.

The adjutant suddenly remembered a phrase in the back of the Spitzbergen burial service, and he exploited it with the triumphant manner of a man who has recalled everything, and can go on.

"O God, have mercy—"

"O God, have mercy—" said Lean.

"Mercy," repeated the adjutant, in quick failure.

"Mercy," said Lean. And then he was moved by some violence of feeling, for he turned upon his two men and tigerishly said, "Throw the dirt in."

The fire of the Rostina sharpshooters was accurate and continuous.

One of the aggrieved privates came forward with his shovel. He lifted his first shovel-load of earth, and for a moment of inexplicable hesitation it was held poised above this corpse, which from its chalk-blue face looked keenly out from the grave. Then the soldier emptied his shovel on—on the feet.

Timothy Lean felt as if tons had been swiftly lifted from off his forehead. He had felt that perhaps the private might empty the shovel on—on the face. It had been emptied on the feet. There was a great point gained there—ha, ha!—the first shovelful had been emptied on the feet. How satisfactory!

The adjutant began to babble. "Well, of course—a man we've messed with all these years—impossible—you can't, you know, leave your intimate friends rotting on the field. Go on, for God's sake, and shovel, you."

The man with the shovel suddenly ducked, grabbed his left arm with his right hand, and looked at his officer for orders. Lean picked the shovel from the ground. "Go to the rear," he said to the wounded man. He also addressed the other private. "You get under cover, too; I'll finish this business."

The wounded man scrambled hard still for the top of the ridge without devoting any glances to the direction from whence the bullets came, and the other man followed at an equal pace; but he was different, in that he looked back anxiously three times.

This is merely the way—often—of the hit and unhit.

Timothy Lean filled the shovel, hesitated, and then, in a movement which was like a gesture of abhorrence, he flung the dirt into the grave, and as it landed it made a sound—plop. Lean suddenly stopped and mopped his brow—a tired laborer.

"Perhaps we have been wrong," said the adjutant. His glance wavered stupidly. "It might have been better if we hadn't buried him just at this time. Of course, if we advance tomorrow the body would have been—"

"Damn you," said Lean, "shut your mouth." He was not the senior officer.

He again filled the shovel and flung the earth. Always the earth made that sound—plop. For a space Lean worked frantically, like a man digging himself out of danger.

Soon there was nothing to be seen but the chalk-blue face. Lean filled the shovel. "Good God," he cried to the adjutant. "Why didn't you turn him somehow when you put him in? This—" Then Lean began to stutter.

The adjutant understood. He was pale to the lips. "Go on, man," he cried, beseechingly, almost in a shout.

Lean swung back the shovel. It went forward in a pendulum curve. When the earth landed it made a sound—plop.

QUESTIONS FOR DISCUSSION

1. Stephen Crane had a strong anti-officer prejudice; his was the voice of the common soldier. The adjutant is an object of scorn in this story. Cite at least four instances which reveal the adjutant's inadequacy.

2. This story is marked by hesitation—hesitation in dialogue and action. During this time, "The fire of the Rostina sharpshooters was accurate and continuous." Explain the effect of the paradoxical combination of threatening rifle fire and hesitation by its intended victims. What does it suggest about the wisdom of the officers' orders? How does it heighten the action?

3. The burial is delayed by a series of problems and concerns affecting the officers. Enumerate the complications confronting the officers. At what point does this progression of complications lead to the climax?

ASSIGNMENT FOR WRITING

Irony may be verbal or dramatic. Select from this story an example of either an ironic statement or an ironic action. In a brief essay, explain in what way the statement or action is ironic. How does the irony relate to the story as a whole?

"God fashioned the ship of the world carefully"

God fashioned the ship of the world carefully.
With the infinite skill of an All-Master
Made He the hull and the sails,
Held He the rudder
Ready for adjustment.
Erect stood He, scanning His work proudly.
Then—at fateful time—a wrong called,
And God turned, heeding.
Lo, the ship, at this opportunity, slipped slyly,
Making cunning noiseless travel down the ways.
So that, for ever rudderless, it went upon the seas
Going ridiculous voyages,
Making quaint progress,
Turning as with serious purpose
Before stupid winds.
And there were many in the sky
Who laughed at this thing.

"A slant of sun on dull brown walls"

A slant of sun on dull brown walls,
A forgotten sky of bashful blue.

Toward God a mighty hymn,
A song of collisions and cries,
Rumbling wheels, hoof-beats, bells,
Welcomes, farewells, love-calls, final moans,
Voices of joy, idiocy, warning, despair,
The unknown appeals of brutes,
The chanting of flowers,
The screams of cut trees,
The senseless babble of hens and wise men—
A cluttered incoherency that says at the stars:
"O God, save us!"

"A god in wrath"

A god in wrath
Was beating a man;
He cuffed him loudly
With thunderous blows
That rang and rolled over the earth.
All people came running.
The man screamed and struggled,
And bit madly at the feet of the god.
The people cried,
"Ah, what a wicked man!"
And—
"Ah, what a redoubtable god!"

"A man said to the universe"

A man said to the universe:
"Sir, I exist!"
"However," replied the universe,
"The fact has not created in me
A sense of obligation."

"A man adrift on a slim spar"

A man adrift on a slim spar
A horizon smaller than the rim of a bottle
Tented waves rearing lashy dark points
The near whine of froth in circles.
                          God is cold.

The incessant raise and swing of the sea
The growl after growl of crest
The sinkings, green, seething, endless
The upheaval half-completed.

       God is cold.

The seas are in the hollow of The Hand;
Oceans may be turned to a spray
Raining down through the stars
Because of a gesture of pity toward a babe.
Oceans may become gray ashes,
Die with a long moan and a roar
Amid the tumult of the fishes
And the cries of the ships,
Because The Hand beckons the mice.
A horizon smaller than a doomed assassin's cap,
Inky, surging tumults
A reeling, drunken sky and no sky
A pale hand sliding from a polished spar.

       God is cold.

The puff of a coat imprisoning air:
A face kissing the water-death
A weary slow sway of a lost hand
And the sea, the moving sea, the sea.

       God is cold.

"To the maiden"

To the maiden
The sea was blue meadow,
Alive with little froth-people
Singing.

To the sailor, wrecked,
The sea was dead gray walls
Superlative in vacancy,
Upon which nevertheless at fateful time
Was written
The grim hatred of nature.

"A newspaper is a collection of half-injustices"

A newspaper is a collection of half-injustices
Which, bawled by boys from mile to mile,
Spreads its curious opinion
To a million merciful and sneering men,
While families cuddle the joys of the fireside
When spurred by tale of dire lone agony.
A newspaper is a court
Where everyone is kindly and unfairly tried
By a squalor of honest men.
A newspaper is a market
Where wisdom sells its freedom
And melons are crowned by the crowd.
A newspaper is a game
Where his error scores the player victory
While another's skill wins death.
A newspaper is a symbol;
It is feckless life's chronicle,
A collection of loud tales
Concentrating eternal stupidities,
That in remote ages lived unhaltered,
Roaming through a fenceless world.

"In the desert"

In the desert
I saw a creature, naked, bestial,
Who, squatting upon the ground,
Held his heart in his hands,
And ate of it.
I said, "Is it good, friend?"
"It is bitter—bitter," he answered;
"But I like it
Because it is bitter,
And because it is my heart."

(Continued on page 481)

The West

GEORGE CALEB BINGHAM: Fur Traders Descending the Missouri, 1845

On the river of Lewis and Clark, where the West begins, a strange trio floats through a vast, misty landscape in a dugout canoe. Mirrored in the water, the quizzical trader in his red shirt and stocking cap, a relic of the days before the steamboat; his companion, a sunny, dreaming youth; the creepy black fox, a malevolent presence, a kind of bad luck mascot. Put them together and you have one of the most unforgettable images in American art. This was the first genre scene of river life that Bingham painted. He followed it up with the popular *Jolly Flatboatman* and *Raftsmen Playing Cards*.

GEORGE CATLIN: Pigeon's Egg Head (The Light) going to and returning from Washington, 1831/32

It was the destiny of Catlin (1796-1872) to do for the Indians of North America what Audubon had done for its birds. He spent seven years making a comprehensive pictorial record of Indian life between the Mississippi and the Rocky Mountains. "I have visited forty-eight different tribes," he was later to claim, "I have brought home safe and in good order, 310 portraits in oil, all painted in their native dress, and in their own wigwams; and also 200 other paintings in oil, containing views of their villages —their wigwams—their games and religious ceremonies—their dances—their ball plays—their buffalo hunting *(below)* . . . and the landscape of the country they live in." He visited the Mandans, Crows, Blackfeet, Crees, Assiniboines, Hidatsas, Arikaras, Sioux, Poncas, Sauks and Foxes, Chippewas, Menominies, Winnebagos, and Iowas. In the Mandan village, Catlin was allowed to witness and record their strange torture ceremonies, part religious rite and part test of bravery. He got there just in time. Five years later virtually the entire tribe was wiped out by smallpox; the rest scattered, and the Mandans completely disappeared from history.

Pigeon's Egg Head *(opposite)* was the son of an Assiniboine chief. Taken to Washington to represent his tribe, he met the Great White Father (Andrew Jackson), saw New York, developed a taste for fire water, and thoroughly enjoyed himself. Catlin met him on the steamboat which was taking him home and sketched him in his suit of full dress American regimentals, top hat with feather, umbrella, fan, and a handy bottle in his pocket. His skeptical tribe refused to believe him when he strutted about telling tales of what he had seen in civilization and finally had him killed as an impossible liar and good-for-nothing.

GEORGE CATLIN: Buffalo Chase with Bows and Lances

ALBERT BIERSTADT: Merced River, Yosemite Valley, 1866

In the 1860's Frederick Church had stiff competition from Albert Bierstadt (1830-1902), who arrived from Humboldt's Germany and applied his native industriousness portraying his adopted country. He had been brought to the United States at the age of one, but had returned to Germany in 1853 to study painting in Düsseldorf. In 1858 Bierstadt began a two-year journey through the Rocky Mountains to California in the party of General Lander. He was immensely impressed by the Rockies, which he compared to the Bernese Alps, and the friendly Indians he met while he was out sketching.

Bierstadt immersed himself in his new subject, and the Hudson River School was gradually transformed into a Rocky Mountain School. He followed the practice of Church in that sketches made on the actual spot were later combined to make the highly finished pictures that issued from his New York studio. The famous *Rocky Mountains* of 1863, spread out over some sixty square feet of canvas, was even more overpowering than a panorama by Church, and the Indian encampment in the foreground, complete with braves, squaws, papooses, horses, dogs, wigwams, and campfires, made a greater concession to the public's weakness for human interest. Despite his success, some critics continued to feel that Bierstadt painted American landscape with a European accent.

The *Yosemite Valley (opposite)*, a more modest effort, records the pristine state of one of the world's most frequented vacation facilities. The lovely valley had only recently been discovered (in 1851) by a company of soldiers in pursuit of an Indian raiding party. *The Buffalo Trail (below)* is another view of the West that was and is no more. Systematic extermination of the buffalo, once numbered between fifty and sixty million, began the year it was painted. The species was able to survive being hunted by Indians (p. 475), but the coming of the white man, his railroad, and his rifles, led to slaughter without limit. By the end of the century there were barely a hundred left.

ALBERT BIERSTADT: The Buffalo Trail: The Impending Storm, 1869

The scene is the Sacramento station of the Central Pacific Railroad in the early 1870's. The artist was born Karl Wilhelm Hahn (1828-1887) in Ebersbach, Germany. He studied painting in the capital city of Dresden, and one of his pictures was purchased by the King; but it was a sojourn in Düsseldorf that prepared him for his main chance. Hahn arrived in California in 1867. For a European, the Far West was about as exotic a spectacle as the world offered, and highly salable bits of local color lay all about. Some titles of Hahn's surviving pictures tell the story: *Logging in California, Miners Playing Cards, The Bear Hunt,* and *Return from the Bear Hunt.* Hahn was in London in 1882 and back in Dresden by 1885.

WILLIAM HAHN: The Sacramento Railroad Station

WILLIAM A. COULTER: Carquinez Straits

Above is a glimpse of San Francisco Bay, with the shipping of the last century, by W. A. Coulter (1849-1936), a California painter who specialized in marine views. It is through the Carquinez Straits that the Sacramento River passes into the storied Bay.

FREDERIC REMINGTON: The Old Stage Coach of the Plains, 1902
Courtesy Amon Carter Museum, Fort Worth, Texas.

Our great-grandfathers had no film or television Westerns, but they got along quite nicely with the aid of Remington (1861-1909), the most accomplished and prolific illustrator in this field. He knew the cowboys, the Indians, and the U.S. Cavalry from firsthand experience, but the pictures were mostly done in his studio in New Rochelle (only forty-five minutes from Broadway), which had doors big enough to accommodate horses. "I paint for boys," he once said, "boys from ten to seventy." Theodore Roosevelt was one of Remington's greatest fans, and some of the boys are still willing to pay incredible sums for the original paintings.

War Is Kind

Do not weep, maiden, for war is kind.
Because your lover threw wild hands toward the sky
And the affrighted steed ran on alone,
Do not weep.
War is kind.

      Hoarse, booming drums of the regiment,
      Little souls who thirst for fight,
      These men were born to drill and die.
      The unexplained glory flies above them,
      Great is the battle-god, great, and his kingdom—
      A field where a thousand corpses lie.

Do not weep, babe, for war is kind.
Because your father tumbled in the yellow trenches,
Raged at his breast, gulped and died,
Do not weep.
War is kind.

      Swift blazing flag of the regiment,
      Eagle with crest of red and gold,
      These men were born to drill and die.
      Point for them the virtue of slaughter,
      Make plain to them the excellence of killing
      And a field where a thousand corpses lie.

Mother whose heart hung humble as a button
On the bright splendid shroud of your son,
Do not weep.
War is kind.

"I explain the silvered passing of a ship at night"

I explain the silvered passing of a ship at night,
The sweep of each sad lost wave,
The dwindling boom of the steel thing's striving,
The little cry of a man to a man,
A shadow falling across the grayer night,
And the sinking of the small star;

Then the waste, the far waste of waters,
And the soft lashing of black waves
For long and in loneliness.

Remember, thou, O ship of love,
Thou leavest a far waste of waters,
And the soft lashing of black waves
For long and in loneliness.

"There was, before me"

There was, before me,
Mile upon mile
Of snow, ice, burning sand.
And yet I could look beyond all this,
To a place of infinite beauty;
And I could see the loveliness of her
Who walked in the shade of the trees.
When I gazed,
All was lost
But this place of beauty and her.
When I gazed,
And in my gazing, desired,
Then came again
Mile upon mile,
Of snow, ice, burning sand.

"Love walked alone"

Love walked alone.
The rocks cut her tender feet,
And the brambles tore her fair limbs.
There came a companion to her,
But, alas, he was no help,
For his name was heart's pain.

"I wonder if sometimes in the dusk"

I wonder if sometimes in the dusk,
When the brave lights that gild thy evenings
Have not yet been touched with flame,
I wonder if sometimes in the dusk
Thou rememberest a time,
A time when thou loved me
And our love was to thee thy all?
Is the memory rubbish now?
An old gown
Worn in an age of other fashions?
Woe is me, oh, lost one,
For that love is now to me
A supernal dream
White, white, white with many suns.

QUESTIONS FOR DISCUSSION

"God fashioned the ship of the world carefully"

1. In what sense is God's turning away from the ship ironic? What do the adjectives describing the ship's voyage, progress, and maneuvering tell us of Crane's view of the world?
2. In what sense is this poem related to the eighteenth-century idea of God the Creator as the "Great Mechanic"?
3. According to the poem, in what sense does the ship share an attitude toward God with those in the sky who laughed?

"A slant of sun on dull brown walls"

1. The opening couplet in this poem is a backdrop for the scene which unfolds. What does the nature of the backdrop lead you to expect?
2. What is the nature of the hymn that rises to God? How does this description make the final plea ironic?

"A god in wrath"

1. One's image of God determines his response to God. Characterize the god being described by the speaker.
2. How does the speaker's image of the god differ from the view of the people? What are the ironic implications of the last four lines?

"A man said to the universe"

1. Describe the tone of voice with which the man addresses the universe. Is the man's assertion presumptuous?
2. Describe the tone of the universe's reply. What does the universe's answer either state or imply about man's stature?
3. Although the universe denies a sense of obligation, man's assertion of his existence implies that there is an obligation. What, if any, is that obligation?

"A man adrift on a slim spar"

1. The poet uses the phrase "God is cold" four times in this poem. What is he trying to achieve by this repetition?
2. What is being described in each of the four-line sections (quatrains) that end with the refrain "God is cold"?
3. How do the subject matter and audience being addressed in lines 9–17 differ from the subject matter and audience in the four quatrains?
4. Why are these nine lines (9–17) connected to the four lines that follow, rather than set off in a stanza by themselves? Does the linking of these lines suggest that the speaker links them in his mind? Does he succeed?
5. What is the speaker's attitude toward the man? Is he concerned and involved in the man's predicament? Is he objective and disinterested, merely reporting an incident?
6. What is the speaker's impression of the sea? What figurative language does he use to describe the sea?
7. What does the speaker mean to suggest about God in the final line of the poem? What is God's relationship to the man? to the sea?

"To the maiden"

1. How do the metaphors in each stanza emphasize the two contrasting images of the sea held by the maiden and by the wrecked sailor?
2. What is the biblical allusion in the reference to "writing on the walls"? In what sense is the sailor in a predicament similar to that of the allusion?

"A newspaper is a collection of half-injustices"

1. Point out all the metaphors for a newspaper. Are they complimentary comparisons? How can you tell?
2. What is the effect of the poet's combining words such as *merciful* and *sneering*, *kindly* and *unfairly*, *wisdom* and *melons*?

3. Keeping in mind that Crane earned much of his living from journalism, what do you think might have been his purpose in writing this poem?

"In the desert"

1. In this poem, do the nakedness and bestiality of the man suggest something in the nature of all men?
2. What is ironic about the man's continuing to eat something bitter? What would occur to a man who actually ate his heart? Does this suggest some deeper irony? Explain your conclusions.

War Is Kind

1. What is the refrain in this poem? What is ironic about its statement?
2. What is the subject of the first, third, and fifth stanzas? How is the refrain related to this subject?
3. What is being described in the second and fourth stanzas? Why are these stanzas set off from the rest of the poem?
4. A poem's mood is established by the use of words rich in connotative power and by the creation of emotion-charged images. Discuss the mood of the indented stanzas and the words and images which produce that mood.
5. The first, third, and fifth stanzas are each addressed to individuals. In what tone should each stanza be spoken? Does the tone differ in each case?
6. How does the mood established in the odd-numbered stanzas fit with the mood of the other two?
7. What is the thrust of the poem as you understand it?

"I explain the silvered passing of a ship at night"

1. Explain how the comparison with the passing ship at sea intensifies the impact of the loss of a lover. Name the specific words and images that produce the sense of intense loss.
2. Images of the sea have also appeared in "God fashioned the ship of the world carefully," "A man adrift on a slim spar," and "To the maiden." What similarities and differences are there between the images in this poem and those in the others?

"There was, before me"

1. List separately the elements of dream and of reality that appear in this poem.
2. The phrases "burning sand" and "shade of the trees" may suggest

the image of an oasis in the desert. Is this an oasis or a mirage? Explain.
3. By combining the two visions of dream and reality within one poem, what is the poet seeking to convey to the reader?

"Love walked alone"

1. The depth of hurt which one experiences in the loss of love is depicted here through personification. How does personification heighten the impact of the poem?
2. Who or what is the companion? How do the mention and the description of a companion help to illustrate the poem?

"I wonder if sometimes in the dusk"

1. What specific images express the speaker's mood and memory? What images suggest his lost lover's memory?
2. Repetition in poetry is often an intensifying agent. How does the repetition in this poem serve such a purpose?
3. Does the speaker's use of the archaic *thy, thou,* and *thee* hinder the effectiveness of his statement?

ASSIGNMENTS FOR WRITING

1. A poet seeks to make a dual impression; he wants both to move us emotionally and to affect us intellectually. This double impact often jars us into action. Write a brief composition in which you describe how the poet made you feel, think, and desire to act as you read "War Is Kind." Be explicit as to what produced your response.
2. Although Crane's poetry seldom uses rhyme, it is nonetheless poetry in its expression of emotion through figurative language. Poetry may also contain dialogue and can be ironic in tone, as some of Crane's poetry demonstrates. Crane's poetry has a certain structure, although it does not always follow the same pattern. Above all, it is succinct. Write a poem of about eight or twelve lines on a subject for which you hold deep feelings. You may want to follow one of Crane's patterns or to use a plan of your own.

Eugene O'Neill

As late as 1920, America yet had no playwright of stature. Although Europe had long known the influence of Norway's Henrik Ibsen and Sweden's August Strindberg, American theater remained unaware of the developments elsewhere. As Professor Alan Downer points out, the American theater was "a wholly commercial operation" which "insisted that its function was to entertain, and it defined entertainment as escapism." To Americans, the theater meant "Broadway" and the row of playhouses just off Times Square.

The new life of the American theater, however, was pulsing in a dingy one-time barn in Greenwich Village, where a group of actors performed as the Provincetown Players. They had taken their name from their founding as a company in Provincetown, the summer resort on the tip of Cape Cod. There in 1916, the greatest name in American drama had first been introduced when Eugene O'Neill's one-act play, *Bound East for Cardiff*, appeared on the summer bill. In November of that year, the Cape Cod company had moved to its New York City stage for the Provincetown Players' initial season there. With it, of course, came O'Neill's plays. Four years later, the name of Eugene O'Neill shone in lights on a Broadway marquee. The play was *Beyond the Horizon;* it won O'Neill his first Pulitzer Prize.

Eugene Gladstone O'Neill was born in 1888 to the theatrical life, a life he abandoned and returned to only after suffering failure and illness. His father, James O'Neill, was one of the most successful touring actors of his day. Although acclaimed for his ability as a Shakespearean actor, he chose instead to play the Count of Monte Cristo in a popular melodramatic version that garnered fabulous financial returns. The father-figure, particularly the father who achieves less than his best, appears often in O'Neill's plays, as in *A Touch of the Poet.* He is frequently Irish and of romantic inclinations; he is also frequently a figure for scorn and despair.

In contrast, O'Neill's mother, Ella Quinlan O'Neill, was of a milder, less ostentatious temperament, and a devoutly religious woman. In marrying an actor, she had been cut off from her outraged family. Her life included the miseries of drug addiction and an infant's death which occurred while she and her husband were on tour. Furthermore, she and her family were always conscious of the ostracism accorded the Irish in America, in spite of her husband's fame. Of lasting consequence to her son, Eugene, was the fact that it was impossible for Mrs. O'Neill to establish a permanent home. Eugene had been born in a New York City hotel; as a child of seven, he was forced to spend the Christmas vacation at the boarding school he attended because once again his parents were touring.

The combination of these personal factors—conflict with his father, alienation as an Irishman, and estrangement from a normal home environment—developed in Eugene O'Neill a restlessness and a sense of life's inevitably tragic decline.

In early manhood, O'Neill drifted from one aimless situation to another. A year at Princeton University ended in suspension for misbehavior. Not unusual for a homeless youth, he married early; but by the time his son was born in 1910, he had already abandoned his wife to seek adventure in Honduras and Argentina. After sampling odd-jobs and the riotous life of a wharf-rat in Buenos Aires, he returned to New York on a tramp steamer. This was followed by further dissipation and seaman's voyages. In 1911, he rejoined his father's troupe briefly for a tour of the West; next he tried journalism, working for a few months as a cub reporter for the New London (Conn.) *Telegraph*. In 1912, his health failed, and suffering with tuberculosis, O'Neill had to be hospitalized in a sanitarium.

The six-month period of confinement became the pivotal point in O'Neill's life, for in the hospital he read and wrote and decided upon his career. Released from the sanitarium in the spring of 1913, he advanced his intentions by renewing his formal education in George Pierce Baker's renowned playwriting classes at Harvard. His seriousness of purpose he conveyed to Professor Baker in a letter of application: "I want to be an artist or nothing." By the end of one year, he had benefited from Baker's encouragement, if nothing more, and he did not return to Harvard.

In the summer of 1916, O'Neill arrived at Provincetown with the scripts of several one-act plays, including *Bound East for Cardiff*. From that point, his career was begun. Between that summer and early 1920, the Provincetown Players produced eleven more of his plays. Then came the Broadway success of *Beyond the Horizon* and national recognition. Three more blockbusters succeeded in rapid file: *The*

Emperor Jones (1920), *Anna Christie* (1921), and *The Hairy Ape* (1922), with a half dozen lesser plays sandwiched in for off-Broadway performances. Never had the American theater known so prolific a playwright of quality. Never had America known such quality, such overwhelming power. Never had a playwright so inexperienced received such uncompromising plaudits from the critics, who called him "the best of American playwrights" and "America's greatest dramatist" after only four Broadway shows.

O'Neill's unparalleled achievement continued throughout the next decade. The titles of some of his greatest plays are *Desire Under the Elms* (1924), the story of a ruthless New England farmer and his son's desperate attraction to his father's young wife; *Strange Interlude* (1928), a five-hour tour of O'Neill's purgatory; and *Mourning Becomes Electra* (1931), a trilogy representing the downfall of an American family, similar to the collapse of Agamemnon, his wife Clytemnestra, and their children, Orestes and Electra.

During this time Eugene O'Neill received the highest acclaim available to a literary artist—three Pulitzer Prizes, an honorary doctorate from Yale, and the ultimate award in 1936, the Nobel Prize for Literature. At the same time, his amazing drive to turn out play after play had begun to subside, and a seriously debilitating illness had taken over, an illness that prevented him from being able to write. After World War II, O'Neill's only major production to be staged was *The Iceman Cometh* (1946). A few frenetic years in search of a lasting cure ended without success, and Eugene O'Neill died in Boston in 1953.

Since O'Neill's death, however, three plays have been produced, bringing about a revival of critical and popular interest in his lasting effect upon the American theater. The plays are *Long Day's Journey into Night* (1956), an autobiographical work which earned a fourth Pulitzer Prize; *A Touch of the Poet* (1957) and *More Stately Mansions* (1962), the only two plays to survive from an intended cycle of eleven entitled "The Tale of the Possessors Self-Dispossessed."

The course of O'Neill's early writing had tended toward the naturalism in vogue in contemporary fiction. Powerful forces at work in human existence determined life's direction. That direction, in O'Neill's view, led inevitably to a tragic end. As he increased in experience, however, O'Neill found himself able to heighten his theatrical effects by turning to the developing European mode called "expressionism." Expressionism sought by means of exaggeration to show its disapproval of the mechanistic society; some of this disapproval was influenced by the popularizing of psychology and by the growth in importance of Marxist economics and politics. In expressionistic drama, character types rather than personal characteristics were emphasized; symbols underscored and blatant, rather than subtle and profound, swarmed through these plays. O'Neill's critics had always been impressed by what Heywood Broun called "the successful approximation of true talk," O'Neill's authenticity of language. As well as concentrating upon diction, O'Neill also insisted upon representing the dialect, tone, and inflection of his speakers. But to the expressionist, language was considered merely one of several means of communication on the stage; as a consequence, the expressionist playwright in general, O'Neill in particular, worried less about exact choices of words. The result for the reader is a not infrequent awkward passage; curiously, the effect upon the listener may be somewhat less infelicitous.

Theme and visual presentation became paramount in O'Neill's subsequent plays. The symbolism of the stage set and the use of lighting received an importance seldom before recognized in the American theater. In *Mourning Becomes Electra,* for instance, the set calls for a pillared New England mansion, suggesting the Grecian backdrop against which the original *Oresteia* of Aeschylus was performed.

The terrifying struggle among family members, first represented in *Desire Under the Elms,* came to dominate O'Neill's later work. In *Long Day's Journey into Night, A Touch of the Poet,* and *More Stately Mansions,* O'Neill shows the essential conflict between idealism and the practicality that confronts and opposes it. The paradoxical tension brings together antagonists as different as their generations and social classes.

Thus what Eugene O'Neill says about life, American life in particular, may well appal the congenital optimist. But to a generation that has experienced the upheaval of its parents' accepted values, O'Neill's message must ring true. Speaking of *A Touch of the Poet* and the other plays in that cycle he had projected, he said, "We talk about the American Dream and want to tell the world about the American Dream, but what is that dream, in most cases, but the dream of material things. I sometimes think that the United States, for this reason, is the greatest failure the world has ever seen." If O'Neill is right, his canon of plays is the chronicle of that failure.

A Touch of the Poet

CHARACTERS

MICKEY MALOY

JAMIE CREGAN

SARA MELODY

NORA MELODY

CORNELIUS MELODY

DAN ROCHE

PADDY O'DOWD

PATCH RILEY

DEBORAH (*Mrs. Henry Harford*)

NICHOLAS GADSBY

ACT ONE

The dining room of Melody's Tavern, in a village a few miles from Boston. The tavern is over a hundred years old. It had once been prosperous, a breakfast stop for the stagecoach, but the stage line had been discontinued and for some years now the tavern has fallen upon neglected days.

The dining room and barroom were once a single spacious room, low-ceilinged, with heavy oak beams and paneled walls—the taproom of the tavern in its prosperous days, now divided into two rooms by a flimsy partition, the barroom being off left. The partition is painted to imitate the old paneled walls but this only makes it more of an eyesore.

At left front, two steps lead up to a closed door opening on a flight of stairs to the floor above. Farther back is the door to the bar. Between these doors hangs a large mirror. Beyond the bar door a small cabinet is fastened to the wall. At rear are four windows. Between the middle two is the street door. At right front is another door, open, giving on a hallway and the main stairway to the second floor, and leading to the kitchen. Farther front at right, there is a high schoolmaster's desk with a stool.

In the foreground are two tables. One, with four chairs, at left center; a larger one, seating six, at right center. At left and right, rear, are two more tables, identical with the ones at right center. All these tables are set with white tablecloths, etc., except the small ones in the foreground at left.

It is around nine in the morning of July 27, 1828. Sunlight shines in through the windows at rear.

MICKEY MALOY *sits at the table at left front, facing right. He is glancing through a newspaper. Maloy is twenty-six, with a sturdy physique and an amiable, cunning face, his mouth usually set in a half-leering grin.*

JAMIE CREGAN *peers around the half-open door to the bar. Seeing Maloy, he comes in. As obviously Irish as Maloy, he is middle-aged, tall, with a lantern-jawed face. There is a scar of a saber cut over one cheekbone. He is dressed neatly but in old, worn clothes. His eyes are bloodshot, his manner sickly, but he grins as he greets Maloy sardonically.*

CREGAN   God bless all here—even the barkeep.

MALOY   (*With an answering grin.*) Top o' the mornin'.

CREGAN   Top o' me head. (*He puts his hand to his head and groans.*) Be the saints, there's a blacksmith at work on it!

MALOY   Small wonder. You'd the divil's own load when you left at two this mornin'.

CREGAN   I must have. I don't remember leaving. (*He sits at right of table.*) Faix, you're takin' it aisy.

MALOY   There's no trade this time o' day.

CREGAN   It was a great temptation, when I saw no one in the bar, to make off with a bottle. A hair av the dog is what I need, but I've divil a penny in my pantaloons.

MALOY   Have one on the house. (*He goes to the cupboard and takes out a decanter of whiskey and a glass.*)

CREGAN   Thank you kindly. Sure, the good Samaritan was a crool haythen beside you.

MALOY   (*Putting the decanter and glass before him.*) It's the same you was drinking last night—his private dew. He keeps it here for emergencies when he don't want to go in the bar.

CREGAN   (*Pours out a big drink.*) Lave it to Con never to be caught dry. (*Raising his glass.*) Your health and inclinations—if they're virtuous! (*He drinks and sighs with relief.*) God bless you, Whiskey, it's you can rouse the dead! Con hasn't been down yet for his morning's morning?

MALOY   No. He won't be till later.

CREGAN   It's like a miracle, me meeting him again. I came to these parts looking for work. It's only by accident I heard talk of a Con Melody and come here to see was it him. Until last night, I'd not seen hide nor hair of him since the war with the French in Spain—after the battle of Salamanca in '12. I was a corporal in the Seventh Dragoons and he was major. (*Proudly.*) I got this cut from a saber at Talavera, bad luck to it!—serving under him. He was a captain then.

MALOY   So you told me last night.

CREGAN   (*With a quick glance at him.*) Did I now? I must have said more than my prayers, with the lashings of whiskey in me.

MALOY   (*With a grin.*) More than your prayers is the truth. (*Cregan glances at him uneasily. Maloy pushes the decanter toward him.*) Take another taste.

CREGAN   I don't like sponging. Sure, my credit ought to be good in this shebeen! Ain't I his cousin?

MALOY   You're forgettin' what himself told you last night as he went up to bed. You could have all the whiskey you could pour down you, but not a penny's worth of credit. This house, he axed you to remember, only gives credit to gentlemen.

CREGAN   Divil mend him!

MALOY   (*With a chuckle.*) You kept thinking about his insults after he'd gone out, getting madder and madder.

CREGAN   God pity him, that's like him. He hasn't changed much. (*He pours out a drink and gulps it down—with a cautious look at Maloy.*) If I was mad at Con, and me blind drunk, I must have told you a power of lies.

MALOY   (*Winks slyly.*) Maybe they wasn't lies.

CREGAN   If I said any wrong of Con Melody—

MALOY   Arrah, are you afraid I'll gab what you said to him? I won't, you can take my oath.

CREGAN   (*His face clearing.*) Tell me what I said and I'll tell you if it was lies.

MALOY   You said his father wasn't of the quality of Galway like he makes out, but a thievin' shebeen keeper who got rich by moneylendin' and squeezin' tenants and every manner of trick. And when he'd enough he married, and bought an estate with a pack of hounds and set up as one of the gentry. He'd hardly got settled when his wife died givin' birth to Con.

CREGAN   There's no lie there.

MALOY   You said none of the gentry would speak to auld Melody, but he had a tough hide and didn't heed them. He made up his mind he'd bring Con up a true gentleman, so he packed him off to Dublin to school, and after that to the College with sloos of money to prove himself the equal of any gentleman's son. But Con found, while there was plenty to drink on him and borrow money, there was few didn't sneer behind his back at his pretensions.

CREGAN   That's the truth, too. But Con wiped the sneer off their mugs when he called one av thim out and put a bullet in his hip. That was his first duel. It gave his pride the taste for revenge and after that he was always lookin' for an excuse to challenge someone.

MALOY   He's done a power av boastin' about his duels, but I thought he was lyin'.

CREGAN   There's no lie in it. It was that brought disgrace on him in the end, right after he'd been promoted to major. He got caught by a Spanish noble making love to his wife, just after the battle of Salamanca, and there was a duel and Con killed him. The scandal was hushed up but Con had to resign from the army. If it wasn't for his fine record for bravery in battle, they'd have court-martialed him. (*Then guiltily.*) But I'm sayin' more than my prayers again.

MALOY   It's no news about his women. You'd think, to hear him when he's drunk, there wasn't one could resist him in Portugal and Spain.

CREGAN   If you'd seen him then, you wouldn't wonder. He was as strong as an ox, and on a thoroughbred horse, in his uniform, there wasn't a handsomer man in the army. And he had the chance he wanted in Portugal and Spain where a British officer was welcome in the gentry's houses. At home, the only women he'd known was whores. (*He adds hastily.*) Except Nora, I mean. (*Lowering his voice.*) Tell me, has he done any rampagin' wid women here?

MALOY   He hasn't. The damned Yankee gentry won't let him come near them, and he considers the few Irish around here to be scum beneath his notice. But once in a while there'll be some Yankee stops overnight wid his wife or daughter and then you'd laugh to see Con, if he thinks she's gentry, sidlin' up to her, playin' the great gentleman and makin' compliments, and then boasting afterward he could have them in bed if he'd had a chance at it, for all their modern Yankee airs.

CREGAN   And maybe he could. If you'd known him in the auld days, you'd nivir doubt any boast he makes about fightin' and women, and gamblin' or any kind av craziness. There nivir was a madder divil.

MALOY   (*Lowering his voice.*) Speakin' av Nora, you nivir mentioned her last night, but I know all about it without you telling me. I used to have my room here, and there's nights he's madder drunk than most when he throws it in her face he had to marry her because—Mind you, I'm not saying anything against poor Nora. A sweeter woman never lived. And I know you know all about it.

CREGAN   (*Reluctantly.*) I do. Wasn't I raised on his estate?

MALOY   He tells her it was the priests tricked him into marrying her. He hates priests.

CREGAN   He's a liar, then. He may like to blame it on them but it's little Con Melody cared what they said. Nothing ever made him do anything, except himself. He married her because he'd fallen in love with her, but he was ashamed of her in his pride at the same time because her folks were only ignorant peasants on his estate, as poor as poor. Nora was as pretty a girl as you'd find in a year's travel, and he'd come to be bitter lonely, with no woman's company but the whores was helpin' him ruin the estate. (*He shrugs his shoulders.*) Well, anyways, he married her and then went off to the war, and left her alone in the castle to have her child, and nivir saw her again till he was sent home from Spain. Then he raised what money he still was able, and took her and Sara here to America where no one would know him.

MALOY   (*Thinking this over for a moment.*) It's hard for me to believe he ever loved her. I've seen the way he treats her now. Well, thank you for telling me, and I take my oath I'll nivir breathe a word of it—for Nora's sake, not his.

CREGAN   (*Grimly.*) You'd better kape quiet for fear of him, too. If he's one-half the man he was, he could bate the lights out of the two av us.

MALOY   He's strong as a bull still for all the whiskey he's drunk. (*He pushes the bottle toward Cregan.*) Have another taste. (*Cregan pours out a drink.*) Drink hearty.

CREGAN   Long life. (*He drinks. Maloy puts the decanter and glass back on the cupboard. A girl's voice is heard from the hall at right. Cregan jumps up—hastily.*) That's Sara, isn't it? I'll get out. She'll likely blame me for Con getting so drunk last night. I'll be back after Con is down.

   He goes out. Maloy starts to go in the bar, as if he too wanted to avoid Sara. Then he sits down defiantly.

MALOY   Be damned if I'll run from her.

   He takes up the paper as SARA MELODY *comes in from the hall at right.*

   Sara is twenty, an exceedingly pretty girl with a mass of black hair, fair skin with rosy cheeks, and beautiful, deep-blue eyes. There is a curious blending in her of what are commonly considered aristocratic and peasant characteristics. She has a fine forehead. Her nose is thin and straight. She has small ears set close to her well-shaped head, and a slender neck. Her mouth, on the other hand, has a touch of coarseness and sensuality and her jaw is too heavy. Her figure is strong and graceful, with full, firm breasts and hips, and a slender waist. But she has large feet and broad, ugly hands with stubby fingers. Her voice is soft and musical, but her speech has at times a self-conscious, stilted quality about it, due to her restraining a tendency to lapse into brogue. Her everyday working dress is of cheap material, but she wears it in a way that gives a pleasing effect of beauty unadorned.

SARA (*With a glance at Maloy, sarcastically.*) I'm sorry to interrupt you when you're so busy, but have you your bar book ready for me to look over?

MALOY (*Surlily.*) I have. I put it on your desk.

SARA Thank you.
> *She turns her back on him, sits at the desk, takes a small account book from it, and begins checking figures.*

MALOY (*Watches her over his paper.*) If it's profits you're looking for, you won't find them—not with all the drinks himself's been treating to. (*She ignores this. He becomes resentful.*) You've got your airs of a grand lady this morning, I see. There's no talkin' to you since you've been playin' nurse to the young Yankee upstairs. (*She makes herself ignore this, too.*) Well, you've had your cap set for him ever since he came to live by the lake, and now's your chance, when he's here sick and too weak to defend himself.

SARA (*Turns on him—with quiet anger.*) I warn you to mind your own business, Mickey, or I'll tell my father of your impudence. He'll teach you to keep your place, and God help you.

MALOY (*Doesn't believe this threat but is frightened by the possibility.*) Arrah, don't try to scare me. I know you'd never carry tales to him. (*Placatingly.*) Can't you take a bit of teasing, Sara?

SARA (*Turns back to her figuring.*) Leave Simon out of your teasing.

MALOY Oho, he's Simon to you now, is he? Well, well (*He gives her a cunning glance.*) Maybe, if you'd come down from your high horse, I could tell you some news.

SARA You're worse than an old woman for gossip. I don't want to hear it.

MALOY When you was upstairs at the back taking him his breakfast, there was a grand carriage with a nigger coachman stopped at the corner and a Yankee lady got out and came in here. I was sweeping and Nora was scrubbing the kitchen. (*Sara has turned to him, all attention now.*) She asked me what road would take her near the lake—

SARA (*Starts.*) Ah.

MALOY So I told her, but she didn't go. She kept looking around, and said she'd like a cup of tea, and where was the waitress. I knew she must be connected someway with Harford or why would she want to go to the lake where no one's ever lived but him. She didn't want tea at all, but only an excuse to stay.

SARA (*Resentfully.*) So she asked for the waitress, did she? I hope you told her I'm the owner's daughter, too.

MALOY I did. I don't like Yankee airs any more than you. I was short with her. I said you was out for a walk, and the tavern wasn't open yet, anyway. So she went out and drove off.

A TOUCH OF THE POET 495

SARA   (*Worriedly now.*) I hope you didn't insult her with your bad manners. What did she look like, Mickey?

MALOY   Pretty, if you like that kind. A pale, delicate wisp of a thing with big eyes.

SARA   That fits what he's said of his mother. How old was she?

MALOY   It's hard to tell, but she's too young for his mother, I'd swear. Around thirty, I'd say. Maybe it's his sister.

SARA   He hasn't a sister.

MALOY   (*Grinning.*) Then maybe she's an old sweetheart looking for you to scratch your eyes out.

SARA   He's never had a sweetheart.

MALOY   (*Mockingly.*) Is that what he tells you, and you believe him? Faix, you must be in love!

SARA   (*Angrily.*) Will you mind your own business? I'm not such a fool! (*Worried again.*) Maybe you ought to have told her he's here sick to save her the drive in the hot sun and the walk through the woods for nothing.

MALOY   Why would I tell her, when she never mentioned him?

SARA   Yes, it's her own fault. But—Well, there's no use thinking of it now—or bothering my head about her, anyway, whoever she was.

> *She begins checking figures again. Her mother appears in the doorway at right.*
> NORA MELODY *is forty, but years of overwork and worry have made her look much older. She must have been as pretty as a girl as Sara is now. She still has the beautiful eyes her daughter has inherited. But she has become too worn out to take care of her appearance. Her black hair, streaked with gray, straggles in untidy wisps about her face. Her body is dumpy, with sagging breasts, and her old clothes are like a bag covering it, tied around the middle. Her red hands are knotted by rheumatism. Cracked working shoes, run down at the heel, are on her bare feet. Yet in spite of her slovenly appearance there is a spirit which shines through and makes her lovable, a simple sweetness and charm, something gentle and sad and, somehow, dauntless.*

MALOY   (*Jumps to his feet, his face lighting up with affection.*) God bless you, Nora, you're the one I was waitin' to see. Will you keep an eye on the bar while I run to the store for a bit av 'baccy?

SARA   (*Sharply.*) Don't do it, Mother.

NORA   (*Smiles—her voice is soft, with a rich brogue.*) Why wouldn't I? "Don't do it, Mother."

MALOY   Thank you, Nora. (*He goes to the door at rear and opens it, burning for a parting shot at Sara.*) And the back o' my hand to you, your Ladyship! (*He goes out, closing the door.*)

SARA   You shouldn't encourage his laziness. He's always looking for excuses to shirk.

NORA   Ah, nivir mind, he's a good lad. (*She lowers herself painfully on the nearest chair at the rear of the table at center front.*) Bad cess to the rheumatism. It has me destroyed this mornin'.

SARA   (*Still checking figures in the book—gives her mother an impatient but at the same time worried glance. Her habitual manner toward her is one of mingled love and pity and exasperation.*) I've told you a hundred times to see the doctor.

NORA   We've no money for doctors. They're bad luck, anyway. They bring death *with them*. (*A pause. Nora sighs.*) Your father will be down soon. I've some fine fresh eggs for his breakfast.

SARA   (*Her face becomes hard and bitter.*) He won't want them.

NORA   (*Defensively.*) You mean he'd drop too much taken last night? Well, small blame to him, he hasn't seen Jamie since—

SARA   *Last* night? What night hasn't he?

NORA   Ah, don't be hard on him. (*A pause—worriedly.*) Neilan sent round a note to me about his bill. He says we'll have to settle by the end of the week or we'll get no more groceries. (*With a sigh.*) I can't blame him. How we'll manage, I dunno. There's the intrist on the mortgage due the first. But that I've saved, God be thanked.

SARA   (*Exasperatedly.*) If you'd only let me take charge of the money.

NORA   (*With a flare of spirit.*) I won't. It'd mean you and himself would be at each other's throats from dawn to dark. It's bad enough between you as it is.

SARA   Why didn't you pay Neilan the end of last week? You told me you had the money put aside.

NORA   So I did. But Dickinson was tormentin' your father with his feed bill for the mare.

SARA   (*Angrily.*) I might have known! The mare comes first, if she takes the bread out of our mouths! The grand gentleman must have his thoroughbred to ride out in state!

NORA   (*Defensively.*) Where's the harm? She's his greatest pride. He'd be heartbroken if he had to sell her.

SARA   Oh yes, I know well he cares more for a horse than for us!

NORA   Don't be saying that. He has great love for you, even if you do be provokin him all the time.

SARA   Great love for me! Arrah, God pity you, Mother!

NORA   (*Sharply*) Don't put on the brogue, now. You know how he hates to hear you. And I do, too. There's no excuse not to cure yourself. Didn't he send you to school so you could talk like a gentleman's daughter?

SARA   (*Resentfully, but more careful of her speech.*) If he did, I wasn't there long.

NORA   It was you insisted on leavin'.

SARA   Because if he hadn't the pride or love for you not to live on your slaving your heart out, I had that pride and love!

NORA   (*Tenderly.*) I know, Acushla. I know.

SARA   (*With bitter scorn.*) We can't afford a waitress, but he can afford to keep a thoroughbred mare to prance around on and show himself off! And he can afford a barkeep when, if he had any decency, he'd do his part and tend the bar himself.

NORA   (*Indignantly.*) Him, a gentleman, tend bar!

SARA   A gentleman! Och, Mother, it's all right for the two of us, out of our own pride, to pretend to the world we believe that lie, but it's crazy for you to pretend to me.

NORA   (*Stubbornly.*) It's no lie. He *is* a gentleman. Wasn't he born rich in a castle on a grand estate and educated in college, and wasn't he an officer in the Duke of Wellington's army—

A TOUCH OF THE POET   497

SARA   All right, Mother. You can humor his craziness, but he'll never make me pretend to him I don't know the truth.

NORA   Don't talk as if you hated him. You ought to be shamed—

SARA   I do hate him for the way he treats you. I heard him again last night, raking up the past, and blaming his ruin on his having to marry you.

NORA   (*Protests miserably.*) It was the drink talkin', not him.

SARA   (*Exasperated.*) It's you ought to be ashamed, for not having more pride! You bear all his insults as meek as a lamb! You keep on slaving for him when it's that has made you old before your time! (*Angrily.*) You can't much longer, I tell you! He's getting worse. You'll have to leave him.

NORA   (*Aroused.*) I'll never! Howld your prate!

SARA   You'd leave him today, if you had any pride!

NORA   I've pride in my love for him! I've loved him since the day I set eyes on him, and I'll love him till the day I die! (*With a strange superior scorn.*) It's little you know of love, and you never will, for there's the same divil of pride in you that's in him, and it'll kape you from ivir givin' all of yourself, and that's what love is.

SARA   I could give all of myself if I wanted to, but—

NORA   If! Wanted to! Faix, it proves how little of love you know when you prate about if's and want-to's. It's when you don't give a thought for all the if's and want-to's in the world! It's when, if all the fires of hell was between you, you'd walk in them gladly to be with him, and sing with joy at your own burnin', if only his kiss was on your mouth! That's love, and I'm proud I've known the great sorrow and joy of it!

SARA   (*Cannot help being impressed—looks at her mother with wondering respect.*) You're a strange woman, Mother. (*She kisses her impulsively.*) And a grand woman! (*Defiant again, with an arrogant toss of her head.*) I'll love—but I'll love where it'll gain me freedom and not put me in slavery for life.

NORA   There's no slavery in it when you love! (*Suddenly her exultant expression crumbles and she breaks down.*) For the love of God, don't take the pride of my love from me, Sara, for without it what am I at all but an ugly, fat woman gettin' old and sick!

SARA   (*Puts her arm around her—soothingly.*) Hush, Mother. Don't mind me. (*Briskly, to distract her mother's mind.*) I've got to finish the bar book. Mickey can't put two and two together without making five. (*She goes to the desk and begins checking figures again.*)

NORA   (*Dries her eyes—after a pause she sighs worriedly.*) I'm worried about your father. Father Flynn stopped me on the road yesterday and tould me I'd better warn him not to sneer at the Irish around here and call thim scum, or he'll get in trouble. Most of thim is in a rage at him because he's come out against Jackson and the Democrats and says he'll vote with the Yankees for Quincy Adams.

SARA   (*Contemptuously.*) Faith, they can't see a joke, then, for it's a great joke to hear him shout against mob rule, like one of the Yankee gentry, when you know what he came from. And after the way the Yanks swindled him when he came here, getting him to buy this inn by telling him a new coach line was going to stop here. (*She laughs with bitter scorn.*) Oh, he's the easiest fool ever came to America! It's that I hold against him as much as anything, that when he came here the chance was before him to make himself all his lies pretended to be. He had education above most Yanks, and he had money enough to start him, and this is a country where you can rise as high as you like, and no one but the fools who envy you care what you rose from, once you've the money and the power goes with it. (*Passionately.*) Oh, if I was a man with the chance he had, there wouldn't be a dream I'd not make come true! (*She looks at her mother, who is staring at the floor dejectedly and hasn't been listening. She is exasperated for a second—then she smiles pityingly.*) You're a fine one to talk to, Mother. Wake up. What's worrying you now?

NORA Father Flynn tould me again I'd be damned in hell for lettin' your father make a haythen of me and bring you up a haythen, too.

SARA (*With an arrogant toss of her head.*) Let Father Flynn mind his own business, and not frighten you with fairy tales about hell.

NORA It's true, just the same.

SARA True, me foot! You ought to tell the good Father we aren't the ignorant shanty scum he's used to dealing with. (*She changes the subject abruptly—closing Mickey's bar book.*) There. That's done. (*She puts the book in the desk.*) I'll take a walk to the store and have a talk with Neilan. Maybe I can blarney him to let the bill go another month.

NORA (*Gratefully.*) Oh, you can. Sure, you can charm a bird out of a tree when you want to. But I don't like you beggin' to a Yankee. It's all right for me but I know how you hate it.

SARA (*Puts her arms around her mother—tenderly.*) I don't mind at all, if I can save you a bit of the worry that' killing you. (*She kisses her.*) I'll change to my Sunday dress so I can make a good impression.

NORA (*With a teasing smile.*) I'm thinkin' it isn't on Neilan alone you want to make an impression. You've changed to your Sunday best a lot lately.

SARA (*Coquettishly.*) Aren't you the sly one! Well, maybe you're right.

NORA How was he when you took him his breakfast?

SARA Hungry, and that's a good sign. He had no fever last night. Oh, he's on the road to recovery now, and it won't be long before he'll be back in his cabin by the lake.

NORA I'll never get it clear in my head what he's been doing there the past year, living like a tramp or a tinker, and him a rich gentleman's son.

SARA Oh, he isn't like his kind, or like anyone else at all. He's a born dreamer with a raft of great dreams, and he's very serious about them. I've told you before he wanted to get away from his father's business, where he worked for a year after he graduated from Harvard College, because he didn't like being in trade, even if it is a great company that trades with the whole world in its own ships.

NORA (*Approvingly.*) That's the way a true gentleman would feel—

SARA He wanted to prove his independence by living alone in the wilds, and build his own cabin, and do all the work, and support himself simply, and feel one with Nature, and think great thoughts about what life means, and write a book about how the world can be changed so people won't be greedy to own money and land and get the best of each other but will be content with little and live in peace and freedom together, and it will be like heaven on earth. (*She laughs fondly—and a bit derisively.*) I can't remember all of it. It seems crazy to me, when I think of what people are like. He hasn't written any of it yet, anyway—only the notes for it. (*She smiles coquettishly.*) All he's written the last few months are love poems.

NORA That's since you began to take long walks by the lake. (*She smiles.*) It's you are the sly one.

SARA (*Laughing.*) Well, why shouldn't I take walks on our own property? (*Her tone changes to a sneer.*) The land our great gentleman was swindled into buying when he came here with grand ideas of owning an American estate!—a bit of farm land no one would work any more, and the rest all wilderness! You couldn't give it away.

NORA (*Soothingly.*) Hush, now. (*Changing the subject.*) Well, it's easy to tell young Master Harford has a touch av the poet in him—(*She adds before she thinks.*) the same as your father.

SARA (*Scornfully.*) God help you, Mother! Do you think Father's a poet because he shows off reciting Lord Byron?

NORA (*With an uneasy glance at the door at left front.*) Whist, now. Himself will be down any moment. (*Changing the subject.*) I can see the Harford lad is falling in love with you.

SARA (*Her face lights up triumphantly.*) Falling? He's fallen head over heels. He's so timid, he hasn't told me yet, but I'll get him to soon.

NORA I know you're in love with him.

SARA (*Simply.*) I am, Mother. (*She adds quickly.*) But not too much. I'll not let love make me any man's slave. I want to love him just enough so I can marry him without cheating him, or myself. (*Determinedly.*) For I'm going to marry him, Mother. It's my chance to rise in the world and nothing will keep me from it.

NORA (*Admiringly.*) Musha, but you've boastful talk! What about his fine Yankee family? His father'll likely cut him off widout a penny if he marries a girl who's poor and Irish.

SARA He may at first, but when I've proved what a good wife I'll be—He can't keep Simon from marrying me. I know that. Simon doesn't care what his father thinks. It's only his mother I'm afraid of. I can tell she's had great influence over him. She must be a queer creature, from all he's told me. She's very strange in her ways. She never goes out at all but stays home in their mansion, reading books, or in her garden. (*She pauses.*) Did you notice a carriage stop here this morning, Mother?

NORA (*Preoccupied—uneasily.*) Don't count your chickens before they're hatched. Young Harford seems a dacent lad. But maybe it's not marriage he's after.

SARA (*Angrily.*) I won't have you wronging him, Mother. He has no thought— (*Bitterly.*) I suppose you're bound to suspect—(*She bites her words back, ashamed.*) Forgive me, Mother. But it's wrong of you to think badly of Simon. (*She smiles.*) You don't know him. Faith, if it came to seducing, it'd be me that'd have to do it. He's that respectful you'd think I was a holy image. It's only in his poems, and in the diary he keeps—I had a peek in it one day I went to tidy up the cabin for him. He's terribly ashamed of his sinful inclinations and the insult they are to my purity. (*She laughs tenderly.*)

NORA (*Smiling, but a bit shocked.*) Don't talk so bould. I don't know if it's right, you to be in his room so much, even if he is sick. There's a power av talk about the two av you already.

SARA Let there be, for all I care! Or all Simon cares, either. When it comes to not letting others rule him, he's got a will of his own behind his gentleness. Just as behind his poetry and dreams I feel he has it in him to do anything he wants. So even if his father cuts him off, with me to help him we'll get on in the world. For I'm no fool, either.

NORA Glory be to God, you have the fine opinion av yourself!

SARA (*Laughing.*) Haven't I though! (*Then bitterly.*) I've had need to have, to hold my head up, slaving as a waitress and chambermaid so my father can get drunk every night like a gentleman!

> The door at left front is slowly opened and CORNELIUS MELODY *appears in the doorway above the two steps. He and Sara stare at each other. She stiffens into hostility and her mouth sets in scorn. For a second his eyes waver and he looks guilty. Then his face becomes expressionless. He descends the steps and bows—pleasantly.*

MELODY Good morning, Sara.

SARA (*Curtly.*) Good morning. (*Then, ignoring him.*) I'm going up and change my dress, Mother. (*She goes out right.*)

> Cornelius Melody *is forty-five, tall, broad-shouldered, deep-chested, and powerful, with long muscular arms, big feet, and large hairy hands. His heavy-boned body is still firm, erect, and soldierly. Beyond shaky nerves, it shows no effects of hard drinking. It has a bull-like, impervious strength, a tough peasant vitality. It is his face that reveals the ravages of dissipation—a ruined face, which was once extraordinarily handsome in a reckless, arrogant fashion. It is still handsome—the face of an embittered Byronic hero, with a finely chiseled nose over a domineering, sensual mouth set in disdain, pale, hollow-cheeked, framed by thick, curly iron-gray hair. There is a look of wrecked distinction about it, of brooding, humiliated pride. His bloodshot gray eyes have an insulting cold stare which anticipates insult. His manner is that of a polished gentleman. Too much so. He overdoes it and one soon feels that he is overplaying a role which has become more real than his real self to him. But in spite of this, there is something formidable and impressive about him. He is dressed with foppish elegance in old, expensive, finely tailored clothes of the style worn by English aristocracy in Peninsular War days.*

MELODY (*Advancing into the room—bows formally to his wife.*) Good morning, Nora. (*His tone condescends. It addresses a person of inferior station.*)

NORA (*Stumbles to her feet—timidly.*) Good mornin', Con. I'll get your breakfast.

MELODY No. Thank you. I want nothing now.

NORA (*Coming toward him.*) You look pale. Are you sick, Con, darlin'?

MELODY No.

NORA (*Puts a timid hand on his arm.*) Come and sit down. (*He moves his arm away with instinctive revulsion and goes to the table at center front, and sits in the chair she had occupied. Nora hovers round him.*) I'll wet a cloth in cold water to put round your head.

MELODY No! I desire nothing—except a little peace in which to read the news. (*He picks up the paper and holds it so it hides his face from her.*)

NORA (*Meekly.*) I'll lave you in peace.

A TOUCH OF THE POET 501

She starts to go to the door at right but turns to stare at him worriedly again. Keeping the paper before his face with his left hand, he reaches out with his right and pours a glass of water from the carafe on the table. Although he cannot see his wife, he is nervously conscious of her. His hand trembles so violently that when he attempts to raise the glass to his lips the water sloshes over his hand and he sets the glass back on the table with a bang. He lowers the paper and explodes nervously.

MELODY For God's sake, stop your staring!

NORA I—I was only thinkin' you'd feel better if you'd a bit av food in you.

MELODY I told you once—! (*Controlling his temper.*) I am not hungry, Nora.

> *He raises the paper again. She sighs, her hands fiddling with her apron. A pause.*

NORA (*Dully.*) Maybe it's a hair av the dog you're needin'.

MELODY (*As if this were something he had been waiting to hear, his expression loses some of its nervous strain. But he replies virtuously.*) No, damn the liquor. Upon my conscience, I've about made up my mind I'll have no more of it. Besides, it's a bit early in the day.

NORA If it'll give you an appetite—

MELODY To tell the truth, my stomach is out of sorts. (*He licks his lips.*) Perhaps a drop wouldn't come amiss. (*Nora gets the decanter and glass from the cupboard and sets them before him. She stands gazing at him with a resigned sadness. Melody, his eyes on the paper, is again acutely conscious of her. His nerves cannot stand it. He throws his paper down and bursts out in bitter anger.*) Well? I know what you're thinking! Why haven't you the courage to say it for once? By God, I'd have more respect for you! I hate the damned meek of this earth! By the rock of Cashel, I sometimes believe you have always deliberately encouraged me to— It's the one point of superiority you can lay claim to, isn't it?

NORA (*Bewilderedly—on the verge of tears.*) I don't—It's only your comfort—I can't bear to see you—

MELODY (*His expression changes and a look of real affection comes into his eyes. He reaches out a shaking hand to pat her shoulder with an odd, guilty tenderness. He says quietly and with genuine contrition.*) Forgive me, Nora. That was unpardonable. (*Her face lights up. Abruptly he is ashamed of being ashamed. He looks away and grabs the decanter. Despite his trembling hand he manages to pour a drink and get it to his mouth and drain it. Then he sinks back in his chair and stares at the table, waiting for the liquor to take effect. After a pause he sighs with relief.*) I confess I needed that as medicine. I begin to feel more myself. (*He pours out another big drink and this time his hand is steadier, and he downs it without much difficulty. He smacks his lips.*) By the Immortal, I may have sunk to keeping an inn but at least I've got a conscience in my trade. I keep liquor a gentleman can drink. (*He starts looking over the paper again—scowls at something—disdainfully, emphasizing his misquote of the line from Byron.*) "There shall he rot—Ambition's dishonored fool!" The paper is full of the latest swindling lies of that idol of the riffraff, Andrew Jackson. Contemptible, drunken scoundrel! But he will be the next President, I predict, for all we others can do to prevent. There is a cursed destiny in these decadent times. Everywhere the scum rises to the top. (*His eyes fasten on the date and*

502 EUGENE O'NEILL

suddenly he strikes the table with his fist.) Today is the 27th! By God, and I would have forgotten!

NORA   Forgot what?

MELODY   The anniversary of Talavera!

NORA   (*Hastily.*) Oh, ain't I stupid not to remember.

MELODY   (*Bitterly.*) I had forgotten myself and no wonder. It's a far cry from this dunghill on which I rot to that glorious day when the Duke of Wellington—Lord Wellesley, then—did me the honor before all the army to commend my bravery. (*He glances around the room with loathing.*) A far cry, indeed! It would be better to forget!

NORA   (*Rallying him.*) No, no, you mustn't. You've never missed celebratin' it and you won't today. I'll have a special dinner for you like I've always had.

MELODY   (*With a quick change of manner—eagerly.*) Good, Nora. I'll invite Jamie Cregan. It's a stroke of fortune he is here. He served under me at Talavera, as you know. A brave soldier, if he isn't a gentleman. You can place him on my right hand. And we'll have Patch Riley to make music and O'Dowd and Roche. If they are rabble, they're full of droll humor at times. But put them over there. (*He points to the table at left front.*) I may tolerate their presence out of charity, but I'll not sink to dining at the same table.

NORA   I'll get your uniform from the trunk, and you'll wear it for dinner like you've done each year.

MELODY   Yes, I must confess I still welcome an excuse to wear it. It makes me feel at least the ghost of the man I was then.

NORA   You're so handsome in it still, no woman could take her eyes off you.

MELODY   (*With a pleased smile.*) I'm afraid you've blarney on your tongue this morning, Nora. (*Then boastfully.*) But it's true, in those days in Portugal and Spain—(*He stops a little shamefacedly, but Nora gives no sign of offense. He takes her hand and pats it gently—avoiding her eyes.*) You have the kindest heart in the world, Nora. And I—(*His voice breaks.*)

NORA   (*Instantly on the verge of grateful tears.*) Ah, who wouldn't, Con darlin', when you—(*She brushes a hand across her eyes—hastily.*) I'll go to the store and get something tasty. (*Her face drops as she remembers.*) But, God help us, where's the money?

MELODY   (*Stiffens—haughtily.*) Money? Since when has my credit not been good?

NORA   (*Hurriedly.*) Don't fret, now. I'll manage.

    He returns to his newspaper, disdaining further interest in money matters.

MELODY   Ha. I see work on the railroad at Baltimore is progressing. (*Lowering his paper.*) By the Eternal, if I had not been a credulous gull and let the thieving Yankees swindle me of all I had when we came here, that's how I would invest my funds now. And I'd become rich. This country, with its immense territory cannot depend solely on creeping canal boats, as short-sighted fools would have us believe. We must have railroads. Then you will see how quickly America will become rich and great! (*His expression changes to one of bitter hatred.*) Great enough to crush England in the next war between them, which I know is inevitable! Would I could live to celebrate that victory! If I have one regret for the past—and there are few things in it that do not call for bitter regret—it is that I shed my blood for a country that thanked me with disgrace. But I will be avenged. This country—my country, now—will drive the English from the face of the earth their shameless perfidy has dishonored!

NORA   Glory be to God for that! And we'll free Ireland!

MELODY   (*Contemptuously.*) Ireland? What benefit would freedom be to her unless she could be freed from the Irish? (*Then irritably.*) But why do I discuss such things with you?

NORA   (*Humbly.*) I know. I'm ignorant.

MELODY   Yet I tried my best to educate you, after we came to America—until I saw it was hopeless.

NORA   You did, surely. And I tried, too, but—

MELODY   You won't even cure yourself of that damned peasant's brogue. And your daughter is becoming as bad.

NORA   She only puts on the brogue to tease you. She can speak as fine as any lady in the land if she wants.

MELODY   (*Is not listening—sunk in bitter brooding.*) But in God's name, who am I to reproach anyone with anything? Why don't you tell me to examine my own conduct?

NORA   You know I'd never.

MELODY   (*Stares at her—again he is moved—quietly.*) No. I know you would not, Nora. (*He looks away—after a pause.*) I owe you an apology for what happened last night.

NORA   Don't think of it.

MELODY   (*With assumed casualness.*) Faith, I'd a drink too many, talking over old times with Jamie Cregan.

NORA   I know.

MELODY   I am afraid I may have—The thought of old times—I become bitter. But you understand, it was the liquor talking, if I said anything to wound you.

NORA   I know it.

MELODY   (*Deeply moved, puts his arm around her.*) You're a sweet, kind woman, Nora—too kind.

    He kisses her.

NORA   (*With blissful happiness.*) Ah, Con darlin', what do I care what you say when the black thoughts are on you? Sure, don't you know I love you?

MELODY   (*A sudden revulsion of feeling convulses his face. He bursts out with disgust, pushing her away from him.*) For God's sake, why don't you wash your hair? It turns my stomach with its stink of onions and stew!

    He reaches for the decanter and shakingly pours a drink. Nora looks as if he had struck her.

NORA   (*Dully.*) I do be washin' it often to plaze you. But when you're standin' over the stove all day, you can't help—

MELODY   Forgive me, Nora. Forget I said that. My nerves are on edge. You'd better leave me alone.

NORA   (*Her face brightening a little.*) Will you ate your breakfast now? I've fine fresh eggs—

MELODY   (*Grasping at this chance to get rid of her—impatiently.*) Yes! In a while. Fifteen minutes, say. But leave me alone now. (*She goes out right. Melody drains his* drink. Then he gets up and paces back and forth, his hands clasped behind him. The third drink begins to work and his face becomes arrogantly self-assured. He catches his reflection in the mirror on the wall at left and stops before it. He brushes a sleeve fastidiously, adjusts the set of his coat, and surveys himself.) Thank God, I still bear the unmistakable stamp of an officer and a gentleman. And so I will remain to the end, in spite of all fate can do to crush my spirit! (He squares his shoulders defiantly. He stares into his eyes in the glass and recites from Byron's "Childe Harold," as if it were an incantation by which he summons pride to justify his life to himself.)

"I have not loved the World, nor the World me;
I have not flattered its rank breath, nor bowed
To its idolatries a patient knee,
Nor coined my cheek to smiles—nor cried aloud
In worship of an echo: in the crowd
They could not deem me one of such—I stood
Among them, but not of them . . ."

(He pauses, then repeats:) "Among them, but not of them." By the Eternal, that expresses it! Thank God for you, Lord Byron—poet and nobleman who made of his disdain immortal music! (Sara appears in the doorway at right. She has changed to her Sunday dress, a becoming blue that brings out the color of her eyes. She draws back for a moment—then stands watching him contemptuously. Melody senses her presence. He starts and turns quickly away from the mirror. For a second his expression is guilty and confused, but he immediately assumes an air of gentlemanly urbanity and bows to her.) Ah, it's you, my dear. Are you going for a morning stroll? You've a beautiful day for it. It will bring fresh roses to your cheeks.

SARA   I don't know about roses, but it will bring a blush of shame to my cheeks. I have to beg Neilan to give us another month's credit, because you made Mother pay the feed bill for your fine thoroughbred mare! (He gives no sign he hears this. She adds scathingly.) I hope you saw something in the mirror you could admire!

MELODY   (In a light tone.) Faith, I suppose I must have looked a vain peacock, preening himself, but you can blame the bad light in my room. One cannot make a decent toilet in that dingy hole in the wall.

SARA   You have the best room in the house, that we ought to rent to guests.

MELODY   Oh, I've no complaints. I was merely explaining my seeming vanity.

SARA   Seeming!

MELODY   (Keeping his tone light.) Faith, Sara, you must have risen the wrong side of the bed this morning, but it takes two to make a quarrel and I don't feel quarrelsome. Quite the contrary. I was about to tell you how exceedingly charming and pretty you look, my dear.

SARA   (With a mocking, awkward, servant's curtsy—in broad brogue.) Oh, thank ye, yer Honor.

MELODY   Every day you resemble your mother more, as she looked when I first knew her.

SARA   Musha, but it's you have the blarneyin' tongue, God forgive you!

MELODY   (In spite of himself, this gets under his skin—angrily.) Be quiet! How dare you talk to me like a common, ignorant—You're my daughter, damn you. (He controls himself and forces a laugh.) A fair hit! You're a great tease, Sara. I shouldn't let you score so easily. Your mother warned me you only did it to provoke me. (*Unconsciously he reaches out for the decanter on the table—then pulls his hand back.*)

SARA (*Contemptuously—without brogue now.*) Go on and drink. Surely you're not ashamed before me, after all these years.

MELODY (*Haughtily.*) Ashamed? I don't understand you. A gentleman drinks as he pleases—provided he can hold his liquor as he should.

SARA A gentleman!

MELODY (*Pleasantly again.*) I hesitated because I had made a good resolve to be abstemious today. But if you insist—(*He pours a drink—a amall one—his hand quite steady now.*) To your happiness, my dear. (*She stares at him scornfully. He goes on graciously.*) Will you do me the favor to sit down? I have wanted a quiet chat with you for some time. (*He holds out a chair for her at rear of the table at center.*)

SARA (*Eyes him suspiciously—then sits down.*) What is it you want?

MELODY (*With a playfully paternal manner.*) Your happiness, my dear, and what I wish to discuss means happiness to you, unless I have grown blind. How is our patient, young Simon Harford, this morning?

SARA (*Curtly.*) He's better.

MELODY I am delighted to hear it. (*Gallantly.*) How could he help but be with such a charming nurse? (*She stares at him coldly. He goes on.*) Let us be frank. Young Simon is in love with you. I can see that with half an eye—and, of course, you know it. And you return his love, I surmise.

SARA Surmise whatever you please.

MELODY Meaning you do love him? I am glad, Sara. (*He becomes sentimentally romantic.*) Requited love is the greatest blessing life can bestow on us poor mortals; and first love is the most blessed of all. As Lord Byron has it: (*He recites.*)
"But sweeter still than this, than these, than all,
Is first and passionate Love—it stands alone,
Like Adam's recollection of his fall. . ."

SARA (*Interrupts him rudely.*) Was it to listen to you recite Byron—?

MELODY (*Concealing discomfiture and resentment—pleasantly.*) No. What I was leading up to is that you have my blessing, if that means anything to you. Young Harford is, I am convinced, an estimable youth. I have enjoyed my talks with him. It has been a privilege to be able to converse with a cultured gentleman again. True, he is a bit on the sober side for one so young, but by way of compensation, there is a romantic touch of the poet behind his Yankee phlegm.

SARA It's fine you approve of him!

MELODY In your interest I have had some enquiries made about his family.

SARA (*Angered—with taunting brogue.*) Have you, indade? Musha, that's cute av you! Was it auld Patch Riley, the Piper, made them? Or was it Dan Roche or Paddy O'Dowd, or some other drunken sponge—

MELODY (*As if he hadn't heard—condescendingly.*) I find his people will pass muster.

SARA Oh, do you? That's nice!

MELODY Apparently, his father is a gentleman—that is, by Yankee standards, insofar as one in trade can lay claim to the title. But as I've become an

American citizen myself, I suppose it would be downright snobbery to hold to old-world standards.

SARA   Yes, wouldn't it be!

MELODY   Though it is difficult at times for my pride to remember I am no longer the master of Melody Castle and an estate of three thousand acres of as fine pasture and woodlands as you'd find in the whole United Kingdom, with my stable of hunters, and—

SARA   (*Bitterly.*) Well, you've a beautiful thoroughbred mare now, at least—to prove you're still a gentleman!

MELODY   (*Stung into defiant anger.*) Yes, I've the mare! And by God, I'll keep her if I have to starve myself so she may eat.

SARA   You mean, make Mother slave to keep her for you, even if she has to starve!

MELODY   (*Controls his anger—and ignores this.*) But what was I saying? Oh, yes, young Simon's family. His father will pass muster, but it's through his mother, I believe, he comes by his really good blood. My information is, she springs from generations of well-bred gentlefolk.

SARA   It would be a great pride to her, I'm sure, to know you found her suitable!

MELODY   I suppose I may expect the young man to request an interview with me as soon as he is up and about again?

SARA   To declare his honorable intentions and ask you for my hand, is that what you mean?

MELODY   Naturally. He is a man of honor. And there are certain financial arrangements Simon's father or his legal representative will wish to discuss with me. The amount of your settlement has to be agreed upon.

SARA   (*Stares at him as if she could not believe her ears.*) My settlement! Simon's father! God pity you—!

MELODY   (*Firmly.*) Your settlement, certainly. You did not think, I hope, that I would give you away without a penny to your name as if you were some poverty-stricken peasant's daughter? Please remember I have my own position to maintain. Of course, it is a bit difficult at present. I am temporarily hard pressed. But perhaps a mortgage on the inn—

SARA   It's mortgaged to the hilt already, as you very well know.

MELODY   If nothing else, I can always give my note at hand for whatever amount—

SARA   You can give it, sure enough! But who'll take it?

MELODY   Between gentlemen, these matters can always be arranged.

SARA   God help you, it must be a wonderful thing to live in a fairy tale where only dreams are real to you. (*Then sharply.*) But you needn't waste your dreams worrying about my affairs. I'll thank you not to interfere. Attend to your drinking and leave me alone. (*He gives no indication that he has heard a word she has said. She stares at him and a look almost of fear comes into her eyes. She bursts out with a bitter exasperation in which there is a strong undercurrent of entreaty.*) Father! Will you never let yourself wake up—not even now when you're sober, or nearly? Is it stark mad you've gone, so you can't tell any more what's dead and a lie, and what's the living truth?

MELODY   (*His face is convulsed by a spasm of pain as if something vital had been stabbed in him—with a cry of tortured appeal.*) Sara! (*But instantly his pain is transformed* into rage. He half rises from his chair threateningly.) Be quiet, damn you! How dare you—! (*She shrinks away and rises to her feet. He forces control on himself and sinks back in his chair, his hands gripping the arms.*)

The street door at rear is flung open and DAN ROCHE, PADDY O'DOWD, *and* PATCH RILEY *attempt to pile in together and get jammed for a moment in the doorway. They all have hangovers, and Roche is talking boisterously. Dan Roche is middle-aged, squat, bowlegged, with a potbelly and short arms lumpy with muscle. His face is flat with a big mouth, protruding ears, and red-rimmed little pig's eyes. He is dressed in dirty, patched clothes. Paddy O'Dowd is thin, round-shouldered, flat-chested, with a pimply complexion, bulgy eyes, and a droopy mouth. His manner is oily and fawning, that of a born sponger and parasite. His clothes are those of a cheap sport. Patch Riley is an old man with a thatch of dirty white hair. His washed-out blue eyes have a wandering, half-witted expression. His skinny body is clothed in rags and there is nothing under his tattered coat but his bare skin. His mouth is sunken in, toothless. He carries an Irish bagpipe under his arm.*

ROCHE (*His back is half turned as he harangues O'Dowd and Riley, and he does not see Melody and Sara.*) And I says, it's Andy Jackson will put you in your place, and all the slave-drivin' Yankee skinflints like you! Take your damned job, I says, and—

O'DOWD (*Warningly, his eyes on Melody.*) Whist! Whist! Hold your prate!

Roche whirls around to face Melody, and his aggressiveness oozes from him, changing to a hangdog apprehension. For Melody has sprung to his feet, his eyes blazing with an anger which is increased by the glance of contempt Sara casts from him to the three men. O'Dowd avoids Melody's eyes, busies himself in closing the door. Patch Riley stands gazing at Sara with a dreamy, admiring look, lost in a world of his own fancy, oblivious to what is going on.

ROCHE (*Placatingly.*) Good mornin' to ye, Major.

O'DOWD (*Fawning.*) Good mornin', yer Honor.

MELODY How dare you come tramping in here in that manner! Have you mistaken this inn for the sort of dirty shebeen you were used to in the old country where the pigs ran in and out the door?

O'DOWD We ask pardon, yer Honor.

MELODY (*To Roche—an impressive menace in his tone.*) You, Paddy. Didn't I forbid you ever to mention that scoundrel Jackson's name in my house or I'd horse-whip the hide off your back? (*He takes a threatening step toward him.*) Perhaps you think I cannot carry out that threat.

ROCHE (*Backs away frightenedly.*) No, no, Major. I forgot—Good mornin' to ye, Miss.

O'DOWD Good mornin', Miss Sara. (*She ignores them. Patch Riley is still gazing at her with dreamy admiration, having heard nothing, his hat still on his head. O'Dowd officiously snatches it off for him—rebukingly.*) Where's your wits, Patch? Didn't ye hear his Honor?

RILEY (*Unheeding—addresses Sara.*) Sure it's you, God bless you, looks like a fairy princess as beautiful as a rose in the mornin' dew. I'll raise a tune for you. (*He starts to arrange his pipes.*)

SARA (*Curtly.*) I want none of your tunes. (*Then, seeing the look of wondering hurt in the old man's eyes, she adds kindly.*) That's sweet of you, Patch. I know you'd raise a beautiful tune, but I have to go out.

Consoled, the old man smiles at her gratefully.

MELODY Into the bar, all of you, where you belong! I told you not to use this entrance! (*With disdainful tolerance.*) I suppose it's a free drink you're after. Well, no one can say of me that I turned away anyone I knew thirsty from my door.

O'DOWD Thank ye, yer Honor. Come along, Dan. (*He takes Riley's arm.*) Come on, Patch.

The three go into the bar and O'Dowd closes the door behind them.

SARA (*In derisive brogue.*) Sure, it's well trained you've got the poor retainers on your American estate to respect the master! (*Then as he ignores her and casts a furtive glance at the door to the bar, running his tongue over his dry lips, she says acidly, with no trace of brogue.*) Don't let me keep you from joining the gentlemen!

She turns her back on him and goes out the street door at rear.

MELODY (*His face again convulsed by a spasm of pain—pleadingly.*) Sara!

Nora enters from the hall at right, carrying a tray with toast, eggs, bacon, and tea. She arranges his breakfast on the table at front center, bustling garrulously.

NORA Have I kept you waitin'? The divil was in the toast. One lot burned black as a naygur when my back was turned. But the bacon is crisp, and the eggs not too soft, the way you like them. Come and sit down now. (*Melody does not seem to hear her. She looks at him worriedly.*) What's up with you, Con? Don't you hear me?

O'DOWD (*Pokes his head in the door from the bar.*) Mickey won't believe you said we could have a drink, yer Honor, unless ye tell him.

MELODY (*Licking his lips.*) I'm coming.

He goes to the bar door.

NORA Con! Have this in your stomach first! It'll all get cauld.

MELODY (*Without turning to her—in his condescendingly polite tone.*) I find I am not the least hungry, Nora. I regret your having gone to so much trouble.

He goes into the bar, closing the door behind him. Nora slumps on a chair at the rear of the table and stares at the breakfast with a pitiful helplessness. She begins to sob quietly.

CURTAIN

ACT TWO

Same as Act One. About half an hour has elapsed. The barroom door opens and Melody comes in. He has had two more drinks and still no breakfast, but this has had no outward effect except that his face is paler and his manner more disdainful. He turns to give orders to the spongers in the bar.

MELODY Remember what I say. None of your loud brawling. And you, Riley, keep your bagpipe silent, or out you go. I wish to be alone in quiet for a while with my memories. When Corporal Cregan returns, Mickey, send him in to me. He, at least, knows Talavera is not the name of a new brand of whiskey.

"He shuts the door contemptuously on Mickey's "Yes, Major." and the obedient murmur of the others. He sits at rear of the table at left front. At first, he poses to himself, striking an attitude—a Byronic hero, noble, embittered, disdainful, defying his tragic fate, brooding over past glories. But he has no audience and he cannot keep it up. His shoulders sag and he stares at the table top, hopelessness and defeat bringing a trace of real tragedy to his ruined, handsome face.

The street door is opened and Sara enters. He does not hear the click of the latch, or notice her as she comes forward. Fresh from the humiliation of cajoling the storekeeper to extend more credit, her eyes are bitter. At sight of her father they become more so. She moves toward the door at right, determined to ignore him, but something unusual in his attitude strikes her and she stops to regard him searchingly. She starts to say something bitter—stops—finally, in spite of herself, she asks with a trace of genuine pity in her voice.

SARA   What's wrong with you, Father? Are you really sick or is it just—
    He starts guiltily, ashamed of being caught in such a weak mood.
MELODY   (*Gets to his feet politely and bows.*) I beg your pardon, my dear. I did not hear you come in. (*With a deprecating smile.*) Faith, I was far away in spirit, lost in memories of a glorious battle in Spain, nineteen years ago today.
SARA   (*Her face hardens.*) Oh. It's the anniversary of Talavera, is it? Well, I know what that means—a great day for the spongers and a bad day for this inn!
MELODY   (*Coldly.*) I don't understand you. Of course I shall honor the occasion.
SARA   You needn't tell me. I remember the other celebrations—and this year, now Jamie Cregan has appeared, you've an excuse to make it worse.
MELODY   Naturally, an old comrade in arms will be doubly welcome—
SARA   Well, I'll say this much. From the little I've seen of him, I'd rather have free whiskey go down his gullet than the others'. He's a relation, too.
MELODY   (*Stiffly.*) Merely a distant cousin. That has no bearing. It's because Corporal Cregan fought by my side—
SARA   I suppose you've given orders to poor Mother to cook a grand feast for you, as usual, and you'll wear your beautiful uniform, and I'll have the honor of waiting on table. Well, I'll do it just this once more for Mother's sake, or she'd have to, but it'll be the last time. (*She turns her back on him and goes to the door at right.*) You'll be pleased to learn your daughter had almost to beg on her knees to Neilan before he'd let us have another month's credit. He made it plain it was to Mother he gave it because he pities her for the husband she's got. But what do you care about that, as long as you and your fine thoroughbred mare can live in style!
    Melody is shaken for a second. He glances toward the bar as if he longed to return there to escape her. Then he gets hold of himself. His face becomes expressionless. He sits in the same chair and picks up the paper, ignoring her. She starts to go out just as her mother appears in the doorway. Nora is carrying a glass of milk.
NORA   Here's the milk the doctor ordered for the young gentleman. It's time for it, and I knew you'd be going upstairs.
SARA   (*Takes the milk.*) Thank you, Mother. (*She nods scornfully toward her father.*) I've just been telling him I begged another month's credit from Neilan, so he needn't worry.
NORA   Ah, thank God for that. Neilan's a kind man.

MELODY   (*Explodes.*) Damn his kindness! By the Eternal, if he'd refused, I'd have—! (*He controls himself, meeting Sara's contemptuous eyes. He goes on quietly, a bitter, sneering antagonism underneath.*) Don't let me detain you, my dear. Take his milk to our Yankee guest, as your mother suggests. Don't miss any chance to play the ministering angel. (*Vindictively.*) Faith, the poor young devil hasn't a chance to escape with you two scheming peasants laying snares to trap him!

SARA   That's a lie! And leave Mother out of your insults!

MELODY   And if all other tricks fail, there's always one last trick to get him through his honor!

SARA   (*Tensely.*) What trick do you mean?
            Nora grabs her arm.

NORA   Hould your prate, now! Why can't you leave him be? It's your fault for provoking him.

SARA   (*Quietly.*) All right, Mother. I'll leave him to look in the mirror, like he loves to, and remember what he said, and be proud of himself.
            Melody winces. Sara goes out right.

MELODY   (*After a pause—shakenly.*) I—She mistook my meaning—It's as you said. She goads me into losing my temper and I say things—

NORA   (*Sadly.*) I know what made you say it. You think maybe she's like I was, and you can't help remembering my sin with you.

MELODY   (*Guiltily vehement.*) No! No! I tell you she mistook my meaning, and now you— (*Then exasperatedly.*) Damn your priests' prating about your sin! (*With a strange, scornful vanity.*) To hear you tell it, you'd think it was you who seduced me! That's likely, isn't it?—remembering the man I was then!

NORA   I remember well. Sure, you was that handsome, no woman could resist you. And you are still.

MELODY   (*Pleased.*) None of your blarney, Nora. (*With Byronic gloom.*) I am but a ghost haunting a ruin. (*Then gallantly but without looking at her.*) And how about you in those days? Weren't you the prettiest girl in all Ireland? (*Scornfully.*) And be damned to your lying, pious shame! You had no shame then, I remember. It was love and joy and glory in you and you were proud!

NORA   (*Her eyes shining.*) I'm still proud and will be to the day I die!

MELODY   (*Gives her an approving look which turns to distaste at her appearance—looks away irritably.*) Why do you bring up the past? I do not wish to discuss it.

NORA   (*After a pause—timidly.*) All the same, you shouldn't talk to Sara as if you thought she'd be up to anything to catch young Harford.

MELODY   I did not think that! She is my daughter—

NORA   She is surely. And he's a dacent lad. (*She smiles a bit scornfully.*) Sure, from all she's told me, he's that shy he's never dared even to kiss her hand!

MELODY   (*With more than a little contempt.*) I can well believe it. When it comes to making love the Yankees are clumsy, fish-blooded louts. They lack savoir-faire. They have no romantic fire! They know nothing of women. (*He snorts disdainfully.*) By the Eternal, when I was his age— (*Then quickly.*) Not that I don't approve of young Harford, mind you. He is a gentleman. When he asks me for Sara's hand I will gladly give my consent, provided his father and I can agree on the amount of the settlement.

NORA   (*Hastily.*). Ah, there's no need to think of that yet. (*Then lapsing into her own dream.*) Yes, she'll be happy because she loves him dearly, a lot more than she admits. And it'll give her a chance to rise in the world. We'll see the day when she'll live in a grand mansion, dressed in silks and satins, and riding in a carriage with coachman and footman.

MELODY   I desire that as much as you do, Nora. I'm done—finished—no future but the past. But my daughter has the looks, the brains—ambition, youth—She can go far. (*Then sneeringly.*) That is, if she can remember she's a gentlewoman and stop acting like a bogtrotting peasant wench! (*He hears Sara returning downstairs.*) She's coming back. (*He gets up—bitterly.*) As the sight of me seems to irritate her, I'll go in the bar a while. I've had my fill of her insults for one morning.

> He opens the bar door. There is a chorus of eager, thirsty welcome from inside. He goes in, closing the door. Sara enters from right. Her face is flushed and her eyes full of dreamy happiness.

NORA   (*Rebukingly.*) Himself went in the bar to be out of reach of your tongue. A fine thing! Aren't you ashamed you haven't enough feeling not to torment him, when you know it's the anniversary—

SARA   All right, Mother. Let him take what joy he can out of the day. I'll even help you get his uniform out of the trunk in the attic and brush and clean it for you.

NORA   Ah, God bless you, that's the way— (*Then, astonished at this unexpected docility.*) Glory be, but you've changed all of a sudden. What's happened to you?

SARA   I'm so happy now—I can't feel bitter against anyone. (*She hesitates—then shyly.*) Simon kissed me. (*Having said this, she goes on triumphantly.*) He got his courage up at last, but it was me made him. I was freshening up his pillows and leaning over him, and he couldn't help it, if he was human. (*She laughs tenderly.*) And then you'd have laughed to see him. He near sank through the bed with shame at his boldness. He began apologizing as if he was afraid I'd be so insulted I'd never speak to him again.

NORA   (*Teasingly.*) And what did you do? I'll wager you wasn't as brazen as you pretend.

SARA   (*Ruefully.*) It's true, Mother. He made me as bashful as he was. I felt a great fool.

NORA   And was that all? Sure, kissing is easy. Didn't he ask you if you'd marry—?

SARA   No. (*Quickly.*) But it was my fault he didn't. He was trying to be brave enough. All he needed was a word of encouragement. But I stood there, dumb as a calf, and when I did speak it was to say I had to come and help you, and the end was I ran from the room, blushing as red as a beet—(*She comes to her mother. Nora puts her arms around her. Sara hides her face on her shoulder, on the verge of tears.*) Oh, Mother, ain't it crazy to be such a fool?

NORA   Well, when you're in love—

SARA   (*Breaking away from her—angrily.*) That's just it! I'm too much in love and I don't want to be! I won't let my heart rule my head and make a slave of me! (*Suddenly she smiles confidently.*) Ah well, he loves me as much, and more, I know that, and the next time I'll keep my wits. (*She laughs happily.*) You can consider it as good as done, Mother. I'm Mrs. Simon Harford, at your pleasure. (*She makes a sweeping bow.*)

NORA (*Smiling.*) Arrah, none of your airs and graces with me! Help me, now, like you promised, and we'll get your father's uniform out of the trunk. It won't break your back in the attic, like it does me.

SARA (*Gaily puts her arm around her mother's waist.*) Come along then.

NORA (*As they go out right.*) I disremember which trunk—and you'll have to help me find the key.

> *There is a pause. Then the bar door is opened and Melody enters again in the same manner as he did at the beginning of the act. There is the same sound of voices from the bar but this time Melody gives no parting orders but simply shuts the door behind him. He scowls with disgust.*

MELODY Cursed ignorant cattle. (*Then with a real, lonely yearning.*) I wish Jamie Cregan would come. (*Bitterly.*) Driven from pillar to post in my own home! Everywhere ignorance—or the scorn of my own daughter! (*Then defiantly.*) But by the Eternal God, no power on earth, nor in hell itself, can break me! (*His eyes are drawn irresistibly to the mirror. He moves in front of it, seeking the satisfying reassurance of his reflection there. What follows is an exact repetition of his scene before the mirror in Act One. There is the same squaring of his shoulders, arrogant lifting of his head, and then the favorite quote from Byron, recited aloud to his own image.*)

"I have not loved the World, nor the World me;
I have not flattered its rank breath, nor bowed
To its idolatries a patient knee,
Nor coined my cheek to smiles,—nor cried aloud
In worship of an echo: in the crowd
They could not deem me one of such—I stood
Among them, but not of them . . ."

> *He stands staring in the mirror and does not hear the latch of the street door click. The door opens and DEBORAH (Mrs. Henry Harford), Simon's mother, enters, closing the door quietly behind her. Melody continues to be too absorbed to notice anything. For a moment, blinded by the sudden change from the bright glare of the street, she does not see him. When she does, she stares incredulously. Then she smiles with an amused and mocking relish.*
>
> *Deborah is forty-one, but looks to be no more than thirty. She is small, a little over five feet tall, with a fragile, youthful figure. One would never suspect that she is the middle-aged mother of two grown sons. Her face is beautiful—that is, it is beautiful from the standpoint of the artist with an eye for bone structure and unusual character. It is small, with high cheekbones, wedge-shaped, narrowing from a broad forehead to a square chin, framed by thick, wavy, red-brown hair. The nose is delicate and thin, a trifle aquiline. The mouth, with full lips and even, white teeth, is too large for her face. So are the long-lashed, green-flecked brown eyes, under heavy, angular brows. These would appear large in any face, but in hers they seem enormous and are made more startling by the pallor of her complexion. She has tiny, high-arched feet and thin, tapering hands. Her slender, fragile body is dressed in white with calculated simplicity. About her whole personality is a curious atmosphere of deliberate detachment, the studied aloofness of an ironically amused spectator. Something perversely assertive about it too, as if she consciously carried her originality to the point of whimsical eccentricity.*

DEBORAH   I beg your pardon.

> *Melody jumps and whirls around. For a moment his face has an absurdly startled, stupid look. He is shamed and humiliated and furious at being caught for a second time in one morning before the mirror. His revenge is to draw himself up haughtily and survey her insolently from head to toe. But at once, seeing she is attractive and a lady, his manner changes. Opportunity beckons and he is confident of himself, put upon his mettle. He bows, a gracious, gallant gentleman. There is seductive charm in his welcoming smile and in his voice.*

MELODY   Good morning, Mademoiselle. It is an honor to welcome you to this unworthy inn. (*He draws out a chair at rear of the larger table in the foreground—bowing again.*) If I may presume. You will find it comfortable here, away from the glare of the street.

DEBORAH   (*Regards him for a second puzzledly. She is impressed in spite of herself by his bearing and distinguished, handsome face.*) Thank you.

> *She comes forward. Melody makes a gallant show of holding her chair and helping her be seated. He takes in all her points with sensual appreciation. It is the same sort of pleasure a lover of horseflesh would have in the appearance of a thoroughbred horse. Meanwhile he speaks with caressing courtesy.*

MELODY   Mademoiselle—(*He sees her wedding ring.*) Pray forgive me, I see it is Madame—Permit me to say again, how great an honor I will esteem it to be of any service. (*He manages, as he turns away, as if by accident to brush his hand against her shoulder. She is startled and caught off guard. She shrinks and looks up at him. Their eyes meet and at the nakedly physical appraisement she sees in his, a fascinated fear suddenly seizes her. But at once she is reassured as he shifts his gaze, satisfied by her reactions to his first attack, and hastens to apologize.*) I beg your pardon, Madame. I am afraid my manners have grown clumsy with disuse. It is not often a lady comes here now. This inn, like myself, has fallen upon unlucky days.

DEBORAH   (*Curtly ignoring this.*) I presume you are the innkeeper, Melody?

MELODY   (*A flash of anger in his eyes—arrogantly.*) I am *Major* Cornelius Melody, one time of His Majesty's Seventh Dragoons, at your service. (*He bows with chill formality.*)

DEBORAH   (*Is now an amused spectator again—apologetically.*) Oh. Then it is I who owe you an apology, Major Melody.

MELODY   (*Encouraged—gallantly.*) No, no, dear lady, the fault is mine. I should not have taken offense. (*With the air of one frankly admitting a praiseworthy weakness.*) Faith, I may was well confess my besetting weakness is that of all gentlemen who have known better days. I have a pride unduly sensitive to any fancied slight.

DEBORAH   (*Playing up to him now.*) I assure you, sir, there was no intention on my part to slight you.

MELODY   (*His eyes again catch hers and hold them—his tone insinuatingly caressing.*) You are as gracious as you are beautiful, Madame. (*Deborah's amusement is gone. She is again confused and, in spite of herself, frightened and fascinated. Melody proceeds with his attack, full of confidence now, the successful seducer of old. His voice takes on a calculated melancholy cadence. He becomes a romantic, tragic figure, appealing for a woman's understanding and loving compassion.*) I am a poor fool, Madame.

I would be both wiser and happier if I could reconcile myself to being the proprietor of a tawdry tavern, if I could abjure pride and forget the past. Today of all days it is hard to forget, for it is the anniversary of the battle of Talavera. The most memorable day of my life, Madame. It was on the glorious field I had the honor to be commended for my bravery by the great Duke of Wellington, himself—Sir Arthur Wellesley, then. So I am sure you can find it in your heart to forgive—(*His tone more caressing.*) One so beautiful must understand the hearts of men full well, since so many must have given their hearts to you. (*A coarse passion comes into his voice.*) Yes, I'll wager my all against a penny that even among the fish-blooded Yankees there's not a man whose heart doesn't catch flame from your beauty! (*He puts his hand over one of her hands on the table and stares into her eyes ardently.*) As mine does now!

DEBORAH (*Feeling herself borne down weakly by the sheer force of his physical strength, struggles to release her hand. She stammers, with an attempt at lightness.*) Is this—what the Irish call blarney, sir?

MELODY (*With a fierce, lustful sincerity.*) No! I take my oath by the living God, I would charge a square of Napoleon's Old Guard singlehanded for one kiss of your lips.

> He bends lower, while his eyes hold hers. For a second it seems he will kiss her and she cannot help herself. Then abruptly the smell of whiskey on his breath brings her to herself, shaken with disgust and coldly angry. She snatches her hand from his and speaks with withering contempt.

DEBORAH Pah! You reek of whiskey! You are drunk, sir! You are insolent and disgusting! I do not wonder your inn enjoys such meager patronage, if you regale all your guests of my sex with this absurd performance!

> Melody straightens up with a jerk, taking a step back as though he had been slapped in the face. Deborah rises to her feet, ignoring him disdainfully. At this moment Sara and her mother enter through the doorway at right. They take in the scene at a glance. Melody and Deborah do not notice their entrance.

NORA (*Half under her breath.*) Oh, God help us!

SARA (*Guesses at once this must be the woman Mickey had told her about. She hurries toward them quickly, trying to hide her apprehension and anger and shame at what she knows must have happened.*) What is it, Father? What does the lady wish?

> Her arrival is a further blow for Melody, seething now in a fury of humiliated pride. Deborah turns to face Sara.

DEBORAH (*Coolly self-possessed—pleasantly.*) I came here to see you, Miss Melody, hoping you might know the present whereabouts of my son, Simon.

> This is a bombshell for Melody.

MELODY (*Blurts out with no apology in his tone but angrily, as if she had intentionally made a fool of him.*) You're his mother? In God's name, Madame, why didn't you say so!

DEBORAH (*Ignoring him—to Sara.*) I've been out to his hermit's cabin, only to find the hermit flown.

SARA (*Stammers.*) He's here, Mrs. Harford—upstairs in bed. He's been sick—

DEBORAH Sick? You don't mean seriously?

SARA (*Recovering a little from her confusion.*) Oh, he's over it now, or almost. It was only a spell of chills and fever he caught from the damp of the lake. I found him there shivering and shaking and made him come here where there's a doctor handy and someone to nurse him.

DEBORAH   (*Pleasantly.*) The someone being you, Miss Melody?

SARA   Yes, me and—my mother and I.

DEBORAH   (*Graciously.*) I am deeply grateful to you and your mother for your kindness.

NORA   (*Who has remained in the background, now comes forward—with her sweet, friendly smile.*) Och, don't be thankin' us, ma'am. Sure, your son is a gentle, fine lad, and we all have great fondness for him. He'd be welcome here if he never paid a penny—

> She stops embarrassedly, catching a disapproving glance from Sara. Deborah is repelled by Nora's slovenly appearance, but she feels her simple charm and gentleness, and returns her smile.

SARA   (*With embarrassed stiffness.*) This is my mother, Mrs. Harford.

> Deborah inclines her head graciously. Nora instinctively bobs in a peasant's curtsy to one of the gentry. Melody, snubbed and seething, glares at her.

NORA   I'm pleased to make your acquaintance, ma'am.

MELODY   Nora! For the love of God, stop—(*Suddenly he is able to become the polished gentleman again—considerately and even a trifle condescendingly.*) I am sure Mrs. Harford is waiting to be taken to her son. Am I not right, Madame?

> Deborah is so taken aback by his effrontery that for a moment she is speechless. She replies coldly, obviously doing so only because she does not wish to create further embarrassment.

DEBORAH   That is true, sir. (*She turns her back on him.*) If you will be so kind, Miss Melody. I've wasted so much of the morning and I have to return to the city. I have only time for a short visit—

SARA   Just come with me, Mrs. Harford. (*She goes to the door at right, and steps aside to let Deborah precede her.*) What a pleasant surprise this will be for Simon. He'd have written you he was sick, but he didn't want to worry you. (*She follows Deborah into the hall.*)

MELODY   Damned fool of a woman! If I'd known—No, be damned if I regret! Cursed Yankee upstart! (*With a sneer.*) But she didn't fool me with her insulted airs! I've known too many women—(*In a rage.*) "Absurd performance," was it? God damn her!

NORA   (*Timidly.*) Don't be cursing her and tormenting yourself. She seems a kind lady. She won't hold it against you, when she stops to think, knowing you didn't know who she is.

MELODY   (*Tensely.*) Be quiet!

NORA   Forget it now, do, for Sara's sake. Sure, you wouldn't want anything to come between her and the lad. (*He is silent. She goes on comfortingly.*) Go on up to your room now and you'll find something to take your mind off. Sara and I have your uniform brushed and laid out on the bed.

MELODY   (*Harshly.*) Put it back in the trunk! I don't want it to remind me— (*With humiliated rage again.*) By the Eternal, I'll wager she believed what I told her of Talavera and the Great Duke honoring me was a drunken liar's boast!

NORA   No, she'd never, Con. She couldn't.

MELODY   (*Seized by an idea.*) Well, seeing would be believing, eh, my fine lady? Yes, by God, that will prove to her—(*He turns to Nora, his self-confidence partly restored.*) Thank you for reminding me of my duty to Sara. You are right. I do owe it to her interests to forget my anger and make a formal apology to Simon's mother for our little misunderstanding. (*He smiles condescendingly.*) Faith, as a gentleman, I should grant it is a pretty woman's privilege to be always right even when she is wrong. (*He goes to the door at extreme left front and opens it.*) If the lady should come back, kindly keep her here on some excuse until I return.

> This is a command. He disappears, closing the door behind him.

NORA   (*Sighs.*) Ah well, it's all right. He'll be on his best behavior now, and he'll feel proud again in his uniform.

> She sits at the end of center table right and relaxes wearily. A moment later Sara enters quickly from right and comes to her.

SARA   Where's Father?

NORA   I got him to go up and put on his uniform. It'll console him.

SARA   (*Bitterly.*) Console *him*? It's me ought to be consoled for having such a great fool for a father!

NORA   Hush now! How could he know who—?

SARA   (*With a sudden reversal of feeling—almost vindictively.*) Yes, it serves her right. I suppose she thinks she's such a great lady anyone in America would pay her respect. Well, she knows better now. And she didn't act as insulted as she might. Maybe she liked it, for all her pretenses. (*Again with an abrupt reversal of feeling.*) Ah, how can I talk such craziness! Him and his drunken love-making! Well, he got put in his place, and aren't I glad! He won't forget in a hurry how she snubbed him, as if he was no better than dirt under her feet!

NORA   She didn't. She had the sense to see he'd been drinking and not to mind him.

SARA   (*Dully.*) Maybe. But isn't that bad enough? What woman would want her son to marry the daughter of a man like—(*She breaks down.*) Oh, Mother, I was feeling so happy and sure of Simon, and now—Why did she have to come today? If she'd waited till tomorrow, even, I'd have got him to ask me to marry him, and once he'd done that no power on earth could change him.

NORA   If he loves you no power can change him, anyway. (*Proudly.*) Don't I know! (*Reassuringly.*) She's his mother, and she loves him and she'll want him to be happy, and she'll see he loves you. What makes you think she'll try to change him?

SARA   Because she hates me, Mother—for one reason.

NORA   She doesn't. She couldn't.

SARA   She does. Oh, she acted as nice as nice, but she didn't fool me. She's the kind would be polite to the hangman, and her on the scaffold. (*She lowers her voice.*) It isn't just to pay Simon a visit she came. It's because Simon's father got a letter telling him about us, and he showed it to her.

NORA   Who did a dirty trick like that?

SARA   It wasn't signed, she said. I suppose someone around here that hates Father—and who doesn't?

NORA   Bad luck to the blackguard, whoever it was!

SARA   She said she'd come to warn Simon his father is wild with anger and he's gone to see his lawyer—But that doesn't worry me. It's only her influence I'm afraid of.

NORA   How do you know about the letter?

SARA   (*Avoiding her eyes.*) I sneaked back to listen outside the door.

NORA   Shame on you! You should have more pride!

SARA   I was ashamed, Mother, after a moment or two, and I came away. (*Then defiantly.*) No, I'm not ashamed. I wanted to learn what tricks she might be up to, so I'll be able to fight them. I'm not ashamed at all. I'll do anything to keep him. (*Lowering her voice.*) She started talking the second she got in the door. She had only a few minutes because she has to be home before dinner so her husband won't suspect she came here. He's forbidden her to see Simon ever since Simon came out here to live.

NORA   Well, doesn't her coming against her husband's orders show she's on Simon's side?

SARA   Yes, but it doesn't show she wants him to marry me. (*Impatiently.*) Don't be so simple, Mother. Wouldn't she tell Simon that anyway, even if the truth was her husband sent her to do all she could to get him away from me?

NORA   Don't look for trouble before it comes. Wait and see, now. Maybe you'll find—

SARA   I'll find what I said, Mother—that she hates me. (*Bitterly.*) Even if she came here with good intentions, she wouldn't have them now, after our great gentleman has insulted her. Thank God, if he's putting on his uniform, he'll be hours before the mirror, and she'll be gone before he can make a fool of himself again. (*Nora starts to tell her the truth—then thinks better of it. Sara goes on, changing her tone.*) But I'd like her to see him in his uniform, at that, if he was sober. She'd find she couldn't look down on him—(*Exasperatedly.*) Och! I'm as crazy as he is. As if she hadn't the brains to see through him.

NORA   (*Wearily.*) Leave him be, for the love of God.

SARA   (*After a pause—defiantly.*) Let her try whatever game she likes. I have brains too, she'll discover. (*Then uneasily.*) Only, like Simon's told me, I feel she's strange and queer behind her lady's airs, and it'll be hard to tell what she's really up to. (*They both hear a sound from upstairs.*) That's her, now. She didn't waste much time. Well, I'm ready for her. Go in the kitchen, will you, Mother? I want to give her the chance to have it out with me alone. (*Nora gets up—then, remembering Melody's orders, glances toward the door at left front uneasily and hesitates. Sara says urgently.*) Don't you hear me? Hurry, Mother!

    Nora sighs and goes out quickly, right. Sara sits at rear of the center table and waits, drawing herself up in an unconscious imitation of her father's grand manner. Deborah appears in the doorway at right. There is nothing in her expression to betray any emotion resulting from her interview with her son. She smiles pleasantly at Sara, who rises graciously from her chair.

DEBORAH   (*Coming to her.*) I am glad to find you here, Miss Melody. It gives me another opportunity to express my gratitude for your kindness to my son during his illness.

SARA   Thank you, Mrs. Harford. My mother and I have been only too happy to do all we could. (*She adds defiantly.*) We are very fond of Simon.

DEBORAH (*A glint of secret amusement in her eyes.*) Yes, I feel you are. And he has told me how fond he is of you. (*Her manner becomes reflective. She speaks rapidly in a remote, detached way, lowering her voice unconsciously as if she were thinking aloud to herself.*) This is the first time I have seen Simon since he left home to seek self-emancipation at the breast of Nature. I find him not so greatly changed as I had been led to expect from his letters. Of course, it is some time since he has written. I had thought his implacably honest discovery that the poetry he hoped the pure freedom of Nature would inspire him to write is, after all, but a crude imitation of Lord Byron's would have more bitterly depressed his spirit. (*She smiles.*) But evidently he has found a new romantic dream by way of recompense. As I might have known he would. Simon is an inveterate dreamer—a weakness he inherited from me, I'm afraid, although I must admit the Harfords have been great dreamers, too, in their way. Even my husband has a dream—a conservative, material dream, naturally. I have just been reminding Simon that his father is rigidly unforgiving when his dream is flouted, and very practical in his methods of defending it. (*She smiles again.*) My warning was the mechanical gesture of a mother's duty, merely. I realized it would have no effect. He did not listen to what I said. For that matter, neither did I. (*She laughs a little detached laugh, as if she were secretly amused.*)

SARA (*Stares at her, unable to decide what is behind all this and how she should react—with an undercurrent of resentment.*) I don't think Simon imitates Lord Byron. I hate Lord Byron's poetry. And I know there's a true poet in Simon.

DEBORAH (*Vaguely surprised—speaks rapidly again.*) Oh, in feeling, of course. It is natural you should admire that in him—now. But I warn you it is a quality difficult for a woman to keep on admiring in a Harford, judging from what I know of the family history. Simon's great-grandfather, Jonathan Harford, had it. He was killed at Bunker Hill, but I suspect the War for Independence was merely a symbolic opportunity for him. His was a personal war, I am sure—for pure freedom. Simon's grandfather, Evan Harford, had the quality too. A fanatic in the cause of pure freedom, he became scornful of our Revolution. It made too many compromises with the ideal to free him. He went to France and became a rabid Jacobin, a worshiper of Robespierre. He would have liked to have gone to the guillotine with his incorruptible Redeemer, but he was too unimportant. They simply forgot to kill him. He came home and lived in a little temple of Liberty he had built in a corner of what is now my garden. It is still there. I remember him well. A dry, gentle, cruel, indomitable, futile old idealist who used frequently to wear his old uniform of the French Republican National Guard. He died wearing it. But the point is, you can have no idea what revengeful hate the Harford pursuit of freedom imposed upon the women who shared their lives. The three daughters-in-law of Jonathan, Evan's half-sisters, had to make a large, greedy fortune out of privateering and the Northwest trade, and finally were even driven to embrace the profits of the slave trade—as a triumphant climax, you understand, of their long battle to escape the enslavement of freedom by enslaving it. Evan's wife, of course, was drawn into this conflict, and became their tool and accomplice. They even attempted to own me, but I managed to escape because there was so little of me in the flesh that aged, greedy fingers could clutch. I am sorry they are dead and cannot know you. They would approve of you, I think. They would see that you are strong and ambitious and determined to take what you want. They would have smiled like senile, hungry serpents and welcomed you into their coils. (*She laughs.*) Evil old witches! Detestable, but I could not help admiring them—pitying them, too—in the end. We had a bond in common. They idolized Napoleon. They used to say he was the only man they would ever have married. And I used to dream I was Josephine—even after my marriage, I'm afraid. The Sisters, as everyone called them, and all of the family accompanied my husband and me on our honeymoon—to Paris to witness the Emperor's coronation. (*She pauses, smiling at her memories.*)

SARA   (*Against her will, has become a bit hypnotized by Deborah's rapid, low, musical, flow of words, as she strains to grasp the implication for her. She speaks in a low, confidential tone herself, smiling naturally.*) I've always admired him too. It's one of the things I've held against my father, that he fought against him and not for him.

DEBORAH   (*Starts, as if awakening—with a pleasant smile.*) Well, Miss Melody, this is tiresome of me to stand here giving you a discourse on Harford family history. I don't know what you must think of me—but doubtless Simon has told you I am a bit eccentric at times. (*She glances at Sara's face—amusedly.*) Ah, I can see he has. Then I am sure you will make allowances. I really do not know what inspired me—except perhaps, that I wish to be fair and warn you, too.

SARA   (*Stiffens.*) Warn me about what, Mrs. Harford?

DEBORAH   Why, that the Harfords never part with their dreams even when they deny them. They cannot. That is the family curse. For example, this book Simon plans to write to denounce the evil of greed and possessive ambition, and uphold the virtue of freeing oneself from the lust for power and saving our souls by being content with little. I cannot imagine you taking that seriously. (*She again flashes a glance at Sara.*) I see you do not. Neither do I. I do not even believe Simon will ever write this book on paper. But I warn you it is already written on his conscience and—(*She stops with a little disdaining laugh.*) I begin to resemble Cassandra with all my warnings. And I continue to stand here boring you with words. (*She holds out her hand graciously.*) Goodbye, Miss Melody.

SARA   (*Takes her hand mechanically.*) Goodbye, Mrs. Harford. (*Deborah starts for the door at rear. Sara follows her, her expression confused, suspicious, and at the same time hopeful. Suddenly she blurts out impulsively.*) Mrs. Harford, I—

DEBORAH   (*Turns on her, pleasantly.*) Yes, Miss Melody? (*But her eyes have become blank and expressionless and discourage any attempt at further contact.*)

SARA   (*Silenced—with stiff politeness.*) Isn't there some sort of cooling drink I could get you before you go? You must be parched after walking from the road to Simon's cabin and back on this hot day.

DEBORAH   Nothing, thank you. (*Then talking rapidly again in her strange detached way.*) Yes, I did find my walk alone in the woods a strangely overpowering experience. Frightening—but intoxicating, too. Such a wild feeling of release and fresh enslavement. I have not ventured from my garden in many years. There, nature is tamed, constrained to obey and adorn. I had forgotten how compelling the brutal power of primitive, possessive nature can be—when suddenly one is attacked by it. (*She smiles.*) It has been a most confusing morning for a tired, middle-aged matron, but I flatter myself I have preserved a philosophic poise, or should I say, pose, as well as may be. Nevertheless, it will be a relief to return to my garden and books and meditations and listen indifferently again while the footsteps of life pass and recede along the street beyond the high wall. I shall never venture forth again to do my duty. It is a noble occupation, no doubt, for those who can presume they know what their duty to others is; but I—(*She laughs.*) Mercy, here I am chattering on again. (*She turns to the door.*) Cato will be provoked at me for keeping him waiting. I've already caused his beloved horses to be half-devoured by flies. Cato is our black coachman. He also is fond of Simon, although since Simon became emancipated he has embarrassed Cato acutely by shaking his hand whenever they meet. Cato was always a self-possessed free man even when he was a slave. It astonishes him that Simon has to prove that he—I mean Simon—is free. (*She smiles.*) Goodbye again, Miss Melody. This time I really am going.

> *Sara opens the door for her. She walks past Sara into the street, turns left, and, passing before the two windows, disappears. Sara closes the door and comes back slowly to the head of the table at center. She stands thinking, her expression puzzled, apprehensive, and resentful. Nora appears in the doorway at right.*

NORA   God forgive you, Sara, why did you let her go? Your father told me—

SARA   I can't make her out, Mother. You'd think she didn't care, but she does care. And she hates me. I could feel it. But you can't tell—She's crazy, I think. She talked on and on as if she couldn't stop—queer blather about Simon's ancestors, and herself, and Napoleon, and Nature, and her garden and freedom, and God knows what—but letting me know all the time she had a meaning behind it, and was warning and threatening me. Oh, she may be daft in some ways, but she's no fool. I know she didn't let Simon guess she'd rather have him dead than married to me. Oh, no, I'm sure she told him if he was sure he loved me and I meant his happiness—But then she'd say he ought to wait and prove he's sure—anything to give her time. She'd make him promise to wait. Yes, I'll wager that's what she's done!

NORA   (*Who has been watching the door at left front, preoccupied by her own worry—frightenedly.*) Your father'll be down any second. I'm going out in the garden. (*She grabs Sara's arm.*) Come along with me, and give him time to get over his rage.

SARA   (*Shakes off her hand—exasperatedly.*) Leave me be, Mother. I've enough to worry me without bothering about him. I've got to plan the best way to act when I see Simon. I've got to be as big a liar as she was. I'll have to pretend I liked her and I'd respect whatever advice she gave him. I mustn't let him see—But I won't go to him again today, Mother. You can take up his meals and his milk, if you will. Tell him I'm too busy. I want to get him anxious and afraid maybe I'm mad at him for something, that maybe his mother said something. If he once has the idea maybe he's lost me—that ought to help, don't you think, Mother?

NORA   (*Sees the door at left front begin to open—in a whisper.*) Oh, God help me! (*She turns in panicky flight and disappears through the doorway, right.*)

The door at left front slowly opens—slowly because Melody, hearing voices in the room and hoping Deborah is there, is deliberately making a dramatic entrance. And in spite of its obviousness, it is effective. Wearing the brilliant scarlet full-dress uniform of a major in one of Wellington's dragoon regiments, he looks extraordinarily handsome and distinguished—a startling, colorful, romantic figure, possessing now a genuine quality he has not had before, the quality of the formidably strong, disdainfully fearless cavalry officer he really had been. The uniform has been preserved with the greatest care. Each button is shining and the cloth is spotless. Being in it has notably restored his self-confident arrogance. Also, he has done everything he can to freshen up his face and hide any effect of his morning's drinks. When he discovers Deborah is not in the room, he is mildly disappointed and, as always when he first confronts Sara alone, he seems to shrink back guiltily within himself. Sara's face hardens and she gives no sign of knowing he is there. He comes slowly around the table at left front, until he stands at the end of the center table facing her. She still refuses to notice him and he is forced to speak. He does so with the air of one who condescends to be amused by his own foibles.

MELODY   I happened to go to my room and found you and your mother had laid out my uniform so invitingly that I could not resist the temptation to put it on at once instead of waiting until evening.

SARA   (*Turns on him. In spite of herself she is so struck by his appearance that the contempt is forced back and she can only stammer a bit foolishly.*) Yes, I—I see you did. (*There is a moment's pause. She stares at him fascinatedly—then blurts out with impulsive admiration.*) You look grand and handsome, Father.

MELODY   (*As pleased as a child.*) Why, it is most kind of you to say that, my dear Sara. (*Preening himself.*) I flatter myself I do not look too unworthy of the man I was when I wore this uniform with honor.

SARA   (*An appeal forced out of her that is both pleading and a bitter reproach.*) Oh, Father, why can't you ever be the thing you can seem to be? (*A sad scorn comes into her voice.*) The man you were. I'm sorry I never knew that soldier. I think he was the only man who wasn't just a dream.

MELODY   (*His face becomes a blank disguise—coldly.*) I don't understand you. (*A pause. He begins to talk in an arrogantly amused tone.*) I suspect you are still holding against me my unfortunate blunder with your future mother-in-law. I would not blame you if you did. (*He smiles.*) Faith, I did put my foot in it. (*He chuckles.*) The devil of it is, I can never get used to these Yankee ladies. I do them the honor of complimenting them with a bit of harmless flattery and, lo and behold, suddenly my lady acts as if I had insulted her. It must be their damned narrow Puritan background. They can't help seeing sin hiding under every bush, but this one need not have been alarmed. I never had an eye for skinny, pale snips of women—(*Hastily.*) But what I want to tell you is I am sorry it happened, Sara, and I will do my best, for the sake of your interests, to make honorable amends. I shall do the lady the honor of tendering her my humble apologies when she comes downstairs. (*With arrogant vanity.*) I flatter myself she will be graciously pleased to make peace. She was not as outraged by half as her conscience made her pretend, if I am any judge of feminine frailty.

SARA   (*Who has been staring at him with scorn until he says this last—impulsively, with a sneer of agreement.*) I'll wager she wasn't for all her airs. (*Then furious at herself and him.*) Ah, will you stop telling me your mad dreams! (*Controlling herself—coldly.*) You'll have no chance to make bad worse by trying to fascinate her with your beautiful uniform. She's gone.

MELODY (*Stunned.*) Gone? (*Furiously.*) You're lying, damn you!

SARA I'm not. She left ten minutes ago, or more.

MELODY (*Before he thinks.*) But I told your mother to keep her here until—(*He stops abruptly.*)

SARA So that's why Mother is so frightened. Well, it was me let her go, so don't take out your rage on poor Mother.

MELODY Rage? My dear Sara, all I feel is relief. Surely you can't believe I could have looked forward to humbling my pride, even though it would have furthered your interests.

SARA Furthered my interests by giving her another reason to laugh up her sleeve at your pretenses? (*With angry scorn, lapsing into broad brogue.*) Arrah, God pity you!

> *She turns her back on him and goes off, right. Melody stands gripping the back of the chair at the foot of the table in his big, powerful hands in an effort to control himself. There is a crack as the chair back snaps in half. He stares at the fragments in his hands with stupid surprise. The door to the bar is shoved open and Mickey calls in.*

MALOY Here's Cregan back to see you, Major.

MELODY (*Startled, repeats stupidly.*) Cregan? (*Then his face suddenly lights up with pathetic eagerness and his voice is full of welcoming warmth as he calls.*) Jamie! My old comrade in arms! (*As Cregan enters, he grips his hand.*) By the Powers, I'm glad you're here, Jamie. (*Cregan is surprised and pleased by the warmth of his welcome. Melody draws him into the room.*) Come. Sit down. You'll join me in a drink, I know.

> *He gets Cregan a glass from the cupboard. The decanter and Melody's glass are already on the table.*

CREGAN (*Admiringly.*) Be God, it's the old uniform, no less, and you look as fine a figure in it as ever you did in Spain.

> *He sits at right of table at left front as Melody sits at rear.*

MELODY (*Immensely pleased—deprecatingly.*) Hardly, Jamie—but not a total ruin yet, I hope. I put it on in honor of the day. I see you've forgotten. For shame, you dog, not to remember Talavera.

CREGAN (*Excitedly.*) Talavera, is it? Where I got my saber cut. Be the mortal, I remember it, and you've a right to celebrate. You was worth any ten men in the army that day!

> *Melody has shoved the decanter toward him. He pours a drink.*

MELODY (*This compliment completely restores him to his arrogant self.*) Yes, I think I may say I did acquit myself with honor. (*Patronizingly.*) So, for that matter, did you. (*He pours a drink and raises his glass.*) To the day and your good health, Corporal Cregan.

CREGAN (*Enthusiastically.*) To the day and yourself, God bless you, Con!

> *He tries to touch brims with Melody's glass, but Melody holds his glass away and draws himself up haughtily.*

MELODY   (*With cold rebuke.*) I said, to the day and your good health, *Corporal Cregan.*

CREGAN   (*For a second is angry—then he grins and mutters admiringly.*) Be God, it's you can bate the world and never let it change you! (*Correcting his toast with emphasis.*) To the day and yourself, *Major Melody.*

MELODY   (*Touches his glass to Cregan's—graciously condescending.*) Drink hearty, Corporal.

CURTAIN

ACT THREE

The same. The door to the bar is closed. It is around eight that evening and there are candles on the center table. Melody sits at the head of this table. In his brilliant uniform he presents more than ever an impressively colorful figure in the room, which appears smaller and dingier in the candlelight. Cregan is in the chair on his right. The other chairs at this table are unoccupied. Riley, O'Dowd, and Roche sit at the table at left front. Riley is at front, but his chair is turned sideways so he faces right. O'Dowd has the chair against the wall, facing right, with Roche across the table from him, his back to Melody. All five are drunk, Melody more so than any of them, but except for the glazed glitter in his eyes and his deathly pallor, his appearance does not betray him. He is holding his liquor like a gentleman. Cregan is the least drunk. O'Dowd and Roche are boisterous. The effect of the drink on Riley is merely to sink him deeper in dreams. He seems oblivious to his surroundings.

An empty and a half-empty bottle of port are on the table before Melody and Cregan, and their glasses are full. The three at the table have a decanter of whiskey.

Sara, wearing her working dress and an apron, is removing dishes and the remains of the dinner. Her face is set. She is determined to ignore them, but there is angry disgust in her eyes. Melody is arranging forks, knives, spoons, saltcellar, etc., in a plan of battle on the table before him. Cregan watches him. Patch Riley gives a few tuning-up quavers on his pipes.

MELODY   Here's the river Tagus. And here, Talavera. This would be the French position on a rise of ground with the plain between our lines and theirs. Here is our redoubt with the Fourth Division and the Guards. And here's our cavalry brigade in a valley toward our left, if you'll remember, Corporal Cregan.

CREGAN   (*Excitedly.*) Remember? Sure I see it as clear as yesterday!

RILEY   (*Bursts into a rollicking song, accompanying himself on the pipes, his voice the quavering ghost of a tenor but still true—to the tune of "Baltiorum."*)
"She'd a pig and boneens,
She'd a bed and a dresser,
And a nate little room
For the father confessor;
With a cupboard and curtains, and something, I'm towld,
That his riv'rance liked when the weather was cowld.
And it's hurroo, hurroo! Biddy O'Rafferty!"

Roche and O'Dowd roar after him, beating time on the table with their glasses—"Hurroo, hurroo! Biddy O'Rafferty!"—and laugh drunkenly. Cregan, too, joins in this chorus. Melody frowns angrily at the interruption, but at the end he smiles with lordly condescension, pleased by the irreverence of the song.

O'DOWD   (*After a cunning glance at Melody's face to see what his reaction is—derisively.*) Och, lave it to the priests, divil mend thim! Ain't it so, Major?

MELODY   Ay, damn them all! A song in the right spirit, Piper. Faith, I'll have you repeat it for my wife's benefit when she joins us. She still has a secret fondness for priests. And now, less noise, you blackguards. Corporal Cregan and I cannot hear each other with your brawling.

O'DOWD   (*Smirkingly obedient.*) Quiet it is, yer Honor. Be quiet, Patch.

He gives the old man, who is lost in dreams, a shove that almost knocks him off his chair. Riley stares at him bewilderedly. O'Dowd and Roche guffaw.

MELODY   (*Scowls at them, then turns to Cregan.*) Where was I, Corporal? Oh, yes, we were waiting in the valley. We heard a trumpet from the French lines and saw them forming for the attack. An aide-de-camp galloped down the hill to us—

SARA   (*Who has been watching him disdainfully, reaches out to take his plate—rudely in mocking brogue.*) I'll have your plate, av ye plaze, Major, before your gallant dragoons charge over it and break it.

MELODY   (*Holds his plate on the table with one hand so she cannot take it, and raises his glass of wine with the other—ignoring her.*) Wet your lips, Corporal. Talavera was a devilish thirsty day, if you'll remember. (*He drinks.*)

CREGAN   (*Glances uneasily at Sara.*) It was that. (*He drinks.*)

MELODY   (*Smacking his lips.*) Good wine, Corporal. Thank God, I still have wine in my cellar fit for a gentleman.

SARA   (*Angrily.*) Are you going to let me take your plate?

MELODY   (*Ignoring her.*) No, I have no need to apologize for the wine. Nor for the dinner, for that matter. Nora is a good cook when she forgets her infernal parsimony and buys food that one can eat without disgust. But I do owe you an apology for the quality of the service. I have tried to teach the waitress not to snatch plates from the table as if she were feeding dogs in a kennel but she cannot learn. (*He takes his hand from the plate—to Sara.*) There. Now let me see you take it properly.

She stares at him for a moment, speechless with anger—then snatches the plate from in front of him.

CREGAN   (*Hastily recalls Melody to the battlefield.*) You were where the aide-de-camp galloped up to us, Major. It was then the French artillery opened on us.

Sara goes out right, carrying a tray laden with plates.

MELODY   We charged the columns on our left—here— (*He marks the tablecloth.*) that were pushing back the Guards. I'll never forget the blast of death from the French squares. And then their chasseurs and lancers were on us! By God, it's a miracle any of us came through!

CREGAN   You wasn't touched except you'd a bullet through your coat, but I had this token on my cheek to remember a French saber by.

MELODY   Brave days, those! By the Eternal, then one lived! Then one forgot! (*He stops—when he speaks again it is bitterly.*) Little did I dream then the disgrace that was to be my reward later on.

CREGAN (*Consolingly.*) Ah well, that's the bad luck of things. You'd have been made a colonel soon, if you'd left the Spanish woman alone and not fought that duel.

MELODY (*Arrogantly threatening.*) Are you presuming to question my conduct in that affair, Corporal Cregan?

CREGAN (*Hastily.*) Sorra a bit! Don't mind me, now.

MELODY (*Stiffly.*) I accept your apology. (*He drinks the rest of his wine, pours another glass, then stares moodily before him. Cregan drains his glass and refills it.*)

O'DOWD (*Peering past Roche to watch Melody, leans across to Roche—in a sneering whisper.*) Ain't he the lunatic, sittin' like a play-actor in his red coat, lyin' about his battles with the French!

ROCHE (*Sullenly—but careful to keep his voice low.*) He'd ought to be shamed he ivir wore the bloody red av England, God's curse on him!

O'DOWD Don't be wishin' him harm, for it's thirsty we'd be without him. Drink long life to him, and may he always be as big a fool as he is this night! (*He sloshes whiskey from the decanter into both their glasses.*)

ROCHE (*With a drunken leer.*) Thrue for you! I'll toast him on that. (*He twists round to face Melody, holds up his glass and bawls.*) To the grandest gintleman ivir come from the shores av Ireland! Long life to you, Major!

O'DOWD Hurroo! Long life, yer Honor!

RILEY (*Awakened from his dream, mechanically raises his glass.*) And to all that belong to ye.

MELODY (*Startled from his thoughts, becomes at once the condescending squire—smiling tolerantly.*) I said, less noise, you dogs. All the same, I thank you for your toast. (*They drink. A pause. Abruptly Melody begins to recite from Byron. He reads the verse well, quietly, with a bitter eloquence.*)
"But midst the crowd, the hum, the shock of men,
To hear, to see, to feel, and to possess,
And roam along, the World's tired denizen,
With none who bless us, none whom we can bless;
Minions of Splendour shrinking from distress!
None that, with kindred consciousness endued,
If we were not, would seem to smile the less,
Of all the flattered—followed—sought, and sued;
This is to be alone—This, this is Solitude!"
(*He stops and glances from one face to another. Their expressions are all blank. He remarks with insulting derisiveness.*) What? You do not understand, my lads? Well, all the better for you. So may you go on fooling yourselves that I am fooled in you. (*Then with a quick change of mood, heartily.*) Give us a hunting song, Patch. You've not forgotten "Modideroo," I'll be bound.

RILEY (*Roused to interest immediately.*) Does a duck forget wather? I'll show ye! (*He begins the preliminary quavers on his pipes.*)

O'DOWD Modideroo!

ROCHE Hurroo!

RILEY (*Accompanying himself, sings with wailing melancholy the first verse that comes to his mind of an old hunting song.*)
"And the fox set him down and looked about,

And many were feared to follow;
'Maybe I'm wrong,' says he, 'but I doubt
That you'll be as gay tomorrow.
For loud as you cry, and high as you ride,
And little you feel my sorrow,
I'll be free on the mountainside
While you'll lie low tomorrow.'
Oh, Modideroo, aroo, aroo!"

Melody, excited now, beats time on the table with his glass along with Cregan, Roche, and O'Dowd, and all bellow the refrain, "Oh, Modideroo, aroo, aroo!"

MELODY (*His eyes alight, forgetting himself, a strong lilt of brogue coming into his voice.*) Ah, that brings it back clear as life! Melody Castle in the days that's gone! A wind from the south, and a sky gray with clouds—good weather for the hounds. A true Irish hunter under me that knows and loves me and would raise to a jump over hell if I gave the word! To hell with men, I say!—and women, too!—with their cowardly hearts rotten and stinking with lies and greed and treachery! Give me a horse to love and I'll cry quits to men! And then away, with the hounds in full cry, and after them! Off with divil a care for your neck, over ditches and streams and stone walls and fences, the fox doubling up the mountainside through the furze and the heather—! (*Sara has entered from right as he begins this longing invocation of old hunting days. She stands behind his chair, listening contemptuously. He suddenly feels her presence and turns his head. When he catches the sneer in her eyes, it is as if cold water were dashed in his face. He addresses her as if she were a servant.*) Well? What is it? What are you waiting for now?

SARA (*Roughly, with coarse brogue.*) What would I be waitin' for but for you to get through with your blather about lovin' horses, and give me a chance to finish my work? Can't you—and the other gintlemen—finish gettin' drunk in the bar and lave me clear the tables?

O'Dowd conceals a grin behind his hand; Roche stifles a malicious guffaw.

CREGAN (*With an apprehensive glance at Melody, shakes his head at her admonishingly.*) Now, Sara, be aisy.

But Melody suppresses any angry reaction. He rises to his feet, a bit stiffly and carefully, and bows.

MELODY (*Coldly.*) I beg your pardon if we have interfered with your duties. (*To O'Dowd and his companions.*) Into the bar, you louts!

O'DOWD The bar it is, sorr. Come, Dan. Wake up, Patch.

He pokes the piper. He and Roche go into the bar, and Riley stumbles vaguely after them. Cregan waits for Melody.

MELODY Go along, Corporal. I'll join you presently. I wish to speak to my daughter.

CREGAN All right, Major.

He again shakes his head at Sara, as if to say, don't provoke him. She ignores him. He goes into the bar, closing the door behind him. She stares at her father with angry disgust.

SARA You're drunk. If you think I'm going to stay here and listen to—

MELODY (*His face expressionless, draws out his chair at the head of the center table for her—politely.*) Sit down, my dear.

SARA   I won't. I have no time. Poor Mother is half dead on her feet. I have to
help her. There's a pile of dishes to wash after your grand anniversary feast!
(*With bitter anger.*) Thank God it's over, and it's the last time you'll ever take
satisfaction in having me wait on table for drunken scum like O'Dowd and—

MELODY   (*Quietly.*) A daughter who takes satisfaction in letting even the scum see
that she hates and despises her father! (*He shrugs his shoulders.*) But no matter.
(*Indicating the chair again.*) Won't you sit down, my dear?

SARA   If you ever dared face the truth, you'd hate and despise yourself! (*Passionately.*) All I pray to God is that someday when you're admiring yourself in
the mirror something will make you see at last what you really are! That
will be revenge in full for all you've done to Mother and me! (*She waits defiantly,
as if expecting him to lose his temper and curse her. But Melody acts as if he had
not heard her.*)

MELODY   (*His face expressionless, his manner insistently bland and polite.*) Sit down, my
dear. I will not detain you long, and I think you will find what I have to
tell you of great interest.

> *She searches his face, uneasy now, feeling a threat hidden behind his cold,
> quiet, gentlemanly tone. She sits down and he sits at rear of table, with an empty
> chair separating them.*

SARA   You'd better think well before you speak, Father. I know the devil that's
in you when you're quiet like this with your brain mad with drink.

MELODY   I don't understand you. All I wish is to relate something which happened
this afternoon.

SARA   (*Giving way to bitterness at her humiliation again—sneeringly.*) When you went
riding on your beautiful thoroughbred mare while Mother and I were sweating
and suffocating in the heat of the kitchen to prepare your Lordship's banquet?
Sure, I hope you didn't show off and jump your beauty over a fence into
somebody's garden, like you've done before, and then have to pay damages
to keep out of jail!

MELODY   (*Roused by mention of his pet—disdainfully.*) The damned Yankee yokels
should feel flattered that she deigns to set her dainty hooves in their paltry
gardens! She's a truer-born, well-bred lady than any of their women—than
the one who paid us a visit this morning, for example.

SARA   Mrs. Harford was enough of a lady to put you in your place and make
a fool of you.

MELODY   (*Seemingly unmoved by this taunt—calmly.*) You are very simple-minded, my
dear, to let yourself be taken in by such an obvious bit of clever acting.
Naturally, the lady was a bit discomposed when she heard you and your
mother coming, after she had just allowed me to kiss her. She had to pretend—

SARA   (*Eagerly.*) She let you kiss her? (*Then disgustedly.*) It's a lie, but I don't doubt
you've made yourself think it's the truth by now. (*Angrily.*) I'm going. I don't
want to listen to the whiskey in you boasting of what never happened—as
usual! (*She puts her hands on the table and starts to rise.*)

MELODY   (*With a quick movement pins hers down with one of his.*) Wait! (*A look of
vindictive cruelty comes into his eyes—quietly.*) Why are you so jealous of the mare,
I wonder? Is it because she has such slender ankles and dainty feet? (*He takes*

his hand away and stares at her hands—with disgust, commandingly.) Keep your thick wrists and ugly, peasant paws off the table in my presence, if you please! They turn my stomach! I advise you never to let Simon get a good look at them—

SARA (*Instinctively jerks her hands back under the table guiltily. She stammers.*) You—you cruel devil! I knew you'd—

MELODY (*For a second is ashamed and really contrite.*) Forgive me, Sara. I didn't mean—the whiskey talking—as you said. (*He adds in a forced tone, a trace of mockery in it.*) An absurd taunt, when you really have such pretty hands and feet, my dear. (*She jumps to her feet, so hurt and full of hatred her lips tremble and she cannot speak. He speaks quietly.*) Are you going? I was about to tell you of the talk I had this afternoon with young Harford. (*She stares at him in dismay. He goes on easily.*) It was after I returned from my ride. I cantered the mare by the river and she pulled up lame. So I dismounted and led her back to the barn. No one noticed my return and when I went upstairs it occurred to me I would not find again such an opportunity to have a frank chat with Harford—free from interruptions. (*He pauses, as if he expects her to be furious, but she remains tensely silent, determined not to let him know her reaction.*) I did not beat about the bush. I told him he must appreciate, as a gentleman, it was my duty as your father to demand he lay his cards on the table. I said he must realize that even before you began nursing him here and going alone to his bedroom, there was a deal of gossip about your visits to his cabin, and your walks in the woods with him. I put it to him that such an intimacy could not continue without gravely compromising your reputation.

SARA (*Stunned—weakly.*) God forgive you! And what did he say?

MELODY What could he say? He is a man of honor. He looked damn embarrassed and guilty for a moment, but when he found his tongue, he agreed with me most heartily. He said his mother had told him the same thing.

SARA Oh, she did, did she? I suppose she did it to find out by watching him how far—

MELODY (*Coldly.*) Well, why not? Naturally, it was her duty as his mother to discover all she could about you. She is a woman of the world. She would be bound to suspect that you might be his mistress.

SARA (*Tensely.*) Oh, would she!

MELODY But that's beside the point. The point is, my bashful young gentleman finally blurted out that he wanted to marry you.

SARA (*Forgetting her anger—eagerly.*) He told you that?

MELODY Yes, and he said he had told his mother, and she had said all she wanted was his happiness but she felt in fairness to you and to himself—and I presume she also meant to both families concerned—he should test his love and yours by letting a decent interval of time elapse before your marriage. She mentioned a year, I believe.

SARA (*Angrily.*) Ah! Didn't I guess that would be her trick!

MELODY (*Lifting his eyebrows—coldly.*) Trick? In my opinion, the lady displayed more common sense and knowledge of the world than I thought she possessed. The reasons she gave him are sound and show a consideration for your good name which ought to inspire gratitude in you and not suspicion.

SARA Arrah, don't tell me she's made a fool of you again! A lot of consideration she has for me!

MELODY She pointed out to him that if you were the daughter of some family in their own little Yankee clique, there would be no question of a hasty marriage, and so he owed it to you—

SARA I see. She's a clever one!

MELODY Another reason was—and here your Simon stammered so embarrassedly I had trouble making him out—she warned him a sudden wedding would look damnably suspicious and start a lot of evil-minded gossip.

SARA (*Tensely.*) Oh, she's clever, all right! But I'll beat her.

MELODY I told him I agreed with his mother. It is obvious that were there a sudden wedding without a suitable period of betrothal, everyone would believe—

SARA I don't care what they believe! Tell me this! Did she get him to promise her he'd wait? (*Before he can answer—bitterly.*) But of course she did! She'd never have left till she got that out of him!

MELODY (*Ignores this.*) I told him I appreciated the honor he did me in asking for your hand, but he must understand that I could not commit myself until I had talked to his father and was assured the necessary financial arrangements could be concluded to our mutual satisfaction. There was the amount of settlement to be agreed upon, for instance.

SARA That dream, again! God pity you! (*She laughs helplessly and a bit hysterically.*) And God help Simon. He must have thought you'd gone out of your mind! What did he say?

MELODY He said nothing, naturally. He is well bred and he knows this is a matter he must leave to his father to discuss. There is also the equally important matter of how generous an allowance Henry Harford is willing to settle on his son. I did not mention this to Simon, of course, not wishing to embarrass him further with talk of money.

SARA Thank God for that, at least! (*She giggles hysterically.*)

MELODY (*Quietly.*) May I ask what you find so ridiculous in an old established custom? Simon is an elder son, the heir to his father's estate. No matter what their differences in the past may have been, now that Simon has decided to marry and settle down his father will wish to do the fair thing by him. He will realize, too, that although there is no more honorable calling than that of poet and philosopher, which his son has chosen to pursue, there is no decent living to be gained by its practice. So naturally he will settle an allowance on Simon, and I shall insist it be a generous one, befitting your position as my daughter. I will tolerate no niggardly trader's haggling on his part.

SARA (*Stares at him fascinatedly, on the edge of helpless, hysterical laughter.*) I suppose it would never occur to you that old Harford might not think it an honor to have his son marry your daughter.

MELODY (*Calmly.*) No, it would never occur to me—and if it should occur to him, I would damned soon disabuse his mind. Who is he but a money-grubbing trader? I would remind him that I was born in a castle and there was a time when I possessed wealth and position, and an estate compared to which any

Yankee upstart's home in this country is but a hovel stuck in a cabbage patch. I would remind him that you, my daughter, were born in a castle!

SARA (*Impulsively, with a proud toss of her head.*) Well, that's no more than the truth. (*Then furious with herself and him.*) Och, what crazy blather! (*She springs to her feet.*) I've had enough of your mad dreams!

MELODY Wait! I haven't finished yet. (*He speaks quietly, but as he goes on there is an increasing vindictiveness in his tone.*) There was another reason why I told young Harford I could not make a final decision. I wished time to reflect on a further aspect of this proposed marriage. Well, I have been reflecting, watching you and examining your conduct, without prejudice, trying to be fair to you and make every possible allowance—(*He pauses.*) Well, to be brutally frank, my dear, all I can see in you is a common, greedy, scheming, cunning peasant girl, whose only thought is money and who has shamelessly thrown herself at a young man's head because his family happens to possess a little wealth and position.

SARA (*Trying to control herself.*) I see your game, Father. I told you when you were drunk like this—But this time, I won't give you the satisfaction—(*Then she bursts out angrily.*) It's a lie! I love Simon, or I'd never—

MELODY (*As if she hadn't spoken.*) So, I have about made up my mind to decline for you Simon Harford's request for your hand in marriage.

SARA (*Jeers angrily now.*) Oh, you have, have you? As if I cared a damn what you—

MELODY As a gentleman, I feel I have a duty, in honor, to Simon. Such a marriage would be a tragic misalliance for him—and God knows I know the sordid tragedy of such a union.

SARA It's Mother has had the tragedy!

MELODY I hold young Harford in too high esteem. I cannot stand by and let him commit himself irrevocably to what could only bring him disgust and bitterness, and ruin to all his dreams.

SARA So I'm not good enough for him, you've decided now?

MELODY That is apparent from your every act. No one, no matter how charitably inclined, could mistake you for a lady. I have tried to make you one. It was an impossible task. God Himself cannot transform a sow's ear into a silk purse!

SARA (*Furiously.*) Father!

MELODY Young Harford needs to be saved from himself. I can understand his physical infatuation. You are pretty. So was your mother pretty once. But marriage is another matter. The man who would be the ideal husband for you, from a standpoint of conduct and character, is Mickey Maloy, my bartender, and I will be happy to give him my parental blessing—

SARA Let you stop now, Father!

MELODY You and he would be congenial. You can match tongues together. He's a healthy animal. He can give you a raft of peasant brats to squeal and fight with the pigs on the mud floor of your hovel.

SARA It's the dirty hut in which your father was born and raised you're remembering, isn't it?

MELODY (*Stung to fury, glares at her with hatred. His voice quivers but is deadly quiet.*) Of course, if you trick Harford into getting you with child, I could not refuse my consent. (*Letting go, he bangs his fist on the table.*) No, by God, even then, when I remember my own experience, I'll be damned if I could with a good conscience advise him to marry you!

SARA (*Glaring back at him with hatred.*) You drunken devil! (*She makes a threatening move toward him, raising her hand as if she were going to slap his face—then she controls herself and speaks with quiet, biting sarcasm.*) Consent or not, I want to thank you for your kind fatherly advice on how to trick Simon. I don't think I'll need it but if the worst comes to the worst I promise you I'll remember—

MELODY (*Coldly, his face expressionless.*) I believe I have said all I wished to say to you. (*He gets up and bows stiffly.*) If you will excuse me, I shall join Corporal Cregan. (*He goes to the bar door. Sara turns and goes quietly out right, forgetting to clear the few remaining dishes on the center table. His back turned, he does not see her go. With his hand on the knob of the bar door, he hesitates. For a second he breaks—torturedly.*) Sara! (*Then quietly.*) There are things I said which I re-gret—even now. I—I trust you will overlook—As your mother knows, it's the liquor talking, not—I must admit that, due to my celebrating the anniversary, my brain is a bit addled by whiskey—as you said. (*He waits, hoping for a word of forgiveness. Finally, he glances over his shoulder. As he discovers she is not there and has not heard him, for a second he crumbles, his soldierly erectness sags and his face falls. He looks sad and hopeless and bitter and old, his eyes wandering dully. But, as in the two preceding acts, the mirror attracts him, and as he moves from the bar door to stand before it he assumes his arrogant, Byronic pose again. He repeats in each detail his pantomime before the mirror. He speaks proudly.*) Myself to the bitter end! No weakening, so help me God! (*There is a knock on the street door but he does not hear it. He starts his familiar incantation quotes from Byron.*)
"I have not loved the World, nor the World me;
I have not flattered its rank breath, nor bowed
To its idolatries a patient knee . . ."
(*The knock on the door is repeated more loudly. Melody starts guiltily and steps quickly away from the mirror. His embarrassment is transformed into resentful anger. He calls.*) Come in, damn you! Do you expect a lackey to open the door for you? (*The door opens and* NICHOLAS GADSBY *comes in. Gadsby is in his late forties, short, stout, with a big, bald head, round, florid face, and small, blue eyes. A rigidly conservativee best-family attorney, he is stiffly correct in dress and manner, dryly portentous in speech, and extremely conscious of his professional authority and dignity. Now, however, he is venturing on unfamiliar ground and is by no means as sure of himself as his manner indicates. The unexpected vision of Melody in his uniform startles him and for a second he stands, as close to gaping as he can be, impressed by Melody's handsome distinction. Melody, in his turn, is surprised. He had not thought the intruder would be a gentleman. He unbends, although his tone is still a bit curt. He bows a bit stiffly, and Gadsby finds himself returning the bow.*) Your pardon, sir. When I called, I thought it was one of the damned riffraff mistaking the barroom door. Pray be seated, sir. (*Gadsby comes forward and takes the chair at the head of the center table, glancing at the few dirty dishes on it with distaste. Melody says.*) Your pardon again, sir. We have been feasting late, which accounts for the disarray. I will summon a servant to inquire your pleasure.

GADSBY   (*Beginning to recover his aplomb—shortly.*) Thank you, but I want nothing, sir. I came here to seek a private interview with the proprietor of this tavern, by name, Melody. (*He adds a bit hesitantly.*) Are you, by any chance, he?

MELODY   (*Stiffens arrogantly.*) I am not, sir. But if you wish to see Major Cornelius Melody, one time of His Majesty's Seventh Dragoons, who served with honor under the Duke of Wellington in Spain, I am he.

GADSBY   (*Dryly.*) Very well, sir. Major Melody, then.

MELODY   (*Does not like his tone—insolently sarcastic.*) And whom have I the *honor* of addressing?

> As Gadsby is about to reply, Sara enters from right, having remembered the dishes. Melody ignores her as he would a servant. Gadsby examines her carefully as she gathers up the dishes. She notices him staring at her and gives him a resentful, suspicious glance. She carries the dishes out, right, to the kitchen, but a moment later she can be seen just inside the hall at right, listening. Meanwhile, as soon as he thinks she has gone, Gadsby speaks.

GADSBY   (*With affected casualness.*) A pretty young woman. Is she your daughter, sir? I seemed to detect a resemblance—

MELODY   (*Angrily.*) No! Do I look to you, sir, like a man who would permit his daughter to work as a waitress? Resemblance to me? You must be blind, sir. (*Coldly.*) I am still waiting for you to inform me who you are and why you should wish to see me.

GADSBY   (*Hands him a card—extremely nettled by Melody's manner—curtly.*) My card, sir.

MELODY   (*Glances at the card.*) Nicholas Gadsby. (*He flips it aside disdainfully.*) Attorney, eh? The devil take all your tribe, say I. I have small liking for your profession, sir, and I cannot imagine what business you have with me. The damned thieves of the law did their worst to me many years ago in Ireland. I have little left to tempt you. So I do not see—(*Suddenly an idea comes to him. He stares at Gadsby, then goes on in a more friendly tone.*) That is, unless—Do you happen by any chance to represent the father of young Simon Harford?

GADSBY   (*Indignant at Melody's insults to his profession—with a thinly veiled sneer.*) Ah, then you were expecting—That makes things easier. We need not beat about the bush. I do represent Mr. Henry Harford, sir.

MELODY   (*Thawing out, in his total misunderstanding of the situation.*) Then accept my apologies, sir, for my animadversions against your profession. I am afraid I may be prejudiced. In the army, we used to say we suffered more casualties from your attacks at home than the French ever inflicted. (*He sits down on the chair on Gadsby's left, at rear of table—remarking with careless pride.*) A word of explanation as to why you find me in uniform. It is the anniversary of the battle of Talavera, sir, and—

GADSBY   (*Interrupts dryly.*) Indeed, sir? But I must tell you my time is short. With your permission, we will proceed at once to the matter in hand.

MELODY   (*Controlling his angry discomfiture—coldly.*) I think I can hazard a guess as to what that matter is. You have come about the settlement?

GADSBY   (*Misunderstanding him, replies in a tone almost openly contemptuous.*) Exactly, sir. Mr. Harford was of the opinion, and I agreed with him that a settlement would be foremost in your mind.

A TOUCH OF THE POET   533

MELODY (*Scowls at his tone but, as he completely misunderstands Gadsby's meaning, he forces himself to bow politely.*) It does me honor, sir, that Mr. Harford appreciates he is dealing with a gentleman and has the breeding to know how these matters are properly arranged. (*Gadsby stares at him, absolutely flabbergasted by what he considers a piece of the most shameless effrontery. Melody leans toward him confidentially.*) I will be frank with you, sir. The devil of it is, this comes at a difficult time for me. Temporary, of course, but I cannot deny I am pinched at the moment—devilishly pinched. But no matter. Where my only child's happiness is at stake, I am prepared to make every possible effort. I will sign a note of hand, no matter how ruinous the interest demanded by the scoundrelly moneylenders. By the way, what amount does Mr. Harford think proper? Anything in reason—

GADSBY (*Listening in utter confusion, finally gets the idea Melody is making him the butt of a joke—fuming.*) I do not know what you are talking about, sir, unless you think to make a fool of me! If this is what is known as Irish wit—

MELODY (*Bewildered for a second—then in a threatening tone.*) Take care, sir, and watch your words or I warn you you will repent them, no matter whom you represent! No damned pettifogging dog can insult me with impunity! (*As Gadsby draws back apprehensively, he adds with insulting disdain.*) As for making a fool of you, sir, I would be the fool if I attempted to improve on God's handiwork!

GADSBY (*Ignoring the insults, forces a placating tone.*) I wish no quarrel with you, sir. I cannot for the life of me see—I fear we are dealing at cross-purposes. Will you tell me plainly what you mean by your talk of settlement?

MELODY Obviously, I mean the settlement I am prepared to make on my daughter. (*As Gadsby only looks more dumfounded, he continues sharply.*) Is not your purpose in coming here to arrange, on Mr. Harford's behalf, for the marriage of his son with my daughter?

GADSBY Marriage? Good God, no! Nothing of the kind!

MELODY (*Dumfounded.*) Then what have you come for?

GADSBY (*Feeling he has now the upper hand—sharply.*) To inform you that Mr. Henry Harford is unalterably opposed to any further relationship between his son and your daughter, whatever the nature of that relationship in the past.

MELODY (*Leans forward threateningly.*) By the Immortal, sir, if you dare insinuate—!

GADSBY (*Draws back again, but he is no coward and is determined to carry out his instructions.*) I insinuate nothing, sir. I am here on Mr. Harford's behalf, to make you an offer. That is what I thought you were expecting when you mentioned a settlement. Mr. Harford is prepared to pay you the sum of three thousand dollars—provided, mark you, that you and your daughter sign an agreement I have drawn up which specifies that you relinquish all claims, of whatever nature. And also provided you agree to leave this part of the country at once with your family. Mr. Harford suggests it would be advisable that you go West—to Ohio, say.

MELODY (*So overcome by a rising tide of savage, humiliated fury, he can only stammer hoarsely.*) So Henry Harford does me the honor—to suggest that, does he?

GADSBY (*Watching him uneasily, attempts a reasonable, persuasive tone.*) Surely you could not have spoken seriously when you talked of marriage. There is such a difference in station. The idea is preposterous. If you knew Mr. Harford, you would realize he would never countenance—

MELODY   (*His pent-up rage bursts out—smashing his fist on the table.*) Know him? By the Immortal God, I'll know him soon! And he'll know me! (*He springs to his feet.*) But first, you Yankee scum, I'll deal with you!

> He draws back his fist to smash Gadsby in the face, but Sara has run from the door at right and she grabs his arm. She is almost as furious as he is and there are tears of humiliated pride in her eyes.

SARA   Father! Don't! He's only a paid lackey. Where is your pride that you'd dirty your hands on the like of him?

> While she is talking the door from the bar opens and Roche, O'Dowd, and Cregan crowd into the room. Mickey stands in the doorway. Nora follows Sara in from right.

ROCHE   (*With drunken enthusiasm.*) It's a fight! For the love of God, clout the damned Yankee, Major!

MELODY   (*Controls himself—his voice shaking.*) You are right, Sara. It would be beneath me to touch such a vile lickspittle. But he won't get off scot-free. (*Sharply, a commander ordering his soldiers.*) Here you, Roche and O'Dowd! Get hold of him!

> They do so with enthusiasm and yank Gadsby from his chair.

GADSBY   You drunken ruffians! Take your hands off me!

MELODY   (*Addressing him—in his quiet, threatening tone now.*) You may tell the swindling trader, Harford, who employs you that he'll hear from me! (*To Roche and O'Dowd.*) Throw this thing out! Kick it down to the crossroads!

ROCHE   Hurroo!

> He and O'Dowd run Gadsby to the door at rear. Cregan jumps ahead, grinning, and opens the door for them.

GADSBY   (*Struggling futilely as they rush him through the door.*) You scoundrels! Take your hands off me! Take—

> Melody looks after them. The two women watch him, Nora frightened, Sara with a strange look of satisfied pride.

CREGAN   (*In the doorway, looking out—laughing.*) Oh, it'd do your heart good, Con, to see the way they're kicking his butt down the street!

> He comes in and shuts the door.

MELODY   (*His rage welling again, as his mind dwells on his humiliation—starting to pace up and down.*) It's with his master I have to deal, and, by the Powers, I'll deal with him! You'll come with me, Jamie. I'll want you for a witness. He'll apologize to me—more than that, he'll come back here this very night and apologize publicly to my daughter, or else he meets me in the morning! By God, I'll face him at ten paces or across a handkerchief! I'll put a bullet through him, so help me, Christ!

NORA   (*Breaks into a dirgelike wail.*) God forgive you, Con, is it a duel again—murtherin' or gettin' murthered?

MELODY   Be quiet, woman! Go back to your kitchen! Go, do you hear me!

> Nora turns obediently toward the door at right, beginning to cry.

SARA   (*Puts an arm around her mother. She is staring at Melody apprehensively now.*) There, Mother, don't worry. Father knows that's all foolishness. He's only talking. Go on now in the kitchen and sit down and rest, Mother.

> Nora goes out right. Sara closes the door after her and comes back.

MELODY   (*Turns on her with bitter anger.*) Only talking, am I? It's the first time in my life I ever heard anyone say Con Melody was a coward! It remains for my own daughter—

SARA   (*Placatingly.*) I didn't say that, Father. But can't you see—you're not in Ireland in the old days now. The days of duels are long past and dead, in this part of America anyway. Harford will never fight you. He—

MELODY   He won't, won't he? By God, I'll make him! I'll take a whip. I'll drag him out of his house and lash him down the street for all his neighbors to see! He'll apologize, or he'll fight, or I'll brand him a craven before the world!

SARA   (*Frightened now.*) But you'll never be let see him! His servants will keep you out! He'll have the police arrest you, and it'll be in the papers about another drunken Mick raising a crazy row! (*She appeals to Cregan.*) Tell him I'm telling the truth, Jamie. You've still got some sober sense in you. Maybe he'll listen to you.

CREGAN   (*Glances at Melody uneasily.*) Maybe Sara's right, Major.

MELODY   When I want your opinion, I'll ask for it! (*Sneeringly.*) Of course, if you've become such a coward you're afraid to go with me—

CREGAN   (*Stung.*) Coward, is ut? I'll go, and be damned to you!

SARA   Jamie, you fool! Oh, it's like talking to crazy men! (*She grabs her father's arm—pleadingly.*) Don't do it, Father, for the love of God! Have I ever asked you anything? Well, I ask you to heed me now! I'll beg you on my knees, if you like! Isn't it me you'd fight about, and haven't I a right to decide? You punished that lawyer for the insult. You had him thrown out of here like a tramp. Isn't that your answer to old Harford that insults him? It's for him to challenge you, if he dares, isn't it? Why can't you leave it at that and wait—

MELODY   (*Shaking off her hand—angrily.*) You talk like a scheming peasant! It's a question of my honor!

SARA   No! It's a question of my happiness, and I won't have your mad interfering—! (*Desperately forcing herself to reason with him again.*) Listen, Father! If you'll keep out of it, I'll show you how I'll make a fool of old Harford! Simon won't let anything his father does keep him from marrying me. His mother is the only one who might have the influence over him to come between us. She's only watching for a good excuse to turn Simon against marrying me, and if you go raising a drunken row at their house, and make a public scandal, shouting you want to murder his father, can't you see what a chance that will give her?

MELODY   (*Raging.*) That damned, insolent Yankee bitch! She's all the more reason. Marry, did you say? You dare to think there can be any question now of your marrying the son of a man who has insulted my honor—and yours?

SARA   (*Defiantly.*) Yes, I dare to think it! I love Simon and I'm going to marry him!

MELODY   And I say you're not! If he wasn't sick, I'd—But I'll get him out of here tomorrow! I forbid you ever to see him again! If you dare disobey me I'll—! (*Beginning to lose all control of himself.*) If you dare defy me—for the sake of the dirty money you think you can beg from his family, if you're his wife—!

SARA   (*Fiercely.*) You lie! (*Then with quiet intensity.*) Yes. I defy you or anyone who tries to come between us!

MELODY You'd sell your pride as my daughter—! (*His face convulsed by fury.*) You filthy peasant slut! You whore! I'll see you dead first—! By the living God, I'd kill you myself! (*He makes a threatening move toward her.*)

SARA (*Shrinks back frightenedly.*) Father! (*Then she stands and faces him defiantly.*)

CREGAN (*Steps between them.*) Con! In the name of God! (*Melody's fit of insane fury leaves him. He stands panting for breath, shuddering with the effort to regain some sort of poise. Cregan speaks, his only thought to get him away from Sara.*) If we're going after old Harford, Major, we'd better go. That thief of a lawyer will warn him—

MELODY (*Seizing on this—hoarsely.*) Yes, let's go. Let's go, Jamie. Come along, Corporal. A stirrup cup, and we'll be off. If the mare wasn't lame, I'd ride alone—but we can get a rig at the livery stable. Don't let me forget to stop at the barn for my whip.

> By the time he finishes speaking, he has himself in hand again and his ungovernable fury has gone. There is a look of cool, menacing vengefulness in his face. He turns toward the bar door.

SARA (*Helplessly.*) Father! (*Desperately, as a last, frantic threat.*) You'll force me to go to Simon—and do what you said!

> If he hears this, he gives no sign of it. He strides into the bar. Cregan follows him, closing the door. Sara stares before her, the look of defiant desperation hardening on her face. The street door is flung open and O'Dowd and Roche pile in, laughing uproariously.

ROCHE Hurroo!

O'DOWD The army is back, Major, with the foe flying in retreat. (*He sees Melody is not there—to Sara.*) Where's himself?

> Sara appears not to see or hear him.

ROCHE (*After a quick glance at her.*) Lave her be. He'll be in the bar. Come on. (*He goes to the bar.*)

O'DOWD (*Following him, speaks over his shoulder to Sara.*) You should have seen the Yank! His coachman had to help him in his rig at the corner—and Roche gave the coachman a clout too, for good measure!

> He disappears, laughing, slamming the door behind him. Nora opens the door at right and looks in cautiously. Seeing Sara alone, she comes in.

NORA Sara. (*She comes over to her.*) Sara. (*She takes hold of her arm—whispers uneasily.*) Where's himself?

SARA (*Dully.*) I couldn't stop him.

NORA I could have told you you was wastin' breath. (*With a queer pride.*) The divil himself couldn't kape Con Melody from a duel! (*Then mournfully.*) It's like the auld times come again, and the same worry and sorrow. Even in the days before ivir I'd spoke a word to him, or done more than make him a bow when he'd ride past on his hunter, I used to lie awake and pray for him when I'd hear he was fightin' a duel in the mornin'. (*She smiles a shy, gentle smile.*) I was in love with him even then. (*Sara starts to say something bitter but what she sees in her mother's face stops her. Nora goes on, with a feeble attempt at boastful confidence.*) But I'll not worry this time, and let you not, either. There wasn't a man in Galway was his equal with a pistol, and what chance will this auld stick av a Yankee have against him? (*There is a noise of boisterous farewells from the bar and the noise of an outer door shutting. Nora starts.*) That's him leavin'! (*Her mouth pulls down pitiably. She starts for the bar with a sob.*) Ah, Con darlin', don't—! (*She stops, shaking her head helplessly.*) But what's the good? (*She sinks on a chair with a weary sigh.*)

SARA (*Bitterly, aloud to herself more than to her mother.*) No good. Let him go his way—and I'll go mine. (*Tensely.*) I won't let him destroy my life with his madness, after all the plans I've made and the dreams I've dreamed. I'll show him I can play at the game of gentleman's honor too! (*Nora has not listened. She is sunk in memories of old fears and her present worry about the duel. Sara hesitates—then, keeping her face turned away from her mother, touches her shoulder.*) I'm going upstairs to bed, Mother.

NORA (*Starts—then indignantly.*) To bed, is it? You can think of sleepin' when he's—

SARA I didn't say sleep, but I can lie down and try to rest. (*Still avoiding looking at her mother.*) I'm dead tired, Mother.

NORA (*Tenderly solicitous now, puts an arm around her.*) You must be, darlin'. It's been the divil's own day for you, with all—(*With sudden remorse.*) God forgive me, darlin'. I was forgettin' about you and the Harford lad. (*Miserably.*) Oh, God help us! (*Suddenly with a flash of her strange, fierce pride in the power of love.*) Never mind! If there's true love between you, you'll not let a duel or anything in the world kape you from each other, whatever the cost! Don't I know!

SARA (*Kisses her impulsively, then looks away again.*) You're going to sit up and wait down here?

NORA I am. I'd be destroyed with fear lying down in the dark. Here, the noise of them in the bar kapes up my spirits, in a way.

SARA Yes, you'd better stay here. Good night, Mother.

NORA Good night, darlin'.

> *Sara goes out at right, closing the door behind her.*

CURTAIN

ACT FOUR

It is around midnight. The room is in darkness except for one candle on the table, center. From the bar comes the sound of Patch Riley's pipes playing a reel and the stamp of dancing feet.

Nora sits at the foot of the table at center. She is hunched up in an old shawl, her arms crossed over her breast, hugging herself as if she were cold. She looks on the verge of collapse from physical fatigue and hours of worry. She starts as the door from the bar is opened. It is Mickey. He closes the door behind him, shutting out an uproar of music and drunken voices. He has a decanter of whiskey and a glass in his hand. He has been drinking, but is not drunk.

NORA (*Eagerly.*) There's news of himself?

MALOY (*Putting the decanter and glass on the table.*) Sorra a bit. Don't be worryin' now. Sure, it's not so late yet.

NORA (*Dully.*) It's aisy for you to say—

MALOY I came in to see how you was, and bring you a taste to put heart in you. (*As she shakes her head.*) Oh, I know you don't indulge, but I've known you once in a while, and you need it this night. (*As she again shakes her head—with kindly bullying.*) Come now, don't be stubborn. I'm the doctor and I highly recommend a drop to drive out black thoughts and rheumatism.

NORA Well—maybe—a taste, only.

MALOY That's the talkin'. (*He pours a small drink and hands it to her.*) Drink hearty, now.

NORA (*Takes a sip, then puts the glass on the table and pushes it away listlessly.*) I've no taste for anything. But I thank you for the thought. You're a kind lad, Mickey.

MALOY Here's news to cheer you. The word has got round among the boys, and they've all come in to wait for Cregan and himself. (*With enthusiasm.*) There'll be more money taken over the bar than any night since this shebeen started!

NORA That's good.

MALOY If they do hate Con Melody, he's Irish, and they hate the Yanks worse. They're all hopin' he's bate the livin' lights out of Harford.

NORA (*With belligerent spirit.*) And so he has, I know that!

MALOY (*Grins.*) That's the talk. I'm glad to see you roused from your worryin'. (*Turning away.*) I'd better get back. I left O'Dowd to tend bar and I'll wager he has three drinks stolen already. (*He hesitates.*) Sara's not been down?

NORA No.

MALOY (*Resentfully.*) It's a wonder she wouldn't have more thought for you than to lave you sit up alone.

NORA (*Stiffens defensively.*) I made her go to bed. She was droppin' with tiredness and destroyed with worry. She must have fallen asleep, like the young can. None of your talk against Sara, now!

MALOY (*Starts an exasperated retort.*) The divil take—(*He stops and grins at her with affection.*) There's no batin' you, Nora. Sure, it'd be the joy av me life to have a mother like you to fight for me—or, better still, a wife like you.

NORA (*A sweet smile of pleased coquetry lights up her drawn face.*) Arrah, save your blarney for the young girls!

MALOY The divil take young girls. You're worth a hundred av thim.

NORA (*With a toss of her head.*) Get along with you!

> Mickey grins with satisfaction at having cheered her up and goes in the bar, closing the door. As soon as he is gone, she sinks back into apprehensive brooding.
>
> Sara appears silently in the doorway at right. She wears a faded old wrapper over her nightgown, slippers on her bare feet. Her hair is down over her shoulders, reaching to her waist. There is a change in her. All the bitterness and defiance have disappeared from her face. It looks gentle and calm and at the same time dreamily happy and exultant. She is much prettier than she has ever been before. She stands looking at her mother, and suddenly she becomes shy and uncertain—as if, now that she'd come this far, she had half a mind to retreat before her mother discovered her. But Nora senses her presence and looks up.

NORA (*Dully.*) Ah, it's you, darlin'! (*Then gratefully.*) Praise be, you've come at last! I'm sick with worry and I've got to the place where I can't bear waitin' alone, listenin' to drunks dancin' and celebratin'. (*Sara comes to her. Nora breaks. Tears well from her eyes.*) It's cruel, it is! There's no heart or thought for himself in divil a one av thim. (*She starts to sob. Sara hugs her and kisses her cheek gently. But she doesn't speak. It is as if she were afraid her voice would give her away. Nora stops sobbing. Her mood changes to resentment and she speaks as if Sara had spoken.*) Don't tell me not to worry. You're as bad as Mickey. The Yankee didn't apologize or your father'd been back her long since. It's a duel, that's certain, and he must have taken a room in the city so he'll be near the ground. I hope he'll sleep, but I'm feared he'll stay up drinkin', and at the dawn he'll have had too much to shoot his best and maybe— (*Then defiantly self-reassuringly.*) Arrah, I'm the fool! It's himself can keep his head clear and his eyes sharp, no matter what he's taken! (*Pushing Sara away—with nervous peevishness.*) Let go of me. You've hardened not to care. I'd rather stay alone. (*She grabs Sara's hand.*) No. Don't heed me. Sit down, darlin'. (*Sara sits down on her left at rear of table. She pats her mother's hand, but remains silent, her expression dreamily happy, as if she heard Nora's words but they had no meaning for her. Nora goes on worriedly again.*) But if he's staying in the city, why hasn't he sent Jamie Cregan back for his duelin' pistols? I know he'd nivir fight with any others. (*Resentful now at Melody.*) Or you'd think he'd send Jamie or someone back with a word for me. He knows well how tormented I'd be waiting. (*Bitterly.*) Arrah, don't talk like a loon! Has he ever cared for anyone except himself and his pride? Sure, he'd never stoop to think of me, the grand gentleman in his red livery av bloody England! His pride, indade! What is it but a lie? What's in his veins, God pity him, but the blood of thievin' auld Ned Melody who kept a dirty shebeen? (*Then is horrified at herself as if she had blasphemed.*) No! I won't say it! I've nivir! It would break his heart if he heard me! I'm the only one in the world he knows nivir sneers at his dreams! (*Working herself to rebellion again.*) All the same, I won't stay here the rist of the night worryin' my heart out for a man who—it isn't only fear over the duel. It's because I'm afraid it's God's punishment, all the sorrow and trouble that's come on us, and I have the black tormint in my mind that it's the fault of the mortal sin I did with him unmarried, and the promise he made me make to leave the Church that's kept me from ever confessin' to a priest. (*She pauses—dully.*) Go to a doctor, you say, to cure the rheumatism. Sure, what's rheumatism but a pain in your body? I could bear ten of it. It's the pain of guilt in my soul. Can a doctor's medicine cure that? No, only a priest of Almighty God— (*With a roused rebellion again.*) It would serve Con right if I took the chance now and broke my promise and woke up the priest to hear my confession and give me God's forgiveness that'd bring my soul peace and comfort so I wouldn't feel the three of us were damned. (*Yearningly.*) Oh, if I only had the courage! (*She rises suddenly from her chair—with brave defiance.*) I'll do it, so I will! I'm going to the priest's, Sara. (*She starts for the street door—gets halfway to it and stops.*)

SARA   (*A strange, tenderly amused smile on her lips—teasingly.*) Well, why don't you go, Mother?

NORA   (*Defiantly.*) Ain't I goin'? (*She takes a few more steps toward the door—stops again—she mutters beatenly.*) God forgive me, I can't. What's the use pretendin'?

SARA   (*As before.*) No use at all, Mother. I've found that out.

NORA   (*As if she hadn't heard, comes back slowly.*) He'd feel I'd betrayed him and my word and my love for him—and for all his scorn, he knows my love is all he has in the world to comfort him. (*Then spiritedly, with a proud toss of her head.*) And it's my honor, too! It's not for his sake at all! Divil mend him, he always prates as if he had all the honor there is, but I've mine, too, as proud as his. (*She sits down in the same chair.*)

SARA   (*Softly.*) Yes, the honor of her love to a woman. I've learned about that too, Mother.

NORA   (*As if this were the first time she was really conscious of Sara speaking, and even now had not heard what she said—irritably.*) So you've found your tongue, have you? Thank God. You're cold comfort, sitting silent like a statue, and me making talk to myself. (*Regarding her as if she hadn't really seen her before—resentfully.*) Musha but it's pleased and pretty you look, as if there wasn't a care in the world, while your poor father—

SARA   (*Dreamily amused, as if this no longer had any importance or connection with her.*) I know it's no use telling you there won't be any duel, Mother, and it's crazy to give it a thought. You're living in Ireland long ago, like Father. But maybe you'll take Simon's word for it, if you won't mine. He said his father would be paralyzed with indignation just at the thought he'd ever fight a duel. It's against the law.

NORA   (*Scornfully.*) Och, who cares for the law? He must be a coward. (*She looks relieved.*) Well, if the young lad said that, maybe it's true.

SARA   Of course it's true, Mother.

NORA   Your father'd be satisfied with Harford's apology and that'd end it.

SARA   (*Helplessly.*) Oh, Mother! (*Then quickly.*) Yes, I'm sure it ended hours ago.

NORA   (*Intent on her hope.*) And you think what's keeping him out is he and Jamie would take a power av drinks to celebrate.

SARA   They'd drink, that's sure, whatever happened. (*She adds dreamily.*) But that doesn't matter now at all.

NORA   (*Stares at her—wonderingly.*) You've a queer way of talking, as if you'd been asleep and was still half in a dream.

SARA   In a dream right enough, Mother, and it isn't half of me that's in it but all of me, body and soul. And it's a dream that's true, and always will be to the end of life, and I'll never wake from it.

NORA   Sure, what's come over you at all?

SARA   (*Gets up impulsively and comes around in back of her mother's chair and slips to her knees and puts her arms about her—giving her a hug.*) Joy. That's what's come over me. I'm happy, Mother. I'm happy because I know now Simon is mine, and no one can ever take him from me.

NORA   (*At first her only reaction is pleased satisfaction.*) God be thanked! It was a great sorrow tormentin' me that the duel would come between you. (*Defiantly.*) Honor or not, why should the children have their lives and their love destroyed!

SARA   I was a great fool to fear his mother could turn him against me, no matter what happened.

NORA   You've had a talk with the lad?

SARA   I have. That's where I've been.

NORA   You've been in his room ever since you went up?

SARA   Almost. After I'd got upstairs it took me a while to get up my courage.

NORA   (*Rebukingly.*) All this time—in the dead of the night!

SARA   (*Teasingly.*) I'm his nurse, aren't I? I've a right.

NORA   That's no excuse!

SARA   (*Her face hardening.*) Excuse? I had the best in the world. Would you have me do nothing to save my happiness and my chance in life, when I thought there was danger they'd be ruined forever? Don't you want me to have love and be happy, Mother?

NORA   (*Melting.*) I do, darlin'. I'd give my life— (*Then rebuking again.*) Were you the way you are, in only a nightgown and wrapper?

SARA   (*Gaily.*) I was—and Simon liked my costume, if you don't, although he turned red as a beet when I came in.

NORA   Small wonder he did! Shame on you!

SARA   He was trying to read a book of poetry, but he couldn't he was that worried hoping I'd come to say goodnight, and being frightened I wouldn't. (*She laughs tenderly.*) Oh, it was the cutest thing I've ever done, Mother, not to see him at all since his mother left. He kept waiting for me and when I didn't come, he got scared to death that his kissing me this morning had made me angry. So he was wild with joy to see me—

NORA   In your bare legs with only your nightgown and wrapper to cover your nakedness! Where's your modesty?

SARA   (*Gaily teasing.*) I had it with me, Mother, though I'd tried hard to leave it behind. I got as red as he was. (*She laughs.*) Oh, Mother, it's a great joke on me. Here I'd gone to his room with my mind made up to be as bold as any street woman and tempt him because I knew his honor would make him marry me right away if— (*She laughs.*) And then all I could do was stand and gape at him and blush!

NORA   Oh. (*Rebukingly.*) I'm glad you had the dacency to blush.

SARA   It was Simon spoke first, and once he started, all he'd been holding back came out. The waiting for me, and the fear he'd had made him forget all his shyness, and he said he loved me and asked me to marry him the first day we could. Without knowing how it happened, there I was with his arms around me and mine around him and his lips on my lips and it was heaven, Mother.

NORA   (*Moved by the shining happiness in Sara's face.*) God bless the two av you.

SARA   Then I was crying and telling him how afraid I'd been his mother hated me, Father's madness about the duel would give her a good chance to come between us; Simon said no one could ever come between us and his mother would never try to, now she knew he loved me, which was what she came over to find out. He said all she wanted was for him to be free to do as he pleased, and she only suggested he wait a year, she didn't make him promise. And Simon said I was foolish to think she would take the duel craziness serious. She'd only be amused at the joke it would be on his father, after he'd been so sure he could buy us off, if he had to call the police to save him.

NORA   (*Aroused at the mention of police.*) Call the police, is it? The coward!

SARA (*Goes on, unheedingly.*) Simon was terribly angry at his father for that. And at Father too when I told how he threatened he'd kill me. But we didn't talk of it much. We had better things to discuss. (*She smiles tenderly.*)

NORA (*Belligerently.*) A lot Con Melody cares for police, and him in a rage! Not the whole dirty force av thim will dare interfere with him!

SARA (*Goes on as if she hadn't heard.*) And then Simon told me how scared he'd been I didn't love him and wouldn't marry him. I was so beautiful, he said, and he wasn't handsome at all. So I kissed him and told him he was the handsomest in the world, and he is. And he said he wasn't worthy because he had so little to offer, and was a failure at what he'd hoped he could be, a poet. So I kissed him and told him he was too a poet, and always would be, and it was what I loved most about him.

NORA The police! Let one av thim lay his dirty hand on Con Melody, and he'll knock him senseless with one blow.

SARA Then Simon said how poor he was, and he'd never accept a penny from his father, even if he offered it. And I told him never mind, that if we had to live in a hut, or sleep in the grass of a field without a roof to our heads, and work our hands to the bone, or starve itself, I'd be in heaven and sing with the joy of our love! (*She looks up at her mother.*) And I meant it, Mother! I meant every word of it from the bottom of my heart!

NORA (*Answers vaguely from her preoccupation with the police—patting Sara's hair mechanically.*) Av course you did, darlin'.

SARA But he kissed me and said it wouldn't be as bad as that, he'd been thinking and he'd had an offer from an old college friend who'd inherited a cotton mill and who wants Simon to be equal partners if he'll take complete charge of it. It's only a small mill and that's what tempts Simon. He said maybe I couldn't believe it but he knows from his experience working for his father he has the ability for trade, though he hates it, and he could easily make a living for us from this mill—just enough to be comfortable, and he'd have time over to write his book, and keep his wisdom, and never let himself become a slave to the greed for more than enough that is the curse of mankind. Then he said he was afraid maybe I'd think it was weakness in him, not wisdom, and could I be happy with enough and no more. So I kissed him and said all I wanted in life was his love, and whatever meant happiness to him would be my only ambition. (*She looks up at her mother again—exultantly.*) And I meant it, Mother! With all my heart and soul!

NORA (*As before, patting her hair.*) I know, darlin'.

SARA Isn't that a joke on me, with all my crazy dreams of riches and a grand estate and me a haughty lady riding around in a carriage with coachman and footman! (*She laughs at herslf.*) Wasn't I the fool to think that had any meaning at all when you're in love? You were right, Mother. I knew nothing of love, or the pride a woman can take in giving everything—the pride in her own love! I was only an ignorant, silly girl boasting, but I'm a woman now, Mother, and I know.

NORA (*As before, mechanically.*) I'm sure you do, darlin'. (*She mutters fumingly to herself.*) Let the police try it! He'll whip them back to their kennels, the dirty curs!

SARA (*Lost in her happiness.*) And then we put out the light and talked about how soon we'd get married, and how happy we'd be the rest of our lives together, and we'd have children—and he forgot whatever shyness was left in the dark and said he meant all the bold things he'd written in the poems I'd seen. And I confessed that I was up to every scheme to get him, because I loved him so much there wasn't anything I wouldn't do to make sure he was mine. And all the time we were kissing each other, wild with happiness. And—(*She stops abruptly and looks down guiltily.*)

NORA (*As before.*) Yes, darlin', I know.

SARA (*Guiltily, keeping her eyes down.*) You—know, Mother?

NORA (*Abruptly comes out of her preoccupation, startled and uneasy.*) I know what? What are you sayin'? Look up at me! (*She pulls Sara's head back so she can look down in her face—falteringly.*) I can see—You let him! You wicked, sinful girl!

SARA (*Defiantly and proudly.*) There was no letting about it, only love making the two of us!

NORA (*Helplessly resigned already but feeling it her duty to rebuke.*) Ain't you ashamed to boast—?

SARA No! There was no shame in it! (*Proudly.*) Ashamed? You know I'm not! Haven't you told me of the pride in your love? Were you ashamed?

NORA (*Weakly.*) I was. I was dead with shame.

SARA You were not! You were proud like me!

NORA But it's a mortal sin. God will punish you—

SARA Let Him! If He'd say to me, for every time you kiss Simon you'll have a thousand years in hell, I wouldn't care, I'd wear out my lips kissing him!

NORA (*Frightenedly.*) Whist, now! He might hear you.

SARA Wouldn't you have said the same—?

NORA (*Distractedly.*) Will you stop! Don't torment me with your sinful questions! I won't answer you!

SARA (*Hugging her.*) All right. Forgive me, Mother. (*A pause—smilingly.*) It was Simon who felt guilty and repentant. If he'd had his way, he'd be out of bed now, and the two of us would be walking around in the night, trying to wake up someone who could marry us. But I was so drunk with love, I'd lost all thought or care about marriage. I'd got to the place where all you know or care is that you belong to love, and you can't call your soul your own any more, let alone your body, and you're proud you've given them to love. (*She pauses—then teasing lovingly.*) Sure, I've always known you're the sweetest woman in the world, Mother, but I never suspected you were a wise woman too, until I knew tonight the truth of what you said this morning, that a woman can forgive whatever the man she loves could do and still love him, because it was through him she found the love in herself; that, in one way, he doesn't count at all, because it's love, your own love, you love in him, and to keep that your pride will do anything. (*She smiles with a self-mocking happiness.*) It's love's slaves we are, Mother, not men's—and wouldn't it shame their boasting and vanity if we ever let them know our secret? (*She laughs—then suddenly looks guilty.*) But I'm talking great nonsense. I'm glad Simon can't hear me. (*She pauses. Nora is worrying and hasn't listened. Sara goes on.*) Yes, I can even understand now—a little anyway—how you can still love Father and be proud of it, in spite of what he is.

NORA (*At the mention of Melody, comes out of her brooding.*) Hush, now! (*Miserably.*) God help us, Sara, why doesn't he come, what's happened to him?

SARA   (*Gets to her feet exasperatedly.*) Don't be a fool, Mother. (*Bitterly.*) Nothing's happened except he's made a public disgrace of himself, for Simon's mother to sneer at. If she wanted revenge on him, I'm sure she's had her fill of it. Well, I don't care. He deserves it. I warned him and I begged him, and got called a peasant slut and a whore for my pains. All I hope now is that whatever happened wakes him from his lies and mad dreams so he'll have to face the truth of himself in that mirror. (*Sneeringly.*) But there's devil a chance he'll ever let that happen. Instead, he'll come home as drunk as two lords, boasting of his glorious victory over old Harford, whatever the truth is!

> *But Nora isn't listening. She has heard the click of the latch on the street door at rear.*

NORA   (*Excitedly.*) Look, Sara! (*The door is opened slowly and Jamie Cregan sticks his head in cautiously to peer around the room. His face is battered, nose red and swollen, lips cut and puffed, and one eye so blackened it is almost closed. Nora's first reaction is a cry of relief.*) Praise be to the Saints, you're back, Jamie!

CREGAN   (*Puts a finger to his lips—cautioningly.*) Whist!

NORA   (*Frightenedly.*) Jamie! Where's himself?

CREGAN   (*Sharply.*) Whist, I'm telling you! (*In a whisper.*) I've got him in a rig outside, but I had to make sure no one was here. Lock the bar door, Sara, and I'll bring him in.

> *She goes and turns the key in the door, her expression contemptuous. Cregan then disappears, leaving the street door half open.*

NORA   Did you see Jamie's face? They've been fightin' terrible. Oh, I'm afraid, Sara.

SARA   Afraid of what? It's only what I told you to expect. A crazy row—and now he's paralyzed drunk.

> *Cregan appears in the doorway at rear. He is half leading, half supporting Melody. The latter moves haltingly and woodenly. But his movements do not seem those of drunkenness. It is more as if a sudden shock or stroke had shattered his coordination and left him in a stupor. His scarlet uniform is filthy and torn and pulled awry. The pallor of his face is ghastly. He has a cut over his left eye, a blue swelling on his left cheekbone, and his lips are cut and bloody. From a big raw bruise on his forehead, near the temple, trickles of dried blood run down to his jaw. Both his hands are swollen, with skinned knuckles, as are Cregan's. His eyes are empty and lifeless. He stares at his wife and daughter as if he did not recognize them.*

NORA   (*Rushes and puts her arm around him.*) Con, darlin! Are you hurted bad? (*He pushes her away without looking at her. He walks dazedly to his chair at the head of the center table. Nora follows him, breaking into lamentation.*) Con, don't you know me? Oh, God help us, look at his head!

SARA   Be quiet, Mother. Do you want them in the bar to know he's come home—the way he is. (*She gives her father a look of disgust.*)

CREGAN   Ay, that's it, Sara. We've got to rouse him first. His pride'd nivir forgive us if we let thim see him dead bate like this.

> *There is a pause. They stare at him and he stares sightlessly at the table top. Nora stands close by his side, behind the table, on his right, Sara behind her on her right, Cregan at right of Sara.*

SARA   He's drunk, isn't that all it is, Jamie?

CREGAN   (*Sharply.*) He's not. He's not taken a drop since we left here. It's the clouts on the head he got, that's what ails him. A taste of whiskey would bring him back, if he'd only take it, but he won't.

SARA   (*Gives her father a puzzled, uneasy glance.*) He won't?

NORA   (*Gets the decanter and a glass and hands them to Cregan.*) Here. Try and make him.

CREGAN   (*Pours out a big drink and puts it before Melody—coaxingly.*) Drink this now, Major, and you'll be right as rain! (*Melody does not seem to notice. His expression remains blank and dead. Cregan scratches his head puzzledly.*) He won't. That's the way he's been all the way back when I tried to persuade him. (*Then irritably.*) Well, if he won't, I will, be your leave. I'm needin' it bad. (*He downs the whiskey, and pours another—to Nora and Sara.*) It's the divil's own rampage we've had.

SARA   (*Quietly contemptuous, but still with the look of puzzled uneasiness at her father.*) From your looks it must have been.

CREGAN   (*Indignantly.*) You're takin' it cool enough, and you seein' the marks av the batin' we got! (*He downs his second drink—boastfully.*) But if we're marked, there's others is marked worse and some av thim is police!

NORA   God be praised! The dirty cowards!

SARA   Be quiet, Mother. Tell us what happened, Jamie.

CREGAN   Faix, what didn't happen? Be the rock av Cashel, I've nivir engaged in a livelier shindy! We had no trouble findin' where Harford lived. It's a grand mansion, with a big walled garden behind it, and we wint to the front door. A flunky in livery answered wid two others behind. A big black naygur one was. That pig av a lawyer must have warned Harford to expect us. Con spoke wid the airs av a lord. "Kindly inform your master," he says, "that Major Cornelius Melody, late of His Majesty's Seventh Dragoons, respectfully requests a word with him." Well, the flunky put an insolent sneer on him. "Mr. Harford won't see you," he says. I could see Con's rage risin' but he kept polite. "Tell him," he says, "if he knows what's good for him he'll see me. For if he don't, I'll come in and see him." "Ye will, will ye?" says the flunky, "I'll have you know Mr. Harford don't allow drunken Micks to come here disturbing him. The police have been informed," he says, "and you'll be arrested if you make trouble." Then he started to shut the door. "Anyway, you've come to the wrong door," he says, "the place for the loiks av you is the servants' entrance."

NORA   (*Angrily.*) Och, the impident divil!

SARA   (*In spite of herself her temper has been rising. She looks at Melody with angry scorn.*) You let Harford's servants insult you! (*Then quickly.*) But it serves you right! I knew what would happen! I warned you!

CREGAN   Let thim be damned! Kape your mouth shut, and lave me tell it, and you'll see if we let them! When he'd said that, the flunky tried to slam the door in our faces, but Con was too quick. He pushed it back on him and lept in the hall, roarin' mad, and hit the flunky a cut with his whip across his ugly mug that set him screaming like a stuck pig!

NORA   (*Enthusiastically.*) Good for you, Con darlin'!

SARA   (*Humiliatedly.*) Mother! Don't! (*To Melody with biting scorn.*) The famous duelist—in a drunken brawl with butlers and coachmen!

But he is staring sightlessly at the table top as if he didn't see her or know her.

CREGAN   (*Angrily, pouring himself another drink.*) Shut your mouth, Sara, and don't be trying to plague him. You're wastin' breath anyway, the way he is. He doesn't know you or hear you. And don't put on lady's airs about fighting when you're the whole cause of it.

SARA   (*Angrily.*) It's a lie! You know I tried to stop—

CREGAN   (*Gulps down his drink, ignoring this, and turns to Nora—enthusiastically.*) Wait till you hear, Nora! (*He plunges into the midst of battle again.*) The naygur hit me a clout that had my head dizzy. He'd have had me down only Con broke the butt av the whip over his black skull and knocked him to his knees. Then the third man punched Con and I gave him a kick where it'd do him least good, and he rolled on the floor, grabbin' his guts. The naygur was in again and grabbed me, but Con came at him and knocked him down. Be the mortal, we had the three av thim licked, and we'd have dragged auld Harford from his burrow and tanned his Yankee hide if the police hadn't come!

NORA   (*Furiously.*) Arrah, the dirthy cowards! Always takin' sides with the rich Yanks against the poor Irish!

SARA   (*More and more humiliated and angry and torn by conflicting emotions—pleadingly.*) Mother! Can't you keep still?

CREGAN   Four av thim wid clubs came behind us. They grabbed us before we knew it and dragged us into the street. Con broke away and hit the one that held him, and I gave one a knee in his belly. And then, glory be, there was a fight! Oh, it'd done your heart good to see himself! He was worth two men, lettin' out right and left, roarin' wid rage and cursin' like a trooper—

MELODY   (*Without looking up or any change in his dazed expression, suddenly speaks in a jeering mumble to himself.*) Bravely done, Major Melody! The Commander of the Forces honors your exceptional gallantry! Like the glorious field of Talavera! Like the charge on the French square! Cursing like a drunken, foulmouthed son of a thieving shebeen keeper who sprang from the filth of a peasant hovel, with pigs on the floor—with that pale Yankee bitch watching from a window, sneering with disgust!

NORA   (*Frightenedly.*) God preserve us, it's crazed he is!

SARA   (*Stares at him startled and wondering. For a second there is angry pity in her eyes. She makes an impulsive move toward him.*) Father! (*Then her face hardening.*) He isn't crazed, Mother. He's come to his senses for once in his life! (*To Melody.*) So she was sneering, was she? I don't blame her! I'm glad you've been taught a lesson! (*Then vindictively.*) But I've taught her one, too. She'll soon sneer from the wrong side of her mouth!

CREGAN   (*Angrily.*) Will you shut your gab, Sara! Lave him be and don't heed him. It's the same crazy blather he's talked every once in a while since they brought him to—about the Harford woman—and speakin' av the pigs and his father one minute, and his pride and honor and his mare the next. (*He takes up the story again.*) Well, anyways, they was too much for us, the four av thim wid clubs. The last thing I saw before I was knocked senseless was three av thim clubbing Con. But, be the Powers, we wint down fightin' to the last for the glory av auld Ireland!

MELODY   (*In a jeering mutter to himself.*) Like a rum-soaked trooper, brawling before a brothel on a Saturday night, puking in the gutter!

SARA   (*Strickenly.*) Don't, Father!

CREGAN   (*Indignantly to Melody.*) We wasn't in conditon. If we had been—but they knocked us senseless and rode us to the station and locked us up. And we'd be there yet if Harford hadn't made thim turn us loose, for he's rich and has influence. Small thanks to him! He was afraid the row would get in the paper and put shame on him.

> *Melody laughs crazily and springs to his feet. He sways dizzily, clutching his head—then goes toward the door at left front.*

NORA   Con! Where are you goin'? (*She starts after him and grabs his arm. He shakes her hand off roughly as if he did not recognize her.*)

CREGAN   He don't know you. Don't cross him now, Nora. Sure, he's only goin' upstairs to bed. (*Wheedlingly.*) You know what's best for you, don't you, Major?

> *Melody feels his way gropingly through the door and disappears, leaving it open.*

SARA   (*Uneasy, but consoling her mother.*) Jamie's right, Mother. If he'll fall asleep, that's the best thing— (*Abruptly she is terrified.*) Oh God, maybe he'll take revenge on Simon— (*She rushes to the door and stands listening—with relief.*) No, he's gone to his room. (*She comes back—a bit ashamed.*) I'm a fool. He'd never harm a sick man, no matter— (*She takes her mother's arm—gently.*) Don't stand there, Mother. Sit down. You're tired enough—

NORA   (*Frightenedly.*) I've never heard him talk like that in all the years—with that crazy dead look in his eyes. Oh, I'm afeered, Sara. Lave go of me. I've got to make sure he's gone to bed.

> *She goes quickly to the door and disappears. Sara makes a move to follow her.*

CREGAN   (*Roughly.*) Stay here, unless you're a fool, Sara. He might come to all av a sudden and give you a hell av a thrashin'. Troth, you deserve one. You're to blame for what's happened. Wasn't he fightin' to revenge the insults to you? (*He sprawls on a chair at rear of the table at center.*)

SARA   (*Sitting down at rear of the small table at left front—angrily.*) I'll thank you to mind your own business, Jamie Cregan. Just because you're a relation—

CREGAN   (*Harshly.*) Och, to hell with your airs! (*He pours out a drink and downs it. He is becoming drunk again.*)

SARA   I can revenge my own insults, and I have! I've beaten the Harfords—and he's only made a fool of himself for her to sneer at. But I've beaten her and I'll sneer last! (*She pauses, a hard, triumphant smile on her lips. It fades. She gives a little bewildered laugh.*) God forgive me, what a way to think of—I must be crazy, too.

CREGAN   (*Drunkenly.*) Ah, don't be talkin'! Didn't the two of us lick them all! And Con's all right. He's all right, I'm sayin'! It's only the club on the head makes him quare a while. I've seen it often before. Ay, and felt it meself. I remember at a fair in the auld country I was clouted with the butt av a whip and I didn't remember a thing for hours, but they told me after I never stopped gabbin' but went around tellin' every stranger all my secrets. (*He pauses. Sara hasn't listened. He goes on uneasily.*) All the same, it's no fun listening to his mad blather about the pale bitch, as he calls her, like she was a ghost, haunting and scorning him. And his gab about his beautiful thoroughbred mare is madder still, raving what a grand, beautiful lady she is, with her slender ankles and dainty feet, sobbin' and beggin' her forgiveness and talkin' of dishonor and death— (*He shrinks superstitiously—then angrily, reaching for the decanter.*) Och, be damned to this night!

> *Before he can pour a drink, Nora comes hurrying in from the door at left front.*

NORA (*Breathless and frightened.*) He's come down! He pushed me away like he didn't see me. He's gone out to the barn. Go after him, Jamie.

CREGAN (*Drunkenly.*) I won't. He's all right. Lave him alone.

SARA (*Jeeringly.*) Sure, he's only gone to pay a call on his sweetheart, the mare, Mother, and hasn't he slept in her stall many a time when he was dead drunk, and she never even kicked him?

NORA (*Distractedly.*) Will you shut up, the two av you! I heard him openin' the closet in his room where he keeps his auld set of duelin' pistols, and he was carryin' the box when he came down—

CREGAN (*Scrambles hastily to his feet.*) Oh, the lunatic!

NORA He'll ride the mare back to Harford's! He'll murther someone! For the love av God, stop him, Jamie!

CREGAN (*Drunkenly belligerent.*) Be Christ, I'll stop him for you, Nora, pistols or no pistols! (*He walks a bit unsteadily out the door at left front.*)

SARA (*Stands tensely—bursts out with a strange triumphant pride.*) Then he's not beaten! (*Suddenly she is overcome by a bitter, tortured revulsion of feeling.*) Merciful God, what am I thinking? As if he hadn't done enough to destroy—(*Distractedly.*) Oh, the mad fool! I wish he was— (*From the yard, off left front, there is the muffled crack of a pistol shot hardly perceptible above the noise in the barroom. But Sara and Nora both hear it and stand frozen with horror. Sara babbles hysterically.*) I didn't mean it, Mother! I didn't!

NORA (*Numb with fright—mumbles stupidly.*) A shot!

SARA You know I didn't mean it, Mother!

NORA A shot! God help us, he's kilt Jamie!

SARA (*Stammers.*) No—not Jamie— (*Wildly.*) Oh, I can't bear waiting! I've got to know— (*She rushes to the door at left front—then stops frightenedly.*) I'm afraid to know! I'm afraid—

NORA (*Mutters stupidly.*) Not Jamie? Then who else? (*She begins to tremble—in a horrified whisper.*) Sara! You think—Oh, God have mercy!

SARA Will you hush, Mother! I'm trying to hear— (*She retreats quickly into the room and backs around the table at left front until she is beside her mother.*) Someone's at the yard door. It'll be Jamie coming to tell us—

NORA It's a lie! He'd nivir. He'd nivir!

> *They stand paralyzed by terror, clinging to each other, staring at the open door. There is a moment's pause in which the sound of drunken roistering in the bar seems louder. Then Melody appears in the doorway with Cregan behind him. Cregan has him by the shoulder and pushes him roughly into the room, like a bouncer handling a drunk. Cregan is shaken by the experience he has just been through and his reaction is to make him drunkenly angry at Melody. In his free*

hand is a dueling pistol. Melody's face is like gray wax. His body is limp, his feet drag, his eyes seem to have no sight. He appears completely possessed by a paralyzing stupor.

SARA (*Impulsively.*) Father! Oh, thank God! (*She takes one step toward him—then her expression begins to harden.*)

NORA (*Sobs with relief.*) Oh, praise God you're alive! Sara and me was dead with fear—(*She goes toward them.*) Con! Con, darlin'!

CREGAN (*Dumps Melody down on the nearest chair at left of the small table—roughly, his voice trembling.*) Let you sit still now, Con Melody, and behave like a gintleman! (*To Nora.*) Here he is for ye, Nora, and you're welcome, bad luck to him!

> *He moves back as Nora comes and puts her arms around Melody and hugs him tenderly.*

NORA Oh, Con, Con, I was so afeered for you!

> *He does not seem to hear or see her, but she goes on crooning to him comfortingly as if he were a sick child.*

CREGAN He was in the stable. He'd this pistol in his hand, with the mate to it on the floor beside the mare. (*He shudders and puts the pistol on the table shakenly.*) It's mad he's grown entirely! Let you take care av him now, his wife and daughter! I've had enoughl I'm no damned keeper av lunatics! (*He turns toward the barroom.*)

SARA Wait, Jamie. We heard a shot. What was it?

CREGAN (*Angrily.*) Ask him, not me! (*Then with bewildered horror.*) He kilt the poor mare, the mad fool! (*Sara stares at him in stunned amazement.*) I found him on the floor with her head in his lap, and her dead. He was sobbing like a soul in hell— (*He shudders.*) Let me get away from the sight of him where there's men in their right senses laughing and singing! (*He unlocks the barroom door.*) And don't be afraid, Sara, that I'll tell the boys a word av this. I'll talk of our fight in the city only, because it's all I want to remember.

> *He jerks open the door and goes in the bar, slamming the door quickly behind him. A roar of welcome is heard as the crowd greets his arrival. Sara locks the door again. She comes back to the center table, staring at Melody, an hysterical, sneering grin making her lips quiver and twitch.*

SARA What a fool I was to be afraid! I might know you'd never do it as long as a drink of whiskey was left in the world! So it was the mare you shot?

> *She bursts into uncontrollable, hysterical laughter. It penetrates Melody's stupor and he stiffens rigidly on his chair, but his eyes remain fixed on the table top.*

NORA Sara! Stop! For the love av God, how can you laugh—!

SARA I can't—help it, Mother. Didn't you hear—Jamie? It was the mare he shot! (*She gives way to laughter again.*)

NORA (*Distractedly.*) Stop it, I'm sayin'! (*Sara puts her hand over her mouth to shut off the sound of her laughing, but her shoulders still shake. Nora sinks on the chair at rear of the table. She mutters dazedly.*) Kilt his beautiful mare? He must be mad entirely.

MELODY (*Suddenly speaks, without looking up, in the broadest brogue, his voice coarse and harsh.*) Lave Sara laugh. Sure, who could blame her? I'm roarin' meself inside me. It's the damnedest joke a man ivir played on himself since time began.

They stare at him. Sara's laughter stops. She is startled and repelled by his brogue. Then she stares at him suspiciously, her face hardening.

SARA What joke? Do you think murdering the poor mare a good joke?

Melody stiffens for a second, but that is all. He doesn't look up or reply.

NORA (*Frightened.*) Look at the dead face on him, Sara. He's like a corpse. (*She reaches out and touches one of his hands on the table top with a furtive tenderness— pleadingly.*) Con, darlin'. Don't!

MELODY (*Looks up at her. His expression changes so that his face loses all its remaining distinction and appears vulgar and common, with a loose, leering grin on his swollen lips.*) Let you not worry, Allanah. Sure, I'm no corpse, and with a few drinks in me, I'll soon be lively enough to suit you.

NORA (*Miserably confused.*) Will you listen to him, Sara—puttin' on the brogue to torment us.

SARA (*Growing more uneasy but sneering.*) Pay no heed to him, Mother. He's play-acting to amuse himself. If he's that cruel and shameless after what he's done—

NORA (*Defensively.*) No, it's the blow on the head he got fightin' the police.

MELODY (*Vulgarly.*) The blow, me foot! That's Jamie Cregan's blather. Sure, it'd take more than a few clubs on the head to darken my wits long. Me brains, if I have any, is clear as a bell. And I'm not puttin' on brogue to torment you, me darlint. Nor playactin', Sara. That was the Major's game. It's quare, surely, for the two av ye to object when I talk in me natural tongue, and yours, and don't put on airs loike the late lamented auld liar and lunatic, Major Cornelius Melody, av His Majesty's Seventh Dragoons, used to do.

NORA God save us, Sara, will you listen!

MELODY But he's dead now, and his last bit av lyin' pride is murthered and stinkin'. (*He pats Nora's hand with what seems to be genuine comforting affection.*) So let you be aisy, darlint. He'll nivir again hurt you with his sneers, and his pretindin' he's a gintleman, blatherin' about pride and honor, and his boastin' av duels in the days that's gone, and his showin' off before the Yankees, and thim laughin' at him, prancing around drunk on his beautiful thoroughbred mare— (*He gulps as if he were choking back a sob.*) For she's dead, too, poor baste.

SARA (*This is becoming unbearable for her—tensely.*) Why—why did you kill her?

MELODY Why did the Major, you mean! Be Christ, you're stupider than I thought you, if you can't see that. Wasn't she the livin' reminder, so to spake, av all his lyin' boasts and dreams? He meant to kill her first wid one pistol, and then himself wid the other. But faix, he saw the shot that killed her had finished him, too. There wasn't much pride left in the auld lunatic, anyway, and seeing her die made an end av him. So he didn't bother shooting himself, because it'd be a mad thing to waste a good bullet on a corpse! (*He laughs coarsely.*)

SARA (*Tensely.*) Father! Stop it!

MELODY Didn't I tell you there was a great joke in it? Well, that's the joke. (*He begins to laugh again but he chokes on a stifled sob. Suddenly his face loses the coarse, leering, brutal expression and is full of anguished grief. He speaks without brogue, not to them but aloud to himself.*) Blessed Christ, the look in her eyes by the lantern light with life ebbing out of them—wondering and sad, but still trustful, not reproaching me—with no fear in them—proud, understanding pride—loving me—she saw I was dying with her. She understood! She forgave me! (*He starts to sob but wrenches himself out of it and speaks in broad, jeering brogue.*) Begorra, if that wasn't the mad Major's ghost speakin'! But be damned to him, he won't haunt me long, if I know it! I intind to live at my ease from now on and not let the dead bother me, but enjoy life in my proper station as auld Nick Melody's son. I'll bury his Major's damned red livery av bloody England deep in the ground and he can haunt its grave if he likes, and boast to the lonely night av Talavera and the ladies of Spain and fightin' the French! (*With a leer.*) Troth, I think the boys is right when they say he stole the uniform and he nivir fought under Wellington at all. He was a terrible liar, as I remember him.

NORA   Con, darlin', don't be grievin' about the mare. Sure, you can get another. I'll manage—

SARA   Mother! Hush! (*To Melody, furiously.*) Father, will you stop this mad game you're playing—?

MELODY   (*Roughly.*) Game, is it? You'll find it's no game. It was the Major played a game all his life, the crazy auld loon, and cheated only himself. But I'll be content to stay meself in the proper station I was born to, from this day on. (*With a cunning leer at Sara.*) And it's meself feels it me duty to give you a bit av fatherly advice, Sara darlint, while my mind is on it. I know you've great ambition, so remember it's to hell wid honor if ye want to rise in this world. Remember the blood in your veins and be your grandfather's true descendant. There was an able man for you! Be Jaysus, he nivir felt anything beneath him that could gain him something, and for lyin' tricks to swindle the bloody fools of gintry, there wasn't his match in Ireland, and he ended up wid a grand estate, and a castle, and a pile av gold in the bank.

SARA   (*Distractedly.*) Oh, I hate you!

NORA   Sara!

MELODY   (*Goes on as if he hadn't heard.*) I know he'd advise that to give you a first step up, darlint, you must make the young Yankee gintleman have you in his bed, and afther he's had you, weep great tears and appeal to his honor to marry you and save yours. Be God, he'll nivir resist that, if I know him, for he's a young fool, full av dacency and dreams, and looney, too, wid a touch av the poet in him. Oh, it'll be aisy for you—

SARA   (*Goaded beyond bearing.*) I'll make you stop your dirty brogue and your play-acting! (*She leans toward him and speaks with taunting vindictiveness, in broad brogue herself.*) Thank you kindly but I've already taken your wise advice, Father. I made him have me in his bed, while you was out drunk fightin' the police!

NORA   (*Frightenedly.*) Sara! Hault your brazen tongue!

MELODY   (*His body stiffens on his chair and the coarse leer vanishes from his face. It becomes his old face. His eyes fix on her in a threatening stare. He speaks slowly, with difficulty keeping his words in brogue.*) Did you now, God bless you! I might have known you'd not take any chance that the auld loon av a Major, going out to revenge an insult to you, would spoil your schemes. (*He forces a horrible grin.*) Be the living God, it's me should be proud this night that one av the Yankee gintry has stooped to be seduced by my slut av a daughter! (*Still keeping his eyes fixed on hers, he begins to rise from his chair, his right hand groping along the table top until it clutches the dueling pistol. He aims it at Sara's heart, like an automaton, his eyes as cold, deadly, and merciless as they must have been in his duels of long ago. Sara is terrified but she stands unflinchingly.*)

NORA (*Horror-stricken, lunges from her chair and grabs his arm.*) Con! For the love av God! Would you be murthering Sara?

        A dazed look comes over his face. He grows limp and sinks back on his chair and lets the pistol slide from his fingers on the table. He draws a shuddering breath—then laughs hoarsely.

MELODY (*With a coarse leer.*) Murtherin' Sara, is it? Are ye daft, Nora? Sure, all I want is to congratulate her!

SARA (*Hopelessly.*) Oh! (*She sinks down on her chair at rear of the center table and covers her face with her hands.*)

NORA (*With pitifully well-meant reassurance.*) It's all right, Con. The young lad wants to marry her as soon as can be, she told me, and he did before.

MELODY Musha, but that's kind of him! Be God, we ought to be proud av our daughter, Nora. Lave it to her to get what she wants by hook or crook. And won't we be proud watchin' her rise in the world till she's a grand lady!

NORA (*Simply.*) We will, surely.

SARA Mother!

MELODY She'll have some trouble, rootin' out his dreams. He's set in his proud, noble ways, but she'll find the right trick! I'd lay a pound, if I had one, to a shilling she'll see the day when she'll wear fine silks and drive in a carriage wid a naygur coachman behind spankin' thoroughbreds, her nose in the air; and she'll live in a Yankee mansion, as big as a castle, on a grand estate av stately woodland and soft green meadows and a lake. (*With a leering chuckle.*) Be the Saints, I'll start her on her way by making her a wedding present av the Major's place where he let her young gintleman build his cabin—the land the Yankees swindled him into buyin' for his American estate, the mad fool! (*He glances at the dueling pistol—jeeringly.*) Speakin' av the departed, may his soul roast in hell, what am I doin' wid his pistol? Be God, I don't need pistols. Me fists, or a club if it's handy, is enough. Didn't me and Jamie lick a whole regiment av police this night?

NORA (*Stoutly.*) You did, and if there wasn't so many av thim—

MELODY (*Turns to her—grinningly.*) That's the talk, darlint! Sure, there's divil a more loyal wife in the whole world— (*He pauses, staring at her—then suddenly kisses her on the lips, roughly but with a strange real tenderness.*) and I love you.

NORA (*With amazed, unthinking joy.*) Oh, Con!·

MELODY (*Grinning again.*) I've meant to tell you often, only the Major, damn him, had me under his proud thumb. (*He pulls her over and kisses her hair.*)

NORA Is it kissn' my hair—!

MELODY I am. Why wouldn't I? You have beautiful hair, God bless you! And don't remember what the Major used to tell you. The gintleman's sneers he put on is buried with him. I'll be a real husband to you, and help ye run this shebeen, instead of being a sponge. I'll fire Mickey and tend the bar myself, like my father's son ought to.

NORA You'll not! I'll nivir let you!

MELODY (*Leering cunningly.*) Well, I offered, remember. It's you refused. Sure, I'm not in love with work, I'll confess, and maybe you're right not to trust me too near the whiskey. (*He licks his lips.*) Be Jaysus, that reminds me. I've not had a taste for hours. I'm dyin' av thirst.

NORA (*Starts to rise.*) I'll get you—

MELODY (*Pushes her back on her chair.*) Ye'll not. I want company and singin' and dancin' and great laughter. I'll join the boys in the bar and help Cousin Jamie celebrate our wonderful shindy wid the police. (*He gets up. His old soldierly bearing is gone. He slouches and his movements are shambling and clumsy, his big hairy hands dangling at his sides. In his torn, disheveled, dirt-stained uniform, he looks like a loutish, grinning clown.*)

NORA You ought to go to bed, Con darlin', with your head hurted.

MELODY Me head? Faix, it was nivir so clear while the Major lived to tormint me, makin' me tell mad lies to excuse his divilments. (*He grins.*) And I ain't tired a bit. I'm fresh as a man new born. So I'll say goodnight to you, darlint. (*He bends and kisses her. Sara has lifted her tear-stained face from her hands and is staring at him with a strange, anguished look of desperation. He leers at her.*) And you go to bed, too, Sara. Troth, you deserve a long, dreamless slape after all you've accomplished this day.

SARA Please! Oh, Father, I can't bear—Won't you be yourself again?

MELODY (*Threatening her good-humoredly.*) Let you kape your mouth closed, ye slut, and not talk like you was ashamed of me, your father. I'm not the Major who was too much of a gintleman to lay hand on you. Faix, I'll give you a box on the ear that'll teach you respect, if ye kape on trying to raise the dead!

       She stares at him, sick and desperate. He starts toward the bar door.

SARA (*Springs to her feet.*) Father! Don't go in with those drunken scum! Don't let them hear and see you! You can drink all you like here. Jamie will come and keep you company. He'll laugh and sing and help you celebrate Talavera—

MELODY (*Roughly.*) To hell wid Talavera! (*His eyes are fastened on the mirror. He leers into it.*) Be Jaysus, if it ain't the mirror the auld loon was always admirin' his mug in while he spouted Byron to pretend himself was a lord wid a touch av the poet— (*He strikes a pose which is a vulgar burlesque of his old before-the-mirror one and recites in mocking brogue.*)
"I have not loved the World, nor the World me;
I have not flatthered uts rank breath, nor bowed
To uts idolatries a pashunt knee,
Nor coined me cheek to smiles,—nor cried aloud
In worship av an echo: in the crowd
They couldn't deem me one av such—I stood
Among thim, but not av thim . . ."
(*He guffaws contemptuously.*) Be Christ, if he wasn't the joke av the world, the Major. He should have been a clown in a circus. God rest his soul in the flames av tormint! (*Roughly.*) But to hell wid the dead. (*The noise in the bar rises to an uproar of laughter as if Jamie had just made some climactic point in his story. Melody looks away from the mirror to the bar door.*) Be God, I'm alive and

in the crowd they *can* deem me one av such! I'll be among thim and av thim, too—and make up for the lonely dog's life the Major led me. (*He goes to the bar door.*)

SARA (*Starts toward him—beseechingly.*) Father! Don't put this final shame on yourself. You're not drunk now. There's no excuse you can give yourself. You'll be as dead to yourself after, as if you'd shot yourself along with the mare!

MELODY (*Leering—with a wink at Nora.*) Listen to her, Nora, reproachin' me because I'm not drunk. Troth, that's a condition soon mended. (*He puts his hand on the knob of the door.*)

SARA Father!

NORA (*Has given way to such complete physical exhaustion, she hardly hears, much less comprehends what is said—dully.*) Lave him alone, Sara. It's best.

MELODY (*As another roar is heard from the bar.*) I'm missin' a lot av fun. Be God, I've a bit of news to tell the boys that'll make them roar the house down. The Major's passin' to his eternal rest has set me free to jine the Democrats, and I'll vote for Andy Jackson, the friend av the common men like me, God bless him! (*He grins with anticipation.*) Wait till the boys hear that! (*He starts to turn the knob.*)

SARA (*Rushes to him and grabs his arm.*) No! I won't let you! It's my pride, too! (*She stammers.*) Listen! Forgive me, Father! I know it's my fault—always sneering and insulting you—but I only meant the lies in it. The truth—Talavera—the Duke praising your bravery—an officer in his army—even the ladies in Spain— deep down that's been my pride, too—that I was your daughter. So don't—I'll do anything you ask—I'll even tell Simon—that after his father's insult to you—I'm too proud to marry a Yankee coward's son!

MELODY (*Has been visibly crumbling as he listens until he appears to have no character left in which to hide and defend himself. He cries wildly and despairingly, as if he saw his last hope of escape suddenly cut off.*) Sara! For the love of God, stop—let me go—!

NORA (*Dully.*) Lave your poor father be. It's best.

In a flash Melody recovers and is the leering peasant again.

SARA (*With bitter hopelessness.*) Oh, Mother! Why couldn't you be still!

MELODY (*Roughly.*) Why can't you, ye mean. I warned ye what ye'd get if ye kept on interferin' and tryin' to raise the dead. (*He cuffs her on the side of the head. It is more of a playful push than a blow, but it knocks her off balance back to the end of the table at center.*)

NORA (*Aroused—bewilderedly.*) God forgive you, Con! (*Angrily.*) Don't you be hittin' Sara now. I've put up with a lot but I won't—

MELODY (*With rough good nature.*) Shut up, darlint. I won't have to again. (*He grins leeringly at Sara.*) That'll teach you, me proud Sara! I know you won't try raisin' the dead any more. And let me hear no more gab out of you about not marryin' the young lad upstairs. Be Jaysus, haven't ye any honor? Ye seduced him and ye'll make an honest gentleman av him if I have to march ye both by the scruff av the neck to the nearest church. (*He chuckles—then leeringly.*) And now with your permission, ladies both, I'll join me good friends in the bar.

He opens the door and passes into the bar, closing the door behind him. There is a roar of welcoming drunken shouts, pounding of glasses on bar and tables, then quiet as if he had raised a hand for silence, followed by his voice greeting them and ordering drinks, and other roars of acclaim mingled with the music of Riley's pipes. Sara remains standing by the side of the center table, her shoulders bowed, her head hanging, staring at the floor.

NORA (*Overcome by physical exhaustion again, sighs.*) Don't mind his giving you a slap. He's still quare in his head. But he'll sing and laugh and drink a power av whiskey and slape sound after, and tomorrow he'll be himself again—maybe.

SARA (*Dully—aloud to herself rather than to her mother.*) No. He'll never be. He's beaten at last and he wants to stay beaten. Well, I did my best. Though why I did, I don't know. I must have his crazy pride in me. (*She lifts her head, her face hardening—bitterly.*) I mean, the late Major Melody's pride. I mean, I did have it. Now it's dead—thank God—and I'll make a better wife for Simon.

> There is a sudden lull in the noise from the bar, as if someone had called for silence—then Melody's voice is plainly heard in the silence as he shouts a toast: "Here's to our next President, Andy Jackson! Hurroo for Auld Hickory, God bless him!" There is a drunken chorus of answering "hurroos" that shakes the walls.

NORA Glory be to God, cheerin' for Andy Jackson! Did you hear him, Sara?

SARA (*Her face hard.*) I heard someone. But it wasn't anyone I ever knew or want to know.

NORA (*As if she hadn't heard.*) Ah well, that's good. They won't all be hatin' him now. (*She pauses—her tired, worn face becomes suddenly shy and tender.*) Did you hear him tellin' me he loved me, Sara? Did you see him kiss me on the mouth—and then kiss my hair? (*She gives a little, soft laugh.*) Sure, he must have gone mad altogether!

SARA (*Stares at her mother. Her face softens.*) No, Mother, I know he meant it. He'll keep on meaning it, too, Mother. He'll be free to, now. (*She smiles strangely.*) Maybe I deserved the slap for interfering.

NORA (*Preoccupied with her own thoughts.*) And if he wants to kape on makin' game of everyone, puttin' on the brogue and actin' like one av thim in there— (*She nods toward the bar.*) Well, why shouldn't he if it brings him peace and company in his loneliness? God pity him, he's had to live all his life alone in the hell av pride. (*Proudly.*) And I'll play any game he likes and give him love in it. Haven't I always? (*She smiles.*) Sure, I have no pride at all—except that.

SARA (*Stares at her—moved.*) You're a strange, noble woman, Mother. I'll try and be like you. (*She comes over and hugs her—then she smiles tenderly.*) I'll wager Simon never heard the shot or anything. He was sleeping like a baby when I left him. A cannon wouldn't wake him. (*In the bar, Riley starts playing a reel on his pipes and there is the stamp of dancing feet. For a moment Sara's face becomes hard and bitter again. She tries to be mocking.*) Faith, Patch Riley don't know it but he's playing a requiem for the dead. (*Her voice trembles.*) May the hero of Talavera rest in peace! (*She breaks down and sobs, hiding her face on her mother's shoulder—bewilderedly.*) But why should I cry, Mother? Why do I mourn for him?

NORA   (*At once forgetting her own exhaustion, is all tender, loving help and comfort.*) Don't, darlin', don't. You're destroyed with tiredness, that' all. Come on to bed, now, and I'll help you undress and tuck you in. (*Trying to rouse her—in a teasing tone.*) Shame on you to cry when you have love. What would the young lad think of you?

CURTAIN

QUESTIONS FOR DISCUSSION

Act I

1.   One of the playwright's obligations is to give the audience enough background to make the action understandable. This informing process is called *exposition.* How does O'Neill use the conversation between Maloy and Cregan to achieve exposition? What information is given to the audience?

2.   Although characters in a play may lie, one of the accepted conventions of the theater is that the exposition be true. Yet O'Neill permits considerable talk between Maloy and Cregan about lies, and later in the play other characters doubt some points in the exposition. What is O'Neill's purpose in suggesting an incredibility to Con Melody's history?

3.   According to Maloy, what is the social hierarchy in Con Melody's mind? Where 'does Melody stand in relation to the "Irish around here" and to "the damned Yankee gentry"? What is Melody's basis for establishing such a caste system? How do political preferences reflect upon this social hierarchy?

4.   In an early speech, Nora says to Sara about Con, "Ah, don't be hard on him." What does this speech tell you about Nora's qualities? How does it exemplify the description of her in the stage directions? How does such a speech contribute to our understanding of her present condition? What value judgment can you place upon this apparently casual remark?

5.   How does O'Neill use the debts owed to Neiland and Dickinson to show Con and Nora's system of values? What is Sara's estimate of those values? What is the tone with which she expresses her estimate? To what extent does Sara's tone reveal her contempt for her father's behavior?

6.   What part does the Irish brogue have in revealing character? Why does Nora say to Sara, "Don't put on the brogue, now. You know how he hates to hear you. And I do, too."? Does Con himself ever

speak with the brogue? Does he engage in "blarney"? For what purposes?

7. In one of her most passionate speeches, Nora gives Sara a lesson in the meaning of love, saying, "givin' all of yourself, and that's what love is. . . ." "That's love, and I'm proud I've known the great sorrow and joy of it!" Discuss Nora's definition of love and contrast it with Sara's inexperienced reply. How do these attitudes compare or contrast with your own ideas of love? Why does Sara's attitude toward her mother change after this speech? Do you agree with Sara that Nora is both "a strange woman . . . and a grand woman"?

8. O'Neill creates the character of Sara so that her complexities and contradictions make her wholly human and believable. In the passages in which she discusses her scorn for her father's foolishness and Father Flynn's threats, Sara shows both her Irish and her anti-Irish feelings. Which lines specifically reveal these two sides? What action intended by Sara suggests a streak of opportunism in her?

9. Nora believes that both Simon Harford and Con have "a touch of the poet" in them. Simon writes poems, Con recites them. In what other sense, however, does Con possess the poetic temperament?

10. Con Melody is an Irishman who served in the English army and is now an American citizen. Discuss his attitudes toward each of these three national affiliations.

Act II

1. By what device does O'Neill manage to have Deborah Harford find her son at the Melodys' tavern? In what other plays is a similar device used? What do you think of the playwright's use of such devices?

2. Once the point of attack has introduced the action of the plot, the playwright must construct reasonable *complications* in the plot to affect its course of action. In the development of the romance between Sara and Simon, what complications have been introduced by the end of Act II? In the plot strand concerning Con Melody, what complications already exist?

3. Look closely at the speech in which Deborah Harford analyzes Simon's condition and speaks of his poetry. What is O'Neill trying to achieve in characterization? Is he successful? What is faulty about the construction and sound of this sentence: "I had thought his implacably honest discovery that the poetry he hoped the pure freedom of Nature would inspire him to write is, after all, but a crude imitation of Lord Byron's would have more bitterly depressed his spirit"?

4. Just before she leaves Sara, Deborah Harford says to her, "I had forgotten how compelling the brutal power of primitive, possessive nature can be—when suddenly one is attacked by it." Of what, in addition to her morning's walk in the woods, is she speaking? Why is Sara right in interpreting Mrs. Harford's remarks as a "warning and threatening"?

5. What part does Deborah Harford have in Con's eventual abandoning of his pose? Why is he so angry when he learns that she has left the tavern? Why does he later call her "that damned, insolent Yankee bitch"?

Act III

1. In the quiet exchanges between Roche and O'Dowd, their real attitude toward Con shows through. What is O'Neill's purpose in delaying a straightforward condemnation by Con's alleged friends until this point in the play?
2. By the device of *foreshadowing*, the playwright prepares his audience for significant, even ironic, events yet to come in the plot. In this play, there are several instances of foreshadowing. For instance, within the several references to Con's prized thoroughbred there is a clear suggestion of the horse's impending death. What is this instance of foreshadowing? Can you find other examples?
3. By what process of reasoning does Con arrive at the decision that for Simon to marry Sara would be "a tragic misalliance for him"? How does he always explain such outbursts of insults to his family?
4. How does the appearance of Gadsby bring together the two strands of the plot? Why is Con so enraged at Gadsby's proposition? What is ironic about Con's defense of his daughter's honor? How does this scene constitute a complication of both plots?

Act IV

1. In Nora's lengthy speech near the beginning of this act, she passes through several stages of worry, fear, anger, resolution, pride, and back to worry. Trace the development of these reactions.
2. In Sara's description of her night with Simon, she reveals some aspects of her love for him that contrast with Con's accusation, that she is "a common, greedy, scheming, cunning peasant girl, whose only thought is money and who has shamelessly thrown herself at a young man's head because his family happens to possess a little wealth and position." Discuss this contrast.
3. Cregan's account of the brawl at Harford's house in interspersed by exclamations by Nora and Sara which demonstrate their mixed reactions to the incident. Analyze their feelings and give examples of the differences in their reactions.
4. Melody's reactions to the brawl cause Sara to say, first, "He isn't crazed, Mother. He's come to his senses for once in his life!" Later in hysterical laughter she says, "Pay no heed to him, Mother. He's play-acting to amuse himself." Explain this important contradiction in Sara's understanding of her father.
5. Con refers to his killing the mare as "the damnedest joke a man ivir

played on himself since time began." What does he mean? What is O'Neill's purpose in having Melody kill the mare? Does this attempt at symbolism succeed? Interpret the symbolism.

6. The skillful playwright constructs his play in such a way that the complications lead to an ultimate point of momentous importance called the *climax*. After the climactic moment in the play, nothing else is as important; the course of action simply unwinds itself in the *denouement*. In *A Touch of the Poet*, what are the points of climax in each plot strand? What is the denouement of each? How are these unified at the end of the play?

7. In killing the mare, Con believes that he has also killed the pose of Major Cornelius Melody, gentleman. To what extent do you accept his word? How do you understand his accusation that his past behavior was the result of the Major's "makin' me tell mad lies to excuse his divilments"? What has happened to his notion that he possessed "a touch of the poet"? What is important about his decision to vote for Andrew Jackson?

ASSIGNMENTS FOR WRITING

1. Simon Harford never appears onstage. Write a character sketch of Simon which blends the impressions obtained by the audience from the speeches of Sara, Deborah Harford, Nora, and Con.

2. Near the end of the play, Nora says of her husband, "God pity him, he's had to live all his life alone in the hell av pride." In an essay discuss the problem that develops when pride creates an illusion and forces one to live up to that illusion. Use examples from other works of literature as evidence to support your argument.

3. You have been appointed to direct a production of *A Touch of the Poet*. At the first meeting of the cast and crew you need to make a statement that presents your interpretation of the play—a critical analysis to show your attitude toward characters and to give the acting company an idea of your treatment. Write such a statement.

4. O'Neill has given detailed descriptions of the characters in this play; yet it would be almost impossible to cast people who would match these descriptions exactly. The obligation of the director, however, is to find actors whose basic differences in physical appearance will seem appropriate. In a paragraph or two, describe the physical differences between the following pairs of characters: Con Melody and Gadsby, Nora and Deborah Harford.

The Genteel Tradition

JOHN SINGER SARGENT: The Daughters of Edward D. Boit, 1882

Sargent, born in Florence, spent his youth moving about Europe with his parents and did not visit the U.S. until he was twenty. It has been suggested that Henry James' story *The Pupil* was inspired by the Sargents' itinerant menage. The Boits, proper Bostonians, were also prone to travel, and even the great blue and white Chinese vases made sixteen trips across the Atlantic. This picture, which recalls Velasquez's *Meninas*, was painted in Paris.

561

JOHN SINGER SARGENT: Madame X (Mme. Gautreau), 1884

JAMES ABBOTT McNEILL WHISTLER: Symphony in White
No. 1: The White Girl, 1862

Whistler (1834-1903), Sargent (1856-1925), and Mary Cassatt (1845-1926) are invariably linked as the three expatriates who dared to compete with European painters on their own ground and triumphantly succeeded. Whistler was born in Lowell, Massachusetts, spent much of his youth in Russia (where his father built a railroad for the Tsar), failed at West Point, studied painting in Paris, and finally settled in London. He soon established himself as the most original, if not the most accepted, painter in England. *The White Girl* (p. 563) is more than just a portrait of his favorite model and mistress, Jo; it is a masterful study of varying white tones and textures. It was the most talked-about picture in the historic Salon des Refusés of 1863.

As a painter, Sargent was something of a child prodigy. At eighteen he entered the Paris studio of Carolus-Duran; by the end of two years he had surpassed his teacher. Sargent created an unwitting scandal at the Salon of 1884 with his portrait of the professional beauty Mme. Gautreau (p. 562). She and her friends hated it, critics attacked it, and the public was shocked by the contrast between her chalky pallor and the boldly cut black gown. The artist was fascinated by the uniform lavender "blotting paper color" of her complexion. At the beach she attracted curious crowds: would it run when she went in the water?

Mary Cassatt was not only our finest woman painter but a major influence on American taste. She persuaded her friends and family to buy the Impressionists, El Grecos, and Japanese screens that eventually passed into museums.

WILLIAM MERRITT CHASE: A Friendly Call, 1895

WINSLOW HOMER: Long Branch, New Jersey, 1869

In this delightful picture *(above)*, Homer combines sunlight, sea breeze, and the latest fashions. Chase (1849-1916) studied in Munich, stronghold of the Old Master brown technique, but he was also an intimate of Whistler. He shows that he was well aware of the pastel palette of the Impressionists and the taste for all things Japanese in this view *(left)* of the studio in his summer home at Shinnecock, Long Island. Chase was a popular and influential teacher for more than thirty years.

Mary Cassatt places two ladies at the tea table (p. 568, below) with her customary finesse. Composition and color, as we see them here, were always her strongest points.

Kenyon Cox (1856-1919) was a successful academic artist, mural painter, and art critic. His memorial portrait (p. 568, *above*) of Saint-Gaudens (1848-1907) was painted after the great sculptor's death. Saint-Gaudens was the author of the Shaw Memorial in Boston, the equestrian monument to General Sherman in New York, and the *Diana* atop the tower of the Old Madison Square Garden.

MARY CASSATT: The Bath (La Toilette), c. 1891

When Mary Cassatt left Pittsburgh to study painting in Paris, it was an unheard-of thing for a wealthy American girl to do. She never married, but in her art she constantly returned to the motif of mother and child. One of the few women friends the caustic Degas could tolerate, she began exhibiting with the Impressionists in 1879.

WILLIAM GLACKENS: Chez Mouquin, 1905

This picture is an undisguised tribute to Renoir, but the scene is not Paris.
Chez Mouquin was a New York restaurant where Glackens (1870-1938)
and his bohemian friends hung out. The man is James B. Moore, a lawyer
and restaurateur, who had an impecunious poet, Edwin Arlington Robinson, living in the garret of his house.

top: KENYON COX: Augustus Saint-Gaudens, 1908
bottom: MARY CASSATT: A Cup of Tea, 1880

Robert Frost

Although Robert Frost is invariably associated with New England, he was born in San Francisco in 1874 and spent most of his childhood there. It was not until Frost was eleven that he was brought to Massachusetts, the land of his forbears. After graduation from Lawrence High School, he enrolled at Dartmouth College, but left before completing a full term. He married Elinor White in 1895, taught briefly at his mother's private school, and concluded his formal education with two years of undergraduate study at Harvard.

In 1900, Frost moved his growing family to a farm in West Derry, New Hampshire. For the next ten years he farmed and wrote poetry, supplementing his meager income by teaching school, first at the Pinkerton Academy in Derry and subsequently at the New Hampshire State Normal School.

In 1912, discouraged by ill-health and the continued lack of interest in his poetry, Frost left for England with his family. A year later his first book, *A Boy's Will*, was accepted by a British publisher, who also published *North of Boston* the following year. When the Frost family returned to the United States in 1915, his reputation was established and a new phase of his career began.

While continuing to write prodigiously, Frost traveled widely and became famous for his provocative lectures. In 1920, he helped found the Bread Loaf School of English at Middlebury College, Vermont, where he lectured for many subsequent summers. Honors came also, most notably four Pulitzer Prizes (1924, 1931, 1937, 1943), many honorary degrees, and the invitation of John F. Kennedy, newly elected to the Presidency, to participate in the inaugural ceremonies of 1961.

Always Frost's base remained New England — first New Hampshire and then Vermont. Because of this he has mistakenly been called a regional writer. But his poetry reveals that Frost's only region is man, and the only boundary limiting this region is Frost's perception of the human condition.

What is called "regional" in Frost is more aptly described as his frame of reference. In a sense it is Frost's equivalent of what T. S. Eliot would later call the "objective correlative," which he defined as "a set of objects, a situation, a chain of events which shall be the formula of [a] *particular* emotion; such that when the external facts, which must terminate in sensory experience, are given, the emotion is immediately evoked."

So, whether the character in a Frost poem is mending stone walls, farming in remote areas, or reacting to a specifically evoked scene or season, the progression of images creates the emotional response Frost desires. And this emotional response is not localized in a region; it is found in all men.

The genius in Frost is his ability to evoke sounds and senses of place and situation while powerfully transmitting an insight into the human dilemma. Insight it usually is, not a carefully shaped solution. There are few solutions in Frost. In their place the reader finds doubts and hesitations and scrupulous fairness to alternative sides of questions.

Frost has said, "The poet's material is words that for all we may say and feel against them are more manageable than men. Get a few words alone in a study and with plenty of time on your hands you can make them say anything you please." While a bit optimistic for most of us, this revel in words is immediately apparent in Frost's poetry. He is a master at manipulating the connotative power of words. Quite often, rather than use a direct comparison, he will position a series of words throughout the poem to balance, reinforce, or intensify each other. The language of "Stopping by Woods," for example, achieves just this purpose in its cumulative effect.

Words require arrangement, and the words Frost arranges seem to fall into patterns that directly approximate the rhythms of speech. Yet Frost is eminently a modern poet in his technical skill in choosing meter and rhyme to fit sound to sense. And he is a master of many forms. Besides endless variations on the basic iambic pentameter line, he has written much in trimeter and tetrameter. He has used the heroic couplet forcefully and experimented with the usually rigid sonnet. But the measure of Frost's mastery of structure is not how carefully he has followed a given meter and rhyme scheme but how he has subtly altered an expected structure and shaped it for his own ends.

America has never imitated England in appointing a poet laureate; yet when Robert Frost died in 1963, his recognition as the premier American poet of his time was so nearly universal as to grant him unofficially the poet's laurel.

Mending Wall

Something there is that doesn't love a wall,
That sends the frozen-ground-swell under it,
And spills the upper boulders in the sun;
And makes gaps even two can pass abreast.
The work of hunters is another thing:
I have come after them and made repair
Where they have left not one stone on a stone,
But they would have the rabbit out of hiding,
To please the yelping dogs. The gaps I mean,
No one has seen them made or heard them made,   10
But at spring mending-time we find them there.
I let my neighbor know beyond the hill;
And on a day we meet to walk the line
And set the wall between us once again.
We keep the wall between us as we go.
To each the boulders that have fallen to each.
And some are loaves and some so nearly balls
We have to use a spell to make them balance:
"Stay where you are until our backs are turned!"
We wear our fingers rough with handling them.   20
Oh, just another kind of out-door game,
One on a side. It comes to little more:
There where it is we do not need the wall:
He is all pine and I am apple orchard.
My apple trees will never get across
And eat the cones under his pines, I tell him.
He only says, "Good fences make good neighbors."
Spring is the mischief in me, and I wonder
If I could put a notion in his head:
"Why do they make good neighbors? Isn't it   30
Where there are cows? But here there are no cows.
Before I built a wall I'd ask to know
What I was walling in or walling out,
And to whom I was like to give offence.
Something there is that doesn't love a wall,
That wants it down." I could say "Elves" to him,
But it's not elves exactly, and I'd rather
He said it for himself. I see him there
Bringing a stone grasped firmly by the top
In each hand, like an old-stone savage armed.   40
He moves in darkness as it seems to me,

Not of woods only and the shade of trees.
He will not go behind his father's saying,
And he likes having thought of it so well
He says again, "Good fences make good neighbors."

Birches

When I see birches bend to left and right
Across the lines of straighter darker trees,
I like to think some boy's been swinging them.
But swinging doesn't bend them down to stay.
Ice-storms do that. Often you must have seen them
Loaded with ice a sunny winter morning
After a rain. They click upon themselves
As the breeze rises, and turn many-colored
As the stir cracks and crazes their enamel.
Soon the sun's warmth makes them shed crystal shells 10
Shattering and avalanching on the snow-crust—
Such heaps of broken glass to sweep away
You'd think the inner dome of heaven had fallen.
They are dragged to the withered bracken by the load,
And they seem not to break; though once they are bowed
So low for long, they never right themselves:
You may see their trunks arching in the woods
Years afterwards, trailing their leaves on the ground
Like girls on hands and knees that throw their hair
Before them over their heads to dry in the sun.   20
But I was going to say when Truth broke in
With all her matter-of-fact about the ice-storm
I should prefer to have some boy bend them
As he went out and in to fetch the cows—
Some boy too far from town to learn baseball,
Whose only play was what he found himself,
Summer or winter, and could play alone.
One by one he subdued his father's trees
By riding them down over and over again
Until he took the stiffness out of them,   30
And not one but hung limp, not one was left
For him to conquer. He learned all there was
To learn about not launching out too soon
And so not carrying the tree away

Clear to the ground. He always kept his poise
To the top branches, climbing carefully
With the same pains you use to fill a cup
Up to the brim, and even above the brim.
Then he flung outward, feet first, with a swish,
Kicking his way down through the air to the ground.   40
So was I once myself a swinger of birches.
And so I dream of going back to be.
It's when I'm weary of considerations,
And life is too much like a pathless wood
Where your face burns and tickles with the cobwebs
Broken across it, and one eye is weeping
From a twig's having lashed across it open.
I'd like to get away from earth awhile
And then come back to it and begin over.
May no fate willfully misunderstand me   50
And half grant what I wish and snatch me away
Not to return. Earth's the right place for love:
I don't know where it's likely to go better.
I'd like to go by climbing a birch tree,
And climb black branches up a snow-white trunk
Toward heaven, till the tree could bear no more,
But dipped its top and set me down again.
That would be good both going and coming back.
One could do worse than be a swinger of birches.

A Considerable Speck

A speck that would have been beneath my sight
On any but a paper sheet so white
Set off across what I had written there.
And I had idly poised my pen in air
To stop it with a period of ink
When something strange about it made me think.
This was no dust speck by my breathing blown,
But unmistakably a living mite
With inclinations it could call its own.
It paused as with suspicion of my pen,   10
And then came racing wildly on again
To where my manuscript was not yet dry;
Then paused again and either drank or smelt—

With loathing, for again it turned to fly.
Plainly with an intelligence I dealt.
It seemed too tiny to have room for feet,
Yet it must have had a set of them complete
To express how much it didn't want to die.
It ran with terror and with cunning crept.
It faltered; I could see it hesitate;   20
Then in the middle of the open sheet
Cower down in desperation to accept
Whatever I accorded it of fate.

I have none of the tenderer-than-thou
Collectivistic regimenting love

With which the modern world is being swept.
But this poor microscopic item now!
Since it was nothing I knew evil of
I let it lie there till I hope it slept.

I have a mind myself and recognize   30
Mind when I meet with it in any guise.
No one can know how glad I am to find
On any sheet the least display of mind.

Spring Pools

These pools that, though in forests, still reflect
The total sky almost without defect,
And like the flowers beside them, chill and shiver,
Will like the flowers beside them soon be gone,
And yet not out by any brook or river,
But up by roots to bring dark foliage on.

The trees that have it in their pent-up buds
To darken nature and be summer woods —
Let them think twice before they use their powers
To blot out and drink up and sweep away   10
These flowery waters and these watery flowers
From snow that melted only yesterday.

A Leaf Treader

I have been treading on leaves all day until I am autumn-
         tired.
God knows all the color and form of leaves I have trodden
         on and mired.
Perhaps I have put forth too much strength and been too
         fierce from fear.
I have safely trodden underfoot the leaves of another year.

All summer long they were overhead, more lifted up
         than I.
To come to their final place in earth they had to pass me by.
All summer long I thought I heard them threatening under
         their breath.
And when they came it seemed with a will to carry me
         with them to death.

They spoke to the fugitive in my heart as if it were leaf
         to leaf.
They tapped at my eyelids and touched my lips with an
         invitation to grief.   10
But it was no reason I had to go because they had to go.
Now up my knee to keep on top of another year of snow.

An Old Man's Winter Night

All out of doors looked darkly in at him
Through the thin frost, almost in separate stars,
That gathers on the pane in empty rooms.
What kept his eyes from giving back the gaze
Was the lamp tilted near them in his hand.
What kept him from remembering the need
That brought him to that creaking room was age.
He stood with barrels round him—at a loss.
And having scared the cellar under him
In clomping there, he scared it once again   10
In clomping off;—and scared the outer night,
Which has its sounds, familiar, like the roar

Of trees and crack of branches, common things,
But nothing so like beating on a box.
A light he was to no one but himself
Where now he sat, concerned with he knew what,
A quiet light, and then not even that.
He consigned to the moon, such as she was,
So late-arising, to the broken moon
As better than the sun in any case   20
For such a charge, his snow upon the roof,
His icicles along the wall to keep;
And slept. The log that shifted with a jolt
Once in the stove, disturbed him and he shifted,
And eased his heavy breathing, but still slept.
One aged man—one man—can't keep a house,
A farm, a countryside, or if he can,
It's thus he does it of a winter night.

Stopping by Woods on a Snowy Evening

Whose woods these are I think I know.
His house is in the village though;
He will not see me stopping here
To watch his woods fill up with snow.

My little horse must think it queer
To stop without a farmhouse near
Between the woods and frozen lake
The darkest evening of the year.

He gives his harness bells a shake
To ask if there is some mistake.   10
The only other sound's the sweep
Of easy wind and downy flake.

The woods are lovely, dark and deep.
But I have promises to keep,
And miles to go before I sleep,
And miles to go before I sleep.

The Gift Outright

The land was ours before we were the land's.
She was our land more than a hundred years
Before we were her people. She was ours
In Massachusetts, in Virginia;
But we were England's, still colonials,
Possessing what we still were unpossessed by,
Possessed by what we now no more possessed.
Something we were withholding made us weak
Until we found out that it was ourselves
We were withholding from our land of living,   10
And forthwith found salvation in surrender.
Such as we were we gave ourselves outright
(The deed of gift was many deeds of war)
To the land vaguely realizing westward,
But still unstoried, artless, unenhanced,
Such as she was, such as she would become.

Acquainted with the Night

I have been one acquainted with the night.
I have walked out in rain—and back in rain.
I have outwalked the furthest city light.

I have looked down the saddest city lane.
I have passed by the watchman on his beat
And dropped my eyes, unwilling to explain.

I have stood still and stopped the sound of feet
When far away an interrupted cry
Came over houses from another street,

But not to call me back or say good-bye;   10
And further still at an unearthly height,
One luminary clock against the sky

Proclaimed the time was neither wrong nor right.
I have been one acquainted with the night.

Mowing

There was never a sound beside the wood but one,
And that was my long scythe whispering to the ground.
What was it it whispered? I knew not well myself;
Perhaps it was something about the heat of the sun,
Something, perhaps, about the lack of sound —
And that was why it whispered and did not speak.
It was no dream of the gift of idle hours,
Or easy gold at the hand of fay or elf:
Anything more than the truth would have seemed too
    weak
To the earnest love that laid the swale in rows,   10
Not without feeble-pointed spikes of flowers
(Pale orchises), and scared a bright green snake.
The fact is the sweetest dream that labor knows.
My long scythe whispered and left the hay to make.

For Once, Then, Something

Others taunt me with having knelt at well-curbs
Always wrong to the light, so never seeing
Deeper down in the well than where the water
Gives me back in a shining surface picture
Me myself in the summer heaven godlike
Looking out of a wreath of fern and cloud puffs.
Once, when trying with chin against a well-curb,
I discerned, as I thought, beyond the picture,
Through the picture, a something white, uncertain,
Something more of the depths — and then I lost it.   10
Water came to rebuke the too clear water.
One drop fell from a fern, and lo, a ripple
Shook whatever it was lay there at bottom,
Blurred it, blotted it out. What was that whiteness?
Truth? A pebble of quartz? For once, then, something.

Provide, Provide

The witch that came (the withered hag)
To wash the steps with pail and rag,
Was once the beauty Abishag,

The picture pride of Hollywood.
Too many fall from great and good
For you to doubt the likelihood.

Die early and avoid the fate.
Or if predestined to die late,
Make up your mind to die in state.

Make the whole stock exchange your own!   10
If need be occupy a throne,
Where nobody can call *you* crone.

Some have relied on what they knew;
Others on being simply true.
What worked for them might work for you.

No memory of having starred
Atones for later disregard,
Or keeps the end from being hard.

Better to go down dignified
With boughten friendship at your side   20
Than none at all. Provide, provide!

Desert Places

Snow falling and night falling fast, oh, fast
In a field I looked into going past,
And the ground almost covered smooth in snow,
But a few weeds and stubble showing last.

The woods around it have it—it is theirs.
All animals are smothered in their lairs.
I am too absent-spirited to count;
The loneliness includes me unawares.

And lonely as it is that loneliness
Will be more lonely ere it will be less—   10

A blanker whiteness of benighted snow
With no expression, nothing to express.

They cannot scare me with their empty spaces
Between stars — on stars where no human race is.
I have it in me so much nearer home
To scare myself with my own desert places.

Design

I found a dimpled spider, fat and white,
On a white heal-all,[1] holding up a moth
Like a white piece of rigid satin cloth —
Assorted characters of death and blight
Mixed ready to begin the morning right,
Like the ingredients of a witches' broth —
A snow-drop spider, a flower like a froth,
And dead wings carried like a paper kite.

What had that flower to do with being white,
The wayside blue and innocent heal-all?   10
What brought the kindred spider to that height,
Then steered the white moth thither in the night?
What but design of darkness to appall? —
If design govern in a thing so small.

Neither Out Far Nor In Deep

The people along the sand
All turn and look one way.
They turn their back on the land.
They look at the sea all day.

As long as it takes to pass
A ship keeps raising its hull;
The wetter ground like glass
Reflects a standing gull.

[1] a wild flower of North America.

The land may vary more;
But wherever the truth may be —   10
The water comes ashore,
And the people look at the sea.

They cannot look out far.
They cannot look in deep.
But when was that ever a bar
To any watch they keep?

The Death of the Hired Man

Mary sat musing on the lamp-flame at the table
Waiting for Warren. When she heard his step,
She ran on tip-toe down the darkened passage
To meet him in the doorway with the news
And put him on his guard. 'Silas is back.'
She pushed him outward with her through the door
And shut it after her. 'Be kind,' she said.
She took the market things from Warren's arms
And set them on the porch, then drew him down
To sit beside her on the wooden steps.   10

'When was I ever anything but kind to him?
But I'll not have the fellow back,' he said.
'I told him so last haying, didn't I?
If he left then, I said, that ended it.
What good is he? Who else will harbor him
At his age for the little he can do?
What help he is there's no depending on.
Off he goes always when I need him most.
He thinks he ought to earn a little pay,
Enough at least to buy tobacco with,   20
So he won't have to beg and be beholden.
"All right," I say, "I can't afford to pay
Any fixed wages, though I wish I could."
"Someone else can." "Then someone else will have to.'
I shouldn't mind his bettering himself
If that was what it was. You can be certain,
When he begins like that, there's someone at him
Trying to coax him off with pocket-money, —
In haying time, when any help is scarce.
In winter he comes back to us. I'm done.'   30

'Sh! not so loud: he'll hear you,' Mary said.

'I want him to: he'll have to soon or late.'

'He's worn out. He's asleep beside the stove.
When I came up from Rowe's I found him here,
Huddled against the barn-door fast asleep,
A miserable sight, and frightening, too —
You needn't smile — I didn't recognize him —
I wasn't looking for him — and he's changed.
Wait till you see.'

        'Where did you say he'd been?'

'He didn't say. I dragged him to the house,   40
And gave him tea and tried to make him smoke.
I tried to make him talk about his travels.
Nothing would do: he just kept nodding off.'

'What did he say? Did he say anything?'

'But little.'

      'Anything? Mary, confess
He said he'd come to ditch the meadow for me.'

'Warren!'

     'But did he? I just want to know.'

'Of course he did. What would you have him say?
Surely you wouldn't grudge the poor old man
Some humble way to save his self-respect.   50
He added, if you really care to know,
He meant to clear the upper pasture, too.
That sounds like something you have heard before?
Warren, I wish you could have heard the way
He jumbled everything. I stopped to look
Two or three times — he made me feel so queer —
To see if he was talking in his sleep.
He ran on Harold Wilson — you remember —
The boy you had in haying four years since.
He's finished school, and teaching in his college.   60
Silas declares you'll have to get him back.
He says they two will make a team for work:
Between them they will lay this farm as smooth!
The way he mixed that in with other things.
He thinks young Wilson a likely lad, though daft

On education—you know how they fought
All through July under the blazing sun,
Silas up on the cart to build the load,
Harold along beside to pitch it on.'

'Yes, I took care to keep well out of earshot.'   70

'Well, those days trouble Silas like a dream.
You wouldn't think they would. How some things linger!
Harold's young college boy's assurance piqued him.
After so many years he still keeps finding
Good arguments he sees he might have used.
I sympathize. I know just how it feels
To think of the right thing to say too late.
Harold's associated in his mind with Latin.
He asked me what I thought of Harold's saying
He studied Latin like the violin   80
Because he liked it—that an argument!
He said he couldn't make the boy believe
He could find water with a hazel prong—
Which showed how much good school had ever done him.
He wanted to go over that. But most of all
He thinks if he could have another chance
To teach him how to build a load of hay—'

'I know, that's Silas' one accomplishment.
He bundles every forkful in its place,
And tags and numbers it for future reference,   90
So he can find and easily dislodge it
In the unloading. Silas does that well.
He takes it out in bunches like big birds' nests.
You never see him standing on the hay
He's trying to lift, straining to lift himself.'

'He thinks if he could teach him that, he'd be
Some good perhaps to someone in the world.
He hates to see a boy the fool of books.
Poor Silas, so concerned for other folk,
And nothing to look backward to with pride,   100
And nothing to look forward to with hope,
So now and never any different.'

Part of a moon was falling down the west,
Dragging the whole sky with it to the hills.
Its light poured softly in her lap. She saw it

And spread her apron to it. She put out her hand
Among the harp-like morning glory strings,
Taut with the dew from garden bed to eaves,
As if she played unheard some tenderness
That wrought on him beside her in the night.   110
'Warren,' she said, 'he has come home to die:
You needn't be afraid he'll leave you this time.'

'Home,' he mocked gently.

                          'Yes, what else but home?
It all depends on what you mean by home.
Of course he's nothing to us, any more
Than was the hound that came a stranger to us
Out of the woods, worn out upon the trail.'

'Home is the place where, when you have to go there,
They have to take you in.'

                          'I should have called it
Something you somehow haven't to deserve.'   120

Warren leaned out and took a step or two,
Picked up a little stick, and brought it back
And broke it in his hand and tossed it by.
'Silas has better claim on us you think
Than on his brother? Thirteen little miles
As the road winds would bring him to his door.
Silas has walked that far no doubt today.
Why doesn't he go there? His brother's rich,
A somebody — director in the bank.'

'He never told us that.'

                          'We know it though.'   130

'I think his brother ought to help, of course.
I'll see to that if there is need. He ought of right
To take him in, and might be willing to —
He may be better than appearances.
But have some pity on Silas. Do you think
If he had any pride in claiming kin
Or anything he looked for from his brother,
He'd keep so still about him all this time?'

'I wonder what's between them.'

                          'I can tell you.

Silas is what he is — we wouldn't mind him —   140
But just the kind that kinsfolk can't abide.
He never did a thing so very bad.
He don't know why he isn't quite as good
As anybody. Worthless though he is,
He won't be made ashamed to please his brother.'

'I can't think Si ever hurt anyone.'

'No, but he hurt my heart the way he lay
And rolled his old head on that sharp-edged chair-back.
He wouldn't let me put him on the lounge.
You must go in and see what you can do.   150
I made the bed up for him there tonight.
You'll be surprised at him — how much he's broken.
His working days are done; I'm sure of it.'

'I'd not be in a hurry to say that.'

'I haven't been. Go, look, see for yourself.
But, Warren, please remember how it is:
He's come to help you ditch the meadow.
He has a plan. You mustn't laugh at him.
He may not speak of it, and then he may.
I'll sit and see if that small sailing cloud   160
Will hit or miss the moon.'

                              It hit the moon.
Then there were three there, making a dim row,
The moon, the little silver cloud, and she.

Warren returned — too soon, it seemed to her,
Slipped to her side, caught up her hand and waited.

'Warren?' she questioned.

                         'Dead,' was all he answered.

Home Burial

He saw her from the bottom of the stairs
Before she saw him. She was starting down,
Looking back over her shoulder at some fear.
She took a doubtful step and then undid it
To raise herself and look again. He spoke

Advancing toward her: "What is it you see
From up there always—for I want to know."
She turned and sank upon her skirts at that,
And her face changed from terrified to dull.
He said to gain time: "What is it you see," 10
Mounting until she cowered under him.
"I will find out now—you must tell me, dear."
She, in her place, refused him any help
With the least stiffening of her neck and silence
She let him look, sure that he wouldn't see,
Blind creature; and a while he didn't see.
But at last he murmured, "Oh," and again, "Oh."

"What is it—what?" she said.

                              "Just that I see."

"You don't," she challenged. "Tell me what it is." 20

"The wonder is I didn't see at once.
I never noticed it from here before.
I must be wonted to it—that's the reason.
The little graveyard where my people are!
So small the window frames the whole of it.
Not so much larger than a bedroom is it?
There are three stones of slate and one of marble,
Broad-shouldered little slabs, there in the sunlight
On the sidehill. We haven't to mind *those*.
But I understand: it is not the stones, 30
But the child's mound—"

                    "Don't, don't, don't, don't," she cried.

She withdrew shrinking from beneath his arm
That rested on the banister, and slid downstairs;
And turned on him with such a daunting look,
He said twice over before he knew himself:
"Can't a man speak of his own child he's lost?"

"Not you! Oh, where's my hat? Oh, I don't need it!
I must get out of here. I must get air.
I don't know rightly whether any man can." 40

"Amy! Don't go to someone else this time.
Listen to me. I won't come down the stairs."
He sat and fixed his chin between his fists.
"There's something I should like to ask you, dear."

"You don't know how to ask it."

"Help me, then."

Her fingers moved the latch for all reply.

"My words are nearly always an offense.
I don't know how to speak of anything
So as to please you. But I might be taught   50
I should suppose. I can't say I see how.
A man must partly give up being a man
With women-folk. We could have some arrangement
By which I'd bind myself to keep hands off
Anything special you're a-mind to name.
Though I don't like such things 'twixt those that love.
Two that don't love can't live together without them.
But two that do can't live together with them."
She moved the latch a little. "Don't—don't go.
Don't carry it to someone else this time.   60
Tell me about it if it's something human.
Let me into your grief. I'm not so much
Unlike other folks as your standing there
Apart would make me out. Give me my chance.
I do think, though, you overdo it a little.
What was it brought you up to think it the thing
To take your mother-loss of a first child
So inconsolably—in the face of love.
You'd think his memory might be satisfied—"

"There you go sneering now!"   70

                              "I'm not, I'm not!
You make me angry. I'll come down to you.
God, what a woman! And it's come to this,
A man can't speak of his own child that's dead."

"You can't because you don't know how to speak.
If you had any feelings, you that dug
With your own hand—how could you?—his little grave;
I saw you from that very window there,
Making the gravel leap and leap in air,
Leap up, like that, like that, and land so lightly   80
And roll back down the mound beside the hole.
I thought, Who is that man? I didn't know you.

And I crept down the stairs and up the stairs
To look again, and still your spade kept lifting.
Then you came in. I heard your rumbling voice
Out in the kitchen, and I don't know why,
But I went near to see with my own eyes.
You could sit there with the stains on your shoes
Of the fresh earth from your own baby's grave
And talk about your everyday concerns.   90
You had stood the spade up against the wall
Outside there in the entry, for I saw it."

"I shall laugh the worst laugh I ever laughed.
I'm cursed. God, if I don't believe I'm cursed."

"I can repeat the very words you were saying.
'Three foggy mornings and one rainy day
Will rot the best birch fence a man can build.'
Think of it, talk like that at such a time!
What had how long it takes a birch to rot
To do with what was in the darkened parlor.   100
You *couldn't* care! The nearest friends can go
With anyone to death, comes so far short
They might as well not try to go at all.
No, from the time when one is sick to death,
One is alone, and he dies more alone.
Friends make pretense of following to the grave,
But before one is in it, their minds are turned
And making the best of their way back to life
And living people, and things they understand.
But the world's evil. I won't have grief so   110
If I can change it. Oh, I won't, I won't!"

"There, you have said it all and you feel better.
You won't go now. You're crying. Close the door.
The heart's gone out of it: why keep it up.
Amy! There's someone coming down the road!"

"*You*—oh, you think the talk is all. I must go—
Somewhere out of this house. How can I make you—"

"If—you—do!" She was opening the door wider.
"Where do you mean to go? First tell me that.
I'll follow and bring you back by force. I *will!*—"   120

'Out, Out—'

The buzz saw snarled and rattled in the yard
And made dust and dropped stove-length sticks of wood,
Sweet-scented stuff when the breeze drew across it.
And from there those that lifted eyes could count
Five mountain ranges one behind the other
Under the sunset far into Vermont.
And the saw snarled and rattled, snarled and rattled,
As it ran light, or had to bear a load.
And nothing happened: day was all but done.
Call it a day, I wish they might have said   10
To please the boy by giving him the half hour
That a boy counts so much when saved from work.
His sister stood beside them in her apron
To tell them 'Supper.' At the word, the saw,
As if to prove saws knew what supper meant,
Leaped out at the boy's hand, or seemed to leap—
He must have given the hand. However it was,
Neither refused the meeting. But the hand!
The boy's first outcry was a rueful laugh.
As he swung toward them holding up the hand   20
Half in appeal, but half as if to keep
The life from spilling. Then the boy saw all—
Since he was old enough to know, big boy
Doing a man's work, though a child at heart—
He saw all spoiled. 'Don't let him cut my hand off—
The doctor, when he comes. Don't let him, sister!'
So. But the hand was gone already.
The doctor put him in the dark of ether.
He lay and puffed his lips out with his breath.
And then—the watcher at his pulse took fright.   30
No one believed. They listened at his heart.
Little—less—nothing!—and that ended it.
No more to build on there. And they, since they
Were not the one dead, turned to their affairs.

The Road Not Taken

Two roads diverged in a yellow wood,
And sorry I could not travel both

And be one traveler, long I stood
And looked down one as far as I could
To where it bent in the undergrowth;

Then took the other, as just as fair,
And having perhaps the better claim,
Because it was grassy and wanted wear,
Though as for that the passing there
Had worn them really about the same,   10

And both that morning equally lay
In leaves no step had trodden black.
Oh, I kept the first for another day!
Yet knowing how way leads on to way,
I doubted if I should ever come back.

I shall be telling this with a sigh
Somewhere ages and ages hence:
Two roads diverged in a wood, and I—
I took the one less traveled by,
And that has made all the difference.   20

QUESTIONS FOR DISCUSSION

Mending Wall

1. In the opening lines of the poem, the speaker contrasts "Something there is that doesn't love a wall" with the work of hunters. What are the implications of this distinction? What is the nature of the "something. . .that doesn't love a wall"?
2. How does sound match sense in line 2?
3. What is revealed about the speaker's character in lines 21–22, 25–26, 30–38?
4. What is the speaker's attitude toward his neighbor? Which specific words and lines demonstrate this?
5. Much as the two men involved in the poem balance rocks, Frost balances words, phrases, and images. Line 16 is a good example of this. What other examples are there in the poem?
6. How would you describe the theme of "Mending Wall"? What is the symbolic significance of the wall?
7. One of Frost's notable strengths is creating a universal emotional response within a regional framework. If the regional framework here is a New England farm in spring, what is the universal emotional climate evoked?

Birches

1. Examine closely the imagery in lines 7–13. How do the following words intensify each other and the total image: *click, colored, cracks, crazes, crystal, crust.*
2. Discuss the effectiveness of the similes Frost uses in lines 17–20, 36–38, 44–47.
3. Describe the subtle shifts in tone between lines 1–3, 21–23, 41–42, 43–47, and 50–54.
4. To be a successful "swinger of birches" what skills must one develop?
5. Why is *Toward* italicized in line 56?
6. Why would it "be good both going and coming back"?
7. How does the meter of "Birches" reinforce the reflective tone of the poem?

A Considerable Speck

1. Since Aesop, writers have delighted in constructing fables — which usually point out analogies between human beings and animals. What are some of the human qualities Frost ascribes to the "speck" in this poem?
2. Why is the speck considerable? What are the denotations and notations of the words *speck* and *considerable*?
3. Hyperbole, or exaggeration for effect, is a factor in this poem's structure. Where specifically does it occur?
4. To what is the poet referring in lines 24–26?
5. How would you describe the tone of the last four lines? Is it compassionate? satiric? ironic? What does the final couplet mean?

Spring Pools

1. The similarity between the flowers and pools Frost senses is suggested in lines 3 and 4 and intensified in line 11. What do they have in common?
2. What attitude of the speaker is suggested in lines 9–10? Discuss how the speaker implies the futility of this admonition by suggesting the inevitability of nature's change.
3. Why are "blot up," "drink up," and "sweep away" particularly apt descriptions?
4. There are overtones of light and dark in the poem. Which images are associated with each?

A Leaf Treader

1. What do autumn and, more particularly, the leaves symbolize for Frost?

2. In stanza 1, the Leaf Treader states directly the emotion he is experiencing. What is it? By the last stanza, has there been any change in his emotional state? Quote lines from the poem to support your answer.
3. In this poem, Frost uses the device of personification. Where, specifically, is personification used? What effect does it produce?
4. What is implied in the line "I have safely trodden underfoot the leaves of another year"?
5. The poem ends with the line "Now up my knee to keep on top of another year of snow." What is the literal action shown here? What is the symbolic action? Why does the poet exaggerate the length of winter here? What attitude toward the future is he revealing?
6. Frost uses "treading" and "trodden" to describe what he does to the leaves, but the leaves only "tap" and "touch" him. Besides relative size, what accounts for this difference in intensity?

An Old Man's Winter Night

1. How does Frost use hyperbole and personification in the first three lines?
2. What is the effect of "darkly" and "thin"? How do they help to set the mood of the poem? What other words and images contribute to the mood of the poem?
3. What is suggested by "broken moon" in line 19?
4. What is the narrator's conclusion in the last three lines? How does the "if" affect the statement?

Stopping by Woods on a Snowy Evening

1. In stanza 1, why is the speaker concerned about being observed?
2. Whose feelings is the horse reflecting in lines 5 and 6?
3. Sound, particularly vowel sound, is especially important in creating the mood of the poem. Which vowel sound predominates, and what does it suggest?
4. What is the cumulative effect created by Frost's use of "darkest," "sweep," "easy," "downy," "lovely," "dark," and "deep"? How do these words reinforce each other?
5. What are the implications of line 14? What conflict and resolution does the word *but* signal?
6. What could the man's strange stop symbolize? How is this intensified by his position ("Between the woods and frozen lake") when he stops? Is it important that the occasion is "the darkest evening of the year"?
7. What is the meter and rhyme scheme of this poem? What effect does the rhyme scheme create?

The Gift Outright

1. Discuss Frost's play on the word *possess* in lines 6–7. What central idea does it emphasize?
2. "The deed of gift was many deeds of war." How do the two "deeds" of this line play against each other? Consider both specific meaning and connotation.
3. In what way does Frost suggest we were withholding ourselves from the land?
4. Discuss the description: "vaguely realizing westward." How is it keyed to the theme of the poem?
5. Robert Frost read this poem during the inaugural ceremonies for John F. Kennedy in 1961. Why was this an appropriate poem for the occasion?
6. Critic Reuben Brower has called this poem "a compact psychological essay on colonialism." Discuss the poem in terms of that interpretation.

Acquainted with the Night

1. What is the total effect of the seven lines beginning in the same straightforward manner ("I have)?
2. What are the characteristics of the night being described in this poem? Do you think Frost intends "night" to be symbolic? If so, of what might it be symbolic?
3. Why, in line 13, is the time "neither wrong nor right"?
4. This poem is written in the strict form of Italian terza rima. Examine the meter and rhyme scheme carefully, and describe the form.

Mowing

1. What does the sound of "my long scythe whispering" contribute to the poem? What consonant sounds are responsible for this effect? Where do these sounds reappear throughout the poem?
2. The poem includes a number of simply stated images. What are they, and how might they relate to the statement made in line 13?
3. What is the effect of placing "Pale orchises" in parentheses?
4. Lines 7 and 8 seem to be at odds with the otherwise natural imagery in the poem. What contrast is Frost making here?

For Once, Then, Something

1. What is the effect created by the imagery in lines 4–6?
2. Beginning with the italicized *Once* in line 7, the imagery and diction suggest greater depth but also greater elusiveness. What words are especially responsible for this shift in perspective?

3. Until he reaches the last line, the reader has been involved in the poet's dramatic telling of a simple incident. Then the word *Truth* implies the "double-layer" Frost is fond of referring to. For what might this incident be an extended metaphor?

Provide, Provide

1. Perhaps in choosing the name Abishag, Frost was referring to the biblical story of Abishag, the beautiful young woman who failed in an attempt to arouse King David when he was dying. In this poem Abishag is a "withered hag." What reflection might Frost be casting on the nature of Hollywood stardom?
2. Compare the kinds of advice offered in stanzas 3, 4, 5, and 7. Which, if any, do you think Frost seriously advocates?
3. What is the general tone of the poem? How is this reinforced by the structure—rhyme and meter?
4. What are the connotations of "simply" in line 14?

Desert Places

1. What is the function of "oh" in the first line?
2. Frost repeats several words in this poem to intensify his mood. What are they, and what total effect do they produce?
3. What is the prevailing consonant sound used? What alliterative value does it have?
4. Who is "They" in line 13?
5. Why is the snow "benighted"?
6. Taken symbolically, to what dilemma of man does the poem refer?

Design

1. What is unusual about the description of the spider in the first line?
2. After the first few lines, there is a change in the nature of the imagery. Cite specific examples of this.
3. Besides similar color, what else binds the spider, heal-all, and moth?
4. Discuss the two similes Frost uses to describe the moth. What do they suggest?
5. After beginning the sestet of this sonnet with a series of questions, what answer does the poet propose?
6. How does the title of the poem also suit its structure? What conventional type of poem is "Design"?

Neither Out Far Nor In Deep

1. Who is the speaker in this poem? What is the difference in attitude between the speaker and "they"?

2. What is the effect of Frost's repetition of "all" in stanza 1?

3. Observe the images presented in stanza 2. How do they relate to the title of the poem?

4. Why do the people look at the sea? What are they looking for?

5. In line 9 the speaker says, "The land may vary more." What may it vary more than? How? What are the symbolic implications of "land," "sea," "far," "deep," "bar," "watch"?

6. What commentary on human nature is made in the last stanza?

7. Frost's rhythm and diction have a basic simplicity and directness. Cite specific examples of this. How does this fit the sense of the poem?

The Death of the Hired Man

1. Frost uses three speaking voices in this poem. Distinguish the three voices by discussing their specific attitudes toward the subject of Silas' return.

2. There are only a few examples of figurative language in this poem, but each one is powerful. Select three examples. Explore the connotations suggested by each—both in terms of what it contributes to the specific speech or description and in terms of what it contributes to the overall brooding mood of the poem.

3. What purpose is served by the alliteration in lines 160–165? Select two other examples of this technique found in the poem. Discuss how Frost's word choices for sound reinforce his meaning.

4. Why did Frost title the poem "The Death of the Hired Man" when 165 of the 166 lines are concerned with his life?

5. When you have finished this poem, you probably know most about the character who does not appear. Using this knowledge, would you agree with Mary's comment in lines 99–102?

6. There are several universal themes explored in this poem. To implement this, Frost uses a series of contrasts: Warren's relationship with Silas; Silas' relationship with Harold Wilson; the implied comparison between Silas and the hound dog; the contrast between Warren and Silas' brother. Discuss how these contrasts reveal specific themes in the poem.

7. In lines 88–102, Warren expresses his appreciation for "Silas' one accomplishment," and Mary agrees. What do these lines show to be the development in the relationship between husband and wife? What is Warren's point about Silas' skill at loading and unloading hay? Does Mary mean that Harold is "the fool of books"?

Home Burial

1. In the opening lines of this poem, Frost sets the scene quite dramatically. What do the setting, position of characters, and voice

tones reveal from the very beginning about the relationship between the man and woman?

2. Lines 41 and 60 suggest something about their previous relationship. How has this contributed to the conflict in the poem?
3. What is implied by the husband's statement "A man must partly give up being a man / With women-folk"?
4. The reasons for the present impasse are revealed primarily through dialogue. How do Frost's sentence structure and word choice emphasize the tension of the deep personal conflict?
5. What is the effect of the dashes placed after "mound" (line 31), "satisfied" (line 69), and "will" (line 120)?
6. A conflict far deeper than that caused by reactions to the death of a child is suggested by what the man says in lines 93–94. How would you explain what is implied here?

Out, Out

1. What is the speaker's attitude toward the boy? How does Frost's choice of words reveal this?
2. How is personification used in Frost's treatment of the saw?
3. To intensify the shock of the narrative, Frost structures this poem in a highly compressed manner. Cite several specific examples of this.
4. In the title of this poem Frost refers to this passage from *Macbeth*:

> Out, out, brief candle!
> Life's but a walking shadow, a poor player
> That struts and frets his hour upon the stage
> And then is heard no more; it is a tale
> Told by an idiot, full of sound and fury,
> Signifying nothing.

Discuss how Shakespeare's lines relate to the action and tone of Frost's poem.
5. From line 27 on, Frost reduces the length of phrases and sentences from what they have been earlier in the poem. What effect is the poet attempting to achieve through this technique? What, for instance, is the effect of the two brief sentences in line 31?
6. Some readers may feel that the dead boy's family is unduly businesslike in lines 32–34. Others may appreciate the wisdom of the family's attitude. What is your opinion? How has your reading of Frost's other poems helped you to speculate on what Frost's own attitude might be toward the death of a loved one?

The Road Not Taken

1. In this, one of Frost's better known poems, how does he rely on symbol and metaphor to make his comment? Give specific illustra-

tions from the poem to support your answer.

2. What is the cumulative effect of Frost's use of such stylized language as "diverged," "as just as fair," "wanted wear," "trodden," "ages and ages hence"?

3. Most readers focus on the title first. Frost's title leads us to speculate on the nature of a decision. Why do you think he directed the reader's attention to the road *not* taken?

4. Frost, like most fine poets, intensifies a word's meaning by his placement of the word within a line. Discuss the placement of the word *I* in lines 18 and 19 as an illustration of this point.

5. The meter of this poem is very regular (iambic tetrameter with anapest variations). However, the last stanza breaks this pattern, forcing the reader to change the stress if he is to avoid an unnatural speech pattern. Speculate on the reasons for Frost's choice of form.

ASSIGNMENTS FOR WRITING

1. At one time Frost said, "Everything written is as good as it is dramatic." Drama implies tension or conflict of some kind. Choose and discuss several poems in this volume that you feel would be "good" according to Frost's own statement.

2. Read A. E. Housman's "To an Athlete Dying Young." In an essay, compare and contrast it with Frost's "Provide, Provide." Concentrate on the tone, attitude, and imagery of the two poets.

3. Discuss a chosen aspect of Frost's use of natural imagery as shown in several of his poems. One aspect of his imagery, for example, is that the similes usually involve simple, rustic comparisons.

4. Frost once remarked, "Instead of a realist — if I must be classified — I think I might better be called a synecdochist, for I am fond of the synecdoche in poetry, that figure of speech in which we use a part for the whole." In an essay, discuss how "The Death of the Hired Man" illustrates this fondness.

5. In "Home Burial" the woman comments:

> No, from the time when one is sick to death,
> One is alone, and he dies more alone.

Compare this attitude with the attitudes expressed in "The Death of the Hired Man."

6. In lines 111–120 of "The Death of the Hired Man," Warren and Mary dispute their definitions of "home." What does "home" mean to you? In a brief essay, explain your understanding of the idea of "home" with examples to illustrate your statements.

F. Scott Fitzgerald

The story of F. Scott Fitzgerald reads like the parabola on a graph—the sudden rise from obscurity to popular success, the equally sudden fall to anonymity and despair. The compass of his life-curve was but forty-four years; the last twenty were spent as a novelist, short story writer, and scenario hack for Hollywood studios. In his time Fitzgerald knew both acclaim and rejection, never artistic recognition. Since his death, however, he has been hailed as a writer of surpassing worth.

Francis Scott Key Fitzgerald was born in St. Paul, Minnesota, on September 24, 1896, into a family which represented the double strands of American society. His father's family traced back to a seventeenth-century Maryland line. His mother's family had been Irish immigrants, whose hard work had resulted in a measure of prosperity. Fitzgerald inherited this mixture of faded aristocracy with what he called "straight 1850 potato famine Irish." Perhaps this conflict helps to explain in part his insatiable drive for respectable wealth and position.

After preparatory school in the East, Fitzgerald enrolled at Princeton University. Socially, he seems to have been successful at Princeton, in spite of a gnawing financial inferiority to some of his associates. His writing was published in college periodicals, his ambition to have a Triangle Club musical produced was fulfilled; he was elected to membership in an exclusive club. Academically, however, he was not so successful, and in November 1917, after having already taken a year's leave of absence Fitzgerald left Princeton to join the Army.

He served for 15 months at different American posts, during which time he worked at revising the manuscript for a novel he had written at Princeton. He also met and fell in love with Miss Zelda Sayre of Montgomery, Alabama. The parallel between his situation and Lieutenant Jay Gatsby's is apparent: the handsome, impoverished officer courting the rich Southern belle. For Fitzgerald, as for his hero Gatsby, there could be no future without the money needed to win the "right" girl. Upon his discharge, Fitzgerald went to New York, working as an advertising copywriter by day and a serious writer of fiction by night. Failing to earn the money he needed, he returned to St. Paul, where in a panic at the probability of losing Miss Sayre, he completed and sold his first novel, *This Side of Paradise.* It was published by Scribner's in 1920; shortly after, he married Zelda Sayre.

This Side of Paradise is an autobiographical account of life in a university. Amory Blaine, the novel's principal character, is the first of a catalogue of Fitzgerald's college men—Dexter Green in "Winter Dreams," Nick Carraway of *The Great Gatsby,* and Anson Hunter in "The Rich Boy" are others—who know little more than the superficialities of life until faced by an ultimate issue. Interestingly, almost all of Fitzgerald's college men are from Yale, especially those he most despises, such as Tom Buchanan in *The Great Gatsby.*

Popular acceptance of his first novel gave Fitzgerald a taste of two by-products of his art, fame and money. He knew that together these were less important than a third objective, critical recognition; in his own way, Fitzgerald never lost sight of its priority. But he was launched on a course of extravagance and dissipation that seemed to take him farther and farther away from the artist's primary goal.

His marriage to Zelda Sayre gave impetus to his natural inclination toward romance and excitement. His bride came from a family of substantial means. Fitzgerald undertook to support her at an economic level to which she was accustomed. For this he had to produce the kind of stories that would sell quickly and often. With a prodigality that ignored the future, the Fitzgeralds flitted from a New York penthouse to a Riviera beach hotel, from an estate in Delaware to an apartment in Paris.

All the while, Fitzgerald was writing feverishly. Zelda became his model for the Southern flapper in "The Ice Palace," a story in *Flappers and Philosophers* (1921), which was a compilation of stories sold to slick magazines, like *The Saturday Evening Post.* In 1922, his second novel appeared, bearing an almost prophetic title: *The Beautiful and Damned.* In it Fitzgerald depicted the absence of any purpose other than self-indulgence as characteristic of the beautiful and damned rich people he knew. His monthly budget for 1923 shows an estimated need for $2396.00 to cover items such as "Wild Parties—$100.00" and "Charity—$4.00" among other domestic items.

There would soon be other expenses. Zelda Fitzgerald's inconsistent behavior suggested a serious mental instability that soon manifested itself. As an unhappy counterpoint to her illness, Fitzgerald developed drinking habits that eventually helped bring about his ruin. In 1924, the Fitzgeralds moved to Europe, settling first on the Riviera and then in Paris, where Fitzgerald met Gertrude Stein and Ernest Hemingway. Much has been written about the relationship among these three: Miss Stein is said to have looked at the young men and remarked, "You are all a lost generation." Hemingway narrated his experiences with Scott and Zelda in *A Moveable Feast*, a record that disqualifies Hemingway as a friend to Fitzgerald. In another instance, both men alluded to the same observation regarding the posture of the wealthy class. In "The Rich Boy," Fitzgerald showed how the very rich are "different from you and me." But in "The Snows of Kilimanjaro," Hemingway derided Fitzgerald under a thin guise of fiction. He wrote,

> The rich were dull and they drank too much, or they played too much backgammon. They were dull and they were repetitious. He remembered poor Julian and his romantic awe of them and how he had stated a story once that began, "The very rich are different from you and me." And how some one had said to Julian, Yes, they have more money. But that was not humorous to Julian. He thought they were a special glamorous race and when he found they weren't it wrecked him just as much as any other thing that wrecked him.

"Julian" was Fitzgerald, and the cruel joke was all Hemingway's.

But Fitzgerald's insight into the barrenness of mere riches proved itself in his next book, *The Great Gatsby* (1925). In this work, his greatest achievement, Fitzgerald created what the critic Malcolm Cowley has called "a sort of moral permanence." This "moral permanence" is the quality of durability that belongs only to great art—the quality empowering a book to survive the unrelenting process of attrition that erodes the literary reputation of a mere bestseller. In *The Great Gatsby*, as perhaps in no other book in our century, America's "vast carelessness" and materialism are demonstrated. The contrast between the dream of the New World and its wretched unfulfillment is exposed—so much so that readers who have never known a speakeasy or set foot in a Long Island mansion can nonetheless sense the loss, the emptiness, when Nick Carraway declares, "The party was over."

Already, the party was over for Fitzgerald, too. Life in Europe was costly. The precariousness of living on his publisher's advances made it necessary for the novelist to turn to various kinds of hack work to pay his bills. He moved to Hollywood in an attempt to learn the scriptwriting techniques of his literary inferiors. He wrote the hated pat-ending, "formula stories" for cheap magazines. In 1930, his

wife's illness became derangement, she was permanently institutionalized, and Scott Fitzgerald's alcoholism worsened. Yet, remarkably,
out of this personal nightmare came the beautiful and tragic novel,
Tender Is the Night (1934).

By this late point, however, the vast accumulation of debts and
a weakened physical constitution had left Fitzgerald with little of his
previous joy for living. Back in Hollywood for a second effort at movie
scriptwriting, he met the columnist Sheilah Graham. Her account of
his last years, *Beloved Infidel,* shows what Fitzgerald's Princeton classmate and friend, the critic Edmund Wilson, calls "the familiar phenomenon of impotence—Fitzgerald must have felt powerless in
Hollywood either to do work that met his own standards or to succeed
on Hollywood's terms—that, with alcohol, breaks out into frenzied
aggression, of self-hatred that seeks for relief by directing its fury
against someone else." In his frustration, Fitzgerald struggled with
two remaining books. *The Last Tycoon,* unfinished at his death on
December 21, 1940, presents a view of the film empire of Monroe
Stahr; *The Crack-Up,* edited by Edmund Wilson and published in 1945,
tells the story of Fitzgerald's collapse from the height of popular
success to the depth of despondency and inertia, lost friendships and
personal disgust.

Fitzgerald coined the phrase, "the Jazz Age," and he was its faithful
chronicler. Not until ten years after his death did his work begin
to receive the critical appraisal that saw beyond the froth into the
substance. The irony of this attention has been to show that Fitzgerald's best work—*The Great Gatsby* and "The Rich Boy"—makes very
clear how well he knew that personal destruction is unavoidable when
a man sets all his values by the standard of riches.

Fitzgerald's greatest assets were his style and his piercing understanding of people. His language is a remarkable combination of fresh
metaphors with concrete impressions. His apprehension of the human
spirit in all of its expectancy and despair demonstrates that Fitzgerald
understood the paradoxical nature of human existence. For example,
Jay Gatsby recalls the night when he faced the choice between Daisy
and an independent career:

> His heart beat faster and faster as Daisy's white face came up to his
> own. He knew that when he kissed this girl, and forever wed his unut-
> terable visions to her perishable breath, his mind would never romp
> again like the mind of God. So he waited, listening for a moment longer
> to the tuning-fork that had been struck upon a star. Then he kissed
> her. At his lips' touch she blossomed for him like a flower and the
> incarnation was complete.

From this vantage, the reader can see that Fitzgerald had been the personification of his rich boy, Anson Hunter. When he died of a heart attack, Fitzgerald was trying to recapture in *The Last Tycoon* the power and vitality of his earlier work. Even his severest critics agree that, had he finished it, this novel might have been his masterpiece.

The Rich Boy

I

Begin with an individual, and before you know it you find that
you have created a type; begin with a type, and you find that you
have created—nothing. That is because we are all queer fish, queerer
behind our faces and voices than we want any one to know or than
we know ourselves. When I hear a man proclaiming himself an
"average, honest, open fellow," I feel pretty sure that he has some
definite and perhaps terrible abnormality which he has agreed to
conceal—and his protestation of being average and honest and open
is his way of reminding himself of his misprision.

There are no types, no plurals. There is a rich boy, and this is
his and not his brothers' story. All my life I have lived among his
brothers but this one has been my friend. Besides, if I wrote about
his brothers I should have to begin by attacking all the lies that the
poor have told about the rich and the rich have told about themselves—such a wild structure they have erected that when we pick
up a book about the rich, some instinct prepares us for unreality.
Even the intelligent and impassioned reporters of life have made the
country of the rich as unreal as fairyland.

Let me tell you about the very rich. They are different from
you and me. They possess and enjoy early, and it does something
to them, makes them soft where we are hard, and cynical where we
are trustful, in a way that, unless you were born rich, it is very difficult
to understand. They think, deep in their hearts, that they are better
than we are because we had to discover the compensations and refuges
of life for ourselves. Even when they enter deep into our world or
sink below us, they still think that they are better than we are. They
are different. The only way I can describe young Anson Hunter is
to approach him as if he were a foreigner and cling stubbornly to
my point of view. If I accept his for a moment I am lost—I have
nothing to show but a preposterous movie.

II

Anson was the eldest of six children who would some day divide a fortune of fifteen million dollars, and he reached the age of reason—is it seven?—at the beginning of the century when daring young women were already gliding along Fifth Avenue in electric "mobiles." In those days he and his brother had an English governess who spoke the language very clearly and crisply and well, so that the two boys grew to speak as she did—their words and sentences were all crisp and clear and not run together as ours are. They didn't talk exactly like English children but acquired an accent that is peculiar to fashionable people in the city of New York.

In the summer the six children were moved from the house on 71st Street to a big estate in northern Connecticut. It was not a fashionable locality—Anson's father wanted to delay as long as possible his children's knowledge of that side of life. He was a man somewhat superior to his class, which composed New York society, and to his period, which was the snobbish and formalized vulgarity of the Gilded Age, and he wanted his sons to learn habits of concentration and have sound constitutions and grow up into right-living and successful men. He and his wife kept an eye on them as well as they were able until the two older boys went away to school, but in huge establishments this is difficult—it was much simpler in the series of small and medium-sized houses in which my own youth was spent—I was never far out of the reach of my mother's voice, of the sense of her presence, her approval or disapproval.

Anson's first sense of his superiority came to him when he realized the half-grudging American deference that was paid to him in the Connecticut village. The parents of the boys he played with always inquired after his father and mother, and were vaguely excited when their own children were asked to the Hunters' house. He accepted this as the natural state of things, and a sort of impatience with all groups of which he was not the center—in money, in position, in authority—remained with him for the rest of his life. He disdained to struggle with other boys for precedence—he expected it to be given him freely, and when it wasn't he withdrew into his family. His family was sufficient, for in the East money is still a somewhat feudal thing, a clan-forming thing. In the snobbish West, money separates families to form "sets."

At eighteen, when he went to New Haven, Anson was tall and thick-set, with a clear complexion and a healthy color from the ordered life he had led in school. His hair was yellow and grew in a funny way on his head, his nose was beaked—these two things kept him from being handsome—but he had a confident charm and a certain brusque style, and the upper-class men who passed him on the street knew without being told that he was a rich boy and had gone to one of the best schools. Nevertheless, his very superiority kept him from being a success in college—the independence was mistaken for egotism, and the refusal to accept Yale standards with the proper awe seemed to belittle all those who had. So, long before he graduated, he began to shift the center of his life to New York.

He was at home in New York—there was his own house with "the kind of servants you can't get any more"—and his own family, of which, because of his good humor and a certain ability to make things go, he was rapidly becoming the center, and the débutante parties, and the correct manly world of the men's clubs, and the occasional wild spree with the gallant girls whom New Haven only knew from the fifth row. His aspirations were conventional enough—they included even the irreproachable shadow he would some day marry, but they differed from the aspirations of the majority of young men in that there was no mist over them, none of that quality which is variously known as "idealism" or "illusion." Anson accepted without reservation the world of high finance and high extravagance, of divorce and dissipation, of snobbery and of privilege. Most of our lives end as a compromise—it was as a compromise that his life began.

He and I first met in the late summer of 1917 when he was just out of Yale, and, like the rest of us, was swept up into the systematized hysteria of the war. In the blue-green uniform of the naval aviation he came down to Pensacola, where the hotel orchestras played "I'm sorry, dear," and we young officers danced with the girls. Every one liked him, and though he ran with the drinkers and wasn't an especially good pilot, even the instructors treated him with a certain respect. He was always having long talks with them in his confident, logical voice—talks which ended by his getting himself, or, more frequently, another officer, out of some impending trouble. He was convivial, bawdy, robustly avid for pleasure, and we were all surprised when he fell in love with a conservative and rather proper girl.

Her name was Paula Legendre, a dark, serious beauty from somewhere in California. Her family kept a winter residence just outside of town, and in spite of her primness she was enormously popular; there is a large class of men whose egotism can't endure humor in a woman. But Anson wasn't that sort, and I couldn't understand the attraction of her "sincerity"—that was the thing to say about her—for his keen and somewhat sardonic mind.

Nevertheless, they fell in love—and on her terms. He no longer joined the twilight gathering at the De Soto bar, and whenever they were seen together they were engaged in a long, serious dialogue, which must have gone on several weeks. Long afterward he told me that it was not about anything in particular but was composed on both sides of immature and even meaningless statements—the emotional content that gradually came to fill it grew up not out of the words but out of its enormous seriousness. It was a sort of hypnosis. Often it was interrupted, giving way to that emasculated humor we call fun; when they were alone it was resumed again, solemn, low-keyed, and pitched so as to give each other a sense of unity in feeling and thought. They came to resent any interruptions of it, to be unresponsive to facetiousness about life, even to the mild cynicism of their contemporaries. They were only happy when the dialogue was going on, and its seriousness bathed them like the amber glow of an open fire. Toward the end there came an interruption they did not resent—it began to be interrupted by passion.

Oddly enough, Anson was as engrossed in the dialogue as she was and as profoundly affected by it, yet at the same time aware that on his side much was insincere, and on hers much was merely simple. At first, too, he despised her emotional simplicity as well, but with his love her nature deepened and blossomed, and he could despise it no longer. He felt that if he could enter into Paula's warm safe life he would be happy. The long preparation of the dialogue removed any constraint—he taught her some of what he had learned from more adventurous women, and she responded with a rapt holy intensity. One evening after a dance they agreed to marry, and he wrote a long letter about her to his mother. The next day Paula told him that she was rich, that she had a personal fortune of nearly a million dollars.

III

It was exactly as if they could say "Neither of us has anything: we shall be poor together"—just as delightful that they should be rich instead. It gave them the same communion of adventure. Yet when Anson got leave in April, and Paula and her mother accompanied him North, she was impressed with the standing of his family in New York and with the scale on which they lived. Alone with Anson for the first time in the rooms where he had played as a boy, she was filled with a comfortable emotion, as though she were pre-eminently safe and taken care of. The pictures of Anson in a skull cap at his first school, of Anson on horseback with the sweetheart of a mysterious forgotten summer, of Anson in a gay group of ushers and bridesmaids at a wedding, made her jealous of his life apart from her in the past, and so completely did his authoritative person seem to sum up and typify these possessions of his that she was inspired with the idea of being married immediately and returning to Pensacola as his wife.

But an immediate marriage wasn't discussed—even the engagement was to be secret until after the war. When she realized that only two days of his leave remained, her dissatisfaction crystallized in the intention of making him as unwilling to wait as she was. They were driving to the country for dinner, and she determined to force the issue that night.

Now a cousin of Paula's was staying with them at the Ritz, a severe, bitter girl who loved Paula but was somewhat jealous of her impressive engagement, and as Paula was late in dressing, the cousin, who wasn't going to the party, received Anson in the parlor of the suite.

Anson had met friends at five o'clock and drunk freely and indiscreetly with them for an hour. He left the Yale Club at a proper time, and his mother's chauffeur drove him to the Ritz, but his usual capacity was not in evidence, and the impact of the steam-heated sitting-room made him suddenly dizzy. He knew it, and he was both amused and sorry.

Paula's cousin was twenty-five, but she was exceptionally naïve, and at first failed to realize what was up. She had never met Anson before, and she was surprised when he mumbled strange information and nearly fell off his chair, but until Paula appeared it didn't occur to her that what she had taken for the odor of a dry-cleaned uniform was really whiskey. But Paula understood as soon as she appeared; her only thought was to get Anson away before her mother saw him, and at the look in her eyes the cousin understood too.

When Paula and Anson descended to the limousine they found two men inside, both asleep; they were the men with whom he had been drinking at the Yale Club, and they were also going to the party. He had entirely forgotten their presence in the car. On the way to Hempstead they awoke and sang. Some of the songs were rough, and though Paula tried to reconcile herself to the fact that Anson had few verbal inhibitions, her lips tightened with shame and distaste.

Back at the hotel the cousin, confused and agitated, considered the incident, and then walked into Mrs. Legendre's bedroom, saying: "Isn't he funny?"

"Who is funny?"

"Why—Mr. Hunter. He seemed so funny."

Mrs. Legendre looked at her sharply.

"How is he funny?"

"Why, he said he was French. I didn't know he was French."

"That's absurd. You must have misunderstood." She smiled: "It was a joke."

The cousin shook her head stubbornly.

No. He said he was brought up in France. He said he couldn't speak any English, and that's why he couldn't talk to me. And he couldn't!"

Mrs. Legendre looked away with impatience just as the cousin added thoughtfully, "Perhaps it was because he was so drunk," and walked out of the room.

This curious report was true. Anson, finding his voice thick and uncontrollable, had taken the unusual refuge of announcing that he spoke no English. Years afterwards he used to tell that part of the story, and he invariably communicated the uproarious laughter which the memory aroused in him.

Five times in the next hour Mrs. Legendre tried to get Hempstead on the phone. When she succeeded, there was a ten-minute delay before she heard Paula's voice on the wire.

"Cousin Jo told me Anson was intoxicated."

"Oh, no. . . ."

"Oh, yes. Cousin Jo says he was intoxicated. He told her he was French, and fell off his chair and behaved as if he was very intoxicated. I don't want you to come home with him."

"Mother, he's all right! Please don't worry about—"

"But I do worry. I think it's dreadful. I want you to promise me not to come home with him."

"I'll take care of it, mother. . . ."

"I don't want you to come home with him."

"All right, mother. Good-by."

"Be sure now, Paula. Ask some one to bring you."

Deliberately Paula took the receiver from her ear and hung it up. Her face was flushed with helpless annoyance. Anson was stretched out asleep in a bedroom upstairs, while the dinner party below was proceeding lamely toward conclusion.

The hour's drive had sobered him somewhat—his arrival was merely hilarious—and Paula hoped that the evening was not spoiled, after all, but two imprudent cocktails before dinner completed the disaster. He talked boisterously and somewhat offensively to the party at large for fifteen minutes, and then slid silently under the table; like a man in an old print—but, unlike an old print, it was rather horrible without being at all quaint. None of the young girls present remarked upon the incident—it seemed to merit only silence. His uncle and two other men carried him upstairs, and it was just after this that Paula was called to the phone.

An hour later Anson awoke in a fog of nervous agony, through which he perceived after a moment the figure of his uncle Robert standing by the door.

"... I said are you better?"

"What?"

"Do you feel better, old man?"

"Terrible," said Anson.

"I'm going to try you on another Bromo-seltzer. If you can hold it down, it'll do you good to sleep."

With an effort Anson slid his legs from the bed and stood up.

"I'm all right," he said dully.

"Take it easy."

"I thin' if you gave me a glassbrandy I could go downstairs."

"Oh, no—"

"Yes, that's the only thin'. I'm all right now.... I suppose I'm in Dutch dow' there."

"They know you're a little under the weather," said his uncle deprecatingly. "But don't worry about it. Schuyler didn't even get here. He passed away in the locker room over at the Links."

Indifferent to any opinion, except Paula's, Anson was nevertheless determined to save the débris of the evening, but when after a cold bath he made his appearance most of the party had already left. Paula got up immediately to go home.

In the limousine the old serious dialogue began. She had known that he drank, she admitted, but she had never expected anything like this—it seemed to her that perhaps they were not suited to each other, after all. Their ideas about life were too different, and so forth. When she finished speaking, Anson spoke in turn, very soberly. Then Paula said she'd have to think it over; she wouldn't decide tonight; she was not angry but she was terribly sorry. Nor would she let him come into the hotel with her, but just before she got out of the car she leaned and kissed him unhappily on the cheek.

The next afternoon Anson had a long talk with Mrs. Legendre while Paula sat listening in silence. It was agreed that Paula was to brood over the incident for a proper period and then, if mother and daughter thought it best, they would follow Anson to Pensacola. On his part he apologized with sincerity and dignity—that was all; with every card in her hand Mrs. Legendre was unable to establish any advantage over him. He made no promises, showed no humility, only delivered a few serious comments on life which brought him off with rather a moral superiority at the end. When they came South three weeks later, neither Anson in his satisfaction nor Paula in her relief at the reunion realized that the psychological moment had passed forever.

IV

He dominated and attracted her, and at the same time filled her with anxiety. Confused by his mixture of solidity and self-indulgence, of sentiment and cynicism—incongruities which her gentle mind was unable to resolve—Paula grew to think of him as two alternating personalities. When she saw him alone, or at a formal party, or with his casual inferiors, she felt a tremendous pride in his strong, attractive presence, the paternal, understanding stature of his mind. In other company she became uneasy when what had been a fine imperviousness to mere gentility showed its other face. The other face was gross, humorous, reckless of everything but pleasure. It startled her mind temporarily away from him, even led her into a short covert experiment with an old beau, but it was no use—after four months of Anson's enveloping vitality there was an anæmic pallor in all other men.

In July he was ordered abroad, and their tenderness and desire reached a crescendo. Paula considered a last-minute marriage—decided against it only because there were always cocktails on his breath now, but the parting itself made her physically ill with grief. After his departure she wrote him long letters of regret for the days of love they had missed by waiting. In August Anson's plane slipped down into the North Sea. He was pulled onto a destroyer after a night in the water and sent to hospital with pneumonia; the armistice was signed before he was finally sent home.

Then, with every opportunity given back to them, with no material obstacle to overcome, the secret weavings of their temperaments came between them, drying up their kisses and their tears, making their voices less loud to one another, muffling the intimate chatter of their hearts until the old communication was only possible by letters, from far away. One afternoon a society reporter waited for two hours in the Hunters' house for a confirmation of their engagement. Anson denied it; nevertheless an early issue carried the report as a leading paragraph—they were "constantly seen together at Southampton, Hot Springs, and Tuxedo Park." But the serious dialogue had turned a corner into a long-sustained quarrel, and the affair was almost played out. Anson got drunk flagrantly and missed an engagement with her, whereupon Paula made certain behavioristic demands. His despair was helpless before his pride and his knowledge of himself: the engagement was definitely broken.

"Dearest," said their letters now, "Dearest Dearest, when I wake up in the middle of the night and realize that after all it was not to be, I feel that I want to die. I can't go on living any more. Perhaps when we meet this summer we may talk things over and decide differently—we were so excited and sad that day, and I don't feel that I can live all my life without you. You speak of other people. Don't you know there are not other people for me, but only you. . . ."

But as Paula drifted here and there around the East she would sometimes mention her gaieties to make him wonder. Anson was too acute to wonder. When he saw a man's name in her letters he felt more sure of her and a little disdainful—he was always superior to such things. But he still hoped that they would some day marry.

Meanwhile he plunged vigorously into all the movement and glitter of post-bellum New York, entering a brokerage house, joining half a dozen clubs, dancing late, and moving in three worlds—his own world, the world of young Yale graduates, and that section of the half-world which rests one end on Broadway. But there was always a thorough and infractible eight hours devoted to his work in Wall Street, where the combination of his influential family connection, his sharp intelligence, and his abundance of sheer physical energy brought him almost immediately forward. He had one of those invaluable minds with partitions in it; sometimes he appeared at his office refreshed by less than an hour's sleep, but such occurrences were rare. So early as 1920 his income in salary and commissions exceeded twelve thousand dollars.

As the Yale tradition slipped into the past he became more and more of a popular figure among his classmates in New York, more popular than he had ever been in college. He lived in a great house, and had the means of introducing young men into other great houses. Moreover, his life already seemed secure, while theirs, for the most part, had arrived again at precarious beginnings. They commenced to turn to him for amusement and escape, and Anson responded readily, taking pleasure in helping people and arranging their affairs.

There were no men in Paula's letters now, but a note of tenderness ran through them that had not been there before. From several sources he heard that she had "a heavy beau," Lowell Thayer, a Bostonian of wealth and position, and though he was sure she still loved him, it made him uneasy to think that he might lose her, after all. Save for one unsatisfactory day she had not been in New York for almost five months, and as the rumors multiplied he became increasingly anxious to see her. In February he took his vacation and went down to Florida.

Palm Beach sprawled plump and opulent between the sparkling sapphire of Lake Worth, flawed here and there by houseboats at anchor, and the great turquoise bar of the Atlantic Ocean. The huge bulks of the Breakers and the Royal Poinciana rose as twin paunches from the bright level of the sand, and around them clustered the Dancing Glade, Bradley's House of Chance, and a dozen modistes and milliners with goods at triple prices from New York. Upon the trellised veranda of the Breakers two hundred women stepped right, stepped left, wheeled, and slid in that then celebrated calisthenic known as the double-shuffle, while in half-time to the music two thousand bracelets clicked up and down on two hundred arms.

At the Everglades Club after dark Paula and Lowell Thayer and Anson and a casual fourth played bridge with hot cards. It seemed to Anson that her kind, serious face was wan and tired—she had been around now for four, five, years. He had known her for three.

"Two spades."

"Cigarette? . . . Oh, I beg your pardon. By me."

"By."

"I'll double three spades."

There were a dozen tables of bridge in the room, which was filling up with smoke. Anson's eyes met Paula's, held them persistently even when Thayer's glance fell between them. . . .

"What was bid?" he asked abstractedly.

"Rose of Washington Square"

sang the young people in the corners:

"I'm withering there
In basement air—"

The smoke banked like fog, and the opening of a door filled the room with blown swirls of ectoplasm. Little Bright Eyes streaked past the tables seeking Mr. Conan Doyle among the Englishmen who were posing as Englishmen about the lobby.

"You could cut it with a knife."

". . . cut it with a knife."

". . . . a knife."

At the end of the rubber Paula suddenly got up and spoke to Anson in a tense, low voice. With scarcely a glance at Lowell Thayer, they walked out the door and descended a long flight of stone steps—in a moment they were walking hand in hand along the moonlit beach.

"Darling, darling. . . ." They embraced recklessly, passionately, in a shadow. . . . Then Paula drew back her face to let his lips say what she wanted to hear—she could feel the words forming as they kissed again. . . . Again she broke away, listening, but as he pulled her close once more she realized that he had said nothing—only *"Darling! Darling!"* in that deep, sad whisper that always made her cry. Humbly, obediently, her emotions yielded to him and the tears streamed down her face, but her heart kept on crying: "Ask me—oh, Anson, dearest, ask me!"

"Paula. . . . *Paula!*"

The words wrung her heart like hands, and Anson, feeling her tremble, knew that emotion was enough. He need say no more, commit their destinies to no practical enigma. Why should he, when he might hold her so, biding his own time, for another year—forever? He was considering them both, her more than himself. For a moment, when she said suddenly that she must go back to her hotel, he hesitated, thinking, first, "This is the moment, after all," and then: "No, let it wait—she is mine. . . ."

He had forgotten that Paula too was worn away inside with the strain of three years. Her mood passed forever in the night.

He went back to New York next morning filled with a certain restless dissatisfaction. Late in April, without warning, he received a telegram from Bar Harbor in which Paula told him that she was engaged to Lowell Thayer, and that they would be married immediately in Boston. What he never really believed could happen had happened at last.

Anson filled himself with whiskey that morning, and going to the office, carried on his work without a break—rather with a fear of what would happen if he stopped. In the evening he went out as usual, saying nothing of what had occurred; he was cordial, humorous, unabstracted. But one thing he could not help—for three days, in any place, in any company, he would suddenly bend his head into his hands and cry like a child.

V

In 1922 when Anson went abroad with the junior partner to investigate some London loans, the journey intimated that he was to be taken into the firm. He was twenty-seven now, a little heavy without being definitely stout, and with a manner older than his years. Old people and young people liked him and trusted him, and mothers felt safe when their daughters were in his charge, for he had a way, when he came into a room, of putting himself on a footing with the oldest and most conservative people there. "You and I," he seemed to say, "we're solid. We understand."

He had an instinctive and rather charitable knowledge of the weaknesses of men and women, and, like a priest, it made him the more concerned for the maintenance of outward forms. It was typical of him that every Sunday morning he taught in a fashionable Episcopal Sunday school—even though a cold shower and a quick change into a cutaway coat were all that separated him from the wild night before.

After his father's death he was the practical head of his family, and, in effect, guided the destinies of the younger children. Through a complication his authority did not extend to his father's estate, which was administrated by his Uncle Robert, who was the horsey member of the family, a good-natured, hard-drinking member of that set which centers about Wheatley Hills.

Uncle Robert and his wife, Edna, had been great friends of Anson's youth, and the former was disappointed when his nephew's superiority failed to take a horsey form. He backed him for a city club which was the most difficult in America to enter—one could only join if one's family had "helped to build up New York" (or, in other words, were rich before 1880)—and when Anson, after his election, neglected it for the Yale Club, Uncle Robert gave him a little talk on the subject. But when on top of that Anson declined to enter Robert Hunter's own conservative and somewhat neglected brokerage house, his manner grew cooler. Like a primary teacher who has taught all he knew, he slipped out of Anson's life.

There were so many friends in Anson's life—scarcely one for whom he had not done some unusual kindness and scarcely one whom he did not occasionally embarrass by his bursts of rough conversation or his habit of getting drunk whenever ahd however he liked. It annoyed him when any one else blundered in that regard—about his own lapses he was always humorous. Odd things happened to him and he told them with infectious laughter.

I was working in New York that spring, and I used to lunch with him at the Yale Club, which my university was sharing until the completion of our own. I had read of Paula's marriage, and one afternoon, when I asked him about her, something moved him to tell me the story. After that he frequently invited me to family dinners at his house and behaved as though there was a special relation between us, as though with his confidence a little of that consuming memory had passed into me.

I found that despite the trusting mothers, his attitude toward girls was not indiscriminately protective. It was up to the girl—if she showed an inclination toward looseness, she must take care of herself, even with him.

"Life," he would explain sometimes, "has made a cynic of me."

By life he meant Paula. Sometimes, especially when he was drinking, it became a little twisted in his mind, and he thought that she had callously thrown him over.

This "cynicism," or rather his realization that naturally fast girls were not worth sparing, led to his affair with Dolly Karger. It wasn't his only affair in those years, but it came nearest to touching him deeply, and it had a profound effect upon his attitude toward life.

Dolly was the daughter of a notorious "publicist" who had married into society. She herself grew up into the Junior League, came out at the Plaza, and went to the Assembly; and only a few old families like the Hunters could question whether or not she "belonged," for her picture was often in the papers, and she had more enviable attention than many girls who undoubtedly did. She was dark-haired, with carmine lips and a high, lovely color, which she concealed under pinkish-gray powder all through the first year out, because high color was unfashionable—Victorian-pale was the thing to be. She wore black, severe suits and stood with her hands in her pockets leaning a little forward, with a humorous restraint on her face. She danced exquisitely—better than anything she liked to dance—better than anything except making love. Since she was ten she had always been in love, and, usually, with some boy who didn't respond to her. Those who did—and there were many—bored her after a brief encounter, but for her failures she reserved the warmest spot in her heart. When she met them she would always try once more—sometimes she succeeded, more often she failed.

It never occurred to this gypsy of the unattainable that there was a certain resemblance in those who refused to love her—they shared a hard intuition that saw through to her weakness, not a weakness of emotion but a weakness of rudder. Anson perceived this when he first met her, less than a month after Paula's marriage. He was drinking rather heavily, and he pretended for a week that he was falling in love with her. Then he dropped abruptly and forgot—immediately he took up the commanding position in her heart.

Like so many girls of that day Dolly was slackly and indiscreetly wild. The unconventionality of a slightly older generation had been simply one facet of a postwar movement to discredit obsolete manners—Dolly's was both older and shabbier, and she saw in Anson the two extremes which the emotionally shiftless woman seeks, an abandon to indulgence alternating with a protective strength. In his character she felt both the sybarite and the solid rock, and these two satisfied every need of her nature.

She felt that it was going to be difficult, but she mistook the reason—she thought that Anson and his family expected a more spectacular marriage, but she guessed immediately that her advantage lay in his tendency to drink.

They met at the large débutante dances, but as her infatuation increased they managed to be more and more together. Like most mothers, Mrs. Karger believed that Anson was exceptionally reliable, so she allowed Dolly to go with him to distant country clubs and suburban houses without inquiring closely into their activities or questioning her explanations when they came in late. At first these explanations might have been accurate, but Dolly's worldly ideas of capturing Anson were soon engulfed in the rising sweep of her emotion. Kisses in the back of taxis and motor cars were no longer enough; they did a curious thing:

They dropped out of their world for a while and made another world just beneath it where Anson's tippling and Dolly's irregular hours would be less noticed and commented on. It was composed, this world, of varying elements—several of Anson's Yale friends and their wives, two or three young brokers and bond salesmen and a handful of unattached men, fresh from college, with money and a propensity to dissipation. What this world lacked in spaciousness and scale it made up for by allowing them a liberty that it scarcely permitted itself. Moreover, it centered around them and permitted Dolly the pleasure of a faint condescension—a pleasure which Anson, whose whole life was a condescension from the certitudes of his childhood, was unable to share.

He was not in love with her, and in the long feverish winter of their affair he frequently told her so. In the spring he was weary—he wanted to renew his life at some other source—moreover, he saw that either he must break with her now or accept the responsibility of a definite seduction. Her family's encouraging attitude precipitated his decision—one evening when Mr. Karger knocked discreetly at the library door to announce that he had left a bottle of old brandy in the dining room, Anson felt that life was hemming him in. That night he wrote her a short letter in which he told her that he was going on his vacation, and that in view of all the circumstances they had better meet no more.

It was June. His family had closed up the house and gone to the country, so he was living temporarily at the Yale Club. I had heard about his affair with Dolly as it developed—accounts salted with humor, for he despised unstable women, and granted them no place in the social edifice in which he believed—and when he told me that night that he was definitely breaking with her I was glad. I had seen Dolly here and there, and each time with a feeling of pity at the hopelessness of her struggle, and of shame at knowing so much about her that I had no right to know. She was what is known as "a pretty little thing," but there was a certain recklessness which rather fascinated me. Her dedication to the goddess of waste would have been less obvious had she been less spirited—she would most certainly throw herself away, but I was glad when I heard that the sacrifice would not be consummated in my sight.

Anson was going to leave the letter of farewell at her house next morning. It was one of the few houses left open in the Fifth Avenue district, and he knew that the Kargers, acting upon erroneous information from Dolly, had foregone a trip abroad to give their daughter her chance. As he stepped out the door of the Yale Club into Madison Avenue the postman passed him, and he followed back inside. The first letter that caught his eye was in Dolly's hand.

He knew what it would be—a lonely and tragic monologue, full of the reproaches he knew, the invoked memories, the "I wonder if's"—all the immemorial intimacies that he had communicated to Paula Legendre in what seemed another age. Thumbing over some bills, he brought it on top again and opened it. To his surprise it was a short, somewhat formal note, which said that Dolly would be unable to go to the country with him for the weekend, because Perry Hull from Chicago had unexpectedly come to town. It added that Anson had brought this on himself: "—if I felt that you loved me as I love you I would go with you at any time, any place, but Perry is *so* nice, and he so much wants me to marry him—"

Anson smiled contemptuously—he had had experience with such decoy epistles. Moreover, he knew how Dolly had labored over this plan, probably sent for the faithful Perry and calculated the time of his arrival—even labored over the note so that it would make him jealous without driving him away. Like most compromises, it had neither force nor vitality but only a timorous despair.

Suddenly he was angry. He sat down in the lobby and read it again. Then he went to the phone, called Dolly and told her in his clear, compelling voice that he had received her note and would call for her at five o'clock as they had previously planned. Scarcely waiting for the pretended uncertainty of her "Perhaps I can see you for an hour," he hung up the receiver and went down to his office. On the way he tore his own letter into bits and dropped it in the street.

He was not jealous—she meant nothing to him—but at her pathetic ruse everything stubborn and self-indulgent in him came to the surface. It was a presumption from a mental inferior and it could not be over looked. If she wanted to know to whom she belonged she would see.

He was on the doorstep at quarter past five. Dolly was dressed for the street, and he listened in silence to the paragraph of "I can only see you for an hour," which she had begun on the phone.

"Put on your hat, Dolly," he said, "we'll take a walk."

They strolled up Madison Avenue and over to Fifth while Anson's shirt dampened upon his portly body in the deep heat. He talked little, scolding her, making no love to her, but before they had walked six blocks she was his again, apologizing for the note, offering not to see Perry at all as an atonement, offering anything. She thought that he had come because he was beginning to love her.

"I'm hot," he said when they reached 71st Street. "This is a winter suit. If I stop by the house and change, would you mind waiting for me downstairs? I'll only be a minute."

She was happy; the intimacy of his being hot, of any physical fact about him, thrilled her. When they came to the iron-grated door and Anson took out his key she experienced a sort of delight.

Downstairs it was dark, and after he ascended in the lift Dolly raised a curtain and looked out through opaque lace at the houses over the way. She heard the lift machinery stop, and with the notion of teasing him pressed the button that brought it down. Then on what was more than an impulse she got into it and sent it up to what she guessed was his floor.

"Anson," she called, laughing a little.

"Just a minute," he answered from his bedroom ... then after a brief delay: "Now you can come in."

He had changed and was buttoning his vest.

"This is my room," he said lightly. "How do you like it?"

She caught sight of Paula's picture on the wall and stared at it in fascination, just as Paula had stared at the pictures of Anson's childish sweethearts five years before. She knew something about Paula—sometimes she tortured herself with fragments of the story.

Suddenly she came close to Anson, raising her arms. They embraced. Outside the area window a soft artificial twilight already hovered, though the sun was still bright on a back roof across the way. In half an hour the room would be quite dark. The uncalculated opportunity overwhelmed them, made them both breathless, and they clung more closely. It was imminent, inevitable. Still holding one another, they raised their heads—their eyes fell together upon Paula's picture, staring down at them from the wall.

Suddenly Anson dropped his arms, and sitting down at his desk tried the drawer with a bunch of keys.

"Like a drink?" he asked in a gruff voice.

"No, Anson."

He poured himself half a tumbler of whiskey, swallowed it, and then opened the door into the hall.

"Come on," he said.

Dolly hesitated.

"Anson—I'm going to the country with you tonight, after all. You understand that, don't you?"

"Of course," he answered brusquely.

In Dolly's car they rode on to Long Island, closer in their emotions than they had ever been before. They knew what would happen—not with Paula's face to remind them that something was lacking, but when they were alone in the still, hot Long Island night they did not care.

The estate in Port Washington where they were to spend the weekend belonged to a cousin of Anson's who had married a Montana copper operator. An interminable drive began at the lodge and twisted under imported poplar saplings toward a huge, pink Spanish house. Anson had often visited there before.

After dinner they danced at the Linx Club. About midnight Anson assured himself that his cousins would not leave before two—then he explained that Dolly was tired; he would take her home and return to the dance later. Trembling a little with excitement, they got into a borrowed car together and drove to Port Washington. As they reached the lodge he stopped and spoke to the night watchman.

"When are you making a round, Carl?"

"Right away."

"Then you'll be here till everybody's in?"

"Yes, sir."

"All right. Listen: if any automobile, no matter whose it is, turns in at this gate, I want you to phone the house immediately." He put a five-dollar bill into Carl's hand. "Is that clear?"

"Yes, Mr. Anson." Being of the Old World, he neither winked nor smiled. Yet Dolly sat with her face turned slightly away.

Anson had a key. Once inside he poured a drink for both of them—Dolly left hers untouched—then he ascertained definitely the location of the phone, and found that it was within easy hearing distance of their rooms, both of which were on the first floor.

Five minutes later he knocked at the door of Dolly's room.

"Anson?" He went in, closing the door behind him. She was in bed, leaning up anxiously with elbows on the pillow; sitting beside her he took her in his arms.

"Anson, darling."

He didn't answer.

"Anson. . . . Anson! I love you. . . . Say you love me. Say it now—can't you say it now? Even if you don't mean it?"

He did not listen. Over her head he perceived that the picture of Paula was hanging here upon this wall.

He got up and went close to it. The frame gleamed faintly with thrice-reflected moonlight—within was a blurred shadow of a face that he saw he did not know. Almost sobbing, he turned around and stared with abomination at the little figure on the bed.

"This is all foolishness," he said thickly. "I don't know what I was thinking about. I don't love you and you'd better wait for somebody that loves you. I don't love you a bit, can't you understand?"

His voice broke, and he went hurriedly out. Back in the salon he was pouring himself a drink with uneasy fingers, when the front door opened suddenly, and his cousin came in.

"Why, Anson, I hear Dolly's sick," she began solicitously. "I hear she's sick. . . ."

"It was nothing," he interrupted, raising his voice so that it would carry into Dolly's room. "She was a little tired. She went to bed."

For a long time afterward Anson believed that a protective God sometimes interfered in human affairs. But Dolly Karger, lying awake and staring at the ceiling, never again believed in anything at all.

VI

When Dolly married during the following autumn, Anson was in London on business. Like Paula's marriage, it was sudden, but it affected him in a different way. At first he felt that it was funny, and had an inclination to laugh when he thought of it. Later it depressed him—it made him feel old.

There was something repetitive about it—why, Paula and Dolly had belonged to different generations. He had a foretaste of the sensation of a man of forty who hears that the daughter of an old flame has married. He wired congratulations and, as was not the case with Paula, they were sincere—he had never really hoped that Paula would be happy.

When he returned to New York, he was made a partner in the firm, and, as his responsibilities increased, he had less time on his hands. The refusal of a life insurance company to issue him a policy made such an impression on him that he stopped drinking for a year, and claimed that he felt better physically, though I think he missed the convivial recounting of those Celliniesque adventures which, in his early twenties, had played such a part in his life. But he never abandoned the Yale Club. He was a figure there, a personality, and the tendency of his class, who were now seven years out of college, to drift away to more sober haunts was checked by his presence.

His day was never too full nor his mind too weary to give any sort of aid to any one who asked it. What had been done at first through pride and superiority had become a habit and a passion. And there was always something—a younger brother in trouble at New Haven, a quarrel to be patched up between a friend and his wife, a position to be found for this man, an investment for that. But his specialty was the solving of problems for young married people. Young married people fascinated him and their apartments were almost sacred to him—he knew the story of their love affair, advised them where to live and how, and remembered their babies' names. Toward young wives his attitude was circumspect: he never abused the trust which their husbands—strangely enough in view of his unconcealed irregularities—invariably reposed in him.

He came to take a vicarious pleasure in happy marriages, and to be inspired to an almost equally pleasant melancholy by those that went astray. Not a season passed that he did not witness the collapse of an affair that perhaps he himself had fathered. When Paula was divorced and almost immediately remarried to another Bostonian, he talked about her to me all one afternoon. He would never love any one as he had loved Paula, but he insisted that he no longer cared.

"I'll never marry," he came to say; "I've seen too much of it, and I know a happy marriage is a very rare thing. Besides, I'm too old."

But he did believe in marriage. Like all men who spring from a happy and successful marriage, he believed in it passionately—nothing he had seen would change his belief, his cynicism dissolved upon it like air. But he did really believe he was too old. At twenty-eight he began to accept with equanimity the prospect of marrying without romantic love; he resolutely chose a New York girl of his own class, pretty, intelligent, congenial, above reproach—and set about falling in love with her. The things he had said to Paula with sincerity, to other girls with grace, he could no longer say at all without smiling, or with the force necessary to convince.

"When I'm forty," he told his friends, "I'll be ripe. I'll fall for some chorus girl like the rest."

Nevertheless, he persisted in his attempt. His mother wanted to see him married, and he could now well afford it—he had a seat on the Stock Exchange, and his earned income came to twenty-five thousand a year. The idea was agreeable: when his friends—he spent most of his time with the set he and Dolly had evolved—closed themselves in behind domestic doors at night, he no longer rejoiced in his freedom. He even wondered if he should have married Dolly.

Not even Paula had loved him more, and he was learning the rarity in a single life, of encountering true emotion.

Just as this mood began to creep over him a disquieting story reached his ear. His Aunt Edna, a woman just this side of forty, was carrying on an open intrigue with a dissolute, hard-drinking young man named Cary Sloane. Every one knew of it except Anson's Uncle Robert, who for fifteen years had talked long in clubs and taken his wife for granted.

Anson heard the story again and again with increasing annoyance. Something of his old feeling for his uncle came back to him, a feeling that was more than personal, a reversion toward that family solidarity on which he had based his pride. His intuition singled out the essential point of the affair, which was that his uncle shouldn't be hurt. It was his first experiment in unsolicited meddling, but with his knowledge of Edna's character he felt that he could handle the matter better than a district judge or his uncle.

His uncle was in Hot Springs. Anson traced down the sources of the scandal so that there should be no possibility of mistake and then he called Edna and asked her to lunch with him at the Plaza next day. Something in his tone must have frightened her, for she was reluctant, but he insisted, putting off the date until she had no excuse for refusing.

She met him at the appointed time in the Plaza lobby, a lovely, faded, gray-eyed blonde in a coat of Russian sable. Five great rings, cold with diamonds and emeralds, sparkled on her slender hands. It occurred to Anson that it was his father's intelligence and not his uncle's that had earned the fur and the stones, the rich brilliance that buoyed up her passing beauty.

Though Edna scented his hostility, she was unprepared for the directness of his approach.

"Edna, I'm astonished at the way you've been acting," he said in a strong, frank voice. "At first I couldn't believe it."

"Believe what?" she demanded sharply.

"You needn't pretend with me, Edna. I'm talking about Cary Sloane. Aside from any other consideration, I didn't think you could treat Uncle Robert—"

"Now look here, Anson—" she began angrily, but his peremptory voice broke through hers:

"—and your children in such a way. You've been married eighteen years, and you're old enough to know better."

"You can't talk to me like that! You—"

"Yes, I can. Uncle Robert has always been my best friend." He was tremendously moved. He felt a real distress about his uncle, about his three young cousins.

Edna stood up, leaving her crab flake cocktail untasted.

"This is the silliest thing—"

"Very well, if you won't listen to me I'll go to Uncle Robert and tell him the whole story—he's bound to hear it sooner or later. And afterward I'll go to old Moses Sloane."

Edna faltered back into her chair.

"Don't talk so loud," she begged him. Her eyes blurred with tears. "You have no idea how your voice carries. You might have chosen a less public place to make all these crazy accusations."

He didn't answer.

"Oh, you never liked me, I know," she went on. "You're just taking advantage of some silly gossip to try and break up the only interesting friendship I've ever had. What did I ever do to make you hate me so?"

Still Anson waited. There would be the appeal to his chivalry, then to his pity, finally to his superior sophistication—when he had shouldered his way through all these there would be the admissions, and he could come to grips with her. By being silent, by being impervious, by returning constantly to his main weapon, which was his own true emotion, he bullied her into frantic despair as the luncheon hour slipped away. At two o'clock she took out a mirror and a handkerchief, shined away the marks of her tears and powdered the slight hollows where they had lain. She had agreed to meet him at her own house at five.

When he arrived she was stretched on a *chaise-longue* which was covered with cretonne for the summer, and the tears he had called up at luncheon seemed still to be standing in her eyes. Then he was aware of Cary Sloane's dark anxious presence upon the cold hearth.

"What's this idea of yours?" broke out Sloane immediately. "I understand you invited Edna to lunch and then threatened her on the basis of some cheap scandal."

Anson sat down.

"I have no reason to think it's only scandal."

"I hear you're going to take it to Robert Hunter, and to my father."

Anson nodded.

"Either you break it off—or I will," he said.

"What God damned business is it of yours, Hunter?"

"Don't lose your temper, Cary," said Edna nervously. "It's only a question of showing him how absurd—"

"For one thing, it's my name that's being handed around," interrupted Anson. "That's all that concerns you, Cary."

"Edna isn't a member of your family."

"She most certainly is!" His anger mounted. "Why—she owes this house and the rings on her fingers to my father's brains. When Uncle Robert married her she didn't have a penny."

They all looked at the rings as if they had a significant bearing on the situation. Edna made a gesture to take them from her hand.

"I guess they're not the only rings in the world," said Sloane.

"Oh, this is absurd," cried Edna. "Anson, will you listen to me? I've found out how the silly story started. It was a maid I discharged who went right to the Chilicheffs—all these Russians pump things out of their servants and then put a false meaning on them." She brought down her fist angrily on the table : "And after Robert lent them the limousine for a whole month when we were South last winter—"

"Do you see?" demanded Sloane eagerly. "This maid got hold of the wrong end of the thing. She knew that Edna and I were friends, and she carried it to the Chilicheffs. In Russia they assume that if a man and a woman—"

He enlarged the theme to a disquisition upon social relations in the Caucasus.

"If that's the case it better be explained to Uncle Robert," said Anson dryly, "so that when the rumors do reach him he'll know they're not true.

Adopting the method he had followed with Edna at luncheon he let them explain it all away. He knew that they were guilty and that presently they would cross the line from explanation into justification and convict themselves more definitely than he could ever do. By seven they had taken the desperate step of telling him the truth—Robert Hunter's neglect, Edna's empty life, the casual dalliance that had flamed up into passion—but like so many true stories it had the misfortune of being old, and its enfeebled body beat helplessly against the armor of Anson's will. The threat to go to Sloane's father sealed their helplessness, for the latter, a retired cotton broker out of Alabama, was a notorious fundamentalist who controlled his son by a rigid allowance and the promise that at his next vagary the allowance would stop forever.

They dined at a small French restaurant, and the discussion continued—at one time Sloane resorted to physical threats, a little later they were both imploring him to give them time. But Anson was obdurate. He saw that Edna was breaking up, and that her spirit must not be refreshed by any renewal of their passion.

At two o'clock in a small night club on 53rd Street, Edna's nerves suddenly collapsed, and she cried to go home. Sloane had been drinking heavily all evening, and he was faintly maudlin, leaning on the table and weeping a little with his face in his hands. Quickly Anson gave them his terms. Sloane was to leave town for six months, and he must be gone within forty-eight hours. When he returned there was to be no resumption of the affair, but at the end of a year Edna might, if she wished, tell Robert Hunter that she wanted a divorce and go about it in the usual way.

He paused, gaining confidence from their faces for his final word.

"Or there's another thing you can do," he said slowly, "if Edna wants to leave her children, there's nothing I can do to prevent your running off together."

"I want to go home!" cried Edna again. "Oh, haven't you done enough to us for one day?"

Outside it was dark, save for a blurred glow from Sixth Avenue down the street. In that light those two who had been lovers looked for the last time into each other's tragic faces, realizing that between them there was not enough youth and strength to avert their eternal parting. Sloane walked suddenly off down the street and Anson tapped a dozing taxi driver on the arm.

It was almost four; there was a patient flow of cleaning water along the ghostly pavement of Fifth Avenue, and the shadows of two night women flitted over the dark façade of St. Thomas's church. Then the desolate shrubbery of Central Park where Anson had often played as a child, and the mounting numbers, significant as names, of the marching streets. This was his city, he thought, where his name had flourished through five generations. No change could alter the permanence of its place here, for change itself was the essential substratum by which he and those of his name identified themselves with the spirit of New York. Resourcefulness and a powerful will—for his threats in weaker hands would have been less than nothing—had beaten the gathering dust from his uncle's name, from the name of his family, from even this shivering figure that sat beside him in the car.

Cary Sloane's body was found next morning on the lower shelf of a pillar of Queensboro Bridge. In the darkness and in his excitement he had thought that it was the water flowing black beneath him, but in less than a second it made no possible difference—unless he had planned to think one last thought of Edna, and call out her name as he struggled feebly in the water.

VII

Anson never blamed himself for his part in this affair—the situation which brought it about had not been of his making. But the just suffer with the unjust, and he found that his oldest and somehow his most precious friendship was over. He never knew what distorted story Edna told, but he was welcome in his uncle's house no longer.

Just before Christmas Mrs. Hunter retired to a select Episcopal heaven, and Anson became the responsible head of his family. An unmarried aunt who had lived with them for years ran the house, and attempted with helpless inefficiency to chaperone the younger girls. All the children were less self-reliant than Anson, more conventional both in their virtues and in their shortcomings. Mrs. Hunter's death had postponed the début of one daughter and the wedding of another. Also it had taken something deeply material from all of them, for with her passing the quiet, expensive superiority of the Hunters came to an end.

For one thing, the estate, considerably diminished by two inheritance taxes and soon to be divided among six children, was not a notable fortune any more. Anson saw a tendency in his youngest sisters to speak rather respectfully of families that hadn't "existed" twenty years ago. His own feeling of precedence was not echoed in them—sometimes they were conventionally snobbish, that was all. For another thing, this was the last summer they would spend on the Connecticut estate; the clamor against it was too loud: "Who wants to waste the best months of the year shut up in that dead old town?" Reluctantly he yielded—the house would go into the market in the fall, and next summer they would rent a smaller place in Westchester County. It was a step down from the expensive simplicity of his father's idea, and, while he sympathized with the revolt, it also annoyed him; during his mother's lifetime he had gone up there at least every other weekend—even in the gayest summers.

Yet he himself was part of this change, and his strong instinct for life had turned him in his twenties from the hollow obsequies of that abortive leisure class. He did not see this clearly—he still felt that there was a norm, a standard of society. But there was no norm, it was doubtful if there ever had been a true norm in New York. The few who still paid and fought to enter a particular set succeeded only to find that as a society it scarcely functioned—or, what was more alarming, that the Bohemia from which they fled sat above them at table.

At twenty-nine Anson's chief concern was his own growing loneliness. He was sure now that he would never marry. The number of weddings at which he had officiated as best man or usher was past all counting—there was a drawer at home that bulged with the official neckties of this or that wedding party, neckties standing for romances that had not endured a year, for couples who had passed completely from his life. Scarf pins, gold pencils, cuff buttons, presents from a generation of grooms had passed through his jewel box and been lost—and with every ceremony he was less and less able to imagine himself in the groom's place. Under his hearty goodwill toward all those marriages there was despair about his own.

And as he neared thirty he became not a little depressed at the inroads that marriage, especially lately, had made upon his friendships. Groups of people had a disconcerting tendency to dissolve and disappear. The men from his own college—and it was upon them he had expended the most time and affection—were the most elusive of all. Most of them were drawn deep into domesticity, two were dead, one lived abroad, one was in Hollywood writing continuities for pictures that Anson went faithfully to see.

Most of them, however, were permanent commuters with an intricate family life centering around some suburban country club, and it was from these that he felt his estrangement most keenly.

In the early days of their married life they had all needed him; he gave them advice about their slim finances, he exorcised their doubts about the advisability of bringing a baby into two rooms and a bath, especially he stood for the great world outside. But now their financial troubles were in the past and the fearfully expected child had evolved into an absorbing family. They were always glad to see old Anson, but they dressed up for him and tried to impress him with their present importance, and kept their troubles to themselves. They needed him no longer.

A few weeks before his thirtieth birthday the last of his early and intimate friends was married. Anson acted in his usual role of best man, gave his usual silver tea service, and went down to the usual *Homeric* to say good-by. It was a hot Friday afternoon in May, and as he walked from the pier he realized that Saturday closing had begun and he was free until Monday morning.

"Go where?" he asked himself.

The Yale Club, of course; bridge until dinner, then four or five raw cocktails in somebody's room and a pleasant confused evening. He regretted that this afternoon's groom wouldn't be along—they had always been able to cram so much into such nights: they knew how to attach women and how to get rid of them, how much consideration any girl deserved from their intelligent hedonism. A party was an adjusted thing—you took certain girls to certain places and spent just so much on their amusement; you drank a little, not much more than you ought to drink, and at a certain time in the morning you stood up and said you were going home. You avoided college boys, sponges, future engagements, fights, sentiment, and indiscretions. That was the way it was done. All the rest was dissipation.

In the morning you were never violently sorry—you made no resolutions, but if you had overdone it and your heart was slightly out of order, you went on the wagon for a few days without saying anything about it, and waited until an accumulation of nervous boredom projected you into another party.

The lobby of the Yale Club was unpopulated. In the bar three very young alumni looked up at him, momentarily and without curiosity.

"Hello, there, Oscar," he said to the bartender. "Mr. Cahill been around this afternoon?"

"Mr. Cahill's gone to New Haven."

"Oh . . . that so?"

"Gone to the ball game. Lot of men gone up."

Anson looked once again into the lobby, considered for a moment, and then walked out and over to Fifth Avenue. From the broad window of one of his clubs—one that he had scarcely visited in five years—a gray man with watery eyes stared down at him. Anson looked quickly away—that figure sitting in vacant resignation, in supercilious solitude, depressed him. He stopped and, retracing his steps, started over 47th Street toward Teak Warden's apartment. Teak and his wife has once been his most familiar friends—it was a household where he and Dolly Karger had been used to go in the days of their affair. But Teak had taken to drink, and his wife had remarked publicly that Anson was a bad influence on him. The remark reached Anson in an exaggerated form—when it was finally cleared up, the delicate spell of intimacy was broken, never to be renewed.

"Is Mr. Warden at home?" he inquired.

"They've gone to the country."

The fact unexpectedly cut at him. They were gone to the country and he hadn't known. Two years before he would have known the date, the hour, come up at the last moment for a final drink, and planned his first visit to them. Now they had gone without a word.

Anson looked at his watch and considered a weekend with his family, but the only train was a local that would jolt through the aggressive heat for three hours. And tomorrow in the country, and Sunday—he was in no mood for porch-bridge with polite undergraduates, and dancing after dinner at a rural roadhouse, a diminutive of gaiety which his father had estimated too well.

"Oh, no," he said to himself. . . . "No."

He was a dignified, impressive young man, rather stout now, but otherwise unmarked by dissipation. He could have been cast for a pillar of something—at times you were sure it was not society, at others nothing else—for the law, for the church. He stood for a few minutes motionless on the sidewalk in front of a 47th Street apartment house; for almost the first time in his life he had nothing whatever to do.

Then he began to walk briskly up Fifth Avenue, as if he had just been reminded of an important engagement there. The necessity of dissimulation is one of the few characteristics that we share with dogs, and I think of Anson on that day as some well-bred specimen who had been disappointed at a familiar back door. He was going to see Nick, once a fashionable bartender in demand at all private dances, and now employed in cooling non-alcoholic champagne among the labyrinthine cellars of the Plaza Hotel.

"Nick," he said, "what's happened to everything?"

"Dead," Nick said.

"Make me a whiskey sour." Anson handed a pint bottle over the counter. "Nick, the girls are different; I had a little girl in Brooklyn and she got married last week without letting me know."

"That a fact? Ha-ha-ha," responded Nick diplomatically. "Slipped it over on you."

"Absolutely," said Anson. "And I was out with her the night before."

"Ha-ha-ha," said Nick, "ha-ha-ha!"

"Do you remember the wedding, Nick, in Hot Springs where I had the waiters and the musicians singing 'God save the king'?"

"Now where was that, Mr. Hunter?" Nick concentrated doubtfully. "Seems to me that was—"

"Next time they were back for more, and I began to wonder how much I'd paid them," continued Anson.

"—seems to me that was at Mr. Trenholm's wedding."

"Don't know him," said Anson decisively. He was offended that a strange name should intrude upon his reminiscences; Nick perceived this.

"Na—aw—" he admitted, "I ought to know that. It was one of *your* crowd—Brakins . . . Baker—"

"Bicker Baker," said Anson responsively. "They put me in a hearse after it was over and covered me up with flowers and drove me away."

"Ha-ha-ha," said Nick. "Ha-ha-ha."

Nick's simulation of the old family servant paled presently and Anson went upstairs to the lobby. He looked around—his eyes met the glance of an unfamiliar clerk at the desk, then fell upon a flower from the morning's marriage hesitating in the mouth of a brass cuspidor. He went out and walked slowly toward the blood-red sun over Columbus Circle. Suddenly he turned around and, retracing his steps to the Plaza, immured himself in a telephone booth.

Later he said that he tried to get me three times that afternoon, that he tried every one who might be in New York—men and girls he had not seen for years, an artist's model of his college days whose faded number was still in his address book—Central told him that even the exchange existed no longer. At length his quest roved into the country, and he held brief disappointing conversations with emphatic butlers and maids. So-and-so was out, riding, swimming, playing golf, sailed to Europe last week. Who shall I say phoned?

It was intolerable that he should pass the evening alone—the private reckonings which one plans for a moment of leisure lose every charm when the solitude is enforced. There were always women of a sort, but the ones he knew had temporarily vanished, and to pass a New York evening in the hired company of a stranger never occurred to him—he would have considered that that was something shameful and secret, the diversion of a traveling salesman in a strange town.

Anson paid the telephone bill—the girl tried unsuccessfully to joke with him about its size—and for the second time that afternoon started to leave the Plaza and go he knew not where. Near the revolving door the figure of a woman, obviously with child, stood sideways to the light—a sheer beige cape fluttered at her shoulders when the door turned and, each time, she looked impatiently toward it as if she were weary of waiting. At the first sight of her a strong nervous thrill of familiarity went over him, but not until he was within five feet of her did he realize that it was Paula.

"Why, Anson Hunter!"

His heart turned over.

"Why, Paula—"

"Why, this is wonderful. I can't believe it, *Anson!*"

She took both his hands, and he saw in the freedom of the gesture that the memory of him had lost poignancy to her. But not to him—he felt that old mood that she evoked in him stealing over his brain, that gentleness with which he had always met her optimism as if afraid to mar its surface.

"We're at Rye for the summer. Pete had to come East on business—you know of course I'm Mrs. Peter Hagerty now—so we brought the children and took a house. You've got to come out and see us."

"Can I?" he asked directly. "When?"

"When you like. Here's Pete." The revolving door functioned, giving up a fine tall man of thirty with a tanned face and a trim mustache. His immaculate fitness made a sharp contrast with Anson's increasing bulk, which was obvious under the faintly tight cutaway coat.

"You oughtn't to be standing," said Hagerty to his wife. "Let's sit down here." He indicated lobby chairs, but Paula hesitated.

"I've got to go right home," she said. "Anson, why don't you—why don't you come out and have dinner with us tonight?" We're just getting settled, but if you can stand that—"

Hagerty confirmed the invitation cordially.

"Come out for the night."

Their car waited in front of the hotel, and Paula with a tired gesture sank back against silk cushions in the corner.

"There's so much I want to talk to you about," she said, "it seems hopeless."

"I want to hear about you."

"Well"—she smiled at Hagerty—"that would take a long time too. I have three children—by my first marriage. The oldest is five, then four, then three." She smiled again. "I didn't waste much time having them, did I?"

"Boys?"

"A boy and two girls. Then—oh, a lot of things happened, and I got a divorce in Paris a year ago and married Pete. That's all—except that I'm awfully happy."

In Rye they drove up to a large house near the Beach Club, from which there issued presently three dark, slim children who broke from an English governess and approached them with an esoteric cry. Abstractedly and with difficulty Paula took each one into her arms, a caress which they accepted stiffly, and they had evidently been told not to bump into Mummy. Even against their fresh faces Paula's skin showed scarcely any weariness—for all her physical languor she seemed younger than when he had last seen her at Palm Beach seven years ago.

At dinner she was preoccupied, and afterward, during the homage to the radio, she lay with closed eyes on the sofa, until Anson wondered if his presence at this time were not an intrusion. But at nine o'clock, when Hagerty rose and said pleasantly that he was going to leave them by themselves for a while, she began to talk slowly about herself and the past.

"My first baby," she said—"the one we call Darling, the biggest little girl—I wanted to die when I knew I was going to have her, because Lowell was like a stranger to me. It didn't seem as though she could be my own. I wrote you a letter and tore it up. Oh, you were *so* bad to me, Anson."

It was the dialogue again, rising and falling. Anson felt a sudden quickening of memory.

"Weren't you engaged once?" she asked—"a girl named Dolly something?"

"I wasn't ever engaged. I tried to be engaged, but I never loved anybody but you, Paula."

"Oh," she said. Then after a moment: "This baby is the first one

I ever really wanted. You see, I'm in love now—at last."

He didn't answer, shocked at the treachery of her remembrance. She must have seen that the "at last" bruised him, for she continued:

"I was infatuated with you, Anson—you could make me do anything you liked. But we wouldn't have been happy. I'm not smart enough for you. I don't like things to be complicated like you do." She paused. "You'll never settle down" she said.

The phrase struck at him from behind—it was an accusation that of all accusations he had never merited.

"I could settle down if women were different," he said. "If I didn't understand so much about them, if women didn't spoil you for other women, if they had only a little pride. If I could go to sleep for a while and wake up into a home that was really mine—why, that's what I'm made for, Paula, that's what women have seen in me and liked in me. It's only that I can't get through the preliminaries any more."

Hagerty came in a little before eleven; after a whiskey Paula stood up and announced that she was going to bed. She went over and stood by her husband.

"Where did you go, dearest?" she demanded.

"I had a drink with Ed Saunders."

"I was worried. I thought maybe you'd run away."

She rested her head against his coat.

"He's sweet, isn't he, Anson?" she demanded.

"Absolutely," said Anson, laughing.

She raised her face to her husband.

"Well, I'm ready," she said. She turned to Anson: "Do you want to see our family gymnastic stunt?"

"Yes," he said in an interested voice.

"All right. Here we go!"

Hagerty picked her up easily in his arms.

"This is called the family acrobatic stunt," said Paula. "He carries me upstairs. Isn't it sweet of him?"

"Yes," said Anson.

Hagerty bent his head slightly until his face touched Paula's.

"And I love him," she said. "I've just been telling you, haven't I, Anson?"

"Yes," he said.

"He's the dearest thing that ever lived in this world; aren't you, darling? . . . Well, good night. Here we go. Isn't he strong?"

"Yes," Anson said.

"You'll find a pair of Pete's pajamas laid out for you. Sweet dreams—see you at breakfast."

"Yes," Anson said.

VIII

The older members of the firm insisted that Anson should go abroad for the summer. He had scarcely had a vacation in seven years, they said. He was stale and needed a change. Anson resisted.

"If I go," he declared, "I won't come back any more."

"That's absurd, old man. You'll be back in three months with all this depression gone. Fit as ever."

"No," He shook his head stubbornly. "If I stop, I won't go back to work. If I stop, that means I've given up—I'm through,"

"We'll take a chance on that. Stay six months if you like—we're not afraid you'll leave us. Why, you'd be miserable if you didn't work."

They arranged his passage for him. They liked Anson—every one liked Anson—and the change that had been coming over him cast a sort of pall over the office. The enthusiasm that had invariably signaled up business, the consideration toward his equals and his inferiors, the lift of his vital presence—within the past four months his intense nervousness had melted down these qualities into the fussy pessimism of a man of forty. On every transaction in which he was involved he acted as a drag and a strain.

"If I go I'll never come back," he said.

Three days before he sailed Paula Legendre Hagerty died in childbirth. I was with him a great deal then, for we were crossing together, but for the first time in our friendship he told me not a word of how he felt, nor did I see the slightest sign of emotion. His chief preoccupation was with the fact that he was thirty years old—he would turn the conversation to the point where he could remind you of it and then fall silent, as if he assumed that the statement would start a chain of thought sufficient to itself. Like his partners, I was amazed at the change in him, and I was glad when the *Paris* moved off into the wet space between the worlds, leaving his principality behind.

"How about a drink?" he suggested.

We walked into the bar with that defiant feeling that characterizes the day of departure and ordered four Martinis. After one cocktail a change came over him—he suddenly reached across and slapped my knee with the first joviality I had seen him exhibit for months.

"Did you see that girl in the red tam?" he demanded, "the one with the high color who had the two police dogs down to bid her good-by."

"She's pretty," I agreed.

"I looked her up in the purser's office and found out that she's alone. I'm going down to see the steward in a few minutes. We'll have dinner with her tonight."

After a while he left me, and within an hour he was walking up and down the deck with her, talking to her in his strong, clear voice. Her red tam was a bright spot of color against the steel-green sea, and from time to time she looked up with a flashing bob of her head, and smiled with amusement and interest, and anticipation. At dinner we had champagne, and were very joyous—afterward Anson ran the pool with infectious gusto, and several people who had seen me with him asked me his name. He and the girl were talking and laughing together on a lounge in the bar when I went to bed.

I saw less of him on the trip than I had hoped. He wanted to arrange a foursome, but there was no one available, so I saw him only at meals. Sometimes, though, he would have a cocktail in the bar, and he told me about the girl in the red tam, and his adventures with her, making them all bizarre and amusing, as he had a way of doing, and I was glad that he was himself again, or at least the self that I knew, and with which I felt at home. I don't think he was ever happy unless some one was in love with him, responding to him like filings to a magnet, helping him to explain himself, promising him something. What it was I do not know. Perhaps they promised that there would always be women in the world who would spend their brightest, freshest, rarest hours to nurse and protect that superiority he cherished in his heart.

QUESTIONS FOR DISCUSSION

1. The first section of the story serves as the formal introduction or apology for the main part that follows. What can you tell about the speaker by the way in which his language characterizes him? How does the speaker's statement, that the very rich are "different from you and me," help to identify the tone with which he addresses his audience? What is his attitude toward Anson Hunter? Be specific in your use of evidence from the text itself.

2. How does the narrator's decision to "cling stubbornly to my point of view" affect Fitzgerald's telling of Anson Hunter's story? In what respects is an understanding of this point of view essential to an appreciation for the narrative?

3. In 1873 Samuel L. Clemens and Charles Dudley Warner wrote a book called *The Gilded Age.* Fitzgerald uses this phrase to describe the New York society of Anson Hunter's childhood. What does the phrase imply? How might it apply to elements of society today?

4. Through frequent personal references, the narrator states that his background has been quite different from Anson Hunter's. How, for example, did his childhood differ from the rich boy's?

5. In many of his works, Fitzgerald shows the division between East and West as the root of America's class struggles. In *The Great Gatsby*, for instance, the narrator says that he and others "were all Westerners, and perhaps we possessed some deficiency in common which made us subtly unadaptable to Eastern life." What indication of this division do you find in "The Rich Boy"?

6. What qualities mark Anson Hunter as an unusual undergraduate at Yale? What does the narrator mean when he says that Anson's aspirations were free of the mist of "idealism" or "illusion"? In what sense had Anson Hunter's life begun as a compromise?

7. What is the narrator's attitude toward Paula Legendre? In what phrases is this attitude shown? Does his opinion of Paula ever change? Why is it important to the revealing of her character to demonstrate that she did not know that Anson Hunter was a wealthy man?

8. The narrator says that Anson Hunter's "moral superiority" prevented Mrs. Legendre from establishing any advantage over him even after his display of drunkenness. What is this "moral superiority"?

9. What is "the psychological moment" that passed forever between the time of Paula and Anson's separation and their reunion three weeks later? In what way does this statement by Fitzgerald at the end of section III anticipate the story's melancholy ending?

10. The opening paragraph of section IV is one of the most important passages in this story. What essential shift in point of view has developed? What is the speaker's source of information?

11. In summarizing the estrangement and Anson's subsequent business and social activities, what details does Fitzgerald cite as representative of Anson's position and esteem? What two details are most significant? What details from contemporary society would you include among the activities of a rich businessman today?

12. For Dolly Karger, Fitzgerald saves his most condemning description. He says she had "a weakness of rudder." What does he mean? How is this deficiency exemplified in her actions? What advantage, nonetheless, does she exert over Anson?

13. Why did Anson believe "that a protective God sometimes interfered in human affairs"? Why does the narrator say that Dolly "never again believed in anything at all"?

14. In section IV, Fitzgerald speaks of Anson Hunter's "taking pleasure in helping people." By section VI, he has found a specialty. What is that specialty? What is ironic about Anson's specialty? What causes this quality of helpfulness to become an abusive weapon? What is the result of his "unsolicited meddling"?

15. How can you tell that the narrator is representing only Anson's attitude, and not his own, toward the Cary Sloane incident? What makes the language of statements like "No change could alter the permanence

...." and "Resourcefulness and a powerful will" seem hollow and meaningless?

16. The narrator refers to Anson Hunter's way of living as "intelligent hedonism." Discuss the meaning of this phrase, using details from the story to assist you in arriving at a satisfactory definition of terms.

17. What is the narrator attempting to show about Anson's life by detailing the events of the day when "for almost the first time in his life he had nothing whatever to do"?

18. Throughout their relationship, Paula and Anson depend a great deal upon what the narrator calls "the dialogue." What is it about their conversation that is so important? Is this a recognizable human trait or is it particular only to the characters in this story? Explain your answer.

19. As the story concludes, Anson Hunter is thirty years old. Another of Fitzgerald's young men, Nick Carraway in *The Great Gatsby*, says of himself, "I'm thirty. I'm five years too old to lie to myself and call it honor." How is Nick different from Anson? What is Anson's essential lie?

20. How does the narrator bring his story around so that the formal introduction is relevant to the story's conclusion? What does the word *superiority* connote for you, after experiencing its use in connection with the life of Anson Hunter?

ASSIGNMENTS FOR WRITING

1. Written one year after *The Great Gatsby*, "The Rich Boy" contains a great number of similarities to the novel—in the device of an objective narrator, in the characterization of a wealthy yet disillusioned young man, in the portrait of Eastern society, in the poignant language of the author. Read or reread *The Great Gatsby* and write a critical essay in which you analyze some point of comparison between the two works.

2. Write a 300–500 word extension of "The Rich Boy," showing what happens to Anson Hunter and the girl in the red tam. Try to retain the mood of the story as provided by the narrator's attempt to intellectualize the experience he is relating.

3. As social commentary, "The Rich Boy" challenges certain conventions in the American upper class from the Gilded Age to the Roaring Twenties. From your reading of history, show how acutely Fitzgerald's story depicts the accepted patterns of behavior. In an essay, show that you understand Fitzgerald's criticism of this mode of living.

4. The character of Anson Hunter, like the society of which he is a part, is full of contradictions, if not hypocrisy. Yet the narrator declines to call these contradictions hypocritical. At the same time, there is no doubt that the narrator disapproves of much that he describes. What is the narrator's method of relating the unsavory aspects and incidents?

How does he avoid taking on a condemning tone? In an essay, analyze the implied characteristics of the narrator as you find them in "The Rich Boy."

5. Another of Fitzgerald's stories, "Winter Dreams," presents his version of "the rich girl." Read "Winter Dreams," and in an essay discuss the similarities and dissimilarities that you find in the two stories. Analyze Fitzgerald's treatment of women. Is he as objective in depicting Judy Jones and Dolly Karger as he is in depicting Dexter Green and Anson Hunter?

6. Almost all of the principal characters in Fitzgerald's stories are graduates of Yale. How does Fitzgerald treat the Ivy League college man? Remembering that Fitzgerald himself attended Princeton, do you find any significance in the Yale references? How do Fitzgerald's characterizations of the Ivy League graduate hold up today? Is he a character or a caricature? Write an informal essay in which you discuss these questions.

Ernest Hemingway

Until the publication, in 1969, of Carlos Baker's thorough biography *Ernest Hemingway: A Life Story*, it had been virtually impossible to separate the man from the myth. So powerful a literary personage as Hemingway had never before been known in America; so vast a reputation for courage, gallantry, romance, stamina, and all the virtues and vices of toughened masculinity had never been combined with such sensitivity to language. In Hemingway many Americans found the apotheosis of the artist.

Hemingway was thoroughly conscious of the spell his manner of living could cast upon the masses of his readers, his admirers and detractors alike. With the skill of the story-teller, he developed the plot of his own life, complicating it with wars and marriages, near-catastrophes and triumphs, until he arrived at its denouement. Then he closed the narrative as he thought best.

Born in Oak Park, Illinois, on July 21, 1899, Ernest Hemingway had been introduced to the out-of-doors as an infant. His father, a medical doctor, owned property in northern Michigan, where the family spent the summers. As a three-year-old, young Hemingway distinguished himself as a child who was "'fraid a nothin'"; hunting, fishing, and hiking were his boyhood sports rather than football and the other conventional athletics. Bob Zuppke, coach at Oak Park High School and later at the University of Illinois, when asked to comment on Hemingway's ability as a football player, replied, "He was a better writer."

At age 18, following high school graduation and a brief time as a cub reporter for the Kansas City *Star*, Hemingway enlisted in the American Field Service's ambulance corps and was sent to the Italian front. On July 8, 1918, he was severely wounded and taken to a Milan hospital where he met a nurse, Agnes von Kurowsky. The romance that followed Hemingway used first as the basis for "A Very

Short Story" (*In Our Time*, 1925) and later expanded for his second novel, *A Farewell to Arms* (1929).

At the Armistice concluding World War I, "the War to end all wars," Hemingway returned to Oak Park. Then he drifted to Michigan to recuperate his damaged equilibrium and begin the laborious process of articulating the experiences of a youth who had seen so much of life. He drew upon the reservoir of his summer experiences as a child, the camaraderie of adolescence, the horrors of war at first hand, and the indescribable psychological tensions of a returning veteran. Patiently over the next few years he worked to find the exact language by which to compress these experiences into narrative form.

In the meantime, he worked as a feature writer for the Toronto *Star*. With his bride Hadley, he went to Paris in 1921, where he came to know the leading literary figures of that day—Gertrude Stein, Ezra Pound, James Joyce, and eventually, F. Scott Fitzgerald. By 1924, however, he was ready to "lay it on the line," to abandon the security of a journalist's position and trust to his art to sustain him and his family. The next year, *In Our Time* exploded upon the world, and thus the myth began— the burly, bearded American sitting at the bistro table, surrounded by bread and wine, writing; the bullfight *aficionado* at Pamplona and Madrid; the amateur boxer willing to take on all comers; the confidante of Scott Fitzgerald, with whom he also quarreled frequently.

The structure of *In Our Time* provides the reader with corridors of time through which to trace and retrace the successive phases of Nick Adams' development. The principal stories deal mainly with Nick's quest for maturity after a childhood trauma, while accompanying his father to an Indian camp in northern Michigan, and his search for restored tranquility on the fishing trip to Big Two-Hearted River. Interspersed between these stories are vignettes, some little more than a few lines long, from Nick's wartime experiences. In one of these, Chapter VI, Hemingway offers the germ for Frederic Henry's desertion from the Italian army, in *A Farewell to Arms*, when Nick tells his companion Rinaldi, "You and me we've made a separate peace." The counterbalance of violence in the vignettes with the essential detachment and calm of the narrator's voice in the principal stories reinforces for the reader the authenticity of this book's vision of life.

The Sun Also Rises (1926) continued Hemingway's initial success with its hard-bitten cynicism, its evocation of all that Gertrude Stein may have meant by "the Lost Generation," those nihilists for whom the world has turned sour. By this time, the famous Hemingway style was also gaining recognition as a phenomenon of its own. Terse and repetitive, true to the rhythms of natural speech, the language maintained an integrity that was to be Hemingway's hallmark. Notice for example, the description of Frederic Henry's wounding in *A Farewell to Arms:*

> I sat up straight and as I did so something inside my head moved like the weights on a doll's eyes and it hit me inside in back of my eyeballs. My legs felt warm and wet and my shoes were wet and warm inside. I knew that I was hit and leaned over and put my hand on my knee. My knee wasn't there. My hand went in and my knee was down on my shin.

This was the style, compounded of plain diction and direct metaphor, that shaped the great stories and novels to come—"The Snows of Kilimanjaro," "The Short Happy Life of Francis Macomber," "A Clean, Well-Lighted Place," *For Whom the Bell Tolls* (1940), and *The Old Man and the Sea* (1952). For these accomplishments he received the 1954 Nobel Prize for literature.

To some it seemed that the almost legendary Hemingway had accomplished everything. Renowned as a big-game hunter, as a fearless war correspondent, as a hedonist whose barroom escapades seemed never to catch up with him, the man Hemingway was increasingly uneasy about his inability to sustain, not the elements of the myth, but the art on which his very life was founded. In fact, his health was poor, undermined by both his prodigality and a succession of near-fatal collisions and plane crashes. The Hemingway who had poured out his energies in mastering his art, who had labored painstakingly at innumerable revisions, now struggled to produce a few sentences. From his home in Cuba, he had moved to Ketchum, Idaho, where he worked on *A Moveable Feast*, the recollection of his early days in Paris. Invited to President Kennedy's inauguration, he was too ill to accept; asked to write an inscription for a book to be presented to the new President, he toiled all one day without success, finally announcing in tears that he could not write anymore.

Awareness of his failing powers left Hemingway, the artist, despondent. Not unpredictably, he chose to end his life. On July 2, 1961, he committed suicide.

Big Two-Hearted River

PART I

The train went on up the track out of sight, around one of the hills of burnt timber. Nick sat down on the bundle of canvas and bedding the baggage man had pitched out of the door of the baggage car. There was no town, nothing but the rails and the burned-over country. The thirteen saloons that had lined the one street of Seney had not left a trace. The foundations of the Mansion House hotel stuck up above the ground. The stone was chipped and split by the fire. It was all that was left of the town of Seney. Even the surface had been burned off the ground.

Nick looked at the burned-over stretch of hillside, where he had expected to find the scattered houses of the town and then walked down the railroad track to the bridge over the river. The river was there. It swirled against the log spiles of the bridge. Nick looked down into the clear, brown water, colored from the pebbly bottom, and watched the trout keeping themselves steady in the current with wavering fins. As he watched them they changed their posttions by quick angles, only to hold steady in the fast water again. Nick watched them a long time.

He watched them holding themselves with their noses into the current, many trout in deep, fast moving water, slightly distorted as he watched far down through the glassy convex surface of the pool, its surface pushing and swelling smooth against the resistance of the log-driven piles of the bridge. At the bottom of the pool were the big trout. Nick did not see them at first. Then he saw them at the bottom of the pool, big trout looking to hold themselves on the gravel bottom in a varying mist of gravel and sand, raised in spurts by the current.

Nick looked down into the pool from the bridge. It was a hot day. A kingfisher flew up the stream. It was a long time since Nick had looked into a stream and seen trout. They were very satisfactory. As the shadow of the kingfisher moved up the stream, a big trout shot upstream in a long angle, only his shadow marking the angle, then lost his shadow as he came through the surface of the water, caught the sun, and then, as he went back into the stream under the surface, his shadow seemed to float down the stream with the current, unresisting, to his post under the bridge where he tightened facing up into the current.

Nick's heart tightened as the trout moved. He felt all the old feeling.

He turned and looked down the stream. It stretched away, pebbly-bottomed with shallows and big boulders and a deep pool as it curved away around the foot of a bluff.

Nick walked back up the ties to where his pack lay in the cinders beside the railway track. He was happy. He adjusted the pack harness around the bundle, pulling straps tight, slung the pack on his back, got his arms through the shoulder straps and took some of the pull off his shoulders by leaning his forehead against the wide band of the tump-line. Still, it was too heavy. It was much too heavy. He had his leather rod-case in his hand and leaning forward to keep the weight of the pack high on his shoulders he walked along the road that paralleled the railway track, leaving the burned town behind in the heat, and then turned off around a hill with a high, fire-scarred hill on either side onto a road that went back into the country. He walked along the road feeling the ache from the pull of the heavy pack. The road climbed steadily. It was hard work walking uphill. His muscles ached and the day was hot, but Nick felt happy. He felt he had left everything behind, the need for thinking, the need to write, other needs. It was all back of him.

From the time he had gotten down off the train and the baggage man had thrown his pack out of the open car door things had been different. Seney was burned, the country was burned over and changed, but it did not matter. It could not all be burned. He knew that. He hiked along the road, sweating in the sun, climbing to cross the range of hills that separated the railway from the pine plains.

The road ran on, dipping occasionally, but always climbing. Nick went on up. Finally the road after going parallel to the burnt hillside reached the top. Nick leaned back against a stump and slipped out of the pack harness. Ahead of him, as far as he could see, was the pine plain. The burned country stopped off at the left with the range of the hills. On ahead islands of dark pine trees rose out of the plain. Far off to the left was the line of the river. Nick followed it with his eye and caught glints of the water in the sun.

There was nothing but the pine plain ahead of him, until the far blue hills that marked the Lake Superior height of land. He could hardly see them, faint and far away in the heat-light over the plain. If he looked too steadily they were gone. But if he only half-looked they were there, the far off hills of the height of land.

Nick sat down against the charred stump and smoked a cigarette. His pack balanced on the top of the stump, harness holding ready, a hollow molded in it from his back. Nick sat smoking, looking out over the country. He did not need to get his map out. He knew where he was from the position of the river.

As he smoked, his legs stretched out in front of him, he noticed a grasshopper walk along the ground and up onto his woolen sock. The grasshopper was black. As he had walked along the road, climbing, he had started many grasshoppers from the dust. They were all black. They were not the big grasshoppers with yellow and black or red and black wings whirring out from their black wing sheathing as they fly up. These were just ordinary hoppers, but all a sooty black in color. Nick had wondered about them as he walked, without really thinking about them. Now, as he watched the black hopper that was nibbling at the wool of his sock with its fourway lip, he realized that they had all turned black from living in the burned-over land. He realized that the fire must have come the year before, but the grasshoppers were all black now. He wondered how long they would stay that way.

Carefully he reached his hand down and took hold of the hopper by the wings. He turned him up, all his legs walking in the air; and looked at his jointed belly. Yes, it was black too, iridescent where the back and head were dusty.

"Go on, hopper," Nick said, speaking out loud for the first time, "fly away somewhere."

He tossed the grasshopper up into the air and watched him sail away to a charcoal stump across the road.

Nick stood up. He leaned his back against the weight of his pack where it rested upright on the stump and got his arms through the shoulder straps. He stood with the pack on his back on the brow of the hill looking out across the country, toward the distant river and then struck down the hillside away from the road. Underfoot the ground was good walking. Two hundred yards down the hillside the fire line stopped. Then it was sweet fern, growing ankle high, to walk through, and clumps of jack pines; a long undulating country with frequent rises and descents, sandy underfoot and the country alive again.

Nick kept his direction by the sun. He knew where he wanted to strike the river and he kept on through the pine plain, mounting small rises to see other rises ahead of him and sometimes from the top of a rise a great solid island of pines off to his right or his left. He broke off some sprigs of the heathery sweet fern, and put them under his pack straps. The chafing crushed it and he smelled it as he walked.

He was tired and very hot, walking across the uneven, shadeless pine plain. At any time he knew he could strike the river by turning off to his left. It could not be more than a mile away. But he kept on toward the north to hit the river as far upstream as he could go in one day's walking.

For some time as he walked Nick had been in sight of one of the big islands of pine standing out above the rolling high ground he was crossing. He dipped down and then as he came slowly up to the crest of the ridge he turned and made toward the pine trees.

There was no underbrush in the island of pine trees. The trunks of the trees went straight up or slanted toward each other. The trunks were straight and brown without branches. The branches were high above. Some interlocked to make a solid shadow on the brown forest floor. Around the grove of trees was a bare space. It was brown and soft underfoot as Nick walked on it. This was the over-lapping of the pine needle floor, extending out beyond the width of the high branches. The trees had grown tall and the branches moved high, leaving in the sun this bare space they had once covered with shadow. Sharp at the edge of this extension of the forest floor commenced the sweet fern.

Nick slipped off his pack and lay down in the shade. He lay on his back and looked up into the pine trees. His neck and back and the small of his back rested as he stretched. The earth felt good against his back. He looked up at the sky, through the branches, and then shut his eyes. He opened them and looked up again. There was a wind high up in the branches. He shut his eyes again and went to sleep.

Nick woke stiff and cramped. The sun was nearly down. His pack was heavy and the straps painful as he lifted it on. He leaned over with the pack on and picked up the leather rod-case and started out from the pine trees across the sweet fern swale, toward the river. He knew it could not be more than a mile.

He came down a hillside covered with stumps into a meadow. At the edge of the meadow flowed the river. Nick was glad to get to the river. He walked upstream through the meadow. His trousers were soaked with the dew as he walked. After the hot day, the dew had come quickly and heavily. The river made no sound. It was too fast and smooth. At the edge of the meadow, before he mounted to a piece of high ground to make camp, Nick looked down the river at the trout rising. They were rising to insects come from the swamp on the other side of the stream when the sun went down. The trout jumped out of water to take them. While Nick walked through the little stretch of meadow alongside the stream, trout had jumped high out of the water. Now as he looked down the river, the insects must be settling on the surface, for the trout were feeding steadily all down the stream. As far down the long stretch as he could see, the trout were rising, making circles all down the surface of the water, as though it were starting to rain.

The ground rose, wooded and sandy, to overlook the meadow, the stretch of river and the swamp. Nick dropped his pack and rod-case and looked for a level piece of ground. He was very hungry and he wanted to make his camp before he cooked. Between two jack pines, the ground was quite level. He took the ax out of the pack and chopped out two projecting roots. That leveled a piece of ground large enough to sleep on. He smoothed out the sandy soil with his hand and pulled all the sweet fern bushes by their roots. His hands smelled good from the sweet fern. He smoothed the up-rooted earth. He did not want anything making lumps under the blankets. When he had the ground smooth, he spread his three blankets. One he folded double, next to the ground. The other two he spread on top.

With the ax he slit off a bright slab of pine from one of the stumps and split it into pegs for the tent. He wanted them long and solid to hold in the ground. With the tent unpacked and spread on the ground, the pack, leaning against a jack pine, looked much smaller. Nick tied the rope that served the tent for a ridge-pole to the trunk of one of the pine trees and pulled the tent up off the ground with the other end of the rope and tied it to the other pine. The tent hung on the rope like a canvas blanket on a clothes line. Nick poked a pole he had cut up under the back peak of the canvas and then made it a tent by pegging out the sides. He pegged the sides out taut and drove the pegs deep, hitting them down into the ground with the flat of the ax until the rope loops were buried and the canvas was drum tight.

Across the open mouth of the tent Nick fixed cheese cloth to keep out mosquitoes. He crawled inside under the mosquito bar with various things from the pack to put at the head of the bed under the slant of the canvas. Inside the tent the light came through the brown canvas. It smelled pleasantly of canvas. Already there was something mysterious and homelike. Nick was happy as he crawled inside the tent. He had not been unhappy all day. This was different though. Now things were done. There had been this to do. Now it was done. It had been a hard trip. He was very tired. That was done. He had made his camp. He was settled. Nothing could touch him. It was a good place to camp. He was there, in the good place. He was in his home where he had made it. Now he was hungry.

He came out, crawling under the cheese cloth. It was quite dark outside. It was lighter in the tent.

Nick went over to the pack and found, with his fingers, a long nail in a paper sack of nails, in the bottom of the pack. He drove it into the pine tree, holding it close and hitting it gently with the flat of the ax. He hung the pack up on the nail. All his supplies were in the pack. They were off the ground and sheltered now.

Nick was hungry. He did not believe he had ever been hungrier. He opened and emptied a can of pork and beans and a can of spaghetti into the frying pan.

"I've got a right to eat this kind of stuff, if I'm willing to carry it," Nick said. His voice sounded strange in the darkening woods. He did not speak again.

He started a fire with some chunks of pine he got with the ax from a stump. Over the fire he stuck a wire grill, pushing the four legs down into the ground with his boot. Nick put the frying pan on the grill over the flames. He was hungrier. The beans and spaghetti warmed. Nick stirred them and mixed them together. They began to bubble, making little bubbles that rose with difficulty to the surface. There was a good smell. Nick got out a bottle of tomato catchup and cut four slices of bread. The little bubbles were coming faster now. Nick sat down beside the fire and lifted the frying pan off. He poured about half the contents out into the tin plate. It spread slowly on the plate. Nick knew it was too hot. He poured on some tomato catchup. He knew the beans and spaghetti were still too hot. He looked at the fire, then at the tent, he was not going to spoil it all by burning his tongue. For years he had never enjoyed fried bananas because he had never been able to wait for them to cool. His tongue was very sensitive. He was very hungry. Across the river in the swamp, in the almost dark, he saw a mist rising. He looked at the tent once more. All right. He took a full spoonful from the plate.

"Chrise," Nick said, "Geezus Chrise," he said happily.

He ate the whole panful before he remembered the bread. Nick finished the second plateful with the bread, mopping the plate shiny. He had not eaten since a cup of coffee and a ham sandwich in the station restaurant at St. Ignace. It had been a very fine experience. He had been that hungry before, but had not been able to satisfy it. He could have made camp hours before if he had wanted to. There were plenty of good places to camp on the river. But this was good.

Nick tucked two big chips of pine under the grill. The fire flared up. He had forgotten to get water for the coffee. Out of the pack he got a folding canvas bucket and walked down the hill, across the edge of the meadow, to the stream. The other bank was in the white mist. The grass was wet and cold as he knelt on the bank and dipped the canvas bucket into the stream. It bellied and pulled hard in the current. The water was ice cold. Nick rinsed the bucket and carried it full up to the camp. Up away from the stream it was not so cold.

Nick drove another big nail and hung up the bucket full of water. He dipped the coffee pot half full, put some more chips under the grill onto the fire and put the pot on. He could not remember which way he made coffee. He could remember an argument about it with Hopkins, but not which side he had taken. He decided to bring it to a boil. He remembered now that was Hopkins's way. He had once argued about everything with Hopkins. While he waited for the coffee to boil, he opened a small can of apricots. He liked to open cans. He emptied the can of apricots out into a tin cup. While he watched the coffee on the fire, he drank the juice syrup of the apricots, carefully at first to keep from spilling, then meditatively, sucking the apricots down. They were better than fresh apricots.

The coffee boiled as he watched. The lid came up and coffee and grounds ran down the side of the pot. Nick took it off the grill. It was a triumph for Hopkins. He put sugar in the empty apricot cup and poured some of the coffee out to cool. It was too hot to pour and he used his hat to hold the handle of the coffee pot. He would not let it steep in the pot at all. Not the first cup. It should be straight Hopkins all the way. Hop deserved that. He was a very serious coffee maker. He was the most serious man Nick had ever known. Not heavy, serious. That was a long time ago. Hopkins spoke without moving his lips. He had played polo. He made millions of dollars in Texas. He had borrowed carfare to go to Chicago, when the wire came that his first big well had come in. He could have wired for money. That would have been too slow. They called Hop's girl the Blonde Venus. Hop did not mind because she was not his real girl. Hopkins said very confidently that none of them would make fun of his real girl. He was right. Hopkins went away when the telegram came. That was on the Black River. It took eight days for the telegram to reach him. Hopkins gave away his .22 caliber Colt automatic pistol to Nick. He gave his camera to Bill. It was to remember him always by. They were all going fishing again next summer. The Hop Head was rich. He would get a yacht and they would all cruise along the north shore of Lake Superior. He was excited but serious. They said good-bye and all felt bad. It broke up the trip. They never saw Hopkins again. That was a long time ago on the Black River.

Nick drank the coffee, the coffee according to Hopkins. The coffee was bitter. Nick laughed. It made a good ending to the story. His mind was starting to work. He knew he could choke it because he was tired enough. He spilled the coffee out of the pot and shook the grounds loose into the fire. He lit a cigarette and went inside the tent. He took off his shoes and trousers, sitting on the blankets, rolled the shoes up inside the trousers for a pillow and got in between the blankets.

(Continued on page 657)

The Country

UNKNOWN: Mahatango Valley Farm, 1860

This delightful view of a typical Pennsylvania farm, by someone who probably knew more about farming than he did about art, is painted on a window shade. It demonstrates one of the advantages of being a primitive artist: a more literal-minded professional would not have been able to show such a far-reaching view of the farm unless he had gone up in a balloon. Here the painter has invented his own rules of perspective and gets everything in right up to the horizon. There is a piquant discrepancy, characteristic of primitives, in the comparative sizes of the men, the horses, and the cattle.

WILLIAM SIDNEY MOUNT: Eel Spearing at Setauket, 1845

Mount (1807-1868) took the rural life of Long Island in the second quarter of the nineteenth century for his artistic preserve and rarely strayed from it. He depicted the local farmers with wry affection and avoided any touch of sentimentality as strenuously as they seem to be avoiding work. Mount picked more enjoyable activities to record: *Bargaining for a Horse, Raffling for a Goose, The Power of Music,* or *Dancing on the Barn Floor.* In *Eel Spearing at Setauket (above),* the masterpiece of his middle years, Mount has painted his birthplace. The afternoon sun casts a pervading golden glow over the scene, a lovely countryside that has been touched by civilization but remains uncorrupted. The group of houses in the trees might have been painted by Corot. Mount refused three offers by wealthy patrons to send him to Europe for a final polishing, but the Paris firm of Goupil made reproductions of his work.

THOMAS HART BENTON: July Hay, 1943

While studying in Paris, Benton (born 1889) "wallowed in every ism that came along" but did not really find himself artistically until he returned to his native Missouri in 1924. Having rediscovered the American landscape, he proceeded to fill it with a host of real and legendary characters in his popular murals and easel paintings.

Between 1866 and 1880, Homer brought American genre painting to its highest level, often paralleling in oil the black and white illustrations he contributed to *Harper's Weekly*. Confronted with a group of rural scenes, Henry James, soon to take up permanent residence in Europe, was driven to a paroxysm of prose: "Before Mr. Homer's little barefoot urchins and little girls in calico sunbonnets, straddling beneath a cloudless sky upon the national rail fence, the whole effort of the critic is instinctively to contract himself, to double himself up, as it were, so that he can creep into the problem and examine it humbly and patiently, if a trifle wonderingly. ... He has chosen the least pictorial range of scenery and civilization; he

WINSLOW HOMER: The Country School, 1871

has resolutely treated them as if they were pictorial, as if they were every inch as good as Capri or Tangiers. . . . Mr. Homer has the merit, moreover, that he naturally sees everything at once with its envelope of light and air. He sees not in lines, but in masses, in gross, broad masses. Things come already modeled to his eye. If his masses were only sometimes a trifle more broken, and his brush a good deal richer—if it had a good many more secrets and mysteries and coquetries, he would be, with his vigorous way of looking and seeing, even if fancy in the matter remained the same dead blank, an almost distinguished painter."

GRANT WOOD: American Gothic, 1930

Wood (1892-1941) used his sister and his dentist as the models for the farm couple in his unforgettable double portrait *(above)*. His *Dinner for Threshers* is a loving reconstruction of the rural Iowa of his boyhood. Conceived as a mural, only the oil version and detailed drawings *(opposite, above)* were completed. Pippin (1888-1946) was one of the most gifted of the American primitives. A natural aptitude for painting was stifled by his unprogressive schooling, but he took it up again in middle age as a disabled veteran of World War I, and fashioned from the experience of being black in America an eloquent personal art *(opposite, below)*.

top: GRANT WOOD: Dinner for Threshers, 1934

bottom: HORACE PIPPIN: Domino Players, 1943

CHARLES SHEELER: Bucks County Barn, 1923

Sheeler (1883-1965) had been a pupil of William Merritt Chase, but he banished from his own work the flashing, expressive brushwork that serves as the artist's comment on the scene. The style he chose for himself pursues a different goal. He is as impersonal as the camera and far more clever. Sheeler could see in an ordinary Pennsylvania barn (*above*) the same beauty that he found in a French cathedral. In his pictures the most unpromising industrial landscapes are redeemed from ugliness by his cool appraisal and deft arrangement of the essential architectural forms. Sheeler's superb photographs, such as his 1929 series of the cathedral of Chartres, would guarantee his reputation, even if he had never painted a single picture.

Out through the front of the tent he watched the glow of the fire, when the night wind blew on it. It was a quiet night. The swamp was perfectly quiet. Nick stretched under the blanket comfortably. A mosquito hummed close to his ear. Nick sat up and lit a match. The mosquito was on the canvas, over his head. Nick moved the match quickly up to it. The mosquito made a satisfactory hiss in the flame. The match went out. Nick lay down again under the blankets. He turned on his side and shut his eyes. He was sleepy. He felt sleep coming. He curled up under the blanket and went to sleep.

Big Two-Hearted River

PART II

In the morning the sun was up and the tent was starting to get hot. Nick crawled out under the mosquito netting stretched across the mouth of the tent, to look at the morning. The grass was wet on his hands as he came out. He held his trousers and his shoes in his hands. The sun was just up over the hill. There was the meadow, the river and the swamp. There were birch trees in the green of the swamp on the other side of the river.

The river was clear and smoothly fast in the early morning. Down about two hundred yards were three logs all the way across the stream. They made the water smooth and deep above them. As Nick watched, a mink crossed the river on the logs and went into the swamp. Nick was excited. He was excited by the early morning and the river. He was really too hurried to eat breakfast, but he knew he must. He built a little fire and put on the coffee pot. While the water was heating in the pot he took an empty bottle and went down over the edge of the high ground to the meadow. The meadow was wet with dew and Nick wanted to catch grasshoppers for bait before the sun dried the grass. He found plenty of good grasshoppers. They were at the base of the grass stems. Sometimes they clung to a grass stem. They were cold and wet with the dew, and could not jump until the sun warmed them. Nick picked them up, taking only the medium sized brown ones, and put them into the bottle. He turned over a log and just under the shelter of the edge were several hundred hoppers. It was a grasshopper lodging house. Nick put about fifty of the medium browns into the bottle. While he was picking up the hoppers the others warmed in the sun and commenced to hop away. They flew when they hopped. At first they made one flight and stayed stiff when they landed, as though they were dead.

Nick knew that by the time he was through with breakfast they would be as lively as ever. Without dew in the grass it would take him all day to catch a bottle full of good grasshoppers and he would have to crush many of them, slamming at them with his hat. He washed his hands at the stream. He was excited to be near it. Then he walked up to the tent. The hoppers were already jumping stiffly in the grass. In the bottle, warmed by the sun, they were jumping in a mass. Nick put in a pine stick as a cork. It plugged the mouth of the bottle enough, so the hoppers could not get out and left plenty of air passage.

He had rolled the log back and knew he could get grasshoppers there every morning.

Nick laid the bottle full of jumping grasshoppers against a pine trunk. Rapidly he mixed some buckwheat flour with water and stirred it smooth, one cup of flour, one cup of water. He put a handful of coffee in the pot and dipped a lump of grease out of a can and slid it sputtering across the hot skillet. On the smoking skillet he poured smoothly the buckwheat batter. It spread like lava, the grease spitting sharply. Around the edges the buckwheat cake began to firm, then brown, then crisp. The surface was bubbling slowly to porousness. Nick pushed under the browned under surface with a fresh pine chip. He shook the skillet sideways and the cake was loose on the surface. I won't try and flop it, he thought. He slid the chip of clean wood all the way under the cake, and flopped it over onto its face. It sputtered in the pan.

When it was cooked Nick regreased the skillet. He used all the batter. It made another big flapjack and one smaller one.

Nick ate a big flapjack and a smaller one, covered with apple butter. He put apple butter on the third cake, folded it over twice, wrapped it in oiled paper and put it in his shirt pocket. He put the apple butter jar back in the pack and cut bread for two sandwiches.

In the pack he found a big onion. He sliced it in two and peeled the silky outer skin. Then he cut one half into slices and made onion sandwiches. He wrapped them in oiled paper and buttoned them in the other pocket of his khaki shirt. He turned the skillet upside down on the grill, drank the coffee, sweetened and yellow brown with the condensed milk in it, and tidied up the camp. It was a nice little camp.

Nick took his fly rod out of the leather rod-case, jointed it, and shoved the rod-case back into the tent. He put on the reel and threaded the line through the guides. He had to hold it from hand to hand, as he threaded it, or it would slip back through its own weight. It was a heavy, double tapered fly line. Nick had paid eight dollars for it a long time ago. It was made heavy to lift back in the air and come forward flat and heavy and straight to make it possible to cast a fly which has no weight. Nick opened the aluminum leader box. The leaders were coiled between the damp flannel pads. Nick had wet the pads at the water cooler on the train up to St. Ignace. In the damp pads the gut leaders had softened and Nick unrolled one and tied it by a loop at the end to the heavy fly line. He fastened a hook on the end of the leader. It was a small hook; very thin and springy.

Nick took it from his hook book, sitting with the rod across his lap. He tested the knot and the spring of the rod by pulling the line taut. It was a good feeling. He was careful not to let the hook bite into his finger.

He started down to the stream, holding his rod, the bottle of grasshoppers hung from his neck by a thong tied in half hitches around the neck of the bottle. His landing net hung by a hook from his belt. Over his shoulder was a long flour sack tied at each corner into an ear. The cord went over his shoulder. The sack flapped against his legs.

Nick felt awkward and professionally happy with all his equipment hanging from him. The grasshopper bottle swung against his chest. In his shirt the breast pockets bulged against him with the lunch and his fly book.

He stepped into the stream. It was a shock. His trousers clung tight to his legs. His shoes felt the gravel. The water was a rising cold shock.

Rushing, the current sucked against his legs. Where he stepped in, the water was over his knees. He waded with the current. The gravel slid under his shoes. He looked down at the swirl of water below each leg and tipped up the bottle to get a grasshopper.

The first grasshopper gave a jump in the neck of the bottle and went out into the water. He was sucked under in the whirl by Nick's right leg and came to the surface a little way down stream. He floated rapidly, kicking. In a quick circle, breaking the smooth surface of the water, he disappeared. A trout had taken him.

Another hopper poked his head out of the bottle. His antennae wavered. He was getting his front legs out of the bottle to jump. Nick took him by the head and held him while he threaded the slim hook under his chin, down through his thorax and into the last segments of his abdomen. The grasshopper took hold of the hook with his front feet, spitting tobacco juice on it. Nick dropped him into the water.

Holding the rod in his right hand he let out line against the pull of the grasshopper in the current. He stripped off line from the reel with his left hand and let it run free. He could see the hopper in the little waves of the current. It went out of sight.

There was a tug on the line. Nick pulled against the taut line. It was his first strike. Holding the now living rod across the current, he brought in the line with his left hand. The rod bent in jerks, the trout pumping against the current. Nick knew it was a small one. He lifted the rod straight up in the air. It bowed with the pull.

He saw the trout in the water jerking with his head and body against the shifting tangent of the line in the stream.

Nick took the line in his left hand and pulled the trout, thumping tiredly against the current, to the surface. His back was mottled the clear, water-over-gravel color, his side flashing in the sun. The rod under his right arm, Nick stooped, dipping his right hand into the current. He held the trout, never still, with his moist right hand, while he unhooked the barb from his mouth, then dropped him back into the stream.

He hung unsteadily in the current, then settled to the bottom beside a stone. Nick reached down his hand to touch him, his arm to the elbow under water. The trout was steady in the moving stream, resting on the gravel, beside a stone. As Nick's fingers touched him, touched his smooth, cool, underwater feeling he was gone, gone in a shadow across the bottom of the stream.

He's all right, Nick thought. He was only tired.

He had wet his hand before he touched the trout, so he would not disturb the delicate mucus that covered him. If a trout was touched with a dry hand, a white fungus attacked the unprotected spot. Years before when he had fished crowded streams, with fly fishermen ahead of him and behind him, Nick had again and again come on dead trout, furry with white fungus, drifted against a rock, or floating belly up in some pool. Nick did not like to fish with other men on the river. Unless they were of your party, they spoiled it.

He wallowed down the stream, above his knees in the current, through the fifty yards of shallow water above the pile of logs that crossed the stream. He did not rebait his hook and held it in his hand as he waded. He was certain he could catch small trout in the shallows, but he did not want them. There would be no big trout in the shallows this time of day.

Now the water deepened up his thighs sharply and coldly. Ahead was the smooth dammed-back flood of water above the logs. The water was smooth and dark; on the left, the lower edge of the meadow; on the right the swamp.

Nick leaned back against the current and took a hopper from the bottle. He threaded the hopper on the hook and spat on him for good luck. Then he pulled several yards of line from the reel and tossed the hopper out ahead onto the fast, dark water. It floated down toward the logs, then the weight of the line pulled the bait under the surface. Nick held the rod in his right hand, letting the line run out through his fingers.

There was a long tug. Nick struck and the rod came alive and dangerous, bent double, the line tightening, coming out of water, tightening, all in a heavy, dangerous, steady pull. Nick felt the moment when the leader would break if the strain increased and let the line go.

The reel ratcheted into a mechanical shriek as the line went out in a rush. Too fast. Nick could not check it, the line rushing out, the reel note rising as the line ran out.

With the core of the reel showing, his heart feeling stopped with the excitement, leaning back against the current that mounted icily his thighs, Nick thumbed the reel hard with his left hand. It was awkward getting his thumb inside the fly reel frame.

As he put on pressure the line tightened into sudden hardness and beyond the logs a huge trout went high out of water. As he jumped, Nick lowered the tip of the rod. But he felt, as he dropped the tip to ease the strain, the moment when the strain was too great; the hardness too tight. Of course, the leader had broken. There was no mistaking the feeling when all spring left the line and it became dry and hard. Then it went slack.

His mouth dry, his heart down, Nick reeled in. He had never seen so big a trout. There was a heaviness, a power not to be held, and then the bulk of him, as he jumped. He looked as broad as a salmon.

Nick's hand was shaky. He reeled in slowly. The thrill had been too much. He felt, vaguely, a little sick, as though it would be better to sit down.

The leader had broken where the hook was tied to it. Nick took it in his hand. He thought of the trout somewhere on the bottom, holding himself steady over the gravel, far down below the light, under the logs, with the hook in his jaw. Nick knew the trout's teeth would cut through the snell of the hook. The hook would imbed itself in his jaw. He'd bet the trout was angry. Anything that size would be angry. That was a trout. He had been solidly hooked. Solid as a rock. He felt like a rock, too, before he started off. By God, he was a big one. By God, he was the biggest one I ever heard of.

Nick climbed out onto the meadow and stood, water running down his trousers and out of his shoes. He went over and sat on the logs. He did not want to rush his sensations any.

He wriggled his toes in the water, in his shoes, and got out a cigarette from his breast pocket. He lit it and tossed the match into the fast water below the logs. A tiny trout rose at the match, as it swung around in the fast current. Nick laughed. He would finish the cigarette.

He sat on the logs, smoking, drying in the sun, the sun warm on his back, the river shallow ahead entering the woods, curving into the woods, shallows, light glittering, big water-smooth rocks, cedars along the bank and white birches, the logs warm in the sun, smooth to sit on, without bark, gray to the touch; slowly the feeling of disappointment left him. It went away slowly, the feeling of disappointment that came sharply after the thrill that made his shoulders ache. It was all right now. His rod lying out on the logs, Nick tied a new hook on the leader, pulling the gut tight until it grimped into itself in a hard knot.

He baited up, then picked up the rod and walked to the far end of the logs to get into the water, where it was not too deep. Under and beyond the logs was a deep pool. Nick walked around the shallow shelf near the swamp shore until he came out on the shallow bed of the stream.

On the left, where the meadow ended and the woods began, a great elm tree was uprooted. Gone over in a storm, it lay back into the woods, its roots clotted with dirt, grass growing in them, rising a solid bank beside the stream. The river cut to the edge of the uprooted tree. From where Nick stood he could see deep channels, like ruts, cut in the shallow bed of the stream by the flow of the current. Pebbly where he stood and pebbly and full of boulders beyond; where it curved near the tree roots, the bed of the stream was marly and between the ruts of deep water green weed fronds swung in the current.

Nick swung the rod back over his shoulder and forward, and the line, curving forward, laid the grasshopper down on one of the deep channels in the weeds. A trout struck and Nick hooked him.

Holding the rod far out toward the uprooted tree and sloshing backward in the current, Nick worked the trout, plunging, the rod bending alive, out of the danger of the weeds into the open river. Holding the rod, pumping alive against the current, Nick brought the trout in. He rushed, but always came, the spring of the rod yielding to the rushes, sometimes jerking under water, but always bringing him in. Nick eased downstream with the rushes. The rod above his head he led the trout over the net, then lifted.

The trout hung heavy in the net, mottled trout back and silver sides in the meshes. Nick unhooked him; heavy sides, good to hold, big undershot jaw, and slipped him, heaving and big sliding, into the long sack that hung from his shoulders in the water.

Nick spread the mouth of the sack against the current and it filled, heavy with water. He held it up, the bottom in the stream, and the water poured out through the sides. Inside at the bottom was the big trout, alive in the water.

Nick moved downstream. The sack out ahead of him, sunk, heavy in the water, pulling from his shoulders.

It was getting hot, the sun hot on the back of his neck.

Nick had one good trout. He did not care about getting many trout. Now the stream was shallow and wide. There were trees along both banks. The trees of the left bank made short shadows on the current in the forenoon sun. Nick knew there were trout in each shadow. In the afternoon, after the sun had crossed toward the hills, the trout would be in the cool shadows on the other side of the stream.

The very biggest ones would lie up close to the bank. You could always pick them up there on the Black. When the sun was down they all moved out into the current. Just when the sun made the water blinding in the glare before it went down, you were liable to strike a big trout anywhere in the current. It was almost impossible to fish then, the surface of the water was blinding as a mirror in the sun. Of course, you could fish upstream, but in a stream like the Black, or this, you had to wallow against the current and in a deep place, the water piled up on you. It was no fun to fish upstream with this much current.

Nick moved along through the shallow stretch watching the banks for deep holes. A beech tree grew close beside the river, so that the branches hung down into the water. The stream went back in under the leaves. There were always trout in a place like that.

Nick did not care about fishing that hole. He was sure he would get hooked in the branches.

It looked deep though. He dropped the grasshopper so the current took it under water, back in under the overhanging branch. The line pulled hard and Nick struck. The trout threshed heavily, half out of water in the leaves and branches. The line was caught. Nick pulled hard and the trout was off. He reeled in and holding the hook in his hand, walked down the stream.

Ahead, close to the left bank, was a big log. Nick saw it was hollow; pointing up river the current entered it smoothly, only a little ripple spread each side of the log. The water was deepening. The top of the hollow log was gray and dry. It was partly in the shadow.

Nick took the cork out of the grasshopper bottle and a hopper clung to it. He picked him off, hooked him and tossed him out. He held the rod far out so that the hopper on the water moved into the current flowing into the hollow log. Nick lowered the rod and the hopper floated in. There was a heavy strike. Nick swung the rod against the pull. It felt as though he were hooked into the log itself, except for the live feeling.

He tried to force the fish out into the current. It came, heavily.

The line went slack and Nick thought the trout was gone. Then he saw him, very near, in the current, shaking his head, trying to get the hook out. His mouth was clamped shut. He was fighting the hook in the clear flowing current.

Looping in the line with his left hand, Nick swung the rod to make the line taut and tried to lead the trout toward the net, but he was gone, out of sight, the line pumping. Nick fought him against the current, letting him thump in the water against the spring of the rod. He shifted the rod to his left hand, worked the trout upstream, holding his weight, fighting on the rod, and then let him down into the net. He lifted him clear of the water, a heavy half circle in the net, the net dripping, unhooked him and slid him into the sack.

He spread the mouth of the sack and looked down in at the two big trout alive in the water.

Through the deepening water, Nick waded over to the hollow log. He took the sack off, over his head, the trout flopping as it came out of water, and hung it so the trout were deep in the water. Then he pulled himself up on the log and sat, the water from his trousers and boots running down into the stream. He laid his rod down, moved along to the shady end of the log and took the sandwiches out of his pocket. He dipped the sandwiches in the cold water. The current carried away the crumbs. He ate the sandwiches and dipped his hat full of water to drink, the water running out through his hat just ahead of his drinking.

It was cool in the shade, sitting on the log. He took a cigarette out and struck a match to light it. The match sunk into the gray wood, making a tiny furrow. Nick leaned over the side of the log, found a hard place and lit the match. He sat smoking and watching the river.

Ahead the river narrowed and went into a swamp. The river became smooth and deep and the swamp looked solid with cedar trees, their trunks close together, their branches solid. It would not be possible to walk through a swamp like that. The branches grew so low. You would have to keep almost level with the ground to move at all. You could not crash through the branches. That must be why the animals that live in swamps were built the way they were, Nick thought.

He wished he had brought something to read. He felt like reading. He did not feel like going on into the swamp. He looked down the river. A big cedar slanted all the way across the stream. Beyond that the river went into the swamp.

Nick did not want to go in there now. He felt a reaction against deep wading with the water deepening up under his armpits, to hook big trout in places impossible to land them. In the swamp the banks were bare, the big cedars came together overhead, the sun did not come through, except in patches; in the fast deep water, in the half light, the fishing would be tragic. In the swamp fishing was a tragic adventure. Nick did not want it. He did not want to go down the stream any further today.

He took out his knife, opened it and stuck it in the log. Then he pulled up the sack, reached into it and brought out one of the trout. Holding him near the tail, hard to hold, alive, in his hand, he whacked him against the log. The trout quivered, rigid. Nick laid him on the log in the shade and broke the neck of the other fish the same way. He laid them side by side on the log. They were fine trout.

Nick cleaned them, slitting them from the vent to the tip of the jaw. All the insides and the gills and tongue came out in one piece. They were both males; long gray-white strips of milt, smooth and clean. All the insides clean and compact, coming out all together. Nick tossed the offal ashore for the minks to find.

He washed the trout in the stream. When he held them back up in the water they looked like live fish. Their color was not gone yet. He washed his hands and dried them on the log. Then he laid the trout on the sack spread out on the log, rolled them up in it, tied the bundle and put it in the landing net. His knife was still standing, blade stuck in the log. He cleaned it on the wood and put it in his pocket.

Nick stood up on the log, holding his rod, the landing net hanging heavy, then stepped into the water and splashed ashore. He climbed the bank and cut up into the woods, toward the high ground. He was going back to camp. He looked back. The river just showed through the trees. There were plenty of days coming when he could fish the swamp.

QUESTIONS FOR DISCUSSION

Part I

1. It is important in understanding this story to know that Nick Adams has returned home from World War I, in which he was wounded. He leaves home for a camping trip in northern Michigan, the scene of earlier stories from *In Our Time*. Why do you think Nick seeks out such a desolate place as Seney, Michigan? Why is it ironically appropriate that Seney should be even more desolate than he had expected?

2. The town is not as Nick had expected to find it, but Hemingway writes, "The river was there," and Nick watches "the trout keeping themselves steady in the current." How do these two elements of nature serve as part of the necessary counterbalance to Nick's own instability?

3. From the outset the reader can sense the rudimentary simplicity of Hemingway's style in this story, for example:

   Nick looked down into the pool from the bridge. It was a hot day. A kingfisher flew up the stream. It was a long time since Nick had looked into a stream and seen trout. They were very satisfactory.

   What mood do you feel the language creates by its plainness and childlike diction? Find several other passages to support your observation.

4. What does Nick notice about the grasshopper? Why is this example of adaptation to environment important as a clue to Nick's experience? Do you remember any other instances in literature in which a creature of nature provides insight for a man?

5. Do you find it significant that Nick must pass through the burned-over land before coming to where he finds "the country alive again"? Explain your answer.

6. After the tent has been erected, the narrator expresses Nick's thoughts in a succession of little sentences:

   Now things were done. There had been this to do. Now it was done. It had been a hard trip. He was very tired. That was done. He had made his camp. He was settled. Nothing could touch him. It was a good place to camp. He was there, in the good place. He was in his home where he had made it. Now he was hungry.

   Explain how Hemingway's diction and syntax produce the mood you sense in this passage.

7. Nick cooks his beans and spaghetti together, and Hemingway writes, "There was a good smell." He does not describe the aroma of the food, just as he has not described the smell of the fern. Why does

the author choose not to describe this sense impression? Is his option more effective or less?

8. Why does Nick remember Hopkins? What effect does this recollection have upon Nick's present experience? In what sense does Hopkins serve as a link with the past that Nick is trying to forget? Why does Nick feel the need to "choke" his mind before it begins to work?

9. The action in Part I is so minimal that one might be tempted to say, "Nothing happens." But this is not so; much happens to Nick from the time he leaves the train to the time he falls asleep. What progression do you notice? What has Nick left behind to make this progression possible?

Part II

10. After breakfast the next morning, Nick thinks "It was a nice little camp." But the narrator has already told us how excited Nick is by "the early morning and the river." What does the phrase "It was a nice little camp" show about Nick's state of mind?

11. What evidence does Hemingway give to show that Nick prides himself on his preparation for trout fishing and prides himself on his knowledge of nature? Why does he not like to fish with men whom he does not know?

12. After almost landing the big trout, Nick feels that "the thrill had been too much." What is happening to Nick now? Is such a reaction to excitement normal or peculiar to someone in Nick's state of mind? What does Hemingway mean when he says that Nick "did not want to rush his sensations any"?

13. Why does Nick not want to enter the swamp? Why does he feel that there "the fishing would be tragic"? Do you see any larger meaning in the distinction between the clear, free-flowing river and the darkened swamp? Does Nick?

14. The story ends with Nick's thought that "there were plenty of days coming when he could fish the swamp." How has his experience in Part II given him this assurance? What does he expect to find in the swamp? How must he prepare himself for this expectation?

15. Earl Rovit says that "Big Two-Hearted River" is a story "which generates its power not from what it actually says, but from what it does not say. . . . This technique, which we may call 'the irony of the unsaid,' is one of Hemingway's favorite tricks and one of his most powerful ways of transmitting the shock of emotion in prose." Discuss this critical observation. How does it apply to "Big Two-Hearted River"?

16. This story depends upon the familiar *journey* theme and so operates at two levels: the literal fishing trip and Nick's journey into his own psychic consciousness. To what other works of literature is "Big Two-Hearted River" similar in this respect? Does the story achieve its purpose at the literal level? at the figurative?

17. In an interview Hemingway said, "Read anything I write for the pleasure of reading it. Whatever else you find will be the measure of what you brought to the reading." Is it possible to enjoy this story fully without being an experienced fisherman? How much of the reader's appreciation for the story depends upon being able to identify with Nick's emotional condition? Is Hemingway right in his analysis of "whatever else" the reader finds in the story?

ASSIGNMENTS FOR WRITING

1. Recall an incident from your experience that you remember as having been tranquil and quiet. Write a paragraph in which you attempt to project that mood to your reader.
2. As an experiment in style imitation, write a continuation of "Big Two-Hearted River, Part II," in which you show Nick returning to camp and cooking his trout for supper. When finished, look back at the passages describing his cooking in Parts I and II. How successful has your imitation been?
3. Carlos Baker has written of "Big Two-Hearted River":

   The story is full of rituals. . . . The whole of the fishing is conducted according to the ritualistic codes of fair play. . . . Down under, in short, the close reader finds a carefully determined order of virtue and simplicity which goes towards explaining from below the oddly satisfying effect of the surface story.

   Write a critical essay in which you offer evidence from the text in support of Professor Baker's comment. If you disagree with his interpretation, argue with it, using evidence from the story.
4. For contrast with "Big Two-Hearted River," read "The End of Something," another Nick Adams story from *In Our Time*. In an essay, discuss Hemingway's use of dialogue (an element of narrative missing from "Big Two-Hearted River") and the differences you notice in the personality of Nick Adams in the company of Marjorie.

William Faulkner

It is easy to discover the biographical facts concerning William Faulkner. Textbooks, biographical dictionaries, encyclopedias, dust jackets, literary magazines and journals, periodicals (especially those dated within the first few weeks after the author's death) carry the essentials regarding his birth and life. Most of them relate, in varying degrees of detail, that Faulkner was born in New Albany, Mississippi, September 25, 1897, the first child of Murray and Maud Butler Falkner; that the family moved to Oxford, Mississippi, in 1902, where Faulkner maintained residence for the rest of his life; that he never completed high school although he took special courses during later years at the University of Mississippi in Oxford; that he joined the Royal Flying Corps in Toronto, Canada, for training in World War I; that he worked briefly in a book store in New York City before returning to Oxford to become first a carpenter and painter-about-town and then the postmaster at the University; that he resigned from his office in 1924, the year in which *The Marble Faun*, his first book, a collection of poems, was published; that he spent the next six months in New Orleans working for a newspaper and contributing to a literary magazine, while, at the same time, establishing friendship with Sherwood Anderson; that here, encouraged by Anderson, who, as a recognized writer on the American scene, was invaluable in guiding Faulkner through the intricacies of getting into print, he wrote his first novel, *Soldier's Pay*; that the success of this novel resulted in a contract for a second book, *Mosquitoes*, which was published in 1927; and that from this time on Faulkner was irretrievably launched into his full-scale career as a writer.

All of the biographical sources continue with the fact of his marriage to Estelle (Oldham) Franklin in 1929, the year in which *Sartoris* and *The Sound and the Fury* were published. William Van

O'Connor defined the latter book as "the work of a major writer." Certainly it marked the beginning of what many critics and Faulkner scholars designate as the most important ten years of his writing career. It was a decade highlighted by such successes as *As I Lay Dying, Sanctuary, These Thirteen* (a collection of short stories), *Light in August, Absalom, Absalom!, The Unvanquished,* and *The Wild Palms.* These were followed by such titles as *The Hamlet, Go Down, Moses, and Other Stories, Intruder in the Dust, Collected Stories of William Faulkner, Requiem for a Nun, A Fable, The Town, Three Famous Short Novels, The Mansion,* and his last book, *The Reivers,* published a month before his death.

Faulkner's power as a writer began to be recognized at home and abroad in the mid-forties, and his place as one of the giants in the American literary tradition was assured by his receiving the Nobel Prize for Literature in 1950. His acceptance speech, delivered at Stockholm in December of that year, is a moving personal credo directed particularly to young writers. He received the Pulitzer Prize for *A Fable* in 1954, and in the position of cultural representative, or special emissary of the State Department, he visited Greece, Japan, and several European countries during the mid-fifties. In the spring semesters of 1957 to 1961 he was writer-in-residence at the University of Virginia in Charlottesville. Taped recordings of his talks and conferences with various student and faculty groups have been collected, edited, and published under the title *Faulkner in the University.* The tapes give insight into his thinking as well as into the short stories and novels about which he was questioned specifically. Faulkner and his wife returned to their home in Oxford for the summer vacation periods, and he died there, following a heart attack, July 6, 1962.

Although it is easy to discover the basic facts concerning William Faulkner, it is not easy to discover the essence of the man. An author usually reveals himself through his writings, but Faulkner made knowledge of his inner self difficult for his readers because of his complex style. Perhaps Robert Penn Warren has expressed it best:

> William Faulkner has written nineteen books which, for range of effect, philosophical weight, originality of style, are without equal in our time and country. Let us grant, even so, that there are grave defects in Faulkner's works. Sometimes the tragic intensity becomes mere emotionalism, the technical virtuosity mere complication, the philosophical weight mere confusion of mind. Let us grant that much, for Faulkner is a very uneven writer. The unevenness is, in

a way, an index to his vitality, his willingness to take risks, to try for new effects, to make new explorations of material and method.

Faulkner himself said in lectures at the University of Virginia, "I don't know anything about style . . . I think a writer with a lot . . . pushing inside him to get out hasn't got time to bother with style. If he just likes to write and hasn't got anything urging him, then he can become a stylist, but the ones with a great deal pushing to get out don't have time to be anything but clumsy." A part of his own clumsiness, as many people scornful of his style point out, is his use of long sentences, which sometimes cover several pages. When asked his purpose in using this particular structure, he explained that "the long sentence is an attempt to get his [a man's or a character's] past and possibly his future into the instant when he does something." Faulkner's appreciation and approval of good writing style, however, are intimated in his rather wistful remark, "I wish that I did have a good, lucid, simple method of telling stories."

But he always defended the writer's, his or any other's, "prerogative to create his own language" *if* he doesn't "insist on anyone understanding it." He explained this statement in the words: "He doesn't have to write it in the way that every idiot can understand it . . . but he's got to use a language which is accepted and in which the words have specific meanings that everybody agrees on." His belief in using words of such import is reflected in his practice of writing in the idiom of his fictional Mississippians. Had he adopted more formal diction, the effect would have been untrue and hence unnatural. He believed in the responsibility of the reader to understand familiar words even in an unfamiliar pattern of usage and thus did not hesitate to make daring use of new techniques. Especially daring was his handling of the stream-of-consciousness method.

More important than an understanding of Faulkner's style, however, are a recognition of the two forces which dominated him and an awareness of the part those forces played in the creation of his fictional characters. The forces were his belief in the "old universal truths . . . love and honor and pity and pride and compassion and sacrifice," which he affirmed in his Nobel Prize acceptance speech, and his liking of people, which he affirmed over and over in countless conversations and interviews. "I'm interested primarily in people, in man in conflict with himself, with his fellow man, or with his time and place, his environment," he said, and, again, "You write a story to tell about people, man in his constant struggle with his own heart, with the hearts of others, or with his environment."

It is difficult, at first, to reconcile the illiterate, depraved, selfish, stubborn, unbalanced, cruel, even dull characters (which many people falsely think were the only kinds that Faulkner created) with the ideals expressed in the Nobel Prize speech. It is easier to understand the relationship, however, when we realize that, in the words of Lawrance Thompson, Faulkner often "defined his positive idealism in terms of negatives." Viewed in this light, the generations of characters with which he peopled his famous fictitious county, Yoknapatawpha, Mississippi, assume an importance which, at first reading, they might not have seemed to warrant. This is Faulkner's challenge, that even such people as these have their place in the struggle of the human heart against those circumstances it finds itself in. And if one accepts the fact that reading Faulkner is not easy, if one nonetheless takes up this task, and if one gives his best efforts and attention to such a study, then he will find the essence of the man.

Faulkner's boldness in attempting new writing forms, his concern with the qualities that are in conflict in the heart of man, fictional or real, and his accomplishment in creating a locale and its inhabitants that have become so familiar that they seem real to thousands of readers assure him a permanent and deserved place in American literary acclaim. It seems no more than appropriate, then, in the light of Thompson's idea, to express the full impact of the man and his works as ". . . no sounding brass . . . no tinkling cymbal." He is more, much more, than these isolated parts of a majestic whole.

A Rose for Emily

When Miss Emily Grierson died, our whole town went to her funeral: the men through a sort of respectful affection for a fallen monument, the women mostly out of curiosity to see the inside of her house, which no one save an old manservant—a combined gardener and cook—had seen in at least ten years.

It was a big, squarish frame house that had once been white, decorated with cupolas and spires and scrolled balconies in the heavily lightsome style of the seventies, set on what had once been our most select street. But garages and cotton gins had encroached and obliterated even the august names of that neighborhood; only Miss Emily's house was left, lifting its stubborn and coquettish decay above the cotton wagons and the gasoline pumps—an eyesore among eyesores. And now Miss Emily had gone to join the representatives of those august names where they lay in the cedar-bemused cemetery among the ranked and anonymous graves of Union and Confederate soldiers who fell at the battle of Jefferson.

Alive, Miss Emily had been a tradition, a duty, and a care; a sort of hereditary obligation upon the town, dating from that day in 1894 when Colonel Sartoris, the mayor—he who fathered the edict that no Negro woman should appear on the streets without an apron—remitted her taxes, the dispensation dating from the death of her father on into perpetuity. Not that Miss Emily would have accepted charity. Colonel Sartoris invented an involved tale to the effect that Miss Emily's father had loaned money to the town, which the town, as a matter of business, preferred this way of repaying. Only a man of Colonel Sartoris' generation and thought could have invented it, and only a woman could have believed it.

When the next generation, with its more modern ideas, became mayors and aldermen, this arrangement created some little dissatisfaction. On the first of the year they mailed her a tax notice. February came, and there was no reply. They wrote her a formal letter, asking her to call at the sheriff's office at her convenience.

A week later the mayor wrote her himself, offering to call or to send his car for her, and received in reply a note on paper of an archaic shape, in a thin, flowing calligraphy in faded ink, to the effect that she no longer went out at all. The tax notice was also enclosed, without comment.

They called a special meeting of the Board of Aldermen. A deputation waited upon her, knocked at the door through which no visitor had passed since she ceased giving china-painting lessons eight or ten years earlier. They were admitted by the old Negro into a dim hall from which a stairway mounted into still more shadow. It smelled of dust and disuse—a close, dank smell. The Negro led them into the parlor. It was furnished in heavy, leather-covered furniture. When the Negro opened the blinds of one window, they could see that the leather was cracked; and when they sat down, a faint dust rose sluggishly about their thighs, spinning with slow motes in the single sun-ray. On a tarnished gilt easel before the fireplace stood a crayon portrait of Miss Emily's father.

They rose when she entered—a small, fat woman in black, with a thin gold chain descending to her waist and vanishing into her belt, leaning on an ebony cane with a tarnished gold head. Her skeleton was small and spare; perhaps that was why what would have been merely plumpness in another was obesity in her. She looked bloated, like a body long submerged in motionless water, and of that pallid hue. Her eyes, lost in the fatty ridges of her face, looked like two small pieces of coal pressed into a lump of dough as they moved from one face to another while the visitors stated their errand.

She did not ask them to sit. She just stood in the door and listened quietly until the spokesman came to a stumbling halt. Then they could hear the invisible watch ticking at the end of the gold chain.

Her voice was dry and cold. "I have no taxes in Jefferson. Colonel Sartoris explained it to me. Perhaps one of you can gain access to the city records and satisfy yourselves."

"But we have. We are the city authorities, Miss Emily. Didn't you get a notice from the sheriff, signed by him?"

"I received a paper, yes," Miss Emily said. "Perhaps he considers himself the sheriff . . . I have no taxes in Jefferson."

"But there is nothing on the books to show that, you see. We must go by the—"

"See Colonel Sartoris. I have no taxes in Jefferson."

"But, Miss Emily—"

"See Colonel Sartoris." (Colonel Sartoris had been dead almost ten years.) "I have no taxes in Jefferson. Tobe!" The Negro appeared. "Show these gentlemen out."

2

So she vanquished them, horse and foot, just as she had vanquished their fathers thirty years before about the smell. That was two years after her father's death and a short time after her sweetheart—the one we believed would marry her—had deserted her. After her father's death she went out very little; after her sweetheart went away, people hardly saw her at all. A few of the ladies had the temerity to call, but were not received, and the only sign of life about the place was the Negro man—a young man then —going in and out with a market basket.

"Just as if a man—any man—could keep a kitchen properly," the ladies said; so they were not surprised when the smell developed. It was another link between the gross, teeming world and the high and mighty Griersons.

A neighbor, a woman, complained to the mayor, Judge Stevens, eighty years old.

"But what will you have me do about it, madam?" he said.

"Why, send her word to stop it," the woman said. "Isn't there a law?"

"I'm sure that won't be necessary," Judge Stevens said. "It's probably just a snake or a rat that nigger of hers killed in the yard. I'll speak to him about it."

The next day he received two more complaints, one from a man who came in diffident deprecation. "We really must do something about it, Judge. I'd be the last one in the world to bother Miss Emily, but we've got to do something." That night the Board of Aldermen met—three graybeards and one younger man, a member of the rising generation.

"It's simple enough," he said. "Send her word to have her place cleaned up. Give her a certain time to do it, and if she don't . . ."

"Dammit, sir," Judge Stevens said, "will you accuse a lady to her face of smelling bad?"

So the next night, after midnight, four men crossed Miss Emily's lawn and slunk about the house like burglars, sniffing along the base of the brickwork and at the cellar openings while one of them performed a regular sowing motion with his hand out of a sack slung from his shoulder. They broke open the cellar door and sprinkled lime there, and in all the outbuildings. As they recrossed the lawn, a window that had been dark was lighted and Miss Emily sat in it, the light behind her, and her upright torso motionless as that of an idol. They crept quietly across the lawn and into the shadow of the locusts that lined the street. After a week or two the smell went away.

That was when people had begun to feel really sorry for her. People in our town, remembering how old lady Wyatt, her great-aunt, had gone completely crazy at last, believed that the Griersons held themselves a little too high for what they really were. None of the young men were quite good enough for Miss Emily and such. We had long thought of them as a tableau, Miss Emily a slender figure in white in the background, her father a spraddled silhouette in the foreground, his back to her and clutching a horse-whip, the two of them framed by the back-flung front door. So when she got to be thirty and was still single, we were not pleased exactly, but vindicated; even with insanity in the family she wouldn't have turned down all of her chances if they had really materialized.

When her father died, it got about that the house was all that was left to her; and in a way, people were glad. At last they could pity Miss Emily. Being left alone, and a pauper, she had become humanized. Now she too would know the old thrill and the old despair of a penny more or less.

The day after his death all the ladies prepared to call at the house and offer condolence and aid, as is our custom. Miss Emily met them at the door, dressed as usual and with no trace of grief on her face. She told them that her father was not dead. She did that for three days, with the ministers calling on her, and the doctors, trying to persuade her to let them dispose of the body. Just as they were about to resort to law and force, she broke down, and they buried her father quickly.

We did not say she was crazy then. We believed she had to do that. We remembered all the young men her father had driven away, and we knew that with nothing left, she would have to cling to that which had robbed her, as people will.

3

She was sick for a long time. When we saw her again, her hair was cut short, making her look like a girl, with a vague resemblance to those angels in colored church windows—sort of tragic and serene.

The town had just let the contracts for paving the sidewalks, and in the summer after her father's death they began the work. The construction company came with niggers and mules and machinery, and a foreman named Homer Barron, a Yankee—a big, dark, ready man, with a big voice and eyes lighter than his face. The little boys would follow in groups to hear him cuss the niggers, and the niggers singing in time to the rise and fall of picks. Pretty soon he knew everybody in town. Whenever you heard a lot of laughing anywhere about the square, Homer Barron would be in the center of the group. Presently we began to see him and Miss Emily on Sunday afternoons driving in the yellow-wheeled buggy and the matched team of bays from the livery stable.

At first we were glad that Miss Emily would have an interest, because the ladies all said, "Of course a Grierson would not think seriously of a Northerner, a day laborer." But there were still others, older people, who said that even grief could not cause a real lady to forget *noblesse oblige*—without calling it *noblesse oblige*. They just said, "Poor Emily. Her kinsfolk should come to her." She had some kin in Alabama; but years ago her father had fallen out with them over the estate of old lady Wyatt, the crazy woman, and there was no communication between the two families. They had not even been represented at the funeral.

And as soon as the old people said, "Poor Emily," the whispering began. "Do you suppose it's really so?" they said to one another. "Of course it is. What else could . . ." This behind their hands rustling of craned silk and satin behind jalousies closed upon the sun of Sunday afternoon as the thin, swift clop-clop-clop of the matched team passed: "Poor Emily."

She carried her head high enough—even when we believed that she was fallen. It was as if she demanded more than ever the recognition of her dignity as the last Grierson; as if it had wanted that touch of earthiness to reaffirm her imperviousness. Like when she bought the rat poison, the arsenic. That was over a year after they had begun to say "Poor Emily," and while the two female cousins were visiting her.

"I want some poison," she said to the druggist. She was over thirty then, still a slight woman, though thinner than usual, with cold, haughty black eyes in a face the flesh of which was strained across the temples and about the eye-sockets as you imagine a lighthouse-keeper's face ought to look. "I want some poison," she said.

"Yes, Miss Emily. What kind? For rats and such? I'd recom—"

"I want the best you have. I don't care what kind."

The druggist named several. "They'll kill anything up to an elephant. But what you want is—"

"Arsenic," Miss Emily said. "Is that a good one?"

"Is . . . arsenic? Yes, ma'am. But what you want—"

"I want arsenic."

The druggist looked down at her. She looked back at him, erect, her face like a strained flag. "Why, of course," the druggist said. "If that's what you want. But the law requires you to tell what you are going to use it for."

Miss Emily just stared at him, her head tilted back in order to look him eye for eye, until he looked away and went and got the arsenic and wrapped it up. The Negro delivery boy brought her the package; the druggist didn't come back. When she opened the package at home there was written on the box, under the skull and bones: "For rats."

4

So the next day we all said, "She will kill herself"; and we said it would be the best thing. When she had first begun to be seen with Homer Barron, we had said, "She will marry him." Then we said, "She will persuade him yet," because Homer himself had remarked—he liked men, and it was known that he drank with the younger men in the Elks' Club—that he was not a marrying man. Later we said, "Poor Emily" behind the jalousies as they passed on Sunday afternoon in the glittering buggy, Miss Emily with her head high and Homer Barron with his hat cocked and a cigar in his teeth, reins and whip in a yellow glove.

Then some of the ladies began to say that it was a disgrace to the town and a bad example to the young people. The men did not want to interfere, but at last the ladies forced the Baptist minister —Miss Emily's people were Episcopal—to call upon her. He would never divulge what happened during that interview, but he refused to go back again. The next Sunday they again drove about the streets, and the following day the minister's wife wrote to Miss Emily's relations in Alabama.

So she had blood-kin under her roof again and we sat back to watch developments. At first nothing happened. Then we were sure that they were to be married. We learned that Miss Emily had been to the jeweler's and ordered a man's toilet set in silver, with the letters H. B. on each piece. Two days later we learned that she had bought a complete outfit of men's clothing, including a nightshirt, and we said, "They are married." We were really glad.

We were glad because the two female cousins were even more Grierson than Miss Emily had ever been.

So we were not surprised when Homer Barron—the streets had been finished some time since—was gone. We were a little disappointed that there was not a public blowing-off, but we believed that he had gone on to prepare for Miss Emily's coming, or to give her a chance to get rid of the cousins. (By that time it was a cabal, and we were all Miss Emily's allies to help circumvent the cousins.) Sure enough, after another week they departed. And, as we had expected all along, within three days Homer Barron was back in town. A neighbor saw the Negro man admit him at the kitchen door at dusk one evening.

And that was the last we saw of Homer Barron. And of Miss Emily for some time. The Negro man went in and out with the market basket, but the front door remained closed. Now and then we would see her at a window for a moment, as the men did that night when they sprinkled the lime, but for almost six months she did not appear on the streets. Then we knew that this was to be expected too; as if that quality of her father which had thwarted her woman's life so many times had been too virulent and too furious to die.

When we next saw Miss Emily, she had grown fat and her hair was turning gray. During the next few years it grew grayer and grayer until it attained an even pepper-and-salt iron-gray, when it ceased turning. Up to the day of her death at seventy-four it was still that vigorous iron-gray, like the hair of an active man.

From that time on her front door remained closed, save for a period of six or seven years, when she was about forty, during which she gave lessons in china-painting. She fitted up a studio in one of the downstairs rooms, where the daughters and granddaughters of Colonel Sartoris' contemporaries were sent to her with the same regularity and in the same spirit that they were sent to church on Sundays with a twenty-five-cent piece for the collection plate. Meanwhile her taxes had been remitted.

Then the newer generation became the backbone and the spirit of the town, and the painting pupils grew up and fell away and did not send their children to her with boxes of color and tedious brushes and pictures cut from the ladies' magazines. The front door closed upon the last one and remained closed for good. When the town got free postal delivery, Miss Emily alone refused to let them fasten the metal numbers above her door and attach a mailbox to it. She would not listen to them.

Daily, monthly, yearly we watched the Negro grow grayer and

more stooped, going in and out with the market basket. Each December we sent her a tax notice, which would be returned by the post office a week later, unclaimed. Now and then we would see her in one of the downstairs windows—she had evidently shut up the top floor of the house—like the carven torso of an idol in a niche, looking or not looking at us, we could never tell which. Thus she passed from generation to generation—dear, inescapable, impervious, tranquil, and perverse.

And so she died. Fell ill in the house filled with dust and shadows, with only a doddering Negro man to wait on her. We did not even know she was sick; we had long since given up trying to get any information from the Negro. He talked to no one, probably not even to her, for his voice had grown harsh and rusty, as if from disuse.

She died in one of the downstairs rooms, in a heavy walnut bed with a curtain, her gray head propped on a pillow yellow and moldy with age and lack of sunlight.

5

The Negro met the first of the ladies at the front door and let them in, with their hushed, sibilant voices and their quick, curious glances, and then he disappeared. He walked right through the house and out the back and was not seen again.

The two female cousins came at once. They held the funeral on the second day, with the town coming to look at Miss Emily beneath a mass of bought flowers, with the crayon face of her father musing profoundly above the bier and the ladies sibilant and macabre; and the very old men—some in their brushed Confederate uniforms—on the porch and the lawn, talking of Miss Emily as if she had been a contemporary of theirs, believing that they had danced with her and courted her perhaps, confusing time with its mathematical progression, as the old do, to whom all the past is not a diminishing road but, instead, a huge meadow which no winter ever quite touches, divided from them now by the narrow bottleneck of the most recent decade of years.

Already we knew that there was one room in that region above stairs which no one had seen in forty years, and which would have to be forced. They waited until Miss Emily was decently in the ground before they opened it.

The violence of breaking down the door seemed to fill this room with pervading dust. A thin, acrid pall as of the tomb seemed to lie everywhere upon this room decked and furnished as for a bridal: upon the valance curtains of faded rose color, upon the rose-shaded lights, upon the dressing table, upon the delicate array of crystal and the man's toilet things backed with tarnished silver, silver so tarnished that the monogram was obscured. Among them lay a collar and tie, as if they had just been removed, which, lifted, left upon the surface a pale crescent in the dust. Upon a chair hung the suit, carefully folded; beneath it the two mute shoes and the discarded socks.

The man himself lay in the bed.

For a long while we just stood there, looking down at the profound and fleshless grin. The body had apparently once lain in the attitude of an embrace, but now the long sleep that outlasts love, that conquers even the grimace of love, had cuckolded him. What was left of him, rotted beneath what was left of the nightshirt, had become inextricable from the bed in which he lay; and upon him and upon the pillow beside him lay that even coating of the patient and biding dust.

Then we noticed that in the second pillow was the indentation of a head. One of us lifted something from it, and leaning forward, that faint and invisible dust dry and acrid in the nostrils, we saw a long strand of iron-gray hair.

QUESTIONS FOR DISCUSSION

1. When Miss Emily died, the men went to her funeral "through a sort of respectful affection for a fallen monument." What do you think the phrase "fallen monument" means? Why should the men feel "respectful affection" for such a symbol? Does it surprise you that their attitude is different from that of the women in the town? Why or why not?

2. Later on in the story the narrator says, "Thus she passed from generation to generation—dear, inescapable, impervious, tranquil, and perverse." Do you feel these are appropriate adjectives to describe Miss Emily? In considering each one, discuss why or why not.

3. When Miss Emily refused for three days to allow the authorities to bury her father, the narrator says: "We believed she had to do that. . . . And we knew that with nothing left, *she would have to cling to that which had robbed her, as people will.*" Explain the meaning of the italicized part of the above quotation. Do you agree with this statement as a general principle? Why or why not?

4. What does the sentence, "Whenever you heard a lot of laughing anywhere about the square, Homer Barron would be in the center of the group," suggest to you about the personality of the man?

5. The spoken word often means one thing to the person who speaks it and another thing to the person who hears it. For example, when Miss Emily bought the poison, she said to the druggist: "I want the best you have." Discuss what you think she meant by the adjective *best* and what you think the druggist, conscious of her position in the town's social scale, assumed her to mean. Explain your answers.

6. If you had no other part of this story than these three sentences: "She will marry," "She will persuade him yet," and "She will kill herself," would you need the remainder of the story in order to have at least a reasonably accurate idea of the action? Explain what benefits there are for the reader in the "fleshing out" of this particular story.

7. What is meant when the narrator reflects that "the two female cousins were even more Grierson than Miss Emily had ever been"?

8. One of Faulkner's talents lay in his ability to compress considerable information into a single sentence or into only a few sentences. Such particularly pithy sentences are the last two in this story. Reread them carefully, and be prepared to discuss what they tell you about Miss Emily's character at the time of her liaison with Homer Barron as well as during the subsequent approximately forty years.

9. Identify what you feel is the *predominant* tone of this story. Explain your answer.

10. Do you feel "A Rose for Emily" is told from the viewpoint of a male or female character? from the viewpoint of one of the younger or older citizens of the town? Explore this question in your mind, and express your conclusions to the class.

ASSIGNMENTS FOR WRITING

1. Write an essay in which you discuss the appropriateness or inappropriateness of the title "A Rose for Emily." You may want to consider the phrase "coming to look at Miss Emily beneath a mass of bought flowers," as you think about the assignment.

2. In your school library, find a copy of Edwin Arlington Robinson's poem "Richard Cory." Read it carefully, and write a theme comparing Richard Cory with Miss Emily Grierson as members of the "aristocracy" in their respective towns. Consider ways in which you find them similar and dissimilar. You may want to suggest that one was more admirable or more pitiful than the other and to explain why you feel as you do.

3. In your school library or in an American literature textbook, look up the poem "My Aunt," by Oliver Wendell Holmes. Then write an essay using *one* of the following ideas:
   a. Compare the fathers of the two ladies described.
   b. Contrast the two ladies.

Wash

Sutpen stood above the pallet bed on which the mother and child lay. Between the shrunken planking of the wall the early sunlight fell in long pencil strokes, breaking upon his straddled legs and upon the riding whip in his hand, and lay across the still shape of the mother, who lay looking up at him from still, inscrutable, sullen eyes, the child at her side wrapped in a piece of dingy though clean cloth. Behind them an old Negro woman squatted beside the rough hearth where a meager fire smoldered.

"Well, Milly," Sutpen said, "too bad you're not a mare. Then I could give you a decent stall in the stable."

Still the girl on the pallet did not move. She merely continued to look up at him without expression, with a young, sullen, inscrutable face still pale from recent travail. Sutpen moved, bringing into the splintered pencils of sunlight the face of a man of sixty. He said quietly to the squatting Negress, "Griselda foaled this morning."

"Horse or mare?" the Negress said.

"A horse. A damned fine colt. . . . What's this?" He indicated the pallet with the hand which held the whip.

"That un's a mare, I reckon."

"Hah," Sutpen said. "A damned fine colt. Going to be the spit and image of old Rob Roy when I rode him North in '61. Do you remember?"

"Yes, Marster."

"Hah." He glanced back towards the pallet. None could have said if the girl still watched him or not. Again his whip hand indicated the pallet. "Do whatever they need with whatever we've got to do it with." He went out, passing out the crazy doorway and stepping down into the rank weeds (there yet leaned rusting against the corner of the porch the scythe which Wash had borrowed from him three months ago to cut them with) where his horse waited, where Wash stood holding the reins.

When Colonel Sutpen rode away to fight the Yankees, Wash did not go. "I'm looking after the Kernel's place and niggers," he would tell all who asked him and some who had not asked—a gaunt, malaria-ridden man with pale, questioning eyes, who looked about thirty-five, though it was known that he had not only a daughter but an eight-year-old granddaughter as well. This was a lie, as most of them—the few remaining men between eighteen and fifty—to whom he told it, knew, though there were some who believed that he himself really believed it, though even these believed that he had better sense than to put it to the test with Mrs. Sutpen or the Sutpen slaves. Knew better or was just too lazy and shiftless to try it, they said, knowing that his sole connection with the Sutpen plantation lay in the fact that for years now Colonel Sutpen had allowed him to squat in a crazy shack on a slough in the river bottom on the Sutpen place, which Sutpen had built for a fishing lodge in his bachelor days and which had since fallen in dilapidation from disuse, so that now it looked like an aged or sick wild beast crawled terrifically there to drink in the act of dying.

The Sutpen slaves themselves heard of his statement. They laughed. It was not the first time they had laughed at him, calling him white trash behind his back. They began to ask him themselves, in groups, meeting him in the faint road which led up from the slough and the old fish camp, "Why ain't you at de war, white man?"

Pausing, he would look about the ring of black faces and white eyes and teeth behind which derision lurked. "Because I got a daughter and family to keep," he said. "Git out of my road, niggers."

"Niggers?" they repeated; "niggers?" laughing now. "Who him, calling us niggers?"

"Yes," he said. "I ain't got no niggers to look after my folks if I was gone."

"Nor nothing else but dat shack down yon dat Cunnel wouldn't *let* none of us live in."

Now he cursed them; sometimes he rushed at them, snatching up a stick from the ground while they scattered before him, yet seeming to surround him still with that black laughing, derisive, evasive, inescapable, leaving him panting and impotent and raging. Once it happened in the very back yard of the big house itself. This was after bitter news had come down from the Tennessee mountains and from Vicksburg, and Sherman had passed through the plantation, and most of the Negroes had followed him. Almost everything else had gone with the Federal troops, and Mrs. Sutpen had sent word to Wash that he could have the scuppernongs ripening in the arbor in the back yard. This time it was a house servant, one of the few Negroes who remained; this time the Negress had to retreat up the kitchen steps, where she turned. "Stop right dar, white man. Stop right whar you is. You ain't never crossed dese steps whilst Cunnel here, and you ain't ghy' do hit now."

This was true. But there was this of a kind of pride: he had never tried to enter the big house, even though he believed that if he had, Sutpen would have received him, permitted him. "But I ain't going to give no black nigger the chance to tell me I can't go nowhere," he said to himself. "I ain't even going to give Kernel the chance to have to cuss a nigger on my account." This, though he and Sutpen had spent more than one afternoon together on those rare Sundays when there would be no company in the house. Perhaps his mind knew that it was because Sutpen had nothing else to do, being a man who could not bear his own company. Yet the fact remained that the two of them would spend whole afternoons in the scuppernong arbor, Sutpen in the hammock and Wash squatting against a post, a pail of cistern water between them, taking drink for drink from the same demijohn. Meanwhile on weekdays he would see the fine figure of the man —they were the same age almost to a day, though neither of them (perhaps because Wash had a grandchild while Sutpen's son was a youth in school) ever thought of himself as being so—on the fine figure of the black stallion, galloping about the plantation. For that moment his heart would be quiet and proud. It would seem to him that that world in which Negroes, whom the Bible told him had been created and cursed by God to be brute and vassal to all men of white skin, were better found and housed and even clothed than he and his; that world in which he sensed always about him mocking echoes of black laughter was but a dream and an illusion, and that the actual world was this one across which his own lonely apotheosis seemed to gallop on the black thoroughbred, thinking how the Book said also that all men were created in the image of God and hence all men made the same image in God's eyes at least; so that he could say, as though speaking of himself, "A fine proud man. If God Himself was to come down and ride the natural earth, that's what He would aim to look like."

Sutpen returned in 1865, on the black stallion. He seemed to have aged ten years. His son had been killed in action the same winter in which his wife had died. He returned with his citation for gallantry from the hand of General Lee to a ruined plantation, where for a year now his daughter had subsisted partially on the meager bounty of the man to whom fifteen years ago he had granted permission to live in that tumbledown fishing camp whose very existence he had at the time forgotten. Wash was there to meet him, unchanged: still gaunt, still ageless, with his pale, questioning gaze, his air diffident, a little servile, a little familiar. "Well, Kernel," Wash said, "they kilt us but they ain't whupped us yit, air they?"

That was the tenor of their conversation for the next five years. It was inferior whisky which they drank now together from a stoneware jug, and it was not in the scuppernong arbor. It was in the rear of the little store which Sutpen managed to set up on the highroad: a frame shelved room where, with Wash for clerk and porter, he dispensed kerosene and staple foodstuffs and stale gaudy candy and cheap beads and ribbons to Negroes or poor whites of Wash's own kind, who came afoot or on gaunt mules to haggle tediously for dimes and quarters with a man who at one time could gallop (the black stallion was still alive; the stable in which his jealous get lived was in better repair than the house where the master himself lived) for ten miles across his own fertile land and who had led troops gallantly in battle; until Sutpen in fury would empty the store, close and lock the doors from the inside. Then he and Wash would repair to the rear and the jug. But the talk would not be quiet now, as when Sutpen lay in the hammock, delivering an arrogant monologue while Wash squatted guffawing against his post. They both sat now, though Sutpen had the single chair while Wash used whatever box or keg was handy, and even this for just a little while, because soon Sutpen would reach that stage of impotent and furious undefeat in which he would rise, swaying and plunging, and declare again that he would take his pistol and the black stallion and ride single-handed into Washington and kill Lincoln, dead now, and Sherman, now a private citizen. "Kill them!" he would shout. "Shoot them down like the dogs they are—"

"Sho, Kernel; sho, Kernel," Wash would say, catching Sutpen as he fell. Then he would commandeer the first passing wagon or, lacking that, he would walk the mile to the nearest neighbor and borrow one and return and carry Sutpen home. He entered the house now. He had been doing so for a long time, taking Sutpen home in whatever borrowed wagon might be, talking him into locomotion with cajoling murmurs as though he were a horse, a stallion himself. The daughter would meet them and hold open the door without a word. He would carry his burden through the once white formal entrance, surmounted by a fanlight imported piece by piece from Europe and with a board now nailed over a missing pane, across a velvet carpet from which all nap was now gone, and up a formal stairs, now but a fading ghost of bare boards between two strips of fading paint, and into the bedroom. It would be dusk by now, and he would let his burden sprawl onto the bed and undress it and then he would sit quietly in a chair beside. After a time the daughter would come to the door. "We're all right now," he would tell her. "Don't you worry none, Miss Judith."

Then it would become dark, and after a while he would lie down on the floor beside the bed, though not to sleep, because after a time—sometimes before midnight—the man on the bed would stir and groan and then speak. "Wash?"

"Hyer I am, Kernel. You go back to sleep. We ain't whupped yit, air we? Me and you kin do hit."

Even then he had already seen the ribbon about his granddaughter's waist. She was now fifteen, already mature, after the early way of her kind. He knew where the ribbon came from; he had been seeing it and its kind daily for three years, even if she had lied about where she got it, which she did not, at once bold, sullen, and fearful. "Sho now," he said. "Ef Kernel wants to give hit to you, I hope yo minded to thank him."

His heart was quiet, even when he saw the dress, watching her secret, defiant, frightened face when she told him that Miss Judith, the daughter, had helped her to make it. But he was quite grave when he approached Sutpen after they closed the store that afternoon, following the other to the rear.

"Get the jug," Sutpen directed.

"Wait," Wash said. "Not yit for a minute."

Neither did Sutpen deny the dress. "What about it?" he said.

But Wash met his arrogant stare; he spoke quietly. "I've knowed you for going on twenty years. I ain't never yit denied to do what you told me to do. And I'm a man nigh sixty. And she ain't nothing but a fifteen-year-old gal."

"Meaning that I'd harm a girl? I, a man as old as you are?"

"If you was ara other man, I'd say you was as old as me. And old or no old, I wouldn't let her keep that dress nor nothing else that come from your hand. But you are different."

"How different?" But Wash merely looked at him with his pale, questioning, sober eyes. "So that's why you are afraid of me?"

Now Wash's gaze no longer questioned. It was tranquil, serene. "I ain't afraid. Because you air brave. It ain't that you were a brave man at one minute or day of your life and got a paper to show hit from General Lee. But you air brave, the same as you air alive and breathing. That's where hit's different. Hit don't need no ticket from nobody to tell me that. And I know that whatever you handle or tech, whether hit's a regiment of men or a ignorant gal or just a hound dog, that you will make hit right."

Now it was Sutpen who looked away, turning suddenly, brusquely. "Get the jug," he said sharply.

"Sho, Kernel," Wash said.

So on that Sunday dawn two years later, having watched the Negro midwife, which he had walked three miles to fetch, enter the crazy door beyond which his granddaughter lay wailing, his heart was still quiet though concerned. He knew what they had been saying—the Negroes in cabins about the land, the white men who loafed all day long about the store, watching quietly the three of them: Sutpen, himself, his granddaughter with her air of brazen and shrinking defiance as her condition became daily more and more obvious, like three actors that came and went upon a stage. "I know what they say to one another," he thought. "I can almost hyear them: *Wash Jones has fixed old Sutpen at last. Hit taken him twenty years, but he has done hit at last.*"

It would be dawn after a while, though not yet. From the house, where the lamp shone dim beyond the warped doorframe, his granddaughter's voice came steadily as though run by a clock, while thinking went slowly and terrifically, fumbling, involved somehow with a sound of galloping hooves, until there broke suddenly free in mid-gallop the fine proud figure of the man on the fine proud stallion, galloping; and then that at which thinking fumbled, broke free too and quite clear, not in justification nor even explanation, but as the apotheosis, lonely, explicable, beyond all fouling by human touch: "He is bigger than all them Yankees that kilt his son and his wife and taken his niggers and ruined his land, bigger than this hyer durn country that he fit for and that has denied him into keeping a little country store; bigger than the denial which hit helt to his lips like the bitter cup in the Book. And how could I have lived this nigh to him for twenty years without being teched and changed by him? Maybe I ain't as big as him and maybe I ain't done none of the galloping. But at least I done been drug along. Me and him kin do hit, if so be he will show me what he aims for me to do."

Then it was dawn. Suddenly he could see the house, and the old Negress in the door looking at him. Then he realized that his granddaughter's voice had ceased. "It's a girl," the Negress said. "You can go tell him if you want to." She reëntered the house.

"A girl," he repeated; "a girl"; in astonishment, hearing the galloping hooves, seeing the proud galloping figure emerge again. He seemed to watch it pass, galloping through avatars which marked the accumulation of years, time, to the climax where it galloped beneath a brandished saber and a shot-torn flag rushing down a sky in color like thunderous sulphur, thinking for the first time in his life that perhaps Sutpen was an old man like himself. "Gittin a gal," he thought in that astonishment; then he thought with the pleased surprise of a child: "Yes, sir. Be dawg if I ain't lived to be a great-grandpaw after all."

He entered the house. He moved clumsily, on tiptoe, as if he no longer lived there, as if the infant which had just drawn breath and cried in light had dispossessed him, be it of his own blood too though it might. But even above the pallet he could see little save the blur of his granddaughter's exhausted face. Then the Negress squatting at the hearth spoke, "You better gawn tell him if you going to. Hit's daylight now."

But this was not necessary. He had no more than turned the corner of the porch where the scythe leaned which he had borrowed three months ago to clear away the weeds through which he walked, when Sutpen himself rode up on the old stallion. He did not wonder how Sutpen had got the word. He took it for granted that this was what had brought the other out at this hour on Sunday morning, and he stood while the other dismounted, and he took the reins from Sutpen's hand, an expression on his gaunt face almost imbecile with a kind of weary triumph, saying, "Hit's a gal, Kernel. I be dawg if you ain't as old as I am—" until Sutpen passed him and entered the house. He stood there with the reins in his hand and heard Sutpen cross the floor to the pallet. He heard what Sutpen said, and something seemed to stop dead in him before going on.

The sun was now up, the swift sun of Mississippi latitudes, and it seemed to him that he stood beneath a strange sky, in a strange scene, familiar only as things are familiar in dreams, like the dreams of falling to one who has never climbed. "I kain't have heard what I thought I heard," he thought quietly. "I know I kain't." Yet the voice, the familiar voice which had said the words was still speaking, talking now to the old Negress about a colt foaled that morning. "That's why he was up so early," he thought. "That was hit. Hit ain't me and mine. Hit ain't even hisn that got him outen bed."

Sutpen emerged. He descended into the weeds, moving with that heavy deliberation which would have been haste when he was younger. He had not yet looked full at Wash. He said, "Dicey will stay and tend to her. You better—" Then he seemed to see Wash facing him and paused. "What?" he said.

"You said—" To his own ears Wash's voice sounded flat and ducklike, like a deaf man's. "You said if she was a mare, you could give her a good stall in the stable."

"Well?" Sutpen said. His eyes widened and narrowed, almost like a man's fists flexing and shutting, as Wash began to advance towards him, stooping a little. Very astonishment kept Sutpen still for the moment, watching that man whom in twenty years he had no more known to make any motion save at command than he had the horse which he rode. Again his eyes narrowed and widened; without moving he seemed to rear suddenly upright. "Stand back," he said suddenly and sharply. "Don't you touch me."

"I'm going to tech you, Kernel," Wash said in that flat, quiet, almost soft voice, advancing.

Sutpen raised the hand which held the riding whip; the old Negress peered around the crazy door with her black gargoyle face of a worn gnome. "Stand back, Wash," Sutpen said. Then he struck. The old Negress leaped down into the weeds with the agility of a goat and fled. Sutpen slashed Wash again across the face with the whip, striking him to his knees. When Wash rose and advanced once more he held in his hands the scythe which he had borrowed from Sutpen three months ago and which Sutpen would never need again.

When he reëntered the house his granddaughter stirred on the pallet bed and called his name fretfully. "What was that?" she said.

"What was what, honey?"

"That ere racket out there."

" 'Twarn't nothing," he said gently. He knelt and touched her hot forehead clumsily. "Do you want ara thing?"

"I want a sup of water," she said querulously. "I been laying here wanting a sup of water a long time, but don't nobody care enough to pay me no mind."

"Sho now," he said soothingly. He rose stiffly and fetched the dipper of water and raised her head to drink and laid her back and watched her turn to the child with an absolutely stonelike face. But a moment later he saw that she was crying quietly. "Now, now," he said, "I wouldn't do that. Old Dicey says hit's a right fine gal. Hit's all right now. Hit's all over now. Hit ain't no need to cry now."

But she continued to cry quietly, almost sullenly, and he rose again and stood uncomfortably above the pallet for a time, thinking as he had thought when his own wife lay so and then his daughter in turn: "Women. Hit's a mystry to me. They seem to want em, and yit when they git em they cry about hit. Hit's a mystry to me. To ara man." Then he moved away and drew a chair up to the window and sat down.

Through all that long, bright sunny forenoon he sat at the window, waiting. Now and then he rose and tiptoed to the pallet. But his granddaughter slept now, her face sullen and calm and weary, the child in the crook of her arm. Then he returned to the chair and sat again, waiting, wondering why it took them so long, until he remembered that it was Sunday. He was sitting there at mid-afternoon when a half-grown white boy came around the corner of the house upon the body and gave a choked cry and looked up and glared for a mesmerized instant at Wash in the window before he turned and fled. Then Wash rose and tiptoed again to the pallet.

The granddaughter was awake now, wakened perhaps by the boy's cry without hearing it. "Milly," he said, "air you hungry?" She didn't answer, turning her face away. He built up the fire on the hearth and cooked the food which he had brought home the day before: fatback it was, and cold corn pone; he poured water into the stale coffee pot and heated it. But she would not eat when he carried the plate to her, so he ate himself, quietly, alone, and left the dishes as they were and returned to the window.

Now he seemed to sense, feel, the men who would be gathering with horses and guns and dogs—the curious, and the vengeful: men of Sutpen's own kind, who had made the company about Sutpen's table in the time when Wash himself had yet to approach nearer to the house than the scuppernong arbor—men who had also shown the lesser ones how to fight in battle, who maybe also had signed papers from the generals saying that they were among the first of the brave; who had also galloped in the old days arrogant and proud on the fine horses across the fine plantations—symbols also of admiration and hope; instruments too of despair and grief.

That was whom they would expect him to run from. It seemed to him that he had no more to run from than he had to run to. If he ran, he would merely be fleeing one set of bragging and evil shadows for another just like them, since they were all of a kind throughout all the earth which he knew, and he was old, too old to flee far even if he were to flee. He could never escape them, no matter how much or how far he ran: a man going on sixty could not run that far. Not far enough to escape beyond the boundaries of earth where such men lived, set the order and the rule of living. It seemed to him that he now saw for the first time, after five years, how it was that Yankees or any other living armies had managed to whip them: the gallant, the proud, the brave; the acknowledged and chosen best among them all to carry courage and honor and pride. Maybe if he had gone to the war with them he would have discovered them sooner. But if he had discovered them sooner, what would he have done with his life since? How could he have borne to remember for five years what his life had been before?

Now it was getting toward sunset. The child had been crying; when he went to the pallet he saw his granddaughter nursing it, her face still bemused, sullen, inscrutable. "Air you hungry yit?" he said.

"I don't want nothing."

"You ought to eat."

This time she did not answer at all, looking down at the child. He returned to his chair and found that the sun had set. "Hit kain't be much longer," he thought. He could feel them quite near now, the curious and the vengeful. He could even seem to hear what they were saying about him, the undercurrent of believing beyond the immediate fury: *Old Wash Jones he come a tumble at last. He thought he had Sutpen, but Sutpen fooled him. He thought he had Kernel where he would have to marry the gal or pay up. And Kernel refused.* "But I never expected that, Kernel!" he cried aloud, catching himself at the sound of his own voice, glancing quickly back to find his granddaughter watching him.

"Who you talking to now?" she said.

"Hit ain't nothing. I was just thinking and talked out before I knowed hit."

Her face was becoming indistinct again, again a sullen blur in the twilight. "I reckon so. I reckon you'll have to holler louder than that before he'll hear you, up yonder at that house. And I reckon you'll need to do more than holler before you get him down here too."

"Sho now," he said. "Don't you worry none." But already thinking was going smoothly on: "You know I never. You know how I ain't never expected or asked nothing from ara living man but what I expected from you. And I never asked that. I didn't think hit would need. I said, *I don't need to. What need has a fellow like Wash Jones to question or doubt the man that General*

Lee himself says in a handwrote ticket that he was brave? Brave,"
he thought. "Better if nara one of them had never rid back home in
'65"; thinking *Better if his kind and mine too had never drawn
the breath of life on this earth. Better that all who remain of us
be blasted from the face of the earth than that another Wash Jones
should see his whole life shredded from him and shrivel away like
a dried shuck thrown onto the fire.*

He ceased, became still. He heard the horses, suddenly and
plainly; presently he saw the lantern and the movement of men,
the glint of gun barrels, in its moving light. Yet he did not stir. It
was quite dark now, and he listened to the voices and the sounds
of underbrush as they surrounded the house. The lantern itself
came on; its light fell upon the quiet body in the weeds and
stopped, the horses tall and shadowy. A man descended and
stooped in the lantern light, above the body. He held a pistol; he
rose and faced the house. "Jones," he said.

"I'm here," Wash said quietly from the window. "That you,
Major?"

"Come out."

"Sho," he said quietly. "I just want to see to my granddaughter."

"We'll see to her. Come on out."

"Sho, Major. Just a minute."

"Show a light. Light your lamp."

"Sho. In just a minute." They could hear his voice retreat into
the house, though they could not see him as he went swiftly to the
crack in the chimney where he kept the butcher knife: the one
thing in his slovenly life and house in which he took pride, since it
was razor sharp. He approached the pallet, his granddaughter's
voice:

"Who is it? Light the lamp, Grandpaw."

"Hit won't need no light, honey. Hit won't take but a minute,"
he said, kneeling, fumbling toward her voice, whispering now.
"Where air you?"

"Right here," she said fretfully. "Where would I be? What
is . . ." His hand touched her face. "What is . . . Grandpaw!
Grand. . . ."

"Jones!" the sheriff said. "Come out of there!"

"In just a minute, Major," he said. Now he rose and moved
swiftly. He knew where in the dark the can of kerosene was, just
as he knew that it was full, since it was not two days ago that he
had filled it at the store and held it there until he got a ride home
with it, since the five gallons were heavy. There were still coals on

the hearth; besides, the crazy building itself was like tinder: the coals, the hearth, the walls exploding in a single blue glare. Against it the waiting men saw him in a wild instant springing toward them with the lifted scythe before the horses reared and whirled. They checked the horses and turned them back toward the glare, yet still in wild relief against it the gaunt figure ran toward them with the lifted scythe.

"Jones!" the sheriff shouted; "stop! Stop, or I'll shoot. Jones! Jones!" Yet still the gaunt, furious figure came on against the glare and roar of the flames. With the scythe lifted, it bore down upon them, upon the wild glaring eyes of the horses and the swinging glints of gun barrels, without any cry, any sound.

QUESTIONS FOR DISCUSSION

1. Explain the remark Colonel Sutpen made to Milly at the beginning of the story: ". . . too bad you're not a mare. Then I could give you a decent stall in the stable."
2. Which was more important to the Colonel, the new child or the new foal? How do you know?
3. Explain, by noting the context, the appropriateness of the italicized terms given below:
    a. ". . . a crazy shack . . . that now . . . looked like an aged or sick wild beast crawled *terrifically* there . . ."
    b. ". . . the actual world was this one across which *his own lonely apotheosis* seemed to gallop . . ."
    c. "this hyer durn country . . . that has *denied* him into keeping a little country store."
    d. ". . . he saw his granddaughter . . . , her face still *bemused*."
    e. ". . . *in wild relief* against it the gaunt figure ran . . ."
4. Colonel Sutpen is described as "being a man who could not bear his own company." What do you think these words mean?
5. In tracing the association of the two men, Wash and the Colonel, notice that before the war Wash squatted against a post in the scuppernong arbor, after the war he sat on "whatever box or keg was handy" in the rear of the Colonel's little store, and then he entered the house and sat beside the Colonel's bed. Do you feel that these changes of physical position indicated to Wash anything of significance in the relationship between this pair? to Colonel Sutpen? to you? In all three cases, defend your answer.
6. When the midwife told Wash that Milly had borne a girl-child, his first reaction was one of astonishment. Why? His second reaction was one of pleasure. Why did his emotion change? Are these two responses typical of what you feel his character to be? Explain.

7. At one point in the story Wash asked himself: "And how could I have lived this nigh to him [the Colonel] for twenty years without being teched and changed by him?" Do you feel he was or was not "teched and changed"? Cite your reasons.
8. Explain the meaning of the remark, "Hit ain't even hisn that got him outen bed."
9. What irony is there in the use of the scythe as the instrument of destruction? Explain your answer.
10. In that period of his life on the Colonel's place before the war and for the five years thereafter that this story spans, Wash thought of Sutpen and men such as he as "the gallant, the proud, the brave." After the Colonel's remarks on the morning of the baby's birth, how did Wash see and describe them? With this new definition in mind, explain the meaning of the question he asked himself, ". . . if he had discovered them sooner . . . How could he have borne to remember for five years what his life had been before?"
11. You will understand this story better if you are familiar with the flashback (a representation during the course of a novel, motion picture, etc., of some previous event or scene). Reread "Wash," and make a simple chart of Faulkner's shifts from the present action of the story (the birth of his great-grandchild) to several past periods of time. You should be able to point out three such segments (which are not necessarily in chronological order). You will find that the author has helped you by naming two specific years.

ASSIGNMENTS FOR WRITING

1. After finding out that the Colonel had been giving gifts to his granddaughter, Wash told him that ". . . you air brave." Then he said, "And I know that whatever you handle or tech, whether hit's a regiment of men or a ignorant gal or just a hound dog, that you will make hit right." Write a theme explaining whether or not you feel rightmindedness is a part of bravery.
2. In a brief essay, discuss whether or not Wash's setting the shack afire is an effective ending to the story.
3. In his Nobel Prize acceptance speech Faulkner identified "love and honor and pity and pride and compassion and sacrifice" as "universal truths." Write a theme in which you examine the character of Wash Jones in relation to these qualities. Identify their presence or note their absence, and indicate the degree to which you feel Faulkner succeeded or failed in making him a commendable figure.

The Nobel Prize Acceptance Speech

I feel that this award was not made to me as a man, but to my work—a life's work in the agony and sweat of the human spirit, not for glory and least of all for profit, but to create out of the materials of the human spirit something which did not exist before. So this award is only mine in trust. It will not be difficult to find a dedication for the money part of it commensurate with the purpose and significance of its origin. But I would like to do the same with the acclaim too, by using this moment as a pinnacle from which I might be listened to by the young men and women already dedicated to the same anguish and travail, among whom is already that one who will some day stand here where I am standing.

Our tragedy today is a general and universal physical fear so long sustained by now that we can even bear it. There are no longer problems of the spirit. There is only the question: When will I be blown up? Because of this, the young man or woman writing today has forgotten the problems of the human heart in conflict with itself which alone can make good writing because only that is worth writing about, worth the agony and the sweat.

He must learn them again. He must teach himself that the basest of all things is to be afraid; and, teaching himself that, forget it forever, leaving no room in his workshop for anything but the old verities and truths of the heart, the old universal truths lacking which any story is ephemeral and doomed—love and honor and pity and pride and compassion and sacrifice. Until he does so, he labors under a curse. He writes not of love but of lust, of defeats in which nobody loses anything of value, of victories without hope and, worst of all, without pity or compassion. His griefs grieve on no universal bones, leaving no scars. He writes not of the heart but of the glands.

Until he relearns these things, he will write as though he stood alone and watched the end of man. I decline to accept the end of man. It is easy enough to say that man is immortal simply because he will endure: that when the last ding-dong of doom has clanged and faded from the last worthless rock hanging tideless in the last red and dying evening, that even then there will still be one more sound: that of his puny inexhaustible voice, still talking.

I refuse to accept this. I believe that man will not merely endure: he will prevail. He is immortal, not because he alone among creatures has an inexhaustible voice, but because he has a soul, a spirit capable of compassion and sacrifice and endurance. The poet's, the writer's, duty is to write about these things. It is his privilege to help man endure by lifting his heart, by reminding him of the courage and honor and hope and pride and compassion and pity and sacrifice which have been the glory of his past. The poet's voice need not merely be the record of man, it can be one of the props, the pillars to help him endure and prevail.

QUESTIONS FOR DISCUSSION

1. Look up in an encyclopedia, textbook, or other reference source the Nobel Prize and explain what it is. What American authors other than Faulkner have been winners of this award?
2. Why is it that Faulkner believes man is immortal? Do you agree? Identify who it is that Faulkner declares can help man to endure, and cite the ways in which such help is possible. List others who you think can be of help, too, to man in his present struggle.
3. This speech was delivered in December 1950. Do you think it is applicable today? to what degree, if any? Explain your answers.
4. Reread the speech, noting carefully its tone. Does the tone give you any idea of how Faulkner felt upon being named the winner? Give reasons for your reply.

ASSIGNMENTS FOR WRITING

1. Write a one-sentence précis of Faulkner's credo. Follow this with a one-sentence précis of your own credo.
2. Think back to some award or recognition which you have received and for which you may or may not have been called upon to make a public response. In either case, write an essay in which you both acknowledge the acclaim and express your feelings on being honored.

A Word to Young Writers

Two years ago President Eisenhower conceived a plan based on an idea which is basically a sound one. This was that world conditions, the universal dilemma of mankind at this moment, are what they are simply because individual men and women of different races and tongues and conditions cannot discuss with one another these problems and dilemmas which are primarily theirs, but must attempt to do so only through the formal organizations of their antagonistic and seemingly irreconcilable governments.

That is, that individual people in all walks of life should be given opportunity to speak to their individual opposite numbers all over the earth—laborer to laborer, scientist to scientist, doctors and lawyers and merchants and bankers and artists to their opposite numbers everywhere.

There was nothing wrong with this idea. Certainly no artist—painter, musician, sculptor, architect, writer—would dispute it because this—trying to communicate man to man regardless of race or color or condition—is exactly what every artist has already spent all his life trying to do, and as long as he breathes will continue to do.

What doomed it in my opinion was symptomized by the phraseology of the President's own concept: laborer to laborer, artist to artist, banker to banker, tycoon to tycoon. What doomed it in my opinion was an evil inherent in our culture itself; an evil quality inherent in (and perhaps necessary though I for one do not believe this last) in the culture of any country capable of enduring and surviving through this period of history. This is the mystical belief, almost a religion, that individual man cannot speak to individual man because individual man can no longer exist. A belief that there is no place anymore where individual man can speak quietly to individual man of such simple things as honesty with oneself and responsibility toward others and protection for the weak and compassion and pity for all, because such individual things as honesty and pity and responsibility and compassion no longer exist and man himself can hope to continue only by relinquishing and denying his individuality into a regimented group of his arbitrary factional kind, arrayed against an opposite opposed arbitrary factional regimented group, both filling the same air at the same time with the same double-barreled abstractions of "peoples' democracy" and "minority rights" and "equal justice" and "social welfare"—all the synonyms which take all the shame out of irresponsibility by not merely inviting but even compelling everyone to participate in it.

So in this case—I mean the President's People-to-People Committee—the artist too, who has already spent his life trying to communicate simply people to people the problems and passions of the human heart and how to survive them or anyway endure them, has in effect been asked by the President of his country to affirm that mythology which he has already devoted his life to denying: the mythology that one single individual man is nothing, and can have weight and substance only when organized into the anonymity of a group where he will have surrendered his individual soul for a number.

It would be sad enough if only at such moments as this—I mean, formal recognition by his country of the validity of his life's dedication—did the artist have to run full-tilt into what might be called almost a universal will to regimentation, a universal will to obliterate the humanity from man even to the extent of relieving him not only of moral responsibility but even of physical pain and mortality by effacing him individually into any, it does not matter which as long as he has vanished into one of them, nationally recognized economic group by profession or trade or occupation or income-tax bracket or, if nothing else offers, finance-company list. His tragedy is that today he must even combat this pressure, waste some part of his puny but (if he is an artist) precious individual strength against this universal will to efface his individual humanity, in order to be an artist. Which comes at last to the idea I want to suggest, which is what seems to me to be the one dilemma in which all young writers today participate.

I think that perhaps all writers, while they are "hot," working at top speed to try to get said all they feel the terrific urgency to say, don't read the writers younger, after, themselves, perhaps for the same reason which the sprinter or the distance runner has: he does not have time to be interested in who is behind him or even up to him, but only in who is in front. That was true in my own case anyway, so there was a gap of about twenty-five years during which I had almost no acquaintance whatever with contemporary literature.

So, when a short time ago I did begin to read the writing being done now, I brought to it not only ignorance but a kind of innocence, freshness, what you might call a point of view and an interest virgin of preconceptions. Anyway, I got from the first story an impression which has repeated itself so consistently since, that I shall offer it as a generalization. This is, that the young writer of today is compelled by the present state of our culture which I tried to describe, to function in a kind of vacuum of the human race. His characters do not function, live, breathe, struggle, in that moil and seethe of simple humanity as did those of our predecessors who were the masters from whom we learned our craft: Dickens, Fielding, Thackeray, Conrad, Twain, Smollett, Hawthorne, Melville, James; their names are legion whose created characters were not just weaned but even spawned into a moil and seethe of simple human beings whose very existence was an affirmation of an incurable and indomitable optimism—men and women like themselves, understandable and comprehensible even when antipathetical, even in the very moment while they were murdering or robbing or betraying you, since theirs too were the same simple human lusts and hopes and fears uncomplicated by regimentation or group compulsion—a moil and seethe of humanity into which they could venture not only unappalled and welcome but with pleasure too and with no threat of harm since the worst that could happen to them would be a head bumped by what was only another human head, an elbow or a knee skinned but that too was only another human knee or elbow which did the skinning—a moil and seethe of mankind which accepted and believed in and functioned according, not to angles, but to moral principles; where truth was not where you were standing when you looked at it but was an unalterable quality or thing which could and would knock your brains out if you did not accept it or at least respect it.

While today the young writer's characters must function not in individuality but in isolation, not to pursue in myriad company the anguishes and hopes of all human hearts in a world of a few simple comprehensible truths and moral principles, but to exist alone inside a vacuum of facts which he did not choose and cannot cope with and cannot escape from like a fly inside an inverted tumbler.

Let me repeat: I have not read all the work of this present generation of writing; I have not had time yet. So I must speak only of the ones I do know. I am thinking now of what I rate the best one: Salinger's *Catcher in the Rye*, perhaps because this one expresses so completely what I have tried to say: a youth, father to what will, must someday be a man, more intelligent than some and more sensitive than most, who (he would not even have called it by instinct because he did not know he possessed it) because God perhaps had put it there, loved man and wished to be a part of mankind, humanity, who tried to join the human race and failed. To me, his tragedy was not that he was, as he perhaps thought, not tough enough or brave enough or deserving enough to be accepted into humanity. His tragedy was that when he attempted to enter the human race, there was no human race there. There was nothing for him to do save buzz, frantic and inviolate, inside the glass walls of his tumbler until he either gave up or was himself by himself, by his own frantic buzzing, destroyed. One thinks of course immediately of Huck Finn, another youth already father to what will some day soon now be a man. But in Huck's case all he had to combat was his small size, which time would cure for him; in time he would be as big as any man he had to cope with; and even as it was, all the adult world could do to harm him was to skin his nose a little; humanity, the human race, would and was accepting him already; all he needed to do was just to grow up in it.

That is the young writer's dilemma as I see it. Not just his, but all our problems, is to save mankind from being desouled as the stallion or boar or bull is gelded; to save the individual from anonymity before it is too late and humanity has vanished from the animal called man. And who better to save man's humanity than the writer, the poet, the artist, since who should fear the loss of it more since the humanity of man is the artist's life's blood.

QUESTIONS FOR DISCUSSION

1. What was the plan of former President Dwight D. Eisenhower's People-to-People Committee? What did Faulkner express in this essay as the one thing wrong with it? Did he believe that artists, as a group, share this "mythology"? Explain your answer.
2. How did Faulkner believe man could continue to exist? Do you or do you not feel that this is the same philosophy as that expressed in his Nobel Prize acceptance speech? What makes you think this way?
3. What is the "tragedy" of the artist as Faulkner defined it in this speech to young authors? Is this the same tragedy of which he spoke in the Nobel Prize acceptance speech in 1950? Cite specific passages from each address to explain your answer.
4. In both the Nobel Prize acceptance speech and this "Word to Young Writers" Faulkner spoke of the writer's duty or problem. Locate the passage in each speech which defines this and cite it for your class.

ASSIGNMENTS FOR WRITING

1. In this essay Faulkner spoke of "almost a universal will to regimentation." There are some who rebel, however, to such an extent that forceful means are used to bring their groups under control. Suppose you are a member of one of these groups. In a brief essay, defend your going to extremes to command attention.
2. Suppose you are a member of a group assigned to control a group of violent protestors. Write a brief essay from this new viewpoint, defending your group's use of force to bring about such "regimentation."

James Baldwin

When *Native Son*, Richard Wright's impassioned novel of the black man's plight in America, was published in 1940, James Baldwin, a teenaged son of a Baptist preacher in Harlem, was struggling to choose his vocation. Then sixteen, James Baldwin was the eldest son of a fanatically strict and contentious man. In his ministerial profession, the elder Baldwin had the unhappy capacity for alienating himself from his congregations and from his fellow-clergymen. His narrow rigidity and doctrinaire opinions led him, his son says, into "an intolerable bitterness of spirit" founded upon both contempt for the white man and a subservience to legalistic religion.

Born on August 3, 1924, James Baldwin had begun by age fourteen to preach occasionally in his father's church and in some of the store-front churches throughout the black ghetto of uptown New York City. If his father's will had prevailed, James Baldwin might well have succeeded to one of the major pulpits, for he is an astonishingly effective orator. But Baldwin was being drawn from preaching by his compulsion to write. "I began plotting novels at about the time I learned to read," he recalls. "I wrote—a great deal—and my first professional triumph, in any case, the first effort of mine to be seen in print, occurred at the age of twelve or thereabouts, when a short story I had written about the Spanish revolution won some sort of prize in an extremely short-lived church newspaper."

In school, Baldwin was active in musical and literary activities. Life in Harlem during the Depression years was particularly bleak; for a youth with imagination, one sure escape was the fantasy of literature and drama. As young Baldwin's interest in secular writing deepened, the rift between father and son broadened. At seventeen, James Baldwin left home. At twenty-one, he had received the Eugene Saxton Literary Fellowship, a grant to young writers of promise. The novel on which Baldwin had been working did not appear until 1953, when he published *Go Tell It on the Mountain,* an autobiographical account of the tensions in a preacher's family.

Actually this first novel was completed in France where Baldwin had gone to live in 1948. From France, he moved to Switzerland for a time. Out of his dual sense of alienation—an American expatriate and a black man in Europe—Baldwin wrote a quartet of searching essays, including "Stranger in the Village," which appeared in his collection, *Notes of a Native Son,* published in 1955. These first two books demonstrated Baldwin's talent both as storyteller and as polemicist; he was yet to attempt the role of dramatist.

This early work also demonstrated Baldwin's richness of style, a fluency of language which can either transport its reader with the rhythm of wit and wonder or transfix the reader and the subject side by side for a flogging. America had been brought face to face with a writer of intense concerns—not merely *social* concerns in the broad and ambiguous use of that phrase, but personal concerns for himself as a black man in America. Here too was a voice honest enough to confess his fears about himself and about his countrymen:

> I don't like people who like me because I'm a Negro; neither do I like people who find in the same accident grounds for contempt. I love America more than any other country in the world, and, exactly for this reason, I insist on the right to criticize her perpetually.

Baldwin's subsequent books served to reinforce his importance as a major contemporary writer. *Giovanni's Room* (1956) and *Another Country* (1961) are novels of moral significance, treating such diverse problems as homosexuality and interracial conflicts. Two more books of essays have followed *Notes of a Native Son; Nobody Knows My Name* (1961) and *The Fire Next Time* (1963). This latter book warns of impending bloodshed unless white America accepts the reality and necessity of the black presence. His only collection of short stories, *Going to Meet the Man,* was issued in 1965.

Like Henry James before him, Baldwin has learned that success as a novelist and essayist does not guarantee success as a playwright. Both his plays, *Blues for Mister Charley* (1964) and *The Amen Corner* (1965), have played in New York without popular acceptance. The first play seems to have been Baldwin's response to the unsolved murders of various Americans, black and white, as such it is less drama than diatribe. The second play, written long before it was produced, imitated *Go Tell It on the Mountain* in treating the theme of childhood reminiscence.

Of all his work, Baldwin is most respected for the vigor of his essays, two of which are represented here. The lengthy memoir, "Notes of a Native Son," shows the poignancy of a son's belated recognition of his father's worth as a human being. The strange parallels of birth and death, funeral and festivity, personal anguish and social upheaval are not overlooked by Baldwin. They provide the underlying structure for his reminiscence, for, as Melville wrote in *Moby-Dick*, "Surely all this is not without meaning." "Stranger in the Village" has been answered in rebuttal by the critic and novelist, Leslie Fiedler whose essay, "Negro and Jew: Encounter in America," takes Baldwin to task for some of his arguments against American society.

Baldwin remains a controversial writer and can by no means be regarded as spokesman for any particular bloc of Negroes. But far above racial concerns, James Baldwin is recognized as one of America's great writers.

Notes of a Native Son

On the 29th of July, in 1943, my father died. On the same day, a few hours later, his last child was born. Over a month before this, while all our energies were concentrated in waiting for these events, there had been, in Detroit, one of the bloodiest race riots of the century. A few hours after my father's funeral, while he lay in state in the undertaker's chapel, a race riot broke out in Harlem. On the morning of the 3rd of August, we drove my father to the graveyard through a wilderness of smashed plate glass.

The day of my father's funeral had also been my nineteenth birthday. As we drove him to the graveyard, the spoils of injustice, anarchy, discontent, and hatred were all around us. It seemed to me that God himself had devised, to mark my father's end, the most sustained and brutally dissonant of codas. And it seemed to me, too, that the violence which rose all about us as my father left the world had been devised as a corrective for the pride of his eldest son. I had declined to believe in that apocalypse which had been central to my father's vision; very well, life seemed to be saying, here is something that will certainly pass for an apocalypse until the real thing comes along. I had inclined to be contemptuous of my father for the conditions of his life, for the conditions of our lives. When his life had ended I began to wonder about that life and also, in a new way, to be apprehensive about my own.

I had not known my father very well. We had got on badly, partly because we shared, in our different fashions, the vice of stubborn pride. When he was dead I realized that I had hardly ever spoken to him. When he had been dead a long time I began to wish I had. It seems to be typical of life in America, where opportunities, real and fancied, are thicker than anywhere else on the globe, that the second generation has no time to talk to the first. No one, including my father, seems to have known exactly how old he was, but his mother had been born during slavery. He was of the first generation of free men. He, along with thousands of other Negroes, came North after 1919 and I was part of that generation which had never seen the landscape of what Negroes sometimes call the Old Country.

He had been born in New Orleans and had been a quite young man there during the time that Louis Armstrong, a boy, was running errands for the dives and honky-tonks of what was always presented to me as one of the most wicked of cities—to this day, whenever I think of New Orleans, I also helplessly think of Sodom and Gomorrah. My father never mentioned Louis Armstrong, except to forbid us to play his records; but there was a picture of him on our wall for a long time. One of my father's strong-willed female relatives had placed it there and forbade my father to take it down. He never did, but he eventually maneuvered her out of the house and when, some years later, she was in trouble and near death, he refused to do anything to help her.

He was, I think, very handsome. I gather this from photographs and from my own memories of him, dressed in his Sunday best and on his way to preach a sermon somewhere, when I was little. Handsome, proud, and ingrown, "like a toe-nail," somebody said. But he looked to me, as I grew older, like pictures I had seen of African tribal chieftains: he really should have been naked, with war-paint on and barbaric mementos, standing among spears. He could be chilling in the pulpit and indescribably cruel in his personal life and he was certainly the most bitter man I have ever met; yet it must be said that there was something else in him, buried in him, which lent him his tremendous power and, even, a rather crushing charm. It had something to do with his blackness, I think—he was very black—and his blackness and his beauty, and with the fact that he knew that he was black but did not know that he was beautiful. He claimed to be proud of his blackness but it had also been the cause of much humiliation and it had fixed bleak boundaries to his life. He was not a young man when we were growing up and he had already suffered many kinds of ruin; in his outrageously demanding and protective way he loved his children, who were black like him and menaced, like him; and all these things sometimes showed in his face when he tried, never to my knowledge with any success, to establish contact with any of us. When he took one of his children on his knee to play, the child always became fretful and began to cry; when he tried to help one of us with our homework the absolutely unabating tension which emanated from him caused our minds and our tongues to become paralyzed, so that he, scarcely knowing why, flew into a rage and the child, not knowing why, was punished. If it ever entered his head to bring a surprise home for his children, it was, almost unfailingly, the wrong surprise and even the big watermelons he often brought home on his back in the summertime led to the most appalling scenes. I do not remember, in all those years, that one of his children was ever glad to see him come home. From what I was able to gather of his early life, it seemed that this inability to establish contact with other people had always marked him and had been one of the things which had driven him out of New Orleans. There was something in him, therefore, groping and tentative, which was never expressed and which was buried with him. One saw it most clearly when he was facing new people and hoping to impress them. But he never did, not for long. We went from church to smaller and more improbable church, he found himself in less and less demand as a minister, and by the time he died none of his friends had come to see him for a long time. He had lived and died in an intolerable bitterness of spirit and it frightened me, as we drove him to the graveyard through those unquiet, ruined streets, to see how powerful and overflowing this bitterness could be and to realize that this bitterness now was mine.

When he died I had been away from home for a little over a year. In that year I had had time to become aware of the meaning of all my father's bitter warnings, had discovered the secret of his proudly pursed lips and rigid carriage: I had discovered the weight of white people in the world. I saw that this had been for my ancestors and now would be for me an awful thing to live with and that the bitterness which had helped to kill my father could also kill me.

He had been ill a long time—in the mind, as we now realized, reliving instances of his fantastic intransigence in the new light of his affliction and endeavoring to feel a sorrow for him which never, quite, came true. We had not known that he was being eaten up by paranoia, and the discovery that his cruelty, to our bodies and our minds, had been one of the symptoms of his illness was not, then, enough to enable us to forgive him. The younger children felt, quite simply, relief that he would not be coming home anymore. My mother's observation that it was he, after all, who had kept them alive all these years meant nothing because the problems of keeping children alive are not real for children. The older children felt, with my father gone, that they could invite their friends to the house without fear that their friends would be insulted or, as had sometimes happened with me, being told that their friends were in league with the devil and intended to rob our family of everything we owned. (I didn't fail to wonder, and it made me hate him, what on earth we owned that anybody else would want.)

His illness was beyond all hope of healing before anyone realized that he was ill. He had always been so strange and had lived, like a prophet, in such unimaginably close communion with the Lord that his long silences which were punctuated by moans and hallelujahs and snatches of old songs while he sat at the living-room window never seemed odd to us. It was not until he refused to eat because, he said, his family was trying to poison him that my mother was forced to accept as a fact what had, until then, been only an unwilling suspicion. When he was committed, it was discovered that he had tuberculosis and, as it turned out, the disease of his mind allowed the disease of his body to destroy him. For the doctors could not force him to eat, either, and, though he was fed intravenously, it was clear from the beginning that there was no hope for him.

In my mind's eye I could see him, sitting at the window, locked up in his terrors; hating and fearing every living soul including his children who had betrayed him, too, by reaching towards the world which had despised him. There were nine of us. I began to wonder what it could have felt like for such a man to have had nine children whom he could barely feed. He used to make little jokes about our poverty, which never, of course, seemed very funny to us; they could not have seemed very funny to him, either, or else our all too feeble response to them would never have caused such rages. He spent great energy and achieved, to our chagrin, no small amount of success in keeping us away from the people who surrounded us, people who had all-night rent parties to which we listened when we should have been sleeping, people who cursed and drank and flashed razor blades on Lenox Avenue. He could not understand why, if they had so much energy to spare, they could not use it to make their lives better. He treated almost everybody on our block with a most uncharitable asperity and neither they, nor, of course, their children were slow to reciprocate.

The only white people who came to our house were welfare workers and bill collectors. It was almost always my mother who dealt with them, for my father's temper, which was at the mercy of his pride, was never to be trusted. It was clear that he felt their very presence in his home to be a violation: this was conveyed by his carriage, almost ludicrously stiff, and by his voice, harsh and vindictively polite. When I was around nine or ten I wrote a play which was directed by a young, white schoolteacher, a woman, who then took an interest in me, and gave me books to read and, in order to corroborate my theatrical bent, decided to take me to see what she somewhat tactlessly referred to as "real" plays. Theater-going was forbidden in our house, but, with the really cruel intuitiveness of a child, I suspected that the color of this woman's skin would carry the day for me. When, at school, she suggested taking me to the theater, I did not, and I might have done if she had been a Negro, find a way of discouraging her, but agreed that she should pick me up at my house one evening. I then, very cleverly, left all the rest to my mother, who suggested to my father, as I knew she would, that it would not be very nice to let such a kind woman make the trip for nothing. Also, since it was a schoolteacher, I imagine that my mother countered the idea of sin with the idea of "education," which word, even with my father, carried a kind of bitter weight.

Before the teacher came my father took me aside to ask *why* she was coming, what *interest* she could possibly have in our house, in a boy like me. I said I didn't know but I, too, suggested that it had something to do with education. And I understood that my father was waiting for me to say something—I didn't quite know what; perhaps that I wanted his protection against this teacher and her "education." I said none of these things and the teacher came and we went out. It was clear, during the brief interview in our living room, that my father was agreeing very much against his will and that he would have refused permission if he had dared. The fact that he did not dare caused me to despise him: I had no way of knowing that he was facing in that living room a wholly unprecedented and frightening situation.

Later, when my father had been laid off from his job, this woman became very important to us. She was really a very sweet and generous woman and went to a great deal of trouble to be of help to us, particularly during one awful winter. My mother called her by the highest name she knew: she said she was a "christian." My father could scarcely disagree but during the four or five years of our relatively close association he never trusted her and was always trying to surprise in her open, Midwestern face the genuine, cunningly hidden, and hideous motivation. In later years, particularly when it began to be clear that this "education" of mine was going to lead me to perdition, he became more explicit and warned me that my white friends in high school were not really my friends and that I would see, when I was older, how white people would do anything to keep a Negro down. Some of them could be nice, he admitted, but none of them were to be trusted and most of them were not even nice. The best thing was to have as little to do with them as possible. I did not feel this way and I was certain, in my innocence, that I never would.

But the year which preceded my father's death had made a great change in my life. I had been living in New Jersey, working in defense plants, working and living among southerners, white and black. I knew about the south, of course, and about how southerners treated Negroes and how they expected them to behave, but it had never entered my mind that anyone would look at me and expect *me* to behave that way. I learned in New Jersey that to be a Negro meant, precisely, that one was never looked at but was simply at the mercy of the reflexes the color of one's skin caused in other people. I acted in New Jersey as I had always acted, that is as though I thought a great deal of myself—I had to *act* that way—with results that were, simply, unbelievable. I had scarcely arrived before I had earned the enmity, which was extraordinarily ingenious, of all my superiors and nearly all my co-workers. In the beginning, to make matters worse, I simply did not know what was happening. I did not know what I had done, and I shortly began to wonder what *anyone* could possibly do, to bring about such unanimous, active, and unbearably vocal hostility. I knew about jim-crow but I had never experienced it. I went to the same self-service restaurant three times and stood with all the Princeton boys before the counter, waiting for a hamburger and coffee; it was always an extraordinarily long time before anything was set before me; but it was not until the fourth visit that I learned that, in fact, nothing had ever been set before me: I had simply picked something up. Negroes were not served there, I was told, and they had been waiting for me to realize that I was always the only Negro present. Once I was told this, I determined to go there all the time. But now they were ready for me and, though some dreadful scenes were subsequently enacted in that restaurant, I never ate there again.

It was the same story all over New Jersey, in bars, bowling alleys, diners, places to live. I was always being forced to leave, silently, or with mutual imprecations. I very shortly became notorious and children giggled behind me when I passed and their elders whispered or shouted—they really believed that I was mad. And it did begin to work on my mind, of course; I began to be afraid to go anywhere and to compensate for this I went places to which I really should not have gone and where, God knows, I had no desire to be. My reputation in town naturally enhanced my reputation at work and my working day became one long series of acrobatics designed to keep me out of trouble. I cannot say that these acrobatics succeeded. It began to seem that the machinery of the organization I worked for was turning over, day and night, with but one aim: to eject me. I was fired once, and contrived, with the aid of a friend from New York, to get back on the payroll; was fired again, and bounced back again. It took a while to fire me for the third time, but the third time took. There were no loopholes anywhere. There was not even any way of getting back inside the gates.

That year in New Jersey lives in my mind as though it were the year during which, having an unsuspected predilection for it, I first contracted some dread, chronic disease, the unfailing symptom of which is a kind of blind fever, a pounding in the skull and fire in the bowels. Once this disease is contracted, one can never be really carefree again, for the fever, without an instant's warning, can recur at any moment. It can wreck more important things than race relations. There is not a Negro alive who does not have this rage in his blood—one has the choice, merely, of living with it consciously or surrendering to it. As for me, this fever has recurred in me, and does, and will until the day I die.

My last night in New Jersey, a white friend from New York took me to the nearest big town, Trenton, to go to the movies and have a few drinks. As it turned out, he also saved me from, at the very least, a violent whipping. Almost every detail of that night stands out very clearly in my memory. I even remember the name of the movie we saw because its title impressed me as being so patly ironical. It was a movie about the German occupation of France, starring Maureen O'Hara and Charles Laughton and called *This Land Is Mine.* I remember the name of the diner we walked into when the movie ended: it was the "American Diner." When we walked in the counter-man asked what we wanted and I remember answering with the casual sharpness which had become my habit: "We want a hamburger and a cup of coffee, what do you think we want?" I do not know why, after a year of such rebuffs, I so completely failed to anticipate his answer, which was, of course, "We don't serve Negroes here." This reply failed to discompose me, at least for the moment. I made some sardonic comment about the name of the diner and we walked out into the streets.

This was the time of what was called the "brown-out," when the lights in all American cities were very dim. When we re-entered the streets something happened to me which had the force of an optical illusion, or a nightmare. The streets were very crowded and I was facing north. People were moving in every direction but it seemed to me, in that instant, that all of the people I could see, and many more than that, were moving toward me, against me, and that everyone was white. I remember how their faces gleamed. And I felt, like a physical sensation, a *click* at the nape of my neck as though some interior string connecting my head to my body had been cut. I began to walk. I heard my friend call after me, but I ignored him. Heaven only knows what was going on in his mind, but he had the good sense not to touch me—I don't know what would have happened if he had—and to keep me in sight. I don't know what was going on in my mind, either; I certainly had no conscious plan. I wanted to do something to crush these white faces, which were crushing me. I walked for perhaps a block or two until I came to an enormous, glittering, and fashionable restaurant in which I knew not even the intercession of the Virgin would cause me to be served. I pushed through the doors and took the first vacant seat I saw, at a table for two, and waited.

I do not know how long I waited and I rather wonder, until today, what I could possibly have looked like. Whatever I looked like, I frightened the waitress who shortly appeared, and the moment she appeared all of my fury flowed towards her. I hated her for her white face, and for her great, astounded, frightened eyes. I felt that if she found a black man so frightening I would make her fright worth-while.

She did not ask me what I wanted, but repeated, as though she had learned it somewhere, "We don't serve Negroes here." She did not say it with the blunt, derisive hostility to which I had grown so accustomed, but, rather, with a note of apology in her voice, and fear. This made me colder and more murderous than ever. I felt I had to do something with my hands. I wanted her to come close enough for me to get her neck between my hands.

So I pretended not to have understood her, hoping to draw her closer. And she did step a very short step closer, with her pencil poised incongruously over her pad, and repeated the formula: ". . . don't serve Negroes here."

Somehow, with the repetition of that phrase, which was already ringing in my head like a thousand bells of a nightmare, I realized that she would never come any closer and that I would have to strike from a distance. There was nothing on the table but an ordinary water-mug half full of water, and I picked this up and hurled it with all my strength at her. She ducked and it missed her and shattered against the mirror behind the bar. And, with that sound, my frozen blood abruptly thawed, I returned from wherever I had been, I *saw*, for the first time, the restaurant, the people with their mouths open, already, as it seemed to me, rising as one man, and I realized what I had done, and where I was, and I was frightened. I rose and began running for the door. A round, potbellied man grabbed me by the nape of the neck just as I reached the doors and began to beat me about the face. I kicked him and got loose and ran into the streets. My friend whispered, *"Run!"* and I ran.

My friend stayed outside the restaurant long enough to misdirect my pursuers and the police, who arrived, he told me, at once. I do not know what I said to him when he came to my room that night. I could not have said much. I felt, in the oddest, most awful way, that I had somehow betrayed him. I lived it over and over and over again, the way one relives an automobile accident after it has happened and one finds oneself alone and safe. I could not get over two facts, both equally difficult for the imagination to grasp, and one was that

I could have been murdered. But the other was that I had been ready to commit murder. I saw nothing very clearly but I did see this: that my life, my *real* life, was in danger, and not from anything other people might do but from the hatred I carried in my own heart.

II

I had returned home around the second week in June—in great haste because it seemed that my father's death and my mother's confinement were both but a matter of hours. In the case of my mother, it soon became clear that she had simply made a miscalculation. This had always been her tendency and I don't believe that a single one of us arrived in the world, or has since arrived anywhere else, on time. But none of us dawdled so intolerably about the business of being born as did my baby sister. We sometimes amused ourselves, during those endless, stifling weeks, by picturing the baby sitting within in the safe, warm dark, bitterly regretting the necessity of becoming a part of our chaos and stubbornly putting it off as long as possible. I understood her perfectly and congratulated her on showing such good sense so soon. Death, however, sat as purposefully at my father's bedside as life stirred within my mother's womb and it was harder to understand why he so lingered in that long shadow. It seemed that he had bent, and for a long time, too, all of his energies towards dying. Now death was ready for him but my father held back.

All of Harlem, indeed, seemed to be infected by waiting. I had never before known it to be so violently still. Racial tensions throughout this country were exacerbated during the early years of the war, partly because the labor market brought together hundreds of thousands of ill-prepared people and partly because Negro soldiers, regardless of where they were born, received their military training in the south. What happened in defense plants and army camps had repercussions, naturally, in every Negro ghetto. The situation in Harlem had grown bad enough for clergymen, policemen, educators, politicians, and social workers to assert in one breath that there was no "crime wave" and to offer, in the very next breath, suggestions as to how to combat it. These suggestions always seemed to involve playgrounds, despite the fact that racial skirmishes were occurring in the playgrounds, too. Playground or not, crime wave or not, the Harlem police force had been augmented in March, and the unrest grew—perhaps, in fact, partly as a result of the ghetto's instinctive hatred of policemen. Perhaps the most revealing news item, out of the steady parade of reports of muggings, stabbings, shootings, assaults, gang wars, and accusations of police brutality, is the item concerning six Negro girls who set upon a white girl in the subway because, as they all too accurately put it, she was stepping on their toes. Indeed she was, all over the nation.

I had never before been so aware of policemen, on foot, on horse-back, on corners, everywhere, always two by two. Nor had I ever been so aware of small knots of people. They were on stoops and on corners and in doorways, and what was striking about them, I think, was that they did not seem to be talking. Never, when I passed these groups, did the usual sound of a curse or a laugh ring out and neither did there seem to be any hum of gossip. There was certainly, on the other hand, occurring between them communication extraordinarily intense. Another thing that was striking was the unex-pected diversity of the people who made up these groups. Usually, for example, one would see a group of sharpies standing on the street corner, jiving the passing chicks; or a group of older men, usually, for some reason, in the vicinity of a barber shop, discussing baseball scores, or the numbers, or making rather chilling observations about women they had known. Women, in a general way, tended to be seen less often together—unless they were church women, or very young girls, or prostitutes met together for an unprofessional instant. But that summer I saw the strangest combinations: large, respectable, churchly matrons standing on the stoops or the corners with their hair tied up, together with a girl in sleazy satin whose face bore the marks of gin and the razor, or heavy-set, abrupt, no-nonsense older men, in company with the most disreputable and fanatical "race" men, or these same "race" men with the sharpies, or these sharpies with the churchly women. Seventh Day Adventists and Methodists and Spiritualists seemed to be hobnobbing with Holyrollers and they were all, alike, entangled with the most flagrant disbelievers; some-thing heavy in their stance seemed to indicate that they had all, incredibly, seen a common vision, and on each face there seemed to be the same strange, bitter shadow.

The churchly women and the matter-of-fact, no-nonsense men had children in the Army. The sleazy girls they talked to had lovers there, the sharpies and the "race" men had friends and brothers there. It would have demanded an unquestioning patriotism, happily as uncommon in this country as it is undesirable, for these people not to have been disturbed by the bitter letters they received, by the newspaper stories they read, not to have been enraged by the posters, then to be found all over New York, which described the Japanese as "yellow-bellied Japs." It was only the "race" men, to be sure, who spoke ceaselessly of being revenged—how this vengeance was to be exacted was not clear—for the indignities and dangers suffered by Negro boys in uniform; but everybody felt a directionless, hopeless bitterness, as well as that panic which can scarcely be suppressed when one knows that a human being one loves is beyond one's reach, and in danger. This helplessness and this gnawing uneasiness does something, at length, to even the toughest mind. Perhaps the best way to sum all this up is to say that the people I knew felt, mainly, a peculiar kind of relief when they knew that their boys were being shipped out of the south, to do battle overseas. It was, perhaps, like feeling that the most dangerous part of a dangerous journey had been passed and that now, even if death should come, it would come with honor and without the complicity of their countrymen. Such a death would be, in short, a fact with which one could hope to live.

It was on the 28th of July, which I believe was a Wednesday, that I visited my father for the first time during his illness and for the last time in his life. The moment I saw him I knew why I had put off this visit so long. I had told my mother that I did not want to see him because I hated him. But this was not true. It was only that I *had* hated him and I wanted to hold on to this hatred. I did not want to look on him as a ruin: it was not a ruin I had hated. I imagine that one of the reasons people cling to their hates so stubbornly is because they sense, once hate is gone, that they will be forced to deal with pain.

We traveled out to him, his older sister and myself, to what seemed to be the very end of a very Long Island. It was hot and dusty and we wrangled, my aunt and I, all the way out, over the fact that I had recently begun to smoke and, as she said, to give myself airs. But I knew that she wrangled with me because she could not bear to face the fact of her brother's dying. Neither could I endure the reality of her despair, her unstated bafflement as to what had happened to her brother's life, and her own. So we wrangled and I smoked and from time to time she fell into a heavy reverie. Covertly, I watched her face, which was the face of an old woman; it had fallen in, the eyes were sunken and lightless; soon she would be dying, too.

In my childhood—it had not been so long ago—I had thought her beautiful. She had been quick-witted and quick-moving and very generous with all the children and each of her visits had been an event. At one time one of my brothers and myself had thought of running away to live with her. Now she could no longer produce out of her handbag some unexpected and yet familiar delight. She made me feel pity and revulsion and fear. It was awful to realize that she no longer caused me to feel affection. The closer we came to the hospital the more querulous she became and at the same time, naturally, grew more dependent on me. Between pity and guilt and fear I began to feel that there was another me trapped in my skull like a jack-in-the-box who might escape my control at any moment and fill the air with screaming.

She began to cry the moment we entered the room and she saw him lying there, all shriveled and still, like a little black monkey. The great, gleaming apparatus which fed him and would have compelled him to be still even if he had been able to move brought to mind, not beneficence, but torture; the tubes entering his arm made me think of pictures I had seen when a child, of Gulliver, tied down by the pygmies on that island. My aunt wept and wept, there was a whistling sound in my father's throat; nothing was said; he could not speak. I wanted to take his hand, to say something. But I do not know what I could have said, even if he could have heard me. He was not really in that room with us, he had at last really embarked on his journey; and though my aunt told me that he said he was going to meet Jesus, I did not hear anything except that whistling in his throat. The doctor came back and we left, into that unbearable train again, and home. In the morning came the telegram saying that he was dead. Then the house was suddenly full of relatives, friends, hysteria, and confusion and I quickly left my mother and the children to the care of those impressive women, who, in Negro communities at least, automatically appear at times of bereavement armed with lotions, proverbs, and patience, and an ability to cook. I went downtown. By the time I returned, later the same day, my mother had been carried to the hospital and the baby had been born.

III

For my father's funeral I had nothing black to wear and this posed a nagging problem all day long. It was one of those problems, simple, or impossible of solution, to which the mind insanely clings in order to avoid the mind's real trouble. I spent most of that day at the downtown apartment of a girl I knew, celebrating my birthday with whiskey and wondering what to wear that night. When planning a birthday celebration one naturally does not expect that it will be up against competition from a funeral and this girl had anticipated taking me out that night, for a big dinner and a night club afterwards. Sometime during the course of that long day we decided that we would go out anyway, when my father's funeral service was over. I imagine I decided it, since, as the funeral hour approached, it became clearer and clearer to me that I would not know what to do with myself when it was over. The girl, stifling her very lively concern as to the possible effects of the whiskey on one of my father's chief mourners, concentrated on being conciliatory and practically helpful. She found a black shirt for me somewhere and ironed it and, dressed in the darkest pants and jacket I owned, and slightly drunk, I made my way to my father's funeral.

The chapel was full, but not packed, and very quiet. There were, mainly, my father's relatives, and his children, and here and there I saw faces I had not seen since childhood, the faces of my father's one-time friends. They were very dark and solemn now, seeming somehow to suggest that they had known all along that something like this would happen. Chief among the mourners was my aunt, who had quarreled with my father all his life; by which I do not mean to suggest that her mourning was insincere or that she had not loved him. I suppose that she was one of the few people in the world who had, and their incessant quarreling proved precisely the strength of the tie that bound them. The only other person in the world, as far as I knew, whose relationship to my father rivaled my aunt's in depth was my mother, who was not there.

It seemed to me, of course, that is was a very long funeral. But it was, if anything, a rather shorter funeral than most, nor, since there were no overwhelming, uncontrollable expressions of grief, could it be called—if I dare to use the word—successful. The minister who preached my father's funeral sermon was one of the few my father had still been seeing as he neared his end. He presented to us in his sermon a man whom none of us had ever seen—a man thoughtful, patient, and forbearing, a Christian inspiration to all who knew him, and a model for his children. And no doubt the children, in their disturbed and guilty state, were almost ready to believe this; he had been remote enough to be anything and, anyway, the shock of the incontrovertible, that it was really our father lying up there in that casket, prepared the mind for anything. His sister moaned and this grief-stricken moaning was taken as corroboration. The other faces held a dark, non-committal thoughtfulness. This was not the man they had known, but they had scarcely expected to be confronted with *him*; this was, in a sense deeper than questions of fact, the man they had not known, and the man they had not known may have been the real one. The real man, whoever he had been, had suffered and now he was dead: this was all that was sure and all that mattered now. Every man in the chapel hoped that when his hour came he, too, would be eulogized, which is to say forgiven, and that all of his lapses, greeds, errors, and strayings from the truth would be invested with coherence and looked upon with charity. This was perhaps the last thing human beings could give each other and it was what they demanded, after all, of the Lord. Only the Lord saw the midnight tears, only He was present when one of His children, moaning and wringing hands, paced up and down the room. When one slapped one's child in anger the recoil in the heart reverberated through heaven and became part of the pain of the universe. And when the children were hungry and sullen and distrustful and one watched them, daily, growing wilder, and further away, and running headlong into danger, it was the Lord who knew what the charged heart endured as the strap was laid to the backside; the Lord alone who knew what one *would* have said if one had had, like the Lord, the gift of the living word. It was the Lord who knew of the impossibility every parent in that room faced: how to prepare the child for the day when the child would be despised and how to *create* in the child—by what means?—a stronger antidote to this poison that one had found for oneself. The avenues, side streets, bars, billiard halls, hospitals, police stations, and even the playgrounds of Harlem—not to mention the houses of correction, the jails, and the morgue—testified to the potency of the poison while remaining silent as to the efficacy of whatever antidote, irrestibly raising the question of whether or not such an antidote existed; raising, which was worse, the question of whatever antidote, irresistibly raising the question of whether or not such an antidote existed; raising, which was worse, the question of whether or not an antidote was desirable; perhaps poison should not to judge the man who had gone down under an impossible burden. It was better to remember: *Thou knowest this man's fall; but thou knowest not his wrassling.*

While the preacher talked and I watched the children—years of changing their diapers, scrubbing them, slapping them, taking them to school, and scolding them had had the perhaps inevitable result of making me love them, though I am not sure I knew this then—my mind was busily breaking out with a rash of disconnected impressions. Snatches of popular songs, indecent jokes, bits of books I had read, movie sequences, faces, voices, political issues—I thought I was going mad; all these impressions suspended, as it were, in the solution of the faint nausea produced in me by the heat and liquor. For a moment I had the impression that my alcoholic breath, inefficiently disguised with chewing gum, filled the entire chapel. Then someone began singing one of my father's favorite songs and, abruptly, I was with him, sitting on his knee, in the hot, enormous, crowded church which was the first church we attended. It was the Abyssinia Baptist Church on 138th Street. We had not gone there long. With this image, a host of others came. I had forgotten, in the rage of my growing up, how proud my father had been of me when I was little. Apparently,

I had had a voice and my father had liked to show me off before the members of the church. I had forgotten what he had looked like when he was pleased but now I remembered that he had always been grinning with pleasure when my solos ended. I even remembered certain expressions on his face when he teased my mother—had he loved her? I would never know. And when had it all begun to change? For now it seemed that he had not always been cruel. I remembered being taken for a haircut and scraping my knee on the footrest of the barber's chair and I remembered my father's face as he soothed my crying and applied the stinging iodine. Then I remembered our fights, fights which had been of the worst possible kind because my technique had been silence.

I remembered the one time in all our life together when we had really spoken to each other.

It was on a Sunday and it must have been shortly before I left home. We were walking, just the two of us, in our usual silence, to or from church. I was in high school and had been doing a lot of writing and I was, at about this time, the editor of the high school magazine. But I had also been a Young Minister and had been preaching from the pulpit. Lately, I had been taking fewer engagements and preached as rarely as possible. It was said in the church, quite truthfully, that I was "cooling off."

My father asked me abruptly, "You'd rather write than preach, wouldn't you?"

I was astonished at his question—because it was a real question. I answered, "Yes."

That was all we said. It was awful to remember that that was all we had *ever* said.

The casket now was opened and the mourners were being led up the aisle to look for the last time on the deceased. The assumption was that the family was too overcome with grief to be allowed to make this journey alone and I watched while my aunt was led to the casket and, muffled in black, and shaking, led back to her seat. I disapproved of forcing the children to look on their dead father, considering that the shock of his death, or, more truthfully, the shock of death as a reality, was already a little more than a child could bear, but my judgment in this matter had been overruled and there they were, bewildered and frightened and very small, being led, one by one, to the casket. But there is also something very gallant about children at such moments. It has something to do with their silence and gravity and with the fact that one cannot help them. Their legs, somehow, seem *exposed*, so that it is at once incredible and terribly clear that their legs are all they have to hold them up.

I had not wanted to go to the casket myself and I certainly had not wished to be led there, but there was no way of avoiding either of these forms. One of the deacons led me up and I looked on my father's face. I cannot say that it looked like him at all. His blackness had been equivocated by powder and there was no suggestion in that casket of what his power had or could have been. He was simply an old man dead, and it was hard to believe that he had ever given anyone either joy or pain. Yet, his life filled that room. Further up the avenue his wife was holding his newborn child. Life and death so close together, and love and hatred, and right and wrong, said something to me which I did not want to hear concerning man, concerning the life of man.

After the funeral, while I was downtown desperately celebrating my birthday, a Negro soldier, in the lobby of the Hotel Braddock, got into a fight with a white policeman over a Negro girl. Negro girls, white policemen, in or out of uniform, and Negro males—in or out of uniform—were part of the furniture of the lobby of the Hotel Braddock and this was certainly not the first time such an incident had occurred. It was destined, however, to receive an unprecedented publicity, for the fight between the policeman and the soldier ended with the shooting of the soldier. Rumor, flowing immediately to the streets outside, stated that the soldier had been shot in the back, an instantaneous and revealing invention, and that the soldier had died protecting a Negro woman. The facts were somewhat different—for example, the soldier had not been shot in the back, and was not dead, and the girl seems to have been as dubious a symbol of womanhood as her white counterpart in Georgia usually is, but no one was interested in the facts. They preferred the invention because this invention expressed and corroborated their hates and fears so perfectly. It is just as well to remember that people are always doing this. Perhaps many of those legends, including Christianity, to which the world clings began their conquest of the world with just some such concerted surrender to distortion. The effect, in Harlem, of this particular legend was like the effect of a lit match in a tin of gasoline. The mob gathered before the doors of the Hotel Braddock simply began to swell and to spread in every direction, and Harlem exploded.

The mob did not cross the ghetto lines. It would have been easy, for example, to have gone over Morningside Park on the west side or to have crossed the Grand Central railroad tracks at 125th Street on the east side, to wreak havoc in white neighborhoods. The mob seems to have been mainly interested in something more potent and real than the white face, that is, in white power, and the principal damage done during the riot of the summer of 1943 was to white business establishments in Harlem. It might have been a far bloodier story, of course, if, at the hour the riot began, these establishments had still been open. From the Hotel Braddock the mob fanned out, east and west along 125th Street, and for the entire length of Lenox, Seventh, and Eighth avenues. Along each of these avenues, and along each major side street—116th, 125th, 135th, and so on—bars, stores, pawnshops, restaurants, even little luncheonettes had been smashed open and entered and looted—looted, it might be added, with more haste than efficiency. The shelves really looked as though a bomb had struck them. Cans of beans and soup and dog food, along with toilet paper, corn flakes, sardines and milk tumbled every which way, and abandoned cash registers and cases of beer leaned crazily out of the splintered windows and were strewn along the avenues. Sheets, blankets, and clothing of every description formed a kind of path, as though people had dropped them while running. I truly had not realized that Harlem *had* so many stores until I saw them all smashed open; the first time the word *wealth* ever entered my mind in relation to Harlem was when I saw it scattered in the streets. But one's first, incongruous impression of plenty was countered immediately by an impression of waste. None of this was doing anybody any good. It would have been better to have left the plate glass as it had been and the goods lying in the stores.

It would have been better, but it would also have been intolerable, for Harlem had needed something to smash. To smash something is the ghetto's chronic need. Most of the time it is the members of the ghetto who smash each other, and themselves. But as long as the ghetto walls are standing there will always come a moment when these outlets do not work. That summer, for example, it was not enough to get into a fight on Lenox Avenue, or curse out one's cronies in the barber shops. If ever, indeed, the violence which fills Harlem's churches, pool halls, and bars erupts outward in a more direct fashion, Harlem and its citizens are likely to vanish in an apocalyptic flood. That this is not likely to happen is due to a great many reasons, most hidden and powerful among them the Negro's real relation to the white American. This relation prohibits, simply, anything as un-complicated and satisfactory as pure hatred. In order really to hate white people, one has to blot so much out of the mind—and the heart —that this hatred itself becomes an exhausting and self-destructive pose. But this does not mean, on the other hand, that love comes easily: the white world is too powerful, too complacent, too ready with gratuitous humiliation, and, above all, too ignorant and too innocent for that. One is absolutely forced to make perpetual qualifications and one's own reactions are always canceling each other out. It is this, really, which has driven so many people mad, both white and black. One is always in the position of having to decide between amputation and gangrene. Amputation is swift but time may prove that the amputation was not necessary—or one may delay the amputation too long. Gangrene is slow, but it is impossible to be sure that one is reading one's symptoms right. The idea of going through life as a cripple is more than one can bear, and equally unbearable is the risk of swelling up slowly, in agony, with poison. And the trouble, finally, is that the risks are real even if the choices do not exist.

"But as for me and my house," my father had said, "we will serve the Lord." I wondered, as we drove him to his resting place, what this line had meant for him. I had heard him preach it many times. I had preached it once myself, proudly giving it an interpretation different from my father's. Now the whole thing came back to me, as though my father and I were on our way to Sunday school and I were memorizing the golden text: *And if it seem evil unto you to serve the Lord, choose you this day whom you will serve; whether the gods which your fathers served that were on the other side of the flood, or the gods of the Amorites, in whose land ye dwell: but as for me and my house, we will serve the Lord.* I suspected in these familiar lines a meaning which had never been there for me before. All of my father's texts and songs, which I had decided were meaningless, were arranged before me at his death like empty bottles, waiting to hold the meaning which life would give them for me. This was his legacy: nothing is ever escaped. That bleakly memorable morning I hated the unbelievable streets and the Negroes and whites who had, equally, made them that way. But I knew that it was folly, as my father would have said, this bitterness was folly. It was necessary to hold on to the things that mattered. The dead man mattered, the new life mattered; blackness and whiteness did not matter; to believe that they did was to acquiesce in one's own destruction. Hatred, which could destroy so much, never failed to destroy the man who hated and this was an immutable law.

It began to seem that one would have to hold in the mind forever two ideas which seemed to be in opposition. The first idea was acceptance, the acceptance, totally without rancor, of life as it is, and men as they are: in the light of this idea, it goes without saying that injustice is a commonplace. But this did not mean that one could be complacent, for the second idea was of equal power: that one must never, in one's own life, accept these injustices as commonplace but must fight them with all one's strength. This fight begins, however, in the heart and it now had been laid to my charge to keep my own heart free of hatred and despair. This intimation made my heart heavy and, now that my father was irrecoverable, I wished that he had been beside me so that I could have searched his face for the answers which only the future would give me now.

QUESTIONS FOR DISCUSSION

1. Baldwin calls the events paralleling his father's death "the most sustained and brutally dissonant of codas" and "a corrective for the pride of his eldest son." A coda is the formal ending of a musical composition. In what sense was the father's end "dissonant"? How does the reference to "a corrective" prepare the reader for the attempt at reconciliation which this essay offers?

2. Baldwin begins the portrait of his father with the familiar explanation of a lack of communication between the generations. But he places the emphasis and the blame on "the second generation." What does he mean?

3. In the paragraph about New Orleans, Baldwin begins to show something of his father's narrowness of view. Explain the references upon which Baldwin depends for his characterization of New Orleans. How does the paragraph's concluding sentence complement the characterization already provided?

4. This essay first appeared in 1955, some time before the phrase, "Black is beautiful," became popular. What would Baldwin's father have thought about the phrase if he had heard it?

5. Baldwin offers several examples to document his father's paranoia, the most important concerning the white schoolteacher. What does the author recall that makes him despise his father for his behavior in this incident? How does this incident illuminate Baldwin's own attitudes toward whites?

6. In relating his experiences with racial discrimination, Baldwin speaks of "jim-crow." What is the meaning of this phrase? What is its origin?

7. Baldwin uses the metaphor of "a kind of blind fever" to describe the effects of discrimination upon a black person. What do you think about his generalization, "There is not a Negro alive who does not have this rage in his blood"? Can the same statement be made about other minority-group members?

8. At the end of Part I, Baldwin narrates in detail his experience in the two restaurants. What does he learn about himself from this experience? How is this related to his father's death and his attitudes toward him?

9. Baldwin makes a point of "the unexpected diversity of the people" who stood together on Harlem street-corners that summer. What were

some of the causes for bringing together all sections of the black community? What was their "common vision"?

10. Part II of this essay consists of only two narrative pictures—the streets of Harlem and the visit to the dying father. How do these two scenes serve this essay?

11. Baldwin presents the paradoxical circumstances of trying to concern oneself with both a funeral and the celebration of a birthday on the same day. How does his use of irony assist his expression of the problem?

12. Baldwin speaks at length about the eulogy given his father by the minister officiating at the funeral. Although he says that the eulogy presented "a man whom none of us had ever seen," Baldwin accepts the validity of the eulogy. Upon what grounds? Why is the praise given his father not discarded as false? Why is this acceptance the mark of a turning point in the author's attitude?

13. What is Baldwin saying in his analogy using amputation and gangrene?

14. What is Baldwin's conclusion? What is the "immutable law" which the twin experiences of his father's funeral and the riot have taught him?

ASSIGNMENTS FOR WRITING

1. Baldwin builds this essay upon a series of significant incidents, from childhood, from his time away from home, and from the events at his father's death. Choose one incident out of your own experience and write a personal narrative showing how this experience led you to a decision.

2. The recent reports of Federal commissions warn us that we are becoming an ever-increasingly divided society, given to violence and riot as our means of expressing grievance. Write an essay in which you discuss what you know of riots in America. What are the causes? What do they accomplish? Whom do they harm? How can they be stopped?

Stranger in the Village

From all available evidence no black man had ever set foot in this tiny Swiss village before I came. I was told before arriving that I would probably be a "sight" for the village; I took this to mean that people of my complexion were rarely seen in Switzerland, and also that city people are always something of a "sight" outside of the city. It did not occur to me—possibly because I am an American—that there could be people anywhere who had never seen a Negro.

It is a fact that cannot be explained on the basis of the inaccessibility of the village. The village is very high, but it is only four hours from Milan and three hours from Lausanne. It is true that it is virtually unknown. Few people making plans for a holiday would elect to come here. On the other hand, the villagers are able, presumably, to come and go as they please—which they do: to another town at the foot of the mountain, with a population of approximately five thousand, the nearest place to see a movie or go to the bank. In the village there is no movie house, no bank, no library, no theater; very few radios, one jeep, one station wagon; and, at the moment, one typewriter, mine, an invention which the woman next door to me here had never seen. There are about six hundred people living here, all Catholic—I conclude this from the fact that the Catholic church is open all year round, whereas the Protestant chapel, set off on a hill a little removed from the village, is open only in the summertime when the tourists arrive. There are four or five hotels, all closed now, and four or five *bistros,* of which, however, only two do any business during the winter. These two do not do a great deal, for life in the village seems to end around nine or ten o'clock. There are a few stores, butcher, baker, *épicerie,* a hardware store, and a money-changer—who cannot change travelers' checks, but must send them down to the bank, an operation which takes two or three days. There is something called the *Ballet Haus,* closed in the winter and used for God knows what, certainly not ballet, during the summer. There seems to be only one schoolhouse in the village, and this for the quite young children; I suppose this to mean that their older brothers and sisters at some point descend from these mountains in order to complete their education—possibly, again, to the town just below. The landscape is absolutely forbidding, mountains towering on all four sides, ice and snow as far as the eye can reach. In this white wilderness, men and women and children move all day, carrying washing, wood, buckets of milk or water, sometimes skiing on Sunday afternoons. All week long boys and young men are to be seen shoveling snow off the roof-tops, or dragging wood down from the forest in sleds.

The village's only real attraction, which explains the tourist season, is the hot spring water. A disquietingly high proportion of these tourists are cripples, or semi-cripples, who come year after year—from other parts of Switzerland, usually—to take the waters. This lends the village, at the height of the season, a rather terrifying air of sanctity, as though it were a lesser Lourdes. There is often something beautiful, there is always something awful, in the spectacle of a person who has lost one of his faculties, a faculty he never questioned until it was gone, and who struggles to recover it. Yet people remain people, on crutches or indeed on deathbeds; and wherever I passed, the first summer I was here, among the native villagers or among the lame, a wind passed with me—of astonishment, curiosity, amusement, and outrage. That first summer I stayed two weeks and never intended to return. But I did return in the winter, to work; the village offers, obviously, no distractions whatever and has the further advantage of being extremely cheap. Now it is winter again, a year later, and I am here again. Everyone in the village knows my name, though they scarcely ever use it, knows that I come from America—though, this, apparently, they will never really believe: black men come from Africa—and everyone knows that I am the friend of the son of a woman who was born here, and that I am staying in their chalet. But I remain as much a stranger today as I was the first day I arrived, and the children shout *Neger! Neger!* as I walk along the streets.

It must be admitted that in the beginning I was far too shocked to have any real reaction. In so far as I reacted at all, I reacted by trying to be pleasant—it being a great part of the American Negro's education (long before he goes to school) that he must make people "like" him. This smile-and-the-world-smiles-with-you routine worked about as well in this situation as it had in the situation for which it was designed, which is to say that it did not work at all. No one, after all, can be liked whose human weight and complexity cannot be, or has not been, admitted. My smile was simply another unheard-of phenomenon which allowed them to see my teeth—they did not, really, see my smile and I began to think that, should I take to snarling, no one would notice any difference. All of the physical characteristics of the Negro which had caused me, in America, a very different and almost forgotten pain were nothing less than miraculous—or infernal—in the eyes of the village people. Some thought my hair was the color of tar, that it had the texture of wire, or the texture of cotton. It was jocularly suggested that I might let it all grow long and make myself a winter coat. If I sat in the sun for more than five minutes some daring creature was certain to come along and gingerly put his fingers on my hair, as though he were afraid of an electric shock, or put his hand on my hand, astonished that the color did not rub off. In all of this, in which it must be conceded there was the charm of genuine wonder and in which there was certainly no element of intentional unkindness, there was yet no suggestion that I was human: I was simply a living wonder.

I knew that they did not mean to be unkind, and I know it now; it is necessary, nevertheless, for me to repeat this to myself each time that I walk out of the chalet. The children who shout *Neger!* have no way of knowing the echoes this sound raises in me. They are brimming with good humor and the more daring swell with pride when I stop to speak with them. Just the same, there are days when I cannot pause and smile, when I have no heart to play with them; when, indeed, I mutter sourly to myself, exactly as I muttered on the streets of a city these children have never seen, when I was no bigger than these children are now: *Your* mother *was a nigger.* Joyce is right about history being a nightmare—but it may be the nightmare from which no one *can* awaken. People are trapped in history and history is trapped in them.

There is a custom in the village—I am told it is repeated in many villages—of "buying" African natives for the purpose of converting them to Christianity. There stands in the church all year round a small box with a slot for money, decorated with a black figurine, and into this box the villagers drop their francs. During the *carnaval* which precedes Lent, two village children have their faces blackened—out of which bloodless darkness their blue eyes shine like ice—and fantastic horsehair wigs are placed on their blond heads; thus disguised, they solicit among the villagers for money for the missionaries in Africa. Between the box in the church and the blackened children, the village "bought" last year six or eight African natives. This was reported to me with pride by the wife of one of the *bistro* owners and I was careful to express astonishment and pleasure at the solicitude shown by the village for the souls of black folk. The *bistro* owner's wife beamed with a pleasure far more genuine than my own and seemed to feel that I might now breathe more easily concerning the souls of at least six of my kinsmen.

I tried not to think of these so lately baptized kinsmen, of the price paid for them, or the peculiar price they themselves would pay, and said nothing about my father, who having taken his own conversion too literally never, at bottom, forgave the white world (which he described as heathen) for having saddled him with a Christ in whom, to judge at least from their treatment of him, they themselves no longer believed. I thought of white men arriving for the first time in an African village, strangers there, as I am a stranger here, and tried to imagine the astounded populace touching their hair and marveling at the color of their skin. But there is a great difference between being the first white man to be seen by Africans and being the first black man to be seen by whites. The white man takes the astonishment as tribute, for he arrives to conquer and to convert the natives, whose inferiority in relation to himself is not even to be questioned; whereas I, without a thought of conquest, find myself among a people whose culture controls me, has even, in a sense, created me, people who have cost me more in anguish and rage than they will ever know, who yet do not even know of my existence. The astonishment with which I might have greeted them, should they have stumbled into my African village a few hundred years ago, might have rejoiced their hearts. But the astonishment with which they greet me today can only poison mine.

And this is so despite everything I may do to feel differently, despite my friendly conversations with the *bistro* owner's wife, despite their three-year-old son who has at last become my friend, despite the *saluts* and *bonsoirs* which I exchange with people as I walk, despite the fact that I know that no individual can be taken to task for what history is doing, or has done. I say that the culture of these people controls me—but they can scarcely be held responsible for European culture. America comes out of Europe, but these people have never seen America, nor have most of them seen more of Europe than the hamlet at the foot of their mountain. Yet they move with an authority which I shall never have; and they regard me, quite rightly, not only as a stranger in their village but as a suspect late-comer, bearing no credentials, to everything they have—however unconsciously— inherited.

For this village, even were it incomparably more remote and incredibly more primitive, is the West, the West onto which I have been so strangely grafted. These people cannot be, from the point of view of power, strangers anywhere in the world; they have made the modern world, in effect, even if they do not know it. The most illiterate among them is related, in a way that I am not, to Dante, Shakespeare, Michelangelo, Aeschylus, Da Vinci, Rembrandt, and Racine; the cathedral at Chartres says something to them which it cannot say to me, as indeed would New York's Empire State Building, should anyone here ever see it. Out of their hymns and dances come

Beethoven and Bach. Go back a few centuries and they are in their full glory—but I am in Africa, watching the conquerors arrive.

The rage of the disesteemed is personally fruitless, but it is also absolutely inevitable; this rage, so generally discounted, so little understood even among the people whose daily bread it is, is one of the things that makes history. Rage can only with difficulty, and never entirely, be brought under the domination of the intelligence and is therefore not susceptible to any arguments whatever. This is a fact which ordinary representatives of the *Herrenvolk,* having never felt this rage and being unable to imagine it, quite fail to understand. Also, rage cannot be hidden, it can only be dissembled. This dissembling deludes the thoughtless, and strengthens rage and adds, to rage, contempt. There are, no doubt, as many ways of coping with the resulting complex of tensions as there are black men in the world, but no black man can hope ever to be entirely liberated from this internal warfare—rage, dissembling, and contempt having inevitably accompanied his first realization of the power of white men. What is crucial here is that, since white men represent in the black man's world so heavy a weight, white men have for black men a reality which is far from being reciprocal; and hence all black men have toward all white men an attitude which is designed, really, either to rob the white man of the jewel of his naïveté, or else to make it cost him dear.

The black man insists, by whatever means he finds at his disposal, that the white man cease to regard him as an exotic rarity and recognize him as a human being. This is a very charged and difficult moment, for there is a great deal of will power involved in the white man's naïveté. Most people are not naturally reflective any more than they are naturally malicious, and the white man prefers to keep the black man at a certain human remove because it is easier for him thus to preserve his simplicity and avoid being called to account for crimes committed by his forefathers, or his neighbors. He is inescapably aware, nevertheless, that he is in a better position in the world than black men are, nor can he quite put to death the suspicion that he is hated by black men therefore. He does not wish to be hated, neither does he wish to change places, and at this point in his uneasiness he can scarcely avoid having recourse to those legends which white men have created about black men, the most usual effect of which is that the white man finds himself enmeshed, so to speak, in his own language which describes hell, as well as the attributes which lead one to hell, as being as black as night.

Every legend, moreover, contains its residuum of truth, and the root function of language is to control the universe by describing it. It is of quite considerable significance that black men remain, in the imagination, and in overwhelming numbers in fact, beyond the disciplines of salvation; and this despite the fact that the West has been "buying" African natives for centuries. There is, I should hazard, an instantaneous necessity to be divorced from this so visibly unsaved stranger, in whose heart, moreover, one cannot guess what dreams of vengeance are being nourished; and, at the same time, there are few things on earth more attractive than the idea of the unspeakable liberty which is allowed the unredeemed. When, beneath the black mask, a human being begins to make himself felt one cannot escape a certain awful wonder as to what kind of human being it is. What one's imagination makes of other people is dictated, of course, by the laws of one's own personality and it is one of the ironies of black-white relations that, by means of what the white man imagines the black man to be, the black man is enabled to know who the white man is.

I have said, for example, that I am as much a stranger in this village today as I was the first summer I arrived, but this is not quite true. The villagers wonder less about the texture of my hair than they did then, and wonder rather more about me. And the fact that their wonder now exists on another level is reflected in their attitudes and in their eyes. There are the children who make those delightful, hilarious, sometimes astonishingly grave overtures of friendship in the unpredictable fashion of children; other children, having been taught that the devil is a black man, scream in genuine anguish as I approach. Some of the older women never pass without a friendly greeting, never pass, indeed, if it seems that they will be able to engage me in conversation; other women look down or look away or rather contemptuously smirk. Some of the men drink with me and suggest that I learn how to ski—partly, I gather, because they cannot imagine what I would look like on skis—and want to know if I am married, and ask questions about my *métier*. But some of the men have accused *le sale nègre*—behind my back—of stealing wood and there is already in the eyes of some of them that peculiar, intent, paranoiac malevolence which one sometimes surprises in the eyes of American white men when, out walking with their Sunday girl, they see a Negro male approach.

There is a dreadful abyss between the streets of this village and the streets of the city in which I was born, between the children who shout *Neger!* today and those who shouted *Nigger!* yesterday—the abyss is experience, the American experience. The syllable hurled behind me today expresses, above all, wonder: I am a stranger here. But I am not a stranger in America and the same syllable riding on the American air expresses the war my presence has occasioned in the American soul.

For this village brings home to me this fact: that there was a day, and not really a very distant day, when Americans were scarcely Americans at all but discontented Europeans, facing a great unconquered continent and strolling, say, into a marketplace and seeing black men for the first time. The shock this spectacle afforded is suggested, surely, by the promptness with which they decided that these black men were not really men but cattle. It is true that the necessity on the part of the settlers of the New World of reconciling their moral assumptions with the fact—and the necessity—of slavery enhanced immensely the charm of this idea, and it is also true that this idea expresses, with a truly American bluntness, the attitude which to varying extents all masters have had toward all slaves.

But between all former slaves and slave-owners and the drama which begins for Americans over three hundred years ago at Jamestown, there are at least two differences to be observed. The American Negro slave could not suppose, for one thing, as slaves in past epochs had supposed and often done, that he would ever be able to wrest the power from his master's hands. This was a supposition which the modern era, which was to bring about such vast changes in the aims and dimensions of power, put to death; it only begins, in unprecedented fashion, and with dreadful implications, to be resurrected today. But even had this supposition persisted with undiminished force, the American Negro slave could not have used it to lend his condition dignity, for the reason that this supposition rests on another: that the slave in exile yet remains related to his past, has some means—if only in memory—of revering and sustaining the forms of his former life, is able, in short, to maintain his identity.

This was not the case with the American Negro slave. He is unique among the black men of the world in that his past was taken from him, almost literally, at one blow. One wonders what on earth the first slave found to say to the first dark child he bore. I am told that there are Haitians able to trace their ancestry back to African kings, but any American Negro wishing to go back so far will find his journey through time abruptly arrested by the signature on the bill of sale which served as the entrance paper for his ancestor. At the time—to say nothing of the circumstances—of the enslavement of the captive black man who was to become the American Negro, there was not the remotest possibility that he would ever take power from his master's hands. There was no reason to suppose that his situation would ever change, nor was there, shortly, anything to indicate that his situation had ever been different. It was his necessity, in the words of E. Franklin Frazier, to find a "motive for living under American culture or die." The identity of the American Negro comes out of this extreme situation, and the evolution of this identity was a source of the most intolerable anxiety in the minds and lives of his masters.

For the history of the American Negro is unique also in this: that the question of his humanity, and of his rights therefore as a human being, became a burning one for several generations of Americans, so burning a question that it ultimately became one of those used to divide the nation. It is out of this argument that the venom of the epithet *Nigger!* is derived. It is an argument which Europe has never had, and hence Europe quite sincerely fails to understand how or why the argument arose in the first place, why its effects are so frequently disastrous and always so unpredictable, why it refuses until today to be entirely settled. Europe's black possessions remained—and do remain—in Europe's colonies, at which remove they represented no threat whatever to European identity. If they posed any problem at all for the European conscience, it was a problem which remained comfortingly abstract: in effect, the black man, *as a man*, did not exist for Europe. But in America, even as a slave, he was an inescapable part of the general social fabric and no American could escape having an attitude toward him. Americans attempt until today to make an abstraction of the Negro, but the very nature of these abstractions reveals the tremendous effects the presence of the Negro has had on the American character.

When one considers the history of the Negro in America it is of the greatest importance to recognize that the moral beliefs of a person, or a people, are never really as tenuous as life—which is not moral—very often causes them to appear; these create for them a frame of reference and a necessary hope, the hope being that when life has done its worst they will be enabled to rise above themselves and to triumph over life. Life would scarcely be bearable if this hope did not exist. Again, even when the worst has been said, to betray a belief is not by any means to have put oneself beyond its power; the betrayal of a belief is not the same thing as ceasing to believe. If this were not so there would be no moral standards in the world at all. Yet one must also recognize that morality is based on ideas and that all ideas are dangerous—dangerous because ideas can only lead to action and where the action leads no man can say. And dangerous in this respect: that confronted with the impossibility of remaining faithful to one's beliefs, and the equal impossibility of becoming free of them, one can be driven to the most inhuman excesses. The ideas on which American beliefs are based are not, though Americans often seem to think so, ideas which originated in America. They came out of Europe. And the establishment of democracy on the American continent was scarcely as radical a break with the past as was the necessity, which Americans faced, of broadening this concept to include black men.

This was, literally, a hard necessity. It was impossible, for one thing, for Americans to abandon their beliefs, not only because these beliefs alone seemed able to justify the sacrifices they had endured and the blood that they had spilled, but also because these beliefs afforded them their only bulwark against a moral chaos as absolute as the physical chaos of the continent it was their destiny to conquer. But in the situation in which Americans found themselves, these beliefs threatened an idea which, whether or not one likes to think so, is the very warp and woof of the heritage of the West, the idea of white supremacy.

Americans have made themselves notorious by the shrillness and the brutality with which they have insisted on this idea, but they did not invent it; and it has escaped the world's notice that those very excesses of which Americans have been guilty imply a certain, unprecedented uneasiness over the idea's life and power, if not, indeed, the idea's validity. The idea of white supremacy rests simply on the fact that white men are the creators of civilization (the present civilization, which is the only one that matters; all previous civilizations are simply "contributions" to our own) and are therefore civilization's guardians and defenders. Thus it was impossible for Americans to accept the black man as one of themselves, for to do so was to jeopardize their status as white men. But not so to accept him was to deny his human reality, his human weight and complexity, and the strain of denying the overwhelmingly undeniable forced Americans into rationalizations so fantastic that they approached the pathological.

At the root of the American Negro problem is the necessity of the American white man to find a way of living with the Negro in order to be able to live with himself. And the history of this problem can be reduced to the means used by Americans—lynch law and law, segregation and legal acceptance, terrorization and concession—either to come to terms with this necessity, or to find a way around it, or (most usually) to find a way of doing both these things at once. The resulting spectacle, at once foolish and dreadful, led someone to make the quite accurate observation that "the Negro-in-America is a form of insanity which overtakes white men."

In this long battle, a battle by no means finished, the unforeseeable effects of which will be felt by many future generations, the white man's motive was the protection of his identity; the black man was motivated by the need to establish an identity. And despite the terrorization which the Negro in America endured and endures sporadically until today, despite the cruel and totally inescapable ambivalence of his status in his country, the battle for his identity has long ago been won. He is not a visitor to the West, but a citizen there, an American; as American as the Americans who despise him, the Americans who fear him, the Americans who love him—the Americans who became less than themselves, or rose to be greater than themselves by virtue of the fact that the challenge he represented was inescapable. He is perhaps the only black man in the world whose relationship to white men is more terrible, more subtle, and more meaningful than the relationship of bitter possessed to uncertain possessor. His survival depended, and his development depends, on his ability to turn his peculiar status in the Western world to his own advantage and, it may be, to the very great advantage of that world. It remains for him to fashion out of his experience that which will give him sustenance, and a voice.

The cathedral at Chartres, I have said, says something to the people of this village which it cannot say to me; but it is important to understand that this cathedral says something to me which it cannot say to them. Perhaps they are struck by the power of the spires, the glory of the windows; but they have known God, after all, longer than I have known him, and in a different way, and I am terrified by the slippery bottomless well to be found in the crypt, down which heretics were hurled to death, and by the obscene, inescapable gargoyles jutting out of the stone and seeming to say that God and the devil can never be divorced. I doubt that the villagers think of the devil when they face a cathedral because they have never been identified with the devil. But I must accept the status which myth, if nothing else, gives me in the West before I can hope to change the myth.

Yet, if the American Negro has arrived at his identity by virtue of the absoluteness of his estrangement from his past, American white men still nourish the illusion that there is some means of recovering the European innocence, of returning to a state in which black men do not exist. This is one of the greatest errors Americans can make. The identity they fought so hard to protect has, by virtue of that battle, undergone a change: Americans are as unlike any other white people in the world as it is possible to be. I do not think, for example, that it is too much to suggest that the American vision of the world—which allows so little reality, generally speaking, for any of the darker forces in human life, which tends until today to paint moral issues in glaring black and white—owes a great deal to the battle waged by Americans to maintain between themselves and black men a human separation which could not be bridged. It is only now beginning to be borne in on us—very faintly, it must be admitted, very slowly, and very much against our will—that this vision of the world is dangerously inaccurate, and perfectly useless. For it protects our moral high-mindedness at the terrible expense of weakening our grasp of reality. People who shut their eyes to reality simply invite their own destruction, and anyone who insists on remaining in a state of innocence long after that innocence is dead turns himself into a monster.

The time has come to realize that the interracial drama acted out on the American continent has not only created a new black man, it has created a new white man, too. No road whatever will lead Americans back to the simplicity of this European village where white men still have the luxury of looking on me as a stranger. I am not, really, a stranger any longer for any American alive. One of the things that distinguishes Americans from other people is that no other people has ever been so deeply involved in the lives of black men, and vice versa. This fact faced, with all its implications, it can be seen that the history of the American Negro problem is not merely shameful, it is also something of an achievement. For even when the worst has been said, it must also be added that the perpetual challenge posed by this problem was always, somehow, perpetually met. It is precisely this black-white experience which may prove of indispensable value to us in the world we face today. This world is white no longer, and it will never be white again.

(Continued on page 745)

The City

MAURICE PRENDERGAST: Central Park, 1900/02

1908 was the year of the historic exhibition of The Eight. They were Robert Henri, a painter and brilliant teacher from Philadelphia; his friends William Glackens (p. 567), John Sloan (p. 740), George Luks, and Everett Shinn, who had all studied with Anshutz at the Pennsylvania Academy and worked as newspaper illustrators; Ernest Lawson, a landscape painter and pupil of Twachtman; Maurice Prendergast of Boston; and Arthur B. Davies, who organized the show and produced nearly unclassifiable fantasies of dreamy maidens in idyllic landscapes. Most of them had run afoul of the current academic ideal of what constituted proper subject matter for painting; their works were rejected by the official annual exhibitions, and they were dubbed "the Ashcan School" and "the Black Gang."

Prendergast (1859-1924) had already formed his personal style of Post-impressionist, tapestry-like painting as a result of his studies in Paris. *Central Park* (*above*) is a watercolor. The white paper showing through the bright patches of color makes an even more sparkling effect than the version in oil.

CHILDE HASSAM: Allies Day, 1917

Hassam (1859-1935), the most prolific of the American Impressionists, did a series of pictures on the theme of Fifth Avenue bedecked with flags. They added still more color and movement to a scene that was hardly static to begin with. A splendid idea, and it was an even better one when Manet and Monet first had it in 1878 and painted similar pictures of Paris decorated with flags for the Fête National, which marked the opening of the World's Fair.

CHARLES SHEELER: Offices, 1922

Sheeler's buildings are not plunked down in the midst of life like those of Hassam but have been withdrawn and schematized into a balanced design of light and dark rectangles. Literally, this is a "cubist" picture, but that term should be saved for pictures in the style of Braque and Picasso, who invented it (p. 811). Sheeler, who also photographed skyscrapers and made a short film, *Manhatta* (with Paul Strand), is properly called a "precisionist."

JOHN SLOAN: The Pigeons, 1910

John Sloan (1871-1951) drew black and white illustrations inspired by Japanese prints, and majestic Art Nouveau females in full color, when he was an illustrator for the Philadelphia *Press*. The colloquial manner of his New York scenes was something else. The New York of Sloan and the New York of O. Henry are identical. The artist came to the city in 1904, the writer in 1902, and his most typical collection of short stories, *The Four Million*, was published in 1906. At this time Sloan was producing the most effective examples of the urban reportage we associate with the Ashcan School.

Sloan loved the neighborhood around lower Sixth Avenue and West Fourteenth Street, and he found some of his best ideas, like the fat blonde proprietor in *Hairdresser's Window*, while prowling the streets. He spied the two women of *Three A.M.*, mysteriously cooking in their nightgowns, from the back windows of his studio. *Pigeons (above)*, which was rejected twice for exhibition, records an age-old feature of tenement life: the raising of homing pigeons on the roof. It was Marlon Brando's hobby in the film *On the Waterfront*. In *Scrubwoman, Astor Library*, and *McSorley's Bar*, Sloan immortalized locales still playing a vital role in the city's cultural life.

Bellows (1882-1925), Henri's most promising student, once considered becoming a professional baseball player. His work, which ranges from action-packed sporting events to Hudson River landscapes, is technically assured and highly accomplished. Bellow's stylistic development can be traced in his prizefight scenes. The early *Stag at Sharkey's* and *Both Members of This Club* are handled with a crusty, satirical brush reminiscent of Sloan and the Ashcan painters. In *Dempsey and Firpo (below)* Bellows made use of the Hambidge system of "dynamic symmetry" to give the composition its underlying geometric framework. Especially tender and revealing are Bellows' pictures of women, above all *Lady Jean,* and other portraits of his own family.

GEORGE BELLOWS: Dempsey and Firpo, 1924

EDWARD HOPPER: Room in Brooklyn, 1932

Hopper (1882-1967) painted in a style of drastically simplified realism which he manipulated with such expressiveness that he succeeded in pleasing the public as well as the critics, without ever losing the respect of his fellow artists. Despite his many pictures of Cape Cod summers, it is his New York that we find so uniquely moving. No one else has so accurately captured the feeling of the deserted city at off-hours or the loneliness of its inhabitants—the customers at an all-night restaurant, a movie palace usherette, a single figure in a window (*above*). Two of his most admired pictures are the brooding *House by the Railroad* (1925), the portrait of a Victorian (or "Charles Addams") mansion, and *Early Sunday Morning* (1930), a row of two-story red brick houses, a fire hydrant, and a barber pole. Light is his accomplice in creating these visions, and he preferred the low sunlight of early morning or late afternoon for its form-molding qualities. His last major work was titled simply *Sun in an Empty Room* (1964).

Tooker (born 1920) has taken that metropolitan necessity, the subway *(below)*, and made it the scene of an urban nightmare. The passengers are sleepwalkers; the endless white tile corridors a sinister maze. Tooker paints in egg tempera, an ancient, painstaking method which produces results that have alarming conviction and solidarity. When he began to paint, in the 1940's, New York was filled with surrealist artists who had fled the war in Europe. Their highly Freudian work has had a lasting influence here.

The Italian futurists despised the art of the past, worshiped the machine, and wanted to make a new art which would reflect the speed and movement of modern life. Joseph Stella (1877-1946), an Italian immigrant who had studied with Chase in New York, was in Paris in 1909 at the exact moment that futurism was launched there. Back home, he found in the Brooklyn Bridge (p. 744) the structural form and symbolic appeal he needed to evoke the spirit of the city in a series of brilliant abstract paintings. The row of oval shapes at the bottom of the picture is supposed to represent the subway. Stella used the colored lights, noise, and excitement of Coney Island as the subject of another series of futurist transformations.

GEORGE TOOKER: The Subway, 1950

JOSEPH STELLA: The Bridge, 1920/22

QUESTIONS FOR DISCUSSION

1. Baldwin speaks of "this white wilderness" in which the black man is a curiosity. To what degree do you think he may be using the Swiss village as a microcosm for the world? Support your answer.

2. Baldwin speaks of the village's industry in treating cripples. How far does he wish his reader to extend the analogy between people on crutches and people crippled by prejudice?

3. What does Baldwin mean when he speaks of "human weight and complexity"? What does it mean to him that, in this village, he is "simply a living wonder"?

4. Baldwin makes a strong comment about history. What does he mean?

5. Discuss the irony with which Baldwin relates his conversation about the missionaries with the bistro owner's wife.

6. Do you accept Baldwin's statement, that "the most illiterate [Swiss villager] is related, in a way that I am not, to Dante, Shakespeare, Michelangelo, Aeschylus, Da Vinci, Rembrandt, and Racine"? Is his reasoning sound or does it have fallacies? What does he mean when he later says that the cathedral at Chartres "says something to me which it cannot say to them"?

7. In the subsequent paragraphs, Baldwin presents the dilemma of the black man who feels "rage, dissembling, and contempt." In Baldwin's terms, what is the nature of this dilemma?

8. How do some manifestations of orthodox Christianity—language, doctrine, foreign missions, for example—compound the black man's ironic position?

9. Baldwin speaks of the white man's "rationalizations so fantastic that they approached the pathological." What are these rationalizations? So far as Baldwin is concerned, what is the white man's ultimate hope regarding the black man?

10. At the essay's end, what conclusion has Baldwin reached? How does this ending bring the essay full-circle, from its introductory description to the argument's conclusion?

ASSIGNMENTS FOR WRITING

1. Read Leslie Fiedler's rebuttal to this essay, "Negro and Jew : Encounter in America," and write an analysis of the clash between these two writers.

2. After reading two essays by James Baldwin, you should be able to comment on his style of writing—his use of language, his choice of diction, his reliance upon irony and understatement. Write an essay, using examples from Baldwin, in which you show why he is recognized as a distinguished stylist.

3. One of Baldwin's arguments for his alienation from European culture is that the art of "Western civilization" is not his art. How far may this argument be taken? Does the Taj Mahal speak only to Indians? Do the pyramids have meaning only for Egyptians? Write an argumentative essay in support of or in rebuttal to Baldwin's point.

Lorraine Hansberry

Not often is a writer considered a major playwright after only one full-length play. In Lorraine Hansberry's case, however, recognition must be won early or not at all, for she died at thirty-four with only one more play to her credit. Her first play was not the work of a typical novice. It was *A Raisin in the Sun*, produced on Broadway in 1959, and later filmed with remarkable attention to the dramatic qualities of the original play. Sidney Poitier played Walter Lee Younger in both versions.

Lorraine Hansberry was born in Chicago on May 19, 1930. Her father was a wealthy realtor and banker; consequently, Miss Hansberry's childhood, unlike James Baldwin's, was not spent in ghetto squalor. In fact, the Hansberry home was in a mostly white neighborhood. After graduating from Englewood High School in Chicago, Lorraine Hansberry enrolled at the University of Wisconsin and also took courses at the Chicago Art Institute.

In 1950, Lorraine Hansberry went to New York and worked at various jobs while studying at the New School for Social Research. She began writing, and although nothing she wrote was published, her work made interesting reading for the few friends to whom she showed her manuscripts. At the age of twenty-six, she began *A Raisin in the Sun*, which she finished in a year. To the astonishment of everyone, the play found backing for a Broadway production and then ran for nineteen months as one of the American theater's most successful dramatic plays. In fact, *A Raisin in the Sun* won the New York Drama Critics' Circle Award as the best play of 1959.

From its opening, on March 11, 1959, and throughout its run, this play evoked mixed reactions, and it still does. Some critics see *A Raisin in the Sun* as a "safe" play, that is a play so innocuous as to offend no one. Such criticism stems from a faulty view of the art of theater, a view which sees drama as mere propaganda. *A Raisin in the Sun* is more than that.

The play takes its title from a poem by Langston Hughes called "Montage on a Dream Deferred," which also serves as the epigraph to the play:

> What happens to a dream deferred?
> Does it dry up
> Like a raisin in the sun?

The theme of the aborted or deferred dream—lost or tarnished by years of unfulfilled longing—runs throughout the play. Each of the principal characters has a dream. Walter Lee Younger wants independence from the loving domination of his mother and a job from which he can obtain some self-respect; his wife Ruth longs for a home of their own, a bedroom for her son Travis, instead of the convertible sofa; most of all, Ruth yearns for the contentment of her husband. Beneatha, Walter Lee's sister, is a student at the University of Chicago, determined to become a doctor. Mama, strong and compassionate, dreams of liberating her children from their ghetto prison and giving new life to her late husband's favorite saying, "Seems like God didn't see fit to give the black man nothing but dreams—but He did give us children to make them dreams seem worthwhile."

Looking back from the 1970's, the reader or playgoer can recognize how encompassing of both old and new ideas Miss Hansberry's play is—how far-sighted her vision. The play does not deal in caricatures or stereotypes but in people whose ideas are enacted before us. Like every work of art, it is timeless. Mama is the traditional matriarch when she slaps Beneatha's face and forces her to repeat the words, "In my mother's house there is still God." But Lena Younger is surprisingly flexible as well, and she can shock her children by her youthfulness and imagination. Beneatha's search for her identity, particularized in her relationship with the African student Asagai, represents one form of black assertiveness; her brother's search for his manhood, particularized in his desire to use his father's insurance money to set up in business for himself, reaches beyond any question of race to the universal problem of a man's self-reliance. So, too, are Ruth's ambitions for a fulfilling life as wife and mother, whether in the Southside Chicago ghetto or in the hostile white suburbs.

Lorraine Hansberry insisted that she was not a Negro playwright; that she was, instead, a playwright who happened to be Negro. This attitude is not acceptable to all black artists, some of whom believe that blackness itself is the soul of their art. As if to demonstrate the difference between her larger view of life and the narrower strictures of black exclusivism, Miss Hansberry's second play concerned persons and problems well removed from Chicago's Southside. Set in Greenwich Village in New York City, *The Sign in Sidney Brustein's Window* is a political play about the conflicts that go on in a city between the advocates of life and powers of death. Because it was her last play—Lorraine Hansberry died of cancer on January 12, 1965, while her play was struggling to survive on Broadway—*The Sign in Sidney Brustein's Window* serves as a special testament to Miss Hansberry's vision of life. In the concluding major speech by the play's central character may be found an accurate description of this gifted woman's belief that:

> death is waste and love is sweet and that the earth turns and men change every day and that rivers run and that people wanna be better than they are and that flowers smell good and that I hurt terribly today, and that hurt is desperation and desperation is—energy and energy can *move* things.

In such simplicity, expressed in the heightened language of her dramatic art, lies the answer to Lorraine Hansberry's greatness.

A Raisin in the Sun

What happens to a dream deferred?
Does it dry up
Like a raisin in the sun?
Or fester like a sore—
And then run?
Does it stink like rotten meat?
Or crust and sugar over—
Like a syrupy sweet?

Maybe it just sags
Like a heavy load.

Or does it explode?

—Langston Hughes

CHARACTERS

RUTH YOUNGER

TRAVIS YOUNGER

WALTER LEE YOUNGER (BROTHER)

BENEATHA YOUNGER

LENA YOUNGER (MAMA)

JOSEPH ASAGAI

GEORGE MURCHISON

KARL LINDNER

BOBO

MOVING MEN

The action of the play is set in Chicago's Southside, sometime between World War II and the present.

ACT I

Scene One

The YOUNGER *living room would be a comfortable and well-ordered room if it were not for a number of indestructible contradictions to this state of being. Its furnishings are typical and undistinguished and their primary feature now is that they have clearly had to accommodate the living of too many people for too many years—and they are tired. Still, we can see that at some time, a time probably no longer remembered by the family (except perhaps for* MAMA*) the furnishings of this room were actually selected with care and love and even hope—and brought to this apartment and arranged with taste and pride.*

That was a long time ago. Now the once loved pattern of the couch upholstery has to fight to show itself from under acres of crocheted doilies and couch covers which have themselves finally come to be more important than the upholstery. And here a table or a chair has been moved to disguise the worn places in the carpet; but the carpet has fought back by showing its weariness, with depressing uniformity, elsewhere on its surface.

Weariness has, in fact, won in this room. Everything has been polished, washed, sat on, used, scrubbed too often. All pretenses but living itself have long since vanished from the very atmosphere of this room.

Moreover, a section of this room, for it is not really a room unto itself, though the landlord's lease would make it seem so, slopes backward to provide a small kitchen area, where the family prepares the meals that are eaten in the living room proper, which must also serve as dining room. The single window that has been provided for these "two" rooms is located in this kitchen area. The sole natural light the family may enjoy in the course of a day is only that which fights its way through this little window.

At left, a door leads to a bedroom which is shared by MAMA *and her daughter,* BENEATHA. *At right, opposite, is a second room (which in the beginning of the life of this apartment was probably a breakfast room) which serves as a bedroom for* WALTER *and his wife,* RUTH.

Time: Sometime between World War II and the present.

Place: Chicago's Southside.

At Rise: It is morning dark in the living room. TRAVIS *is asleep on the make-down bed at center. An alarm clock sounds from within the bedroom at right, and presently* RUTH *enters from that room and closes the door behind her. She crosses sleepily toward the window. As she passes her sleeping son she reaches down and shakes him a little. At the window she raises the shade and a dusky Southside morning light comes in feebly. She fills a pot with water and puts it on to boil. She calls to the boy, between yawns, in a slightly muffled voice.*

RUTH *is about thirty. We can see that she was a pretty girl, even exceptionally so, but now it is apparent that life has been little that she expected, and disappointment has already begun to hang in her face. In a few years, before thirty-five even, she will be known among her people as a "settled woman."*

She crosses to her son and gives him a good, final, rousing shake.

RUTH   Come on now, boy, it's seven thirty! (*Her son sits up at last, in a stupor of sleepiness*) I say hurry up, Travis! You ain't the only person in the world got to use a bathroom! (*The child, a sturdy, handsome little boy of ten or eleven, drags himself out of the bed and almost blindly takes his towels and "today's clothes" from drawers and a closet and goes out to the bathroom, which is in an outside hall and which is shared by another family or families on the same floor.* RUTH *crosses to the bedroom door at right and opens it and calls in to her husband)* Walter Lee! . . . It's after seven thirty! Lemme see you do some waking up in there now! *(She waits)* You better get up from there, man! It's after seven thirty I tell you. *(She waits again)* All right, you just go ahead and lay there and next thing you know Travis be finished and Mr. Johnson'll be in there and you'll be fussing and cussing round here like a mad man! And be late too! *(She waits, at the end of patience)* Walter Lee—it's time for you to get up!

> *She waits another second and then starts to go into the bedroom, but is apparently satisfied that her husband has begun to get up. She stops, pulls the door to, and returns to the kitchen area. She wipes her face with a moist cloth and runs her fingers through her sleep-disheveled hair in a vain effort and ties an apron around her housecoat. The bedroom door at right opens and her husband stands in the doorway in his pajamas, which are rumpled and mismated. He is a lean, intense young man in his middle thirties, inclined to quick nervous movements and erratic speech habits—and always in his voice there is a quality of indictment.*

WALTER Is he out yet?

RUTH What you mean *out*? He ain't hardly got in there good yet.

WALTER *(Wandering in, still more oriented to sleep than to a new day)* Well, what was you doing all that yelling for if I can't even get in there yet? *(Stopping and thinking)* Check coming today?

RUTH They *said* Saturday and this is just Friday and I hopes to God you ain't going to get up here first thing this morning and start talking to me 'bout no money—'cause I 'bout don't want to hear it.

WALTER Something the matter with you this morning?

RUTH No—I'm just sleepy as the devil. What kind of eggs you want?

WALTER Not scrambled. *(RUTH starts to scramble eggs)* Paper come? *(RUTH points impatiently to the rolled up* Tribune *on the table, and he gets it and spreads it out and vaguely reads the front page)* Set off another bomb yesterday.

RUTH *(Maximum indifference)* Did they?

WALTER *(Looking up)* What's the matter with you?

RUTH Ain't nothing the matter with me. And don't keep asking me that this morning.

WALTER Ain't nobody bothering you. *(Reading the news of the day absently again)* Say Colonel McCormick is sick.

RUTH *(Affecting tea-party interest)* Is he now? Poor thing.

WALTER *(Sighing and looking at his watch)* Oh, me. *(He waits)* Now what is that boy doing in that bathroom all this time? He just going to have to start getting up earlier. I can't be being late to work on account of him fooling around in there.

RUTH *(Turning on him)* Oh, no he ain't going to be getting up no earlier no such thing! It ain't his fault that he can't get to bed no earlier nights 'cause he got a bunch of crazy good-for-nothing clowns sitting up running their mouths in what is supposed to be his bedroom after ten o'clock at night . . .

WALTER That's what you mad about, ain't it? The things I want to talk about with my friends just couldn't be important in your mind, could they?

He rises and finds a cigarette in her handbag on the table and crosses to the little window and looks out, smoking and deeply enjoying this first one.

RUTH (*Almost matter of factly, a complaint too automatic to deserve emphasis*) Why you always got to smoke before you eat in the morning?

WALTER (*At the window*) Just look at 'em down there ... Running and racing to work ... (*He turns and faces his wife and watches her a moment at the stove, and then, suddenly*) You look young this morning, baby.

RUTH (*Indifferently*) Yeah?

WALTER Just for a second—stirring them eggs. It's gone now—just for a second it was—you looked real young again. (*Then, drily*) It's gone now—you look like yourself again.

RUTH Man, if you don't shut up and leave me alone.

WALTER (*Looking out to the street again*) First thing a man ought to learn in life is not to make love to no colored woman first thing in the morning. You all some evil people at eight o'clock in the morning.

    TRAVIS *appears in the hall doorway, almost fully dressed and quite wide awake now, his towels and pajamas across his shoulders. He opens the door and signals for his father to make the bathroom in a hurry.*

TRAVIS (*Watching the bathroom*) Daddy, come on!

    WALTER *gets his bathroom utensils and flies out to the bathroom.*

RUTH Sit down and have your breakfast, Travis.

TRAVIS Mama, this is Friday. (*Gleefully*) Check coming tomorrow, huh?

RUTH You get your mind off money and eat your breakfast.

TRAVIS (*Eating*) This is the morning we supposed to bring the fifty cents to school.

RUTH Well, I ain't got no fifty cents this morning.

TRAVIS Teacher say we have to.

RUTH I don't care what teacher say. I ain't got it. Eat your breakfast, Travis.

TRAVIS I *am* eating.

RUTH Hush up now and just eat!

    The boy gives her an exasperated look for her lack of understanding, and eats grudgingly.

TRAVIS You think Grandmama would have it?

RUTH No! And I want you to stop asking your grandmother for money, you hear me?

TRAVIS (*Outraged*) Gaaaleee! I don't ask her, she just gimme it sometimes!

RUTH Travis Willard Younger—I got too much on me this morning to be—

TRAVIS Maybe Daddy—

RUTH *Travis!*

    The boy hushes abruptly. They are both quiet and tense for several seconds.

TRAVIS (*Presently*) Could I maybe go carry some groceries in front of the supermarket for a little while after school then?

RUTH Just hush, I said. (*Travis jabs his spoon into his cereal bowl viciously, and rests his head in anger upon his fists*) If you through eating, you can get over there and make up your bed.

    The boy obeys stiffly and crosses the room, almost mechanically, to the bed and more or less carefully folds the covering. He carries the bedding into his mother's room and returns with his books and cap.

TRAVIS   (*Sulking and standing apart from her unnaturally*) I'm gone.

RUTH   (*Looking up from the stove to inspect him automatically*) Come here. (*He crosses to her and she studies his head*) If you don't take this comb and fix this here head, you better! (TRAVIS *puts down his books with a great sigh of oppression, and crosses to the mirror. His mother mutters under her breath about his "slubbornness"*) 'Bout to march out of here with that head looking just like chickens slept in it! I just don't know where you get your slubborn ways . . . And get your jacket, too. Looks chilly out this morning.

TRAVIS   (*With conspicuously brushed hair and jacket*) I'm gone.

RUTH   Get carfare and milk money—(*Waving one finger*)—and not a single penny for no caps, you hear me?

TRAVIS   (*With sullen politeness*) Yes'm.

> He turns in outrage to leave. His mother watches after him as in his frustration he approaches the door almost comically. When she speaks to him, her voice has become a very gentle tease.

RUTH   (*Mocking; as she thinks he would say it*) Oh, Mama makes me so mad sometimes, I don't know what to do! (*She waits and continues to his back as he stands stock-still in front of the door*) I wouldn't kiss that woman good-bye for nothing in this world this morning! (*The boy finally turns around and rolls his eyes at her, knowing the mood has changed and he is vindicated; he does not, however, move toward her yet*) Not for nothing in this world! (*She finally laughs aloud at him and holds out her arms to him and we see that it is a way between them, very old and practiced. He crosses to her and allows her to embrace him warmly but keeps his face fixed with masculine rigidity. She holds him back from her presently and looks at him and runs her fingers over the features of his face. With utter gentleness—*) Now—whose little old angry man are you?

TRAVIS   (*The masculinity and gruffness start to fade at last*) Aw gaalee—Mama . . .

RUTH   (*Mimicking*) Aw gaaaaalleeeee, Mama! (*She pushes him, with rough playfulness and finality, toward the door*) Get on out of here or you going to be late.

TRAVIS   (*In the face of love, new aggressiveness*) Mama, could I *please* go carry groceries?

RUTH   Honey, it's starting to get so cold evenings.

WALTER   (*Coming in from the bathroom and drawing a make-believe gun from a make-believe holster and shooting at his son*) What is it he wants to do?

RUTH   Go carry groceries after school at the supermarket.

WALTER   Well, let him go . . .

TRAVIS   (*Quickly, to the ally*) I *have* to—she won't gimme the fifty cents . . .

WALTER   (*To his wife only*) Why not?

RUTH   (*Simply, and with flavor*) 'Cause we don't have it.

WALTER   (*To RUTH only*) What you tell the boy things like that for? (*Reaching down into his pants with a rather important gesture*) Here, son—

> He hands the boy the coin, but his eyes are directed to his wife's. TRAVIS takes the money happily.

TRAVIS   Thanks, Daddy.

> He starts out. RUTH watches both of them with murder in her eyes. WALTER stands and stares back at her with defiance, and suddenly reaches into his pocket again on an afterthought.

WALTER   (*Without even looking at his son, still staring hard at his wife*) In fact, here's another fifty cents . . . Buy yourself some fruit today—or take a taxicab to school or something!

TRAVIS Whoopee—

> *He leaps up and clasps his father around the middle with his legs, and they face each other in mutual appreciation; slowly* WALTER LEE *peeks around the boy to catch the violent rays from his wife's eyes and draws his head back as if shot.*

WALTER You better get down now—and get to school, man.

TRAVIS (*At the door*) O.K. Goodbye.

> *He exits.*

WALTER (*After him, pointing with pride*) That's my boy. (*She looks at him in disgust and turns back to her work*) You know what I was thinking 'bout in the bathroom this morning?

RUTH No.

WALTER How come you always try to be so pleasant!

RUTH What is there to be pleasant 'bout!

WALTER You want to know what I was thinking 'bout in the bathroom or not!

RUTH I know what you thinking 'bout.

WALTER (*Ignoring her*) 'Bout what me and Willy Harris was talking about last night.

RUTH (*Immediately—a refrain*) Willy Harris is a good-for-nothing loud mouth.

WALTER Anybody who talks to me has got to be a good-for-nothing loud mouth, ain't he? And what you know about who is just a good-for-nothing loud mouth? Charlie Atkins was just a "good-for-nothing loud mouth" too, wasn't he! When he wanted me to go in the dry-cleaning business with him. And now—he's grossing a hundred thousand a year. A hundred thousand dollars a year! You still call *him* a loud mouth!

RUTH (*Bitterly*) Oh, Walter Lee . . .

> *She folds her head on her arms over the table.*

WALTER (*Rising and coming to her and standing over her*) You tired, ain't you? Tired of everything. Me, the boy, the way we live—this beat-up hole—everything. Ain't you? (*She doesn't look up, doesn't answer*) So tired—moaning and groaning all the time, but you wouldn't do nothing to help, would you? You couldn't be on my side that long for nothing, could you?

RUTH Walter, please leave me alone.

WALTER A man needs for a woman to back him up . . .

RUTH Walter—

WALTER Mama would listen to you. You know she listen to you more than she do me and Bennie. She think more of you. All you have to do is just sit down with her when you drinking your coffee one morning and talking 'bout things like you do and—(*He sits down beside her and demonstrates graphically what he thinks her methods and tone should be*)—you just sip your coffee, see, and say easy like that you been thinking 'bout that deal Walter Lee is so interested in, 'bout the store and all, and sip some more coffee, like what you saying ain't really that important to you— And the next thing you know, she be listening good and asking you questions and when I come home—I can tell her the details. This ain't no fly-by-night proposition, baby. I mean we figured it out, me and Willy and Bobo.

RUTH (*With a frown*) Bobo?

WALTER   Yeah. You see, this little liquor store we got in mind cost seventy-five thousand and we figured the initial investment on the place be 'bout thirty thousand, see. That be ten thousand each. Course, there's a couple of hundred you got to pay so's you don't spend your life just waiting for them clowns to let your license get approved—

RUTH   You mean graft?

WALTER   (*Frowning impatiently*) Don't call it that. See there, that just goes to show you what women understand about the world. Baby, don't *nothing* happen for you in this world 'less you pay *somebody* off!

RUTH   Walter, leave me alone! (*She raises her head and stares at him vigorously—then says, more quietly*) Eat your eggs, they gonna be cold.

WALTER   (*Straightening up from her and looking off*) That's it. There you are. Man say to his woman: I got me a dream. His woman say: Eat your eggs. (*Sadly, but gaining in power*) Man say: I got to take hold of this here world, baby! And a woman will say: Eat your eggs and go to work. (*Passionately now*) Man say: I got to change my life, I'm choking to death, baby! And his woman say—(*In utter anguish as he brings his fists down on his thighs*)—Your eggs is getting cold!

RUTH   (*Softly*) Walter, that ain't none of our money.

WALTER   (*Not listening at all or even looking at her*) This morning, I was lookin' in the mirror and thinking about it . . . I'm thirty-five years old; I been married eleven years and I got a boy who sleeps in the living room—(*Very, very quietly*)—and all I got to give him is stories about how rich white people live . . .

RUTH   Eat your eggs, Walter.

WALTER   *Damn my eggs . . . damn all the eggs that ever was!*

RUTH   Then go to work.

WALTER   (*Looking up at her*) See—I'm trying to talk to you 'bout myself—(*Shaking his head with the repetition*)—and all you can say is eat them eggs and go to work.

RUTH   (*Wearily*) Honey, you never say nothing new. I listen to you every day, every night and every morning, and you never say nothing new. (*Shrugging*) So you would rather *be* Mr. Arnold than be his chauffeur. So—I would *rather* be living in Buckingham Palace.

WALTER   That is just what is wrong with the colored woman in this world . . . Don't understand about building their men up and making 'em feel like they somebody. Like they can do something.

RUTH   (*Drily, but to hurt*) There *are* colored men who do things.

WALTER   No thanks to the colored woman.

RUTH   Well, being a colored woman, I guess I can't help myself none.

   She rises and gets the ironing board and sets it up and attacks a huge pile of rough-dried clothes, sprinkling them in preparation for the ironing and then rolling them into tight fat balls.

WALTER   (*Mumbling*) We one group of men tied to a race of women with small minds.

   His sister BENEATHA enters. She is about twenty, as slim and intense as her brother. She is not as pretty as her sister-in-law, but her lean, almost intellectual face has a handsomeness of its own. She wears a bright-red flannel nightie, and her thick hair stands wildly about her head. Her speech is a mixture of many *things; it is different from the rest of the family's insofar as education has permeated her sense of English—and perhaps the Midwest rather than the South has finally—at last—won out in her inflection; but not altogether, because over all of it is a soft slurring and transformed use of vowels which is the decided influence of the Southside. She passes through the room without looking at either* RUTH *or* WALTER *and goes to the outside door and looks, a little blindly, out to the bathroom. She sees that it has been lost to the Johnsons. She closes the door with a sleepy vengeance and crosses to the table and sits down a little defeated.*

BENEATHA   I am going to start timing those people.

WALTER   You should get up earlier.

BENEATHA   (*Her face in her hands. She is still fighting the urge to go back to bed*) Really— would you suggest dawn? Where's the paper?

WALTER   (*Pushing the paper across the table to her as he studies her almost clinically, as though he has never seen her before*) You a horrible-looking chick at this hour.

BENEATHA   (*Drily*) Good morning, everybody.

WALTER   (*Senselessly*) How is school coming?

BENEATHA   (*In the same spirit*) Lovely. Lovely. And you know, biology is the greatest. (*Looking up at him*) I dissected something that looked just like you yesterday.

WALTER   I just wondered if you've made up your mind and everything.

BENEATHA   (*Gaining in sharpness and impatience*) And what did I answer yesterday morning—and the day before that?

RUTH   (*From the ironing board, like someone disinterested and old*) Don't be so nasty, Bennie.

BENEATHA   (*Still to her brother*) And the day before that and the day before that!

WALTER   (*Defensively*) I'm interested in you. Something wrong with that? Ain't many girls who decide—

WALTER *and* BENEATHA   (*In unison*) —"to be a doctor."
       Silence.

WALTER   Have we figured out yet just exactly how much medical school is going to cost?

RUTH   Walter Lee, why don't you leave that girl alone and get out of here to work?

BENEATHA   (*Exits to the bathroom and bangs on the door*) Come on out of there, please! *She comes back into the room.*

WALTER   (*Looking at his sister intently*) You know the check is coming tomorrow.

BENEATHA   (*Turning on him with a sharpness all her own*) That money belongs to Mama, Walter, and it's for her to decide how she wants to use it. I don't care if she wants to buy a house or a rocket ship or just nail it up somewhere and look at it. It's hers. Not ours—*hers.*

WALTER   (*Bitterly*) Now ain't that fine! You just got your mother's interest at heart, ain't you, girl? You such a nice girl—but if Mama got that money she can always take a few thousand and help you through school too—can't she?

BENEATHA   I have never asked anyone around here to do anything for me!

WALTER   No! And the line between asking and just accepting when the time comes is big and wide—ain't it!

BENEATHA   (*With fury*) What do you want from me, Brother—that I quit school or just drop dead, which!

WALTER   I don't want nothing but for you to stop acting holy 'round here. Me and Ruth done made some sacrifices for you—why can't you do something for the family?

RUTH Walter, don't be dragging me in it.

WALTER You are in it—Don't you get up and go work in somebody's kitchen for the last three years to help put clothes on her back?

RUTH Oh, Walter—that's not fair . . .

WALTER It ain't that nobody expects you to get on your knees and say thank you, Brother; thank you, Ruth; thank you, Mama—and thank you, Travis, for wearing the same pair of shoes for two semesters—

BENEATHA (*Dropping to her knees*) Well—I *do*—all right?—thank everybody . . . and forgive me for ever wanting to be anything at all . . . forgive me, forgive me!

RUTH Please stop it! Your mama'll hear you.

WALTER Who the hell told you you had to be a doctor? If you so crazy 'bout messing 'round with sick people—then go be a nurse like other women—or just get married and be quiet . . .

BENEATHA Well—you finally got it said . . . It took you three years but you finally got it said. Walter, give up; leave me alone—it's Mama's money.

WALTER *He was my father, too!*

BENEATHA So what? He was mine, too—and Travis' grandfather—but the insurance money belongs to Mama. Picking on me is not going to make her give it to you to invest in any liquor stores—(*Underbreath, dropping into a chair*)—and I for one say, God bless Mama for that!

WALTER (*To* RUTH) See—did you hear? Did you hear!

RUTH Honey, please go to work.

WALTER Nobody in this house is ever going to understand me.

BENEATHA Because you're a nut.

WALTER Who's a nut?

BENEATHA You—you are a nut. Thee is mad, boy.

WALTER (*Looking at his wife and his sister from the door, very sadly*) The world's most backward race of people, and that's a fact.

BENEATHA (*Turning slowly in her chair*) And then there are those prophets who would lead us out of the wilderness—(WALTER *slams out of the house*)—into the swamps!

RUTH Bennie, why you always gotta be pickin' on your brother? Can't you be a little sweeter sometimes? (*Door opens.* WALTER *walks in*)

WALTER (*To Ruth*) I need some money for carfare.

RUTH (*Looks at him, then warms; teasing, but tenderly*) Fifty cents? (*She goes to her bag and gets money*) Here, take a taxi.

> WALTER *exits.* MAMA *enters. She is a woman in her early sixties, full-bodied and strong. She is one of those women of a certain grace and beauty who wear it so unobtrusively that it takes a while to notice. Her dark-brown face is surrounded by the total whiteness of her hair, and, being a woman who has adjusted to many things in life and overcome many more, her face is full of strength. She has, we can see, wit and faith of a kind that keep her eyes lit and full of interest and expectancy. She is, in a word, a beautiful woman. Her bearing is perhaps most like the noble bearing of the women of the Hereros of Southwest Africa—rather as if she imagines that as she walks she still bears a basket or a vessel upon her head. Her speech, on the other hand, is as careless as her carriage is precise—she*

is inclined to slur everything—but her voice is perhaps not so much quiet as simply soft.

MAMA Who that 'round here slamming doors at this hour?

    She crosses through the room, goes to the window, opens it, and brings in a feeble little plant growing doggedly in a small pot on the window sill. She feels the dirt and puts it back out.

RUTH That was Walter Lee. He and Bennie was at it again.

MAMA My children and they tempers. Lord, if this little old plant don't get more sun than it's been getting it ain't never going to see spring again. (*She turns from the window*) What's the matter with you this morning, Ruth? You looks right peaked. You aiming to iron all them things? Leave some for me. I'll get to 'em this afternoon. Bennie honey, it's too drafty for you to be sitting 'round half dressed. Where's your robe?

BENEATHA In the cleaners.

MAMA Well, go get mine and put it on.

BENEATHA I'm not cold, Mama, honest.

MAMA I know—but you so thin . . .

BENEATHA (*Irritably*) Mama, I'm not cold.

MAMA (*Seeing the make-down bed as* TRAVIS *has left it*) Lord have mercy, look at that poor bed. Bless his heart—he tries, don't he?

    She moves to the bed TRAVIS *has sloppily made up.*

RUTH No—he don't half try at all 'cause he knows you going to come along behind him and fix everything. That's just how come he don't know how to do nothing right now—you done spoiled that boy so.

MAMA Well—he's a little boy. Ain't supposed to know 'bout housekeeping. My baby, that's what he is. What you fix for his breakfast this morning?

RUTH (*Angrily*) I feed my son, Lena!

MAMA I ain't meddling—(*Underbreath; busy-bodyish*) I just noticed all last week he had cold cereal, and when it starts getting this chilly in the fall a child ought to have some hot grits or something when he goes out in the cold—

RUTH (*Furious*) I gave him hot oats—is that all right!

MAMA I ain't meddling. (*Pause*) Put a lot of nice butter on it? (RUTH *shoots her an angry look and does not reply*) He likes lots of butter.

RUTH (*Exasperated*) Lena—

MAMA (*To* BENEATHA, MAMA *is inclined to wander conversationally sometimes*) What was you and your brother fussing 'bout this morning?

BENEATHA It's not important, Mama.

    She gets up and goes to look out at the bathroom, which is apparently free, and she picks up her towels and rushes out.

MAMA What was they fighting about?

RUTH Now you know as well as I do.

MAMA (*Shaking her head*) Brother still worrying hisself sick about that money?

RUTH You know he is.

MAMA You had breakfast?

RUTH Some coffee.

MAMA Girl, you better start eating and looking after yourself better. You almost thin as Travis.

RUTH   Lena—

MAMA   Un-hunh?

RUTH   What are you going to do with it?

MAMA   Now don't you start, child. It's too early in the morning to be talking about money. It ain't Christian.

RUTH   It's just that he got his heart set on that store—

MAMA   You mean that liquor store that Willy Harris want him to invest in?

RUTH   Yes—

MAMA   We ain't no business people, Ruth. We just plain working folks.

RUTH   Ain't nobody business people till they go into business. Walter Lee say colored people ain't never going to start getting ahead till they start gambling on some different kinds of things in the world—investments and things.

MAMA   What done got into you, girl? Walter Lee done finally sold you on investing.

RUTH   No. Mama, something is happening between Walter and me. I don't know what it is—but he needs something—something I can't give him any more. He needs this chance, Lena.

MAMA   (*Frowning deeply*) But liquor, honey—

RUTH   Well—like Walter say—I spec people going to always be drinking themselves some liquor.

MAMA   Well—whether they drinks it or not ain't none of my business. But whether I go into business selling it to 'em *is,* and I don't want that on my ledger this late in life. (*Stopping suddenly and studying her daughter-in-law*) Ruth Younger, what's the matter with you today? You look like you could fall over right there.

RUTH   I'm tired.

MAMA   Then you better stay home from work today.

RUTH   I can't stay home. She'd be calling up the agency and screaming at them, "My girl didn't come in today—send me somebody! My girl didn't come in!" Oh, she just have a fit . . .

MAMA   Well, let her have it. I'll just call her up and say you got the flu—

RUTH   (*Laughing*) Why the flu?

MAMA   'Cause it sounds respectable to 'em. Something white people get, too. They know 'bout the flu. Otherwise they think you been cut up or something when you tell 'em you sick.

RUTH   I got to go in. We need the money.

MAMA   Somebody would of thought my children done all but starved to death the way they talk about money here late. Child, we got a great big old check coming tomorrow.

RUTH   (*Sincerely, but also self-righteously*) Now that's your money. It ain't got nothing to do with me. We all feel like that—Walter and Bennie and me—even Travis.

MAMA   (*Thoughtfully, and suddenly very far away*) Ten thousand dollars—

RUTH   Sure is wonderful.

MAMA   Ten thousand dollars.

RUTH   You know what you should do, Miss Lena? You should take yourself a trip somewhere. To Europe or South America or someplace—

MAMA   (*Throwing up her hands at the thought*) Oh, child!

RUTH   I'm serious. Just pack up and leave! Go on away and enjoy yourself some. Forget about the family and have yourself a ball for once in your life—

MAMA (*Drily*) You sound like I'm just about ready to die. Who'd go with me? What I look like wandering 'round Europe by myself?

RUTH Shoot—these here rich white women do it all the time. They don't think nothing of packing up they suitcases and piling on one of them big steamships and—swoosh!—they gone, child.

MAMA Something always told me I wasn't no rich white woman.

RUTH Well—what are you going to do with it then?

MAMA I ain't rightly decided. (*Thinking. She speaks now with emphasis*) Some of it got to be put away for Beneatha and her schoolin'—and ain't nothing going to touch that part of it. Nothing. (*She waits several seconds, trying to make up her mind about something, and looks at* RUTH *a little tentatively before going on*) Been thinking that we maybe could meet the notes on a little old two-story somewhere, with a yard where Travis could play in the summertime, if we use part of the insurance for a down payment and everybody kind of pitch in. I could maybe take on a little day work again, few days a week—

RUTH (*Studying her mother-in-law furtively and concentrating on her ironing, anxious to encourage without seeming to*) Well, Lord knows, we've put enough rent into this here rat trap to pay for four houses by now . . .

MAMA (*Looking up at the words "rat trap" and then looking around and leaning back and sighing—in a suddenly reflective mood—*) "Rat trap"—yes, that's all it is. (*Smiling*) I remember just as well the day me and Big Walter moved in here. Hadn't been married but two weeks and wasn't planning on living here no more than a year. (*She shakes her head at the dissolved dream*) We was going to set away, little by little, don't you know, and buy a little place out in Morgan Park. We had even picked out the house. (*Chuckling a little*) Looks right dumpy today. But Lord, child, you should know all the dreams I had 'bout buying that house and fixing it up and making me a little garden in the back— (*She waits and stops smiling*) And didn't none of it happen.

Dropping her hands in a futile gesture.

RUTH (*Keeps her head down, ironing*) Yes, life can be a barrel of disappointments, sometimes.

MAMA Honey, Big Walter would come in here some nights back then and slump down on that couch there and just look at the rug, and look at me and look at the rug and then back at me—and I'd know he was down then . . . really down. (*After a second very long and thoughtful pause; she is seeing back to times that only she can see*) And then, Lord, when I lost that baby—little Claude—I almost thought I was going to lose Big Walter too. Oh, that man grieved hisself! He was one man to love his children.

RUTH Ain't nothin' can tear at you like losin' your baby.

MAMA I guess that's how come that man finally worked hisself to death like he done. Like he was fighting his own war with this here world that took his baby from him.

RUTH He sure was a fine man, all right. I always liked Mr. Younger.

MAMA Crazy 'bout his children! God knows there was plenty wrong with Walter Younger—hard-headed, mean, kind of wild with women—plenty wrong with him. But he sure loved his children. Always wanted them to have something—be something. That's where Brother gets all these notions, I reckon. Big Walter used to say, he'd get right wet in the eyes sometimes, lean his head back with the water standing in his eyes and say, "Seem like God didn't see fit to give the black man nothing but dreams—but He did give us children to make them dreams seem worth while." (*She smiles*) He could talk like that, don't you know.

RUTH   Yes, he sure could. He was a good man, Mr. Younger.

MAMA   Yes, a fine man—just couldn't never catch up with his dreams, that's all.

        BENEATHA *comes in, brushing her hair and looking up to the ceiling, where the sound of a vacuum cleaner has started up.*

BENEATHA   What could be so dirty on that woman's rugs that she has to vacuum them every single day?

RUTH   I wish certain young women 'round here who I could name would take inspiration about certain rugs in a certain apartment I could also mention.

BENEATHA   (*Shrugging*) How much cleaning can a house need, for Christ's sakes.

MAMA   (*Not liking the Lord's name used thus*) Bennie!

RUTH   Just listen to her—just listen!

BENEATHA   Oh, God!

MAMA   If you use the Lord's name just one more time—

BENEATHA   (*A bit of a whine*) Oh, Mama—

RUTH   Fresh—just fresh as salt, this girl!

BENEATHA   (*Drily*) Well—if the salt loses its savor—

MAMA   Now that will do. I just ain't going to have you 'round here reciting the scriptures in vain—you hear me?

BENEATHA   How did I manage to get on everybody's wrong side by just walking into a room?

RUTH   If you weren't so fresh—

BENEATHA   Ruth, I'm twenty years old.

MAMA   What time you be home from school today?

BENEATHA   Kind of late. (*With enthusiasm*) Madeline is going to start my guitar lessons today.

        MAMA *and* RUTH *look up with the same expression.*

MAMA   Your *what* kind of lessons?

BENEATHA   Guitar.

RUTH   Oh, Father!

MAMA   How come you done taken it in your mind to learn to play the guitar?

BENEATHA   I just want to, that's all.

MAMA   (*Smiling*) Lord, child, don't you know what to do with yourself? How long it going to be before you get tired of this now—like you got tired of that little play-acting group you joined last year? (*Looking at Ruth*) And what was it the year before that?

RUTH   The horseback-riding club for which she bought that fifty-five-dollar riding habit that's been hanging in the closet ever since!

MAMA   (*To* BENEATHA) Why you got to flit so from one thing to another, baby?

BENEATHA   (*Sharply*) I just want to learn to play the guitar. Is there anything wrong with that?

MAMA   Ain't nobody trying to stop you. I just wonders sometimes why you has to flit so from one thing to another all the time. You ain't never done nothing with all that camera equipment you brought home—

BENEATHA   I don't flit! I—I experiment with different forms of expression—

RUTH   Like riding a horse?

BENEATHA   —People have to express themselves one way or another.

MAMA   What is it you want to express?

BENEATHA   (*Angrily*) Me! (MAMA *and* RUTH *look at each other and burst into raucous laughter*) Don't worry—I don't expect you to understand.

MAMA   (*To change the subject*) Who you going out with tomorrow night?

BENEATHA   (*With displeasure*) George Murchison again.

MAMA   (*Pleased*) Oh—you getting a little sweet on him?

RUTH   You ask me, this child ain't sweet on nobody but herself—(*Underbreath*) Express herself!

> They laugh.

BENEATHA   Oh—I like George all right, Mama. I mean I like him enough to go out with him and stuff, but—

RUTH   (*For devilment*) What does *and stuff* mean?

BENEATHA   Mind your own business.

MAMA   Stop picking at her now, Ruth. (*A thoughtful pause, and then a suspicious sudden look at her daughter as she turns in her chair for emphasis*) What *does* it mean?

BENEATHA   (*Wearily*) Oh, I just mean I couldn't ever really be serious about George. He's—he's so shallow.

RUTH   Shallow—what do you mean he's shallow? He's *Rich!*

MAMA   Hush, Ruth.

BENEATHA   I know he's rich. He knows he's rich, too.

RUTH   Well—what other qualities a man got to have to satisfy you, little girl?

BENEATHA   You wouldn't even begin to understand. Anybody who married Walter could not possibly understand.

MAMA   (*Outraged*) What kind of way is that to talk about your brother?

BENEATHA   Brother is a flip—let's face it.

MAMA   (*To* RUTH, *helplessly*) What's a flip?

RUTH   (*Glad to add kindling*) She's saying he's crazy.

BENEATHA   Not crazy. Brother isn't really crazy yet—he—he's an elaborate neurotic.

MAMA   Hush your mouth!

BENEATHA   As for George. Well. George looks good—he's got a beautiful car and he takes me to nice places and, as my sister-in-law says, he is probably the richest boy I will ever get to know and I even like him sometimes—but if the Youngers are sitting around waiting to see if their little Bennie is going to tie up the family with the Murchisons, they are wasting their time.

RUTH   You mean you wouldn't marry George Murchison if he asked you someday? That pretty, rich thing? Honey, I knew you was odd—

BENEATHA   No I would not marry him if all I felt for him was what I feel now. Besides, George's family wouldn't really like it.

MAMA   Why not?

BENEATHA   Oh, Mama—The Murchisons are honest-to-God-real-*live*-rich colored people, and the only people in the world who are more snobbish than rich white people are rich colored people. I thought everybody knew that. I've met Mrs. Murchison. She's a scene!

MAMA   You must not dislike people 'cause they well off, honey.

BENEATHA   Why not? It makes just as much sense as disliking people 'cause they are poor, and lots of people do that.

RUTH   (*A wisdom-of-the-ages manner. To* MAMA) Well, she'll get over some of this—

BENEATHA   Get over it? What are you talking about, Ruth? Listen, I'm going to be a doctor. I'm not worried about who I'm going to marry yet—if I ever get married.

MAMA *and* RUTH   If!

MAMA   Now, Bennie—

BENEATHA   Oh, I probably will . . . but first I'm going to be a doctor, and George, for one, still thinks that's pretty funny. I couldn't be bothered with that. I am going to be a doctor and everybody around here better understand that!

MAMA   (*Kindly*) 'Course you going to be a doctor, honey, God willing.

BENEATHA   (*Drily*) God hasn't got a thing to do with it.

MAMA   Beneatha—that just wasn't necessary.

BENEATHA   Well—neither is God. I get sick of hearing about God.

MAMA   Beneatha!

BENEATHA   I mean it! I'm just tired of hearing about God all the time. What has He got to do with anything? Does he pay tuition?

MAMA   You 'bout to get your fresh little jaw slapped!

RUTH   That's just what she needs, all right!

BENEATHA   Why? Why can't I say what I want to around here, like everybody else?

MAMA   It don't sound nice for a young girl to say things like that—you wasn't brought up that way. Me and your father went to trouble to get you and Brother to church every Sunday.

BENEATHA   Mama, you don't understand. It's all a matter of ideas, and God is just one idea I don't accept. It's not important. I am not going out and be immoral or commit crimes because I don't believe in God. I don't even think about it. It's just that I get tired of Him getting credit for all the things the human race achieves through its own stubborn effort. There simply is no blasted God—there is only man and it is he who makes miracles!

> MAMA *absorbs this speech, studies her daughter and rises slowly and crosses to* BENEATHA *and slaps her powerfully across the face. After, there is only silence and the daughter drops her eyes from her mother's face, and* MAMA *is very tall before her.*

MAMA   Now—you say after me, in my mother's house there is still God. (*There is a long pause and* BENEATHA *stares at the floor wordlessly.* MAMA *repeats the phrase with precision and cool emotion*) In my mother's house there is still God.

BENEATHA   In my mother's house there is still God.

> *A long pause.*

MAMA   (*Walking away from* BENEATHA, *too disturbed for triumphant posture. Stopping and turning back to her daughter*) There are some ideas we ain't going to have in this house. Not long as I am at the head of this family.

BENEATHA   Yes, ma'am.

> MAMA *walks out of the room.*

RUTH   (*Almost gently, with profound understanding*) You think you a woman, Bennie— but you still a little girl. What you did was childish—so you got treated like a child.

BENEATHA   I see. (*Quietly*) I also see that everybody thinks it's all right for Mama to be a tyrant. But all the tyranny in the world will never put a God in the heavens!

> She picks up her books and goes out.

RUTH   (*Goes to* MAMA's *door*) She said she was sorry.

MAMA   (*Coming out, going to her plant*) They frightens me, Ruth. My children.

RUTH   You got good children, Lena. They just a little off sometimes—but they're good.

MAMA   No—there's something come down between me and them that don't let us understand each other and I don't know what it is. One done almost lost his mind thinking 'bout money all the time and the other done commence to talk about things I can't seem to understand in no form or fashion. What is it that's changing, Ruth?

RUTH   (*Soothingly, older than her years*) Now . . . you taking it all too seriously. You just got strong-willed children and it takes a strong woman like you to keep 'em in hand.

MAMA   (*Looking at her plant and sprinkling a little water on it*) They spirited all right, my children. Got to admit they got spirit—Bennie and Walter. Like this little old plant that ain't never had enough sunshine or nothing—and look at it . . .

> She has her back to RUTH, who has had to stop ironing and lean against something and put the back of her hand to her forehead.

RUTH   (*Trying to keep* MAMA *from noticing*) You . . . sure . . . loves that little old thing, don't you? . . .

MAMA   Well, I always wanted me a garden like I used to see sometimes at the back of the houses down home. This plant is close as I ever got to having one. (*She looks out of the window as she replaces the plant*) Lord, ain't nothing as dreary as the view from this window on a dreary day, is there? Why ain't you singing this morning, Ruth? Sing that "No Ways Tired." That song always lifts me up so—(*She turns at last to see that* RUTH *has slipped quietly into a chair, in a state of semiconsciousness*) Ruth! Ruth honey—what's the matter with you . . . Ruth!

Curtain

Scene Two

It is the following morning; a Saturday morning, and house cleaning is in progress at the YOUNGERS. *Furniture has been shoved hither and yon and* MAMA *is giving the kitchen-area walls a washing down.* BENEATHA, *in dungarees, with a handkerchief tied around her face, is spraying insecticide into the cracks in the walls. As they work, the radio is on and a Southside disk-jockey program is inappropriately filling the house with a rather exotic saxophone blues.* TRAVIS, *the sole idle one, is leaning on his arms, looking out of the window.*

TRAVIS   Grandmama, that stuff Bennie is using smells awful. Can I go downstairs, please?

MAMA   Did you get all them chores done already? I ain't seen you doing much.

TRAVIS   Yes'm—finished early. Where did Mama go this morning?

MAMA   (*Looking at* BENEATHA) She had to go on a little errand.

TRAVIS   Where?

MAMA   To tend to her business.

TRAVIS   Can I go outside then?

MAMA   Oh, I guess so. You better stay right in front of the house, though . . . and keep a good lookout for the postman.

TRAVIS   Yes'm. (*He starts out and decides to give his* AUNT BENEATHA *a good swat on the legs as he passes her*) Leave them poor little old cockroaches alone, they ain't bothering you none.

   He runs as she swings the spray gun at him both viciously and playfully.
   WALTER *enters from the bedroom and goes to the phone.*

MAMA   Look out there, girl, before you be spilling some of that stuff on that child!

TRAVIS   (*Teasing*) That's right—look out now!

   He exits.

BENEATHA   (*Dryly*) I can't imagine that it would hurt him—it has never hurt the roaches.

MAMA   Well, little boys' hides ain't as tough as Southside roaches.

WALTER   (*Into phone*) Hello—Let me talk to Willy Harris.

MAMA   You better get over there behind the bureau. I seen one marching out of there like Napoleon yesterday.

WALTER   Hello, Willy? It ain't come yet. It'll be here in a few minutes. Did the lawyer give you the papers?

BENEATHA   There's really only one way to get rid of them, Mama—

MAMA   How?

BENEATHA   Set fire to this building.

WALTER   Good. Good. I'll be right over.

BENEATHA   Where did Ruth go, Walter?

WALTER   I don't know.

   He exits abruptly.

BENEATHA   Mama, where did Ruth go?

MAMA   (*Looking at her with meaning*) To the doctor, I think.

BENEATHA   The doctor? What's the matter? (*They exchange glances*) You don't think—

MAMA   (*With her sense of drama*) Now I ain't saying what I think. But I ain't never been wrong 'bout a woman neither.

   The phone rings.

BENEATHA   (*At the phone*) Hay-lo . . . (*Pause, and a moment of recognition*) Well—when did you get back! . . . And how was it? . . . Of course I've missed you—in my way . . . This morning? No . . . house cleaning and all that and Mama hates it if I let people come over when the house is like this . . . You *have?* Well, that's different . . . What is it—Oh, what the hell, come on over . . . Right, see you then.

   She hangs up.

MAMA   (*Who has listened vigorously, as is her habit*) Who is that you inviting over here with this house looking like this? You ain't got the pride you was born with!

BENEATHA   Asagai doesn't care how houses look, Mama—he's an intellectual.

MAMA   *Who?*

BENEATHA   Asagai—Joseph Asagai. He's an African boy I met on campus. He's been studying in Canada all summer.

MAMA   What's his name?

BENEATHA   Asagai, Joseph. Ah-sah-guy . . . He's from Nigeria.

MAMA   Oh, that's the little country that was founded by slaves way back . . .

BENEATHA   No, Mama—that's Liberia.

MAMA   I don't think I never met no African before.

BENEATHA   Well, do me a favor and don't ask him a whole lot of ignorant questions about Africans. I mean, do they wear clothes and all that—

MAMA   Well, now, I guess if you think we so ignorant 'round here maybe you shouldn't bring your friends here—

BENEATHA   It's just that people ask such crazy things. All anyone seems to know about when it comes to Africa is Tarzan—

MAMA   (*Indignantly*) Why should I know anything about Africa?

BENEATHA   Why do you give money at church for the missionary work?

MAMA   Well, that's to help save people.

BENEATHA   You mean save them from *heathenism*—

MAMA   (*Innocently*) Yes.

BENEATHA   I'm afraid they need more salvation from the British and the French.

> RUTH *comes in forlornly and pulls off her coat with dejection. They both turn to look at her.*

RUTH   (*Dispiritedly*) Well, I guess from all the happy faces—everybody knows.

BENEATHA   You pregnant?

MAMA   Lord have mercy, I sure hope it's a little old girl. Travis ought to have a sister.

> BENEATHA *and* RUTH *give her a hopeless look for this grandmotherly enthusiasm.*

BENEATHA   How far along are you?

RUTH   Two months.

BENEATHA   Did you mean to? I mean did you plan it or was it an accident?

MAMA   What do you know about planning or not planning?

BENEATHA   Oh, Mama.

RUTH   (*Wearily*) She's twenty years old, Lena.

BENEATHA   Did you plan it, Ruth?

RUTH   Mind your own business.

BENEATHA   It is my business—where is he going to live, on the *roof?* (*There is silence following the remark as the three women react to the sense of it*) Gee—I didn't mean that, Ruth, honest. Gee, I don't feel like that at all. I—I think it is wonderful.

RUTH   (*Dully*) Wonderful.

BENEATHA   Yes—really.

MAMA   (*Looking at* RUTH, *worried*) Doctor say everything going to be all right?

RUTH   (*Far away*) Yes—she says everything is going to be fine . . .

MAMA   (*Immediately suspicious*) "She"—What doctor you went to?

> RUTH *folds over, near hysteria.*

MAMA   (*Worriedly hovering over* RUTH) Ruth honey—what's the matter with you—you sick?

RUTH *has her fists clenched on her thighs and is fighting hard to suppress a scream that seems to be rising in her.*

BENEATHA   What's the matter with her, Mama?

MAMA   (*Working her fingers in* RUTH's *shoulder to relax her*) She be all right. Women gets right depressed sometimes when they get her way. (*Speaking softly, expertly, rapidly*) Now you just relax. That's right . . . just lean back, don't think 'bout nothing at all . . . nothing at all—

RUTH   I'm all right . . .

The glassy-eyed look melts and then she collapses into a fit of heavy sobbing. The bell rings.

BENEATHA   Oh, my God—that must be Asagai.

MAMA   (*To* RUTH) Come on now, honey. You need to lie down and rest awhile . . . then have some nice hot food.

They exit, RUTH's *weight on her mother-in-law.* BENEATHA, *herself profoundly disturbed, opens the door to admit a rather dramatic-looking young man with a large package.*

ASAGAI   Hello, Alaiyo—

BENEATHA   (*Holding the door open and regarding him with pleasure*) Hello . . . (*Long pause*) Well—come in. And please excuse everything. My mother was very upset about my letting anyone come here with the place like this.

ASAGAI   (*Coming into the room*) You look disturbed too . . . Is something wrong?

BENEATHA   (*Still at the door, absently*) Yes . . . we've all got acute ghetto-itus. (*She smiles and comes toward him, finding a cigarette and sitting*) So—sit down! How was Canada?

ASAGAI   (*A sophisticate*) Canadian.

BENEATHA   (*Looking at him*) I'm very glad you are back.

ASAGAI   (*Looking back at her in turn*) Are you really?

BENEATHA   Yes—very.

ASAGAI   Why—you were quite glad when I went away. What happened?

BENEATHA   You went away.

ASAGAI   Ahhhhhhhh.

BENEATHA   Before—you wanted to be so serious before there was time.

ASAGAI   How much time must there be before one knows what one feels?

BENEATHA   (*Stalling this particular conversation. Her hands pressed together, in a deliberately childish gesture*) What did you bring me?

ASAGAI   (*Handing her the package*) Open it and see.

BENEATHA   (*Eagerly opening the package and drawing out some records and the colorful robes of a Nigerian woman*) Oh, Asagai! . . . You got them for me! . . . How beautiful . . . and the records too! (*She lifts out the robes and runs to the mirror with them and holds the drapery up in front of herself*)

ASAGAI   (*Coming to her at the mirror*) I shall have to teach you how to drape it properly. (*He flings the material about her for the moment and stands back to look at her*) Ah—Oh-pay-gay-day, oh-gbah-mu-shay. (*A Yoruba exclamation for admiration*) You wear it well . . . very well . . . mutilated hair and all.

BENEATHA   (*Turning suddenly*) My hair—what's wrong with my hair?

ASAGAI   (*Shrugging*) Were you born with it like that?

BENEATHA   (*Reaching up to touch it*) No . . . of course not.

She looks back to the mirror, disturbed.

ASAGAI   (*Smiling*) How then?

BENEATHA   You know perfectly well how . . . as crinkly as yours . . . that's how.

ASAGAI   And it is ugly to you that way?

BENEATHA   (*Quickly*) Oh, no—not ugly . . . (*More slowly, apologetically*) But it's so hard to manage when it's, well—raw.

ASAGAI   And so to accommodate that—you mutilate it every week?

BENEATHA   It's not mutilation!

ASAGAI   (*Laughing aloud at her seriousness*) Oh . . . please! I am only teasing you because you are so very serious about these things. (*He stands back from her and folds his arms across his chest as he watches her pulling at her hair and frowning in the mirror*) Do you remember the first time you met me at school? . . . (*He laughs*) You came up to me and you said—and I thought you were the most serious little thing I had ever seen—you said: (*He imitates her*) "Mr. Asagai—I want very much to talk with you. About Africa. You see, Mr. Asagai, I am looking for my *identity!*"

    He laughs.

BENEATHA   (*Turning to him, not laughing*) Yes—

    Her face is quizzical, profoundly disturbed.

ASAGAI   (*Still teasing and reaching out and taking her face in his hands and turning her profile to him*) Well . . . it is true that this is not so much a profile of a Hollywood queen as perhaps a queen of the Nile—(*A mock dismissal of the importance of the question*) But what does it matter? Assimilationism is so popular in your country.

BENEATHA   (*Wheeling, passionately, sharply*) I am not an assimilationist!

ASAGAI   (*The protest hangs in the room for a moment and* ASAGAI *studies her, his laughter fading*) Such a serious one. (*There is a pause*) So—you like the robes? You must take excellent care of them—they are from my sister's personal wardrobe.

BENEATHA   (*With incredulity*)You—you sent all the way home—for me?

ASAGAI   (*With charm*) For you—I would do much more . . . Well, that is what I came for. I must go.

BENEATHA   Will you call me Monday?

ASAGAI   Yes . . . We have a great deal to talk about. I mean about identity and time and all that.

BENEATHA   Time?

ASAGAI   Yes. About how much time one needs to know what one feels.

BENEATHA   You never understood that there is more than one kind of feeling which can exist between a man and a woman—or, at least, there should be.

ASAGAI   (*Shaking his head negatively but gently*) No. Between a man and a woman there need be only one kind of feeling. I have that for you . . . Now even . . . right this moment . . .

BENEATHA   I know—and by itself—it won't do. I can find that anywhere.

ASAGAI   For a woman it should be enough.

BENEATHA   I know—because that's what it says in all the novels that men write. But it isn't. Go ahead and laugh—but I'm not interested in being someone's little episode in America or—(*With feminine vengeance*)—one of them! (ASAGAI *has burst into laughter again*) That's funny as hell, huh!

ASAGAI   It's just that every American girl I have known has said that to me. White—black—in this you are all the same. And the same speech, too!

A RAISIN IN THE SUN 769

BENEATHA (Angrily) Yuk, yuk, yuk!

ASAGAI It's how you can be sure that the world's most liberated women are not liberated at all. You all talk about it too much!

      MAMA *enters and is immediately all social charm because of the presence of a guest.*

BENEATHA Oh—Mama—this is Mr. Asagai.

MAMA How do you do?

ASAGAI (Total politeness to an elder) How do you do, Mrs. Younger. Please forgive me for coming at such an outrageous hour on a Saturday.

MAMA Well, you are quite welcome. I just hope you understand that our house don't always look like this. (Chatterish) You must come again. I would love to hear all about—(Not sure of the name)—your country. I think it's so sad the way our American Negroes don't know nothing about Africa 'cept Tarzan and all that. And all that money they pour into these churches when they ought to be helping you people over there drive out them French and Englishmen done taken away your land.

      The mother flashes a slightly superior look at her daughter upon completion of the recitation.

ASAGAI (Taken aback by this sudden and acutely unrelated expression of sympathy) Yes . . . yes . . .

MAMA (Smiling at him suddenly and relaxing and looking him over) How many miles is it from here to where you come from?

ASAGAI Many thousands.

MAMA (Looking at him as she would WALTER) I bet you don't half look after yourself, being away from your mama either. I spec you better come 'round here from time to time and get yourself some decent home-cooked meals . . .

ASAGAI (Moved) Thank you. Thank you very much. (They are all quiet, then—) Well . . . I must go. I will call you Monday, Alaiyo.

MAMA What's that he call you?

ASAGAI Oh—"Alaiyo." I hope you don't mind. It is what you would call a nickname, I think. It is a Yoruba word. I am a Yoruba.

MAMA (Looking at BENEATHA) I—I thought he was from—

ASAGAI (Understanding) Nigeria is my country. Yoruba is my tribal origin—

BENEATHA You didn't tell us what Alaiyo means . . . for all I know, you might be calling me Little Idiot or something . . .

ASAGAI Well . . . let me see . . . I do not know how just to explain it . . . The sense of a thing can be so different when it changes languages.

BENEATHA You're evading.

ASAGAI No—really it is difficult . . . (Thinking) It means . . . it means One for Whom Bread—Food—Is Not Enough. (He looks at her) Is that all right?

BENEATHA (Understanding, softly) Thank you.

MAMA (Looking from one to the other and not understanding any of it) Well . . . that's nice . . . You must come see us again—Mr.—

ASAGAI Ah-sah-guy . . .

MAMA Yes . . . Do come again.

ASAGAI Good-bye.

      He exits.

MAMA   (*After him*) Lord, that's a pretty thing just went out here! (*Insinuatingly, to her daughter*) Yes, I guess I see why we done commence to get so interested in Africa 'round here. Missionaries my aunt Jenny!

> *She exits.*

BENEATHA   Oh, Mama!. . .

> *She picks up the Nigerian dress and holds it up to her in front of the mirror again. She sets the headdress on haphazardly and then notices her hair again and clutches at it and then replaces the headdress and frowns at herself. Then she starts to wriggle in front of the mirror as she thinks a Nigerian woman might.* TRAVIS *enters and regards her.*

TRAVIS   You cracking up?

BENEATHA   Shut up.

> *She pulls the headdress off and looks at herself in the mirror and clutches at her hair again and squinches her eyes as if trying to imagine something. Then, suddenly, she gets her raincoat and kerchief and hurriedly prepares for going out.*

MAMA   (*Coming back into the room*) She's resting now. Travis, baby, run next door and ask Miss Johnson to please let me have a little kitchen cleanser. This here can is empty as Jacob's kettle.

TRAVIS   I just came in.

MAMA   Do as you told. (*He exits and she looks at her daughter*) Where you going?

BENEATHA   (*Halting at the door*) To become a queen of the Nile!

> *She exits in a breathless blaze of glory.* RUTH *appears in the bedroom doorway.*

MAMA   Who told you to get up?

RUTH   Ain't nothing wrong with me to be lying in no bed for. Where did Bennie go?

MAMA   (*Drumming her fingers*) Far as I could make out—to Egypt. (RUTH *just looks at her*) What time is it getting to?

RUTH   Ten twenty. And the mailman going to ring that bell this morning just like he done every morning for the last umpteen years.

> TRAVIS *comes in with the cleanser can.*

TRAVIS   She say to tell you that she don't have much.

MAMA   (*Angrily*) Lord, some people I could name sure is tight-fisted! (*Directing her grandson*) Mark two cans of cleanser down on the list there. If she that hard up for kitchen cleanser, I sure don't want to forget to get her none!

RUTH   Lena—maybe the woman is just short on cleanser—

MAMA   (*Not listening*) —Much baking powder as she done borrowed from me all these years, she could of done gone into the baking business!

> *The bell sounds suddenly and sharply and all three are stunned—serious and silent—mid-speech. In spite of all the other conversations and distractions of the morning, this is what they have been waiting for, even* TRAVIS, *who looks helplessly from his mother to his grandmother.* RUTH *is the first to come to life again.*

RUTH   (*To* TRAVIS) Get down them steps, boy!

> TRAVIS *snaps to life and flies out to get the mail.*

MAMA   (*Hes eyes wide, her hand to her breast*) You mean it done really come?

RUTH   (*Excited*) Oh, Miss Lena!

MAMA   (*Collecting herself*) Well . . . I don't know what we all so excited about 'round here for. We known it was coming for months.

RUTH   That's a whole lot different from having it come and being able to hold it in your hands . . . a piece of paper worth ten thousand dollars . . . (TRAVIS *bursts back into the room. He holds the envelope high above his head, like a little dancer, his face is radiant and he is breathless. He moves to his grandmother with sudden slow ceremony and puts the envelope into her hands. She accepts it, and then merely holds it and looks at it*) Come on! Open it . . . Lord have mercy, I wish Walter Lee was here!

TRAVIS   Open it, Grandmama!

MAMA   (*Staring at it*) Now you all be quiet. It's just a check.

RUTH   Open it . . .

MAMA   (*Still staring at it*) Now don't act silly . . . We ain't never been no people to act silly 'bout no money—

RUTH   (*Swiftly*) We ain't never had none before—*open it!*

> MAMA *finally makes a good strong tear and pulls out the thin blue slice of paper and inspects it closely. The boy and his mother study it raptly over* MAMA's *shoulders.*

MAMA   Travis! (*She is counting off with doubt*) Is that the right number of zeros?

TRAVIS   Yes'm . . . ten thousand dollars. Gaalee, Grandmama, you rich.

MAMA   (*She holds the check away from her, still looking at it. Slowly her face sobers into a mask of unhappiness*) Ten thousand dollars. (*She hands it to* RUTH) Put it away somewhere, Ruth. (*She does not look at* RUTH; *her eyes seem to be seeing something somewhere very far off*) Ten thousand dollars they give you. Ten thousand dollars.

TRAVIS   (*To his mother, sincerely*) What's the matter with Grandmama—don't she want to be rich?

RUTH   (*Distractedly*) You go on out and play now, baby. (TRAVIS *exits.* MAMA *starts wiping dishes absently, humming intently to herself.* RUTH *turns to her, with kind exasperation*) You've gone and got yourself upset.

MAMA   (*Not looking at her*) I spec if it wasn't for you all . . . I would just put that money away or give it to the church or something.

RUTH   Now what kind of talk is that? Mr. Younger would just be plain mad if he could hear you talking foolish like that.

MAMA   (*Stopping and staring off*) Yes . . . he sure would. (*Sighing*) We got enough to do with that money, all right. (*She halts then, and turns and looks at her daughter-in-law hard;* RUTH *avoids her eyes and* MAMA *wipes her hands with finality and starts to speak firmly to* RUTH) Where did you go today, girl?

RUTH   To the doctor.

MAMA   (*Impatiently*) Now, Ruth . . . you know better than that. Old Doctor Jones is strange enough in his way but there ain't nothing 'bout him make somebody slip and call him "she"—like you done this morning.

RUTH   Well, that's what happened—my tongue slipped.

MAMA   You went to see that woman, didn't you?

RUTH   (*Defensively, giving herself away*) What woman you talking about?

MAMA   (*Angrily*) That woman who—

> WALTER *enters in great excitement.*

WALTER   Did it come?

MAMA   (*Quietly*) Can't you give people a Christian greeting before you start asking about money?

WALTER (*To* RUTH) Did it come? (RUTH *unfolds the check and lays it quietly before him, watching him intently with thoughts of her own.* WALTER *sits down and grasps it close and counts off the zeros*) Ten thousand dollars—(*He turns suddenly, frantically to his mother and draws some papers out of his breast pocket*) Mama—look. Old Willy Harris put everything on paper—

MAMA Son—I think you ought to talk to your wife . . . I'll go on out and leave you alone if you want—

WALTER I can talk to her later—Mama, look—

MAMA Son—

WALTER WILL SOMEBODY PLEASE LISTEN TO ME TODAY!

MAMA (*Quietly*) I don't 'low no yellin' in this house, Walter Lee, and you know it—(WALTER *stares at them in frustration and starts to speak several times*) And there ain't going to be no investing in no liquor stores. I don't aim to have to speak on that again.

    A long pause.

WALTER Oh—so you don't aim to have to speak on that again? So *you* have decided . . . (*Crumpling his papers*) Well, *you* tell that to my boy tonight when you put him to sleep on the living-room couch . . . (*Turning to* MAMA *and speaking directly to her*) Yeah—and tell it to my wife, Mama, tomorrow when she has to go out of here to look after somebody else's kids. And tell it to *me*, Mama, every time we need a new pair of curtains and I have to watch *you* go out and work in somebody's kitchen. Yeah, you tell me then!

    WALTER *starts out.*

RUTH Where you going?

WALTER I'm going out!

RUTH Where?

WALTER Just out of this house somewhere—

RUTH (*Getting her coat*) I'll come too.

WALTER I don't want you to come!

RUTH I got something to talk to you about, Walter.

WALTER That's too bad.

MAMA (*Still quietly*) Walter Lee—(*She waits and he finally turns and looks at her*) Sit down.

WALTER I'm a grown man, Mama.

MAMA Ain't nobody said you wasn't grown. But you still in my house and my presence. And as long as you are—you'll talk to your wife civil. Now sit down.

RUTH (*Suddenly*) Oh, let him go on out and drink himself to death! He makes me sick to my stomach! (*She flings her coat against him*)

WALTER (*Violently*) And you turn mine too, baby! (RUTH *goes into their bedroom and slams the door behind her*) That was my greatest mistake—

MAMA (*Still quietly*) Walter, what is the matter with you?

WALTER Matter with me? Ain't nothing the matter with *me*!

MAMA Yes there is. Something eating you up like a crazy man. Something more than me not giving you this money. The past few years I been watching it happen to you. You get all nervous acting and kind of wild in the eyes—(WALTER *jumps up impatiently at her words*) I said sit there now, I'm talking to you!

WALTER Mama—I don't need no nagging at me today.

MAMA Seem like you getting to a place where you always tied up in some kind

A RAISIN IN THE SUN 773

of knot about something. But if anybody ask you 'bout it you just yell at 'em and bust out the house and go out and drink somewheres. Walter Lee, people can't live with that. Ruth's a good, patient girl in her way—but you getting to be too much. Boy, don't make the mistake of driving that girl away from you.

WALTER   Why—what she do for me?

MAMA   She loves you.

WALTER   Mama—I'm going out. I want to go off somewhere and be by myself for a while.

MAMA   I'm sorry 'bout your liquor store, son. It just wasn't the thing for us to do. That's what I want to tell you about—

WALTER   I got to go out, Mama—

      He rises.

MAMA   It's dangerous, son.

WALTER   What's dangerous?

MAMA   When a man goes outside his home to look for peace.

WALTER   (*Beseechingly*) Then why can't there never be no peace in this house then?

MAMA   You done found it in some other house?

WALTER   No—there ain't no woman! Why do women always think there's a woman somewhere when a man gets restless. (*Coming to her*) Mama—Mama—I want so many things . . .

MAMA   Yes, son—

WALTER   I want so many things that they are driving me kind of crazy . . . Mama— look at me.

MAMA   I'm looking at you. You a good-looking boy. You got a job, a nice wife, a fine boy and—

WALTER   A job. (*Looks at her*) Mama, a job? I open and close car doors all day long. I drive a man around in his limousine and I say, "Yes, sir; no, sir; very good, sir; shall I take the Drive, sir?" Mama, that ain't no kind of job . . . that ain't nothing at all. (*Very quietly*) Mama, I don't know if I can make you understand.

MAMA   Understand what, baby?

WALTER   (*Quietly*) Sometimes it's like I can see the future stretched out in front of me—just plain as day. The future, Mama. Hanging over there at the edge of my days. Just waiting for me—a big, looming blank space—full of *nothing.* Just waiting for *me.* (*Pause*) Mama—sometimes when I'm downtown and I pass them cool, quiet-looking restaurants where them white boys are sitting back and talking 'bout things . . . sitting there turning deals worth millions of dollars . . . sometimes I see guys don't look much older than me—

MAMA   Son—how come you talk so much 'bout money?

WALTER   (*With immense passion*) Because it is life, Mama!

MAMA   (*Quietly*) Oh—(*Very quietly*) So now it's life. Money is life. Once upon a time freedom used to be life—now it's money. I guess the world really do change . . .

WALTER   No—it was always money, Mama. We just didn't know about it.

MAMA   No . . . something has changed. (*She looks at him*) You something new, boy. In my time we was worried about not being lynched and getting to the North if we could and how to stay alive and still have a pinch of dignity too . . . Now here come you and Beneatha—talking 'bout things we ain't never even thought about hardly, me and your daddy. You ain't satisfied or proud of nothing we done. I mean that you had a home; that we kept you out of trouble till you was grown; that you don't have to ride to work on the back of nobody's streetcar—You my children—but how different we done become.

WALTER   You just don't understand, Mama, you just don't understand.

MAMA   Son—do you know your wife is expecting another baby? (WALTER *stands, stunned, and absorbs what his mother has said*) That's what she wanted to talk to you about. (WALTER *sinks down into a chair*) This ain't for me to be telling—but you ought to know. (*She waits*) I think Ruth is thinking 'bout getting rid of that child.

WALTER   (*Slowly understanding*) No—no—Ruth wouldn't do that.

MAMA   When the world gets ugly enough—a woman will do anything for her family. *The part that's already living.*

WALTER   You don't know Ruth, Mama, if you think she would do that.

RUTH *opens the bedroom door and stands there a little limp.*

RUTH   (*Beaten*) Yes I would too, Walter. (*Pause*) I gave her a five-dollar down payment.

There is total silence as the man stares at his wife and the mother stares at her son.

MAMA   (*Presently*) Well—(*Tightly*) Well—son, I'm waiting to hear you say something ... I'm waiting to hear how you be your father's son. Be the man he was ... (*Pause*) Your wife say she going to destroy your child. And I'm waiting to hear you talk like him and say we a people who give children life, not who destroys them—(*She rises*) I'm waiting to see you stand up and look like your daddy and say we done give up one baby to poverty and that we ain't going to give up nary another one ... I'm waiting.

WALTER   Ruth—

MAMA   If you a son of mine, tell her! (WALTER *turns, looks at her and can say nothing. She continues, bitterly*) You . . . you are a disgrace to your father's memory. Somebody get me my hat.

Curtain

ACT II

Scene I

Time: Later the same day.

At rise: RUTH *is ironing again. She has the radio going. Presently* BENEATHA's *bedroom door opens and* RUTH's *mouth falls and she puts down the iron in fascination.*

RUTH   What have we got on tonight!

BENEATHA   (*Emerging grandly from the doorway so that we can see her thoroughly robed in the costume Asagai brought*) You are looking at what a well-dressed Nigerian woman wears—(*She parades for* RUTH, *her hair completely hidden by the headdress; she is coquettishly fanning herself with an ornate oriental fan, mistakenly more like Butterfly than any Nigerian that ever was*) Isn't it beautiful? (*She promenades to the radio and, with an arrogant flourish, turns off the good loud blues that is playing*) Enough of this assimilationist junk! (RUTH *follows her with her eyes as she goes to the phonograph and puts on a record and turns and waits ceremoniously for the music to come up. Then, with a shout—*) OCOMOGOSIAY!

> RUTH *jumps. The music comes up, a lovely Nigerian melody.* BENEATHA *listens, enraptured, her eyes far away—"back to the past." She begins to dance.* RUTH *is dumfounded.*

RUTH   What kind of dance is that?

BENEATHA   A folk dance.

RUTH   (*Pearl Bailey*) What kind of folks do that, honey?

BENEATHA   It's from Nigeria. It's a dance of welcome.

RUTH   Who you welcoming?

BENEATHA   The men back to the village.

RUTH   Where they been?

BENEATHA   How should I know—out hunting or something. Anyway, they are coming back now . . .

RUTH   Well, that's good.

BENEATHA   (*With the record*)

> Alundi, alundi
> Alundi alunya
> Jop pu a jeepua
> Ang gu sooooooooooo
> Ai yai yae . . .
> Ayehaye—alundi . . .

> WALTER *comes in during this performance; he has obviously been drinking. He leans against the door heavily and watches his sister, at first with distaste. Then his eyes look off—"back to the past"—as he lifts both his fists to the roof, screaming.*

WALTER   YEAH . . . AND ETHIOPIA STRETCH FORTH HER HANDS AGAIN! . . .

RUTH   (*Drily, looking at him*) Yes—and Africa sure is claiming her own tonight. (*She gives them both up and starts ironing again*)

WALTER   (*All in a drunken, dramatic shout*) Shut up . . . I'm digging them drums . . . them drums move me! . . . (*He makes his weaving way to his wife's face and leans in close to her*) In my heart of hearts—(*He thumps his chest*)—I am much warrior!

RUTH   (*Without even looking up*) In your heart of hearts you are much drunkard.

WALTER   (*Coming away from her and starting to wander around the room, shouting*) Me and Jomo . . . (*Intently, in his sister's face. She has stopped dancing to watch him in this unknown mood*) That's my man, Kenyatta. (*Shouting and thumping his chest*) FLAMING SPEAR! HOT DAMN! (*He is suddenly in possession of an imaginary spear and actively spearing enemies all over the room*) OCOMOGOSIAY . . . THE LION IS WAKING . . . OWIMOWEH! (*He pulls his shirt open and leaps up on a table and gestures with his spear. The bell rings.* RUTH *goes to answer*)

BENEATHA   (*To encourage* WALTER, *thoroughly caught up with this side of him*) OCOMO-GOSIAY, FLAMING SPEAR!

WALTER (*On the table, very far gone, his eyes pure glass sheets. He sees what we cannot, that he is a leader of his people, a great chief, a descendant of Chaka, and that the hour to march has come*) Listen, my black brothers—

BENEATHA OCOMOGOSIAY!

WALTER —Do you hear the waters rushing against the shores of the coastlands—

BENEATHA OCOMOGOSIAY!

WALTER —Do you hear the screeching of the cocks in yonder hills beyond where the chiefs meet in council for the coming of the mighty war—

BENEATHA OCOMOGOSIAY!

WALTER —Do you hear the beating of the wings of the birds flying low over the mountains and the low places of our land—

    RUTH *opens the door.* GEORGE MURCHISON *enters.*

BENEATHA OCOMOGOSIAY!

WALTER —Do you hear the singing of the women, singing the war songs of our fathers to the babies in the great houses ... singing the sweet war songs? OH, DO YOU HEAR, MY BLACK BROTHERS!

BENEATHA (*Completely gone*) We hear you, Flaming Spear—

WALTER Telling us to prepare for the greatness of the time—(*To* GEORGE) Black Brother!

    He extends his hand for the fraternal clasp.

GEORGE Black Brother, hell!

RUTH (*Having had enough, and embarrassed for the family*) Beneatha, you got company—what's the matter with you? Walter Lee Younger, get down off that table and stop acting like a fool ...

    WALTER *comes down off the table suddenly and makes a quick exit to the bathroom.*

RUTH He's had a little to drink ... I don't know what her excuse is.

GEORGE (*To* BENEATHA) Look honey, we're going *to* the theatre—we're not going to be *in* it ... so go change, huh?

RUTH You expect this boy to go out with you looking like that?

BENEATHA (*Looking at* GEORGE) That's up to George. If he's ashamed of his heritage—

GEORGE Oh, don't be so proud of yourself, Bennie—just because you look eccentric.

BENEATHA How can something that's natural be eccentric?

GEORGE That's what being eccentric means—being natural. Get dressed.

BENEATHA I don't like that, George.

RUTH Why must you and your brother make an argument out of everything people say?

BENEATHA Because I hate assimilationist Negroes!

RUTH Will somebody please tell me what assimila-who-ever means!

GEORGE Oh, it's just a college girl's way of calling people Uncle Toms—but that isn't what it means at all.

RUTH Well, what does it mean?

BENEATHA (*Cutting* GEORGE *off and staring at him as she replies to* RUTH) It means someone who is willing to give up his own culture and submerge himself completely in the dominant, and in this case, *oppressive* culture!

GEORGE Oh, dear, dear, dear! Here we go! A lecture on the African past! On our Great West African Heritage! In one second we will hear all about the great Ashanti empires; the great Songhay civilizations; and the great sculpture of

Bénin—and then some poetry in the Bantu—and the whole monologue will end with the word *heritage!* (*Nastily*) Let's face it, baby, your heritage is nothing but a bunch of raggedy-assed spirituals and some grass huts!

BENEATHA *Grass huts!* (RUTH *crosses to her and forcibly pushes her toward the bedroom*) See there . . . you are standing there in your splendid ignorance talking about people who were the first to smelt iron on the face of the earth! (RUTH *is pushing her through the door*) The Ashanti were performing surgical operations when the English—(RUTH *pulls the door to, with* BENEATHA *on the other side, and smiles graciously at* GEORGE. BENEATHA *opens the door and shouts the end of the sentence defiantly at* GEORGE)—were still tattooing themselves with blue dragons . . . (*She goes back inside*)

RUTH Have a seat, George. (*They both sit.* RUTH *folds her hands rather primly on her lap, determined to demonstrate the civilization of the family*) Warm, ain't it? I mean for September. (*Pause*) Just like they always say about Chicago weather: If it's too hot or cold for you, just wait a minute and it'll change. (*She smiles happily at this chiché of clichés*) Everybody say it's got to do with them bombs and things they keep setting off. (*Pause*) Would you like a nice cold beer?

GEORGE No, thank you. I don't care for beer. (*He looks at his watch*) I hope she hurries up.

RUTH What time is the show?

GEORGE It's an eight-thirty curtain. That's just Chicago, though. In New York standard curtain time is eight forty.

He is rather proud of this knowledge.

RUTH (*Properly appreciating it*) You get to New York a lot?

GEORGE (*Offhand*) Few times a year.

RUTH Oh—that's nice. I've never been to New York.

WALTER *enters. We feel he has relieved himself, but the edge of unreality is still with him.*

WALTER New York ain't got nothing Chicago ain't. Just a bunch of hustling people all squeezed up together—being "Eastern."

He turns his face into a screw of displeasure.

GEORGE Oh—you've been?

WALTER *Plenty* of times.

RUTH (*Shocked at the lie*) Walter Lee Younger!

WALTER (*Staring her down*) Plenty! (*Pause*) What we got to drink in this house? Why don't you offer this man some refreshment. (*To* GEORGE) They don't know how to entertain people in this house, man.

GEORGE Thank you—I don't really care for anything.

WALTER (*Feeling his head; sobriety coming*) Where's Mama?

RUTH She ain't come back yet.

WALTER (*Looking* MURCHISON *over from head to toe, scrutinizing his carefully casual tweed sports jacket over cashmere V-neck sweater over soft eyelet shirt and tie, and soft slacks, finished off with white buckskin shoes*) Why all you college boys wear them fairyish-looking white shoes?

RUTH Walter Lee!

GEORGE MURCHISON *ignores the remark.*

WALTER (*To* RUTH) Well, they look crazy as hell—white shoes, cold as it is.

RUTH (*Crushed*) You have to excuse him—

WALTER No he don't! Excuse me for what? What you always excusing me for! I'll excuse myself when I needs to be excused! (*A pause*) They look as funny as them black knee socks Beneatha wears out of here all the time.

RUTH It's the college *style*, Walter.

WALTER Style, hell. She looks like she got burnt legs or something!

RUTH Oh, Walter—

WALTER (*An irritable mimic*) Oh, Walter! Oh, Walter! (*To* MURCHISON) How's your old man making out? I understand you all going to buy that big hotel on the Drive? (*He finds a beer in the refrigerator, wanders over to* MURCHISON, *sipping and wiping his lips with the back of his hand, and straddling a chair backwards to talk to the other man*) Shrewd move. Your old man is all right, man. (*Tapping his head and half winking for emphasis*) I mean he knows how to operate. I mean he thinks *big*, you know what I mean, I mean for a *home*, you know? But I think he's kind of running out of ideas now. I'd like to talk to him. Listen, man. I got some plans that could turn this city upside down. I mean I think like he does. *Big*. Invest big, gamble big, hell, lose *big* if you have to, you know what I mean. It's hard to find a man on this whole Southside who understands my kind of thinking—you dig? (*He scrutinizes* MURCHISON *again, drinks his beer, squints his eyes and leans in close, confidential, man to man*) Me and you ought to sit down and talk sometimes, man. Man, I got me some ideas . . .

MURCHISON (*With boredom*) Yeah—sometimes we'll have to do that, Walter.

WALTER (*Understanding the indifference, and offended*) Yeah—well, when you get the time, man. I know you a busy little boy.

RUTH Walter, please—

WALTER (*Bitterly, hurt*) I know ain't nothing in this world as busy as you colored college boys with your fraternity pins and white shoes . . .

RUTH (*Covering her face with humiliation*) Oh, Walter Lee—

WALTER I see you all all the time—with the books tucked under your arms—going to your (*British A—a mimic*) "clahsses." And for what! What the hell you learning over there? Filling up your heads—(*Counting off on his fingers*)—with the sociology and the psychology—but they teaching you how to be a man? How to take over and run the world? They teaching you how to run a rubber plantation or a steel mill? Naw—just to talk proper and read books and wear white shoes . . .

GEORGE (*Looking at him with distaste, a little above it all*) You're all wacked up with bitterness, man.

WALTER (*Intently, almost quietly, between the teeth, glaring at the boy*) And you—ain't you bitter, man? Ain't you just about had it yet? Don't you see no stars gleaming that you can't reach out and grab? You happy?—You contented son-of-a-bitch—you happy? You got it made? Bitter? Man, I'm a volcano. Bitter? Here I am a giant—surrounded by ants! Ants who can't even understand what it is the giant is talking about.

RUTH (*Passionately and suddenly*) Oh, Walter—ain't you with nobody!

WALTER (*Violently*) No! 'Cause ain't nobody with me! Not even my own mother!

RUTH Walter, that's a terrible thing to say!

BENEATHA *enters, dressed for the evening in a cocktail dress and earrings.*

GEORGE Well—hey, you look great.

BENEATHA Let's go, George. See you all later.

RUTH Have a nice time.

GEORGE Thanks. Good night. (*To* WALTER, *sarcastically*) Good night, *Prometheus.*

BENEATHA *and* GEORGE *exit.*

WALTER (*To* RUTH) Who is Prometheus?

RUTH I don't know. Don't worry about it.

WALTER (*In fury, pointing after* GEORGE) See there—they get to a point where they can't insult you man to man—they got to go talk about something ain't nobody never heard of!

RUTH How do you know it was an insult? (*To humor him*) Maybe Prometheus is a nice fellow.

WALTER Prometheus! I bet there ain't even no such thing! I bet that simple-minded clown—

RUTH Walter—

She stops what she is doing and looks at him.

WALTER (*Yelling*) Don't start!

RUTH Start what?

WALTER Your nagging! Where was I? Who was I with? How much money did I spend?

RUTH (*Plaintively*) Walter Lee—why don't we just try to talk about it . . .

WALTER (*Not listening*) I been out talking with people who understand me. People who care about the things I got on my mind.

RUTH (*Wearily*) I guess that means people like Willy Harris.

WALTER Yes, people like Willy Harris.

RUTH (*With a sudden flash of impatience*) Why don't you all just hurry up and go into the banking business and stop talking about it!

WALTER Why? You want to know why? 'Cause we all tied up in a race of people that don't know how to do nothing but moan, pray and have babies!

The line is too bitter even for him and he looks at her and sits down.

RUTH Oh, Walter . . . (*Softly*) Honey, why can't you stop fighting me?

WALTER (*Without thinking*) Who's fighting you? Who even cares about you?

This line begins the retardation of his mood.

RUTH Well—(*She waits a long time, and then with resignation starts to put away her things*) I guess I might as well go on to bed . . . (*More or less to herself*) I don't know where we lost it . . . but we have . . . (*Then, to him*) I—I'm sorry about this new baby, Walter. I guess maybe I better go on and do what I started . . . I guess I just didn't realize how bad things was with us . . . I guess I just didn't really realize—(*She starts out to the bedroom and stops*) You want some hot milk?

WALTER Hot milk?

RUTH Yes—hot milk.

WALTER Why hot milk?

RUTH 'Cause after all that liquor you come home with you ought to have something hot in your stomach.

WALTER I don't want no milk.

RUTH   You want some coffee then?

WALTER   No, I don't want no coffee. I don't want nothing hot to drink. (*Almost plaintively*) Why you always trying to give me something to eat?

RUTH   (*Standing and looking at him helplessly*) What else can I give you, Walter Lee Younger?

>   She stands and looks at him and presently turns to go out again. He lifts his head and watches her going away from him in a new mood which began to emerge when he asked her "Who cares about you?"

WALTER   It's been rough, ain't it, baby? (*She hears and stops but does not turn around and he continues to her back*) I guess between two people there ain't never as much understood as folks generally thinks there is. I mean like between me and you—(*She turns to face him*) How we gets to the place where we scared to talk softness to each other. (*He waits, thinking hard himself*) Why you think it got to be like that? (*He is thoughtful, almost as a child would be*) Ruth, what is it gets into people ought to be close?

RUTH   I don't know, honey. I think about it a lot.

WALTER   On account of you and me, you mean? The way things are with us. The way something done come down between us.

RUTH   There ain't so much between us, Walter ... Not when you come to me and try to talk to me. Try to be with me ... a little even.

WALTER   (*Total honesty*) Sometimes ... sometimes ... I don't even know how to try.

RUTH   Walter—

WALTER   Yes?

RUTH   (*Coming to him, gently and with misgiving, but coming to him*) Honey ... life don't have to be like this. I mean sometimes people can do things so that things are better ... You remember how we used to talk when Travis was born ... about the way we were going to live ... the kind of house ... (*She is stroking his head*) Well, it's all starting to slip away from us ...

>   MAMA *enters, and* WALTER *jumps up and shouts at her.*

WALTER   Mama, where have you been?

MAMA   My—them steps is longer than they used to be. Whew! (*She sits down and ignores him*) How you feeling this evening, Ruth?

>   RUTH *shrugs, disturbed some at having been prematurely interrupted and watching her husband knowingly.*

WALTER   Mama, where have you been all day?

MAMA   (*Still ignoring him and leaning on the table and changing to more comfortable shoes*) Where's Travis?

RUTH   I let him go out earlier and he ain't come back yet. Boy, is he going to get it!

WALTER   Mama!

MAMA   (*As if she has heard him for the first time*) Yes, son?

WALTER   Where did you go this afternoon?

MAMA   I went downtown to tend to some business that I had to tend to.

WALTER   What kind of business?

MAMA   You know better than to question me like a child, Brother.

WALTER   (*Rising and bending over the table*) Where were your, Mama? (*Bringing his fists down and shouting*) Mama, you didn't go do something with that insurance money, something crazy?

> *The front door opens slowly, interrupting him, and* TRAVIS *peeks his head in, less than hopefully.*

TRAVIS (*To his mother*) Mama, I—

RUTH "Mama I" nothing! You're going to get it, boy! Get on in that bedroom and get yourself ready!

TRAVIS But I—

MAMA Why don't you all never let the child explain hisself.

RUTH Keep out of it now, Lena

> MAMA *clamps her lips together, and* RUTH *advances toward her son menacingly.*

RUTH A thousand times I have told you not to go off like that—

MAMA (*Holding out her arms to her grandson*) Well—at least let me tell him something. I want him to be the first one to hear ... Come here, Travis. (*The boy obeys, gladly*) Travis—(*She takes him by the shoulder and looks into his face*)—you know that money we got in the mail this morning?

TRAVIS Yes'm—

MAMA Well—what you think your grandmama gone and done with that money?

TRAVIS I don't know, Grandmama.

MAMA (*Putting her finger on his nose for emphasis*) She went out and she bought you a house! (*The explosion comes from* WALTER *at the end of the revelation and he jumps up and turns away from all of them in a fury.* MAMA *continues, to* TRAVIS) You glad about the house? It's going to be yours when you get to be a man.

TRAVIS Yeah—I always wanted to live in a house.

MAMA All right, gimme some sugar then—(TRAVIS *puts his arms around her neck as she watches her son over the boy's shoulder. Then, to* TRAVIS, *after the embrace*) Now when you say your prayers tonight, you thank God and your grandfather—'cause it was him who give you the house—in his way.

RUTH (*Taking the boy from* MAMA *and pushing him toward the bedroom*) Now you get out of here and get ready for your beating.

TRAVIS Aw, Mama—

RUTH Get on in there—(*Closing the door behind him and turning radiantly to her mother-in-law*) So you went and did it!

MAMA (*Quietly, looking at her son with pain*) Yes, I did.

RUTH (*Raising both arms classically*) Praise God! (*Looks at* WALTER *a moment, who says nothing. She crosses rapidly to her husband*) Please, honey—let me be glad ... you be glad too. (*She has laid her hands on his shoulders, but he shakes himself free of her roughly, without turning to face her*) Oh, Walter ... a home ... a home. (*She comes back to* MAMA) Well—where is it? How big is it? How much it going to cost?

MAMA Well—

RUTH When we moving?

MAMA (*Smiling at her*) First of the month.

RUTH (*Throwing back her head with jubilance*) Praise God!

MAMA (*Tentatively, still looking at her son's back turned against her and* RUTH) It's—it's a nice house too ... (*She cannot help speaking directly to him. An imploring quality in her voice, her manner, makes her almost like a girl now*) Three bedrooms—nice big one for you and Ruth ... Me and Beneatha still have to share our room, but Travis have one of his own—and (*With difficulty*) I figure if the—new baby—is a boy, we could get one of them double-decker outfits ... And there's a yard with a little patch of dirt where I could maybe get to grow me a few flowers ... And a nice big basement ...

RUTH   Walter honey, be glad—

MAMA   (*Still to his back, fingering things on the table*) 'Course I don't want to make it sound fancier than it is ... It's just a plain little old house—but it's made good and solid—and it will be *ours*. Walter Lee—it makes a difference in a man when he can walk on floors that belong to *him* ...

RUTH   Where is it?

MAMA   (*Frightened at this telling*) Well—well—it's out there in Clybourne Park—

> RUTH's radiance fades abruptly, and WALTER finally turns slowly to face his mother with incredulity and hostility.

RUTH   Where?

MAMA   (*Matter-of-factly*) Four o six Clybourne Street, Clybourne Park.

RUTH   Clybourne Park? Mama, there ain't no colored people living in Clybourne Park.

MAMA   (*Almost idiotically*) Well, I guess there's going to be some now.

WALTER   (*Bitterly*) So that's the peace and comfort you went out and bought for us today!

MAMA   (*Raising her eyes to meet his finally*) Son—I just tried to find the nicest place for the least amount of money for my family.

RUTH   (*Trying to recover from the shock*) Well—well—'course I ain't one never been 'fraid of no crackers, mind you—but—well, wasn't there no other houses nowhere?

MAMA   Them houses they put up for colored in them areas way out all seem to cost twice as much as other houses. I did the best I could.

RUTH   (*Struck senseless with the news, in its various degrees of goodness and trouble, she sits a moment, her fists propping her chin in thought, and then she starts to rise, bringing her fists down with vigor, the radiance spreading from cheek to cheek again*) Well—well!—All I can say is—if this is my time in life—*my time*—to say good-bye—(*And she builds with momentum as she starts to circle the room with an exuberant, almost tearfully happy release*)—to these Goddamned cracking walls!—(*She pounds the walls*)—and these marching roaches!—(*She wipes at an imaginary army of marching roaches*)—and this cramped little closet which ain't now or never was no kitchen! ... then I say it loud and good, Hallelujah! and good-bye misery ... I don't never want to see your ugly face again! (*She laughs joyously, having practically destroyed the apartment, and flings her arms up and lets them come down happily, slowly, reflectively, over her abdomen, aware for the first time perhaps that the life therein pulses with happiness and not despair*) Lena?

MAMA   (*Moved, watching her happiness*) Yes, honey?

RUTH   (*Looking off*) Is there—is there a whole lot of sunlight?

MAMA   (*Understanding*) Yes, child, there's a whole lot of sunlight.

> Long pause.

RUTH   (*Collecting herself and going to the door of the room* TRAVIS *is in*) Well—I guess I better see 'bout Travis. (*To* MAMA) Lord, I sure don't feel like whipping nobody today!

> She exits.

MAMA *(The mother and son are left alone now and the mother waits a long time, considering deeply, before she speaks)* Son—you—you understand what I done, don't you? (WALTER *is silent and sullen)* I—I just seen my family falling apart today . . . just falling to pieces in front of my eyes . . . We couldn't of gone on like we was today. We was going backwards 'stead of forwards—talking 'bout killing babies and wishing each other was dead . . . When it gets like that in life—you just got to do something different, push on out and do something bigger . . . *(She waits)* I wish you say something, son . . . I wish you'd say how deep inside you you think I done the right thing—

WALTER *(Crossing slowly to his bedroom door and finally turning there and speaking measuredly)* What you need me to say you done right for? *You* the head of this family. You run our lives like you want to. It was your money and you did what you wanted with it. So what you need for me to say it was all right for? *(Bitterly, to hurt her as deeply as he knows is possible)* So you butchered up a dream of mine—you—who always talking 'bout your children's dreams . . .

MAMA Walter Lee—

     He just closes the door behind him. MAMA *sits alone, thinking heavily.*

Curtain

Scene II

  Time: Friday night. A few weeks later.
  At rise: Packing crates mark the intention of the family to move. BENEATHA *and* GEORGE *come in, presumably from an evening out again.*

GEORGE O.K. . . . O.K., whatever you say . . . *(They both sit on the couch. He tries to kiss her. She moves away)* Look, we've had a nice evening; let's not spoil it, huh? . . .

     He again turns her head and tries to nuzzle in and she turns away from him, not with distaste but with momentary lack of interest; in a mood to pursue what they were talking about.

BENEATHA I'm *trying* to talk to you.

GEORGE We always talk.

BENEATHA Yes—and I love to talk.

GEORGE *(Exasperated; rising)* I know it and I don't mind it sometimes . . . I want you to cut it out, see—The moody stuff, I mean. I don't like it. You're a nice-looking girl . . . all over. That's all you need, honey, forget the atmosphere. Guys aren't going to go for the atmosphere—they're going to go for what they see. Be glad for that. Drop the Garbo routine. It doesn't go with you. As for myself, I want a nice—*(Groping)*—simple *(Thoughtfully)*—sophisticated girl . . . not a poet—O.K.?

     She rebuffs him again and he starts to leave.

BENEATHA Why are you angry?

GEORGE Because this is stupid! I don't go out with you to discuss the nature of "quiet desperation" or to hear all about your thoughts—because the world will go on thinking what it thinks regardless—

BENEATHA   Then why read books? Why go to school?

GEORGE   (*With artificial patience, counting on his fingers*) It's simple. You read books—to learn facts—to get grades—to pass the course—to get a degree. That's all—it has nothing to do with thoughts.

> *A long pause.*

BENEATHA   I see. (*A longer pause as she looks at him*) Good night, George.

> GEORGE *looks at her a little oddly, and starts to exit. He meets* MAMA *coming in.*

GEORGE   Oh—hello, Mrs. Younger.

MAMA   Hello, George, how you feeling?

GEORGE   Fine—fine, how are you?

MAMA   Oh, a little tired. You know them steps can get you after a day's work. You all have a nice time tonight?

GEORGE   Yes—a fine time. Well, good night.

MAMA   Good night. (*He exits.* MAMA *closes the door behind her*) Hello, honey. What you sitting like that for?

BENEATHA   I'm just sitting.

MAMA   Didn't you have a nice time?

BENEATHA   No.

MAMA   No? What's the matter?

BENEATHA   Mama, George is a fool—honest. (*She rises*)

MAMA   (*Hustling around unloading the packages she has entered with. She stops*) Is he, baby?

BENEATHA   Yes.

> BENEATHA *makes up* TRAVIS' *bed as she talks.*

MAMA   You sure?

BENEATHA   Yes.

MAMA   Well—I guess you better not waste your time with no fools.

> BENEATHA *looks up at her mother, watching her put groceries in the refrigerator. Finally she gathers up her things and starts into the bedroom. At the door she stops and looks back at her mother.*

BENEATHA   Mama—

MAMA   Yes, baby—

BENEATHA   Thank you.

MAMA   For what?

BENEATHA   For understanding me this time.

> *She exits quickly and the mother stands, smiling a little, looking at the place where* BENEATHA *just stood.* RUTH *enters.*

RUTH   Now don't you fool with any of this stuff, Lena—

MAMA   Oh, I just thought I'd sort a few things out.

> *The phone rings.* RUTH *answers.*

RUTH   (*At the phone*) Hello—Just a minute. (*Goes to door*) Walter, it's Mrs. Arnold. (*Waits. Goes back to the phone. Tense*) Hello. Yes, this is his wife speaking . . . He's lying down now. Yes . . . well, he'll be in tomorrow. He's been very sick. Yes—I know we should have called, but we were so sure he'd be able to come in today. Yes—yes, I'm very sorry. Yes . . . Thank you very much. (*She hangs up.* WALTER *is standing in the doorway of the bedroom behind her*) That was Mrs. Arnold.

WALTER (*Indifferently*) Was it?

RUTH She said if you don't come in tomorrow that they are getting a new man . . .

WALTER Ain't that sad—ain't that crying sad.

RUTH She said Mr. Arnold has had to take a cab for three days . . . Walter, you ain't been to work for three days! (*This is a revelation to her*) Where you been, Walter Lee Younger? (WALTER *looks at her and starts to laugh*) You're going to lose your job.

WALTER That's right . . .

RUTH Oh, Walter, and with your mother working like a dog every day—

WALTER That's sad too—Everything is sad.

MAMA What you been doing for these three days, son?

WALTER Mama—you don't know all the things a man what got leisure can find to do in this city . . . What's this—Friday night? Well—Wednesday I borrowed Willy Harris' car and I went for a drive . . . just me and myself and I drove and drove . . . Way out . . . way past South Chicago, and I parked the car and I sat and looked at the steel mills all day long. I just sat in the car and looked at them big black chimneys for hours. Then I drove back and I went to the Green Hat. (*Pause*) And Thursday—Thursday I borrowed the car again and I got in it and I pointed it the other way and I drove the other way—for hours—way, way up to Wisconsin, and I looked at the farms. I just drove and looked at the farms. Then I drove back and I went to the Green Hat. (*Pause*) And today—today I didn't get the car. Today I just walked. All over the Southside. And I looked at the Negroes and they looked at me and finally I just sat down on the curb at Thirty-ninth and South Parkway and I just sat there and watched the Negroes go by. And then I went to the Green Hat. You all sad? You all depressed? And you know where I am going right now—

>   RUTH *goes out quietly.*

MAMA Oh, Big Walter, is this the harvest of our days?

WALTER You know what I like about the Green Hat? (*He turns the radio on and a steamy, deep blues pours into the room*) I like this little cat they got there who blows a sax . . . He blows. He talks to me. He ain't but 'bout five feet tall and he's got a conked head and his eyes is always closed and he's all music—

MAMA (*Rising and getting some papers out of her handbag*) Walter—

WALTER And there's this other guy who plays the piano . . . and they got a sound. I mean they can work on some music . . . They got the best little combo in the world in the Green Hat . . . You can just sit there and drink and listen to them three men play and you realize that don't nothing matter worth a damn, but just being there—

MAMA I've helped do it to you, haven't I, son? Walter, I been wrong.

WALTER Naw—you ain't never been wrong about nothing, Mama

MAMA Listen to me, now. I say I been wrong, son. That I been doing to you what the rest of the world been doing to you. (*She stops and he looks up slowly at her and she meets his eyes pleadingly*) Walter—what you ain't never understood is that I ain't got nothing, don't own nothing, ain't never really wanted nothing that wasn't for you. There ain't nothing as precious to me . . . There ain't nothing worth holding on to, money, dreams, nothing else—if it means—if it means it's going to destroy my boy. (*She puts her papers in front of him and he watches her without speaking or moving*) I paid the man thirty-five hundred dollars down on the house. That leaves sixty-five hundred dollars. Monday morning I want you to take this money and take three thousand dollars and put it in a savings account for Beneatha's medical schooling. The rest you put in a checking account—with your name on it. And from now on any penny that comes out of it or that go in it is for you to look after. For you to decide. (*She drops her hands a little helplessly*) It ain't much, but it's all I got in the world and I'm putting it in your hands. I'm telling you to be the head of this family from now on like you supposed to be.

WALTER   (*Stares at the money*) You trust me like that, Mama?

MAMA   I ain't never stop trusting you. Like I ain't never stop loving you.

> She goes out and WALTER sits looking at the money on the table as the music continues in its idiom, pulsing in the room. Finally, in a decisive gesture, he gets up, and, in mingled joy and desperation, picks up the money. At the same moment, TRAVIS enters for bed.

TRAVIS   What's the matter, Daddy? You drunk?

WALTER   (*Sweetly, more sweetly than we have ever known him*) No, Daddy ain't drunk. Daddy ain't going to never be drunk again . . .

TRAVIS   Well, good night, Daddy.

> The FATHER has come from behind the couch and leans over, embracing his son.

WALTER   Son, I feel like talking to you tonight.

TRAVIS   About what?

WALTER   Oh, about a lot of things. About you and what kind of man you going to be when you grow up. . . . Son—son, what do you want to be when you grow up?

TRAVIS   A bus driver.

WALTER   (*Laughing a little*) A what? Man, that ain't nothing to want to be!

TRAVIS   Why not?

WALTER   'Cause, man—it ain't big enough—you know what I mean.

TRAVIS   I don't know then. I can't make up my mind. Sometimes Mama asks me that too. And sometimes when I tell her I just want to be like you—she says she don't want me to be like that and sometimes she says she does. . . .

WALTER   (*Gathering him up in his arms*) You know what, Travis? In seven years you going to be seventeen years old. And things is going to be very different with us in seven years, Travis. . . . One day when you are seventeen I'll come home—home from my office downtown somewhere—

TRAVIS   You don't work in no office, Daddy.

WALTER   No—but after tonight. After what your daddy gonna do tonight, there's going to be offices—a whole lot of offices . . .

TRAVIS   What you gonna do tonight, Daddy?

WALTER   You wouldn't understand yet, son, but your daddy's gonna make a transaction . . . a business transaction that's going to change our lives. . . . That's how come one day when you 'bout seventeen years old I'll come home and I'll be pretty tired, you know what I mean, after a day of conferences and secretaries getting things wrong the way they do ... 'cause an executive's life is hell, man—(*The more he talks the farther away he gets*) And I'll pull the car up on the driveway ... just a plain black Chrysler, I think, with white walls—no—black tires. More elegant. Rich people don't have to be flashy ... though I'll have to get something a little sportier for Ruth—maybe a Cadillac convertible to do her shopping in. ... And I'll come up the steps to the house and the gardener will be clipping away at the hedges and he'll say, "Good evening, Mr. Younger." And I'll say, "Hello, Jefferson, how are you this evening?" And I'll go inside and Ruth will come downstairs and meet me at the door and we'll kiss each other and she'll take my arm and we'll go up to your room to see you sitting on the floor with the catalogues of all the great schools in America around you. ... All the great schools in the world! And—and I'll say, all right son—it's your seventeenth birthday, what is it you've decided? ... Just tell me where you want to go to school and you'll *go*. Just tell me, what it is you want to be—and you'll *be* it. ... Whatever you want to be—Yessir! (*He holds his arms open for* TRAVIS) You just name it, son ... (TRAVIS *leaps into them*) and I hand you the world!

WALTER's *voice has risen in pitch and hysterical promise and on the last line he lifts* TRAVIS *high.*

Blackout

Scene III

Time: Saturday, moving day, one week later.

Before the curtain rises, RUTH's *voice, a strident, dramatic church alto, cuts through the silence.*

It is, in the darkness, a triumphant surge, a penetrating statement of expectation: "Oh, Lord, I don't feel no ways tired! Children, oh, glory hallelujah!"

As the curtain rises we see that RUTH *is alone in the living room, finishing up the family's packing. It is moving day. She is nailing crates and tying cartons.* BENEATHA *enters, carrying a guitar case, and watches her exuberant sister-in-law.*

RUTH   Hey!

BENEATHA   (*Putting away the case*) Hi.

RUTH   (*Pointing at a package*) Honey—look in that package there and see what I found on sale this morning at the South Center. (RUTH *gets up and moves to the package and draws out some curtains*) Lookahere—hand-turned hems!

BENEATHA   How do you know the window size out there?

RUTH   (*Who hadn't thought of that*) Oh—Well, they bound to fit something in the whole house. Anyhow, they was too good a bargain to pass up. (RUTH *slaps her head, suddenly remembering something*) Oh, Bennie—I meant to put a special note on that carton over there. That's your mama's good china and she wants 'em to be very careful with it.

BENEATHA I'll do it.

> BENEATHA *finds a piece of paper and starts to draw large letters on it.*

RUTH You know what I'm going to do soon as I get in that new house?

BENEATHA What?

RUTH Honey—I'm going to run me a tub of water up to here ... (*With her fingers practically up to her nostrils*) And I'm going to get in it—and I am going to sit ... and sit ... and sit in that hot water and the first person who knocks to tell *me* to hurry up and come out—

BENEATHA Gets shot at sunrise.

RUTH (*Laughing happily*) You said it, sister! (*Noticing how large* BENEATHA *is absent-mindedly making the note*) Honey, they ain't going to read that from no airplane.

BENEATHA (*Laughing herself*) I guess I always think things have more emphasis if they are big, somehow.

RUTH (*Looking up at her and smiling*) You and your brother seem to have that as a philosophy of life. Lord, that man—done changed so 'round here. You know—you know what we did last night? Me and Walter Lee?

BENEATHA What?

RUTH (*Smiling to herself*) We went to the movies. (*Looking at* BENEATHA *to see if she understands*) We went to the movies. You know the last time me and Walter went to the movies together?

BENEATHA No.

RUTH Me neither. That's how long it been. (*Smiling again*) But we went last night. The picture wasn't much good, but that didn't seem to matter. We went—and we held hands.

BENEATHA Oh, Lord!

RUTH We held hands—and you know what?

BENEATHA What?

RUTH When we come out of the show it was late and dark and all the stores and things was closed up ... and it was kind of chilly and there wasn't many people on the streets ... and we was still holding hands, me and Walter.

BENEATHA You're killing me.

> WALTER *enters with a large package. His happiness is deep in him; he cannot keep still with his new-found exuberance. He is singing and wiggling and snapping his fingers. He puts his package in a corner and puts a phonograph record, which he has brought in with him, on the record player. As the music comes up he dances over to* RUTH *and tries to get her to dance with him. She gives in at last to his raunchiness and in a fit of giggling allows herself to be drawn into his mood and together they deliberately burlesque an old social dance of their youth.*

BENEATHA (*Regarding them a long time as they dance, then drawing in her breath for a deeply exaggerated comment which she does not particularly mean*) Talk about—olddddddddddd-fashionedddddddd—Negroes!

WALTER (*Stopping momentarily*) What kind of Negroes? (*He says this in fun. He is not angry with her today, nor with anyone. He starts to dance with his wife again*)

BENEATHA Old-fashioned.

WALTER (*As he dances with* RUTH) You know, when these *New Negroes* have their convention—(*Pointing at his sister*)—that is going to be the chairman of the Committee on Unending Agitation. (*He goes on dancing, then stops*) Race, race, race! ... Girl, I do believe you are the first person in the history of the entire human race to successfully brainwash yourself. (BENEATHA *breaks up and he goes on dancing. He stops again, enjoying his tease*) Damn, even the N double A C P takes a holiday sometimes! (BENEATHA *and* RUTH *laugh. He dances with* RUTH *some more and starts to laugh and stops and pantomimes someone over an operating table*) I can just see that chick someday looking down at some poor cat on an operating table before she starts to slice him, saying ... (*Pulling his sleeves back maliciously*) "By the way, what are your views on civil rights down there? ..."

> *He laughs at her again and starts to dance happily. The bell sounds.*

BENEATHA   Sticks and stones may break my bones but ... words will never hurt me!

> BENEATHA *goes to the door and opens it as* WALTER *and* RUTH *go on with the clowning.* BENEATHA *is somewhat surprised to see a quiet-looking middle-aged white man in a business suit holding his hat and a briefcase in his hand and consulting a small piece of paper.*

MAN   Uh—how do you do, miss. I am looking for a Mrs.—(*He looks at the slip of paper*) Mrs. Lena Younger?

BENEATHA   (*Smoothing her hair with slight embarrassment*) Oh—yes, that's my mother. Excuse me (*She closes the door and turns to quiet the other two*) Ruth! Brother! Somebody's here. (*Then she opens the door. The man casts a curious quick glance at all of them*) Uh—come in please.

MAN   (*Coming*) Thank you.

BENEATHA   My mother isn't here just now. Is it business?

MAN   Yes ... well, of a sort.

WALTER   (*Freely, the Man of the House*) Have a seat. I'm Mrs. Younger's son. I look after most of her business matters.

> RUTH *and* BENEATHA *exchange amused glances.*

MAN   (*Regarding* WALTER, *and sitting*) Well—My name is Karl Lindner ...

WALTER   (*Stretching out his hand*) Walter Younger. This is my wife—(RUTH *nods politely*)—and my sister.

LINDNER   How do you do.

WALTER   (*Amiably, as he sits himself easily on a chair, leaning with interest forward on his knees and looking expectantly into the newcomer's face*) What can we do for you, Mr. Lindner!

LINDNER   (*Some minor shuffling of the hat and briefcase on his knees*) Well—I am a representative of the Clybourne Park Improvement Association—

WALTER   (*Pointing*) Why don't you sit your things on the floor?

LINDNER   Oh—yes. Thank you. (*He slides the briefcase and hat under the chair*) And as I was saying—I am from the Clybourne Park Improvement Association and we have had it brought to our attention at the last meeting that you people—or at least your mother—has bought a piece of residential property at—(*He digs for the slip of paper again*)—four o six Clybourne Street ...

WALTER   That's right. Care for something to drink? Ruth, get Mr. Lindner a beer.

LINDNER   (*Upset for some reason*) Oh—no, really. I mean thank you very much, but no thank you.

RUTH (*Innocently*) Some coffee?

LINDNER Thank you, nothing at all.

      BENEATHA *is watching the man carefully.*

LINDNER Well, I don't know how much you folks know about our organization. (*He is a gentle man; thoughtful and somewhat labored in his manner*) It is one of these community organizations set up to look after—oh, you know, things like block upkeep and special projects and we also have what we call our New Neighbors Orientation Committee . . .

BENEATHA (*Drily*) Yes—and what do they do?

LINDNER (*Turning a little to her and then returning the main force to* WALTER) Well—it's what you might call a sort of welcoming committee, I guess. I mean they, we, I'm the chairman of the committee—go around and see the new people who move into the neighborhood and sort of give them the lowdown on the way we do things out in Clybourne Park.

BENEATHA (*With appreciation of the two meanings, which escape* RUTH *and* WALTER) Uh-huh.

LINDNER And we also have the category of what the association calls—(*He looks elsewhere*)—uh—special community problems . . .

BENEATHA Yes—and what are some of those?

WALTER Girl, let the man talk.

LINDNER (*With understated relief*) Thank you. I would sort of like to explain this thing in my own way. I mean I want to explain to you in a certain way.

WALTER Go ahead.

LINDNER Yes. Well. I'm going to try to get right to the point. I'm sure we'll all appreciate that in the long run.

BENEATHA Yes.

WALTER Be still now!

LINDNER Well—

RUTH (*Still innocently*) Would you like another chair—you don't look comfortable.

LINDNER (*More frustrated than annoyed*) No, thank you very much. Please. Well—to get right to the point I—(*A great breath, and he is off at last*) I am sure you people must be aware of some of the incidents which have happened in various parts of the city when colored people have moved into certain areas—(BENEATHA *exhales heavily and starts tossing a piece of fruit up and down in the air*) Well—because we have what I think is going to be a unique type of organization in American community life—not only do we deplore that kind of thing—but we are trying to do something about it. (BENEATHA *stops tossing and turns with a new and quizzical interest to the man*) We feel—(*gaining confidence in his mission because of the interest in the faces of the people he is talking to*)—we feel that most of the trouble in this world, when you come right down to it—(*He hits his knee for emphasis*)—most of the trouble exists because people just don't sit down and talk to each other.

RUTH (*Nodding as she might in church, pleased with the remark*) You can say that again, mister.

LINDNER (*More encouraged by such affirmation*) That we don't try hard enough in this world to understand the other fellow's problem. The other guy's point of view.

RUTH Now that's right.

      BENEATHA *and* WALTER *merely watch and listen with genuine interest.*

LINDNER   Yes—that's the way we feel out in Clybourne Park. And that's why I was elected to come here this afternoon and talk to you people. Friendly like, you know, the way people should talk to each other and see if we couldn't find some way to work this thing out. As I say, the whole business is a matter of *caring* about the other fellow. Anybody can see that you are a nice family of folks, hard working and honest I'm sure. (BENEATHA *frowns slightly, quizzically, her head tilted regarding him*) Today everybody knows what it means to be on the outside of *something*. And of course, there is always somebody who is out to take the advantage of people who don't always understand.

WALTER   What do you mean?

LINDNER   Well—you see our community is made up of people who've worked hard as the dickens for years to build up that little community. They're not rich and fancy people; just hard-working, honest people who don't really have much but those little homes and a dream of the kind of community they want to raise their children in. Now, I don't say we are perfect and there is a lot wrong in some of the things they want. But you've got to admit that a man, right or wrong, has the right to want to have the neighborhood he lives in a certain kind of way. And at the moment the overwhelming majority of our people out there feel that people get along better, take more of a common interest in the life of the community, when they share a common background. I want you to believe me when I tell you that race prejudice simply doesn't enter into it. It is a matter of the people of Clybourne Park believing, rightly or wrongly, as I say, that for the happiness of all concerned that our Negro families are happier when they live in their *own* communities.

BENEATHA   (*With a grand and bitter gesture*) This, friends, is the Welcoming Committee!

WALTER   (*Dumfounded, looking at* LINDNER) Is this what you came marching all the way over here to tell us?

LINDNER   Well, now we've been having a fine conversation. I hope you'll hear me all the way through.

WALTER   (*Tightly*) Go ahead, man.

LINDNER   You see—in the face of all things I have said, we are prepared to make your family a very generous offer . . .

BENEATHA   Thirty pieces and not a coin less!

WALTER   Yeah?

LINDNER   (*Putting on his glasses and drawing a form out of the briefcase*) Our association is prepared, through the collective effort of our people, to buy the house from you at a financial gain to your family.

RUTH   Lord have mercy, ain't this the living gall!

WALTER   All right, you through?

LINDNER   Well, I want to give you the exact terms of the financial arrangement—

WALTER   We don't want to hear no exact terms of no arrangements. I want to know if you got any more to tell us 'bout getting together?

LINDNER   (*Taking off his glasses*) Well—I don't suppose that you feel . . .

WALTER   Never mind how I feel—you got any more to say 'bout how people ought to sit down and talk to each other? . . . Get out of my house, man.

He turns his back and walks to the door.

LINDNER   (*Looking around at the hostile faces and reaching and assembling his hat and briefcase*) Well—I don't understand why you people are reacting this way. What do you think you are going to gain by moving into a neighborhood where you just aren't wanted and where some elements—well—people can get awful worked up when they feel that their whole way of life and everything they've ever worked for is threatened.

WALTER Get out.

LINDNER (*At the door, holding a small card*) Well—I'm sorry it went like this.

WALTER Get out.

LINDNER (*Almost sadly regarding* WALTER) You just can't force people to change their hearts, son.

> He turns and puts his card on a table and exits. WALTER *pushes the door to with stinging hatred, and stands looking at it.* RUTH *just sits and* BENEATHA *just stands. They say nothing.* MAMA *and* TRAVIS *enter.*

MAMA Well—this all the packing got done since I left out of here this morning. I testify before God that my children got all the energy of the dead. What time the moving men due?

BENEATHA Four o'clock. You had a caller, Mama.

> *She is smiling, teasingly.*

MAMA Sure enough—who?

BENEATHA (*Her arms folded saucily*) The Welcoming Committee.

> WALTER *and* RUTH *giggle.*

MAMA (*Innocently*) Who?

BENEATHA The Welcoming Committee. They said they're sure going to be glad to see you when you get there.

WALTER (*Devilishly*) Yeah, they said they can't hardly wait to see your face.

> *Laughter.*

MAMA (*Sensing their facetiousness*) What's the matter with you all?

WALTER Ain't nothing the matter with us. We just telling you 'bout the gentleman who came to see you this afternoon. From the Clybourne Park Improvement Association.

MAMA What he want?

RUTH (*In the same mood as* BENEATHA *and* WALTER) To welcome you, honey.

WALTER He said they can't hardly wait. He said the one thing they don't have, that they just *dying* to have out there is a fine family of colored people! (*To* RUTH *and* BENEATHA) Ain't that right!

RUTH *and* BENEATHA (*Mockingly*) Yeah! He left his card in case—

> *They indicate the card, and* MAMA *picks it up and throws it on the floor—understanding and looking off as she draws her chair up to the table on which she has put her plant and some sticks and some cord.*

MAMA Father, give us strength. (*Knowingly—and without fun*) Did he threaten us?

BENEATHA Oh—Mama—they don't do it like that any more. He talked Brotherhood. He said everybody ought to learn how to sit down and hate each other with good Christian fellowship.

> *She and* WALTER *shake hands to ridicule the remark.*

MAMA (*Sadly*) Lord, protect us . . .

RUTH You should hear the money those folks raised to buy the house from us. All we paid and then some.

BENEATHA What they think we going to do—eat 'em?

RUTH   No, honey, marry 'em.

MAMA   (*Shaking her head*) Lord, Lord, Lord . . .

RUTH   Well—that's the way the crackers crumble. Joke.

BENEATHA   (*Laughingly noticing what her mother is doing*) Mama, what are you doing?

MAMA   Fixing my plant so it won't get hurt none on the way . . .

BENEATHA   Mama, you going to take *that* to the new house?

MAMA   Un-huh—

BENEATHA   That raggedy-looking old thing?

MAMA   (*Stopping and looking at her*) It expresses *me*.

RUTH   (*With delight, to* BENEATHA) So there, Miss Thing!

> WALTER *comes to* MAMA *suddenly and bends down behind her and squeezes her in his arms with all his strength. She is overwhelmed by the suddenness of it and, though delighted, her manner is like that of* RUTH *with* TRAVIS.

MAMA   Look out now, boy! You make me mess up my thing here!

WALTER   (*His face lit, he slips down on his knees beside her, his arms still about her*) Mama . . . you know what it means to climb up in the chariot?

MAMA   (*Gruffly, very happy*) Get on away from me now . . .

RUTH   (*Near the gift-wrapped package, trying to catch* WALTER'S *eye*) Psst—

WALTER   What the old song say, Mama . . .

RUTH   Walter—Now?

> She is pointing at the package.

WALTER   (*Speaking the lines, sweetly, playfully, in his mother's face*)
> I got wings . . . you got wings . . .
> All God's children got wings . . .

MAMA   Boy—get out of my face and do some work . . .

WALTER
> When I get to heaven gonna put on my wings,
> Gonna fly all over God's heaven . . .

BENEATHA   (*Teasingly, from across the room*) Everybody talking 'bout heaven ain't going there!

WALTER   (*To* RUTH, *who is carrying the box across to them*) I don't know, you think we ought to give her that . . . Seems to me she ain't been very appreciative around here.

MAMA   (*Eying the box, which is obviously a gift*) What is that?

WALTER   (*Taking it from* RUTH *and putting it on the table in front of* MAMA) Well—what you all think? Should we give it to her?

RUTH   Oh—she was pretty good today.

MAMA   I'll good you—

> She turns her eyes to the box again.

BENEATHA   Open it, Mama.

> She stands up, looks at it, turns and looks at all of them, and then presses her hands together and does not open the package.

WALTER   (*Sweetly*) Open it, Mama, It's for you. (MAMA *looks in his eyes. It is the first present in her life without its being Christmas. Slowly she opens her package and lifts out, one by one, a brand-new sparkling set of gardening tools.* WALTER *continues, prodding*) Ruth made up the note—read it . . .

MAMA   (*Picking up the card and adjusting her glasses*) "To our own Mrs. Miniver—Love from Brother, Ruth and Beneatha." Ain't that lovely . . .

TRAVIS   (*Tugging at his father's sleeve*) Daddy, can I give her mine now?

WALTER   All right, son. (TRAVIS *flies to get his gift*) Travis didn't want to go in with the rest of us, Mama. He got his own. (*Somewhat amused*) We don't know what it is . . .

TRAVIS   (*Racing back in the room with a large hatbox and putting it in front of his grandmother*) Here!

MAMA   Lord have mercy, baby. You done gone and bought your grandmother a hat?

TRAVIS   (*Very proud*) Open it!

> *She does and lifts out an elaborate, but very elaborate, wide gardening hat, and all the adults break up at the sight of it.*

RUTH   Travis, honey, what is that?

TRAVIS   (*Who thinks it is beautiful and appropriate*) It's a gardening hat! Like the ladies always have on in the magazines when they work in their gardens.

BENEATHA   (*Giggling fiercely*) Travis—we were trying to make Mama Mrs. Miniver—not Scarlet O'Hara!

MAMA   (*Indignantly*) What's the matter with you all! This here is a beautiful hat! (*Absurdly*) I always wanted me one just like it!

> *She pops it on her head to prove it to her grandson, and the hat is ludicrous and considerably oversized.*

RUTH   Hot dog! Go, Mama!

WALTER   (*Doubled over with laughter*) I'm sorry, Mama—but you look like you ready to go out and chop you some cotton sure enough!

> *They all laugh except* MAMA, *out of deference to* TRAVIS' *feelings.*

MAMA   (*Gathering the boy up to her*) Bless your heart—this is the prettiest hat I ever owned—(WALTER, RUTH *and* BENEATHA *chime in—noisily, festively and insincerely congratulating* TRAVIS *on his gift*) What are we all standing around here for? We ain't finished packin' yet. Bennie, you ain't packed one book.

> *The bell rings.*

BENEATHA   That couldn't be the movers . . . it's not hardly two o'clock yet—

> BENEATHA *goes into her room.* MAMA *starts for door.*

WALTER   (*Turning, stiffening*) Wait—wait—I'll get it.

> *He stands and looks at the door.*

MAMA   You expecting company, son?

WALTER   (*Just looking at the door*) Yeah—yeah . . .

> MAMA *looks at* RUTH, *and they exchange innocent and unfrightened glances.*

MAMA   (*Not understanding*) Well, let them in, son.

BENEATHA   (*From her room*) We need some more string.

MAMA   Travis—you run to the hardware and get me some string cord.

> MAMA *goes out and* WALTER *turns and looks at* RUTH. TRAVIS *goes to a dish for money.*

RUTH   Why don't you answer the door, man?

WALTER   (*Suddenly bounding across the floor to her*) 'Cause sometimes it hard to let the future begin! (*Stooping down in her face*)

> I got wings! You got wings!
> All God's children got wings!

> *He crosses to the door and throws it open. Standing there is a very slight little man in a not too prosperous business suit and with haunted frightened eyes*

and a hat pulled down tightly, brim up, around his forehead. TRAVIS passes between
the men and exits. WALTER leans deep in the man's face, still in his jubilance.

When I get to heaven gonna put on my wings,
Gonna fly all over God's heaven . . .

(The little man just stares at him)

Heaven—

(Suddenly he stops and looks past the little man into the empty hallway) Where's Willy,
man?

BOBO He ain't with me.

WALTER (Not disturbed) Oh—come on in. You know my wife.

BOBO (Dumbly, taking off his hat) Yes—h'you, Miss Ruth.

RUTH (Quietly, a mood apart from her husband already, seeing BOBO) Hello, Bobo.

WALTER You right on time today . . . Right on time. That's the way! (He slaps
BOBO on his back) Sit down . . . lemme hear.

  RUTH stands stiffly and quietly in back of them, as though somehow she senses
  death, her eyes fixed on her husband.

BOBO (His frightened eyes on the floor, his hat in his hands) Could I please get a drink
of water, before I tell you about it, Walter Lee?

  WALTER does not take his eyes off the man. RUTH goes blindly to the tap and
  gets a glass of water and brings it to BOBO.

WALTER There ain't nothing wrong, is there?

BOBO Lemme tell you—

WALTER Man—didn't nothing go wrong?

BOBO Lemme tell you—Walter Lee. (Looking at RUTH and talking to her more than
to WALTER) You know how it was. I got to tell you how it was. I mean first
I got to tell you how it was all the way . . . I mean about the money I put
in, Walter Lee . . .

WALTER (With taut agitation now) What about the money you put in?

BOBO Well—it wasn't much as we told you—me and Willy—(He stops) I'm sorry,
Walter. I got a bad feeling about it. I got a real bad feeling about it . . .

WALTER Man, what you telling me about all this for? . . . Tell me what happened
in Springfield . . .

BOBO Springfield.

RUTH (Like a dead woman) What was supposed to happen in Springfield?

BOBO (To her) This deal that me and Walter went into with Willy—Me and Willy
was going to go down to Springfield and spread some money 'round so's
we wouldn't have to wait so long for the liquor license . . . That's what we
were going to do. Everybody said that was the way you had to do, you
understand, Miss Ruth?

WALTER Man—what happened down there?

BOBO (A pitiful man, near tears) I'm trying to tell you, Walter.

WALTER (Screaming at him suddenly) THEN TELL ME, GODDAMMIT . . . WHAT'S
THE MATTER WITH YOU?

BOBO Man . . . I didn't go to no Springfield, yesterday.

WALTER (Halted, life hanging in the moment) Why not?

BOBO (The long way, the hard way to tell) 'Cause I didn't have no reasons to . . .

WALTER Man, what are you talking about!

BOBO   I'm talking about the fact that when I got to the train station yesterday morning—eight o'clock like we planned ... Man—*Willy didn't never show up.*

WALTER   Why ... where was he ... where is he?

BOBO   That's what I'm trying to tell you ... I don't know ... I waited six hours ... I called his house ... and I waited ... six hours ... I waited in that train station six hours ... (*Breaking into tears*) That was all the extra money I had in the world ... (*Looking up at* WALTER *with the tears running down his face*) Man, *Willy is gone.*

WALTER   Gone, what you mean Willy is gone? Gone where? You mean he went by himself. You mean he went off to Springfield by himslf—to take care of getting the license—(*Turns and looks anxiously at* RUTH) You mean maybe he didn't want too many people in on the business down there? (*Looks to* RUTH *again, as before*) You know Willy got his own ways. (*Looks back to* BOBO) Maybe you was late yesterday and he just went on down there without you. Maybe— maybe—he's been callin' you at home tryin' to tell you what happened or something. Maybe—maybe—he just got sick. He's somewhere—he's got to be somewhere. We just got to find him—me and you got to find him. (*Grabs* BOBO *senselessly by the collar and starts to shake him*) We got to!

BOBO   (*In sudden angry, frightened agony*) What's the matter with you, Walter! *When a cat take off with your money he don't leave you no maps!*

WALTER   (*Turning madly, as though he is looking for* WILLY *in the very room*) Willy! ...Willy ... don't do it ... Please don't do it ... Man, not with that money ... Man, please, not with that money ... Oh, God ... Don't let it be true ... (*He is wandering around, crying out for* WILLY *and looking for him or perhaps for help from God*) Man ... I trusted you ... Man, I put my life in your hands ... (*He starts to crumple down on the floor as* RUTH *just covers her face in horror.* MAMA *opens the door and comes into the room, with* BENEATHA *behind her*) Man ... (*He starts to pound the floor with his fists, sobbing wildly*) *That money is made out of my father's flesh ...*

BOBO   (*Standing over him helplessly*) I'm sorry, Walter ... (*Only* WALTER's *sobs reply.* BOBO *puts on his hat*) I had my life staked on this deal, too ...

        He exits.

MAMA   (*To* WALTER) Son—(*She goes to him, bends down to him, talks to his bent head*) Son ... Is it gone? Son, I gave you sixty-five hundred dollars. Is it gone? All of it? Beneatha's money too?

WALTER   (*Lifting his head slowly*) Mama ... I never ... went to the bank at all ...

MAMA   (*Not wanting to believe him*) You mean ... your sister's school money ... you used that too ... Walter? ...

WALTER   Yessss! ...All of it ... It's all gone ...

        There is total silence. RUTH *stands with her face covered with her hands;* BENEATHA *leans forlornly against a wall, fingering a piece of red ribbon from the mother's gift.* MAMA *stops and looks at her son without recognition and then, quite without thinking about it, starts to beat him senselessly in the face.* BENEATHA *goes to them and stops it.*

BENEATHA   Mama!

        MAMA *stops and looks at both of her children and rises slowly and wanders vaguely, aimlessly away from them.*

MAMA   I seen ... him ... night after night ... come in ... and look at that rug ... and then look at me ... the red showing in his eyes ... the veins moving in his head ... I seen him grow thin and old before he was forty ... working and working and working like somebody's old horse ... killing himself ... and you—you give it all away in a day ...

BENEATHA   Mama—

MAMA   Oh, God ... (*She looks up to Him*) Look down here—and show me the strength.

BENEATHA   Mama—

MAMA   (*Folding over*) Strength ...

BENEATHA   (*Plaintively*) Mama ...

MAMA   Strength!

Curtain

ACT III

An hour later.

At curtain, there is a sullen light of gloom in the living room, gray light not unlike that which began the first scene of Act One. At left we can see WALTER *within his room, alone with himself. He is stretched out on the bed, his shirt out and open, his arms under his head. He does not smoke, he does not cry out, he merely lies there, looking up at the ceiling, much as if he were alone in the world.*

In the living room BENEATHA *sits at the table, still surrounded by the now almost ominous packing crates. She sits looking off. We feel that this is a mood struck perhaps an hour before, and it lingers now, full of the empty sound of profound disappointment. We see on a line from her brother's bedroom the sameness of their attitudes. Presently the bell rings and* BENEATHA *rises without ambition or interest in answering. It is* ASAGAI, *smiling broadly, striding into the room with energy and happy expectation and conversation.*

ASAGAI   I came over ... I had some free time. I thought I might help with the packing. Ah, I like the look of packing crates! A household in preparation for a journey! It depresses some people ... but for me ... it is another feeling. Something full of the flow of life, do you understand? Movement, progress ... It makes me think of Africa.

BENEATHA   Africa!

ASAGAI   What kind of a mood is this? Have I told you how deeply you move me?

BENEATHA   He gave away the money, Asagai ...

ASAGAI   Who gave away what money?

BENEATHA   The insurance money. My brother gave it away.

ASAGAI   Gave it away?

BENEATHA   He made an investment! With a man even Travis wouldn't have trusted.

ASAGAI And it's gone?

BENEATHA Gone!

ASAGAI I'm very sorry ... And you, now?

BENEATHA Me? ... Me? ... Me I'm nothing ... Me. When I was very small ... we used to take our sleds out in the wintertime and the only hills we had were the ice-covered stone steps of some houses down the street. And we used to fill them in with snow and make them smooth and slide down them all day ... and it was very dangerous you know ... far too steep ... and sure enough one day a kid named Rufus came down too fast and hit the sidewalk ... and we saw his face just split open right there in front of us ... And I remember standing there looking at his bloody open face thinking that was the end of Rufus. But the ambulance came and they took him to the hospital and they fixed the broken bones and they sewed it all up ... and the next time I saw Rufus he just had a little line down the middle of his face ... I never got over that ...

> WALTER *sits up, listening on the bed. Throughout this scene it is important that we feel his reaction at all times, that he visibly respond to the words of his sister and* ASAGAI.

ASAGAI What?

BENEATHA That that was what one person could do for another, fix him up—sew up the problem, make him all right again. That was the most marvelous thing in the world ... I wanted to do that. I always thought it was the one concrete thing in the world that a human being could do. Fix up the sick, you know—and make them whole again. This was truly being God ...

ASAGAI You wanted to be God?

BENEATHA No—I wanted to cure. It used to be so important to me. I wanted to cure. It used to matter. I used to care. I mean about people and how their bodies hurt ...

ASAGAI And you've stopped caring?

BENEATHA Yes—I think so.

ASAGAI Why?

> WALTER *rises, goes to the door of his room and is about to open it, then stops and stands listening, leaning on the door jamb.*

BENEATHA Because it doesn't seem deep enough, close enough to what ails mankind—I mean this thing of sewing up bodies or administering drugs. Don't you understand? It was a child's reaction to the world. I thought that doctors had the secret to all the hurts. ... That's the way a child sees things—or an idealist.

ASAGAI Children see things very well sometimes—and idealists even better.

BENEATHA I know that's what you think. Because you are still where I left off—you still care. This is what you see for the world, for Africa. You with the dreams of the future will patch up all Africa—you are going to cure the Great Sore of colonialism with Independence—

ASAGAI Yes!

BENEATHA Yes—and you think that one word is the penicillin of the human spirit: "Independence!" But then what?

ASAGAI That will be the problem for another time. First we must get there.

A RAISIN IN THE SUN 799

BENEATHA   And where does it end?

ASAGAI   End? Who even spoke of an end? To life? To living?

BENEATHA   An end to misery!

ASAGAI   (*Smiling*) You sound like a French intellectual.

BENEATHA   No! I sound like a human being who just had her future taken right out of her hands! While I was sleeping in my bed in there, things were happening in this world that directly concerned me—and nobody asked me, consulted me—they just went out and did things—and changed my life. Don't you see there isn't any real progress, Asagai, there is only one large circle that we march in, around and around, each of us with our own little picture—in front of us—our own little mirage that we think is the future.

ASAGAI   That is the mistake.

BENEATHA   What?

ASAGAI   What you just said—about the circle. It isn't a circle—it is simply a long line—as in geometry, you know, one that reaches into infinity. And because we cannot see the end—we also cannot see how it changes. And it is very odd but those who see the changes are called "idealists"—and those who cannot, or refuse to think, they are the "realists." It is very strange, and amusing too, I think.

BENEATHA   You—you are almost religious.

ASAGAI   Yes ... I think I have the religion of doing what is necessary in the world—and of worshipping man—because he is so marvelous, you see.

BENEATHA   Man is foul! And the human race deserves its misery!

ASAGAI   You see: *you* have become the religious one in the old sense. Already, and after such a small defeat, you are worshipping despair.

BENEATHA   From now on, I worship the truth—and the truth is that people are puny, small and selfish. ...

ASAGAI   Truth? Why is it that you despairing ones always think that only you have the truth? I never thought to see *you* like that. You! Your brother made a stupid, childish mistake—and you are grateful to him. So that now you can give up the ailing human race on account of it. You talk about what good is struggle; what good is anything? Where are we all going? And why are we bothering?

BENEATHA   *And you cannot answer it!* All your talk and dreams about Africa and Independence. Independence and then what? What about all the crooks and petty thieves and just plain idiots who will come into power to steal and plunder the same as before—only now they will be black and do it in the name of the new Independence—You cannot answer that.

ASAGAI   (*Shouting over her*) *I live the answer!* (*Pause*) In my village at home it is the exceptional man who can even read a newspaper ... or who ever *sees* a book at all. I will go home and much of what I will have to say will seem strange to the people of my village ... But I will teach and work and things will happen, slowly and swiftly. At times it will seem that nothing changes at all ... and then again ... the sudden dramatic events which make history leap into the future. And then quiet again. Retrogression even. Guns, murder, revolution. And I even will have moments when I wonder if the quiet was not better than all that death and hatred. But I will look about my village at the illiteracy and disease and ignorance and I will not wonder long. And perhaps ... perhaps I will be a great man ... I mean perhaps I will hold on to the substance of truth and find my way always with the right course ... and perhaps for it I will be butchered in my bed some night by the servants of empire ...

BENEATHA *The martyr!*

ASAGAI ... or perhaps I shall live to be a very old man, respected and esteemed in my new nation ... And perhaps I shall hold office and this is what I'm trying to tell you, Alaiyo; perhaps the things I believe now for my country will be wrong and outmoded, and I will not understand and do terrible things to have things my way or merely to keep my power. Don't you see that there will be young men and women, not British soldiers then, but my own black countrymen ... to step out of the shadows some evening and slit my then useless throat? Don't you see they have always been there ... that they always will be. And that such a thing as my own death will be an advance? They who might kill me even ... actually replenish me!

BENEATHA Oh, Asagai, I know all that.

ASAGAI Good! Then stop moaning and groaning and tell me what you plan to do.

BENEATHA Do?

ASAGAI I have a bit of a suggestion.

BENEATHA What?

ASAGAI (*Rather quietly for him*) That when it is all over—that you come home with me—

BENEATHA (*Slapping herself on the forehead with exasperation born of misunderstanding*) Oh—Asagai—at this moment you decide to be romantic!

ASAGAI (*Quickly understanding the misunderstanding*) My dear, young creature of the New World—I do not mean across the city—I mean across the ocean; home—to Africa.

BENEATHA (*Slowly understanding and turning to him with murmured amazement*) To—to Nigeria?

ASAGAI Yes! ... (*Smiling and lifting his arms playfully*) Three hundred years later the African Prince rose up out of the seas and swept the maiden back across the middle passage over which her ancestors had come—

BENEATHA (*Unable to play*) Nigeria?

ASAGAI Nigeria. Home. (*Coming to her with genuine romantic flippancy*) I will show you our mountains and our stars; and give you cool drinks from gourds and teach you the old songs and the ways of our people—and, in time, we will pretend that—(*Very softly*)—you have only been away for a day—

　　　She turns her back to him, thinking. He swings her around and takes her full in his arms in a long embrace which proceeds to passion.

BENEATHA (*Pulling away*) You're getting me all mixed up—

ASAGAI Why?

BENEATHA Too many things—too many things have happened today. I must sit down and think. I don't know what I feel about anything right this minute.

　　　She promptly sits down and props her chin on her fist.

ASAGAI (*Charmed*) All right, I shall leave you. No—don't get up. (*Touching her, gently sweetly*) Just sit awhile and think . . . Never be afraid to sit awhile and think. (*He goes to door and looks at her*) How often I have looked at you and said, "Ah—so this is what the New World hath finally wrought . . ."

> *He exits.* BENEATHA *sits on alone. Presently* WALTER *enters from his room and starts to rummage through things, feverishly looking for something. She looks up and turns in her seat.*

BENEATHA (*Hissingly*) Yes—just look at what the New World hath wrought!. . . Just look! (*She gestures with bitter disgust*) There he is! *Monsieur le petit bourgeois noir*—himself! There he is—Symbol of a Rising Class! Entrepreneur! Titan of the system! (WALTER *ignores her completely and continues frantically and destructively looking for something and hurling things to floor and tearing things out of their place in his search.* BENEATHA *ignores the eccentricity of his actions and goes on with the monologue of insult*) Did you dream of yachts on Lake Michigan, Brother? Did you see yourself on that Great Day sitting down at the Conference Table, surrounded by all the mighty bald-headed men in America? All halted, waiting, breathless, waiting for your pronouncements on industry? Waiting for you— Chairman of the Board? (WALTER *finds what he is looking for—a small piece of white paper—and pushes it in his pocket and puts on his coat and rushes out without ever having looked at her. She shouts after him*) I look at you and I see the final triumph of stupidity in the world!

> *The door slams and she returns to just sitting again.* RUTH *comes quickly out of* MAMA'S *room.*

RUTH Who was that?

BENEATHA Your husband.

RUTH Where did he go?

BENEATHA Who knows—maybe he has an appointment at U.S. Steel.

RUTH (*Anxiously, with frightened eyes*) You didn't say nothing bad to him, did you?

BENEATHA Bad? Say anything bad to him? No—I told him he was a sweet boy and full of dreams and everything is strictly peachy keen, as the ofay kids say!

> MAMA *enters from her bedroom. She is lost, vague, trying to catch hold, to make some sense of her former command of the world, but it still eludes her. A sense of waste overwhelms her gait; a measure of apology rides on her shoulders. She goes to her plant, which has remained on the table, looks at it, picks it up and takes it to the window sill and sits it outside, and she stands and looks at it a long moment. The she closes the window, straightens her body with effort and turns around to her children.*

MAMA Well—ain't it a mess in here, though? (*A false cheerfulness, a beginning of something*) I guess we all better stop moping around and get some work done. All this unpacking and everything we got to do. (RUTH *raises her head slowly in response to the sense of the line; and* BENEATHA *in similar manner turns very slowly to look at her mother*) One of you all better call the moving people and tell 'em not to come.

RUTH Tell 'em not to come?

MAMA Of course, baby. Ain't no need in 'em coming all the way here and having to go back. They charges for that too. (*She sits down, fingers to her brow, thinking*) Lord, ever since I was a little girl, I always remembers people saying, "Lena— Lena Eggleston, you aims too high all the time. You needs to slow down and see life a little more like it is. Just slow down some." That's what they always used to say down home—"Lord, that Lena Eggleston is a high-minded thing. She'll get her due one day!"

RUTH   No, Lena . . .

MAMA   Me and Big Walter just didn't never learn right.

RUTH   Lena, no! We gotta go. Bennie—tell her . . . (*She rises and crosses to* BENEATHA *with her arms outstretched.* BENEATHA *doesn't respond*) Tell her we can still move . . . the notes ain't but a hundred and twenty-five a month. We got four grown people in this house—we can work . . .

MAMA   (*To herself*) Just aimed too high all the time—

RUTH   (*Turning and going to* MAMA *fast—the words pouring out with urgency and desperation*) Lena—I'll work . . . I'll work twenty hours a day in all the kitchens in Chicago . . . I'll strap my baby on my back if I have to and scrub all the floors in America and wash all the sheets in America if I have to—but we got to move . . . We got to get out of here . . .

     MAMA *reaches out absently and pats* RUTH's *hand.*

MAMA   No—I sees things differently now. Been thinking 'bout some of the things we could do to fix this place up some. I seen a second-hand bureau over on Maxwell Street just the other day that could fit right there. (*She points to where the new furniture might go.* RUTH *wanders away from her*) Would need some new handles on it and then a little varnish and then it look like something brand-new. And—we can put up them new curtains in the kitchen . . . Why this place be looking fine. Cheer us all up so that we forget trouble ever came . . . (*To* RUTH) And you could get some nice screens to put up in your room round the baby's bassinet . . . (*She looks at both of them, pleadingly*) Sometimes you just got to know when to give up some things . . . and hold on to what you got.

     WALTER *enters from the outside, looking spent and leaning against the door, his coat hanging from him.*

MAMA   Where you been, son?

WALTER   (*Breathing hard*) Made a call.

MAMA   To who, son?

WALTER   To The Man.

MAMA   What man, baby?

WALTER   The Man, Mama. Don't you know who The Man is?

RUTH   Walter Lee?

WALTER   *The Man.* Like the guys in the streets say—The Man. Captain Boss—Mistuh Charley . . . Old Captain Please Mr. Bossman . . .

BENEATHA   (*Suddenly*) Lindner!

WALTER   That's right! That's good. I told him to come right over.

BENEATHA   (*Fiercely, understanding*) For what? What do you want to see him for!

WALTER   (*Looking at his sister*) We going to do business with him.

MAMA   What you talking 'bout, son?

WALTER   Talking 'bout life, Mama. You all always telling me to see life like it is. Well—I laid in there on my back today . . . and I figured it out. Life just like it is. Who gets and who don't get. (*He sits down with his coat on and laughs*) Mama, you know it's all divided up. Life is. Sure enough. Between the takers and the "tooken." (*He laughs*) I've figured it out finally. (*He looks around at them*) Yeah. Some of us always getting "tooken." (*He laughs*) People like Willy Harris, they don't never get "tooken." And you know why the rest of us do? 'Cause we all mixed up. Mixed up bad. We get to looking 'round for the right and the wrong; and we worry about it and cry about it and stay up nights trying to figure out 'bout the wrong and the right of things all the time ... And all the time, man, them takers is out there operating, just taking and taking. Willy Harris? Shoot—Willy Harris don't even count. He don't even count in the big scheme of things. But I'll say one thing for old Willy Harris ... he's taught me something. He's taught me to keep my eye on what counts in this world. Yeah—(*Shouting out a little*) Thanks, Willy!

RUTH What did you call that man for, Walter Lee?

WALTER Called him to tell him to come on over to the show. Gonna put on a show for the man. Just what he wants to see. You see, Mama, the man came here today and he told us that them people out there where you want us to move—well they so upset they willing to pay us not to move out there. (*He laughs again*) And—and oh, Mama—you would of been proud of the way me and Ruth and Bennie acted. We told him to get out ... Lord have mercy! We told the man to get out. Oh, we was some proud folks this afternoon, yeah. (*He lights a cigarette*) We were still full of that old-time stuff ...

RUTH (*Coming toward him slowly*) You talking 'bout taking them people's money to keep us from moving in that house?

WALTER I ain't just talking 'bout it, baby—I'm telling you that's what's going to happen.

BENEATHA Oh, God! Where is the bottom! Where is the real honest-to-God bottom so he can't go any farther!

WALTER See—that's the old stuff. You and that boy that was here today. You all want everybody to carry a flag and a spear and sing some marching songs, huh? You wanna spend your life looking into things and trying to find the right and the wrong part, huh? Yeah. You know what's going to happen to that boy someday—he'll find himself sitting in a dungeon, locked in forever—and the takers will have the key! Forget it, baby! There ain't no causes—there ain't nothing but taking in this world, and he who takes most is smartest—and it don't make a damn bit of difference *how*.

MAMA You making something inside me cry, son. Some awful pain inside me.

WALTER Don't cry, Mama. Understand. That white man is going to walk in that door able to write checks for more money than we ever had. It's important to him and I'm going to help him ... I'm going to put on the show, Mama.

MAMA Son—I come from five generations of people who was slaves and sharecroppers—but ain't nobody in my family never let nobody pay 'em no money that was a way of telling us we wasn't fit to walk the earth. We ain't never been that poor. (*Raising her eyes and looking at him*) We ain't never been that dead inside.

BENEATHA Well—we are dead now. All the talk about dreams and sunlight that goes on in this house. All dead.

WALTER What's the matter with you all! I didn't make this world! It was give to me this way! Hell, yes, I want me some yachts someday! Yes, I want to hang some real pearls 'round my wife's neck. Ain't she supposed to wear no pearls? Somebody tell me—tell me, who decides which women is suppose to wear pearls in this world. I tell you I am a *man*—and I think my wife should wear some pearls in this world!

> *This last line hangs a good while and* WALTER *begins to move about the room. The word "Man" has penetrated his consciousness; he mumbles it to himself repeatedly between strange agitated pauses as he moves about.*

MAMA   Baby, how you going to feel on the inside?

WALTER   Fine! . . . Going to feel fine . . . a man . . .

MAMA   You won't have nothing left then, Walter Lee.

WALTER   (*Coming to her*) I'm going to feel fine, Mama. I'm going to look that son-of-a-bitch in the eyes and say—(*He falters*)—and say, "All right, Mr. Lindner— (*He falters even more*)—that's your neighborhood out there. You got the right to keep it like you want. You got the right to have it like you want. Just write the check and—the house is yours." And, and I am going to say—(*His voice almost breaks*) And you—you people just put the money in my hand and you won't have to live next to this bunch of stinking niggers! . . . (*He straightens up and moves away from his mother, walking around the room*) Maybe—maybe I'll just get down on my black knees . . . (*He does so;* RUTH *and* BENNIE *and* MAMA *watch him in frozen horror*) Captain, Mistuh, Bossman. (*He starts crying*) A-hee-hee-hee! (*Wringing his hands in profoundly anguished imitation*) Yassssuh! Great White Father, just gi' ussen de money, fo' God's sake, and we's ain't gwine come out deh and dirty up yo' white folks neighborhood . . .

> *He breaks down completely, then gets up and goes into the bedroom.*

BENEATHA   That is not a man. That is nothing but a toothless rat.

MAMA   Yes—death done come in this here house. (*She is nodding, slowly, reflectively*) Done come walking in my house. On the lips of my children. You what supposed to be my beginning again. You—what supposed to be my harvest. (*To* BENEATHA) You—you mourning your brother?

BENEATHA   He's no brother of mine.

MAMA   What you say?

BENEATHA   I said that that individual in that room is no brother of mine.

MAMA   That's what I thought you said. You feeling like you better than he is today? (BENEATHA *does not answer*) Yes? What you tell him a minute ago? That he wasn't a man? Yes? You give him up for me? You done wrote his epitaph too—like the rest of the world? Well, who give you the privilege?

BENEATHA   Be on my side for once! You saw what he just did, Mama! You saw him—down on his knees. Wasn't it you who taught me—to despise any man who would do that. Do what he's going to do.

MAMA   Yes—I taught you that. Me and your daddy. But I thought I taught you something else too . . . I thought I taught you to love him.

BENEATHA   Love him? There is nothing left to love.

MAMA   There is always something left to love. And if you ain't learned that, you ain't learned nothing. (*Looking at her*) Have you cried for that boy today? I don't mean for yourself and for the family 'cause we lost the money. I mean for him; what he been through and what it done to him. Child, when do you think is the time to love somebody the most; when they done good and made things easy for everybody? Well then, you ain't through learning—because that ain't the time at all. It's when he's at his lowest and can't believe in hisself 'cause the world done whipped him so. When you starts measuring somebody, measure him right, child, measure him right. Make sure you done taken into account what hills and valleys he come through before he got to wherever he is.

TRAVIS *bursts into the room at the end of the speech, leaving the door open.*

TRAVIS Grandmama—the moving men are downstairs! The truck just pulled up.

MAMA (*Turning and looking at him*) Are they, baby? They downstairs?

She sighs and sits. LINDNER *appears in the doorway. He peers in and knocks lightly, to gain attention, and comes in. All turn to look at him.*

LINDNER (*Hat and briefcase in hand*) Uh—hello . . .

RUTH *crosses mechanically to the bedroom door and opens it and lets it swing open freely and slowly as the lights come up on* WALTER *within, still in his coat, sitting at the far corner of the room. He looks up and out through the room to* LINDNER.

RUTH He's here.

A long minute passes and WALTER *slowly gets up.*

LINDNER (*Coming to the table with efficiency, putting his briefcase on the table and starting to unfold papers and unscrew fountain pens*) Well, I certainly was glad to hear from you people. (WALTER *has begun the trek out of the room, slowly and awkwardly, rather like a small boy, passing the back of his sleeve across his mouth from time to time*) Life can really be so much simpler than people let it be most of the time. Well—with whom do I negotiate? You, Mrs. Younger, or your son here? (MAMA *sits with her hands folded on her lap and her eyes closed as* WALTER *advances.* TRAVIS *goes close to* LINDNER *and looks at the papers curiously*) Just some official papers, sonny.

RUTH Travis, you go downstairs.

MAMA (*Opening her eyes and looking into* WALTER's) No. Travis, you stay right here. And you make him understand what you doing, Walter Lee. You teach him good. Like Willy Harris taught you. You show where our five generations done come to. Go ahead, son—

WALTER (*Looks down into his boy's eyes.* TRAVIS *grins at him merrily and* WALTER *draws him beside him with his arm lightly around his shoulders*) Well, Mr. Lindner. (BENEATHA *turns away*) We called you—(*There is a profound, simple groping quality in his speech*)—because, well, me and my family (*He looks around and shifts from one foot to the other*) Well—we are very plain people . . .

LINDNER Yes—

WALTER I mean—I have worked as a chauffeur most of my life—and my wife here, she does domestic work in people's kitchens. So does my mother. I mean—we are plain people . . .

LINDNER Yes, Mr. Younger—

WALTER (*Really like a small boy, looking down at his shoes and then up at the man*) And—uh—well, my father, well, he was a laborer most of his life.

LINDNER (*Absolutely confused*) Uh, yes—

WALTER (*Looking down at his toes once again*) My father almost beat a man to death once because this man called him a bad name or something, you know what I mean?

LINDNER No, I'm afraid I don't.

WALTER (*Finally straightening up*) Well, what I mean is that we come from people who had a lot of pride. I mean—we are very proud people. And that's my sister over there and she's going to be a doctor—and we are very proud—

LINDNER Well—I am sure that is very nice, but—

WALTER (*Starting to cry and facing the man eye to eye*) What I am telling you is that we called you over here to tell you that we are very proud and that this is—this is my son, who makes the sixth generation of our family in this country, and that we have all thought about your offer and we have decided to move into our house because my father—my father—he earned it. (MAMA *has her eyes closed and is rocking back and forth as though she were in church, with her head nodding the amen yes*) We don't want to make no trouble for nobody or fight no causes—but we will try to be good neighbors. That's all we got to say. (*He looks the man absolutely in the eyes*) We don't want your money.

> He turns and walks away from the man.

LINDNER (*Looking around at all of them*) I take it then that you have decided to occupy.

BENEATHA That's what the man said.

LINDNER (*To* MAMA *in her reverie*) Then I would like to appeal to you, Mrs. Younger. You are older and wiser and understand things better I am sure . . .

MAMA (*Rising*) I am afraid you don't understand. My son said we was going to move and there ain't nothing left for me to say. (*Shaking her head with double meaning*) You know how these young folks is nowadays, mister. Can't do a thing with 'em. Good-bye.

LINDNER (*Folding up his materials*) Well—if you are that final about it . . . There is nothing left for me to say. (*He finishes. He is almost ignored by the family, who are concentrating on* WALTER LEE. *At the door* LINDNER *halts and looks around*) I sure hope you people know what you're doing.

> He shakes his head and exits.

RUTH (*Looking around and coming to life*) Well, for God's sake—if the moving men are here—LET' GET THE HELL OUT OF HERE!

MAMA (*Into action*) Ain't it the truth! Look at all this here mess. Ruth, put Travis' good jacket on him . . . Walter Lee, fix your tie and tuck your shirt in, you look just like somebody's hoodlum. Lord have mercy, where is my plant? (*She flies to get it amid the general bustling of the family, who are deliberately trying to ignore the nobility of the past moment*) You all start on down . . . Travis child, don't go empty-handed . . . Ruth, where did I put that box with my skillets in it? I want to be in charge of it myself . . . I'm going to make us the biggest dinner we ever ate tonight . . . Beneatha, what's the matter with them stockings? Pull them things up, girl . . .

> The family starts to file out as two moving men appear and begin to carry out the heavier pieces of furniture, bumping into the family as they move about.

BENEATHA Mama, Asagai—asked me to marry him today and go to Africa—

MAMA (*In the middle of her getting-ready activity*) He did? You ain't old enough to marry nobody—(*Seeing the moving men lifting one of her chairs precariously*) Darling, that ain't no bale of cotton, please handle it so we can sit in it again. I had that chair twenty-five years . . .

> The movers sigh with exasperation and go on with their work.

BENEATHA (*Girlishly and unreasonably trying to pursue the conversation*) To go to Africa, Mama—be a doctor in Africa . . .

MAMA (*Distracted*) Yes, baby—

WALTER   Africa! What he want you to go to Africa for?

BENEATHA   To practice there . . .

WALTER   Girl, if you don't get all them silly ideas out your head! You better marry yourself a man with some loot . . .

BENEATHA   (*Angrily, precisely as in the first scene of the play*) What have you got to do with who I marry!

WALTER   Plenty. Now I think George Murchison—

> *He and* BENEATHA *go out yelling at each other vigorously;* BENEATHA *is heard saying that she would not marry* GEORGE MURCHISON *if he were Adam and she were Eve, etc. The anger is loud and real till their voices diminish.* RUTH *stands at the door and turns to* MAMA *and smiles knowingly.*

MAMA   (*Fixing her hat at last*) Yeah—they something all right, my children . . .

RUTH   Yeah—they're something. Let's go, Lena.

MAMA   (*Stalling, starting to look around at the house*) Yes—I'm coming. Ruth—

RUTH   Yes?

MAMA   (*Quietly, woman to woman*) He finally come into his manhood today, didn't he? Kind of like a rainbow after the rain . . .

RUTH   (*Biting her lip lest her own pride explode in front of* MAMA) Yes, Lena.

> WALTER'S *voice calls for them raucously.*

MAMA   (*Waving* RUTH *out vaguely*) All right, honey—go on down. I be down directly.

> RUTH *hesitates, then exits.* MAMA *stands, at last alone in the living room, her plant on the table before her as the lights start to come down. She looks around at all the walls and ceilings and suddenly, despite herself, while the children call below, a great heaving thing rises in her and she puts her fist to her mouth, takes a final desperate look, pulls her coat about her, pats her hat and goes out. The lights dim down. The door opens and she comes back in, grabs her plant, and goes out for the last time.*

Curtain

(*Continued on page 817*)

The Modern
Movement

JAMES ABBOTT McNEILL WHISTLER: Nocturne in Black and Gold:
The Falling Rocket, c. 1874

This night scene of fireworks was beyond the grasp of the critic Ruskin.
He wrote that he had never seen a work "in which the ill-educated conceit of the artist so nearly approached the aspect of willful imposture. . . .
I never expected to hear a coxcomb ask two hundred guineas for flinging
a pot of paint in the public's face." Whistler sued him for libel and was
awarded damages of one farthing.

"America's most brilliant virtuoso of the brush" was a descendant of Copley's *Epes Sargent* (p. 34). In the *Rehearsal (below)* we have an example of how far Sargent had gone by the time he was twenty. The first Impressionist exhibition had taken place in 1874, and he had absorbed the new freedom and fluidity as easily as he breathed the Paris air. Throughout his life, Sargent was to paint oil sketches of interiors, informal scenes of his friends picnicking or relaxing out of doors, and watercolors of the landscapes he saw on his travels. They were the other side of the coin, the relief from the exigencies of his professional career as the top portrait painter of Edwardian London's glittering society and its counterpart in Boston.

JOHN SINGER SARGENT: Rehearsal of the Pasdeloup Orchestra at the Cirque d'Hiver, 1876

MAX WEBER: Chinese Restaurant, 1915

New ideas from Europe continued to be felt in American art, and some of the best work of our painters was the result of this process of cross-fertilization. Weber (1881-1961) spent three years in Paris, knew the sophisticated Picasso and Matisse as well as the imperturbably naive Rousseau, and came back stimulated by African sculpture and the great memorial exhibition of Cézanne. In the picture above, he hit upon the ideal subject to show off what he had learned about cubism. Weber explained it this way: "On entering a Chinese restaurant from the darkness of the night outside, a maze and a blaze of light seemed to split into fragments the interior and its contents, the human and inanimate. For the time being the static became the transient and fugitive—oblique planes and contours took vertical and horizontal positions, and the horizontal and vertical became oblique, the light so piercing and so luminous, the color so liquid and the life and movement so enchanting! To express this, kaleidoscopic means had to be chosen."

MARSDEN HARTLEY: Portrait of a German Officer, 1914

Hartley (1877-1943) had his first show at Stieglitz's "291" in 1909. In 1913, the most notorious exhibit in the Armory Show was Marcel Duchamp's cubist *Nude Descending a Staircase,* irreverently dubbed "explosion in a shingle factory." Viewers who couldn't see the lady would be equally baffled by Hartley's *German Officer (opposite)* in a highly effective cubist-expressionist style he developed during his prewar years in Berlin. He was to abandon abstraction shortly afterwards, and did not paint so well again until he returned to his native Maine in the 1930's and adapted his somewhat ponderous style to its rugged landscape and people.

Davis (1894-1964) was consistent throughout his career. He developed his own very American form of pop-cubism and stuck to it. He once explained his style in these words: "Paris school, abstraction, escapism? Nope, just color-space composition celebrating the resolution in art of stresses set up by some aspect of the American scene." In 1927/28 he spent a whole year painting a still life series featuring an egg beater, an electric fan, and a rubber glove. The year of his death Davis won a competition for the design of the first abstract U.S. postage stamp, and it is a toss-up whether the greater honor belonged to the artist or the Post Office Department.

STUART DAVIS: House and Street, 1931

STANTON MACDONALD-WRIGHT:
"Oriental." Synchromy in Blue-Green, 1918

Two young Americans in Paris, Stanton Macdonald-Wright (born 1890) and Morgan Russell, decided to found their own avant-garde art movement. They called it "synchromism." It was a purely abstract art which took advantage of the full spectrum of color and its emotional overtones (unlike contemporary cubism, which tended toward earth colors). The first synchromist exhibition was held in Munich in 1913 and was pronounced the most original American contribution to art since Whistler. Blue-green *(above)*, according to the artist, should be used for a "subject that is serious, has many rich relationships of parts, not too sonorous, not too solidly set upon a base, but replete with sudden changes, great contrasts and a certain strength underlying its seeming playfulness." Emotionally, blue-green has a "quality of remembered things, of sadness; and sadness always implies feeling." When he is not in Florence or a Zen Buddhist monastery in Kyoto, Macdonald-Wright lives in southern California, his home since 1900.

Georgia O'Keeffe (born 1887) lives in New Mexico and draws much of the inspiration for her unique art from the stark beauty of the desert landscape. She did a famous series of flowers, blown up to gigantic size, trying to push beyond the borders of the picture; another explored the decorative possibilities of a bleached cow's skull; and, from the very beginning, she has made pictures which are purely abstract *(below)*. The human figure does not interest her as a subject, and she once said that she wished people were trees, for then she could enjoy them better. After studying in Chicago and New York, she was public school art supervisor in Amarillo, Texas. In 1915 an excited Stieglitz saw some of her drawings and exclaimed, "Finally a woman on paper." He exhibited them in the 291 gallery, and she moved to New York. They were married in 1924. O'Keeffe is still active, and her interests include oriental philosophy and bullfighting. She rivals Cassatt as our finest woman painter.

GEORGIA O'KEEFFE: Only One, 1959

CHARLES HENRY DEMUTH: I Saw the Figure 5 in Gold, 1928

THE GREAT FIGURE

Among the rain
and lights
I saw the figure 5
in gold
on a red
firetruck
moving

tense
unheeded
to gong clangs
siren howls
and wheels rumbling
through the dark city.

WILLIAM CARLOS WILLIAMS

QUESTIONS FOR DISCUSSION

Act I

1. How does the author use the Younger family's sleeping accommodations and bathroom facilities to create empathy in the audience?
2. Money is very important in this play. How does Travis' attitude toward money reflect the attitudes of the adults with whom he lives? What is each adult's attitude toward money?
3. The first signs of tension between Walter Lee and his wife Ruth come during their conversation about Willy Harris. What are Ruth's objections to her husband's friends and their plan?
4. What causes the tensions between Walter Lee and his sister Beneatha?
5. Even before we meet Mama, we can tell that Walter Lee is a man living in a woman-dominated household. What is his attitude toward these women? What is significant about his having to return to ask for carfare money?
6. In *Orientation to the Theater,* Theodore Hatlen writes: "The realist uses symbols which have a direct and immediate reference to life." In the terms of this statement, what is symbolic about Mama's plant?
7. There are almost no speeches given entirely to an expository purpose; instead, the background to the play's action must be inferred from several speeches. What facts do you know about the Younger family—each member—by the end of Act I, scene 1?
8. What does Joseph Asagai represent to Beneatha? to her family? What does Asagai think of Americans in general? of Beneatha in particular? How does Mama surprise Beneatha upon meeting Asagai?
9. Aristotle defines one of the major features of serious drama as "crisis of feeling" or "sufferings engendered among the affections." What crisis of feeling develops between Walter Lee and Ruth and between Walter Lee and Mama in Act I, scene 2?

Act II

1. Jomo Kenyatta was the leader of the Mau Mau movement and later president of Kenya. Among his people he was known as "The Flaming Spear" and "The Lion." What prompts Walter Lee to play the Kenyatta role? How sincere is he? What is his wife's reaction?
2. In what ways does George Murchison contrast with Joseph Asagai? Why does Walter Lee speak so abusively to George? Why does he object to George's white buckskin shoes?

3. By the end of Act II, scene 1, Mama has put a down payment on the house. How do Ruth and Walter Lee's reactions drive them even farther apart?

4. Act II, scene 2 introduces a second theme to the play: Mama's attempt to turn Walter Lee into a man. What is his first reaction to being trusted with $6500? How does the playwright use the conversation with Travis to show Walter Lee's immaturity?

5. In Act II, scene 3, the arrival of Karl Lindner provides the Younger family with a common enemy in the form of community bigotry. What phrases in Lindner's speeches can rightly be interpreted as veiled expressions of racial discrimination? Why does he continually refer to the Younger family as "you people"? Who first understands the purpose of Lindner's visit? Who is last to recognize it? Why?

6. What is the effect of Lindner's visit upon the family? How does the playwright use their reaction to contrast with the arrival of Bobo?

Act III

1. Why is Asagai's conversation with Beneatha, in Act III, important to Walter Lee's decision to sell the house?

2. Why is Walter Lee's plan so offensive to Mama? What is her argument against it?

3. What causes Walter Lee to change his mind? Do you accept the change as reasonable? Has the playwright adequately prepared her audience for the change? How?

4. Why does Walter Lee recommend that Beneatha marry George Murchison rather than Asagai?

5. What has the Younger family learned through this experience? What have you learned from the play?

ASSIGNMENTS FOR WRITING

1. Read carefully Langston Hughes' poem at the beginning of the play and write an essay to show the appropriateness of the poem as an epigraph to this play.

2. What is the role a mother plays in the development of her family? Choose one or two other mothers in literature and compare or contrast their roles with that performed by Lena Younger. Show how each woman's character was or was not sufficient for the needs of her family.

3. *A Raisin in the Sun* ends with the Younger family moving from the Southside ghetto to Clybourne Park, the all-white suburb. What happened to them there? Write a narrative in which you tell the continuing story of Walter Lee, Ruth, Travis, Mama, and Beneatha.
4. *A Raisin in the Sun* is the author's first major work. As such it may well be flawed. What are its imperfections? Write a critical evaluation of the play as though you were a reviewer commenting on its first performance.